PAUL TILLICH

A History of Christian Thought

From Its Judaic and Hellenistic Origins to Existentialism

Edited by Carl E. Braaten

A Touchstone Book

Published by Simon and Schuster

Contents

PART II

Preface to the Touchstone Edition

This history of Christian thought combines into one volume two books of Paul Tillich's lectures that have been previously published. The first part appeared under the title *A History of Christian Thought*, beginning with the Graeco-Roman preparations for Christianity and ending with the post-Reformation development in Protestant theology. The second part first appeared as *Perspectives on Nineteenth and Twentieth Century Protestant Theology*, beginning with the rise of the Enlightenment and ending with the theology of Karl Barth and modern existentialism.* *A History of Christian Thought* originated as lectures delivered by Tillich at Union Theological Seminary in New York, stenographically recorded and transcribed by Peter N. John and distributed by him in a small first edition. A second edition appeared shortly thereafter, in which Peter John corrected a number of errors. At that time he acknowledged the need for a thorough revision of the text for matters of style and content. This I tried to accomplish in the first published edition by Harper & Row, 1968. This edition now appears unaltered in this volume.

The second part of this volume contains tape-recorded lectures which Paul Tillich delivered at the Divinity School of the University of Chicago during the spring quarter of the 1962-63 school year and is based entirely on his spoken words.

Tillich's history of the Christian tradition appears at a time when interest in new theological fads that come and go quickly has faded dramatically. The demise of Tillich's thought was prematurely nnounced. In the world of English-speaking theology no move ent has yet arisen to eclipse the influence of Paul Tillich. The wider dissemination of this influence, to a new generation of college and seminary students, as well as to theologians

---

* A comprehensive German edition of these volumes, edited by Ingeborg C. Hennel, was published in 1971.

who have a lot of catching up to do, is very much to be desired. Tillich introduces students to the roots of their own religious traditions, making the symbols of their faith more meaningful for today. He was and is a truly great teacher of theology.

CARL E. BRAATEN
Chicago, Illinois
March 1972

Paul Tillich and the

Classical Christian Tradition

by Carl E. Braaten

THE RADICALISM OF PAUL TILLICH

It has been said that the real Tillich is the radical Tillich but the radicalism which moved Paul Tillich was not the iconoclastic spirit of those who wish to create *de novo* an original brand of Christianity; rather, it was the radicalism which moved the great prophetic spirits of the religious tradition. Tillich's term for it was the "Protestant principle." This radical principle was to be used not against but for the sake of the "catholic substance" of the Christian tradition. One question which Tillich posed for his own theological effort was this: "How can the radicalism of prophetic criticism which is implied in the principles of genuine Protestantism be united with the classical tradition of dogma, sacred law, sacraments, hierarchy, cult, as preserved in the Catholic churches?"[1] Tillich also saw the danger in prophetic criticism. The prophet hopes to get to the heart of the matter with his knife of radical protest; the false prophet is known in the tradition as one who cuts out the heart itself. It was the true radicalism rooted in Biblical prophetism

[1] Tillich, "The Conquest of Intellectual Provincialism: Europe and America," *Theology of Culture* (New York: Oxford University Press, 1959), p. 169.

which drove Tillich to criticize our religious and cultural forms of tradition. Thus, like the Old Testament prophets, his criticism *of* the tradition was always *from* the tradition, from some deeper level in it, not from some arbitrary, neutral or alien standpoint outside the "theological circle."[2]

Most of Tillich's commentators and critics in America have had the impression that Tillich was a radical, perhaps even dangerous, innovator.[3] The chief reason for this impression was often cited by Tillich himself. Americans—and perhaps moderns in general—have little sense of history. They are not aware of the sources of tradition from which they come. Europeans possess a more vivid historical consciousness than Americans, and for this reason European theologians are much less inclined to stress the innovating features of Tillich's thought. Many of Tillich's favorite ideas and terms, which sounded utterly novel to American students, came originally from a long line of honored ancestors. His basic categories and concepts, the style and structure of his thinking, were not unprecedented in the Christian tradition—to those who knew their history of thought. Tillich's uniqueness, his creativity and originality, lay in his power of thought, the comprehensive scope of his vision, his depth of insight, the systematic consistency with which he developed the internal relations of the various elements of his philosophy and theology, and the daring he displayed in crossing borders into new fields. He could be so actively immersed in the currents of his time and exert such vital influence on the shape of things to come because his roots were deeply embedded in and nourished by the classical traditions of the Christian Church.

DIALOGUE WITH THE CLASSICAL TRADITION

Tillich was a son of the whole tradition of the church in a measure that can hardly be said of any other theologian since the Reformation.

[2] To be in the "theological circle" is to have made an existential decision, to be in the situation of faith. Cf. Tillich, *Systematic Theology* (Chicago: The University of Chicago Press, 1951), Vol. II, pp. 6, 8, 9–11.

[3] See Tillich's answer to a student's question, "Is Paul Tillich a dangerous man?" in *Ultimate Concern*, edited by D. Mackenzie Brown (New York: Harper & Row, 1965), pp. 188–93.

Although Tillich confessed he was a Lutheran "by birth, education, religious experience, and theological reflection,"[4] he did not rest comfortably within any traditional form of Lutheranism. He transcended so far as possible every limiting feature of his immediate heritage. The transconfessional style of his theology made it difficult for many of his Lutheran contemporaries to recognize him as a member of the same family.[5] He did not have to *try* to be ecumenical; for the substance of his thinking was drawn from the whole sweep of the classical tradition. His theology was a living dialogue with great men and ideas of the past, with the fathers of the ancient church, both Greek and Latin, with the schoolmen and mystics of the medieval period, with Renaissance humanists and Protestant reformers, with the theologians of liberalism and their neo-orthodox critics. His method of handling the tradition was eminently dialectical, in the spirit of the *Sic et Non* of Abelard.

Tillich's systematic theology was built up through the rhythm of raising and answering existential questions. Each of the five parts of the system contains two sections, one in which the human question is developed, the other in which the theological answer is given. He admitted that there could very well have been an intermediate section which places his theological answer more explicitly within the context of the tradition.[6] The dialogue with the tradition mediated through the Scriptures and the church, the sort of thing which appears in small print in Karl Barth's *Church Dogmatics*, thus receded pretty much into the background of the *Systematic Theology*. This sacrifice of explicit attention to the historical tradition had the result, I believe, in gaining for Tillich the reputation in some circles as a speculative theologian who arbitrarily projected ideas whether or not they squared with the central thrusts of the church's tradition. If that was the result, it is unfortunate. It conceals the catholicity of Tillich's mind and the extent

[4] Tillich, *The Interpretation of History* (New York: Charles Scribner's Sons, 1936), p. 54.
[5] Cf. my brief article, "Paul Tillich as a Lutheran Theologian," in *The Chicago Lutheran Theological Seminary Record* (August, 1962), Vol. 67, No. 3. See also the chapter by Jaroslav Pelikan, "Ein deutscher lutherischer Theologe in Amerika: Paul Tillich und die dogmatische Tradition," in *Gott ist am Werk*, the *Festschrift* for Hanns Lilje, edited by Heinz Brunotte and Erich Ruppel (Hamburg: Furche Verlag, 1959), pp. 27–36.
[6] *Systematic Theology*, I, p. 66.

to which his systematic ideas were won through an intense intellectual struggle with the sources of the tradition.

To reveal more of this living background of Tillich's systematic theology, it has seemed important to us to publish some of his lectures on the history of thought. Seldom did he publish in the field of historical theology. He had a fear of being judged by the strict canons of scientific historiography. On the occasion of the Tillich Memorial Service in Chicago, Mircea Eliade was not exaggerating when he stated: "But, of course, Paul Tillich would never have become a historian of religions nor, as a matter of fact, a *historian* of anything else. He was interested in the existential meaning of history—*Geschichte*, not *Historie*."[7] Yet, very few minds were so laden with the consciousness of history, with memories of the classical tradition. Tillich's students were awed by his ability to trace from memory the history of an idea through its main stages of development, observing even subtle shifts in the nuances of meaning at the main turning points. In fact, a great part of Tillich's career in teaching theology was devoted to lectures and seminars in the history of thought. Students who were privileged to study under Tillich at Union, Harvard, or Chicago reminisce today about their most memorable courses, such as the basic sequence in The History of Christian Thought, or The History of Christian Mysticism, or The Pre-Socratics, or German Classical Idealism. Even students from backgrounds uncongenial to Tillich's views on the Christian faith could not fail to learn from him as an interpreter of the Christian tradition. Many were liberated from the strait jacket of a given denominational tradition to become more open to the fullness of the common Christian heritage.

THE INTERPRETATION OF HISTORY

The key to an understanding of Tillich's handling of the tradition is his fundamental proposition that every interpretation is a creative union of the interpreter and the interpreted in a third beyond both of them.

[7] Eliade, "Paul Tillich and the History of Religions," in *The Future of Religions,* by Paul Tillich, edited by Jerald C. Brauer (New York: Harper & Row, 1966), p. 33.

The ideal of unbiased historical research to report only the "naked facts" without any admixture of subjective interpretation Tillich called "a questionable concept."[8] Without a union of the historian with the material he interprets there can be no real understanding of history. "The historian's task is to 'make alive' what has 'passed away.' "[9] The dimension of interpretation is made unavoidable because history itself is more than a series of facts. An historical event "is a syndrome (i.e., a running-together) of facts and interpretation."[10] Furthermore, the historian himself is unavoidably a member of a group which has a living tradition of memories and values. "Nobody writes history on a 'place above all places.' "[11] The element of empathic participation in history is basic to the act of interpreting history.

Tillich was too much influenced by both the existentialist and the Marxist understandings of history to imagine that one could grasp the meaning of history by surveying the past in cool detachment. In a crucial passage Tillich emphatically states: "Only full involvement in historical action can give the basis for an interpretation of history. Historical activity is the key to understanding history."[12] This dynamic view of history arose out of Tillich's own struggle with the historical actualities of his situation. In one of his autobiographies he acknowledged that many of his most important concepts, such as the Protestant principle, *kairos,* the demonic, the *Gestalt* of grace, and the trio of theonomy, heteronomy, autonomy, were worked out for the sake of a new interpretation of history. "History became the central problem of my theology and philosophy," he said, "because of the historical reality as I found it when I returned from the first World War."[13] With prophetic zeal he sounded forth the theme of *kairos,* that moment in time when the eternal breaks into history, issuing to his contemporaries a summons to a consciousness of history in the sense of the *kairos.* He

[8] *Systematic Theology,* III, p. 301.
[9] *Systematic Theology,* I, p. 104.
[10] *Systematic Theology,* III, p. 302.
[11] *Ibid.,* p. 301.
[12] *Ibid.,* p. 349.
[13] Tillich, *The Protestant Era,* translated by James Luther Adams (Chicago: The University of Chicago Press, 1948), xvii.

allied himself in these years with religious socialism, and was no doubt the main theoretician of this movement.

When Tillich turned toward the past he had little interest in it for its own sake. His involvement in the present and his sense of responsibility for the future drove him to search out meanings from the past. "Whoever would maintain the idea of pure observation must content himself with numbers and names, statistics and newspaper clippings. He might collect thousands of things which could be verified but he would not for that reason be able to understand what is actually happening in the present. One is enabled to speak of that which is most vital in the present, of that which makes the present a generative force, only insofar as one immerses oneself in the creative process which brings the future forth out of the past."[14] To act in the present, one must understand oneself and one's situation; to understand this, one has to recapitulate the process by which the present situation has evolved. In the "Introduction" of this volume Tillich states that the primary purpose of his lectures on Protestant theology is to show "how we have arrived at the present situation," or in other words, "to understand ourselves."[15] The fascination for the past on its own account is given as a second and subordinate purpose. We have tried to indicate the primacy of Tillich's existential interest in the historical tradition by characterizing these lectures as "perspectives." The term "history," which Tillich requested us not to use, would have suggested to many people a historiographical treatment less preponderantly interpretative.

TILLICH AND EARLY CATHOLICISM

The knowledge of Tillich's theology could serve as a prerequisite to an advanced course in patristic studies, or vice versa. There are many bridges in Tillich's theology to the traditions of the ancient church. One immediately thinks, of course, of the centrality of the trinitarian and christological doctrines in Tillich as well as in the leading church fathers. No doubt it was Tillich's love for Greek philosophy which pre-

[14] Tillich, *The Religious Situation,* translated by H. Richard Niebuhr (Cleveland: Meridian Books, 1956), p. 34.
[15] Cf. *infra,* p. 1.

pared him for a sympathetic understanding of the development of these dogmas. Quite unlike the great historians of dogma in the Ritschlian school, especially Adolf von Harnack, Tillich esteemed the classic dogmas of the Trinity and the Christ very highly as the appropriate reception of the Christian message in the categories of Hellenistic philosophy. Harnack's thesis that the "Hellenization of Christianity" was an intellectualistic distortion of the New Testament gospel resulted, Tillich claimed, from a misinterpretation of Greek thought. What Harnack did not understand was that "Greek thought is existentially concerned with the eternal, in which it seeks for eternal truth and eternal life."[16] On the other hand, Tillich did not believe that the conciliar formulations of the ancient church were binding on all future theology. The categories that were used then are not unquestionably valid for our time. His reconstructions of these dogmas in his *Systematic Theology* are serious efforts to get beneath the outer crust of the old formulas to clear the way for an understanding of the reality which originally they were meant to protect from heretical attacks. Critical essays and books have been and will continue to be written for a long time to come to assess to what extent Tillich succeeded in reinterpreting the old doctrines of the church.

The concept of the Logos in the early Greek fathers also found one of its stanchest allies in Tillich. Of all the leading contemporary theologians, Tillich was the only one who integrated the Logos doctrine into his own theological system. Without it he could not have been the apologetic theologian he was. When Tillich referred to himself as an apologetic theologian, he had in mind the example of the great second-century apologist, Justin Martyr, for whom the Logos doctrine was, as for Tillich, the universal principle of the divine self-manifestation. If the apologist is to answer the questions and accusations of the despisers of Christianity, he must discover some common ground. The common ground for both Justin and Tillich was the presence of the Logos beyond the boundaries of the church, making it possible for men in all religions and cultures to have a partial grasp of the truth, a love of beauty, and a moral sensitivity. Tillich could stand "on the

[16] *Systematic Theology*, III, p. 287.

boundary"[17] between theology and philosophy, church and society, religion and culture, because the Logos who became flesh was the same Logos who was universally at work in the structures of human existence. Tillich's apologetic writing demonstrates how he shared the conviction of the Apologists that Christians by no means have a monopoly on the truth, and that the truth, wherever it may be found, essentially belongs to us Christians. The Logos doctrine saved Tillich's theology from a false particularism that has hampered so much of the ecclesiastical tradition.

Tillich was never under any illusion that the first five centuries of the church provide any clear support for Protestantism against Roman Catholicism. What he stressed instead was *how early* the formative principles of Catholicism developed, especially in the defense against the onslaughts of Gnosticism. The closing of the canon, defining the apostolic tradition, the rule of faith, the formation of creeds, and also episcopal authority were developments which occurred very early, and cannot be written off as aberrations of the "Dark Ages." Of course, Tillich was never able to endorse the rise of early Catholicism as an unambiguously salutary occurrence. In the light of the "Protestant principle" he could point out that the church paid a dear price in its struggle against heresies. What he called the heteronomous structures of an authoritarian church, which later resulted in the church of the Inquisition, had their beginnings in the anti-Gnostic response of Orthodoxy. Also every definition entails exclusion. When the church was pressed by heresies to defend itself, it had to define itself. This self-definition, Tillich believes, inevitably has a narrowing result. "The whole history of Christian dogma is a continuing narrowing down, but at the same time a *defining*. And the definition is important, because without it many elements would have undercut the whole church, would have denied its existence. The dogma, therefore, the dogmatic development, is not something merely lamentable or evil. It was the necessary form by which the church kept its very identity. . . . The tragic element in all history is that if something like this must be

---

[17] Tillich's autobiographical sketch by this title, *On the Boundary* (New York: Charles Scribner's Sons, 1966). This edition is both a revision and a new translation of Part I of *The Interpretation of History*.

done, it immediately has the consequence of narrowing down and excluding very valuable elements."[18] The theologian today has the onerous task of breaking through the definitions to recover if possible those valuable elements which for *tragically necessary* reasons were temporarily excluded. With this sort of dialectical insight Tillich could affirm that the church was basically correct in each instance in which it rejected a major heresy, but wrong when its self-defining formulations became rigid, as in the case of post-Tridentine Roman Catholicism and Protestant Orthodoxy. There is no solution to this problem of self-reduction through self-definition except by the continual reformation of the church (*ecclesia semper reformanda*).

The two theologians of the ancient church who had the greatest influence on Tillich were Origen and Augustine. Clearly it was their common bond of Neo-Platonism which attracted Tillich to their way of thinking. When Tillich expounded the doctrines of Origen and Augustine, it was often difficult to distinguish Tillich's own doctrine from theirs.[19] This was not simply a case of Tillich reading his own ideas into Origen and Augustine; I think it was rather that he had read such ideas out of them, probably at first backtracking his way from Schelling, through Boehme, German mysticism, medieval Augustinianism, and early Christian Platonism. At any rate, whatever occasioned his interest in Origen and Augustine, he felt at home in them.

Origen's mysticism, his understanding of the symbolic significance of religious language, his doctrines of the Logos, the Trinity, creation, the transcendental fall, and his eschatology, especially its universalism, were all features which Tillich was able to adapt to his own systematic theology. I do not suggest that Tillich did this uncritically. In particular, it was evident that despite his kindred feeling for Augustine, Tillich rejected his conservative philosophy of history, namely that aspect of it which resulted in the ecclesiastical interpretation of the Kingdom of God as ruling on earth through the church's hierarchy and its sacramental mediations. This is a decisive deviation from Augustine. It meant that Tillich could ally himself more with the prophetic in-

[18] Brown, ed., *Ultimate Concern,* pp. 64–65.

[19] Tillich's lectures on the history of Christian thought have been recorded and edited by Peter H. John, and have circulated on a limited scale among Tillich's students. A new edition of these lectures will be published soon.

terpretation of history, receiving its impulses from Joachim of Floris, the radical Franciscans, and the left-wing Reformers. His own doctrine of the *kairos* could hardly be accommodated by the traditional, ecclesiastical interpretation of history, with its antichiliastic, nonutopian character. For Tillich and the prophetic line of interpretation the future may be pregnant with a decisively new meaning for which the past and the present are merely preparations. The conservative ecclesiastical tendency has always managed to quash too vivid expectations of the future; such expectations are the spawning bed of revolutionary attitudes toward the present situation and the church's place in it.

Theonomy and Mysticism in the Middle Ages

Moving on to Tillich's interpretation of the Middle Ages, our first observation must be that he made important contributions toward overcoming the deep-seated rationalistic and Protestant prejudices against the so-called "Dark Ages." The one thousand years from Pope Gregory the Great to Doctor Martin Luther have often been pictured with contempt as a monolithic age of ignorance, priestly tyranny, and religious superstition. Directly against this stands the idealized image of the Middle Ages in Romanticism. Tillich was no romanticist, but he was influenced by its outlook on the Middle Ages. Christian romanticists look back to the Middle Ages as an ideal unity of religion and culture, as an organism in which the religious center irradiates through all forms of cultic, legal, moral, and aesthetic activities. Tillich could not share the hope of Romanticism to re-create a society according to the pattern of an idealized Middle Ages. On the other hand, Tillich drew the inspiration for his own concept of theonomy from this romanticist outlook on medieval society. "Protestantism cannot accept the medieval pattern either in Romantic or in Roman terms. It must look forward to a new theonomy. Yet, in order to do so, it must know what theonomy means, and this it can find in the Middle Ages."[20]

Tillich was able to give a sweeping overview of historical periods in terms of the principles of autonomy, heteronomy, and theonomy. "Theonomy can characterize a whole culture and give a key to the inter-

[20] *Systematic Theology,* I, p. 149.

pretation of history."[21] The ideal of a theonomous culture can never be fully realized on earth because of man's existential estrangement that runs through all history. But there may be partial realizations. Such a culture is one in which the inner potentialities of man are being fulfilled through the driving presence of the Spirit, giving power, meaning, and direction to the autonomous forms of life. Autonomy describes a situation which cuts itself off from the transcendent source and aim of life. Examples of more or less autonomous periods are those of skepticism in Greek philosophy, the Renaissance, the Enlightenment, and present-day secularism. Heteronomy represents the attempt to impose an alien law upon the autonomous structures of life, demanding unconditional obedience to finite authorities, splitting the conscience and the inner life. The struggle between the independence of autonomy and the coercions of heteronomy can only be overcome through a new theonomy. This is a situation in which religion and culture are not divorced, where instead, according to one of Tillich's most famous formulations, culture provides the form of religion, and religion the substance of culture.

Applying these principles to the Middle Ages, Tillich emphasized, not their homogeneous nature, but the great diversities and transitions within medieval culture. He contrasted the relative openness of the medieval church toward a variety of ways of thinking to the narrowness of the church of the counter-Reformation. The high point of the Middle Ages was attained in the thirteenth century in the great systems of the Scholastics. Particularly, the Augustinian line from Anselm of Canterbury to Bonaventura represented a theonomous style of theologizing. Here, beginning with faith, the mind was opened to perceive the reflections of the divine presence in all realms and facets of life. The end of the Middle Ages was characterized by nominalism and heteronomy. The world was split; the realms of religion and culture were separated. The double-truth theory was invented as a way of maintaining philosophy and theology side by side, in a state of mutual contradictoriness. A statement that is true in theology may be false in philosophy and one that is true in philosophy may be false in theology. Adherence to the creeds of the church can be maintained only on

[21] *Systematic Theology*, III, p. 250.

the basis of an absolute authority. This positivistic notion of authority came to clear expression in Duns Scotus and William of Ockham. The concept of authority became heteronomous and was applied more and more in a heteronomous way by the church.

What seems unique in Tillich's interpretation of the Middle Ages is the fact that he attributed the disintegration of theonomy and the emerging gap between scientific autonomy and ecclesiastical heteronomy to none other than Thomas Aquinas. In one of his most self-revealing essays, "The Two Types of the Philosophy of Religion,"[22] he traces the roots of the modern split between faith and knowledge back to the Thomistic denial of the Augustinian belief in the immediate presence of God in the act of knowing. For Thomas, God is first in the order of being but last in the order of knowledge. The knowledge of God is the end result of a line of reasoning, not the presupposition of all our knowing. Where reason leaves off, faith takes over. The act of faith, however, becomes the movement of the will to accept truth on authority. Tillich's verdict is clear: "This is the final outcome of the Thomistic *dis*solution of the Augustinian *solution.*"[23]

This essay on "The Two Types of the Philosophy of Religion" reveals how alive the philosophical debates of the Middle Ages were in Tillich's own thinking. He saw that fundamental issues were being decided with tremendous consequences for world history. When Tillich lectured on this period, he was no impartial observer of the debates; he was definitely a passionate participant. On most issues he took the side of the Augustinians against the Thomists, the Franciscans against the Dominicans, the realists against the nominalists, etc. The background to all these controversies was what Tillich called the eternal dialogue that continues in history between Plato and Aristotle. It is the dialogue between a philosophy of wisdom (*sapientia*) and a philosophy of science (*scientia*), or as Tillich put it, between the ontological and the cosmological approaches to God.

Tillich's alliance with the Middle Ages appears also in his high evaluation of its mysticism. For Tillich there is an ineliminable element of mysticism in every religion. A question he often posed to his students

[22] *Theology of Culture,* pp. 10–29.
[23] *Ibid.,* p. 19.

was whether "mysticism can be baptized by Christianity." His answer was "yes," provided we distinguish between the abstract type of mysticism of Hinduism and the concrete mysticism of Christianity. Concrete mysticism is Christ-mysticism. Such a mysticism may be taken up into Christianity as an historical religion. Without the mystical element in religion Tillich observed that it becomes reduced to intellectualism or moralism. True doctrines or good morals become the essence of a religion without the mystical dimension. In this he agreed basically with Schleiermacher and Rudolf Otto against Kant and Albrecht Ritschl. He never joined Karl Barth and Emil Brunner in their wholesale rejection of Christian mysticism. In this regard both Barth and Brunner were still clinging to the Ritschlian prejudice that Christianity and mysticism are irreconcilable opposites.

The eradication of all mystical elements in the Christian tradition would leave us but a torso. In Tillich's judgment this would require getting rid of half of the apostle Paul's theology, its Spirit-mysticism; the Christ-mysticism of men like Bernard of Clairvaux whom Luther prized so highly would have to go; indeed, much of the theology of the young Luther would have to be cut out, and along with it his understanding of faith. The Christian tradition would be a vast wasteland without its enrichment through mysticism. Of all the labels that have been applied to Tillich's theology, none of them come close to fitting unless they bring out the mystical ontology which undergirds his whole way of thinking. This is why it is not very revealing to label Tillich an existentialist as popularly done; it tends to obscure the underlying essentialism of his reflections on existence. Tillich's doctrine of existence is cradled within the framework of his mystical ontology. Only from this perspective should we understand many of Tillich's expressions which have created either offense or puzzlement, such as "God beyond the God of theism," "Being itself," "absolute faith," "ecstatic naturalism," "belief-ful realism," "symbolic knowledge," "essentialization," etc. These terms are echoes of the mystical side of Tillich and of the Christian tradition.

participatio Christi

The Rediscovery of the Prophetic Tradition

The mystical side of Tillich's thought was always kept in tension with the prophetic aspect. Some of his sharpest judgments were made against mysticism as a way of self-elevation to the divine through ascetic exercises. In the name of the *sola gratia* principle of the Reformation he condemned mysticism as a method of self-salvation. The enigma many have sensed in Paul Tillich is due to this polygenous character of his thinking. Although his roots were planted deeply in the soil of neo-Platonic mysticism, German idealism, and nineteenth-century Protestant liberalism, nevertheless, Tillich placed this entire heritage under the criticism of the "Protestant principle." This principle he derived from the Pauline-Lutheran tradition. The estrangement between God and man is overcome solely on the basis of divine grace, without any merit or worthiness on man's part. The existential power and theological relevance of the Reformation doctrine of justification by grace alone through faith alone was mediated to Paul Tillich by his teacher Martin Kähler. Tillich, however, radicalized it to meet even the situation of the doubter. "Not only he who is in sin but also he who is in doubt is justified through faith. The situation of doubt, even of doubt about God, need not separate us from God."[24]

Tillich bemoaned the fact that modern man can scarcely understand the meaning of justification. For this reason he exchanged the legal imagery taken from the courtroom for new expressions borrowed from the psychoanalytic situation in which the therapist accepts the patient *as he is*. Justification by grace through faith is interpreted as our being accepted *in spite of* the fact we are unacceptable. The whole gospel is contained in the phrase "in spite of." In spite of our sin and guilt, in spite of our condemnation and unbelief, in spite of our doubts and our total unworthiness, the miracle of the good news is for just such people. "Justification is the paradox that man the sinner is justified, that man the unrighteous is righteous; that man the unholy is holy, namely, in the judgment of God, which is not based on any human achievements but only on the divine, self-surrendering grace. Where this

[24] *The Protestant Era*, xiv.

paradox of the divine-human relationship is understood and accepted, all ideologies are destroyed. Man does not have to deceive himself about himself, because he is accepted as he is, in the total perversion of his existence."[25]

An important part of Paul Tillich's mission to American Protestantism was to reinterpret in contemporary terms the message of the Reformation. He felt that American Protestantism had scarcely been touched by the prophetic message of Luther and Calvin. Lectures he delivered at The Washington Cathedral Library, Washington, D.C., in 1950, dealt with "The Recovery of the Prophetic Tradition in the Reformation" and are now published in Volume VII of the collected works of Paul Tillich in German.[26] The great doctrines of the Reformation, which have become mummified for many of its heirs, are in Tillich's treatment living symbols of the new relationship to God which provided the explosive power of Luther's reformatory work. The poignancy of Tillich's own prophetic criticism of American Protestantism's pseudo-orthodoxies, shallow liberalisms, and puritan moralisms was due to his grasp of Luther's message. His observation on Protestant preaching in America was that it too often tends to make the grace of God, that is, God's attitude toward man, depend on the individual's moral earnestness, religious devotion, or true beliefs. The formula "justification by faith" has been retained, to be sure, but then, as Tillich rightly pointed out, faith is transformed into a work which a man is exhorted to perform on his own conscious decision. To avoid this Pelagianizing implication Tillich suggested that it might help to say justification *through* faith instead of *by* faith. This would mean that faith does not *cause* but *mediates* God's grace. Tillich's little book, *Dynamics of Faith*,[27] was written in part to overcome dreadful distortions of the concept of faith. Faith is distorted when it is conceived anthropocentrically as either a knowing (intellectualism) or a doing (moralism) or a feeling

---

[25] *Ibid.*, p. 170.

[26] "Die Wiederentdeckung der prophetischen Tradition in der Reformation," *Der Protestantismus als Kritik und Gestaltung* (Stuttgart: Evangelisches Verlagswerk, 1962), Gesammelte Werke, VII, pp. 171–215. An English version of these lectures was published; the German edition, however, is by Tillich's request the authoritative one.

[27] New York: Harper & Row, 1957.

(emotionalism). Tillich's own definition of faith as a state of being grasped by an ultimate concern was an attempt to use an expression which suggests that faith involves both the depths and the totality of the self, and is therefore not merely the function of a particular faculty of the mind.

The extent of Luther's influence on Tillich's mind cannot be detailed here. Several connections may, however, be worth a brief mention. Luther said that what makes a theologian is his ability to distinguish rightly between law and gospel. This means that like the two natures of Christ, law and gospel must be differentiated without being separated (Nestorianism) or being confused (Monophysitism). Tillich rarely ever used the categories of law and gospel as an explicit theological formula. The structure of his thinking is, however, clearly patterned after this feature of Luther's theology. It makes its appearance in Tillich's system as the methodological principle of correlation. He does not develop a doctrine *about* law and gospel; instead all his thinking is structured in terms of it. His essays dealing with theology and culture, the plan of his *Systematic Theology,* and all his sermons show that before he would announce the Christian answer, the kerygma, he would carefully describe the human predicament. The description of the human predicament is man's existence *under the law;* the presentation of the Christian answer offers the new possibility of life *under the gospel.* The sequence is always law before gospel, that is, always the posing of the question before the attempt to answer. For Tillich this is the proper theological method, and at just this point he deviated from Karl Barth who placed the gospel before the law, who spoke of Christ before turning to the analysis of the actual human situation as man today experiences it. Tillich's plea for a fruitful correlation between philosophy and theology also rests upon this law/gospel basis. When he states that philosophy raises the question which theology must answer, he is saying in another way that the gospel is the divine response to the questionability of human existence under the law. Philosophy functions analogously to the law as theology does to the gospel.

Tillich believed that the "law of contrasts" in Luther's doctrine of God can help to counter the trend in Protestant theology to rationalize and moralize the picture of God. This law of contrasts is expressed in a series of terms that must be maintained in a relation of dialectical tension to each other: e.g., the hiddenness of God and the revealedness of God, the wrath of God and the love of God, the strange work of God (*opus alienum*) and the proper work of God (*opus proprium*), God's kingdom on the left hand and his kingdom on the right hand, etc. This style of thinking in terms of dialectical tension between contrasting concepts also characterized Tillich's theology. One can see shades of this in Tillich's analysis of the ontological polarities in the depth of the divine life and in his trinitarian principles. The difference, of course, between Tillich and Luther must also be acknowledged. Between them stood Jacob Boehme who through German classical idealism, especially Schelling, provided Tillich with a powerful model of dialectical thinking in mystical-ontological categories. Thus, for example, Luther's idea of the devil as the agent of God's wrath makes its appearance in the tradition of mystical theology, running from Boehme through Schelling to Tillich, as a negative principle, as the principle of nonbeing, gnawing at the foundations of reality. Also the mystical feeling for depth is brought out by the idea of the abyss in the divine life, the *Ungrund* in Boehme's language. Tillich saw that both Luther and Boehme's ideas of God had their common background in late medieval mysticism as expressed, for example, in the *Theologia Germanica*. He drew upon this tradition in protesting the reduction of the picture of God in late nineteenth-century Protestantism to the simple image of a loving father. Hence, for Tillich the symbol of the wrath of God was not merely an outdated notion of primitive mythology that can be excised from our picture of God. Tillich was always grateful to Rudolf Otto's book, *The Idea of the Holy*, for making him more deeply aware of the abysmal mystery of God, the *mysterium tremendum et fascinosum*. And on this point he was convinced that Otto was a better interpreter of Luther's theology than the leading Ritschlians had been.

From Orthodoxy to Neo-Orthodoxy

The rest of the story of Tillich as an interpreter of the Christian tradition can be had by reading this book. Although its title promises to bring out Tillich's perspectives on theology in the nineteenth and twentieth centuries, he actually reaches back to the period of Protestant

Orthodoxy to begin his account of the development. He lays out the main principles of theology in the seventeenth and eighteenth centuries. The period of Protestant Scholasticism did not evoke in Tillich, as in many of his contemporaries, a feeling of revulsion. He ranked it as part of the "classical tradition," not as an aberration from which we have nothing to learn. Not the theologians of Orthodoxy but their modern imitators were the butt of Tillich's scorn. The original pietists, men like Spener and Zinzendorf, were likewise not to be disparaged, only their followers who tried to make a method out of their piety. In numerous places in Tillich's writings he shows how he would mediate between Orthodoxy and Pietism on the question whether theology could be done only by those who are regenerated.[28] His answer was that the Pietists were right in stressing that theology involves existential commitment, but wrong in making that commitment a matter of absolute certainty. This leads to subjectivism in theology against which the Orthodox theologians rightly protested.

One of Tillich's most provocative theses in this book states that mysticism is the mother of rationalism. Both have in common a subjectivist outlook; the "inner light," by a slight shift of emphasis, becomes the autonomous reason. This hypothesis can perhaps best be tested by examining to see to what extent the pietists and the rationalists allied themselves in the attack on Orthodoxy and to what extent rationalism prospered most where Pietism had gained the strongest foothold. The exact nature of the alliance would be an interesting subject for careful historical research.

The sections on Schleiermacher and Hegel are revealing of Tillich's indebtedness to them. It must be remembered that Tillich kept alive the memory of these figures at a time when it was generally popular in theology to debunk them. Schleiermacher was glibly dismissed as a mystic and Hegel as a speculative philosopher. Søren Kierkegaard's verdict on Hegel was accepted by many as the last word, and Emil Brunner's book on Schleiermacher charged the ills of modern Protestantism to his account.[29] Tillich used to recall how hostile the reaction was during the twenties and thirties to his seminars on these men. It

[28] *Systematic Theology*, I, p. 11.
[29] *Die Mystik und das Wort* (Tübingen: J. C. B. Mohr, 1924).

is to Tillich's credit that he maintained for himself and imparted to others a sense of balance toward the era of liberalism. Today there is a renewed interest in the thought of both Schleiermacher and Hegel, not only for historical reasons, but also for their constructive theological significance. The new affirmation of Hegel, that is, the early Hegel, in German theology is a movement with which he was not intimately acquainted, but with which, nonetheless, his own theology has certain strong affinities.[30]

Tillich's attitude toward liberalism was dialectical. When he first became known in America, he tended to be classified with the neo-orthodox movement. He shared its critique of the liberal doctrine of progress and sounded similar notes on man's radical estrangement. He attacked the illusory schemes of self-salvation and pointed to the grace of God, to the new being in Christ, and to the Kingdom of God beyond history as the source of man's hope for a real fulfillment. The brand of liberalism he most readily rejected was the reduction of Christianity to the religion of Jesus. Liberalism's attempt to apply the methods of higher criticism to recover the historical Jesus beneath the various apostolic portraitures of Jesus as the Christ provided no adequate basis for Christian faith. He pronounced the search for the historical Jesus a failure, and believed that Bultmann's skepticism toward the sources was largely justified. In his student days the ascendant form of liberalism was the Ritschlian school. Tillich could never share the basic outlook of the Ritschlian theologians, neither their antimetaphysical bias nor their rejection of mysticism, neither their "back to Kant" posture nor their ethicization of Christianity. The University of Marburg was the center of the Kant-Ritschl sphere of influence. Tillich came from the University of Halle, where the traditions of German classical idealism and the theology of revivalism or pietism were mediated to him by his professors of philosophy and theology, the most often acknowledged of whom was Martin Kähler. This difference between Halle and Marburg symbolizes, perhaps even accounts for, the opposition between Tillich and Bultmann, the Marburg professor of New Testament. Bultmann was trained under Wilhelm Herrmann, who tended to teach dogmatics in

[30] *Inter alia,* Jürgen Moltmann, Wolf-Dieter Marsch, also Wolfhart Pannenberg.

the form of ethics. Tillich criticized Bultmann's demythologizing of the New Testament because only its ethical symbolism remains in his existentialist interpretation. The cosmic symbolism drops out of sight; it is removed as so much primitive mythology. Tillich, the ontologist *par excellence*, was passionately interested in the cosmic symbols. Therefore, demythologizing for Tillich did not mean the removal of such symbols, but deliteralization and interpretation. Since ethics is the focus of Bultmann's interpretation, the basic appeal is for decision; his is a theology of decision. By marked contrast Tillich's interpretation is in terms of ontological categories; he spoke of participation in the reality becoming transparent through the symbols. The idea of participation suggests that even the dimension of the unconscious is involved in the religious act; the idea of decision confines the religious act to the level of consciousness. In this light we can understand why Tillich's thinking was thoroughly sacramental; the decisionism of existentialist theology, on the other hand, leaves no room for the sacramental aspects of religion.

The main body of this volume deals with the great prophetic voices of the nineteenth century. Many of these were on the fringes of the Christian tradition, some even among its most bitter opponents. Tillich's selective treatment of this period focuses on the critical thrust from the philosophical side. He leaves largely out of account the developments in historical criticism, the investigation of the origins of primitive Christianity; also he pays little attention to the reconstructions of church doctrine that were being advanced by professional theologians. The reason for this selectivity is Tillich's conviction that the impetus to historical research and doctrinal reformulation came from changes in philosophical outlook. One has only to think of the dependence of historical critics like David F. Strauss and Ferdinand C. Baur on Hegel's philosophy of history, or of the dependence of dogmatic theologians like Alexander Schweizer and J. C. K. von Hofmann on Schleiermacher's philosophy of religion. The greatness of Tillich's interpretation lies in his masterful ability to detect and trace out the repercussions of a philosophical concept upon the subsequent course of things.

The more immediate reason, however, for slanting the selection toward the *philosophical challenges* to Christian theology was Tillich's own mind-set and vocational self-understanding. He communicated best with persons of a philosophical orientation and he had an almost evangelistic zeal to recommend the Christian message to the intellectual doubters and scoffers of the faith. His account of the nineteenth-century critics of Christianity is simultaneously a revelation of Tillich's intellectual autobiography; it serves as a mirroring of Tillich's dialogue with the radical questions which modern culture places on the theological agenda. I think it provides documentary evidence of the assertion that Tillich was a *radical* theologian who searched into the depths of the *tradition* to find positive answers to the questions of modern man. One of his last statements confirms this estimate of his own theological intention: "I presuppose in my theological thinking the entire history of Christian thought up until now, and I consider the attitude of those people who are in doubt or estrangement or opposition to everything ecclesiastical and religious, including Christianity. And I have to speak to them. My work is with those who ask questions, and for them I am here."[31]

Tillich's career was begun when liberal theology was on the wane; he lived through the transitions of theology from the rise of "crisis" theology to its transformation by Barth into neo-orthodoxy, and from the decline of Barth's influence to the paramountcy of Bultmannianism after World War II. In half a century theology had gone a full cycle; Tillich observed the signs of the revival of liberalism. In his last Chicago address entitled "The Significance of the History of Religions for the Systematic Theologian," Tillich turned to the question of the future of theology. He saw that we were standing at a kind of crossroads. Theology could go with the secular group down a road strewn with the paradoxes of "a religion of non-religion" or of a "theology-without-God language,"[32] or it could take an opposite route toward a theology of the history of religions. Tillich's hope for the future of theology was the latter. He saw no promising future for theology if it clings to the exclusive attitudes of neo-orthodoxy or joins the "death of God" group. Theology would have to meet a new challenge: "Therefore, as theologians, we have to break through two barriers against a

---

[31] Brown, ed., *Ultimate Concern*, p. 191.
[32] *The Future of Religions*, p. 80.

free approach to the history of religions: the orthodox-exclusive one and the secular-rejective one."[33] A theology fully informed by the universal revelation of God in the history of religions and purified by the concrete event on which Christianity as a particular religion is based points to a way beyond these two barriers. A religion which combines both the universal and concrete aspects Tillich called "The Religion of the Concrete Spirit."[34]

Tillich's vision of the future of theology was formed in part through his association with Professor Mircea Eliade in their joint seminars on "History of Religions and Systematic Theology" in 1964. Eliade reports how Tillich opened his mind to the new stimulus from the side of the history of religions. For Tillich, Eliade states, this was an occasion for the "renewal of his own Systematic Theology."[35] He did not ask his theological students to look upon his system of theology as an achievement that could not be transcended. To the end Tillich displayed an amazing freedom to press beyond the limits of his own system and to point out new options for theology. Eliade's picture of Tillich in their seminars is the way Tillich himself would have had us remember him; it is the picture of "how Tillich was fighting his way to a new understanding of systematic theology."[36]

[33] *Ibid.*, p. 83.
[34] *Ibid.*, p. 87.
[35] "Paul Tillich and the History of Religions," *op. cit.*, p. 33.
[36] *Ibid.*, p. 35.

PART I

Introduction:
The Concept of Dogma

ALL human experience implies the element of thought, simply because the intellectual or spiritual life of man is embodied in his language. Language is thought expressed in words spoken and heard. There is no human existence without thought. The emotionalism that is so rampant in religion is not more but less than thinking, and reduces religion to the level of sub-human experience of reality.

Schleiermacher emphasized the function of "feeling" in religion and Hegel emphasized "thought", giving rise to the tension between them. Hegel said that even dogs have feeling, but man has thought. This was based on an unintentional misunderstanding of what Schleiermacher meant by "feeling", one that we often find repeated even today. Yet it expresses the truth that man cannot be without thought. He must think even if he is a most pious Christian without any theological education. Even in religion we give names to special objects; we distinguish acts of the divine; we relate symbols to each other and explain their meanings. There is language in every religion, and where there is language there are universals or concepts that one must use even at the most primitive level of thought. It is interesting that this conflict between Hegel and Schleiermacher was anticipated already in the third century by Clement of Alexandria who said that if animals had a religion, it would be mute, without words.

Reality precedes thought; it is equally true, however, that thought shapes reality. They are interdependent; one cannot be abstracted from the other. We should remember this when we come to the discussions on the trinity and christology. Here on the basis of much thought the church fathers made decisions which have influenced the life of all Christians ever since, even the most primitive.

There is also the development of methodological thought which proceeds according to the rules of logic and uses methods in order to deal with experiences. When this methodological thought is expressed in speaking or writing and communicated to other people, it produces theological doctrines. This is a development beyond the more primitive use of thought. Ideally such a development leads to a theological system. Now a system is not something in which to dwell. Everyone who dwells within a system feels after some time that it becomes a prison. If you produce a systematic theology, as I have done, you try to go beyond it in order not to be imprisoned in it. Nevertheless, the system is necessary because it is the form of consistency. I have found that students who express the greatest misgivings about the systematic character of my theology are the very ones who are most impatient when discovering two of my statements that contradict each other. They are unhappy to find one point in which the hidden system has a gap. But when I develop the system further to close this gap, they feel that is a mean attempt on my part to imprison them. This is a very interesting double reaction. Yet it is understandable, because if the system is taken as a final answer, it becomes even worse than a prison. If we understand the system, however, as an attempt to bring theological concepts to a consistent form of expression in which there are no contradictions, then we cannot avoid it. Even if you think in fragments, as some philosophers and theologians (and some great ones) have done, then each fragment implicitly contains a system. When you read the fragments of Nietzsche—in my opinion the greatest fragmentist in philosophy—you can find implied in each of them a whole system of life. So a system cannot be avoided unless you choose to make nonsensical or self-contradictory statements. Of course, this is sometimes done.

The system has the danger not only of becoming a prison, but also of moving within itself. It may separate itself from reality and become something which is, so to speak, above the reality it is supposed to describe. Therefore, my interest is not so much in the systems as such, but in their power to express the reality of the church and its life.

The doctrines of the church have been called dogmas. In

former times this type of course used to be called "the history of dogma". Now we call it "the history of Christian thought", but this is only a change in name. Actually, nobody would dare to present a complete history of what every theologian in the Christian Church has thought. That would be an ocean of contradictory ideas. The purpose of this course is quite different, namely, to show those thoughts which have become accepted expressions of the life of the church. This is what the word "dogma" originally meant.

The concept of dogma is one of those things which stand between the church and the secular world. Most secular people are afraid of the dogmas of the church, and not only secular people but also members of the churches themselves. "Dogma" is like a red cloth waved before the bull in a bull fight; it provokes anger or aggressiveness, and in some cases flight. I think the latter is most often the case with secular people in relation to the church. To understand this we have to examine the history of the concept of dogma, which is very interesting.

The first step in this history is the use of "dogma" derived from the Greek word *dokein*, which means "to think, imagine, or hold an opinion". In the schools of Greek philosophy preceding Christianity *dogmata* were the doctrines which differentiated the various schools from each other, the Academics (Plato), the Peripatetics (Aristotle), the Stoics, the Skeptics, and the Pythagoreans. Each of these schools had its own fundamental doctrines. If someone wanted to become a member of one of these schools, he had to accept at least the basic presuppositions which distinguished that school from the others. So even the philosophical schools were not without their *dogmata*.

In similar fashion the Christian doctrines were understood as *dogmata* which distinguished the Christian school from the philosophical schools. This was accepted as natural; it was not like a red cloth which produces anger. The Christian dogma in the early period was the expression of what Christians accepted when they entered Christian congregations, at great risk and with a tremendous transformation of their lives. So a dogma was never just a theoretical statement by an individual; it was the expression of a reality, the reality of the church.

Secondly, all dogmas were formulated negatively, that is, as reactions against misinterpretations from inside the church.

This is true even of the Apostles' Creed. Take the first article of the Creed, "I believe in God the Father Almighty, Maker of heaven and earth." This is not simply a statement that says something in itself. It is at the same time the rejection of dualism, formulated after a life-and-death struggle of a hundred years. The same is true of the other dogmas. The later they are, the more clearly they show this negative character. We may call them protective doctrines, for they were intended to protect the substance of the biblical message. To an extent the substance was fluid; of course, there was a fixed core, the confession that Jesus was the Christ. But beyond this everything was in motion. When new doctrines arose which seemed to undercut the fundamental confession, the protective doctrines were added to it. In this way the dogmas arose. Luther recognized this fact that the dogmas were not the result of a theoretical interest, but arose from the need to protect the Christian substance.

Since each new protective statement was itself subject to misinterpretation, there was always the need for sharper theoretical formulations. In order to do this it was necessary to use philosophical terms. This is how the many philosophical concepts entered into the Christian dogmas. It was not that people were interested in them as philosophical concepts. Luther was very frank about this; he openly declared that he disliked terms like "trinity", "*homoousios*", etc., but he admitted that they must be used, however unfortunate, because we have no better ones. Theoretical formulations must be made when other people formulate doctrines theoretically in such a way that the substance seems to be endangered.

The next step in the history of this concept was for dogmas to become accepted as canon law by the church. Law according to the canon is the rule of thought or behavior. Canon law is the ecclesiastical law to which everybody who belongs to the church must subject himself. Thus the dogma receives a legal sanction. In the Roman Church the dogma is part of canon law; its authority comes from the legal realm. This is in line with the general development of the Roman Church; the word "Roman" has the connotation of legalistic development.

However, the tremendous reaction against dogma in the last four centuries would perhaps not have been created without one further step: the ecclesiastical law became accepted as civil law by medieval society. This meant that the person who breaks the canonic law of doctrines is not only a heretic, one who disagrees with the fundamental doctrines of the church, but he is also a criminal against the state. It is this last point which has produced the radical reaction in modern times against dogma. Since the heretic undermines not only the church but also the state, he must be not only excommunicated but also delivered into the hands of the civil authorities to be punished as a criminal. It was this state of the dogma against which the Enlightenment was fighting. The Reformation itself was still pretty much in line with the prior development of dogma. But certainly since the Enlightenment all liberal thinking has been characterized by the attempt to avoid dogma. This trend was also supported by the development of science. Science and philosophy had to be given complete freedom in order to make possible their creative growth.

In his famous *History of Dogma* Adolph von Harnack raised the question whether dogma has not come to an end in view of its dissolution in the early period of the Enlightenment. He concedes that there is still dogma in orthodox Protestantism, but he believes that the last step in the history of dogma was reached when the Protestant dogma was dissolved by the Enlightenment. Since then there is really no dogma in Protestantism. Now this implies a very narrow concept of dogma, and Harnack is aware that he is using the concept in a narrow sense, namely, in the sense of the christological-trinitarian doctrine of the ancient church. Reinhold Seeberg emphasized that, on the contrary, the dogmatic development did not end with the coming of the Enlightenment, but is still going on.

Here we face a very important systematic question. Are there any dogmas in present-day Protestantism? Those of you who enter the ministry must take some kind of examination by the church, which is not so much an examination of knowledge as of faith. The churches want to know whether you agree with their fundamental dogmatic tenets. They often conduct these examinations in a very narrow way, without much understanding of the developments in theology since Protestant Orthodoxy. Many students have an inner revolt against these examinations of faith, but you should not forget that you are entering a particular group which is different from other groups. First of all, it is a Christian and not a pagan group; or it is a Protestant and not a

Catholic group; and within Protestantism it could be either an Episcopalian or a Baptist group. Now this means that the church has a justified interest in having those who represent it show some acceptance of its foundations. Every baseball team demands that its members accept its rules and standards. Why should the church leave it completely to the arbitrary feelings of the individual? This is impossible.

It is one of the tasks of systematic theology to help the churches to solve this problem in a way which is not too narrow-minded and not dependent on the sixteenth- and seventeenth-century theologians. There is some fundamental point which is accepted if somebody accepts the church. I believe that it is not a matter of the church requiring its ministers to accept a series of dogmas. How could they honestly say that they have no doubts about any of these dogmas? If they had no doubts, they would hardly be very good Christians, because the intellectual life is as ambiguous as the moral life. And who would call himself morally perfect? How then could someone call himself intellectually perfect? The element of doubt is an element in faith itself. What the church should do is to accept someone who says that the faith for which the church stands is a matter of his ultimate concern, which he wants to serve with all his strength. But if he is asked to say what he believes about this or that doctrine, he is driven into a kind of dishonesty. If he says he agrees completely with a given doctrine, for example, the doctrine of the Virgin Birth, either he is dishonest or he must cease to think. If he cannot cease to think, he must also doubt. That is the problem. I think the only solution on Protestant soil is to say that this whole set of doctrines represents one's own ultimate concern, that one desires to serve in this group which has this basis as its ultimate concern. But one can never promise not to doubt any one of these particular doctrines.

The dogma should not be abolished but interpreted in such a way that it is no longer a suppressive power which produces dishonesty or flight. Instead it is a wonderful and profound expression of the actual life of the church. In this sense I will try to show that in discussing these dogmas, even when they are expressed in the most abstract formulations by means of difficult Greek concepts, we are dealing with those things which the church believed to be the most adequate expression for its life and devotion in its life-and-death struggle against the pagan and

Jewish worlds outside, and against all the disintegrating tendencies which appeared inside. My conclusion is that we should estimate the dogma very highly; there is something great about it. But it should not be taken as a set of particular doctrines to which one must subscribe. This is against the spirit of the dogma, against the spirit of Christianity.

CHAPTER I

The Preparation for Christianity

A. THE *Kairos*

ACCORDING to the apostle Paul there does not always exist the possibility that that can happen which, for example, happened in the appearance of Jesus as the Christ. This happened in one special moment of history when everything was ready for it to happen. We will now discuss the "readiness". Paul speaks of the *kairos* in describing the feeling that the time was ripe, mature, or prepared. This Greek word is an example of the richness of the Greek language in comparison with the poverty of modern languages. We have only one word for "time". The Greeks had two words, *chronos* and *kairos*. *Chronos* is clock time, time which is measured, as we have it in words like "chronology" and "chronometer". *Kairos* is not the quantitative time of the clock, but the qualitative time of the occasion, the right time. (Cf. its use in some of the Gospel stories.) There are things that happen when the right time, the *kairos*, has not yet come. *Kairos* is the time which indicates that something has happened which makes an action possible or impossible. We all experience moments in our lives when we feel that now is the right time to do something, now we are mature enough, now we can make the decision. This is the *kairos*. It was in this sense that Paul and the early church spoke of the *kairos*, the right time for the coming of the Christ. The early church, and Paul to a certain extent, tried to show why the time in which Christ appeared was the right time, how his appearance was made possible by a providential constellation of factors.

What we must do now is to show the preparation for Christian theology in the world situation into which Jesus came. We will do this from a theological point of view—there are others— and thus provide an understanding of the possibilities of a Christian theology. It is not as if the revelation from Christ fell down like a stone from heaven, as some theologians seem to believe. "Here it is; you must take it or leave it." This is contrary to Paul. Actually there is a universal revelatory power going through all history and preparing for that which Christianity considers to be the ultimate revelation.

B. The Universalism of the Roman Empire

The actual situation into which the New Testament event came was the universalism of the Roman Empire. This meant something negative and positive at the same time. Negatively it meant the breakdown of national religions and cultures. Positively it meant that the idea of mankind as a whole could be conceived at that time. The Roman Empire produced a definite consciousness of world history, in contrast to accidental national histories. World history is now not only a purpose which will be actualized in history, in the sense of the prophets; instead it has become an empirical reality. This is the positive meaning of Rome. Rome represents the universal monarchy in which the whole known world is united. This idea has been taken over by the Roman Church, but applied to the pope. It is still actual in the Roman Church; it means that Rome still claims the monarchic power over all the world, following the Roman Empire in this. It is perhaps an important remark generally that we should never forget that the Roman Church is *Roman*, that the development of this church is influenced not only by Christianity but also by the Roman Empire, by its greatness and by its idea of law. The Roman Church took over the heritage of the Roman Empire. We should never forget this fact. If we are tempted to evaluate the Roman Church more highly than we should, we ought to ask ourselves: how many Roman elements are in it, and to what extent are they valid for us in our culture? We should do the same thing with the Greek philosophical concepts which created the Christian dogma. To what degree are they valid today? Of course, it is not necessary to reject something simply because it happens to be Roman or Greek, but neither is it necessary to accept something which the church has derived from Rome or Greece, even if sanctioned by a dogmatic decision.

C. HELLENISTIC PHILOSOPHY

Within this realm of one world, of a world history and monarchy created by Rome, we have Greek thought. This is the Hellenistic period of Greek philosophy. We distinguish the classical period of Greek thought, which ends with the death of Aristotle, from the Hellenistic period which includes the Stoics, Epicureans, Neo-Pythagoreans, Skeptics, and Neo-Platonists. This Hellenistic period is the immediate source of much of Christian thought. It was not so much classical Greek thinking but Hellenistic thought which influenced early Christianity.

Again I want to distinguish the negative and the positive elements in Greek thought in the period of the *kairos*, the period of the ancient world coming to an end. The negative side is what we would call Skepticism. Skepticism, not only in the school of the Skeptics but also in the other schools of Greek philosophy, is the end of the tremendous and admirable attempt to build a world of meaning on the basis of an interpretation of reality in objective and rational terms. Greek philosophy had undercut the ancient mythological and ritual traditions. At the time of Socrates and the Sophists it became obvious that these traditions were not valid any more. Sophism is the revolution of the subjective mind against the old traditions. But life must go on; the meaning of life in all realms had yet to be probed, in politics, law, art, social relations, knowledge, religion, etc. This the Greek philosophers tried to do. They were not people sitting behind their desks writing philosophical books. If they had done nothing but philosophize about philosophy, we would have forgotten their names long ago. But they were people who took upon themselves the task of creating a spiritual world by observing reality objectively as it was given to them, interpreting it in terms of analytic and synthetic reason.

1. *Skepticism*

This great attempt of the Greek philosophers to create a world of meaning broke down at the end of the ancient world and produced what I call the skeptical end of the ancient development. Originally *skepsis* meant "observing" things. But it has received the negative sense of looking at every dogma, even the *dogmata* of the Greek schools of philosophy, and thereby undercutting them. The Skeptics were those who doubted the statements of all schools of philosophy. What is perhaps even more important is that these schools of philosophy, for example, the Platonic Academy, took a lot of these skeptical elements into themselves. Skepticism did not go beyond probabilism, while the other schools became pragmatic. Thus a skeptical mood entered all the schools and permeated the whole life of the later ancient world. This skepticism was a very serious matter of life. Again it was not a matter of sitting behind one's desk and finding out that everything can be doubted. That is comparatively easy. Rather, it was an inner breakdown of all convictions. The consequence was— and this was very characteristic of the Greek mind—that if they were no longer able to render theoretical judgments, they believed that they could not act practically either. Therefore, they introduced the doctrine of *epochē*, which meant "restraining, keeping down, neither making a judgment nor acting, deciding neither theoretically nor practically." This doctrine of *epochē* meant the resignation of judgment in every respect. For this reason these people went into the desert with a suit or gown. The later Christian monks followed them in this respect, because they also were in despair over the possibility of living in this world. Some of the skeptics of the ancient church were very serious people, and drew the consequences which our snobbistic skeptics today are usually unwilling to do, who have a very good time while doubting everything. The Greek skeptics retired from life in order to be consistent.

This element of skepticism was an important preparation for Christianity. The Greek schools, the Epicureans, Stoics, Academics, Peripatetics, Neo-Pythagoreans, were not only schools in the sense in which we today speak of philosophical schools, for example, the school of Dewey or Whitehead. A Greek philosophical school was also a cultic community; it was half-ritual and half-philosophical in character. These people wanted to live according to the doctrines of their masters. During this period when the skeptical mood permeated the ancient world, they wanted certainty above all; they demanded it in order to live.

Their answer was that their great teachers, Plato or Aristotle, Zeno the Stoic or Epicurus, and at a later time, Plotinus, were not merely thinkers or professors, but they were inspired men. Long before Christianity the idea of inspiration was developed in these Greek schools; the founders of these schools were inspired. When members of these schools later entered into discussion with Christians, they said, for example, that Heraclitus, not Moses, was inspired. This doctrine of inspiration gave Christianity also a chance to enter into the world. Pure reason alone is not able to build up a reality in which one can live.

What was said about the character of the founders of these philosophical schools was very similar to what the Christians also said about the founder of their church. It is interesting that a man like Epicurus—who later was so much attacked by the Christians that only some of his fragments remain—was called *soter* by his pupils. This is the Greek word which the New Testament uses and which we translate as "savior". Epicurus the philosopher was called a savior. What does this mean? He is usually regarded as a man who always had a good time in his beautiful gardens and who taught an anti-Christian hedonistic philosophy. The ancient world thought quite differently about Epicurus. He was called *soter* because he did the greatest thing anyone could do for his followers: he liberated them from anxiety. Epicurus, with his materialistic system of atoms, liberated them from the fear of demons which permeated the whole life of the ancient world. This shows what a serious thing philosophy was at that time.

Another consequence of this skeptical mood was what the Stoics called *apatheia* (apathy), which means being without feelings toward the vital drives of life such as desires, joys, pains, and instead being beyond all these in the state of wisdom. They knew that only a few people could reach this state. Those who went into the desert as Skeptics showed that they were able to do so to a certain extent. Behind all this, of course, stands the earlier criticism of the mythological gods and the traditional rites. The criticism of mythology happened in Greece about the same time that Second Isaiah did it in Judea. It was a very similar kind of criticism and had the effect of undercutting the belief in the gods of polytheism.

2. *The Platonic Tradition*

We have dealt with the negative side in Greek thought at the time of the *kairos*. But there were also some positive elements. First we will take up the Platonic tradition. The idea of transcendence, that there is something that surpasses empirical reality, was prepared for Christian theology in the Platonic tradition. Plato spoke of essential reality, of "ideas" (*ousia*) as the true essences of things. At the same time we find in Plato, and even stronger in later Platonism and Neo-Platonism, a trend toward the devaluation of existence. The material world has no ultimate value in comparison with the essential world. Also in Plato the inner aim of human existence is described—somewhere in the *Philebus*, but also practically everywhere in Plato—as becoming similar to God as much as possible. God is the spiritual sphere. The inner *telos* of human existence is participation in the spiritual, divine sphere as much as possible. This element in the Platonic tradition was used especially by the Cappadocian Fathers of the church to describe the ultimate aim of human existence.

A third doctrine besides the idea of transcendence and the *telos* of human existence described the soul as falling down from an eternal participation in the essential or spiritual world, being on earth in a body, then trying to get rid of its bondage to the body, and finally reaching an elevation above the material world. This happens in steps and degrees. This element was also taken into the church, not only by all Christian mystics, but also by the official church fathers to a great extent.

The fourth point in which the Platonic tradition was important was its idea of providence. This seems to us to be a Christian idea, but it was already formulated by Plato in his later writings. It was a tremendous attempt to overcome the anxiety of fate and death in the ancient world. In the late ancient world the anxiety of accident and necessity, or fate, as we would call it today, represented by the Greek goddesses *Tychē* and *Haimarmene*, was a very powerful thing. In Romans 8, where we have the greatest hymn of triumph in the New Testament, we hear that it is the function of Christ to overcome the demonic forces of fate. The fact that Plato anticipated this situation by his doctrine of providence is one of his greatest contributions. This providence, coming from the highest god, gives us the courage to escape the vicissitudes of fate.

A fifth element was added to the Platonic tradition which came from Aristotle. The divine is a form without matter, perfect in itself. This is the profoundest idea in Aristotle. This highest form, called "God", is moving the world, not causally by pushing it from the outside, but by driving everything finite toward him by means of love. In spite of his apparently scientific attitude toward reality, Aristotle developed one of the greatest systems of love. He said that God, the highest form, or pure actuality (*actus purus*), as he called it, moves everything by being loved by everything. Everything has the desire to unite itself with the highest form, to get rid of the lower forms in which it lives, where it is in the bondage of matter. Later the Aristotelian God, as the highest form, entered into Christian theology and exerted a tremendous influence upon it.

3. *The Stoics*

The Stoics were more important than Plato and Aristotle together for the life of the late ancient world. The life of the educated man in the ancient world at this time was shaped mostly by the Stoic tradition. In my book, *The Courage to Be*, I have dealt with the Stoic idea of the courage to take fate and death upon oneself. There I show that Christianity and the Stoics are the great competitors in the whole Western world. But here I want to show something else. Christianity took from its great competitor many fundamental ideas. The first is the doctrine of the Logos, a doctrine that may bring you to despair when you study the history of trinitarian and christological thought. The dogmatic development of Christianity cannot be understood without it.

Logos means "word". But it also refers to the meaning of a word, the reasonable structure which is indicated by a word. Therefore, Logos can also mean the universal law of reality. This is what Heraclitus meant by it, who was the first to use this word philosophically. The Logos for him was the law which determines the movements of all reality.

For the Stoics the Logos was the divine power which is present in everything that is. There are three aspects to it, all of which become extremely important in the later development. The first is the law of nature. The Logos is the principle according to which all natural things move. It is the divine seed, the creative divine power, which makes anything what it is. And it is the creative power of movement of all things. Secondly, Logos means the moral law. With Immanuel Kant we could call this the "practical reason", the law which is innate in every human being when he accepts himself as a personality, with the dignity and greatness of a person. When we see the term "natural law" in classical books, we should not think of physical laws, but of moral laws. For example, when we speak of the "rights of man" as embodied in the American Constitution, we are speaking of natural law.

Thirdly, Logos also means man's ability to recognize reality; we could call it "theoretical reason". It is man's ability to reason. Because man has the Logos in himself, he can discover it in nature and history. From this it follows for Stoicism that the man who is determined by the natural law, the Logos, is the *logikos*, the wise man. But the Stoics were not optimists. They did not believe that everybody was a wise man. Perhaps there were only a few who ever reached this ideal. All the others were either fools or stood somewhere between the wise and the foolish. So Stoicism held a basic pessimism about the majority of human beings.

Originally the Stoics were Greeks; later they were Romans. Some of the most famous Stoics were Roman emperors, for example, Marcus Aurelius. They applied the concept of the Logos to the political situation for which they were responsible. The meaning of the natural law was that every man participates in reason by virtue of the fact that he is a human being. From this basis they derived laws far superior to many that we find in the Christian Middle Ages. They gave universal citizenship to every human being because everyone potentially participates in reason. Of course, they did not believe that people were actually reasonable, but they presupposed that through education they could become so. Granting Roman citizenship to all citizens of the conquered nations was a tremendous equalizing step. Women, slaves, and children, who were regarded as inferior beings under the old Roman law, became equalized by the laws of the Roman emperors. This was done not by Christianity but by the Stoics, who derived this idea from their belief in the universal Logos in which everyone participates. (Of course, Christianity holds the same idea on a different basis: all human beings are the children of God the Father.) Thus the Stoics conceived of the idea of a state embracing the whole world, based on the common rationality of everybody. This was something which Christianity could take up and develop. The difference was that the Stoics did not have the concept of sin. They had the concept of foolishness, but not sin. Therefore, salvation in Stoicism is a salvation through reaching wisdom. In Christianity salvation is brought about by divine grace. These two approaches are in conflict with each other to the present day.

4. Eclecticism

Eclecticism is another reality which was taken over by the Christian Church. This comes from a Greek word meaning to choose some possibilities out of many. Americans should not have contempt for this because in this respect as in so many others they are like the ancient Romans. The Eclectics were not creative philosophers like the Greeks. The Roman thinkers were often at the same time politicians and statesmen. As Eclectics they did not create new systems. Instead, they chose (Cicero, for example) the most important concepts from the classical Greek systems which they thought would be pragmatically useful for Roman citizens. From a pragmatic point of view they chose what would make possible the best way of living for a Roman citizen, as a citizen of the world state. The main ideas which they chose, which we find again in the eighteenth-century Enlightenment, were the following: the idea of providence, which provides a feeling of safety to the life of the people; the idea of God as innate in everybody, which induces fear of God and discipline; the idea of moral freedom and responsibility, which makes it possible to educate and to hold people accountable for moral failure; and finally the idea of immortality, which threatens with another world those who escape punishment in this one. All these ideas were in some way a preparation for the Christian mission.

D. THE INTER-TESTAMENTAL PERIOD

We come now to the Hellenistic period of the Jewish religion. In Judaism during the inter-testamental period there developed ideas and attitudes which deeply influenced the apostolic age, that is, Jesus, the apostles, and the writers of the New Testament.

The development in the idea of God during this period between the Testaments was toward a radical transcendence. God becomes more and more transcendent, and for this reason he becomes more and more universal. But a God who is both absolutely transcendent and absolutely universal has lost many of the concrete traits which the God of a nation has. For this reason names were introduced to preserve some of the concreteness of the divinity, names like "heaven". For example, in the New Testament we often find the term "kingdom of heaven" in place of "kingdom of God". At the same time, the abstraction is carried on under two influences: (1) the prohibition against using the name of God; (2) the struggle against anthropomorphisms, that is, seeing God in the image (*morphē*) of man (*anthropos*). Consequently the passions of the God of the Old Testament disappear and the abstract oneness is emphasized. This made it possible for the Greek philosophers, who had introduced the same radical abstraction with respect to God, and the Jewish universalists to unite on the idea of God. It was Philo of Alexandria, in particular, who carried through this union.

When God becomes abstract, however, it is not sufficient to hypostasize some of his qualities, such as heaven, height, glory, etc. Mediating beings must appear between God and man. During the inter-testamental period these mediating beings became more and more important for practical piety. First, there were the angels, deteriorated gods and goddesses from surrounding paganism. During the period when the prophets fought against polytheism, they could not play any role. When the danger of polytheism was completely overcome, as it was in later Judaism, the angels could reappear without much danger of a relapse into it. Even so, however, the New Testament is aware of this danger and warns against the cult of the angels.

The second type of figure was the Messiah. The Messiah became a transcendent being, the king of paradise. In the Book of Daniel, which is dependent on Persian religion, the Messiah is also called the "Son of Man" who will judge the world. In Daniel this term is probably used for Israel, but later it became the figure of the "man from above" as described by Paul in I Corinthians 15. Thirdly, the names of God are increased and become almost living figures. The most important of these figures is the Wisdom of God, which appears already in the Old Testament. Wisdom created the world, appeared in it, and then returned to heaven since it did not find a place among men. This is very close to the idea in the Prologue of the Fourth Gospel.

Another of these powers between God and man is the *shekinah*, the dwelling of God on earth. Another is the *memra'*, the Word of God, which later became so important in the Fourth Gospel. Still another is the "Spirit of God", which in the Old Testament means God in action. Now, however, it became a partly independent figure between the most high God and man. The Logos became most important for it united the Jewish *memra'* with the Greek philosophical *logos*. Logos in Philo is the *protogenēs huios theou*, the first-born Son of God. These mediating beings between the most high God and man to some extent replace the immediacy of the relationship to God. As in Christianity, particularly in Roman Catholic Christianity, the ever more transcendent idea of God was made acceptable to the popular mind by the introduction of the saints into practical piety. The official doctrine remained monotheistic; the saints were to receive only veneration, never adoration.

Between man and God there arose also another world of beings having great power, namely, the realm of demons. There were evil as well as good angels. These evil angels are not only the agencies of temptation and punishment under God's direction, but they are also a realm of power in opposition to God. This comes out clearly in Jesus' conversation with the Pharisees concerning the divine or demonic power in connection with his exorcism of demons. This belief in demons permeated the daily life of that time and was also the subject of the highest speculations. Although there was an element of dualism here, it never reached the state of an ontological dualism. Here again Judaism was able to introduce a number of ideas from Persia, including the demonology of Persian religion in which the demons have the same status as the gods, but it never lapsed into an ontological dualism. All the demonic powers derive their power from the one God; they have no standing on their own in an ultimate sense. This comes out in the mythology of the fallen angels. The evil angels as created beings are good, but as fallen they are evil angels, and therefore they are responsible and punishable. They are not simply creations of an anti-divine being. Here we have the first anti-pagan dogma.

Another influence from this period on the New Testament is the elevation of the future into a coming aeon. In the late apocalyptic period of Jewish history, world history was divided into two aeons, into this aeon in which we are living (*aiōn houtos*) and the coming aeon which is expected (*aiōn mellon*). This aeon is evaluated very pessimistically, while the coming aeon is awaited with ecstasy. The coming aeon is not only a political idea; it goes beyond the political hopes of the Maccabean period in which the Maccabees defended the Jewish people against tyranny. Nor was it a statement of the prophetic message; the prophetic message was much more historical and this-worldly. These apocalyptic ideas were cosmological; the whole cosmos participates in these two aeons. This aeon is controlled by demonic forces; the world, even nature itself, is ageing and fading away. One of the reasons for this is that man has subjected himself to the demonic forces and is disobedient against the law. Adam's fall has produced the universal destiny of death. This idea was developed from the brief story of the fall in Genesis into a system as we find it in Paul. This fall is confirmed by every individual through his actual sin. This aeon is under a tragic fate, but in spite of that the individual is responsible for it.

During this inter-testamental period the piety of the law gains in importance, in part replacing the piety of the cult. Of course, the temple still exists, but the synagogue is developed alongside it as a religious school. The synagogue becomes the form in which the decisive religious life develops. The law was not evaluated in the negative way in which we usually do it; for the Jews it was a gift and a joy. The law was eternal, always in God and pre-existent in the same way that later Christian theology said that Jesus was pre-existent. The contents of the law provided for the organization of the whole of life, down to the smallest functions. Every moment of life was under God. This was the profound idea of the legalism of the Pharisees which Jesus attacked so vigorously. For this legalism produces an intolerable burden. There are always two possibilities in religion if an intolerable burden is placed on thought and action; the first is the way of compromise, which is the way of the majority. This means that the burden is reduced to the point that it can be endured. The second is the way of despair, which was the way of people like Paul, Augustine, and Luther. In IV Esdras we read: "We who have received the law shall be lost because of our sins, but the law never will be lost." Here a mood is expressed which is reflected in many Pauline sayings, a mood that permeated late Judaism during the period between the Testaments. Many of these ideas left their imprint on the New Testament.

E. The Mystery Religions

The mystery religions were also influential on early Christian theology. These mystery religions should not be equated with mysticism as such. Mysticism is something that we find in Philo, for example. He developed a doctrine of ecstasy, or *ek-stasis*, which means "standing outside oneself". This is the highest form of piety which lies beyond faith. This mysticism unites prophetic ecstasy with "enthusiasm", a word which comes from *en-theos-mania*, meaning to possess the divine. From this there comes finally the fully developed mystical system of the Neo-Platonists, for example, of Dionysius the Areopagite. In this mystical system the ecstasy of the individual person leads to a union with the One, with the Absolute, with God.

But besides this development of mysticism we have the even more important development of the concrete mystery gods. These mystery gods are in a sense monotheistic, that is, the person who is initiated into a given mystery has a concrete god who is, at the same time, the only god. However, it was possible to be initiated into more than one mystery. This means that the figures of the mystery gods were exchangeable. There is lacking here the exclusiveness of Yahweh in the Old Testament.

These mystery gods greatly influenced the Christian cult and theology. If someone is initiated into a mystery, as later the Christians initiated their members into the congregations by steps, he participates in the mystery god and in the experiences of that deity. In Romans 6 Paul describes such experiences with respect to Jesus in terms of participation in his death and resurrection. An ecstatic experience is produced in the mystery activities. Those who participate are brought into a state of deep sorrow over the death of the god, and then after a time they have an ecstatic experience of the god resurrected. The suffering god is described in these mysteries. Ever since the Delphic Apollo we have the idea of the participation of God in the suffering of man. Apollo at Delphi had to pay for the guilt of slaying the powers of the underworld which have their own rights. Then there are the methods of introduction through psychological means. Intoxication is brought about by a change of light and darkness, by ascetic fasting, by incense, sounds, music, etc.

These mysteries also had an esoteric character. Initiation could only follow upon a harsh process of selection and preparation. In this way the mystery of the performances was protected against profanation. Later in the Christian congregations a similar thing took place in order to protect against betrayal to the pagan persecutors.

F. The Method of the New Testament

All of the elements we have discussed were a preparation for the rise of Christianity. The decisive preparation, however, was the event which is documented in the New Testament. Here we cannot present a New Testament theology, but we can show, by means of a few examples, how the New Testament received from the surrounding religions categories of interpretation and transformed them in the light of the reality of Jesus as the Christ. This means that there were always two steps, reception and transformation. The categories which had developed in the various religions, in the Old Testament, and in the inter-testamental period, were used to interpret the event of Jesus' appearance, but the meanings of these categories were transformed in being applied to him.

With respect to christology, for example, Messiah is the ancient prophetic symbol. This symbol was applied to Jesus by the early disciples, perhaps at the very beginning of their encounter with him. This was a great paradox. On the one hand, it was adequate because Jesus brings the new being; on the other hand, it was inadequate because many of the connotations of the term "Messiah" go beyond the actual appearance of Jesus. According to the records, Jesus himself realized the difficulty of this double judgment. Therefore, he prohibited his disciples to use this term. Now it may be that this is a later construction of the records;

but however that may be, it does mirror the double judgment that this category is both adequate and inadequate.

The same thing is true of the "Son of Man" concept. On the one hand, it is adequate, and perhaps used by Jesus himself, for it points to the divine power present in him to bring the new aeon. On the other hand, it is inadequate because the Son of Man was supposed to appear in power and glory.

The term "Son of David" was also used. It is adequate since he was supposed to be the fulfiller of all the prophecies. Yet it is inadequate because David was a king, so "Son of David" can indicate a political leader and king. Jesus resisted this misunderstanding when he said that David himself called the Messiah his Lord.

The "Son of God" is an adequate term because of the special relationship and intimate communion between Jesus and God. At the same time it is inadequate because "Son of God" is a very familiar pagan concept. The pagan gods propagated sons on earth. Because of this the words "only begotten" were added and he was called "eternal". The Jews had difficulty with this term because of its pagan connotations. They could speak of Israel as "Son of God" but they could not apply it to an individual.

The title "kyrios" means Lord; it is adequate because of its use in the Old Testament where it is an expression of divine power. At the same time it is inadequate because the mystery gods were also *kyrioi*, lords, and, furthermore, Jesus was pictured concretely as a finite being. It was adequate because the mystery gods were objects of mystical union, and so was Jesus. For Paul especially, a person could be in Christ (*en Christō*), that is, in the power, holiness, and fear of his being.

Finally, the concept "Logos" was adequate insofar as it expressed the universal self-manifestation of God in all forms of reality. In Greek philosophy and Jewish symbolism it is the cosmic principle of creation. Yet it is inadequate because the Logos is a universal principle, whereas Jesus is a concrete reality. His is a concrete personal life described by this term. This is expressed in the great paradox of Christianity: the Logos became flesh. Here we have a perfect example of how the meaning of a term, with all the connotations it had from the past, can be transformed in expressing the Christian message. The idea that the universal Logos became flesh could never have been derived from the

Greek thought. Therefore, the church fathers emphasized again and again that while the Greek philosophers possessed the idea of the universal Logos, what was peculiarly Christian was that the Logos became flesh in a personal life.

The greatness of the New Testament is that it was able to use words, concepts, and symbols which had developed in the history of religions and at the same time preserve the picture of Jesus who was interpreted by them. The spiritual power of the New Testament was great enough to take all these concepts into Christianity, with all their pagan and Jewish connotations, without losing the basic reality, namely, the event of Jesus as the Christ, which these concepts were supposed to interpret.

CHAPTER II

Theological Developments in the Ancient Church

A. The Apostolic Fathers

We come now to the apostolic fathers, the earliest post-biblical writers we know of, some of them even earlier than the later books of the New Testament. These apostolic fathers, Ignatius of Antioch, Clement of Rome, "The Shepherd" of Hermas, and others, were more dependent on a Christian conformism that had gradually developed than on the outspoken position of Paul in his Letters. Paul's influence during this period was felt more indirectly through John and Ignatius. The reason for this, at least in part, was that the controversy with the Jews was a matter of the past; Paul's conflict with the Jewish Christians did not have to be continued. Instead of that, the positive elements in the faith which could provide an understandable content for the pagans had to be brought out. In general one could say that in the period of the apostolic fathers the great visions of the first ecstatic breakthrough had disappeared, leaving in their place a given set of ideas which produced a kind of ecclesiastical conformity, and making the missionary work possible. Some people have complained about this development, deploring that so early after the second generation of Christians the power of the Spirit was on the wane. This is an unavoidable thing, however, in all creative periods. One needs only to think of the Reformation. After the breakthrough and after the second generation which received the breakthrough, a fixation or concentration on some special points begins. There are the educational needs to preserve what was given earlier.

Nevertheless, this period of the apostolic fathers is extremely important, even though it may have considerably lost its spiritual power in comparison with the preceding period of the apostles, since it preserved what was needed for the life of the congregations. The first question to be asked was: Where could one find the expression of the common spirit of the congregation? Originally the real mediators of the message were those who were bearers of the Spirit, the "pneumatics", those who had the *pneuma*. But as we know from Paul's first letter to the Corinthians, especially chapter 12, he already encountered difficulties with the bearers of the Spirit because they produced disorder. So he laid stress on order together with the Spirit. In the Pastoral Epistles, which were attributed to Paul, the emphasis on ecclesiastical order became increasingly important. By the time of the apostolic fathers the ecstatic spirit had almost disappeared. It was considered dangerous. And why, they asked, do we need it? Everything the Spirit had to say has already been classically expressed in Scripture and tradition. Therefore, instead of the prophets who traveled from place to place as the apostles did, we now have definite norms and authorities arising in the Christian congregations. What were these norms and authorities?

The first and basic authority was the Old Testament. Next to that was the earliest collection of writings which are now in the New Testament. The limits of the New Testament had not yet been definitely set. It took more than two hundred years for the church to make a final decision on all the books in the New Testament canon.

Besides these writings there was already a complex of dogmatic and ethical doctrines which had become traditional. In I Clement these are called "the canon of our tradition". This tradition had various names, like truth, gospel, doctrine, and commandments. This, however, was a large amount of material; it had to be narrowed down for those who were to be baptized. So a creed was created which they could confess when they became members of the church. This creed had a similarity to our present Apostles' Creed, because its center was also christological. Christology was at the center because this is what distinguished the Christian communities from Judaism as well as paganism.

Baptism was the sacrament of entrance into the church. The baptized person, who at that time, of course, was a pagan adult, had to confess that he would accept the implications of his baptism. Then he was baptized in the name of Christ. Later on the names of God the Father and the Spirit were added. As yet there were no accompanying explanations; this was faith and liturgy, not yet theology.

All these things were going on in the church. This church was the *ekklesia*, the assembly of God or Christ. The original meaning of *ekklesia* was "called out". They were called out of the houses and nations to form the church universal; they were called out of the barbarians, out of the Greeks and the Jews, to become the true people of God. Of course, the Jews anticipated this and were a kind of *ekklesia* themselves. But they were not the true people of God, for the true people of God are universally called out of all the nations. If this is the case, it becomes necessary for those called together unto the conformity of the ecclesiastical creed to distinguish themselves from those outside and from heretics inside. How can this be done? How is it possible to determine whether a doctrine conforms to the doctrines of the church instead of being introduced from barbarian, Greek, or Jewish teachings? The answer was that this can be done only by the bishop who is the "overseer" of the congregation. The bishop represents the Spirit who is supposed to be within the whole congregation. In the struggle against pagans, Jews, barbarians, and heretics, the bishop became more and more important. In his letter to the Smyrneans Ignatius wrote: "Where the bishop is, there the congregation should be." Prophets who appear may be right or wrong, but the bishop is right. The bishops were representatives of the true doctrine. Originally the bishops were not distinguished from the presbyters or elders. Gradually, however, the bishop became a monarch among the elders, giving rise to the monarchical episcopate. This is a natural development. If the authority which guarantees truth is embodied in human beings, it is almost unavoidable that there will be a tendency to narrow down upon one individual who holds the final decision. In Clement of Rome we already find traces of the idea of apostolic succession, that is, that the bishop represents the apostles. This shows clearly how early the problem of authority became decisive in the church and started a trend toward its fuller development in the Roman Church.

We shall now take up some of the special doctrines of this period. In view of the pagan world in which these Christians lived it was essential to emphasize above all a monotheistic idea of God. Thus the Shepherd of Hermas says: "First of all, believe that God is one, who has made all things, bringing them out of nothing into being." The doctrine of creation out of nothing is expressed here. Although we cannot find this doctrine explicitly in the Old Testament, it might be said to be implicit there, and certainly was expressed prior to Christianity by the Jewish theologians during the inter-testamental period. This doctrine was decisive for the separation of the early church from paganism.

Along the same line was the emphasis on the almighty God, the *despotēs*, as he was called, the powerful ruling Lord. Clement exclaims, "O great demiurge", speaking of him as the great builder of the universe and the Lord of everything. These concepts which seem so natural to us were important because they were a defense against paganism. Creation out of nothing means that God did not find an already pre-existent matter when he started to create. There was no matter which resists form, as it was in Neo-Platonic paganism, and which must therefore be transcended. Instead, the material world is an object of God's creation; it is good and must not be disparaged for the sake of salvation. The word "demiurge" was used in Plato and Gnosticism for something below the highest God. The highest God is beyond doing such a lowly thing as creating the world, and so he leaves that to the demiurge. This means that the divine reality is not present in the act of creation. Against this notion Clement says that the great demiurge is God himself; there is no dichotomy between the highest God and the maker of the world. Creation is an absolute act out of nothing. This implies God's almighty power. To say that God is almighty does not mean that God is one who sits on a throne and can do anything he wants to do like an arbitrary tyrant. Rather, almightiness means that God is the sole ground of everything created, and that there is no such thing as matter which resists him. This is the meaning of the first article of the Apostles' Creed: "I believe in God the Father Almighty, Maker of heaven and earth." We should read this with great awe, because by this confession Christianity separated itself from the dualistic interpretation of reality in paganism. There are not two eternal principles, an evil principle of matter as eternal as a good principle of form. The first article of the Creed is the great wall which Christianity erected against paganism. Without this wall

form-good - (Aristotle)

matter evil

christology inevitably deteriorates into gnosticism in which Christ is one of the cosmic powers alongside others, although perhaps the highest among them. Only in the light of the first article is the second article of the Creed meaningful. Do not reduce God to the second Person of the Trinity.

As the ruler of everything God has a plan of salvation. Ignatius in particular develops this idea of a plan of salvation. In his letter to the Ephesians he speaks of the "economy towards the new man". This is a wonderful summary of the Christian message. Economy here means "building a house". It is used for the structure of the relationships between God and the world. There is an economy of trinitarian thinking: Father, Son, and Spirit. Only all three together are God. There is an economy of salvation, that is the building up of the different periods which finally lead to the new man. This idea of the new man, the new creature or new being, as the aim of the history of salvation is an important contribution of these theologians. This economy of salvation is already present in the period of the Old Testament. So Ignatius says: "Judaism has believed towards Christianity." The Christ, the new man, is the perfect fulfillment in which the disruption of the old man is overcome and death is dissolved. This leads to Christology.

Generally one can say that Jesus as the Christ was considered to be a pre-existent spiritual being who had transformed the historical Jesus into an agent of his saving activity. The Spirit is a *hypostasis* in God, an independent power in complete union with God. The Son came into the realm of flesh. "Flesh" here always means historical reality. He accepted flesh; or the flesh co-operated with the Spirit in him. The Holy Spirit dwelt in the flesh which he chose. He became the Son of God by his service.

Alongside this there was another idea. One could also say that the first Spirit, the *proton pneuma*, became flesh. For instance, Ignatius said: "Christ is God and perfect man at the same time. He comes from the Spirit and the seed of David." This means that he is not only some spiritual power which has accepted flesh, but that he as the spiritual power has become flesh.

Another term that was used was *iatros*, physician. Salvation was still understood here as healing. This physician heals both fleshly and spiritually. Very mixed ideas were used to emphasize that something paradoxical has happened, that a divine spiritual power has appeared under the conditions of humanity and existence. Thus, he is depicted as one having genesis and at the same time without genesis; he has come into the flesh; he has entered into death. But he is God who came into flesh and in death has eternal life. He is both from Mary and from God; he is able to suffer and not able to suffer, because of his elevation to God.

Ignatius could say: "For there is one God who made himself manifest through Jesus Christ his Son, who is his logos, proceeding from his silence." And II Clement: "Being the first Spirit, the head of the angels, he became flesh. Being he who appears in human form, Christ is the word proceeding out of the silence." He proceeds from silence, *apo sigēs*. The Christ breaks the eternal silence of the divine ground. As such he is both God and complete man. The same historical reality is the one as well as the other, both as one person. One could speak of a double message (a *diplon kerygma*), the message that this same being is both God *and* man.

Here we see the chief religious interest of this whole period, the interest, as Clement says, to speak theologically of Christ as of God. "Brothers, so we must think about Jesus Christ as about God, for if we think small things about him, we can hope to receive small things only." The absoluteness of salvation demands an absolute divine Savior. We are confronted here by the problem of two possible ways of thinking: Did Christ come into the flesh, accepting it? Or did he come as the Logos, being transformed into it? Both types of christology already appear, taking on flesh, or being transformed into it.

The idea of the divine Logos breaking the silence of God is very profound. It means that the divine abyss in itself is without word, form, object, and voice. It is the infinite silence of the eternal. But out of this divine silence, the Logos breaks forth and opens up what is hidden in this silence. He reveals the divine ground.

The christology we find here is not a theoretical problem; rather, the christological problem is one side of the soteriological problem. The interest is to have a safe salvation; the desire is to get the courage which overcomes the anxiety of being lost. The question of salvation is the basis of the christological question. What is this salvation? The work of Christ is twofold, first, *gnōsis* (knowledge) and secondly *zōē* (life). This is the way salvation was conceived of in the early Greek church. Christ brings knowledge and life. Sometimes the two things are combined in the phrase *athanatos gnōsis,* immortal knowledge, knowledge of that which is immortal and which makes immortal.

Christ called us from darkness into light; he made us serve the Father of truth. He called us who had no being and willed that we have being, out of his new being. This means that knowledge brings being. Knowledge and being belong together; so do lie and non-being. Truth is being; new truth is new being. Whoever has this knowledge of being has saving knowledge. This has to be emphasized against a gross misunderstanding. Harnack and his followers viewed ancient Christianity as being infected by Greek intellectualism. There are two things wrong in this viewpoint. First, Greek intellectualism is an inappropriate term because the Greeks were extremely interested in truth. With but some exceptions, the truth they wanted to have was existential truth, truth concerning their existence, truth that saves them out of this distorted existence and elevates them to the immovable One. The early Christian congregations understood truth in the same way. Truth is not theoretical knowledge about objects, but cognitive participation in a new reality that has appeared in the Christ. Without this participation no truth is possible, and knowledge is abstract and meaningless. This is what they meant when they combined knowledge and being. Participating in the new being is participation in truth, in the true knowledge.

This identity of truth and being mediates life. Christ gives immortal knowledge, the knowledge which gives immortality. He is the Savior and leader of immortality. In his own being he is our imperishable life. He gives both the knowledge of immortality and the drug of immortality, which is the sacrament. Ignatius called the Lord's Supper the remedy against our having to die, the *antidoton tō mē apothanein.* There is a very profound meaning in this idea that the sacramental materials of the Lord's Supper are, so to speak, drugs or remedies which produce immortality. First of all, it shows that the apostolic fathers did not believe in the immortality of the soul. There is no natural immortality, otherwise it would be meaningless for them to speak about immortal life which Christ offers. They believed that man is naturally mortal, just as the Old Testament held that in paradise man was able to eat from the food of the gods, called the "tree of life", and to keep alive by participating in this divine power. Similarly the apostolic fathers taught that with the coming of Christ the situation of paradise has been re-established. Again we may participate in the food of eternity, which is the body and the blood of Christ. In doing this we build into ourselves a counter-balance to our natural having to die. Death is the wages of sin only insofar as sin is separation from God. Because of this sin God's power to overcome our natural having to die does not work any more. But with Christ's coming it works again. It works in a sacramentally realistic way in the materials of the sacrament of the Lord's Supper. In the light of this we can conclude that our traditional way of speaking of the immortality of the soul is not classically Christian doctrine, but a distortion of it, not in a genuine, but in a pseudo-Platonic sense.

B. THE APOLOGETIC MOVEMENT

The Apologetic movement can rightly be called the birthplace of a developed Christian theology. Christianity needed apologetics for different reasons. An *apologia* means a reply or answer to a judge in the court, if someone should accuse you. Socrates' *apologia*, for instance, was his answer to those who accused him. Likewise, Christianity expressed itself in terms of answers to particular accusations. Those who did this systematically are called the Apologists.

Answers were needed because of a double accusation against Christianity: (1) Christianity was a threat to the Roman Empire. This was a political accusation; Christianity undermines the structure of the empire; (2) Christianity was, philosophically speaking, nonsense, a superstition mixed with philosophical fragments. These two attacks supported each other. The philosophical attack was taken over by the political authorities and used in their accusations. Thus the philosophical attacks became dangerous in terms of their political consequences. Celsus, the physician and philosopher, was the most important representative of these attacks. It is important to know his thinking if we want to see how Christianity was regarded at that time by an educated Greek philosopher and scientist. Celsus saw Christianity as a mixture of fanatic superstition and piecemeal philosophy. According to him the historical reports in the Bible are contradictory and lack any certain evidence. Here for the first time we have historical criticism of the Old and New Testaments, something which will be repeated later again and again. In Celsus it is criticism motivated by hate. Later, in the eighteenth century, we witness a criticism moved by a love toward the reality which lies behind these reports.

In turning to Celsus' attack on Christianity, we find that one of the main points is the resurrection of Jesus. Celsus observed that this event, which is supposed to be so important, was witnessed only by adherents of the faith, and at first only by a few ecstatic women. The deification of Jesus is not any different from the processes of deification which we know of elsewhere in history. For example, Euhemerus, the Cynic, has given enough examples of the way in which a human being, a king or hero, was deified. What is particularly disgusting, Celsus said, is that when the stories are most incredible, as many of the Old Testament stories, they are explained away allegorically. Of course, this was actually done. An element of anti-Judaism is visible in Celsus' criticism of the Old Testament miracle stories. This is understandable because Celsus was directing his criticisms against the Jews as much as against the Christians.

Celsus charged that the descent of God contradicts the unchangeable character of God which the Christian writers had also strongly emphasized. But if the divine Being has descended to earth, why did this happen in a despised corner of the world, and why did it happen only once? Particularly disgusting to the educated pagan—and we have here another element of anti-Judaistic feeling—is the fight between the Jews and Christians whether the Messiah has or has not appeared. The argument from prophecy to fulfillment that was used so much by Christians is also a stupid one. Celsus was historically educated enough to see that the prophet did not anticipate a fulfillment in the terms in which the fulfillment happened. This is an especially sore point in all of church history. For the sound idea of a universal preparatory revelation was distorted into a mechanism of "foreseeing" events which later happened.

Celsus' deepest criticism of Christianity was neither scientific with respect to history nor philosophical with respect to the idea of incarnation; instead, it was one which arose out of a basically religious feeling. He said that the demonic powers which, according to Paul, had been conquered by Christ are actually ruling the world. The world has not changed since the beginning of Christianity. And Celsus adds that there is no sense in trying to overcome these powers; they are the real rulers of the world. Therefore, one should be obedient to the Roman rulers on earth; at least they have reduced the power of the demons to some extent—which is also a Pauline idea. They have established a certain order in which the demonic forces are limited. However questionable the Roman emperors may be as persons, they must be obeyed and venerated, for Rome has become great through obedience to the orders of this world, to the necessities of law and nature. Christians are guilty of undermining the greatness and the glory of Rome, and thus undercut the only power that can prevent the world from falling into chaos and the demons from having a complete victory.

That was a serious attack, one which has been heard frequently in the history of Christianity. Christians who had the same philosophical education that Celsus had tried to answer for the church. The Apologists did not answer the attacks so much on the level of historical criticism as on the philosophical level. They did it in a way which shows three things that characterize every apologetic. First of all, if you want to speak meaningfully with someone, there must be a common basis of some mutually accepted ideas. The truth that is common to both Christians and pagans must first be elaborated. If they have nothing in common, no conversation is possible and no meaningful address to the pagans is possible. A rule for all Christian missionary work is that the other one must understand what you say; but understanding involves at least partial participation. If the missionary speaks an absolutely different language, no understanding is possible. Thus, the Apologists had to show that there is something in common.

Secondly, the Apologists had to point out defects in the ideas of paganism. There are things which contradict the pagan ideas. It can be shown that for centuries pagan philosophers have brought forth criticisms of these ideas. This is the second step of apologetics, namely, showing the negativity in the other. Thirdly, it must be shown that one's own position is not to be accepted as something from the outside, but rather that Christianity is the fulfillment of a longing and desire in paganism. This is the apologetic form of theology which I use in my own systematic theology, that is, the correlation between question and answer.

There is, however, one danger in apologetics; the common ground may be overemphasized at the expense of the differences. Then you merely accept the other as he is, without giving him anything different. A way must be found between the two extremes of either throwing indigestible material at the other from an external position, or telling him what he already knows. The latter is the way liberal theology has often acted, while the former is the way of fundamentalism and orthodoxy.

1. *The Christian Philosophy*

Justin Martyr was perhaps the most important of the Apologists. In speaking of Christianity he said: "This is the only philosophy which I have found certain and adequate." What does this mean? Some anti-apologetic theologians interpret this as evidence that Christianity was dissolved into a philosophy. They say further that this is what every apologetic theology does to Christianity. But when Justin said that Christianity was a philosophy, we must understand what he meant by philosophy. Philosophy at that time referred to the spiritual, non-magical and non-superstitious character of a movement. So Justin was saying that Christianity is the only certain and adequate philosophy because it is not magical or superstitious. For the later Greeks philosophy was not only a theoretical but more a practical matter. It was a matter of existential interpretation of life, a matter of life and death for the existence of the people at that time. To be a philosopher ordinarily meant to belong to a philosophical school, a sort of ritual community in which the founder of the school was supposed to have had a revelatory insight into the truth. Acceptance into such a school was not a matter of having a Ph.D., but of being personally initiated into the atmosphere of this school.

Justin taught that this Christian philosophy is universal; it is the all-embracing truth about the meaning of existence. From this it follows that wherever truth appears, it belongs to the Christians. Truth concerning existence, wherever it appears, is Christian truth. "What anybody has said about the truth belongs to us, the Christians." This is not sheer arrogance. He does not mean that

Christians now possess all the truth, or that they alone discovered it. He means, in terms of the Logos doctrine, that there cannot be truth anywhere which is not in principle included in Christian truth. This is what the Fourth Gospel says: the Logos appeared, full of truth and grace.

And vice versa, Justin said: "Those who live according to the logos are Christians." He included people like Socrates, Heraclitus, and Elijah. He added, however, that the total logos which appeared in Christ has become body, mind, and soul. Therefore, the philosophers apart from Christianity are partly in error and even partly subjected to demonic inspirations which come from the pagan gods. The gods of the heathen are not non-existent; they are real demonic forces and have destructive power.

What does all this mean? It removes the impression that these Christians felt themselves to be just another religion. Actually we find here the negation of the concept of religion with respect to Christianity, as though it were one religion among others, and as though Christianity is right and all other religions wrong. The Apologists would not say that their *religion* is right, the others wrong, but that the Logos has appeared on which their religion is based. He is the full Logos of God himself, appearing in the center of his being, appearing in his totality. This is more than religion. This is truth appearing in time and space. So the word "Christianity" is understood not as a religion but as the negation of *all* religions. In virtue of its universality Christianity is able to embrace them all. Justin said what I think is absolutely necessary to say. If anywhere in the world there were an existential truth which could not be received by Christianity as an element of its own thinking, Jesus would not be the Christ. He would be merely one teacher alongside other teachers, all of whom are limited and partly in error. But that is not what the early Christians said. They said—and we should say—that if we call Jesus the Christ, or the Logos as the Apologists called him, this means that by definition there cannot be any truth which cannot in principle be taken into Christianity. Otherwise the application of the term "Logos" to Jesus as the Christ would not have been possible. This does not mean that this *Logos* knew all the truth; that would be nonsense and would destroy his humanity. But it does mean that the fundamental truth which has appeared in him is essentially universal, and therefore can take in every other truth. For this reason the early theologians did not hesitate to take in as much Greek philosophical truth as they could, and also as much Oriental mysticism as they could.

The appearance of the Logos in Christ makes it possible for even the most uneducated human being to receive the full existential truth. In contrast, the philosophers may lose it in discussing it. In other words, the Apologists are saying that Christianity is far superior to all philosophy. Since philosophy presupposes education, only a few human beings have access to its truth. Others are excluded from truth in its philosophical form. However, they are not excluded from the truth that is manifest through the Logos in a living person. The message of Jesus as the Christ is universal in embracing all mankind, all classes, groups, and social stratifications of mankind.

Another argument that was used in defense of Christianity was the moral power and action of those who belong to the church. Therefore, the Christian congregations could not be dangerous to the Roman Empire. They help to prevent the world from falling into chaos. Even more than the Roman Empire itself, they are supporters of world order. So Justin could say: "The world lives from the prayers of the Christians and from the obedience of the Christians to the law of the state. The Christians preserve the world, and on the other hand, for their sake God preserves the world."

2. *God and the Logos*

The philosophical idea of God is inborn in every human being. All the characteristics which Parmenides attributed to Being are here attributed to God—eternal, without beginning, needing nothing, beyond passions, indestructible, unchangeable, and invisible. There is, however, one point of difference between classical Greek philosophy and Justin's doctrine of God. This difference comes from the Old Testament and changes everything. It is the statement that God is the Almighty Creator! The moment this statement is made, the personal element enters the abstract and mystical description of God's identity. God as Creator is acting, and as the Almighty he is the acting power behind everything which moves.

It is interesting to observe that in such a statement about God,

Christian monotheism oscillates between the transpersonal element of Being and the personal element of God as Creator and, of course, also as Savior. This oscillation is necessary as soon as the idea of God is made an object of thought. One cannot escape some elements of the eternal, the unconditional, the unchangeable, etc. On the other hand, practical piety and our experience of creatureliness presuppose a person-to-person relationship. Christianity must oscillate between these two elements, because both elements are in God himself.

Between God and man there are angels and powers, some good and some evil. But their mediating power is insufficient. The Logos is the real mediator. It is difficult to explain what the word "logos" means, especially to those who are nominalists from birth. It is difficult because this concept is not the description of an individual being, but of a universal principle. If one is not used to thinking in terms of universals as powers of being, such a concept as Logos remains impossible to understand. The concept of the Logos can be explained best against the background of Platonism or medieval realism.

Logos is the principle of the self-manifestation of God. The Logos is God manifest to himself in himself. Therefore, whenever God appears, either to himself or to others outside himself, it is the Logos which appears. This Logos is in Jesus as the Christ in a unique way. And this, according to the Apologists, is the greatness of Christianity and the basis of its claim about salvation. For if the divine Logos in its fullness had not appeared in Jesus as the Christ, no salvation would be possible. This is an argument from existence, not from speculation. This means that the classical theologians start from the experience of salvation, and then proceed to speak of Jesus as the Christ in terms of the Logos.

The Logos is the first "work" or generation of God as Father. The Father, being eternal mind, has the Logos in himself; he is "eternally logical", as Athenagoras, one of the Apologists, said. Here "logical" does not mean that he can argue well; he leaves that to us. As "logikos" he is adequate to the principles of meaning and truth. God is not irrational will; he is called eternal *nous* (mind), and this means he has within himself the power of self-manifestation. This analogy is taken from our experience. There is no mental process that is going on in some way or other except in silent words. Likewise, the inner spiritual life of God includes the silent word in him.

There is a spiritual procession that goes out from the Father to the world in which he manifests himself to himself and to the world. But this procession does not produce separation. The Word is not the same thing of which it is the Word. On the other hand, the Word cannot be separated from that of which it is the Word. The Word of God is not identical with God; it is the self-manifestation of God. But if you separate it from God, it becomes empty, without content. This is an attempt to describe the meaning of the term "Logos," in analogy with the mental processes of man. The process of generation of the Logos in God—eternally, of course—does not make God small. He is not less than he was by the fact that he generates his Word. So Justin can say: "The Logos is different from God according to number, but not according to concept." He is God; he is not *the* God, but he is one with God in essence. Justin used also the Stoic doctrines of the immanent and the transcendent Logos. The Logos in God is *logos endiathetos*, that is the indwelling Logos. This eternal, indwelling Logos, the Word in which God expresses himself to himself, becomes with the creation the *logos prophorikos*, the proceeding, outgoing Logos. The Logos is then a word that is spoken toward the outside, toward the creature, through the prophets and the wise men. Logos means both word and reason. If one thinks in Old Testament terms, one would prefer to translate *logos* by "word"; if one thinks in Greek terms, as the Apologists did on the whole, then one would translate *logos* by "reason". "Reason" here does not mean "reasoning", but refers to the meaningful structure of reality.

As the immediate self-expression of the divine, the Word (the Logos, form, or reason) is less than the divine abyss, because the divine abyss is always the beginning, and out of the depths of divinity his self-manifestation toward the world comes. The Logos is the beginning of the generations of God; he has, so to speak, a diminished transcendence or divinity. But if this is so, how can he reveal God fully? This became a problem for later times. As soon as the Apologists used the term "logos" the problem arose and could not be silenced any more. If the Logos is the self-expression of God in movement, is he less than God or fully God? One continued to call Christ God, but how could the statement be made understandable to pagans that a historical individual who lived and died is to be called "God"? The difficulty was not the incarnation as such. "Incarnation" is one of the most ordinary events in Greek mythology and in all mythology. Gods come to earth; they take on animal, human, or plant form; they do certain things and then return to their divinity. Such a concept, however, could not be accepted by Christianity. The difficulty was that *this* Son of God, who was a historical man and not a mythical figure, is supposed to be the absolute and unique incarnation of God.

The incarnation is a once-for-all event; and it is not a particular element or characteristic of God which becomes incarnate. Rather, it is the very center of divinity which becomes incarnate, and to express this the idea of the Logos was used. The problem was to combine monotheism, which was emphasized so strongly against pagan polytheism, with the idea of Christ's divinity. Both aspects of Christ, his humanity and his universality, had to be kept together. This was the need of that time which the Apologists fulfilled. And therefore they were successful.

In the Apologists the incarnation is not the union of the divine Spirit with the man Jesus; rather, the Logos really *becomes* man. This transformation christology becomes increasingly important through the Logos doctrine. Through the will of God the pre-existent Logos has become man. He has been made *flesh*. Here we have the first clear decision for the transformation christology over against the adoptionist christology. If the Logos (or Spirit) adopted the man Jesus, then we have quite a different kind of christology from the idea that the Logos is transformed into flesh.

The saving gifts of the Logos are gnōsis (knowledge) of God, of the law, and of the resurrection. As the Logos Christ is, first of all, a teacher; not a teacher who teaches us many things he knows better than we, but a teacher in the Socratic sense of giving us existential power of being. The Logos gives us truth about God and moral laws which we are to fulfill through freedom. Thus a kind of intellectualization and some educational elements come into the doctrine of the Christ. This was a possible consequence of the Logos doctrine, and for this reason there have always been reactions against it.

C. GNOSTICISM

The Apologists defended Christianity against the philosophers and emperors. However, the threats to Christianity did not come only from the outside. A much greater danger came from the inside; this was the danger of gnosticism. The term "gnosticism" is derived from the Greek word *gnōsis*, meaning "knowledge". It does not mean scientific knowledge. *Gnōsis* is used in three ways: (1) as knowledge in general terms; (2) as mystical communion; (3) as sexual intercourse. All three meanings can be found in the New Testament. *Gnōsis* is a knowledge by participation. It is as intimate as the relation between husband and wife. It is not the knowledge resulting from analytic and synthetic research. It is a knowledge of union and of salvation, existential knowledge in contrast to scientific knowledge. The Gnostics were the Greek intellectuals; but they understood the cognitive function of man in terms of participation in the divine.

The Gnostics were not a sect; if anything, they were many sects. Actually, however, gnosticism was a widespread religious movement in the late ancient world. This movement is usually called syncretism. It was a mixture of all the religious traditions of that time. It spread all over the world, and was strong enough to penetrate Greek philosophy and the Jewish religion. Philo of Alexandria was a typical forerunner of gnosticism. It was also strong enough to penetrate Roman law and Christian theology.

The basic elements of this religious mixture are the following: (1) The destruction of the national religions by the conquests of Alexander and Rome. The great world empires undercut the national religions. This is the negative presupposition. (2) The philosophical interpretation of mythology. When you read the systems of the Gnostics, you have the feeling that they have rationalized mythology. And this feeling is accurate. (3) The renewal of the ancient mystery traditions. (4) The revival of the psychic and magical elements which appeared in the religious propaganda of the East. While the political movement went from West to East, the religious movement went from East to West. Hence, gnosticism was an attempt to combine all the religious traditions which had lost their genuine roots, and to unite them in a system of a half-philosophical, half-religious character.

There were many similarities and differences between the gnostic groups and original Christianity. Against the public tradition of the Christian churches, they claimed to possess secret traditions known only to the initiated. They rejected the Old Testament because it contradicted many of the their fundamental tenets, especially their dualistic and ascetic tendencies. The New Testament was not rejected but purged. Marcion was the man who tried to purge the New Testament, leaving the ten main Letters of Paul and the Gospel of Luke, which most clearly bears Pauline influence. Presumably, they did not contain elements which contradicted the basic ideas of gnosticism, as did the other Epistles and Gospels in the New Testament.

Marcion was not primarily a speculative philosopher, but a religious reformer. He founded congregations of followers which lasted for a long time. The title of his book is *Antitheses.* He was a Gnostic in his distinction between the God of the Old Testament and the God of the New Testament, the God of the law and the God of the gospel. He rejected the former and accepted the latter. This problem should not be seen in terms of the fantastic idea of two gods. Rather, it should be seen in terms of the problem with which Harnack wrestled at the end of his life. That is the problem whether the Old and New Testaments are not so different that they cannot be combined. Marcionism is a form of radical Paulinism which exists throughout church history. In the modern period we have it in the Barthian school, when the God of revelation is placed against the God of natural law. In natural law and in history man is thought to be by himself. Of course, this school does not speak of a second God; such a fantastic mythology would be impossible today. Rather, it speaks of a radical tension between the natural world of reason and of morality and the religious realm of revelation which stands against all other realms. This was Marcion's problem, and he solved it by a radical separation in terms of a gnostic dualism.

For the Gnostics the created world is evil; it was created by an evil god whom they equated with the God of the Old Testament. Therefore, salvation is liberation from the world, and had to be accomplished through ascetic means. There is no place for eschatology in this dualistic world view, for the end of the world is seen in the light of a dualism. A dualistic fulfillment is not a fulfillment; it implies a split in God himself.

The Savior is one of the heavenly powers, called "aeons" or "eternities". The word "eternity" does not have the connotation of timelessness here, but of cosmic power. The higher aeon, the savior aeon, the savior power of being, descends to earth and takes on human flesh. It is self-evident, however, that a divine power cannot suffer. So he takes on either a strange body, or a body which only seems to be a body, but he does not *become* flesh. (The early Christians rejected the Gnostics on this point.) The Savior descends to the different realms in which the various astrological powers rule. This has special reference to the planets, which were considered as astrological powers long after the Renaissance, even in Protestantism. He reveals the hidden weapons of these demonic powers by trespassing their realm and overcoming them on his descent. He brings down the seals of their power, their names and their characters. If you have the name of a demonic power, you are superior to it; if you call it by name, it falls down. One of the Gnostic texts says: "Having the seals, I shall descend, going through all aeons. I shall recognize all mysteries. I shall show the shape of the gods. And the hidden things of the holy path, called gnōsis, I shall deliver." Here we see the claim of the good God, of the power of mystery which comes down to earth.

The demonic powers are the representatives of fate. The human soul which has fallen into their hands is liberated by the Savior and by the knowledge he brings. One could say: What the Savior does in gnosticism is somehow to use white magic against the black magic of the planetary powers, the same powers of whom Paul in Romans 8 speaks when he says they have been subjected by Christ. Therefore, the magic power of the sacraments is acknowledged. The highest power comes to earth in them.

Besides these speculative and sacramental features, gnosticism had ethical values of community and asceticism. The ascent of the soul is demanded, following the Savior who has ascended. The Savior liberates from demonic powers for the sake of union with the fullness, the *plērōma*, the spiritual word. On the upward way the human soul meets these rulers; the soul tells the rulers what it knows about them. He knows their names, and therefore their mysterious power, the structure of evil they represent. When he tells them their names, they fall down and tremble and cannot stop the soul on its way any more. These poetic images show that gnosticism was a religion of salvation from the demonic powers. This was the problem of the whole period, both in and outside of Christianity. Somehow man is better than his creator. Man must be saved from the powers of the demiurge, the one who created the world. But not all men are able to be saved. There are three classes of human beings: the *pneumatikoi*, i.e., the spiritual ones; the *psychikoi*, i.e., those who follow the soul; and the *sarkikoi*, i.e., those who follow the flesh. The *sarkikoi* are lost; the *pneumatikoi* are saved; but the middle group, the *psychikoi*, can go either way. In order to be elevated on high, man must participate in the mysteries. These are mostly mysteries of purification, and usually connected with baptism. The Spirit in baptism enters the sacramental water and dwells in it. The Spirit is brought down by a special formula of initiation.

These ideas formed a great temptation to Christianity. Christ remained in the center of history as the bringer of salvation; but he was put into the framework of the dualistic world view of Hellenism. The religious mood of this period is beautifully expressed in the Acts of Andrew, one of the apocryphal writings. "Blessed is our generation. We are not thrown down, for we have been recognized by the light. We do not belong to time, which would dissolve us. We are not a product of motion, which would destroy us again. We belong to the greatness toward which we are striving. We belong to him who has mercy towards us, to the light which has expelled the darkness, to the One from whom we have turned away, to the Manifold, to the Super-heavenly, by whom we have understood the earthly. If we praise him, it is because we are recognized by him." This is really religious piety, not mere speculation, as the critics of gnosticism have said.

There are many people today who would like to renew gnostic religion as their own daily expression of religious experience, not because of the fantastic speculation, but because of the real piety expressed in it. Gnosticism was a great danger for Christianity. If Christian theology had succumbed to this temptation, the particular character of Christianity would have been lost. Its unique basis in the person of Jesus would have become meaningless. The Old Testament would have disappeared, and with it the historical picture of the Christ. All of this was avoided because of the work of the men whom we call the anti-gnostic fathers. These fathers fought against gnosticism and expelled it from the church.

D. THE ANTI-GNOSTIC FATHERS

The first great Christian theologians developed their systems in opposition to—and partly in acceptance of—the ideas of gnosticism. Their defense against attacks from the outside was made in terms of the Logos doctrine. However, some of the spirit of the world which was conquered by Christianity entered into Christianity itself. The fight then had to be waged against a Christianized paganism. Such a fight, however, is never simply a negation, but always involves reception as well. The result of this partial rejection and partial reception of the religious mood of that time is what we call "early Catholicism". The theologians with whom we now have to deal are important because they represent this early Catholicism. They express ideas which grew out of a rejection and an acceptance of the pagan religious movement of their time. To do this they accepted the Logos doctrine which had been developed by the Apologists. But now they brought it constructively—not only apologetically—into a framework of Bible and tradition. In doing this they deprived this doctrine, at least partly, of its dangerous implications, one of them, of course, being a relapse into polytheism, tritheism, or ditheism. The greatness of theologians like Irenaeus and Tertullian is that they saw this danger, and used the Logos doctrine to develop constructive theological ideas in relation to the religious movements of their own period.

Irenaeus was the greatest of the anti-gnostic fathers, religiously speaking. He understood the spirit of Paul and had a feeling for what Paul's theology meant for the Christian Church. However, the Pauline doctrine that was important for Irenaeus was not so much the one with which Paul fought against Judaism —the doctrine of justification by grace through faith—but it was more the center of Paul's own teaching, his doctrine of the Holy Spirit. In some ways Irenaeus' theology stands closer to Protestant Christianity than most of early Catholicism; yet he was the father of early Catholicism—and ultimately not a Protestant—

inasmuch as the Pauline doctrine of justification through faith, which I like to call the "corrective side" in Paul's theology, was not at the center of Irenaeus' thought.

Tertullian was another anti-gnostic father, the master of Latin rhetoric. He was the creator of ecclesiastical terminology in the Latin language. He had a juristic mind, although not a jurist himself. He was possessed of a very aggressive temperament and a strong character. He understood the primacy of faith and the paradox of Christianity. But he was not artificially primitive, for he accepted the Stoic philosophy and with it the idea that the human soul is by nature Christian—*anima naturaliter christiana*. He also accepted the Logos doctrine of the Apologists, because he did not only accept the paradox of Christianity but, having a sharp rational mind, he believed that Greek philosophy could not surpass Christianity in rational sharpness and clarity.

The third anti-gnostic theologian was Hippolytus, more scholarly than the other two. He carried on polemics against the gnostic movement in his exegetical works and writings on church history. These three theologians saw clearly the situation of the early church. It is important for Protestants to see how early the main fundamentals of the later Roman system were already present in the third century.

1. *The System of Authorities*

The problem which the Gnostics posed for the church was in the realm of authority, the question whether the Holy Scriptures were decisive as over against the secret teachings of the Gnostics. The gnostic teachers said that Jesus had passed on secret insights to them during the forty days after his resurrection when he was together with his disciples. These insights formed the content of gnostic philosophy and theology. Against this notion the anti-gnostic fathers had to establish a doctrine of Scripture.

The Holy Scripture is given by the Logos through the divine Spirit. Therefore, it became necessary to fix the canon. The very foundations of the church were threatened by the intrusion of secret traditions which asserted quite different things from what the biblical writings said. Thus, the decision to fix the canon arose out of the life-and-death struggle with gnosticism. This meant that the church must always return to the classical period, namely, the apostolic period of Christianity. What was written at that time is valid for all later times; anything really new that comes later can never be canonical. This is one of the reasons that so many of the books in the Bible go under apostolic names even though they were written during the post-apostolic period.

That which is canonical, it was felt, must be canonical in an absolute sense, including the letters of the text. Here Christianity simply followed the legalistic interpretation of the law in Judaism in which every Hebrew letter in the Old Testament text has an open and a hidden meaning, and is absolutely inspired. This, of course, was not enough, because the Bible must be interpreted. This is true whenever the Bible is made an absolute norm. The Gnostics interpreted the Scriptures differently from the official church. Therefore, the principle of tradition was bound to come up. The tradition was identified with the *regula fidei*, the rule of faith. When this happened, not the Bible but the rule of faith became decisive, just as the confessional documents written after the Reformation became the decisive canon for theological instruction, and not the Bible.

The rule of faith was also called the canon of truth; something is true because it comes from the apostles. It is apostolic tradition (*traditio apostolica*) which is mediated through presbyters or bishops. This, however, is still too indefinite; there are too many elements in the tradition, ethical and dogmatic. So a concentrated summary of the Bible and the rule of faith was needed in connection with the confession at baptism, the main sacrament at that time. This, of course, presupposes that the bishops who are responsible for the rule of faith and the baptismal creed have the gift of truth. They have it because they are the successors of the apostles. Here already we have a clear expression of the episcopal doctrine of apostolic succession. The apostolic succession is most visible in the Roman Church, which was founded by Peter and Paul, according to these anti-gnostic fathers. Irenaeus says about this church: "To this church all nations must come, because of its greater principality, the church in which the apostolic tradition has been always preserved."

Thus we have a very impressive system of authorities: the Bible, the apostolic tradition, the rule of faith, the baptismal creed, and the bishops, created in the struggle against the Gnostics. What is astonishing is how early all this happened.

2. The Montanist Reaction

A reaction set in against the developing order, a reaction of the Spirit against the order, represented by a man named Montanus. This reaction was very serious, as evident in the fact that Tertullian himself later became a Montanist. This Montanistic reaction against ecclesiastical fixation of Christianity runs throughout church history in one form or other.

The Montanists had two basic ideas: the Spirit and the "end". The Spirit was suppressed by the organized church. There was a fear of spiritual movements because the Gnostics had claimed to have the Spirit. It was denied that prophets necessarily have an ecstatic character. A churchman at this time wrote a pamphlet to the effect that it is unnecessary for a prophet to speak in ecstasy. The church was unable to understand the prophetic Spirit any more. It was understandably afraid of the Spirit because in the name of the Spirit all kinds of disruptive elements entered into the church.

The other idea was that of the "end". After the expectation of Jesus and the apostles that the end was very imminent had been disappointed, the apostolic fathers began to establish themselves in the world. The disappointment that the end did not come caused great difficulties and led to the necessity of creating a worldly church, a church that is able to live in the world. Montanism was a reaction against this worldly church. But the Montanists experienced what the earlier Christians had experienced; the end they expected did not come. So they also had to establish themselves in the world; they also became a church. It was a church with a strict discipline, and to a certain extent it was an anticipation of the sectarian type of church which arose during the Reformation and in later Protestantism. The Montanists believed that they represented the period of the Paraclete, following the periods of the Father and the Son. The sectarian revolutionary movements in the church have generally made the same claim; they represent the age of the Spirit.

It happens, however, that when the attempt is made to fix the content of what the Spirit teaches, the result is extreme poverty. This happened, for example, to the Quakers after their initial ecstatic period. When the content is fixed it turns out that there is nothing new, or what is new is more or less some form of a rational moralism. This happened to George Fox and his followers, and to all ecstatic sects. In the second generation they become rational, moralistic, and legalistic; the ecstatic element disappears; not much remains that is creative compared to the classical period of apostolic Christianity. The Montanists fixed their poor contents in new books; they adopted the idea of a prophetic succession. Of course, this is self-contradictory, because succession is an organizational principle, whereas prophecy is an anti-organizational principle. The attempt to combine them was unsuccessful, and will always be unsuccessful.

The Christian Church excluded Montanism. However, its victory over Montanism also resulted in loss. This loss is visible in four ways: (1) The canon was victorious against the possibility of new revelations. The solution of the Fourth Gospel that there will be new insights, always standing under the criticism of the Christ, was at least reduced in power and meaning. (2) The traditional hierarchy was confirmed against the prophetic spirit. This meant that the prophetic spirit was more or less excluded from the organized church and had to flee into sectarian movements. (3) Eschatology became less significant than it had been in the apostolic age. The ecclesiastical establishment became much more important. The expectation of the end was reduced to an appeal to each individual to be prepared for his end which can come at any moment. The idea of an end of history was not important in the church after that. (4) The strict discipline of the Montanists was lost, giving way to a growing laxity in the church. Here again something happened which has frequently happened in the history of the church. Small groups arise with a strict discipline; they are regarded with suspicion by the church; they form themselves into larger churches; then they lose their original disciplinary power in themselves.

3. *God the Creator*

We must now deal with what the anti-gnostic fathers taught within the framework of the strict safeguards which they built up against gnosticism. The Gnostics had contrasted God the Father and God the Savior. Now the gnostic theory was called a *blasphemia creatoris*, a blasphemy of the Creator. This ought to be kept in mind by all neo-orthodox theologians today. There is much gnostic Marcionism in them, that is, a dualistic blasphemy of the Creator God. They put the Savior God in such opposition to the Creator God that, although they never fall into any real heresy, they implicitly blaspheme the divine creation by identifying it with the sinful state of reality. Against this tendency Irenaeus said that God is one; there is no duality in him. Law and gospel, creation and salvation, are derived from the same God.

This one God is known to us not speculatively but existentially. He expresses this in saying: "Without God, you cannot know God." God is never an object. In all knowledge it is he who knows in us and through us. Only he can know himself; we may participate in his knowledge of himself. But he is not an object whom we can know from the outside. God is unknown according to his greatness, his absoluteness, his unconditional character. He is known according to his love in which he comes to us. Therefore, in order to know God, you must be within God; you must participate in him. You can never look at him as an object outside yourself. This God has created the world out of nothing. This phrase "out of nothing" is not a description of the way God created, but a protective concept that is only negatively meaningful. It means that there is no prior resisting matter out of which God created the world, as in paganism. In creating the world God is not dependent on a matter which resisted the form which the demiurge, the world-builder, wanted to impose on it. The Christian idea is that everything is created directly by God without any resisting matter. God is the cause of everything. His purpose, the immanent *telos* of everything, is the salvation of mankind. The result is that the creation is good, and the Creator God is the same as the Savior God. We should see that the blasphemy of the Creator, new or old, is always based on a confusion of the created goodness of the world with its distortion.

This one God is a *trias*, a trinity. The word *trinitas* appears first in Tertullian. Although God is one, he is never alone. Irenaeus says: "There is always with him the word and the wisdom, the Son and the Spirit, through which he has made everything freely and spontaneously." God is always a living God and, therefore, never alone, never a dead identity with himself. He always has his word and his wisdom with himself. These are symbols of his spiritual life, his self-manifestation and his self-actualization. The motive of the doctrine of the trinity is to speak of God as living and to make understandable the presence of the divine as a living, creative ground. According to Irenaeus, these three are one God because they have one *dynamis*, one power of being, essence, or potentiality. "Potentiality" and "dynamics" are the Latin and Greek terms respectively for what we can best translate as "power of being".

Tertullian spoke of the one divine substance which develops itself in the triadic economy. "Economy" means "building-up". The divinity builds up eternally in a unity. Any polytheistic interpretation of the trinity is sharply rejected. On the other hand, God is established as a living God, not as a dead identity. Thus Tertullian used the formula *una substantia, tres personae* to speak of God.

Contrary to gnosticism, man is created good. He has fallen by his own freedom. Man who is mortal by nature was supposed to become immortal through obedience to God, remaining in paradise and participating in the food of the gods, in the tree of life. But he lost this power by disobedience to God. So it must be regained. Immortality, as we said before, is not a natural quality but something which must be received as a gift from the realm of the eternal. There is no other way to get it. Sin is spiritual as well as carnal. Adam has lost the possible *similitudo* (similitude) to God, namely, immortality, but he has not lost the natural image, because the natural image makes him human. Here we have Irenaeus' famous distinction between *similitudo* and *imago*. These two words are used in the Vulgate translation of Genesis 1:26, which states that God made man in his *image*, after his *likeness*. Irenaeus places a theological interpretation on these two words. Every man has the natural image of God; man as man, as a finite, rational being, is able to have a relationship to God. *Similitudo* means that man has the possibility of becoming similar to God. The main point in this similarity with God is eternal life. If someone gets eternal life, he overcomes his natural mortality and participates in the eternal life as a gift of God.

4. *The History of Salvation*

The history of salvation was described in three or four covenants. The first covenant is that which is given with creation.

This is the natural law which is ultimately the law of love innate in man. Secondly, the law is reinstated after it faded away when man lost his immediate innocent participation in it. The third stage is law as it is re-established in Christ, after Judaism distorted the law of Sinai. The law is the same throughout, namely, the law of love innate in man by nature. God does not give arbitrary commandments, but he restates those commandments which are identical with man's essential nature and which are, therefore, valid under all circumstances. Then, in Tertullian, we have a fourth covenant, because he became a Montanist. This is the covenant with the Paraclete, the divine Spirit, who gives the new law at the end of the days. This means that the history of salvation was understood as the education of mankind in terms of a law. This made it possible to understand why the Old Testament belongs to the Christian Scriptures and why philosophy belongs to Christianity. They are all stages in the one history of salvation. They are not negated but confirmed by the revelation in Christ. The problems connected with a dualism were solved in terms of a history of salvation in different covenants. There is not only one revelation. The biblical idea of *kairos* means that there is a revelation adapted to each new covenant situation, first, that of paradise, then that of the elected nation, then that of the followers of Christ, and, sometimes, that of the divine Spirit. In each case there is a different *kairos*, a different "right time". This kind of thinking liberates Christianity from a narrowness in which its own revelation is declared to be the only one and is not viewed within the whole context of the history of revelation. Such a narrowness leads, as in the case of Marcion and, partly at least, in the Barthian school, to an isolation of revelation over against the whole history of mankind.

Turning to christology, Irenaeus said: "The invisible of the Son is the Father; the visible of the Father is the Son." This is eternally so. There is always something which is potentially visible in God, and there is always something which remains as mystery and abyss in God. These are two sides which symbolically are distinguished as Father and Son. The Son who is eternally the visible of the Father becomes manifest in the personal appearance of Jesus as the Christ. The anti-gnostic fathers emphasized the monotheistic aspect in Christianity more strongly than the Apologists because they had to deal with Christian polytheistic tendencies. The Apologists, with their Logos doctrine, were drawn into a dangerous approximation to polytheistic thinking, or tritheistic, if the Spirit is handled in the same way as the Logos. In the line of thought which leads from John to Ignatius and Irenaeus, the Logos is not so much a lesser hypostasis, an inferior form or power of being in God, but is much more God himself as revealer, as his self-manifestation.

Irenaeus called salvation *anakephalaiōsis*, or *recapitulatio*, meaning recapitulation. He was pointing to Ephesians 1.10 which speaks of all things in heaven and earth being gathered up into Christ. Irenaeus built his idea of the history of salvation on these words in Ephesians. It means that the development which was broken in Adam is resumed by Christ and fulfilled in him. In Christ the new mankind has started. That which mankind was supposed to become, once disrupted by Adam, has finally reached its fulfillment in Christ. However, not only mankind but the whole cosmos finds its fulfillment in the appearance of the Christ. In order to accomplish this, Christ had to participate in the nature of Adam. Thus Christ is the beginning of the living as Adam is the beginning of the dead. Adam is fulfilled in Christ; this means that Christ is the essential man, the man Adam was to become but did not actually become. Adam was not in a state of fulfillment from the beginning; he lived in childish innocence. Here we have a profound doctrine of what I call a transcendent humanism, a humanism which says that Christ is the fulfillment of essential man, of the Adamic nature. Such a fulfillment became necessary because a break occurred in the development of man; Adam fell away from what he was to become. The childish innocence of Adam has been lost; but the second Adam can become what he was to become, fully human. And we can become fully human through participation in this full humanity which has appeared in Christ. This includes eternal life, similitude with God with respect to participation in infinity.

When I go into these matters, I am always surprised how much better the theology of the ancient church was than the popular theology which developed in the nineteenth century, how much profounder and more adequate to the paradox of Christianity, without becoming irrationalistic, nonsensical, or absurd. Of course, there were absurd elements on the borderline, on the edges, with respect to miracles, etc. But the central position was utterly profound, namely, the understanding of Christ, not as an accidental event or a transmutation of a highest being, but as fulfilled or essential humanity, therefore always related to Adam, to man's essential being and to his fallen state.

5. *Trinity and Christology*

Tertullian provided the fundamental formula for the trinity and christology. He used juristic language in a skillful way so that it became decisive for the future. The formulae of Tertullian entered the Latin creeds of the Roman Catholic Church. "Let us preserve the mystery of the divine economy which disposes the unity into trinity, the Father, the Son and the Holy Spirit, three not in essence but in grade, not in substance but in form." Here we have for the first time the word *trinitas*, introduced by Tertullian into ecclesiastical language. He also spoke of the unity in the trinity, denying any form of tritheistic tendencies. Instead, he speaks of "economy", an important word in ancient Christian theology. To speak of divine economy is to speak of God "building up" his manifestations in periods of history. In a living and dynamic way the trinity is built up in historical manifestations. But in this trinity there is but one divine essence. If we translate "essence" by "power of being", we have what this word meant. There is one divine power of being, and each of the three economic manifestations of the power of being participates in the full power of being.

God has eternally the *ratio* (reason) or *logos* in himself. It is an inner word. This is, of course, the characteristic of spiritual existence. If we say God is Spirit, we must also say he is trinitarian; he has the word within himself and has the unity with his self-objectivation. The word proceeds from God just as the beam proceeds from the sun. In the moment of creation the Son becomes a second person, and the Spirit a third person. The divine substance or essence, meaning power of being, is in all three persons. Tertullian's term "persona" does not mean the same as our word "person". You and I are persons because we are able to reason, to decide, to be responsible, etc. Such a concept of person was not applied to God at all, nor to the three *hypostases* in God. What then does *persona* mean? *Persona*, like the Greek word *prosōpon*, is the mask of the actor through which a special character is acted out. Thus we have three faces, three countenances, three characteristic expressions of the divine, in the process of divine self-explication. These are the classical formulae of trinitarian monotheism.

Tertullian also provided basic formulae with respect to christology. He said: "We see a double essence, not confused but united in one person, in God and the man Jesus." In this statement we have the formula of the doctrine of the two natures, or powers of being, in the one person of Christ. Here *persona* means one individual face or being of personal character, namely, Jesus. In this person two different powers of being are united, one divine and one human. Each of these powers is independent; neither is confused with the other; yet they are united in one person. If we ask how this is possible, we are anticipating the later discussions.

On the question whether the incarnation is a metamorphosis, that is, God *becoming* man, or the acceptance of a human essence, Tertullian decides for the latter. Like most of the theologians Tertullian is certain that God is ultimately unchangeable, and that the two powers of being must be preserved in their respective identities. Jesus as man is not a transformed God; he is a real man, true man. He can be true God also, but he is not a mixture of both. If the Logos were transfigured or transformed into something else, he would have changed his nature; but the Logos remains Logos in the man Jesus. So Tertullian thinks more in terms of the Logos adopting a human nature instead of the mythological idea of transmutation.

According to Irenaeus the saving power is the divine Spirit who dwells in the church and renews the members out of what is old into the newness in Christ. Christ gives them life (*zōē*) and light (*phōs*); he gives them the new reality. This is God's work in man, accepted by faith. Therefore, no law is needed since we love God and the neighbor. That is the Pauline element, but it is not strong enough to overcome the anti-Pauline elements. Ultimately, the new being is mystical and ethical. In this sense Irenaeus' conception is the highest form of early Catholicism, but it is not Protestant. In Protestantism the renewal takes place by justification through faith.

Irenaeus thinks of the process of salvation in terms of a mystical regeneration into immortality. In contrast to this, Tertullian

speaks of a wholesome discipline as the content of the Christian
life. He speaks of a process of education by the law, and the
reality of obedience to it is eternal life. Here we have Tertullian,
the Roman juristic mind, who likes the law, and at the same time
the ascetic pietist, who became a Montanist. In Irenaeus we
have mystical participation, in Tertullian subjection to the law.
These are the two sides of early Catholicism. The second aspect,
subjection to law, became decisive just before the Protestant
breakthrough. But the Protestant movement denied also the
Irenaean form, and returned to the other side of Paul, namely,
justification through faith.

In Tertullian we have the Roman Catholic form of Jewish
legalism. The relationship to God is legal. Christianity is merely
the new law. Christianity returns to the religion of the law, but
is prevented from becoming simply another Jewish system of
laws and rules by the sacramental salvation. Therefore, he could
say: "the *evangelium*, the Gospel, is our special law." Trans-
gressing the law means that guilt is produced and punishment is
required. "But if we do his will, he will make himself our debtor.
Then we can gain merits." There are two classes of demands:
precepts and counsels. In this way every man can acquire a
treasury of holiness in which he returns to Christ what Christ
has given him. The virtue of the Christian is crowned. The
sacrifice of asceticism and martyrdom moves God to do good to
us. "In the measure in which you do not spare yourselves, in this
measure, believe me, God will spare you." Here at the end of the
second century we meet many ideas that were to become important in later Roman Catholicism. Already we have the idea
that while the precepts are for everybody, there are special
counsels for monks; and we already have the idea of Christ as
the new law. Roman Catholicism emerged quickly in Christianity.
The reason for this is that Roman Catholicism was the form in
which Christianity could be readily received, including all the
Roman and Greek forms of thinking and living.

6. *The Sacrament of Baptism*

At this time baptism is still the most important sacrament. It
removes past sins. Baptism has two meanings: it means the wash-
ing away of sins and the reception of the divine Spirit. This, of

course, presupposed the baptismal confession of the creed, the consciousness of one's sins and the certainty of the Savior.

The practice of baptism had three characteristics: (1) One lays the hand on the candidate for baptism, and gives him sacred oil, the medium which makes the reception of the Spirit possible. (2) One rejects the devil, with all his pomp and angels. One leaves the demonic sphere; this meant the end of one's participation in paganism. This was not simply a moralistic formula; it went much deeper. It was breaking away from the demons which ruled the world, the rejection of polytheistic paganism. (3) The third element in baptism is the unity of forgiveness and regeneration. The pagan existence has come to an end, and the Christian existence begins. At baptism the preparatory stage of introduction into the church has come to an end. Those who are baptized are called the *teleioi*, the perfect ones. For they have reached the *telos*, the inner aim, of man's existence itself.

The theory of baptism in the anti-gnostic fathers was that the Spirit is united with the water, as it was in the gnostic mysteries. It was easy for Tertullian, with his Stoic background, to think of the Spirit as a material force in the water. This force somehow physically extinguishes the former sins and physically gives the Spirit. Here we see what has been called Tertullian's "materialism". This is important because it made infant baptism possible. If the water is the saving power, the child can be saved as much as the adult. It was not without some hesitation that Tertullian accepted this doctrine. But Christianity had to accept it as soon as it ceased to baptize individuals, one by one, called out of paganism, but baptized "all nations". Then the children cannot be excluded. However, if children are to be included, it is necessary to have a completely objective theory of baptism, because infants are not subjects who can decide.

The Lord's Supper was for Irenaeus the physical mediation of immortality. In it the union with heavenly and divine elements takes place.

These ideas are the making of the Roman Church; in the long run they were to become very influential. The Catholic Church was ready around the year A.D. 300. For this reason we cannot say that Protestantism is a restatement of the early centuries. The Catholic features were powerful very early. This is one of the reasons that the "middle way" of Anglicanism, which in itself would be an ideal solution to the schism of the churches, does not work. The so-called agreement of the first five centuries is by no means an agreement with the principles of the Reformation. Therefore, if someone says that we should unite by going back to the development which runs from Irenaeus to Dionysius the Areopagite, I would say that he had better become a Catholic, because Protestantism cannot do that. In these first centuries there are many elements which Protestantism cannot accept, for example, in the doctrine of the church, the system of authorities, the theory of the sacraments, not so much with respect to trinity and christology, although the implications are present there also.

E. NEO-PLATONISM

The end of Greek philosophy reached a state in which philosophy had become religion, and religion had become mystical philosophy. So when philosophers now became Christian, they could use a philosophy which was already half-religious. Philosophy at this time was not the philosophy taught today by empiricists, logical positivists, or naturalists. In the period of the New Testament philosophy itself included a religious attitude. This is why Christianity had to deal with philosophy, for it was a rival religion. The name of this religious philosophy was Neo-Platonism. In Neo-Platonism, Platonic, Stoic, and Aristotelian ideas were brought into a system which was philosophical and religious at the same time. Neo-Platonism expressed the longing of the ancient world for a new religion. It expressed the dissolution of all particular religions and at the same time the collapse of autonomous reason, the impossibility for reason to create by itself a new content of life. Therefore, these philosophers became mystics and, as mystics, they tried to create a new religion under the imperial protection of Julian the Apostate. In doing this they had to clash with Christianity. The great Alexandrian theologians, Clement and Origen, met the challenge of Neo-Platonism, and used its concepts to express Christianity.

Neo-Platonism is important not only because of its influence on Origen, who produced the first great theological system, but because through Dionysius the Areopagite it influenced all later forms of Christian mysticism and most forms of classical Christian theology, especially with respect to the doctrines of God, the world, and the soul. It is impossible to understand the further development of Christian theology without knowing something about Neo-Platonism, the last great attempt of paganism to express itself in terms of a philosophical theology, which was both science and life for the ancient mind.

Plotinus was the philosopher most responsible for the system of Neo-Platonism. There is not only a scientific and a religious side to it, but also a political aspect. The emperor, Julian the Apostate, tried to introduce the Neo-Platonic system against Christianity, which shows that he considered it not only as science or philosophy, but as an all-embracing system of religious elevation of the soul.

For Plotinus God is the transcendent One; he is the one who transcends every number, even the number "one" inasmuch as it is a number which includes 2, 3, 4, 5, etc. It is that which is beyond number, and for this he uses the word "one". Thus, whenever we hear the word "one" in mystical language, it is not to be understood as one number alongside others, but as that which transcends all numbers. The One points in particular to that which is beyond the basic cleavages of reality, the cleavage between subject and object, and between the self and the world. Therefore, the divine is the abyss of everything specific, the abyss in which everything definite disappears. But this abyss is not simply something negative; it is the most positive of all because it contains everything that is. When you read in mystical literature about "transcendent nothingness", do not interpret this as "nothing" but as "no-thing", that is, nothing definite, nothing finite, but the ground of everything finite and definite. Since it is without differentiation within itself, it is immovable, unchangeable, and eternal. Out of this eternal ground of everything, in which everything disappears, all things have their origin at the same time. The whole system is a description of the way in which the world and all its forms originate in the ultimate ground of being. The first thing which is originated, like the light which is radiated out of the sun, is what in Greek is called the *nous*, which can be translated as "mind" or "spirit". It is the second principle after the ultimate principle, after the ground of being from which it has emanated. This second principle, the *nous*, is that in which the first principle, the eternal ground, looks at itself. It is the principle of the self-intuition of the eternal. God is manifest to himself in the principle of the *nous*. This self-intuition of the divine in the *nous* is the source of all forms and structures, of all possibilities and of what Plato called "ideas". These "ideas" are the essential potentialities of being. Everything true and beautiful is contained in the *nous*, in the divine mind and his eternal self-intuition. Not only are the universal essences—treehood, redness, etc.—in the eternal mind, but also the essences of the individuals. In God is the form of each of us, independent of the changes in every moment of our lives, that form which a great painter would see and express in his portrait of us.

But there is a third principle which Plotinus called the "soul". The soul is the principle of life in all Greek thinking. It is not primarily an immortal substance, but the principle of movement. It is the principle which moves the stars, so the stars have souls; the principle which moves the animals and plants, so they also have souls; the principle which moves our bodies, so we have souls; the principle which moves the whole universe, so there is a world-soul. This soul-principle is midway between the *nous* and the bodily reality. It is the productive power of the existing world; it forms and controls matter, as our life-principle forms and controls every cell in our body. The soul of the world actualizes itself in many individual souls. Everything has an individual soul. These individual souls give movement and life to everything, but they all have their common principle in the world-soul.

This principle of soul, universally and individually, is the principle of ambiguity. Plotinus knew that life is ambiguous, that ambiguity is a definite characteristic of life. The soul is turned both toward the spirit (or *nous*) and toward matter. It looks in two directions, so to speak; it looks always to meaningful contents. In our language we call this man's spiritual life, expressed in knowledge, ethics, aesthetics, etc. At the same time it looks to our bodily existence and the whole world of material embodiment.

In this system of hierarchies, coming down from the ultimate to the mind and soul and matter, everything which is has a place. In this way Plotinus could place the whole mythological world into his system, after it was purified by philosophy. The gods of the pagans become limited powers of being which have their place in the whole of reality. This world is harmonious; it is directed by the principle of providence. This union of providence and harmony—the main principle of the Enlightenment and of the modern belief in progress—forms the basis of an optimistic world-view. This optimism immediately makes itself felt in another statement of Plotinus, namely, that the planetary forces, the demonic forces, are an illusion. They have no independent power; they are subjected to providence, just as Paul described it in Romans 8. The difference is that Plotinus derived this statement from his philosophy of cosmic harmony, while Paul derived it from the victorious triumph of Christ over the demons.

There are many different souls in the cosmos: mortal souls, such as plants, animals, and human beings, and immortal souls, such as the half-divine and divine beings of ancient mythology. These mythological gods are re-established in this system as powers of being. They do not contradict each other but have their definite place in this system of hierarchies.

The principle which orders this whole world, in terms of providence, is the logos. The logos is the rational side of the *nous* or mind. It is not another hierarchy but is only the dynamic side of the *nous*; it is the principle of reason which organizes everything providentially and gives it its place. To use a modern expression, it is the natural law to which everything is subjected, in physics and living bodies. The *nous* is not the logos; it is the source of all contents, but the logos gives order to them. The logos is the more dynamic principle, the providentially working power which directs the natural and moral laws.

Because of its ambiguity the soul is able to turn away from the *nous*, and with it from its eternal source in the abysmal One. It can separate itself from its eternal origin and turn to the lower realms. Nature is the realm of the unconscious; it stands between matter and the conscious soul. But nature has unconscious souls; in man alone the soul is completely conscious. This turning away of the soul from the *nous* toward matter, toward the bodily realm, is the source of evil. Evil is not a positive power; it is the negation of the spiritual. It is participation in matter, in non-being, in that which has no power of being by itself. Evil arises when the soul turns to non-being. Neither Greeks nor Christians could admit that evil is an ontological reality. The idea that there is a divine ground of evil, a divine being which produces evil, is the Manichaean heresy. Evil is non-being. When this statement is made, whether by Plotinus, Augustine, or myself, the charge is made that this means that sin is not taken seriously, that sin is nothing. The sound of the word "non-being" conveys the impression to some that sin is imaginary, not real. However, a distortion of something which has being is as real as the undistorted state of that being, only it is not ontologically real. If sin were ontologically real, this would mean that there is a creative principle of evil, as in Manichaeism; but this is what the Christian doctrine of creation denies. Augustine said, "*Esse qua esse bonum est*", being as being is good. Evil is the distortion of the good creation.

Plotinus described this non-being (*mē on*) as that which is matter and can become being. This non-being of which he speaks is that which as yet has no being and which resists against having being. He calls it that which lacks measure, limit, form. It is always in want, indefinite, hungry; it is the absolute poverty. In other words, evil is the presence of this non-being in our bodily existence. It is the absence of the power of being, the power of the good.

The soul turned toward this non-being because it believed that with its help it could stand upon itself. Thus, it separated itself from the ground and from the *nous* toward which it looked originally. But the soul looks back and yearns for the ground from which it came. Lovingly the soul ascends to that which is worth being loved, namely, the ground and origin of being itself. When the soul reaches the ultimate aim of its longing, it becomes like God. He who has the ultimate intuition of the divine has become one with God. But this way is hard. This way goes first through the virtues, next to the ascetic purification. The ultimate union with God cannot be reached either by morals or by asceticism in this life. It can only be reached by grace, that is, when the divine power of the transcendent One grasps the mind in ecstasy. This happens only rarely, only in great experiences which cannot be forced.

In the highest ecstasy there happens what Plotinus calls the flight of the one to the One, that is, of us who are individual ones to the ultimate One who is beyond number. What is the *telos*, the inner aim, the goal, the purpose, of man's being? Plato had already given the answer: *homoiōsis tou theou kata to dynaton*, that is, becoming similar to God as much as possible. This was also the aim of the mystery religions, in which the soul was supposed to participate in the eternal One. This is the Alexandrian scheme of thought. It is a circle which starts in the abysmal One, descending by emanation through the hierarchies until the ambiguous situation of the soul is reached, then through the soul falling into the power of the material world, which is determined by non-being. The circle continues then through the elevation of the soul, back through all these different grades up to the highest one, and in ecstasy this goal is reached. We must keep this system in mind, for we cannot understand the relationship of Christianity to mysticism and to Greek philosophy apart from it.

F. CLEMENT AND ORIGEN OF ALEXANDRIA

1. *Christianity and Philosophy*

The Neo-Platonic system was developed in Alexandria. Ammonius Saccas was the teacher of both Plotinus and Origen. Origen was the great theologian and philosopher of the school in Alexandria. This was a catechetical school, a kind of theological seminary. The first great teacher in this school was Clement of Alexandria. Clement used the Logos doctrine in a radical way. In this respect he was more dependent on Stoicism than on the Platonic school. God is the One who is beyond numbers. The Logos, however, is the mediator of everything in which the divine becomes manifest. The Logos, he said, is the man-loving organ of God, and therefore the educator of mankind in past and present. The Logos, as the self-manifestation of the divine, is always working in human minds. The Logos prepared the Jews by the law, and the Greeks by their philosophy. He has prepared all nations in some way. The Logos is never absent from people.

When Clement speaks of philosophy, he does not have in mind a particular philosophy, but that which is true in all philosophers. In his thought many elements from Greek philosophy are mixed with biblical materials. He quoted whole sections from Stoic sources. He introduced Christianity not only into philosophy but also into a philosophical way of life. *Philosophein* was defined by Clement as a striving for a perfect life. Living a philosophical life in the late Greek development was striving to become as near to God as possible. Clement's idea was to live according to the

Logos, a *logikon* life; perhaps we could translate this as a "meaningful life", a life in terms of objective meanings. Christians start first with faith, *pistis*. *Pistis* is not adequately translated by "faith". It is a state of being in faith. In this sense faith is a state of participation in the reality of the new being. It includes conversion, ascetic tendencies, passions, and hope. This is the presupposition of everything else in Christianity, and here Clement deviates from the Greek philosophers. Living according to the Logos means participation in the realm of faith and love, that is, in the realm of the church. The Alexandrian theologians were not independent philosophers, but members of the Christian Church. Therefore, they participated in the state of faith which is presupposed by all knowledge. However, the state of faith is insufficient since it is understood only as assent and obedience. A real participation demands something more, a drive toward knowledge or *gnōsis*. The Christian is the perfect "gnostic". *Gnōsis* is a cognitive faith, a faith which develops its contents cognitively. It is a scientific explanation of the traditions of faith. "Scientific" here is used not in the sense of the natural sciences but in the methodological sense. Everybody is on the way of this development, but only a few reach the aim. The perfect ones are only those who are, as Clement says, "gnostics according to the ecclesiastical canon". This means that philosophers are bound by the ecclesiastical tradition which they accepted when they entered the church. The highest good for these perfect gnostics is the knowledge of God. This knowledge is not a theoretical knowledge in terms of arguments and analyses, but a participation in God. It is not *epistēmē*, that is, scientific knowledge; it is *gnōsis*, that is, mystical or participating knowledge. It is not a *gnōsis* of free speculation but of participation in the congregation and in God. The tradition remains the canon, that is, the criterion, and the church is the mother without which *gnōsis* is unattainable.

Clement's thought is a great example of a synthesis of Christian thinking and Greek philosophy. Christianity had to cope with Neo-Platonism as a universal and extremely impressive system. All the values of the past were united in it. Christianity had to use it and conquer it at the same time. This was done by the school of Alexandria. Christianity was elevated to a state of highest education.

Porphyry was one of the most important Neo-Platonists. He

acknowledged the high educational standing of the Alexandrian school, especially of Origen. He expressed regrets, however, that Origen would live in a barbaric and irrational way as a Christian. Participation in the Christian congregation was incomprehensible to him as a Neo-Platonist. Porphyry acknowledged Origen's philosophical creativity; he said that Origen "hellenized" by interpreting the strange myths of the Bible by Greek thought. Clement and Origen were both Greek philosophers, and at the same time faithful and obedient members of the Christian Church. They had no doubt that it is possible to combine these two things.

Origen begins his system with the question of sources. He takes the sources much more seriously than Clement. The sources are the biblical writings and their summary in the ecclesiastical teaching and preaching. The ancient "rule of faith" provided the systematic scheme of his thought, but the Scriptures are the basis of its contents. The first step for the true theologian is the acceptance of the biblical message. Nobody can be a theologian who does not belong to the church. A free-soaring philosopher is not a Christian theologian. But more than this is required of the theologian. He must also try to understand things philosophically, and that means for Origen in terms of Neo-Platonic philosophy.

2. *The Allegorical Method*

The basic authority for Origen was Scripture. He introduced the famous distinction between three meanings of the Scripture. (1) The *somatic*, literal or philological sense. Everybody can understand the somatic sense (from *sōma*, meaning "body"); it is identical with the literal historical meaning. (2) The *psychic* or moral sense. The moral sense means the application of the biblical text to our situation, its existential application to ourselves. (3) The *pneumatic* or spiritual sense. It is understandable only to those who are perfect, not in the moral sense but in the mystical sense. There are some cases in which the biblical text has only a mystical meaning; then this coincides with the literal sense. Ordinarily, however, the mystical sense has to be distinguished from the literal meaning. The mystical sense is to be found through the allegorical method; this is a method of finding the hidden meaning behind the texts.

This doctrine of the allegorical method, or the idea of a mystical meaning in the texts, was strongly attacked by the sixteenth-century reformers, and it is alien to our realistic philological mind. What is the reason behind the allegorical method? This is easily understood. It arose in order to make a text that is absolutely authoritative applicable to the situation of the interpreter. It became necessary to find a meaning other than the literal one. Every sermon does this with the biblical texts. Today it is done by those interpreters of the Old Testament who find the christological pronouncements of the New Testament in it. It is almost inescapable; if you have a text that is an absolute authority, and its literal meaning does not say anything to you, then consciously or unconsciously you use a method which transfers the original meaning into an existential meaning. Of course, this can lead to a complete undercutting of the authority of the text. For this reason the Lutheran Reformation re-established the genuine, literal, philological text as the real authority. But when we examine the dogmatic statements and their proofs derived from the Bible that we find in orthodox or fundamentalist authors, we notice immediately that they do exactly what Origen did; they use a method which interprets the Bible beyond itself. Only if you are completely honest can you have the literal text, and then say, "This does not say anything to us," or "We must say something else; we recommend *beyond* the text, and we do not mean to express a hidden meaning in the text." I think this is the only consistent attitude. But think of another example—the American Constitution and its Amendments. They have absolute, legal validity, but in order to make them applicable, there is the Supreme Court which interprets them. Interpreting always means applying something to the present situation. The justices of the Supreme Court do not apply the allegorical method; instead they speak of the "spirit" of the law, and the spirit of the law may often contradict the letter of the law.

There are two classes of Christians: (1) The many simple ones, who accept on authority the biblical message and the teachings of the church without understanding them fully. They take the myths literally. As Origen said, they prefer the healing miracles to the story of Jesus going with his three apostles to the mount of transfiguration, which is an allegorical or metaphorical expression for those who go beyond the literal meaning to a transformed interpretation of it. Origen referred to the attitude of the primitive believers as "mere faith". This represents a lower degree of Christian perfection. All Christians begin at this level. (2) There are those to whom the charisma of *gnōsis*, the grace of knowledge, is given. In this way the converted, educated Greek becomes the perfect Christian, but he always does it on the basis of faith. This concept of faith is different from the meaning of faith in Protestantism. Here faith means the acceptance of doctrines, whereas in Protestantism faith is acceptance of the re-uniting grace of God. For Origen the first step is the acceptance of authority; the second is the autonomous rational understanding of the biblical message. The second step does not do away with the first step, but is possible only on the basis of it.

3. *The Doctrine of God*

The first doctrine in Origen's system was the doctrine of God. God is being-itself, and therefore beyond everything that is. He is beyond knowledge, because knowledge presupposes the cleavage between subject and object. He is beyond change and passion. He is the source of everything. But he has his *Logos*, his inner word, his self-manifestation. This *Logos* makes God manifest first to himself and then to the world. The Logos is the creative power of being; all powers of being are united in him. The whole spiritual world is united in the Logos. It is the universal principle of everything in particular, of anything that has being. This divine Logos radiates eternally from the ground of being, from the divine abyss, as splendor radiates from the source of light. Therefore, one is not supposed to say: "There was a time when the Son did not exist." To say this is to deny the eternity of the Logos. There never was a time in which the Son, the eternal Logos, did not exist.

The eternal Logos is eternally generated out of the divine substance. He is not created "out of nothing"; he is not finite. He has the same substance with the Father. Here the formula *homoousios tō patri* (being of one substance with the Father) first arises. In spite of the eternity of the Logos, however, the Logos is less than the Father. Only the Father is without origin; he is not even generated. He is *auto theos*, God by himself, whereas the Son is God by the Father. The Son is the picture of the goodness or essence or nature of God, but not God himself.

Thus, we have two trends in this Origenistic thinking. First, the Son is co-eternal with the Father; secondly, the Son has a kind of lesser validity and power of being than the Father. The Son is the highest of all generated realities, but he is less than the Father. The same thing is true of the Spirit, who is working in the souls of the saints. Although the religious tradition of the congregations demands that the *trias* (the three) be the object of adoration, the Spirit is called less than the Son and the Son less than the Father. And sometimes the highest spiritual beings are even called gods. This means that two principles are in conflict in Origen's thought. The one is the divinity of the Savior; he must be divine in order to be able to save. The other is the scheme of emanation. There are degrees of emanation from the absolute, the Father, down to the lowest levels. The line of division between the highest three (Father, Son and Spirit) and the rest of spiritual beings is somewhat arbitrary.

The rational natures, or spirits, which are eternal were originally equal and free, but they fell away from their unity with God in different degrees of distance. As result of their revolt in heaven against God, they may have fallen into material bodies. This is their punishment and at the same time the way of their purification. The human soul is the mediation between these fallen spirits and the human body. The human soul is the spirit which has become cold. That is, the intensive fire, which is the symbol for the divine Spirit, is reduced to a life process. The fall is a transcendent fall. It precedes our existence in time and space. And it is a free fall; it is decided in freedom. The freedom is not lost by the fall, but it is actual and present in all concrete actions. In these concrete actions the transcendent fall becomes historical reality. We could say that the individual act represents the eternal nature of the fall. In other words, our individual existence in time and space has a prelude in heaven. The decisive thing about us has already happened when we appear on earth. This has particular reference to sin. Sin is based on the transcendent fall. This doctrine of the transcendent fall is difficult to understand for people who have grown up in nominalistic thinking. It is understandable only if one realizes that transcendent powers are realities and not individual things. There is a profound meaning in this doctrine which makes it necessary as a symbol in Christian theology. It means that our human existence and the existence of reality as a whole are considered not only as creation but also as guilt and judgment. When we look at the world, we see that it is universally fallen. Its fallenness penetrates through everything, even through nature outside of man. If we ask: Where did it come from? Why is the fall universal? Why are there no exceptions? Then the answer is: Because the fall precedes the creation, just as the fall follows the creation. Origen has two myths of the fall. The one is transcendent; mythologically speaking, it is not in space. It is the eternal transition from union with God to separation from God. The other is the immanent, inner-historical fall. The transcendent fall becomes actual through special acts on the historical plane. Sin is spiritual, but the bodily and social existence strengthens sin. It is transcendent and a destiny which, like every destiny, is united with freedom.

As in Plotinus, sin for Origen is a turning away from God. It is not something positive. Being evil means being without goodness. Sin, therefore, has a double relation to creation. With respect to the creation of the free and equal spirits, creation precedes the fall; with respect to the bodily world, creation follows the fall and follows the freedom of the spirits. On account of the freedom of the spirits, it is possible for the fall to happen again even in eternity. The end of the world process is not necessarily the end of history. The fall may repeat itself, and then the whole process starts over again. In these ideas we see the cyclical thinking of Greek philosophy with respect to history. This way of thinking was not overcome by Origen, as it was done later by Augustine.

4. *Christology*

The most difficult part of Origen's thought has to do with his christology. The Logos unites itself with the soul of Jesus, who is an eternal spirit as everyone else is. He is pre-existent as all souls are. But the Logos unites himself with just this soul. The soul of the man Jesus has received the Logos completely. The soul of Jesus has merged into the power and the light of the Logos. This is a mystical union which can be emulated in all saints. The soul mediates between the Logos of God and the body of man. In this way there are two sharply separated natures united in Jesus. The statement of the Fourth Gospel that the *Logos became flesh* is a literal way of speaking. The truth is that the Logos took on flesh so much that it could be said that he had become it. This is more like adoptionistic thinking. Popular feeling in the East, on the other hand, wanted to have a God on earth who walks with us, not a divine transcendent power who merely takes on flesh, and then returns after he has taken it on. But for Origen this idea was unacceptable because the Logos can never cease to be also outside of Jesus. The Logos is the form of everything that has form. After the incarnation the Logos ceased to be a man, but this is somehow the case with all spiritual beings, who for this reason are called gods. But if they are gods, where does the dividing line come between them and the third person of the trinity? This problem was not solved, and could not be solved on the basis of the doctrine of emanation. In the doctrine of emanation there is a continuous going down and returning. Christianity, however, belonged to monotheism. How can monotheism be maintained if there are two emanations which are lower than God and at the same time divine?

When men follow the example of the Logos, they themselves become *logikoi*, that is, determined by meaning, reason, and creative power. They are led back to deification. However, Jesus had to do something else to make this possible for men. He had to give his body as a sacrifice. To whom did he give it? To Satan, as a ransom! Satan demands such a price for letting the others go free; but Satan was betrayed. Satan was unable to keep Jesus, because Jesus was pure and therefore not within the pale of Satan's power. This idea of the betrayal of Satan was not only a theological notion in Origen but was also to be found in popular piety. The Middle Ages was full of stories of how the peasants, especially their wives, betrayed the devil when he came, so he had to leave them alone. To us this seems to be a grotesque mythological idea, and it certainly is if taken literally. But it contains a profound religious insight, namely, that the negative element can never ultimately prevail; it cannot prevail because it lives from the positive. When Satan takes Jesus into his power, he cannot keep in his power that from which he himself lives, namely, the divine nature. This shows the ultimate futility of sin. It cannot indefinitely keep in its control the positive power of being, because this power of being is derived from the good. The good and the power of being are one and the same thing. So the meaning of Origen's doctrine is that it is impossible for Satan to prevail ultimately, because he lives from that against which he strives to prevail.

Origen's interpretation of the Song of Songs in terms of the mystical love of the soul with Christ introduced into practical piety an idea which had a tremendous effect on later church history. The human soul is the bride of the Logos; this is the meaning of this love song. The soul receives the bridegroom in herself; she is sometimes visited by the Logos. That is, the divine Spirit is sometimes experienced by us, sometimes the soul is left alone, and no one visits her from the eternal. This is the first mystical interpretation of the Song of Songs that is directly related to the individual. In Judaism it was interpreted in terms of the relation between God and the synagogue. Here we see an example of the necessity for allegorical interpretation. The Song of Songs itself is nothing more than a Jewish love song, perhaps a wedding song which was performed at weddings or festivals. Yet it is in the canon and has divine authority. What can be done with it? The answer of the Jews was that it concerns the relationship between God and the nation. And in my old Luther Bible, which I love dearly because I received it for my baptism, there is something that is said in the superscription of the Song of Songs about the relationship between God and the church. But Origen interpreted it in terms of the mystical marriage between Christ and the soul. This is, of course, an example of mysticism, but it is a transformation of non-Christian mysticism. It is concrete mysticism. The soul, being grasped by the Spirit of God, does not go beyond itself into the abyss of the divine, but the Logos, the concreteness of the divine, comes into the soul. This is the first step in what I call the "baptizing" of mysticism. Mysticism could be introduced into the church by becoming concrete. If Origen, and later on Bernard of Clairvaux, speaks of the mystical marriage between the Logos and the soul, the centered personality is not destroyed. It is preserved, as in a marriage there is a complete union in which the persons are not destroyed.

5. *Eschatology*

The last point in Origen's theology is the doctrine of the final end of history and the world. He interprets this end spiritualistically. The primitive imagery is interpreted in spiritual terms.

The second coming of Christ is the spiritual appearance of Christ in the souls of the pious. He comes back to earth again and again, not in a dramatic appearance in physical terms, but into our souls. The pious people are fulfilled in a spiritual experience. The "spiritual body" of which Paul speaks is the essence or the idea of the material body. It is that which is painted by a great portrait painter. This is what partcipation of the body in the eternal means.

The punishment for sin is hell. Hell is the fire which burns in our conscience, the fire of despair because of our separation from God. This, however, is a temporary state of purging our souls. At the end everyone and everything will become spiritualized; the bodily existence will vanish. This famous doctrine of Origen is called *apokatastasis tōn pantōn*, the restitution of all things. Because freedom is never cancelled out, there is the possibility that the whole process could start over again. Origen was a thoroughgoing philosopher of freedom, and this is what distinguishes him from Augustine.

This spiritualization of eschatology was at least part of the reason that Origen became a heretic in the Christian Church, although he was its greatest theologian. The simple ones revolted against this great system of scientific theology. Monks and others did not want to yield their literalism with respect to the future life, the final catastrophe, the eternal judgment, etc. The motives of the simple ones were mixed. Partly this reaction to Origen's doctrine was due to a Jewish type of realism of bodily existence, against a Greek dualism, and partly it was motivated by the idea of revenge against those who were better off on earth. So they fought for a very realistic and literalistic idea of judgment, final catastrophe, and heaven. The church took their side and condemned the heretical side of Origen.

G. Dynamic and Modalistic Monarchianism

The simple ones revolted also against Origen's Logos christology which he had received from the Apologists. The laymen, the simple ones, were not interested in the cosmological speculations of the Logos concept. They wanted to have God himself on earth in Christ. This group was called the Monarchians, from *monarchia*, meaning "one man's rule". They wanted to have only one ruler, one God not three, as they felt was entailed by the Logos christology. Against the Logos as a second God, they stressed the "monarchy" of the Father. This movement was a monotheistic reaction against the tritheistic danger of the Logos doctrine. The Logos doctrine hypostasized the Son beside God, and the Spirit beside both of them.

A man named Theodotus, a craftsman from Rome, thought that Jesus was a man on whom the divine Spirit descended in baptism, giving him the power of his messianic vocation. But this did not make him God. People of this type of thinking were most interested in those passages in the Gospels which deal with Jesus as a man. There is perhaps a connection between Theodotus and a group in Asia Minor called the *Alogoi*, so called because they denied the doctrine of the Logos. And since the Logos idea appeared in the Fourth Gospel, they rejected it. They tried to establish the true text and to stress its literal interpretation against allegorizing. They were in a sense predecessors of many later movements in church history which emphasized the humanity of Jesus, from the school of Antioch through medieval adoptionism to modern liberal theology, over against the Logos as God becoming man. This is called the adoptionistic or dynamic christology. The man Jesus is adopted; he is filled by the Logos or the Spirit, but he is not God himself. This is the one wing of the monarchic, monotheistic reaction against the Logos Christology.

1. *Paul of Samosata*

Paul of Samosata, a bishop of Antioch, was in the line of thinking we have just presented. He said that the Logos and Spirit are qualities of God, but not persons. They are eternal powers or potentialities in God, but not persons in the sense of independent beings. Jesus is a man who was inspired by this power from above. The power of the Logos inhabited Jesus as in a vessel, or as we live in houses. The unity that Jesus has with God is the unity of will and love; it is not a unity of nature, because nature has no meaning with respect to God. The more that Jesus developed in his own being, the more he received of the Spirit. Finally he achieved eternal union with God, and then he became the judge and received the status of God. He became God, but somehow he had to deserve to become God. Such an idea is, of course, the negation of the divine nature of the Savior. This denial is what made him a heretic, although many people of his time and even today would prefer to follow his way of thinking.

The Monarchian movement itself was split. The one side followed the adoptionist christology. It says that God, or the Logos, or the Spirit, adopted a fully human individual, made him into Christ, and gave him the possibility of becoming fully divine in his resurrection. In the West we find this way of thinking in Theodotus of Rome and in the East in Paul of Samosata. This christology started with human existence, then it emphasized those biblical statements which refer to the humanity of Christ, and finally it showed that Jesus was driven by the Spirit while on earth and in the end elevated into the divine sphere. The other side of Monarchianism is called modalistic Monarchianism; it was more in line with the basic feeling of the masses of Christians. "Modalism" means that God himself appears in different modes, in different ways. It was also called *Patripassianism*, which means that the Father himself suffered in Christ. Another name for this movement is Sabellianism, from its leading representative, Sabellius. This became a widespread movement in the East and the West, and was a real danger to the Logos christology.

In the West there was a man named Praxeas with whom Tertullian was fighting. His idea was that God the Father himself was born through the Virgin Mary, that God the Father himself, the only God, suffered and died. To be God means to be the universal Father of everything. If we say that God was in Jesus, this means that the Father was in him. Therefore, Praxeas and his followers attacked the so-called *ditheoi*, those who believed in two Gods, and the *tritheoi*, those who believed in three Gods. They fought for the monarchy of God and for the full divinity of Christ in whom the Father himself appeared. Both notions had great popular support because the popular mind wanted to have God himself present on earth, a God who is with us, who participates in our fate, and whom we can see and hear when we see and hear Jesus.

2. Sabellius

Sabellius was the leader of the modalistic Monarchians. He said: "The same is the Father, the same is the Son, the same is the

Holy Spirit. They are three names, but names for the same reality. Do we have one or three Gods?" Father, Son, and Spirit are names, they are *prosōpa* (countenances, faces), but they are not independent beings. They are effective in consecutive energies; one follows the other, but the same God appears in different faces. It is the same God acting in history in three countenances. The *prosōpon* (countenance) of the Father appears in his work as creator and law-giver. The *prosōpon* of the Son appears from the birth to the ascension of Jesus. Since the ascension of Jesus the countenance of the Spirit appears as the life-giver. Through all appearances it is the same monarchic Father-God. Therefore, it is not adequate to speak of a *trias* in heaven. There is no transcendent, heavenly trinity. Instead of being transcendent, the trinity is historical or "economically", in the sense of *oikonomia*, building a house. The trinity is built up in history.

When Sabellius says that the same God is essentially in the Father, Son, and the Spirit, that there are only differences of faces, appearances, or manifestations, he is saying that they are all *homoousios*. That is, they all have the same essence, the same divine power of being. They are not three beings, but they have the same power of being in three manifestations. Although this trend of thinking was condemned, it has never disappeared. It reappeared as a strong monotheistic trend in Augustine and through him in Western theology in general. This modalistic thinking was in opposition to the Logos christology. If you are able to distinguish these two basic trends, you have an insight into what was involved in these seemingly incomprehensible struggles over an iota in *homoousios* and *homoiousios*. This was not a fight over abstract concepts, but it was a conflict between a monotheistic trend and the attempt to establish divine hierarchies between God and man. The East in general, dependent as it was on Plato, Plotinus, and Origen, was interested in hierarchical essences between God and man. This, of course, would make of Christ a demi-god, as we shall see. The West, and some groups in the East, were interested in the divine monarchy, on the one side, and in the humanity of Jesus, on the other. For us as Westerners, the problem of hierarchies is an abstract one, not a problem of living realities.

H. The Trinitarian Controversy

First we must see how the trinitarian problem developed after Origen. Origen was so powerful in his constructive thinking that he conquered all rivals, also the Monarchian and Sabellian theologians. And his christology was so impregnated with mystical piety that his statements could become formulae of a creed. We must not forget that when the Greek thinkers produced a confession or creed, it may seem like abstract philosophy to us, but to them it was the mystical intuition of essences, of powers of being. For instance, in Caesarea a creed was used in baptism which had added mystical formulae from Origen: "We believe in Jesus Christ, the Logos of God, God from God, Light from Light, Life from Life, first-born of all creatures, generated out of the Father before all generations." This is both philosophy and mysticism. It is Hellenistic and not classical Greek philosophy. Hellenistic philosophy was united with the mystical traditions of the East. Therefore, seemingly abstract philosophical concepts could become mystical confessions.

This combination of mystical philosophy with a Christian confession was endangered when the emanation system of Origen was called into question from the point of view of Christian conformism. For example, the eternity and the pre-existence of all spirits, the idea of the transcendent fall, the spiritual body-less resurrection, and the spiritualized eschatology, were all questioned. The place of the Logos was also questioned. Common-sense conformism, supported by the Monarchian reaction, demanded nothing less than God on earth. The theory of emanation by degrees, in hierarchies of powers of being, demanded something less than that which is ultimately transcendent, the One which is beyond everything given.

Out of this conflict a division occurred in the school of Origen between a left wing and a right wing of Origenistic thinking. The right wing said: Nothing is created or subordinate in the *trias*; nothing has been added which is not in the trinity from the beginning. The Son is not inferior to the Father, nor the Spirit to the Son. Representatives of this position wanted what is today called a "high christology". The Son in Jesus is not less than the Father himself.

The left wing opposed the traditionalism of the right wing; it was "scientific" and modernistic. This position held that the Son is essentially strange to the Father; he was a created being; he had no being before he was generated. This means that the Logos christology is developed in hierarchical terms. First, there is God the Father, the highest hierarchy, the eternal One beyond everything; then there is the Logos, the second hierarchy and inferior to the first; the Spirit is the third hierarchy, and inferior to the second. The immortal spirits form the fourth hierarchy, lower than the three others. These are the two wings involved in a great struggle which almost ruined the Christian Church.

Besides theological differences politics became involved in the trinitarian controversy. The attempt was made to find a practical way to solve the problem without going into its theoretical depths. This was the way of Roman eclecticism, something like our American pragmatism. Rome provided the direction for a practical solution which avoided the depths of Greek thinking. Dionysius, the pope in Rome, declared: "Two things must be preserved: the divine *trias* and the holy message of monarchy." These were the two main terms of the two wings, the one affirming the holy message of the monarchy, which stood against the Logos christology, the other affirming the divine *trias*, which expressed the Logos christology. So the pope took the main formulae of both groups and said they must both be preserved. But he did not say how that was possible. This was practical church politics, an approach which finally prevailed, as we shall see. But it prevailed only after a tremendous conflict of almost eighty years. This conflict, which we call the Arian controversy, had a lasting effect on the church, and the decision which was finally reached became valid for all periods of Christianity.

1. *Arianism*

The Arian controversy was a unique and classical struggle which was caused by many motives. The politics of the emperors was involved in it. They needed a unity in the church because Christianity had by this time become the favored religion of the Roman Empire. This threatening division in the church would split the whole empire into pieces, it was feared. Personal feuds between bishops and theologians were involved. There was also a conflict between a narrow traditionalism and an unrestrained speculation. A strong emphasis on theoretical solutions to problems collided with popular monastic fanaticism. But that is not the whole story. The really decisive issue, its basic meaning and permanent significance, had to do with the question: How is salvation possible in a world of darkness and mortality? This has been the central question ever since the apostolic fathers, and it was the question involved in the great trinitarian and christological controversies.

Athanasius, the great foe of Arius, answered that salvation was possible only on one condition, namely, that the Son of God was made man in Jesus so that we might become God. This is possible only if the Logos is eternal, if it is really God who has appeared to us in Jesus. God is Father only because he is the Father of the Son. Thus, the Son is without beginning; eternally the Father has the Son. The Son is the eternal Son of the Father; and the Father is the eternal Father of the Son. Only if they are co-eternal can Jesus, in whom the Logos is present, give us eternity. He can make us like God, which always means to make us immortal, and to give us eternal knowledge, the knowledge of eternal life. Not even the highest of all created spirits can give us a real salvation. A created spirit, even the highest, is less than God. But we are separated from God. We are dependent on God and must return to him. So God himself must save us.

According to Arius, a presbyter from Alexandria, only God the Father is eternal and unoriginated. The Logos, the pre-existent Christ, is a creature. He is created out of nothing; there was a time when he was not. Origen had made the statement that there was no time in which he was not. Against this the left-wing Origenistic theology said that there was a time in which he was not. This time was prior to our temporal existence, but it was not eternity. The Logos is not eternal. The power of God at work in Jesus is not the eternal divine power itself, but is a limited and lower hierarchy. This Logos is strange to the divine nature and dissimilar in every respect from the Father's essence. The Logos can neither see nor know the Father completely and exactly. He becomes God only in the way in which every saint may become deified. This deification happened, as it happens in every saint, through his freedom. The Logos had the freedom to turn away from God, but he did not do that. This Logos, a half-divine power, is the soul of Jesus. This means that Jesus is not fully man with a natural human soul. Mary gives birth to this half-God, who is neither fully God nor fully man. This solution of Arius is in line with the hero cults of the ancient world. This world is full of half-gods, gods who even in heaven (i.e., Olympus) are not fully gods but derived forms of God. Jesus is one of these gods, but he is not God himself.

2. The Council of Nicaea

Arius' christology was rejected at the Council of Nicaea, A.D. 325. The Nicene Creed begins: "We believe in one God, the Father Almighty, Maker of all things visible and invisible." *ideas* These are important words. The word "invisible" has reference to the Platonic "ideas". God is the creator not only of the things on earth, but of the "essences" as they appear in Plato's philosophy. The Creed continues: "And in one Lord, Jesus Christ, the Son of God, begotten of the Father, the only-begotten of the essence of the Father, God of God, and Light of Light, true God of true God, begotten not made, being of one substance [*homoousios*] with the Father, by whom all things were made in heaven and on earth, who for us men and our salvation came down and was incarnate and was made man. He suffered and the third day he rose again, ascended into heaven. From thence he comes to judge the quick and the dead. And in the Holy Ghost." Then it goes on to say: "And those who say there was a time when he was not, or he was not before he was made, and he was made out of nothing, and out of another substance or thing, or the Son of God is created or changeable, or alterable, they are condemned by the Catholic Church." This is the fundamental Christian confession. The central phrase is "of one substance with the Father". Nothing like this is said of the Holy Ghost. And this was the reason for further struggles and decisions. The condemnations are interesting; the all-embracing one is directed against the Arians: "Those who say there was a time when he was not . . . are condemned by the Catholic Church."

Now we will present the significance of the decision of Nicaea for world history and the history of the church:

(1) The most serious Christian heresy was overcome. Christ is not one of the many half-gods; he is not a hero. He is God

himself appearing in divine essence within a historical person. It meant a definite negation of paganism. In Arius paganism again raised its head after it had been defeated in the anti-gnostic struggle. The victory of Arianism would have made Christianity only one of many possible religions.

(2) The confession of Nicaea was expressed in terms more pleasing to Rome and the West than to the East. The East did not like the *homoousios*; instead it wanted a ladder of hierarchies. Rome and her allies in the East insisted on the *homoousios*. For this reason the decision of Nicaea was immediately attacked. A sixty-year struggle ensued until in A.D. 381 a settlement was reached more satisfying to the East.

(3) The decisive statement is: "Being of one substance with the Father." This is not in the scheme of emanation but in the scheme of Monarchianism. Consequently it was accused of being Sabellian; and so were the main defenders, Athanasius and Marcellus.

(4) The negative character of the decision is especially evident in the condemnations. The creatureliness of Christ is negated. He has no other *ousia* than the Father; but what the *homoousios* is was not explained. It was not decided whether the three *prosōpa* are really differences in God, and if so whether they are eternal or historical. And no doctrine of the Spirit was given. Only one thing was determined: Jesus Christ is not an incarnated half-god; he is not a creature above all others; he is God. And God is creator and unconditioned. This negative decision is the truth and the greatness of the Council of Nicaea.

(5) There were some other implications. The statements were made in philosophical, non-biblical terms. Some Greek concepts were taken into the dogma, not so much as classical philosophy but as mystical philosophy of religion.

(6) From now on the unity of the church is identical with the majority of the bishops. A conciliarism had developed in hierarchical terms; the majority of the bishops replace all other authorities. Only much later did the claim of the Roman bishop to a special status among the bishops become dominant, until finally the authority of the majority of the bishops was abolished.

(7) The church had become a state church. This was the price which had to be paid for unity. The emperor did not command the content of the dogma, but he exercised pressure. When there were revolts against the dogma, the emperors after Constantine

had to exert even more pressure. This means that a new development in church history, indeed, of world history, had begun.

3. *Athanasius and Marcellus*

The chief defender of the decision of Nicaea was Athanasius. He was primarily a great religious personality. His basic religious conviction was unalterable, and therefore he was able to use a variety of scientific means and political ways to advance his cause. His style was clear; he was consistent and cautious, although at times he could be compromising in his terminology. Several times he was expelled from his episcopal see in Alexandria. He was persecuted, but in the end he was victorious over heretics and emperors. Athanasius saved the decision of Nicaea, but in order to do so he had to compromise with a more Origenistic interpretation of the Nicene formulae.

For Athanasius sin is overcome by forgiveness, and death, which is the curse of sin, is overcome by the new life. Both are given by Christ. The new life includes communion with God, moral renewal, and eternal life as a present possession. Positively speaking, eternal life is deification, becoming like God as much as possible. Thus, two things are needed, a victory over finitude and a victory over sin. There must be both participation in the infinity of God and participation in the holiness of God. How can this be provided? Only by Christ who, as true man, suffers the curse of sin and, as true God, overcomes death. No half-god, no hero, no limited and relative power of being can do that. Only as historical man could God change history, and only as divine could he give eternity. There is no such thing as a half-forgiveness or half-eternity. If our sins are forgiven, they must be fully forgiven; if we are eternal, we must be fully eternal. No half-god could be the Savior. Salvation is the problem of christology.

The Christ who performs this work of salvation is not understandable to the human mind except through the divine Spirit. Only through the Spirit can we come into unity with the Christ. This implies that the Spirit of Christ must be as divine as Christ himself. Groups arose after the Nicene decision to deny the divinity of the Spirit. Athanasius fought against them too, and said: They are wrong, for they want to make the Spirit into a creature. But if the Spirit of Christ is a creature, then Christ also is a creature. The Spirit of Christ is not the human spirit of the man Jesus; the Spirit of Christ is not a psychological function. The Spirit of Christ is God himself in Jesus and through him in us. In this way the trinitarian formula which remained unfinished at Nicaea was finally completed. In order to be able to unite us with Christ, the Spirit must be as divine as Christ himself, not half-divine, but fully God.

One of Athanasius' supporters was Marcellus, by whom the Monarchian tradition entered the discussion. Although he was an intimate friend of Athanasius, Marcellus was condemned by the more Origenistic theologians who did not like his Monarchian tendencies. Marcellus' emphasis was on monotheism. Before the creation God was a *monas*, a unity without differentiation. His Logos was in him, but only as a potential power for creation, but not yet as an actual power. Only with the creation does the Logos proceed and become the acting energy of God in all things, through whom all things have been made. At the moment of creation the divine *monas* has become a *dyas*, the unity has become a duality. In the incarnation, the act in which the Logos took on flesh, the second "economy" is performed. An actual separation occurs between Father and Son, in spite of the remaining potential unity, so that now it is possible for the "eyes of faith" to see the Father in the Son. Then a further broadening of the *monas* and of the *dyas* occurs, when after the resurrection of Christ the Spirit becomes a relatively independent power in the Christian Church. But these separations are only preliminary; the independence of the Spirit and of the Son is not final. The Son and the Spirit will finally return into the unity with the Father, and then the flesh of Jesus will wither away. The potential or eternal Logos should not be called the Son; he becomes the Son only through the incarnation and the resurrection. In Jesus a new man, a new manhood, appears, united with the Logos by love.

What we have described is a dynamic Monarchian system. The trinity is dynamized, is put into movement, approaches history, and has lost the static character it has in genuine Origenistic thinking. But this system was rejected. It was accused of being Sabellian, of representing that kind of Monarchianism in which God the Father himself appears on earth. The Origenistic system of degrees and hierarchies triumphed against Marcellus.

But the struggle continued. The Origenistic protest against the *homoousios* led not only to conflict with people like Athanasius or Marcellus, but also against the Nicaenum itself. This happened in the East, of course. The Origenists who had been overwhelmed by the pressure of the emperor at Nicaea gathered their forces again and insisted, against the Nicaenum, on three substances in the trinity. This was, so to speak, a pluralistic interpretation of the trinity, in the scheme of emanation, of hierarchies and powers of being. The trinity is seen in degrees, but only the Father is unconditioned and unlimited. He alone is the source of everything eternal and temporal. This was the mood of the Eastern theologians and the popular piety in the East. This mood prevailed again and again, in some cases with strong support of the emperor, who defied the decision of his predecessor Constantine and tried to press the supporters of Nicaea against the Nicaenum.

There was, however, a shortcoming in Eastern theology; it was united only negatively and not on a positive decision. So it was easy to split it and reduce its power of resistance against the Nicaenum. There were some in the East who practically returned to Arius; they were called the *anomoioi* (Anomoeans), which means "the Son is unlike the Father in all things". He is completely a creature. There were still others who mediated between the Nicaenum and the mood of the East. They were called the *homoiousianoi*, for they accepted the *homoiousios*, but not the *homoousios*. *Homoiousios* is derived from *homoios* which means "similar". This means that the Son is similar in essence to the Father. So now we have the struggle between the *homoousios* and the *homoiousios*. The hostile pagans in Alexandria cracked jokes about this fight going on in the streets, barbershops, and stores, in which Christians were arguing over an iota, the smallest letter in the alphabet, the only letter that distinguishes *homoiousios* from *homoousios*. But this was more than a fight over an iota; a different piety lay behind it. For the *homoiousianoi* the Father and Son are equal in every respect, but they do not have the identical substance. This group interpreted the Nicene formula *homoousios*, which they could not remove any more, in the sense of *homoiousios*. And even Athanasius and the West finally agreed that this could be done, if only the formula itself were accepted. The West in turn accepted the eternal generation of the Son, a formula which derived from Origen and which the

West did not like, and with it the West accepted the inner-divine, eternal trinity, which is a non-historical (non-economic) view of the trinity. The East, on the other hand, accepted the *homoousios* after it was possible to interpret it in the light of the *homoiousios*. And under these same conditions the East also accepted the *homoousia* of the Spirit.

This means that theological formulae were discovered which were able to resolve the struggle, but theological terms are never able to overcome the religious difference itself. We shall see how this worked itself out in the later developments of the Eastern and Western churches, in the coming fights and struggles and in the final separation. But for the time being the Synod of Constantinople, A.D. 381, was able to make a decision in which both East and West agreed, in which the *homoousios* and the *homoiousios* could come together. Before this was possible, however, new theological developments had to occur. These developments are represented by the three great Cappadocian theologians.

4. *The Cappadocian Theologians*

The three Cappadocian theologians were Basil the Great, Gregory of Nyssa, his brother, and Gregory of Nazianzus. Basil the Great was the bishop of Caesarea; he was many things, a churchman, bishop, the great reformer of monasticism, a preacher, and a moralist. He fought against the old and neo- and semi-Arians, against everything which followed the idea that Christ is a half-god and a half-man. Basil died, however, before the favorable decision of Constantinople was reached.

Basil's younger brother, Gregory of Nyssa, was called "the theologian". He continued the Origenistic tradition and its "scientific" methods. After Christianity became victorious under Constantine and after the Nicene dogma became fixed, it was possible now again for theology to attempt a union of Greek philosophy and Christian dogma. But this theology no longer had the freshness of the first great attempts made by the Apologists and Origen. It was much more determined by the ecclesiastical situation and the Creed of Nicaea; thus, it was more a matter of formulae than of material creativity. Gregory of Nazianzus created the definitive formulae for the doctrine of the trinity. He had become an intimate friend of Basil when both of them were

students in Athens. They were united not only in their common
theological convictions but also in their common asceticism.
Gregory of Nazianzus became bishop and was president of the
synod of Constantinople for a certain period.

These Cappadocian Fathers, especially Gregory of Nazianzus,
made sharper distinctions between the concepts that were used
in the trinitarian dogma. Two series of concepts were used: the
first is one divinity, one essence (*ousia*), one nature (*physis*); the
second series is three substances (*hypostaseis*), three properties
(*idiōtētes*), three persons (*prosōpa, personae*). The divinity is
one essence or nature in three forms, three independent realities.
All three have the same will, the same nature and essence. Nevertheless, the number three is real; each of the three has its special
characteristics or properties. The Father has the property of
being ungenerated; he is from eternity to eternity. The Son has
the characteristic of being generated. The Spirit has the characteristic of proceeding from the Father and the Son. But these
characteristics are not differences in the divine essence, but only
in their relations to each other. This is complex and abstract
philosophy, but it offered the formula which made the reunion of
the church possible. The Council of Constantinople removed the
condemnations which had been added to the Creed of Nicaea,
because they did not apply to the new terminology any more. It
also said something about the Holy Spirit which was not included
at Nicaea: "And in the Holy Spirit, the Lord and Giver of life,
who proceedeth from the Father, who with the Father and the
Son together is worshipped and glorified." These phrases have
mystical power and could be used liturgically.

This decision ends the trinitarian struggle. Arius and Sabellius
and their many followers were excluded. The negative side of
this decision is clear, but its positive implications for developing
the doctrine of the trinity pose extreme difficulties. I shall point
out four of them.

(1) On the one hand, the Father is the ground of divinity; on
the other hand, he is a special *persona*, a particular *hypostasis*.
Now, if these two points of view are taken together, it is possible
to speak of a quaternity instead of a trinity. It is possible to speak
of the divine substance as the one divine ground, and of the three
persons, Father, Son, and Spirit, as the manifestations of the
ground. Then we have a quaternity rather than a trinity. There

was always an inclination in this direction, and Thomas Aquinas still had to fight against it. As a rule theology said: The Father is both the source of all divinity and of each of the manifestations.

(2) The distinctions in the eternal trinity are empty. The doctrine of the trinity was created in order to understand the historical Jesus. As long as this was kept in mind, the difference between God and Jesus was evident. But how can differences be maintained in the realm of a transcendent trinity? Distinctions are made by words like non-generated, generated, and proceeding. And what do such words mean? They are words without content, because there is no perception of any kind which can confirm their meaning. To anticipate a bit, Augustine said these differences are *not* expressed because something is said by them, but in order not to remain silent. This means that if the motives for the doctrine of the trinity are forgotten, the formulae become empty.

(3) The Holy Spirit even now remains an abstraction. The Spirit can be brought in concretely only if he is defined as the Spirit of Christ, of Jesus as the Christ; but if he is placed into the transcendent trinity, he is more an abstraction than a person. For this reason the Spirit was never very important for Christian piety. In the moment in which he was deified in the same sense that Christ was considered divine, the Spirit was replaced in actual piety by the Holy Virgin. The Virgin who gave birth to God acquired divinity herself to a certain extent, at least for popular piety.

(4) The idea of three *hypostaseis*, three different *personae*, could lead to tritheism. This danger became much more real when the philosophy of Aristotle replaced that of Plato. Plato's philosophy was always the background of mystical realism in the Middle Ages. In this philosophy the universals are more real than their individual exemplars. In Aristotle the matter is quite different. Aristotle called the individual thing the *telos*, the inner aim, of all natural development. If this is the case, the three powers of being in God become three independent realities, or more exactly, the three manifestations of God become independent powers of being, independent persons. Those who are nominalists by education have a great difficulty in understanding the trinitarian dogma. For nominalism everything which is must be a definite thing, limited and separated from all other things.

For mystical realism, as we have it in Plato, Origen, and the Middle Ages, the power of being in a *universal* can be something quite superior to and different from the power of being in the individuals. Therefore, the danger of tritheism was very minimal as long as the trinitarian dogma was interpreted in terms of the Platonic philosophy. Tritheism became a danger as soon as the Aristotelian categories came to predominate, and with it the nominalistic trend which placed great emphasis on the individual realities. Then the Son and the Spirit could become, so to speak, special individual beings; then we are in the realm of tritheism.

The great theologian in the East, John of Damascus, protested against this consequence. He emphasized the unity of action and being among the three manifestations of God. However, something else happened. For practical piety the trinitarian dogma became just the opposite of what it was originally supposed to be. It was supposed to be an interpretation of Jesus as the Christ; it was supposed to mediate this understanding to the Greeks with the help of the Logos doctrine. But the consequences of the Logos doctrine had become so dangerous in Arius, in particular, that traditional theology reacted against it. When it was still used, its philosophical meaning had been broken. In this way the trinitarian dogma became a sacred mystery. The sacred mystery was placed on the altar, so to speak, and adored. It was introduced into the icons, the pictures which are so important for the cult in the Eastern church, into liturgical formulae and hymns, and there the mystery has lived ever since. However, it lost its power to interpret the meaning of the living God.

I. The Christological Problem

The christological problem is historically a consequence of the trinitarian controversy. In principle, however, it is the other way around. The trinity is the answer to the christological problem. It is an answer whose final formulae seem to deny the basis on which it arose. The question was: If the Son is of one substance with the Father, how can the historical Jesus be understood? This was the purpose of the whole trinitarian dogma. But with the trinitarian dogma formulated as it was at Nicaea, is it still possible to make Jesus understandable? How can he who is of divine nature, without any restriction, be a real man at the same time? The christological controversy, which lasted for several centuries and brought the church once again to the edge of self-destruction, was an attempt to answer this question.

There were always two main types of christological thought: Either God as Father (or as Logos or Spirit) used the man Jesus of Nazareth, begetting, inspiring, and adopting him as his Son, or a divine being (the Logos or eternal Son) *became* man in an act of transformation. The Creed of Nicaea, with its *homoousios* and its Monarchian tendency, favors the former solution. And so does the Roman theology. The emphasis on the divinity of the eternal Son makes the emphasis on the humanity of the historical Son much easier. A half-god can be transformed into man; God himself can only adopt man. But this former solution was not in the line of Origenism. In Origen the eternal Logos is inferior to the Father and has, by his union with the soul of Jesus, in eternity the traits of the historical Jesus. Therefore, he can easily be transformed into Jesus with the help of the body, and a transformation christology can result. No sharp distinction between these two possibilities was made. The *homoousios* could be interpreted closer to Sabellius or to Arius. This means that the christological interpretations that followed Nicaea could be either in the sense of adoption or in the sense of transformation. This uncertainty was soon discovered by some theologians. It became a matter of controversy when a man arose to do what Arius had done in the trinitarian struggle, namely, to draw out the consequences of the Origenistic position, but now in the sphere of christology. This man was Apollinarius of Laodicea.[1]

1. *The Antiochean Theology*

The West never followed the Alexandrian line, of which Apollinarius was the most radical expression. The religious interest of the Alexandrians really had to do with the problem of salvation. How is salvation possible unless the humanity of Jesus is more or less swallowed up into the divinity, so that we can adore him as a whole, so that his mind is identical with the divine

[1] Editor's note: At this point in Tillich's lectures, Father Georges Florovsky delivered two lectures on Apollinarius and on Cyril of Alexandria. For this reason Tillich did not himself deal with their positions at any length.

Logos? The answer is: It would be impossible. Therefore, the general trend moves in the direction of what was later called Monophysitism. According to Monophysitism there is only one nature; the divine nature has swallowed up the human nature.

The West and the school of Antioch protested against this tendency in Alexandrian theology. One of the first theologians of this school was Theodore of Mopsuestia. The Antiochean school has definite characteristics which distinguish it from the school of Alexandria, and which make this school the predecessor of the emphasis on the historical Jesus in modern theology.

(1) The school of Antioch had a strong philological interest and wanted an exact interpretation and emphasis on the historical picture of Christ. In this way it anticipated the historical criticism developed in the modern period.

(2) The school had a rational tendency—just as liberal theology also had—in the sense of Alexandrian philosophy.

(3) The Antiochean theologians also had strong ethical-personalistic—instead of mystical-ontological—interests, just as Rome and the Stoics had.

Rome and the West were not always on the side of Antiochean theology, but on the whole Antioch represented the main trends of the West. In alliance with Antioch in the East, it was possible for Rome, with its emphasis on history and personality, to become victorious over the mystical ontological interest of the East. Popular religion, however, was on the whole on the side of Alexandria and against Antioch. Antioch could not prevail for a number of reasons. The basic structure of the dogma was against it, coming as it did from Origen and being much more in line with Alexandrian thinking. Politics was against it and there was also a lack of moral resistance against the superstitions which had developed widely in Christianity at that time. The personalities were not great enough to resist the demands of the people for a magically working God who walks on earth and whose human nature is only a gown for his divine nature. Nevertheless, Antioch, in alliance with Rome, saved the human picture of Christ in its religious significance. Without Antioch the church would probably have lost entirely the human picture, and the historical consciousness of the West would not have been able to develop.

Antioch defended the church against the Monophysites for whom the human character of Christ was swallowed up in divinity and who also gave rise to numerous magical and superstitious ideas. Thus, Antioch paved the way for the christological emphasis of the West. It is perhaps impossible for someone from the West fully to understand the religious meaning of the East. This is even more difficult for Americans than for Europeans, because Europe is much closer to the East, not only geographically but historically. The mystical-ontological elements permeate the whole of Western culture in Europe. This is not the case in the United States. Your heritage is indebted to the Antiochean school and to Rome which, in alliance with this school, saved the kind of attitude which is natural to you.

Theodore of Mopsuestia emphasized against Apollinarius that in Christ there is a perfect nature of man in union with the perfect nature of God. He said: "A complete man, in his nature, is Christ, consisting of a rational soul and human flesh; complete is the human person; complete also the person of the divinity in him. It is wrong to call one of them impersonal." It was common in the East, in Monophysitism, to hold that only one nature is personal, the divine nature and not the human. Therefore, Theodore said: "One should not say that the Logos *became* flesh." For Theodore this was a vague, metaphorical way of speaking and should not be used as a precise formula. Instead, one should say: "He took on humanity." The Logos was not transformed into flesh. This idea of transformation, or transmutation, was felt by him to be pagan, so he rejected it. The pagan spirit of superstition wanted to have a transformed God walking on earth. But then Theodore was confronted by a difficult problem. If the human and divine sides of Christ are themselves persons, is he not then a being with two personal centers? Is he not a combination of two sons, a monster with two heads, as Theodore's enemies put it? Theodore tried to show the unity of the two persons. He rejected the unity in essence or nature. In essence they are absolutely different because the divine nature cannot be confined to an individual man. The Logos is universally present. Even when Jesus lived, the flowers were blooming, animals were living, men were walking, and culture was going on. The Logos was active in all this. He said that it is impossible for the Logos to be only the man Jesus. He spoke, therefore, of a unity by the Holy Spirit, which is a unity of grace and will. In this way he established in Jesus an analogy with the prophets, who were driven by the Spirit. How-

ever, this is a unique event in Jesus, for in the prophets the
Spirit was limited, whereas in Jesus the Spirit was unlimited.

The union of the two natures started in the womb of Mary. In
it the Logos connected himself with a perfect man in a mysterious
way. This Logos directed the development, the inner growth, of
Jesus, but never by coercion. As every man Jesus had grace, even
unlimited grace. Grace never works through coercion but through
the personal center. By the grace of God Jesus increased in
perfection. In this way, he said, there is one person in Jesus, but
the natures are not mixed. He denied that he spoke of two sons;
instead, he said, he affirmed two natures. The divine nature does
not change the human nature in its essence. Jesus had a human
nature which by grace could follow the divine nature. Thus, one
could speak of Mary giving birth to God. This was the decisive
formula. It was against the tradition of the Antiocheans, but they
could not deny the phrase *theotokos* (Mother of God). He justified
the acceptance of this phrase by saying that Mary also gave birth
to a man. This is a direct and adequate way of speaking; the
other, that Mary gave birth to God, is only indirectly adequate,
because the body of Jesus was united with the Logos of God.

In the same way Theodore agreed that the human nature must
be adored and, conversely, that God had suffered. These things
can be said only of the unity of the person. Of this unity one can
say these things because what can be said of the unity can be
said of the whole being. But he rejected the idea of a transformation of the Logos into a human being. The Western theologians
said that the oneness of nature is reached only when Christ is
elevated to the throne of God at the resurrection, with the body
and the human soul being glorified and transformed. This event
of the human side being swallowed up is a transcendent event
which happens in heaven, not on earth. So Theodore said that
only the flesh, that is, the historical person, suffered and died,
not the divine nature in him. It is blasphemy to say that divinity
and flesh belong to one nature. Ambrose said that though Christ
had two natures, he suffered only in his human nature. The same
grace which accepted the human nature in Christ and made him
the Son of God also justified us before God and made us his children.

Thus we see here two allies: Rome, with her empirical, personal, and historical interest; Antioch, having the same interest,

but using it for philological studies and philosophical considerations. This alliance of Rome and Antioch might have led perhaps
to a full victory of the Antiocheans over the Alexandrians. But
this did not happen. For Rome had more of a political than a
theological interest. Rome was the great center of the church and
as such it did not want to surrender Christianity on account of a
theological formula.

Nestorius was one of the leaders of the Antiochean school. In
A.D. 429 he preached against the doctrine of *theotokos*, that the
Virgin Mary gave birth to God. Nestorius taught that Mary gave
birth to a man who became the organ of divinity. Not the divinity
but the humanity of Christ suffered. Thus, one could say that
Mary is *christotokos*. Later Nestorius admitted that indirectly one
could speak of Mary as *theotokos* in the sense that God the Logos
came down and united himself with the man to whom Mary gave
birth. But this was not a divine being coming down to become
a man in terms of a transmutation myth.

The two natures of Christ preserve their qualities in the personal union. They are connected without being mixed in the
humanity of Jesus. The term "man" describes the one nature in
him, the term "God" or "Logos" the other nature. These ideas
brought the charge of heresy against Nestorius. They were
generally present in the Antiochean tradition, but with Nestorius
they became suspect and finally repudiated. If we say that
Nestorius became a heretic, we could say that he was the most
innocent of all heretics. Actually he was a victim of the struggle
between Byzantium and Alexandria.

2. The Alexandrian Theology

There were other developments which supported the Alexandrian cause.

(1) For a long time the Mary-legend, for which there is little
basis in the Bible, had grown out of the pious imagination. The
figure of Mary attracted the novelistic mind.

(2) The second reason for the predominance of Alexandria over
Antioch was the high valuation placed on virginity strengthening
the trend toward asceticism.

(3) There was also a spiritual vacuum in the religious life of
that period. The empty space which wanted to be filled was the

desire to have a female element in the center of religion. Egypt had such an element in its myth of Isis and Osiris, the goddess and her son, but Christianity did not. In this it followed Judaism, which discarded every female element. The Spirit was not able to replace the female element. First of all, the Spirit appears, in the stories of Jesus' birth, as the male factor. Secondly, the Spirit is an abstract concept. Thus, in the popular mind the Spirit could never replace the different forms of male-centered religion which came from the Old Testament.

(4) The transformation christology of Alexandria had a popular appeal. Imagine a simple-minded human being who wants to have God. If you tell her: "There is God, on the altar; go and have him there", then she will go. But how is this possible? Because of the incarnation, for in the incarnation God *became* something which we can have, whom we can see, with whom we can walk, etc. This is popular feeling, and this feeling became decisive against the Antiocheans.

Cyril of Alexandria wanted to show that the human nature was taken into the unity of the Logos, who remained what he was. So he could say that the Logos himself experienced death, since he received into himself the body of Jesus. In his formula, "out of two natures, one", he accepted the abstract distinction of the natures, but in actuality there is no difference between the two natures. This made it possible for him to be the protagonist in the fight for the *theotokos*. His religious motive was this: It is not a man who has become King over us, but God himself who appeared in the form of a man. If Nestorius were right, then only a man, and not the Logos, would have died for us; if he were right, then in the Lord's Supper we eat the flesh of a man. What the people wanted was the physical presence of the divine.

At first it seemed that the Antiocheans and the Alexandrians could be united. Then, however, the Alexandrians reacted so vigorously and victoriously that Rome took the side of Antioch. Rome put a condition to the Antiocheans; they had to remove Nestorius because he was under too much suspicion. After a compromise was worked out at the Council of Ephesus (A.D. 431) and a number of other synods, including the famous *Latrocinium* of Ephesus (the synod of robbers), a final settlement was reached at the Council of Chalcedon (A.D. 451). Here the alliance of Rome and Antioch proved its strength. They were helped by the

fact that one from the opposition, Eutyches, a monk in Constantinople, put forth such a radically Monophysitic position that he
was condemned. This was both a condemnation of Alexandria
and a victory for Antioch.

3. *The Council of Chalcedon*

Pope Leo I wrote a letter which became decisive for the outcome at Chalcedon. It said that the properties of each nature and
substance were preserved entire, and came together to form one
person. Humility was assumed by majesty, weakness by strength,
mortality by eternity. There was one true God in the entire and
perfect nature of true man. The Son of God therefore came down
from his throne, from heaven, without withdrawing from his
Father's glory, and entered this lower world, because of the unity
of the person in each nature, which can be understood that the
Son of Man came from heaven, and conversely that the Son of
God has been crucified and buried. Here we have the same
phenomenon as in the theology of Antioch. A radical statement is
combined rather easily with traditional ideas. The decision of
Chalcedon was made on this basis. In significance it was not
surpassed by Nicaea, and together with Nicaea it surpasses all
other synodal decisions. No one can study systematic theology
today without knowing something about this decision at Chalcedon. The substance of it was expressed in paradoxical formulae.

(1) "Therefore, following the holy Fathers, we all with one
consent teach men to confess one and the same Son, our Lord
Jesus Christ, the same complete in Godhead and also complete
in manhood."

(2) "True God, and at the same time true man, of a reasonable
soul and body."

(3) He is "consubstantial with the Father, according to his Godhead, and consubstantial with us according to his manhood; in
all things like unto us, apart from sin."

(4) He is "begotten before all ages of the Father according to
the Godhead, and in these latter days, for us and for our salvation, born of the Virgin Mary, the God-bearer (*theotokos*), according to the manhood."

(5) "One and the same Jesus Christ, Son, Lord, Only-begotten,
in two natures. These two natures must not be confused, and they

are natures without any change, without division, without separation."

(6) "The distinction of natures being by no means annulled by
the union, but rather the characteristic of each being preserved
and coming together to form one person and one substance. He
is not parted or divided into two persons but one and the same
Son and Only-begotten, God the Word, the Lord Jesus Christ."

In this document, as in similar ones, we see how readily philosophical terms could have a transition into liturgical and poetic
language. The negative side of these statements is clear. The positive side is more doubtful. The position of Rome was victorious,
but different interpretations were possible. The East was disappointed by the decision; the delegates from Alexandria did not
subscribe. If they had subscribed to something so contrary to
popular demand back home, they would have been beaten to
death by the fanatic monks on their return. The reaction of the
East against Chalcedon, in its radical aspects, was strong enough
to divide the East from Rome to such a degree that it became
an easy prey to the Islamic puritan reaction. This is especially
true of the Monophysitic churches of Egypt and neighboring
countries. They were all swallowed up by the reaction of Islam,
which I would call a puritan reaction, that is, a reaction against
the sacramental superstitious form into which Christianity had
fallen more and more. I have a thesis—I do not know whether
Father Florovsky would agree with it—that the attacks of Islam
would never have been successful if Eastern Christianity had
taken into itself the elements of personality and history. Instead,
Christianity in this region fell deeper and deeper into popular
superstition, and so became vulnerable to the Islamic type of
reaction.

The decision of Chalcedon was partly denied, partly set aside.
From A.D. 482–519 the first schism occurred between the East
and the West. Chalcedon was maintained by the West; the East
either rejected it or veered toward a Monophysitic interpretation
of it. After the reunion under Emperor Justin (519), Monophysitism became victorious in Alexandria. It was a radical
return to Cyril and his emphasis on the unity of the natures. After
the union in the incarnation only one nature is present. Christ
is one, according to his composite nature, according to his person,
according to his will. After the union there is no duality of natures

or energies. The more radical Monophysites said that Chalcedon and Pope Leo, who asserted two natures and two energies, should be condemned. These Monophysites taught that with the conception in Mary the flesh of Christ became progressively deified. That really made Mary a goddess. The radicals said their enemies adored something mortal. They wanted nothing less than God on earth, without human relativity.

4. *Leontius of Byzantium*

Emperor Justinian wanted a reunion of the Chalcedonians and the Monophysites. He was aided in this by the teaching of a monastic theologian, Leontius of Byzantium. By combining Cyril and Leo with a new scholastic idea he found a solution to the christological problem which endured in the East for a long time. Leontius said that the human nature in Christ does not have its own *hypostasis*; it is *anhypostasis* (without *hypostasis*). Here *hypostasis* means being an "independent being". Instead, the human nature is *enhypostasis*, which means that the human nature is *in* the *hypostasis* of the divine Logos. Here we have reached scholasticism. When it comes to the formula *enhypostasis*, we do not really know what that means. But the reason it was invented is clear. The question was: Can two natures exist without an independent head, an *hypostasis*? The answer was, they cannot. Therefore, Christ has one *hypostasis* representing the two natures.

The being of the human nature is in the Logos. This meant that the theology of Antioch had to be condemned, including Theodore. The religious meaning of this Byzantine theology became visible in the fight about the suffering of God which was expressed in liturgical and theological formulae. The *treis-hagion* (thrice holy) was also enlarged to the formula: "Holy God . . . Almighty . . . immortal, who for us was crucified, have mercy upon us." One of the holy *trias* has suffered in the flesh. This was carried through and dogmatized in A.D. 553, at the Fifth Ecumenical Council in Constantinople, in spite of protests from Rome. The Council expressed itself in fourteen anathemas. The two natures are distinguished only in theory, not in practice. The person of the Logos has become the personal center of a man. The human nature has no personal characteristics of its own. This was the decisive point, because if this is the case, how can he help us? The Crucified is the true God and Lord of glory, and one of the trinity. The identification of Jesus Christ with the Logos is complete. As in the icons in which Christ appears in gold-ground setting, the human personality has disappeared.

But the West could not be so easily conquered. A new reaction of the West occurred. The question arose whether the one person of Jesus Christ has one or two wills. This time the fight was between the *Monothelites* and the *Dyothelites*. This time the West prevailed. Christ who has two natures also has two wills. The human nature is not swallowed up by the divine. This whole development can be grasped only if we realize that the key to it is the problem of how salvation is related to the individual, to history, and to personal life. On this point the West was clear, the East was not.

The last controversy in the East had to do with the icons. *Eikōn* means "image". Icons were the images of the fathers and saints in the churches. The icons deserve veneration and not adoration. However, if one asks what this distinction actually means, we must say that in popular understanding veneration always develops into adoration.

We have been surveying the rise and further fate of the christological doctrine as formulated at the Council of Chalcedon. Through all this there has probably been a hidden protest against this emphasis on the Eastern church. This is understandable because it does not have the same vital significance to you as, let us say, the Reformation or modern theology. However, the situation is such that if you know the fundamentals of the early development, and really understand it, everything else becomes comparatively easy. If, on the other hand, you know only the contemporary situation, and not the foundations, then everything is in the air. It is like a house built from the roof rather than from the foundations. I believe that the developments in ancient Christian theology are really foundations, foundations that must be considered immediately after the biblical foundations.

The doctrine of Chalcedon, whatever we think of the use of Greek terms in Christian theology, saved the human side of the picture of Jesus for our Western theology, and even for the East. The human side was on the verge of being completely swallowed up by the divine nature, so that succeeding developments in the

West, including the Reformation, would not have been possible. This is the importance of the Council of Chalcedon and its decision, which the East never really accepted, but transformed it and let it become swallowed up in its sacramental way of thinking and acting.

To understand the steps in the christological doctrine, always keep in mind two pictures: (1) The being with the two heads, God and man, where there is no unity; (2) The being in which one head has disappeared, but also humanity has disappeared. The one remaining head is the head of the Logos, of God himself, so that when Jesus acts, it is not the unity of something divine and something human, but it is the Logos who is acting. Thus, all the struggles, the uncertainties, the despair and loneliness, which the Gospels present, were only seemingly experienced by Jesus, but not really. They are inconsequential. This was the danger in the Eastern development. The fact that this danger was overcome is due to the decision of Chalcedon. We must be grateful to the Eastern church that it was able to do this against its own basic feeling. The power of the Old Testament and the power of the full picture of the human side of Jesus prevented the East from failing in this respect.

J. Pseudo-Dionysius the Areopagite

Dionysius the Areopagite is the classic Christian mystic, one of the most interesting figures in Eastern church history. He was also of extreme importance to the West. In Acts 17.34 we read of a man called Dionysius who followed Paul after he had preached in the Areopagus. His name was used by a writer who lived around A.D. 500. In the tradition this man was accepted as the real Dionysius who talked with Paul. He wrote his books under the name of Dionysius. What seems to us now a falsification was a custom in ancient writing. It was not a betrayal in any technical or moral sense to launch one's books under famous names. Not until the fifteenth century was this falsification historically established. It is an established historical fact that the man who wrote these books wrote around A.D. 500 and used the name of Paul's companion in Athens in order to lend authority to his books. He was translated into Latin by John Scotus Eriugena, a great theologian of the West, around 840. This Latin translation was used throughout the Middle Ages and had many scholastic commentators. Dionysius represents the main characteristics of the Byzantine end of the Greek development. He is the mediator of Neo-Platonism and Christianity, and the father of most of Christian mysticism. His concepts underlie most Christian mysticism in the East as well as the West. Some of his concepts, such as that of hierarchy, entered the ordinary language and helped greatly to form the Western hierarchical system of Rome.

We have two basic works of his, *On the Divine Names* and *On the Hierarchies*. The latter book is divided into the heavenly and the ecclesiastical hierarchies. The word "hierarchy" was probably created by him; at least we do not know whether anyone else had used it before. The word is derived from *hieros*, meaning "holy, sacred" and *archē*, meaning "principle, power, beginning". Thus, hierarchy is defined by Dionysius as a "holy system of degrees with respect to knowledge and efficacy". This characterizes all Catholic thinking to a great extent; it is not only ontological, but also epistemological; there are degrees not only in being, but also in knowledge. The system of holy degrees is taken from Neo-Platonism, where it was first fully developed after Aristotle and Plato (*Symposium*). The man who is most important is Proclus, a Neo-Platonic philosopher who has often been compared with Hegel. He has the same kind of triadic thinking—thesis, antithesis, and synthesis—and brings all reality into such a system of holy degrees.

The surprising thing about Dionysius is that this system, which was the end of the Greek world and summarized everything Greek wisdom had to say about life, was introduced into Christianity and used by it. A short time before, this system had been used by Julian the Apostate in order to combat Christianity. Thus, Julian and the Christian theologians who fought against each other in a life-and-death struggle were united in a Greek Christian mystic and theologian, Pseudo-Dionysius.

The other book is *On the Divine Names*. The term "Divine Names" is also a Neo-Platonic term, which the Neo-Platonists used when they brought all the gods of the pagans into their system. How could they do this? Because they followed the philosophical criticism in terms of which no educated Greek of that time believed literally in the pagan gods. Still there was the tradition, there was popular religion, and so something had to be done about these divine names. They tried to show that the qualities of the divine were expressed in these names. These names express different degrees and powers in the divine ground and divine emanation. They point to principles of power, of love, of energy, and other virtues, but they cannot be taken as names for special beings. This means that they discovered, in present-day terminology, the symbolic character of all our speaking about God. Writings on the divine names can be found throughout the medieval period. The theologians wrote on the symbolic meaning of everything we say about God. They did not use the word "symbol" at that time, but they spoke of "name" as an expression of a characteristic or quality. If we follow the insight of classical theology in this respect, we will not say, as is often done, that our speaking of God is *only* symbolic. This "only" is very wrong! The wrong is on our side when we fall into a literalism, against which also the Reformers, especially Calvin, fought.

The symbolic interpretation of everything we say about God corresponds to the idea of God which Dionysius developed. How can we know about God? Dionysius answered: There are two ways of recognizing God. First, there is the way of positive or affirmative theology. All names, so far as they are positive, must be attributed to God because he is the ground of everything. So he is designated by everything; everything points to him. God must be named with all names. Secondly, however, there is the way of negative theology which denies that he can be named by anything whatsoever. God is beyond even the highest names which theology has given to him. He is beyond spirit, beyond the good. God is, as Dionysius says, super-essential. He is beyond the Platonic ideas, the essences, beyond all the superlatives. He is not the highest being but beyond any possible highest being. He is supra-divinity, beyond God, if we speak of God as a divine being. Therefore, he is "unspeakable darkness". By this combination of words he denies that God, in view of his nature, can be either spoken of or seen. Thus, all the names must disappear after they have been attributed to God, even the holy name "God" itself. Perhaps this is the source—unconsciously—of what I said at the end of my book, *The Courage to Be*, about the "God above God", namely, the God above God who is the real ground of everything that is, who is above any special name we can give to even the highest being.

It is important that the positive and the negative ways lead to the same end. In both cases the forms of the word are negated. If you say everything about God, you can just as well say that you say nothing about him, that is, not anything special. This is the first thing, of course, which must be said about God, because it is this which makes him God, namely, that which transcends everything finite. In this sense even the problem of unity and trinity disappears in the abyss of God. Since that which is super-essential, beyond the Platonic ideas, is also beyond all numbers, it is even beyond the number "one"—so that there is no difference between three or one or many in this respect. Whenever it is said that God is One, translate this to mean that God is beyond all numbers, even the number "one". Only on this basis can we then speak of "trinity", and of the infinite self-expression in the world.

From this abysmal One, which is the source and substance of all being, the light emanates, and the light is the good in all things. Light is a symbol not only for knowing but also for being. It is as the Greek philosopher Parmenides said, that where there is being there is also the *logos* of being. This light, which is the power of being and knowledge, is identical with itself; it is unshaken and everlasting. There is a way downward and a way upward. We have this already in Heraclitus who said that in everything there is a trend from earth over water over fire to air, and an opposite trend from the air to earth. That is, there is a fundamental tension in every living being, a tension of the creative power of being going down, and the saving power of being going up. The three stages of the way upward are purgation, illumination, and union. Purgation is purification in the ethical-ascetic realm; illumination is in the realm of mystical understanding; union is the state of perfection, the return into unity with God. In this last stage something takes place which Dionysius called the mystical ignorance. The same thing was mediated to the modern world through Nicholas of Cusa in his idea of learned ignorance (*docta ignorantia*). These two men say that this is the only ultimate true knowledge. This word "ignorance" says that we do not know anything special any more when we have penetrated into the ground of everything that is. And since everything special is changing, it cannot be ultimate reality and truth. If you penetrate from everything changing to the ultimate, you reach the rock of eternity; you have the truth which can rest on this rock alone.

This fundamental reality is represented in degrees called hierarchies. The line from above to below is the line of emanation. The line from below to above is the line of salvation. The hierarchies represent both ways. They are the way in which the divine abyss emanates. At the same time, they are the revelations of the divine abyss, so far as it can be revealed, in the upward way of saving union with God. From the point of view of the way upward, the hierarchies have the purpose to create the greatest possible similarity and union of all beings with God. The old Platonic formula, "being equal to God as much as possible", was used also by the Areopagite—coming nearer and nearer to God and finally uniting with him.

Every hierarchy receives its light from the higher one and passes it down to the lower one. In this way each hierarchy is active and passive at the same time. It receives the divine power of being and gives it in a restrictive way to those which are lower than it. However, this system of degrees is ultimately dualistic. There are two fundamentally different hierarchies, the heavenly and the earthly. The heavenly hierarchies are the Platonic essences or ideas above which there is God. These are the first emanations from God, which Dionysius interpreted as hierarchies of angels. This is a development which had already occurred in later Judaism (the inter-testamental period). The concept of angels—which is a symbolic personalistic concept—amalgamates with the concept of hypostatized essences or powers of being. They become one and the same being and represent the heavenly hierarchies. If you want to interpret the concept of angels in a meaningful way today, interpret them as the Platonic essences, as the powers of being, not as special beings. If you interpret them in the latter way, it all becomes crude mythology. On the other hand, if you interpret them as emanations of the divine power of being in essences, in powers of being, the concept of angels becomes meaningful and perhaps important. The sentimental picture of angels as winged babies has nothing to do with the great concept of divine emanations in terms of powers of being.

The ecclesiastical hierarchy on earth is an image of the heavenly hierarchy. The angels are the spiritual mirrors of the divine abyss. They always look at him and are the immediate recipients of his power of being. They are always longing to become equal with him and to return to him. With respect to us, they are the first revealers. If we understand the matter in this way, we can understand what it means that they are the essences in which the divine ground expresses itself first. There are three times three orders of angels—which is, of course, a scholastic play—making it possible to give a kind of analogy to the earthly hierarchies. The earthly hierarchies are powers of spiritual being. Here we can learn something about medieval realism. The earthly hierarchies are:

(1) The three sacraments: baptism, the Lord's Supper, confirmation;

(2) The three degrees of the clergy: deacons, priests, bishops;

(3) The three degrees of non-clergy: the imperfect, who are not even members of the congregation, the laymen, and the monks, who have a special function.

These nine earthly hierarchies mediate the return of the soul to God. They are all equally necessary and are all equally powers of being. As children of nominalism, you will immediately ask: What does it mean that sacraments are equal with people (clergy, laity) as hierarchies? This can be understood only if you realize that the people here function as bearers of sacramental power, as bearers of the power of being. The same is true of the sacraments. This is what makes it possible for Dionysius to call all nine of them hierarchies. They are all sacred powers of being, some of them embodied in persons, some in sacraments, and some in persons who only have the functions of being believers in the congregation.

This brings the earthly world into a hierarchical system, because earthly things such as sounds, colors, forms, stone, etc. are used, especially in the sacraments, to express the ecclesiastical hierarchy. All reality belongs to the ecclesiastical reality, because the ecclesiastical reality is the hierarchical reality as expressed in the different degrees of being and knowledge of God. In the mystery of the church all things are interpreted in terms of their symbolic power to express the abyss of divinity. They express it and they guide everything back to it. The ecclesiastical mysteries penetrate into the interior divinity, into the divine ground of all things. Thus, a system of symbols in which everything is potentially included is established. This is the principle of

Byzantine culture, namely, to transform reality into something which points to the eternal, not to *change* reality as in the Western world.

Hence, hierarchical thinking in the East is much more in the vertical line, interpreting reality by penetrating into its depths, whereas the kingdom of God concept, as in Protestantism, belongs to a horizontal theology. Looking at the situation in terms of East and West, the East lacked the ability to work in the historical line of transforming reality, and therefore became first the victim of the Islamic attack, and then a victim of the Marxist attack. On the other hand, when we look at our culture we can say without much doubt that we have lost the vertical dimension to a great extent. We always go ahead; we never have time to stand somewhere and to look above and below.

To understand what I mean by making everything transparent for the divine ground, we should look for a moment at art. We have the most translucent religious art in the Byzantine mosaics. These mosaics have no tendency at all to describe anything which happens in the horizontal line. They want to express the presence of the divine through everything which appears on the horizontal level of reality, on the place of time and space, by making everything a symbol pointing to its own depths. This is the greatness of the mosaics. There are a few examples of them in the New York Metropolitan Museum of Art. There you have the expression of divine transcendence, even when the subjects are completely earthly—animals, trees, men of politics, women of the court. Every expression has its ultimate symbolic meaning. The last great controversy in the Byzantine church had to do with icons, or pictures, because the Byzantine culture believed in the power of pictures to express the divine ground of things. The danger was very great that popular belief would confuse the transparency of the pictures with the power of the divine itself, which is effective through the pictures but is never identical with them. The whole conflict was over the meaning of the transparent power of the pictures. For the East this was essential; therefore, most of the great art came from there, and then conquered the West. The danger then became so great in the West that after Rome had partly capitulated, it finally was attacked again by Protestantism, especially Reformed Protestantism, in a way which removed the pictures from the churches altogether. Thus, in

Seienu possible

Calvinism natural objects lost their transparency. This is the meaning of all iconoclastic (image-destroying) movements. This is understandable as a reaction to the superstitious way in which many Catholics prayed *to* their pictures, etc. When we realize, however, that by the same act all natural objects lost their transparency, one cannot be so sure about it. Things become merely objects of technical activity, nature becomes dedivinized, and its function to represent the divine becomes lost. We can say that what the Byzantine culture effected was the spiritualization of all reality. That is not to be confused with idealization, which is something quite different. Hofmann's picture of Jesus is an idealization. A Byzantine picture of Jesus has transparency, but it is not an idealized picture. The divine majesty is visible throughout, not a nice human being with ideal, manly handsomeness. So I would say that the Eastern church represents something which we have lost. Therefore, I am especially happy that Eastern Orthodox churches could be taken into the World Council of Churches, thus making communication with them possible again. We should not imagine that we have nothing to learn from them. It may happen that with centuries of more intimate contact, the dimension of depth may again enter Western thinking.

The system of Dionysius was received by the West. There were two things which made this possible, which Christianized or baptized this mysticism. First, the emanation was understood not in a natural but in a personal picture. God has given existence to all beings because of his benevolence. This goes beyond pagan thinking. Here the personalistic element comes in and the Neo-Platonic dualism is removed. Secondly, the system of hierarchies was built around Christ and around the church. All things have their power of illuminating and uniting only in relationship to the church and to the Christ. Christ is not one hierarchy alongside others. This was prevented by Nicaea. But Christ is God manifest, who appears in every hierarchy and works through each one. In this way the system of pagan deities and mysteries, which lived in Neo-Platonism, was overcome, and in this way the Western church could receive the system of hierarchies and mysteries. As a result medieval mysticism was not in opposition to the ecclesiastical hierarchy. They worked together; only much later did conflicts arise.

K. TERTULLIAN AND CYPRIAN

The two men in the West with whom we must deal first are Tertullian and Cyprian. We already discussed Tertullian to some extent in connection with the Montanist movement of radical spiritualism and radical eschatology. He was its greatest theological representative. We also spoke of him in terms of his ability to create those trinitarian and christological formulae which, under pressure from Rome, finally conquered all the other suggestions made by the East. Further, we saw that he was a Stoic philosopher, and as such he used reason to develop his rational system in a radical way. The same Tertullian, however, was also aware of the fact that in Christianity there is also the element of paradox. He who said that the human soul is naturally Christian (*anima naturaliter christiana*) is the same one who is supposed to have said—though he did not actually say it—"I believe because it is absurd" (*credo quia absurdum est*). What Tertullian actually said was: "The son of God died: it is by all means to be believed, because it is absurd. And he was buried, and rose again; the fact is certain, because it is impossible." This *paradoxa* is a mixture of two factors: first, it expresses the surprising, unexpected reality of the appearance of God under the conditions of existence; secondly, it is a rhetorical expression of this idea in the way in which Roman orators used the Latin language. It must not be taken as a literal expression, but by means of a paradox a pointing to the incredible reality of the appearance of Christ. Now, people added to this the formula, *credo quia absurdum est*, but Tertullian himself never said this. With such a view he never would have been able to present such clear dogmatic formulae and, as a Stoic, believe in the ruling power of the Logos.

In Tertullian there also appeared an emphasis on sin, which was to become important in the West later. He spoke of the *vicium originis*, the original vice, and identified it with sexuality. In this way he anticipated a long development in Roman Christianity, the depreciation of sex and the idea of the universality of sinfulness.

For Tertullian the Spirit is a kind of fine substance, as it was also in Stoic philosophy. The fine substance is called Spirit, or grace or love. They are actually the same thing in Catholic theology. Thus,

Roman Catholic theology can speak of *gratia infusa*, infused grace, infused like a liquid, a very fine substance, into the soul of man and transforming it. This is the non-personalistic element in Roman Catholic sacramental thought. This grace can be infused sacramentally into the oil of extreme unction, into the water of baptism, into the bread of the Lord's Supper, and thus into the soul. This is one of the sources of this kind of "spiritual materialism", so to speak, which played such a great role in the Roman Church.

Finally, Tertullian represented the idea that asceticism, the self-denial of the vital reality of oneself, is the way to receive this substantial grace of God. He used the juristic term "compensation" for sin; asceticism is the compensation for the negative character of sin. And he used the term "satisfaction". By good works we can "satisfy" God. And he spoke of "self-punishment". To the degree that we will punish ourselves, God will not punish us. All of this is legalistic thinking, although Tertullian was not himself a jurist. But every Roman orator and philosopher used the legal categories. This was in general a fundamental characteristic of the West and it became decisive for the later development of the Roman Church.

Cyprian, bishop of North Africa, had his greatest influence on the doctrine of the church. The problem of the church which Cyprian discussed was a very existential one. There were the persecutions as a result of which there were those who were called the *lapsi*, those who fell away either by recanting the faith or by surrendering books to the searching servants of the pagan authorities or by denouncing fellow Christians in a trial. This was a matter of great concern to the church. These people wanted to return to the church and overcome the weakness which had caused them to fall. Who should be readmitted to the church? The church could not accept those who had fallen out of sheer malignancy. Who should make the decision as to who is eligible to return? The ordinary teaching was that it shall be done by those who were "spirituals", that is, those who had become martyrs or in some other way had proved that they were fully responsible Christians. This method, however, was a sort of remnant from the past in which the "spirit" was still dominant over the "office". But now the office wanted to set aside this remnant of the past and to take over this decision too. The bishop, who is the church, must make the decision on the *lapsi*. And he should decide in a very liberal way; he should accept those who fell even more than once, in the same way that other mortal sinners are received.

On the other hand, the teaching was still powerful that the Spirit must decide whether or not someone can belong to the church. So Cyprian said that the bishops are the spirituals, those who have the Spirit, namely, the Spirit of succession from the early apostles, apostolic succession. In this way the Spirit became the qualification of the office. This was the greatest triumph of the office, that now the Spirit is bound to the office, and the Spirit is called the Spirit of succession. This was a transition to the idea that the clergy are endowed with the graces by virtue of ordination, and that the highest of all clergy, the pope himself, embodies the grace of God on earth.

Another existential problem was what to do with people who are baptized by heretics and schismatics. I hope the difference is clear. Heretics are those who have a different faith, those who have deviated from the doctrinal order of the Christian Church. Schismatics are those who follow a special line of church-political development, those who split away from the church, motivated perhaps by a conflict between bishops or by an unwillingness to accept the bishop of Rome. Hence, the separation of the Eastern and Western churches is called a schism. The Eastern church is considered by Rome not as a heretical church but as a schismatic church. Protestantism is considered by Rome as a heretical movement, because the very foundations of faith are at stake and not only the refusal to acknowledge the bishop of Rome.

Now the question arose as to how it was possible to receive into one's own congregation persons who had been baptized by one of these groups. The answer that was given was in terms of the objective character of baptism. The validity of baptism does not depend on the person who performed it. We shall see how Augustine carried this through. Cyprian's idea of the church stood behind all this.

(1) "He who does not have the church as Mother cannot have God as Father." "There is no salvation outside the church" (*extra ecclesiam nulla salus*). The church is the institution in which salvation is attained. This represents a change from the early

Christian period in which the church was a community of saints and not an institution for salvation. Of course, in this period too salvation was happening in the church; people who were being saved from paganism and from the demons gathered in the church. But the church itself was not considered as an institution of salvation but as a community of the saints. This emphasis in Cyprian is very consistent with the legal thinking of the West.

(2) The church is built on the episcopate. This is according to divine law and is, therefore, an object of faith. "Therefore you must know that the bishop is in the church and the church is in the bishop, and that if somebody is not with the bishop, he is not in the church." This is the purest form of episcopalianism, although somewhat different from what that word means today.

(3) The unity of the church is correspondingly rooted in the unity of the episcopate. All bishops represent this unity. However, in spite of the equality of all of them, there is one representative of this unity; that is Peter and his See. The See of Peter is the church "from which the priestly unity has arisen, the womb and the root of the Catholic Church." This is said prior to Augustine. The consequence of this, although not yet in Cyprian's mind, was unavoidably the principate of Rome in a much more radical way than he expressed it.

(4) The bishop is *sacerdos*—the Latin word for "priest". The main function of the priest is sacrificial. The priest sacrifices the elements in the Lord's Supper and thus repeats the sacrifice on Golgotha. "He imitates what Christ did; he offers a true and perfect sacrifice to God the Father within the church." Here again this is not yet the same thing as the Catholic Mass, but it would unavoidably lead to it, the more so in the primitive nations, with their realistic thinking and their tendency to take as real what is symbolic. Many of the fundamentals of the Roman Church existed as early as about A.D. 250, when Cyprian lived. Whatever we say against the Roman Church, we should not forget that the early developments in Christianity led this way. And when today one speaks of the agreement of the first five centuries, this is entirely misleading. Of course, Protestants, Catholics, and Orthodox agree on the major synodal decisions, but this is only an apparent agreement, because the living meaning of these things was absolutely different from what the Reformers built up as Protestant

doctrine. If you look at a man like Cyprian, you can see the difference. No Protestant can accept any of these points.

Let me sum up some of the points of the Occidental tradition.

(1) One could mention first the general practical, activistic tendency in the West, the legal relations between God and man, the much stronger ethical impulses for the average Christian, not with respect to himself but with respect to the world. And we can include in this point the eschatological interest, without mystagogical and mystical emphasis. In short, we could say that law more than participation characterizes the West from the very beginning.

(2) The idea of sin, even original sin, is almost exclusively Occidental. The main concerns of the East dealt with death and immortality, error and truth. The main focus of the West was on sin and salvation. In St. Ambrose, for example, the apostle Paul, the main teacher on sin and salvation, is held in high esteem. Ambrose has been called the *doctor gentium*, the teacher of the nations. Paul has the keys of knowledge; Peter has the keys of power. Throughout the history of the Middle Ages there continued a struggle between Peter and Paul, so to speak, between the keys of knowledge which finally prevailed in the Reformation, and the keys of power which always prevailed in the Roman Church. Therefore, according to St. Ambrose grace is primarily understood as the forgiveness of sins and not as deification, as we have it in the Platonic attitude in the East.

(3) The latter point has the following consequences: Western Christianity emphasizes the historical humanity of Christ, his humility and not his glory. For example, on the door of St. Sabina in Rome, before which I stood with great awe, you find in woodcut relief the first picture or sculpture of the crucifixion. The door is world-famous, coming from the fourth century. Here the West shows that it deviates from the Christ of glory which you find in all mosaics; this is more symptomatic of the difference between East and West than many theological formulae. Of course, the same thing is also expressed in theological formulae. What we said when we dealt with Chalcedon can now be illustrated by contrasting a mosaic in, let us say, Ravenna, which was under Byzantine influence at that time, with the door in St. Sabina. There you find the two christologies clearly expressed in picture. In the one you have the tremendously powerful Lord

of the universe, the Judge of the world in all glory, or as the risen One, in his majesty surrounded by angels, men, animals, and inorganic parts of nature, all of which participate in his glory. In the other you have this wonderful—from another aspect, poor—presentation of the suffering Christ. The former is Alexandrian christology, which portrays a Christ whose bodily existence is swallowed up by the divine form. The latter is Antiochean, Roman christology, which emphasizes the humanity of Christ more than anything else, including his suffering humanity. This gives an example of the difference in feeling. Thus, we have in the whole history of painting in the West the most wonderful, the most cruel, and the most destructive representations of the crucifixion. The early Gothic crucifixes, of which there are many, are such that perhaps trustees of a modern church would not permit them to be hung; they are so ugly. As if the crucifixion were a beautiful thing! It was ugly—and that is what the West accepted and could understand.

(4) The idea of the church is emphasized much more in the West than in the East. Somehow the church is built according to the legal structure of the Roman state, with the principle of authority, with the double law—the canonic and the civil law. The hierarchical power is centralized in the pope; and everyone personally participates, even the monks, in the sacrament of penance.

L. THE LIFE AND THOUGHT OF AUGUSTINE

Now we come to the man who is more than anyone else the representative of the West; he is the foundation of everything the West had to say. Augustine lived from A.D. 354 to 430. His influence overshadows not only the next thousand years but all periods ever since. In the Middle Ages his influence was such that even those who struggled against him in theological terminology and method—the Dominicans, with the help of Aristotle—quoted him often. Thomas Aquinas, who was the great opponent of Augustinianism in the Middle Ages, quoted him affirmatively most frequently.

In Augustine we also have the man to whom all the Reformers referred in their fight with the Roman Church. He influenced modern philosophy in a profound way insofar as it was Platonic, for example, Descartes and his school, including Spinoza. He has influenced modern theology as well. I would say, almost un-ambiguously, that I myself, and my whole theology, stand much more in the line of the Augustinian than in the Thomistic tradi-tion. We can trace a line of thought from Augustine to the Fran-ciscans in the Middle Ages, to the Reformers, to the philosophers of the seventeenth and eighteenth centuries, to the German clas-sical philosophers, including Hegel, to the present-day philosophy of religion, to the extent it is not empirical philosophy of religion, which I think is a contradiction in terms, but a philosophy of religion which is based on the immediacy of the truth in every human being.

1. *The Development of Augustine*

To understand Augustine we must trace his development in seven different steps, and then an eighth step which is a nega-tive one with respect to content.

(a) The first of these seven steps, which may help us to under-stand the immense influence of this greatest of all church fathers, is Augustine's dependence on the piety of his mother. This means, at the same time, that he is dependent on the Christian tradition. This reminds us of Plato's situation. When Plato wrote, he also wrote out of a tradition, the aristocratic tradition of the Athenian gentry to which he belonged. However, this tradition had come to an end in the self-destructive Peloponnesian War; the masses took over, and then, as always, followed the tyrants. The aristo-cracy was killed, not only as human beings, but as the principle of aristocracy itself. So what Plato saw in his mind was an ideal form of political and philosophical existence; it was a vision which had no reality any more. Therefore, I must warn you about a mistake! The name of Plato overshadows everything else in Greek thought, even Aristotle. However, do not imagine that Plato was the most influential man in the later ancient world. To be sure, he did have some influence and his book, *Timaeus*, was almost the "bible" of the later ancient world. But he could not exercise real influence because everything he developed was in the realm of pure es-sences, and no longer had historical foundations. Here I am thinking in terms of pure economic materialism. If the social and economic conditions no longer exist, if a civilization has reached a certain state, it cannot be influenced, much less transformed, by the ideal form of ideas which come from the past. There is a parallel to this in our day in the longing for the Middle Ages; the increasing power of the Roman Church has something to do with this situation. But it cannot succeed. We cannot go back to the Middle Ages, although this is the hope of every Catholic. Thus, when Plato wrote his *Republic* and later on his *Laws*, implying in these writings all elements of his philosophical thought—which included at the same time his social, psychological, and religious thought—he was acting in some sense as a reactionary. By reactionary we mean that he was driving toward something which was a matter of the past, and could not be re-established any more in the period of the Roman Empire. This produced again a kind of emptiness in which the Cynics, Skeptics, and Stoics were much more important than Plato, because they were adequate to the situation. Stoicism, not Platonism, governed the later ancient world. Plato, however, returned in the Middle Ages.

Augustine was in quite the opposite situation. Whereas in Plato a great aristocratic tradition came to an end, a new tradition started in Augustine. He had a pagan father and a Christian mother. The pagan father made it possible for him to participate in what was greatest in paganism at that time, and his Christian mother made it possible for him to enter into another tradition, a new archaism.

(b) Augustine discovered the problem of truth. This second step is connected with the fact that he read Cicero's book, *Hortensius*. In it Cicero dealt with the question of truth. For Cicero this meant choosing between existing ways of truth, between the different philosophies. Cicero, a great Roman statesman, answered in terms of a kind of eclectic philosophy, as I believe every American statesman would do if he were to write a book on truth. He would choose those elements in philosophy which are most relevant to the political situation in which he found himself. Likewise, Cicero was interested in truth from a practical point of view. He was not an original philosopher. After the catastrophe of Greek philosophy this was impossible. Hence, from a pragmatic point of view he held that what enhances good citizenship in the Roman Empire is of philosophical value. The ideas which enhance are providence, God, freedom, immortality, rewards, etc. Augustine was in the same situation, only for him it was the City of God, not the *civitas terrena*, which he had in mind. So he developed a pragmatic philosophy, with Platonic and other elements, on the basis of the need of the Christian life, not on the basis of Roman citizenship. The basic form was pragmatic and eclectic, as in Cicero. Augustine also was not an original philosopher in the sense in which Plato or the Stoics were. He was a philosopher in whom the great synthesis between the Old Testament idea of Yahweh and the Parmenidean idea of being was achieved. More than anyone else in the history of the church Augustine was responsible for the communion of Jerusalem with Athens.

(c) The third point was his Manichaeism. The Persian religion was dualistic and in the Hellenistic period produced a movement called Manichaeism, named after its leader Mani. It was a Hellenized Parsism, dualistic in character. We can consider it a mixture between the prophecy of Zoroaster, the prophet of the Persian religion, and Platonism in the form of the gnostic thinking in the late ancient world.

The Manichaeans were for a long time the main competitors of Christianity. They asserted that they represented the truly scientific theology of their time. Augustine was attracted to it for this reason, and also because the dualism of the Manichaeans made it possible to explain sin rationally. This is the reason that the Manichaeans have always had some influence in the history of Christianity. In the Middle Ages there were always some sects influenced by Manichaean ideas, and there are many Manichaean ideas around today without our knowing them as such. Whenever sin is explained in terms of two ultimate principles, that is Manichaean; the evil principle is as positive as the good. For ten years Augustine was attracted to Manichaeism. There were reasons for this. First of all, for this group truth was not a merely theoretical issue, a matter of logical analysis, but it was a religious issue, a matter of practical or existential concern. Secondly, truth was saving truth. Manichaeism was a system of salvation. The elements of the good, which are captivated by the evil principle, are saved from it. Thirdly, truth lies in the struggle between good and bad, which gives one the possibility of interpreting history.

Augustine always remained under the influence of Manichaeism. He left the group and fought against it, but his thinking and even more his feeling were colored by its profound pessimism about reality. His doctrine of sin is probably not understandable apart from his Manichaean period. Augustine left Manichaeism under the influence of astronomy. Astronomy showed him the perfect motion of the stars, that is, the fundamental elements in the structure of the universe. This made any dualistic principle impossible. If the universe has a structure of regular mathematical forms which can be calculated and which are harmonious, where can you find the effect of the demonic creation in the world? The world as created in its basic structure is good; this is what he derived from astronomy. This means that he used the Greek Pythagorean idea of the cosmos. He used the principles of form and harmony as expressed in mathematics.

This Greek European principle overcame for Augustine the Asiatic dualism and negativity. Thus, the separation of Augustine from the Manichaean philosophy was a symbolic event. It meant the liberation of modern natural science, mathematics, and technology from the Asiatic dualistic pessimism and negation of reality. This was extremely important for the future of Europe. The later medieval Augustinian philosophers and theologians were always men who emphasized astronomy and mathematics more than anything else. Modern natural science is born, as are Platonism and Augustinianism, on the basis of a belief in a harmonious cosmos determined by mathematical rules. This was also the world-view of the Renaissance. If we look deeper into the movements of thought, we can see that this anecdote about Augustine leaving the Manichaeans because of astronomy, after he had joined them because of its explanation of sin and evil, becomes a world-historical symbol for the relationship of the Asiatic East and the European West.

(d) After Augustine left the Manichaean group, he fell into skepticism, as often happens if you are disillusioned about a system of truth. You may fall into doubt about every possibility of truth. At this time the mood of skepticism was widespread. Even in the later Academy, the Platonic school, skepticism about knowledge existed in what was called probabilism. Only probable statements are possible; no certainty is possible. All of Augustine's earlier philosophical writings deal with the problem of certainty. He wanted to overcome the skeptical philosophy; he wanted certainty. This is an important element in his thinking because it presupposed the negative end of the Greek development. The heroic Greek attempt to build a world on the basis of philosophical reason came to a catastrophic end in skepticism. The attempt to create a new world in terms of a doctrine of essences ended in skepticism. It is on this basis that the emphasis on revelation must be understood. Skepticism, the end of Greek philosophy, was the negative presupposition of the way in which Christianity received the idea of revelation. Skepticism is very often the basis for a doctrine of revelation. Those people who emphasize revelation in the most absurd supernaturalistic terms are those who enjoy being skeptical about everything. Skepticism and dogmatism about revelation are correlated. The way that Christianity emphasized revelation up to the Renaissance is related to the tremendous shock Western mankind experienced when all the attempts of the Greek philosophers to bring certainty proved to be in vain.

Skepticism also gave rise to a new doctrine of knowledge, a new epistemology, which Augustine created. It starts with the *inner* man instead of the experience of the external world. Skepticism, which was the end of all attempts to build a world in the objective realm, in the realm of things and objects, had the effect of throwing Augustine upon himself to find therein the place of truth. Thus, we have two consequences of his participation in skepticism: the one is that he accepted revelation, the other that to find certainty as a philosopher he looked into the innermost center of his soul, in the subject himself. Augustine stood between skepticism and the new authority, that of the church, just as Plato stood between the old authority and the beginning of skepticism. Here again we have the end of the archaic period in Plato and the beginning of a new archaic period in Augustine.

(e) Augustine's liberation from skepticism in the philosophical realm was brought about by his Neo-Platonic period. While skepticism was at one end of Greek thinking, Neo-Platonism was at the other. Skepticism was the negative, Neo-Platonism the mystical, way that Greek philosophy came to its finish. Augustine became a Neo-Platonic philosopher and used this philosophy as the basis for a new certainty, the immediate certainty of God. In Neo-Platonism you have the immediacy of truth in the inner soul, and from this he got his new certainty of the divine.

Neo-Platonism also gave Augustine the basis for his interpretation of the relationship of God and the world; God is the creative ground of the world in terms of *amor* (love). Then, from a psychological point of view it gave him an entrance into himself, although this had to be supported by his Christian experience. But now Augustine did something which later on all Renaissance philosophers also did—he turned the meaning of Neo-Platonism into its opposite. Neo-Platonism was a negative philosophy, a philosophy of escape from the world. The elevation of the soul out of the material world into the ultimate is the meaning of Neo-Platonism. Augustine changed this emphasis; he dropped the idea of degrees, and instead used Neo-Platonism for the immediate experience of the divine in everything, but especially in his soul.

(f) Augustine overcame skepticism not only philosophically with the help of the Neo-Platonists, but also with the help of the authority of the church. This happened under the influence of St. Ambrose, bishop of Milan, in whom the authority of the church was represented. The principle of authority was a form in which the new archaism, or the new archaic period which starts with the church tradition, became conscious of itself. The catastrophe of skepticism drove Augustine more and more to authority, to the authority of revelation, concretely given to him by the authority of the church.

The entire medieval development had an underlying anxiety of skepticism, the anxiety of meaninglessness, as we would call it, over against which the acceptance of revelation and authority stood. Authority for Augustine meant the impressive, imposing, overwhelming power of the church and its great representatives. The phenomenon of authority was not a problem of heteronomy, as it is for us, that is, subjection to what someone else tells us to accept. For Augustine it was the answer to the question implied in ancient skepticism. Therefore, he did not experience it as heteronomy but as theonomy, and somehow rightly so at that time.

(g) Another thing which impressed Augustine profoundly was Christian asceticism, as represented by monks and saints. He experienced the tension between the mystical ideal and his own sensual nature. In Augustine's time the sphere of sexuality was profanized in a terrible way. Neither Stoic reason nor Neo-Platonism was able to overcome this profanation on a large scale. The natural forms of love, sanctified by tradition and faith in the archaic periods of Greece and the other countries, had been destroyed. An unrestrained naturalism of sex prevailed.

None of the preaching of the Stoics, Cynics, or Skeptics was able to help against this, because they preached the law, and the law is powerless against a naturalistically distorted libido. Augustine found a new principle of sanctification which proved the solution for himself and for others in this realm. It had the same tension in itself as we met in the Christian Neo-Platonism in Dionysius, that is, both affirmation and negation of the world. Christianity affirms creation and sanctifies existence through the historical appearance of the divine in Christ. Neo-Platonism negates creation; in fact, it has no real creation. And it negates the historical appearance of God, or makes it a universal event which always is happening. Augustine was divided; insofar as he was a Christian, with his roots in the Old Testament, he valued family and sex, to the extent that sex was kept within the family. Being influenced by Neo-Platonism and the ancient negativity toward the world, he denied sex and praised asceticism. This conflict went on through the whole history of the church. We find it even in the Reformers, although the Reformation was basically on the positive side of Augustine, affirming the body in dependence on Old Testament prophetism. On the other hand, the suspicion of libido was so deeply rooted in the Christian tradition that in spite of their radicalism, the Reformers were unable to eradicate the remnants of Neo-Platonic asceticism, and were suspicious of everything sexual. This is still true of Protestants in countries under Calvinist influence.

(h) It is important not only to understand these seven steps in the development of Augustine, but also to notice what is missing among these major influences on him. Aristotle is missing, not entirely, of course, because Plotinus had taken much of Aristotle into his system. Yet, Aristotle was not directly important for Augustine. This means that Augustine did not include in his philosophy and theology the concern for Greek science. Not only Greek natural science, but also political science was not really implied in his thinking. This is significant for the further development in the Middle Ages.

(1) What Aristotle did was to construct a system of mediation, not a system of dualism, as we have in Plato and Plotinus. The system of mediation could not be used by Augustine because for him the dualistic world-view seemed to be the adequate expression of Christianity.

(2) The emphasis in Aristotle on the importance of the individual provides a basis for tendencies which are far removed from Augustine, who wanted the *community* of the church.

(3) Aristotle speaks about the middle way between the extremes. He denies anything like the erotic and ascetic ecstasies of Augustine. Again, it is a quasi-bourgeois attitude. The consequences of this later on become very explicit in Protestantism.

(4) Aristotle represents the special sciences which deal with things in their rational and horizontal relationship. Augustine denies the importance of such things. What is important is the knowledge of God and the soul, not knowledge of the natural things.

(5) Aristotle was a logician. Augustine had no particular interest in logic. The intuitive and voluntaristic character of his thinking made him disinterested in the abstractions of pure logic.

(6) Aristotle was an inductive thinker, an empiricist. He started from the given reality in time and space and went up from there to the highest abstractions. Augustine, following Plato, was an intuitive thinker; he started from above and went down to the empirical realities.

Now, these two different attitudes were due to clash as soon as Aristotle was rediscovered in the thirteenth century. For this reason this is the greatest century of Christian theology; it is completely determined by the tension between Aristotle and Augustine. This tension continues through all the succeeding centuries. If anyone wishes to place a label on me, he can call me an "Augustianian", and in this sense "anti-Aristotelian" and "anti-Thomistic". I am in basic agreement with Augustine with respect to the philosophy of religion, but not necessarily in other things. For example, as a *Gestalt* theologian or philosopher I am closer to Aristotle than to Augustine or Plato, because the idea of the living structure of an organism is Aristotelian, whereas the atomistic, mechanical, mathematical science is Augustinian and Platonic.

2. *Augustine's Epistemology*

The purpose and the way of knowledge are expressed in Augustine's famous words: "I wish to know God and the soul." "Nothing else?" "Nothing at all." God and the soul! This means that the soul is the place where God appears to man. He wants to know the soul because only there can he know God, and in no other place. This implies, of course, that God is not an object beside other objects. God is seen in the soul. He is in the center of man, before the split into subjectivity and objectivity. He is not a strange being whose existence or non-existence one might discuss. Rather, he is our own *a priori*; he precedes ourselves in dignity, reality, and logical validity. In him the split between the subject and object, and the desire of the subject to know the object, are overcome. There is no such gap. God is given to the subject as nearer to itself than it is to itself.

In the Augustianian tradition the source of all philosophy of religion is the immediacy of the presence of God in the soul or, as I prefer to say it, the experience of the unconditional, of the ultimate, in terms of an ultimate or unconditional concern. This is the *prius* of everything. This is not a matter of discussing whether or not somebody exists. Augustine connects this with the problem of certainty. He says that we have immediate evidence of two things, first, the logical form—because even the question of evidence presupposes the logical form—and secondly, the immediate sense experience, which should really be called "sense impression" because "experience" is too ambiguous. What he means is this: I now say that I see blue. Objectively the color may be not blue but green—sometimes I confuse these two, especially in ladies' dresses, to the horror of Mrs. Tillich. In any case, the sense impression I have is blue. This is absolutely certain, even if the dress is not blue. This is what he means with immediacy. I may see a man, but as I come nearer, it is in reality a tree. This often happens when you are walking in a fog. This means there is no certainty about the objective element in it; but there is absolute certainty about the impression I have as such. There is skepticism about everything real. Logical forms are not real; they are structures which make questions possible. Therefore, they are immediate and necessary. And sense experiences are not real, except insofar as I have them. Whether they are more than this, I do not know. Thus, these two evidences—of the logic and of the perception—do not overcome skepticism.

How then can doubt about reality be overcome? First, we must start with the general doubt; we must doubt about everything. It was not Descartes who first said this. It was said even before

Augustine. But Augustine also said it. Is there a point of certainty somewhere? He said: "You know that you are thinking." "Do not go outside; go into yourself," namely, where you are thinking. "The truth dwells in the interior of man, for a mind knows nothing except what is present to the mind. But nothing is more present to the mind than the mind itself." That is to say, the immediate self-consciousness of the asking skeptic is the fixed point. The truth which was lost in the exterior world, where everything fell under skepticism, is found again in the interior world. The soul is the inner realm, in contrast to Greek philosophy in which it is the power of life. The discovery of soul in this sense is one of the most important consequences of Christianity. It includes the world as the sum of all appearances. In contrast to the Greeks, where the soul is a part of all things, the world now becomes an object. The world is an appearance for the soul, which is the only real thing.

Now these ideas—go into your inner reality and there you will find truth—sound very much like Descartes' *cogito ergo sum* (I think, therefore I am). The difference is that in Descartes the self-certainty of the ego is the principle of mathematical evidence —he derives from this his rational system of nature—whereas for Augustine the inner evidence is the immediacy of having God. So Augustine says: After going into your soul, transcend yourself. This means that in your soul there is something which transcends your soul, something immutable, namely, the divine ground. He refers here to the immediate awareness of that which is unconditional. This is certainly not an argument for the existence of God, but a way of showing that God is presupposed in the situation of doubt about him. "While not seeing what we believe, we see the belief in ourselves." That is, we see the situation of being grasped by something unconditional.

There were people whom Augustine met who said: Why truth at all? Truth as such is not necessary. Why not stick to probabilities? Why not restrict oneself to pragmatic answers, answers which work? Augustine replied that this is not sufficient, because it leads to a complete emptiness of life. Without something unconditional or ultimate, the preliminary meanings lose their significance. This cannot be counteracted by saying that the human situation is not one of *having* truth but of searching for truth. Augustine replies that searching for truth is no answer to the question of truth, because if we are searching for truth, we must at least have some intuition of truth, we must know when we approach truth that we are approaching it. In order to know that we are approaching truth, we must already have some criterion, namely, truth itself. He is saying that in every relativism, however radical it may be, an absolute norm is presupposed, even if it cannot be expressed in propositions. Since truth is something which we can find only in the interior of the human soul, physics is useless for ultimate truth. It does not contribute to the knowledge of God. He says that while angels have knowledge of divine things, the lower demons recognize the world of bodies. A knowledge of the bodily world involves participation in it. Knowledge is union; union implies love; and he who deals cognitively with the bodies loves them and participates in them. This means that he is distracted from the highest, divine knowledge; it means that he is in untruth. The natural sciences have meaning only insofar as they show the divine causes in nature and show the traces of the trinity in flowers and animals; they have no meaning in themselves. The consequence of this is that for the greater part of the Middle Ages the natural sciences were reduced in significance and were not really furthered at all. The technical relation to nature is of no interest to Augustine, nor the analytic character of controlling knowledge. This makes the attitude of the Middle Ages to the natural sciences understandable. If the people of the Middle Ages loved nature, it was because they could see it as an embodiment of the trinity. This, of course, gave them the possibility of artistic production, which is much higher than most of what we produce under the power of controlling knowledge. Go to the Cloisters (Museum) and look at the carpets on the walls there; what you see there is not a representation of nature in terms of natural science. None of the flowers or animals is naturalistically exact; but they are all painted in order to show the traces of the trinity, that is, the movement of life to separation and reunion in the natural objects. They try to show the divine ground in nature, and that gives them their beauty. To understand these creations, you must see their *intentio*, that which is really meant.

Augustine said that the Neo-Platonists and Plato himself were nearest to Christianity. He saw trinitarian elements in their thought, especially the Logos doctrine. Then he says—an important statement for revealing the relationship of theology and philosophy—that one thing which philosophy could not affirm is that the Logos has become flesh. Philosophy makes it possible for theologians to speak of the Logos, but when theology says the Logos became flesh, this is a theological statement based on a religious message that distinguished Christianity from classical philosophy. The statement about the Logos becoming flesh is a matter of revelation, not philosophy. The Logos as the universal principle of the cosmos appears in historical form. This is a unique, incomparable historical event.

3. *The Idea of God*

Augustine's idea of love is the power which unites the mystical and ethical elements in his idea of God. Let us first deal with his idea of love before taking up the problem of God. Anders Nygren, the Swedish theologian who wrote *Agape and Eros*, criticized Augustine, as he did Christian theology in general, for combining *erōs* and *agapē* in a synthesis. Nygren is right that in Augustine there are both elements. *Agapē* is the element of love in the New Testament sense of the personal, forgiving character of God. *Erōs* represents the longing of all creatures for God as the highest good, the desire to be united with it, to fulfill itself by intuiting eternally the divine abundance. The *agapē* element is emphasized when we speak of God moving down to man in *caritas*—I prefer the Latin word to the much distorted word "charity"—of becoming humble in Christ, exercising grace and mercy, participating in the lowest and elevating it to the highest. *Erōs*, on the other side, drives from below to above; it is a longing, striving, being moved by the highest, being grasped by it in its fullness and abundance. The Logos becoming flesh, that is *agapē*. But all flesh (all natural and historical reality) is desirous for God; this is *erōs*. In my *Systematic Theology* I have shown that if you remove *erōs*, you cannot speak of love toward God any more, because this is love toward that which is the highest power of being in which we are fulfilled.

God is *summa essentia*, ultimate being, beyond all categories, beyond all temporal and spatial things. Even the categories of substance cannot be used. Essence and existence, being and quality, functions and acts, these cannot be distinguished in this side of God. The negative theology which we found in Dionysius is present also here; both were dependent on Neo-Platonism. On the other hand, there is the positive way. God is the unity of all forms; he is the principle of all beauty. Unity is the form of all beauty and God is the unity of all forms. All ideas, all essences, or power, or principles of things, are in the mind of God. Individual things come to pass and return to God through the ideas.

Here we have the two elements in the idea of God. Insofar as God is beyond any difference, he is beyond subject and object. Love is not a subjective feeling directed toward an object. It is not that objects are ultimately loved, but through our love toward them love itself is loved. *Amor amatur*, love is loved; this means that the divine ground of being is love. Love is beyond the separation of subject and object. It is the pure essence, blessedness, which is the divine ground in all things. If we love things in the right way, including ourselves, we love the divine substance in them. If we love things for their own sake, in separation from the divine ground in them, we love them in the wrong way; then we are separated from God. There is thus for Augustine a right kind of self-love; this is to love yourself as loved by God, or to love God, the divine ground of everything, through yourself.

Augustine is also in the personalistic tradition of the Old and New Testaments and the early church. This is more important for him than for the Eastern theologians, like Origen. He sides completely with the West in the trinitarian discussion. He is more interested in the unity of God than in the different *hypostaseis*, the three *personae*, in God. He expresses this in terms which make it clear he is one of those responsible for our present-day inclination to apply the term *persona* to God, instead of applying it individually to the Father, Son, and Spirit. Of course, Augustine never became heterodox in this respect, although he leaned, as did the West generally, toward a Monarchian view. That he was inclined in this direction is evident by the analogy he sees between the trinity and the personal life of man. He says: "Father, Son, and Spirit are analogous to *amans* (he who loves), *quod amatur* (that which is loved), and *amor* (the power of love)." Or: "The trinity is analogous to memory, intelligence, and will." This means that he uses the trinity in order to give analogically a description of God as person. Since God is a person, and that means a unity, all acts of God toward the outside (*ad extra*) are always acts of the whole trinity, even the act of the incarnation. None of the three *personae* or *hypostaseis* acts for himself. Since the substance of all things is love, in its threefold appearance as *amans, quod amatur,* and *amor,* everything which is created by the divine ground bears the traces of the trinity. This gives a theonomous character to the immediate world. The forms of life are not denied or broken but theonomously filled with divine substance.

On the relation of God to the world, Augustine expressed very clearly the doctrine of creation out of nothing. There is no matter which precedes creation; creation is done without an independent substance. This means there is a continuous threat of finitude. I believe that when our modern existentialist thinkers, including myself, say that finitude is the mixture of being and non-being, or that non-being is present in everything finite, this has something to do with Augustine's statement that everything is in danger of the fathomless abyss of nothingness. The world is created in every moment by the divine will, which is the will of love. Therefore, Augustine concluded—and the Reformers followed him—that the creation and preservation are the same thing; the world is at no moment independent of God. The forms, laws, and structures of reality do not make it an independent reality. God is the supporting power of being, which has the character of love. This makes every deistic fixation of the two realities—God and the world—impossible. God is the continuous, carrying ground of the world.

All of this is in agreement with Augustine's famous doctrine of time. Philosophically speaking, this is his greatest achievement, because here he really starts a new era of thinking about the concept of time. (Cf. his prayer, Book II of the *Confessions.*) Time is not an objective reality in the sense in which a thing is. Therefore it is not valid for God. The question how time was before creation is meaningless. Time is created *with* the world; it is the form of the world. Time is the form of the finitude of things, as is space also. Both world and space/time have eternity only insofar as they are subjects of the eternal will to creation. That means they are potentially present in the divine life, but they are not eternal as real; as real they are finite; they have a beginning and an end. According to Augustine there is only one world process.

This is the decisive statement by which he denies the Greek concept, held by Aristotle and the Stoics, that the world is cyclical, that there are cycles of birth and rebirth which repeat themselves infinitely. For Augustine there is a definite beginning and a definite end; only eternity is before and after this beginning and end. For the Greeks space was finite and time was infinite, or better, endless. For Augustine neither time nor space is infinite. He agrees with the Greeks on the finitude of space. They could not understand the infinity of space because they were all potential sculptors; their world-view was plastic; they wanted to see bodies in space. The infinity of space would have disrupted the plastic form of reality, expressed in mathematical forms by the Pythagoreans. Augustine, however, said time was finite. This finitude of time is necessary if time is to have an ultimate meaning. In Greek thought it does not; instead it is the form of decay and repetition. Time has no meaning of itself in creative terms. The endlessly recurring times of nature are meaningless. Meaningful time is historical time, and historical time is not a matter of quantity. The six thousand years of world history about which Augustine speaks *are* the meaning of time. And if, instead, there were one hundred thousand years or even a few billion years, this could not take away the meaning of time. Meaning is a qualitative, not a quantitative, concept. The measure of time is not clock time. Clock time is physical time; it tends to repeat itself. But the meaning of time is the *kairos*, the historical moment, which is the qualitative characteristic of time.

There is one world whose center is the earth, and one history whose center is the Christ. This one process is eternally intended by God, but eternity is not time before time, nor is it timelessness. It is something beyond all these categories. However, although the world is intended eternally, it is neither eternal nor infinite; it is finite and meaningful. Infinite meaning is actualized in the finite moment. This feeling of finitude makes the Middle Ages understandable to us. People then felt that they lived in one process which has a definitely known beginning with the days of creation a few thousand years before our time and which will have a definite end with the days of judgment a few years or a few thousand years ahead of us. We live within this period, and what we are doing in it is extremely important—it is the meaning of the whole world process. We are in the center of everything that happens, and Christ is in the center of everything that we are. This was the medieval world-view. You can imagine how far we are removed from it if you realize what this means not in terms of words but in terms of a feeling toward reality, an awareness of one's existence.

4. *The Doctrine of Man*

Augustine said that the decisive function in man is the will. It is present in memory and in intellect, and has the quality of love, namely, the desire toward reunion. This predominance of will was another of the great ideas by which the West overcame the East, and which produced the great medieval struggle between voluntarism and intellectualism. The two basic activities of the soul—knowledge and love, or will, which is the same—have an ambiguous character. They are directed partly toward themselves and partly beyond themselves. They are directed toward one's self in self-knowledge and self-love. "We are, we know that we are, and we love this our being and knowing." This means we are self-related and self-affirming. We affirm ourselves in knowledge and in will.

On the other hand, love and knowledge transcend ourselves and go to the other beings. Love participates in the eternal; this is its own eternity. The soul has transtemporal dimensions. This participation is not what is usually called immortality, but it is the participation in the divine life, in the divine loving ground of being. However, this idea is in tension with another in Augustine. One could say that this mystical element is in tension with an educational element. The souls are not only eternal in their essence, but also immortal in the technical sense of continuation in time. As a result those who are excluded from eternity because they are separated from God are still immortal; this immortality means their punishment and damnation. They are excluded from God; this means they are excluded from love—love is the ground of being—and they deserve no pity. There is no unity of love between them and the others. If this is the case, however, one must ask how there can then be unity of being, if being is love. Here we see one of those conflicts between mystical-ontological thinking and ethical-educational thinking. We saw the same conflict in Origen when he spoke about the *apokatastasis tōn pantōn*, the return of everything to God, the final salvation of every-thing that has being, a teaching which the church rejected. In this sort of conflict esoteric theology, philosophy, or mysticism always chooses the one side, specifically the side of the eternal and the union with God in eternity. Ecclesiastical, educational or ethical thinking always chooses the other side, namely, the per-sonal possibility of being eternally condemned and punished. Logically this is impossible to hold, because the very concept of the eternal excludes continuation in time, and the ontological concept of love, which is so strong in Augustine, excludes being which is not in unity with love. The educational view exercises a continual threat over everyone. Therefore, the church has always maintained it, accepting the logical contradiction in order to produce the threat of the eternal (i.e., endless) condemnation. Ontological mysticism and educational moralism contradict each other on such matters.

I am reminded here of another problem which is perhaps much more concrete in our time. Anybody who seriously reflects on it, or at least carries on his reflection within the Christian or exis-tentialist tradition, will no doubt agree that the idea is utopian that at a certain time the kingdom of God, or the classless society, will be established on earth, without power or compul-sion. Utopian means literally (from *ou-topos*, no place) that there is "no place" for this in time and space. But if this is admitted, then we diminish the fanatical will toward political revolution and the transformation of society. Some will tell you they know this is utopian, but if they tell the people, they will no longer fight for the transformation of society. They can fight only if they believe the final stage is at hand, if the kingdom of God is at hand. Only this conviction releases the power to act. What are we to answer? Here we have the same problem. The ethical, in this case the social-educational, point of view contradicts the insight into the relation of time and eternity. So many say, we know this is utopianism, but we must affirm it, otherwise people will not act. Others say, and I belong to this latter group, the disappointment which follows utopianism always and necessarily makes it impos-sible to speak like this to people, if you know better, because the disappointment is worse than the weakening of fanaticism. This would be my decision, and yet it is a very questionable one.

In Augustine even the unbaptized children are not condemned

to hell but to the *limbus infantium* where they are excluded from
the eternal blessedness, from the divine love. Such an idea might
have had a tremendous educational and ecclesiastical value in
certain periods of history, but not for us any more. Very often it
produces—this is especially true of the personal fear of condemnation—neurotic stages, and therefore we cannot say that it
is superior.

5. *Philosophy of History*

Augustine's philosophy of history is based—as philosophy of
history usually is—on a dualism, not an ontological dualism, of
course, which is impossible, but a dualism in history. On the one
hand, there is the city of God, on the other the city of earth or the
devil. The city of God is the actualization of love. It is present in
the church, but the church is a *corpus mixtum*, a mixed body,
with some people who belong to it essentially and spiritually and
others who do not. Then there is a mediation between these two
characteristics of the church, the one wherein it represents the
kingdom of God and the other wherein it is a mixed body, and
this is the hierarchy. The hierarchy, those who have the consecra-
tions, mediates between the two. In them Christ rules the church
and Christ is present. Thus, the Catholic Church could use
Augustine in both ways. It could identify the kingdom of God
with the church to such a degree that the church became abso-
lutized; this was the one development which actually happened.
On the other hand, the difference could be made very clear, and
this is what the sectarian movements and the Protestants did.
There is a dialectical relationship between the kingdom of God
and the church in Augustine. It was ambiguous enough to be useful for different points of view. But one thing was clear for him:
there is no thousand-year stage in world history, no third age.
Chiliasm or millennialism was denied by him. Christ rules the
church in this present time; these are the thousand years. There
is no stage of history beyond the one in which we are living. The
kingdom of God rules through the hierarchy, and the chiliasts are
wrong. We should not look beyond the present period in which
the kingdom of God is present in terms of history.

The kingdom of the earth has the same ambiguity. On the one
hand, it is the state of power, compulsion, arbitrariness, tyranny;

Augustine called it the "gangster state". It possesses all the imperialistic characteristics that we see in all states. On the other hand, there is the unity which overcomes the split of reality, and from this point of view it is a work of love. If this is understood by the emperor, he can become a Christian ruler. Here again we have the ambiguous valuation: the state is partly identical with the kingdom of the devil and it is partly different from it because it restricts the devilish powers.

History has three periods: that before the law, that under the law, and that after the law. In this way we have a fully developed interpretation of history. We are in the last period, in the third stage; it is a sectarian heresy to say that another state must still be expected. The medieval sects, of course, expressed this heresy. In this light the struggle becomes visible between the revolutionary attempts of the sectarian movements and the conservatism of Augustine's philosophy of history.

6. *The Pelagian Controversy*

We touched on Augustine's doctrine of man when speaking of the voluntaristic character of his thinking, his idea that the center of man is not the intellect but the will. In this he began a development which goes through the whole Western world, represented by theologians and philosophers for whom the will is the center of man. When we come to the medieval philosophers and theologians, and to the modern ones, we will see how this influence was continually maintained in creative tension with the tendencies coming from Aristotle. The tension between Augustine and Aristotle is the decisive power which moves the medieval history of thought; almost everything can be seen in relation to this tension.

So far this has been only a description of man in his essential relationship. If man is seen in his essential relationship to God, to himself, and to others, then he is seen by Augustine as a will whose substance is love. This love is the creative ground of everything that is. This is an idea of love in which *agapē* and *erōs* are united. However, this essential nature of man is not his existential nature; it is not actual in time and space. On the contrary, this essential nature of man is distorted by what Augustine calls sin, especially original sin, in line with the tradition of the New Testament and the church. His doctrine of sin, the center of his doctrine of man, was developed in his controversy with Pelagius.

Augustine's conflict with Pelagius is one of the great struggles in church history, comparable to the trinitarian and christological controversies. It is one which repeats itself again and again in the history of the church. Already in the New Testament there was the tension between Paul and the writers of the "catholic" Letters; we have it between Augustine and Pelagius, somehow also between Thomas Aquinas and the Franciscans, and finally between Karl Barth and the present-day liberals. One point is always decisive. Usually it is discussed in terms of the concept of freedom, but this is misleading because freedom has so many connotations not relevant for this question. The decisive point is the relationship of religion and ethics. The question is whether the moral imperative is dependent on the divine grace for its actualization, or whether divine grace is dependent on the fulfillment of the moral imperative.

Pelagius was not an isolated heretic. He represented the ordinary doctrine of people who were educated in Greek thinking, especially in Stoic traditions, and for whom freedom is the essential nature of man. Man is a rational being, and a rational being has freedom of deliberation and decision. This alone would not have made him a heretic, because most of the Eastern church had exactly the same idea of freedom. But Pelagius developed this concept in a way which brought him into conflict with Augustine. When this conflict was resolved, Augustine was at least partly victorious and Pelagius was an arch-heretic, whose name still stands for one of the classic Christian heresies.

For Pelagius death is a natural event, not a result of the fall. Since death belongs to finitude, it would have happened even if Adam had not fallen into sin. The same idea, we have already seen, was expressed in Ignatius and Irenaeus, namely, that man is naturally finite and destined to die as everything natural. However, according to the story of paradise it is possible for man to overcome his essential finitude through participation in the food of the divine. What Pelagius does is to leave out the second possibility and to affirm only the first as true and in accord with the Christian tradition.

The sin of Adam belongs to him alone and not to the human race as such. In this sense original sin does not exist. Original sin would make sin into a natural category, but man is a moral being. Therefore, the contradiction of the moral demand must be an event of freedom and not a natural event. Everybody must sin in order to be a sinner. The simple dependence on Adam does not make anyone a sinner. Here again Pelagius is saying something that is universally Christian, that there is no sin without personal participation in sin. On the other hand, he does not see that Christianity also stresses the tragic universality of sin, thus making it a destiny of the human race. The relationship to Adam as the one presupposed as the first man is, of course, mythological, but in this myth the Christian Church—whether it took it literally or not—has preserved the tragic element which we also find in the Greek world-view. Pelagius had a point, but he did not see the profundity of the Christian description of the human situation.

When children are born they are in the state of Adam before the fall; they are innocent. Of course, Pelagius could not close his eyes to the fact that the evil surroundings and customs distort their innocence. This is akin to the modern psychoanalytic theory of the relationship to the parents or their representatives which determines the complexes and other negativities in the depths of the soul. Today there is even another theory, the biological theory that the distortion is inherited and cannot be avoided even if you place the child in the best possible surroundings. There is some distortion in its very nature from birth. However, Pelagius wanted to avoid the idea of hereditary sin. Sin is not a universally tragic necessity, but a matter of freedom. America is very much in favor of this Pelagian idea that every individual can always make a new beginning, that he is able by his individual freedom to make decisions for or against the divine. The tragic element, on the other hand, is very much known in Europe, and is not so near to the heart of Americans. In Europe the negative side of Augustinianism—we could call it existentialism—has emphasized the tragic element and has reduced the ethical zeal and impact that Pelagianism can have.

The function of Christ under these circumstances is a double one: to provide the forgiveness of sins in baptism to those who believe, and to give an example of a sinless life not only by avoiding sins but also by avoiding the occasions of sins through asceticism. Jesus was an example of asceticism, a kind of first monk; Pelagius himself was a monk. Grace is identical with the general remission of sins in baptism. Grace has no meaning after this because then man is able to do everything himself. Only in the situation of baptism does man receive the grace of forgiveness.

We can say that Pelagianism has a strong ethical emphasis with many ascetic elements, but the tragic aspect of life has been entirely lost. Do not take him lightly; take him seriously. I do not say that we are all born Pelagians—as I say about nominalism—but I would say that Pelagianism is very near to all of us, especially in those countries which are dependent on sectarian movements, as America so strongly is. It is always effective in us when we try to force God down to ourselves. This is what we usually call "moralism", a much abused term. Pelagius said that good and evil are performed by us; they are not given. If this is true, then religion is in danger of being transformed into morality.

Against these views of Pelagius we have Augustine's doctrine of sin. Augustine agreed with Pelagius that freedom is the original, essential quality of man, so that Adam was free when he fell. Originally man's freedom was directed toward the good, and the good is the love with which God loves himself. In this sense everybody is free. But this freedom is dangerous, so dangerous that man could change his direction toward God and direct himself instead toward particular things in time and space. Augustine saw that the danger of freedom was so great that he created the famous doctrine of *adjutorium gratiae*, the helping power of grace, which was given to Adam before he fell. He was not in pure nature (*in puris naturalibus*). The assisting power of grace made it possible for Adam to continue indefinitely in directing his will toward God. It made it *possible* for him. This, however, was a point on which the Reformers disagreed with Augustine. This *adjutorium gratiae*, this assisting power of grace, implied indirectly that nature in itself cannot be good; it must be fulfilled by supernature. It implied that man *in puris naturalibus*, in his purely natural state, is so endangered that actually he must fall, unless supernature helps him. The Reformers placed such an emphasis on human nature—very similar to the Renaissance at this point—that they declined this idea of a *donum superadditum*, a gift of grace that is added to man's nature. This is a very profound distinction, and behind this seemingly Scholastic terminology there is hidden the question of the valuation of creation. In the doctrine of the *donum superadditum* there is something of the Greek valuation of matter as the resisting power. An element of the Greek tragic feeling enters here in contrast to the Jewish and Protestant affirmation of nature as good in itself.

Augustine held that the first man, Adam, had the freedom not to fall, not to die, not to turn away from the good. In this state he was at peace with himself—a profound remark in view of our modern depth psychology; he was at peace with all things and all men. There was no cupidity, no desire, not even in sexual life. There was no pain in this state, not even in the event of childbirth. It was easy for Adam not to fall; there was no real reason for it. Yet, astonishingly, he did fall. And since there was no external reason for his fall, it started in his inner life. Sin, according to Augustine, is in its very inception spiritual sin. Man wanted to be in himself; he had all the good possibilities; there was nothing for him to endure from which he would have to turn away; he had everything he needed. However, he wanted to have all this by himself; he wanted to stay in himself. Therefore he turned away from God and fell. This is what Reinhold Niebuhr calls "pride" and what I prefer to call *hybris*, self-elevation. In this way man lost the assistance of grace and was left alone. Man wanted to be autonomous and to stand upon himself. This meant a wrong love of himself which cut off the proper love toward God. Augustine said: "The beginning of all sin is pride; the beginning of pride is man's turning away from God." If you say *hybris* instead of pride, it is profounder because pride often has the connotation of a special psychological attitude. But that is not what is meant here. The most humble people in a psychological sense can have the greatest pride.

Now these statements show first of all that Augustine was aware that sin is something which happens in the spiritual realm —turning away from the ground of being to whom one belongs. It is not a naturalistic doctrine of sin. Even more important than this, Augustine shows clearly the religious character of sin. Sin for him is not moral failure; it is not even disobedience. Disobedience is a consequence, not the cause of sin. The cause is turning away from God, from God as the highest good, as the love with which God loves himself through us. Since this is the nature of sin, it ought to be kept distinct from "sins", which refer to moral acts. Sin is primarily and basically the power of turning away from God. For this reason no moral remedy is possible. Only one remedy is adequate—a return to God. This, of course, is possible only in the power of God, a power which man under the conditions of existence has lost.

The immediate consequence of man's turning away from his highest good is the loss of this good. This loss is the essential punishment of man. Punishments in terms of educational or juristic terminology are secondary. For Augustine the basic punishment is ontological. If God is everything positive, the ultimate good, or the power of being overcoming non-being, the only real punishment that is possible is the intrinsic one of losing this power of being, of not participating any more in the ultimate good. Augustine described it thus: "The soul died when it was left alone by God, as a body will die when it is left by the soul." The soul which is dead, religiously speaking, has lost its control over the body. When this happened, the other side of sin became actual. The beginning is pride, *hybris*, turning to oneself, becoming separate from God. The consequence is concupiscence, the infinite endless desire. The word *concupiscentia*, desire or libido (in the ways in which modern psychology uses it) has two meanings in Augustine: the universal meaning, the turning toward the movable goods, those goods which change and disappear, and the narrower meaning of natural, sexual desire, which is accompanied by shame. This ambiguity of the term "concupiscence" is to be found also in Freud's concept of libido. Both terms are meant universally, the desire to fulfill one's own being with the abundance of reality, and both have the meaning of sexual desire. Innumerable consequences followed from this ambiguity. For example, in Freud there followed his puritanism, his depreciation of sex, his bourgeois suppression, and on the other hand, the revelation of this situation. But Freud never found a solution to this problem, either by suppressing or getting rid of the desire. And since you cannot get rid of it, you have, according to Freud, the desire unto death, the death instinct, as he calls it, which is the necessary answer to the endlessness of desire. In Protestantism, as in all of Catholicism earlier, the ambiguity of the term "concupiscence" had all sorts of ascetic consequences, including the most extreme and disgusting forms. The Reformers tried to reestablish the dignity of the sexual, but they succeeded only in a limited way. They never completely followed through on their own principles against the Roman Church. Therefore, anyone who knows anything about the history of moral behavior and the history of ethical theory in Protestantism will see that Christianity has been very uncertain on this point and has produced no satisfactory answer to this question implied in human existence.

Adam's sin is original sin for two reasons. We all existed potentially in Adam, in his procreative power, and in this way we participated in his free decision and thus are guilty. This is myth, of course, and a very questionable one. Secondly, Adam introduced libido, desire, into the process of sexual generation, and this element was passed on by heredity to all posterity. Everyone is born out of the evil of sexual desire. Original sin is primarily spiritual, sin of the soul, in Adam as in everyone else. But it is also bodily sin. Augustine had great difficulty in uniting the spiritual character of sin in everybody with the hereditary character of sin which derives from Adam.

Because of original, hereditary sin, everybody belongs to a "mass of perdition", to a unity of negativity. The most striking consequence of this is that even infants who die early are lost. Since everyone belongs to the mass of perdition, nobody can be saved except by a special act of God. This is the most powerful emphasis on the solidarity of mankind in the tragedy of sin. Thus, he denies most radically—almost in a Manichaean sense—the freedom in the individual personality. The all-embracing unity of mankind makes us what we are. Now, in the light of our modern research into depth psychology and sociology we are probably able to understand better than our fathers what Augustine meant, namely, the inescapable participation of everyone in human existence, in a social structure, and in an individual psychological structure, whether neurotic or otherwise. The question which arises, however, is: What about the participation of the individual in guilt? There is no answer to this in the context of Augustine.

Man has lost his possibility to turn toward the ultimate good because of his universal sinfulness. We are under the law of servitude, the bondage of the will. Therefore, grace is first of all *gratia data*, grace given without merit. It is given by God to a certain number of people who cannot be augmented or dimin-

ished; they belong to him eternally. The rest of the people are left
to the damnation which they deserve. There is no reason in man
for the predestination of the one group or the rejection of the
other. The reason is in God alone; it is a mystery. Thus, one cannot speak of prescience, of foreseeing what man would do, as is
often done in the doctrine of freedom. This is impossible since
God's willing and knowing are identical. God can never look at
something as though it were not carried by his power of being,
that is, his will. God always wills what he knows. "He has
elected us not because we would be holy, but in order to have us
become holy." There is no reason in man for predestination. God
does both the willing and the fulfilling.

Augustine was nevertheless not a determinist in the technical
psychological sense. Predestination does not exclude man's will.
The psychological will of man is preserved and distinguished
from external forces, or from compulsory elements in man. But
the direction of the will toward God is dependent on God's predestination, and his predestinating will cannot be explored. Grace
is given to everybody who becomes a Christian. The forgiveness
of sins, which is given first, happens in baptism and is received
by faith. Here Augustine continues the general tradition. But
beyond this, forgiving is a real participation in the ultimate
good. This ultimate good has appeared in Jesus as the Christ,
without which neither good thinking nor good acting nor loving
is possible. He describes this side of grace as the inspiration of
the good will, or he speaks of the inspiration of love, primarily
the love toward God. "The Spirit helps", he says, "by inspiring in
the place of bad concupiscence, good concupiscence, that is,
diffusing *caritas* (*agapē*) within our hearts." Justification, therefore, is an inspiration of love. Faith is the means to receive it.
But faith by that time already had the deteriorated sense—
which makes Christian preaching about faith almost impossible
today—of an acceptance of doctrines which are unbelievable. So
Augustine distinguished between two forms of faith. The one
form of faith he called *credere deo aut christo*, believing directed
toward God or Christ, that is, accepting their words and commands; the other is *credere in deum aut christum*, believing *into*
God and *into* Christ. The first is an intellectual acknowledgment,
without hope and love. The second is a personal communion
which is created by grace, or by the Holy Spirit, or by love.

This alone is the faith which justifies, because it makes him who is justified just.

Those who are predestined are not able to fall away again. They receive the gift of perseverance, the gift of not losing the grace which they have received. None of this depends on any merit, not even on the merit of not resisting grace, since grace for Augustine is irresistible when it comes to you.

With these ideas Augustine attacked Pelagius. In all respects it is the opposite of Pelagius' teachings. Augustine's doctrine, however, was never completely accepted by the church, although he was considered the greatest teacher of the church. Pelagianism was rejected, and even semi-Pelagianism, which cropped up later, was condemned a hundred years later. Yet, this rejection did not prevent it from creeping back into the church. Historians sometimes refer to this as crypto-semi-Pelagianism. It cannot be denied that especially in the Augustinian school, in the later Franciscans, semi-Pelagianism was very much alive. It was, of course, out of the question to repeat Pelagius' teachings in the official church. But semi-Pelagianism, which denied the irresistibility of grace and stressed the necessity to work to keep grace, crept back into the church to make Augustine's doctrine educationally possible. We spoke about this problem before. You cannot have such a doctrine as Augustine's in an institution of education, and the Christian Church was the only institution of education for a thousand years. In such a situation you must appeal to the free will of those to be educated. An extreme doctrine cannot be presented in a direct way to most people. Thus, the ultimate tragic element was not lost entirely, but it was to a certain extent restricted for the sake of the educational needs. This was the situation when the Reformers came upon the scene. In their time the tragic element had been reduced almost to nothing by the educational, ethical, and ascetic emphases which were dominant in the church. The churches with only some exceptions are usually very suspicious of any doctrine of predestination—at least the Catholic Church was—because that makes the ultimate relation to God independent of the church, or at least it tends to do so. So here again we have one of those tensions of which I spoke in connection with Origen and other theologians, the tension between the ultimate theological and the penultimate educational points of view. You always have these two elements in tension in religious instruction, in counseling, as well as in preaching. The great struggle between Augustine and Pelagius is perhaps the classic example of the problem in the Christian Church.

7. *The Doctrine of the Church*

Augustine's doctrine of the church has had a great influence on all Christian churches, not only the Roman, and therefore we must deal with it. We have already shown that in Cyprian the church is defined as an institution of salvation, largely replacing the concept of the church as the communion of saints (*communio sanctorum*). The consequence of regarding the church as an institution was a change in the idea of the holiness of the church. In this situation Augustine entered into conflict with the Donatist movement. Originally there was an emphasis on the sanctification of the individual members and the group as a whole. This emphasis gave way to the sacramental reality of the church. Now the holiness of the church is identical with the sacramental gifts, especially with the sacramental power of the clergy. The idea of *sanctus* (holy, saint) no longer refers to someone who is personally sanctified, but to one who has the sacramental power. This represents a fundamental change in meaning from the subjective to the objective element, from personal holiness to institutional holiness.

There were people in North Africa where Augustine was a bishop who did not go along with this development and who were interested in the actual sanctification of the church and its members, especially of the clergy. The issues which were involved were the following:

(1) the discipline in the act of penance;

(2) the question whether baptism is valid if performed by heretics;

(3) the question whether ordination is valid if performed by *traditores*, traitors, who either delivered over holy books during the persecutions, or denied they were Christians.

Are the objective graces valid if they are mediated by persons who are not subjectively holy? The Donatists excluded them and did not allow them to become ministers because for them the holiness of the church is the personal holiness of its representatives. The consequence of this would be to make individual

Christians dependent on the moral and religious status of the clergy. They would be dependent on the inner holiness of the ministers. Now, Augustine was clear about the fact that it is impossible to make a judgment of this kind, that any attempt to do so would lead to terrible consequences—to assume the role of God who alone can look into the hearts of people. He wanted to save the objectivity of the church in face of the demand for subjective holiness of its representatives. Here he followed the lead of Cyprian. To do this he introduced the distinction between faith (including hope) and love. Faith and hope are possible outside the church because they are determined by their content. You may live among heretics, you may even be one yourself, but if you satisfy the formula of baptism in the right way, then the content is decisive and not your personally heretical or morally unworthy status. The formulae are the same as they are in the Catholic Church. Thus, if the heretical churches use these same formulae, their objective contents make their sacramental actions valid.

Love, on the other hand, is something which cannot be found where there is not the right faith. Love is the principle which unites the church. This is not a simple moral goodness, which can be found everywhere, but it is the agapeic relationship of individuals to each other. This spirit of love, which is embodied in the church as the unity of peace, as the re-establishment of the original divine unity which is disrupted in the state of existence, is something that can be found only in the church. For this reason there is salvation only in the church. Salvation is impossible without the inpouring of *agapē*, that grace given like a fluid into the hearts of men. Although there may be valid sacraments outside the church, salvation can only be had within it.

This distinction between faith and love is of extreme importance and makes the church the only place of salvation for Catholics. From this there follows the distinction between the validity and the effectiveness of the sacraments. The sacraments of the heretics are valid if they are performed in terms of the orthodox tradition. This means nobody has to be rebaptized. On the other hand, the sacraments have no effectiveness within the heretical groups, but only within the church. For example, baptism always gives a *character indelebilis*, as the technical term stated; it is a quality coming from God, which one has throughout one's life whatever one does. This was very important because it enabled the medieval church to treat the pagans and Jews differently from the baptized Christians. The baptized Christians were subjected to the laws of heresy, while pagans and Jews were not. Even though baptized Christians should try to become Jews or pagans or Muslims, they could not because the very act of baptism conferred an indelible character upon them, no matter who performed the act, whether orthodox or heretical.

In the same way ordination is always valid. Priests who are fallen and excommunicated are forbidden to administer the sacraments, but if they should do it, the sacraments are valid. If in prison a medieval priest who happens to be excommunicated should marry a couple, the marriage is valid in spite of the fact that he was forbidden to do so. And no re-ordination is needed if the priest is absolved and rejoins the clergy, because ordination is and remains valid.

All of this made the people in the church completely independent of the quality of the priest. Nobody can know this quality for sure anyway. Of course, priests who committed mortal sins that were publicly visible were excommunicated and forbidden to perform sacramental acts, but this is different. What he does is valid in any case. What we have here is the hierarchical institution of salvation, which as an institution is independent of the character of those who function in its behalf, and within this institution there is the spiritual community of the faithful. According to Catholic doctrine the first is the condition of the second; according to sectarian beliefs the second, if anything, is the condition of the first. These two concepts of the church have been in conflict throughout the history of the church.

CHAPTER III

Trends in the Middle Ages

FIRST we shall present a survey of the main ideas and trends of the Middle Ages from beginning to end, and only after that take up a few of the leading figures.

The basic problem of the Middle Ages, one which we find in all its periods, is that of a transcendent reality, manifest and embodied in a special institution, in a special sacred society, leading the culture and interpreting the nature. If you keep this in mind, you can understand everything going on in the Middle Ages. Without it you cannot understand anything, because then you would measure the Middle Ages by your own standards of today. The Middle Ages do not permit this. If you consider the distorted pictures of the Middle Ages, a common judgment is that they were the "Dark Ages"; the implication is that we live in the age of illumination, so we look back upon this period of terrible superstition with a kind of contempt. But nothing of this sort is true. The Middle Ages were one form in which the great problem of human existence in the light of the eternal was solved. The people who lived during this thousand-year period did not live worse than we live in many respects, and in other respects they lived better than we do. There is no reason to look back upon the Middle Ages with any form of contempt. On the other hand, I am not a romanticist; I do not want to measure our own situation by standards taken from the Middle Ages as romanticism does.

The Middle Ages were not so uniform as our ignorance about them allows us to believe. They were very much differentiated. We can distinguish the following periods:

(1) The period of transition, A.D. 600–1000. The year 600 marks the papacy of Gregory the Great, a man in whom the ancient

tradition was still alive, but in whom the Middle Ages had already begun. During this period we have the years of preservation—as much as could be was preserved, which was comparatively little—and of reception; the tribes which ruled Europe, the Germanic-Romanic tribes, were taken in. It was the period of transition from the ancient to the medieval world, a transitional period which is sometimes called the "Dark Ages", particularly the ninth and tenth centuries. But they were not so dark as they seem. Great things happened then which prepared a new world out of which we all have come, even though we have forgotten it.

(2) The early Middle Ages, A.D. 1000–1200. During this time new and original forms developed which were decisively different from the ancient world. This is a creative and profound period, represented by Romanesque art.

(3) The high Middle Ages, A.D. 1200–1300. Here all the basic motifs are elaborated and brought into the great systems of the scholastics, of Gothic art, and of feudal life.

(4) The late Middle Ages, A.D. 1300–1450. From 1300 on we enter the period in which the Middle Ages disintegrate. But if we speak of "disintegration" we do not wish to depreciate the tremendous surge of new motifs which developed during this period and which made both the Renaissance and the Reformation possible.

A. Scholasticism, Mysticism, Biblicism

The first series of problems we shall discuss are the main cognitive attitudes, or the main theological attitudes. There were three of them that were always present and influential: scholasticism, mysticism, and biblicism.

Scholasticism was the determinative cognitive attitude of the whole Middle Ages. It is the methodological explanation of Christian doctrine. This term is derived from "school" and means "school philosophy"—philosophy as it was treated in the school. Today "school" has connotations of separation from life and "scholasticism" even more so. When we hear this word we think of lifeless systems—"as heavy as a horse", as was said by one of the scholastics. No one can read them, since they have nothing to do with reality. Scholasticism became distorted in the late Middle Ages; but the real intention of scholasticism was the theological interpretation of all problems of life. We have an extremely rich scholastic literature that had a tremendous influence on the spiritual life of the Middle Ages.

There was one limit to this: a scholastic education was given only to a small upper class. All the scholastic books were written in Latin, a language which only the educated of that time knew. Of course, the masses could not even read or write. So the question was how to bring the message discussed in these scholastic systems to the people. There were two ways: participation in the church services, the liturgies, pictures, hearing the music, and receiving other sense impressions, which do not require much intellectual activity but give the feeling of the numinous and some kind of moral guidance. However, this does not mean that these objective things were really personal experiences. This is what mysticism meant in the Middle Ages; it introduced personal experience into the religious life.

The meaning of mysticism has been misinterpreted by Protestant theology which began with Ritschl and is still alive in Barthian theology. It is misleading when people identify this mysticism with either Asiatic mysticism of the Vedanta type, or with Neo-Platonic mysticism (Plotinus). Forget about this when you approach the Middle Ages. Every medieval scholastic was a mystic; that is, he experienced what he was talking about as personal experience. This is what mysticism originally meant in the realm of scholasticism. There was no opposition between mysticism and scholasticism. Mysticism was the experience of the scholastic message. The basis of the dogma was unity with the divine in devotion, prayer, contemplation, and ascetic practices. If you know this, it may be hoped that you will not fall into the trap of removing mysticism from Christianity, which would mean to reduce the latter to an intellectualized faith and a moralized love. This is what has happened since the Ritschlian school became dominant in Protestantism. Do not make the mistake of identifying this type of mysticism with the absolute or abstract mysticism in which the individual disappears in the abyss of the divine. Mysticism—the Protestant Orthodox theologians called it *unio mystica*—is the immediate union with God in his presence. Even for the people of Orthodoxy this was the highest form of the relationship to God. In the Middle Ages mysticism and scholasticism belonged together.

The third attitude besides scholasticism and mysticism is biblicism. Biblicism is strong in the later Middle Ages and helps to prepare the way for the Reformation. Biblicism is not something exclusively Protestant, for there were always biblicistic reactions during the Middle Ages. These reactions were sometimes very critical of the scholastic systems and also of mysticism. Usually, however, these biblicistic reactions were united with mysticism, and often also with scholasticism. Biblicism was an attempt to use the Bible as the basis for a practical Christianity, especially a lay Christianity. Biblicism in the later Middle Ages was predominant and made it possible for many laymen even to read the Bible before the Reformation.

These three attitudes, scholasticism, mysticism, and biblicism, were in most cases united in the same person. They could also stand in tension with each other. For example, scholasticism and mysticism were in tension in the conflict between Bernard of Clairvaux and Abelard. But neither of these attitudes prevailed. Both gave what they had to give to the medieval church. And the biblicistic criticisms were simply appropriated as the biblical foundation of the scholastic system and the mystical experiences. Scholasticism was the theology of that time; mysticism was the personal experiential piety, and biblicism was the continuous critical reaction coming from the biblical tradition and entering the two other attitudes, finally overcoming both of them in the Reformation.

B. THE SCHOLASTIC METHOD

Scholasticism had one basic problem, that of authority and reason. What was the medieval authority? It was the substantive tradition on which medieval life was based. Authority was first of all the tradition of the church as it was expressed in the acknowledged church fathers, in the creeds and councils, and in the Bible. When we hear of "authority" today, we tend to think of it in terms of a tyrant, be it a father, a king, a dictator, or even a teacher. We should not read this meaning into the word *auctoritas* (authority) when we see it in the medieval sources; nor should we identify it with the pope at that time, which is a much later development, toward the end of the Middle Ages. In the earlier and high Middle Ages authority is the living tradition. The question arose: What was the relation of reason to the living tradition of the church in which everyone was living? There was no other tradition. This living tradition was as natural to them as the air we breathe is to us. This analogy may help us understand what living tradition meant in the Middle Ages.

The tradition, however, was composed of many elements, not all of which said the same thing. Upon inquiry into them, it became necessary to choose from among them. The Middle Ages experienced this first of all in the realm of practical decisions, that is, of canon law. Canon law was the basis of medieval life; the dogma was one of the canon laws, and this gave it its legal authority within the church. Thus, practical needs created a class of people whose task it was to harmonize the different authorities on the meaning of the canon laws, as they appear in the many collections of canon law. This harmonizing method was a dialectical method, the method of "yes and no", as it was called. Reason in the Middle Ages was the tool for this purpose. Reason combines and harmonizes the sentences of the fathers and of the councils, first practically and then in the theoretical realm of theological statements. The function of reason was thus to collect, to harmonize, and to comment on the given sentences of the fathers. The man who did this most successfully was Peter the Lombard, whose *Four Books of Sentences* was the handbook of all medieval scholasticism. His *Sentences* were commented on by others when they wrote their own systems.

The next function of reason was to interpret the meaning of the given tradition which was expressed in the sentences. This means that the contents of faith had to be interpreted, but faith was presupposed. Out of this situation came the slogan: *credo ut intelligam*, I believe in order to know. This means that the substance of faith was given; it was something in which one participated. In the Middle Ages one did not exert a will-to-believe. The creed was given just as nature is given. Natural science does not create nature; instead, the natural scientist calculates the structures and movements of the given nature. Similarly, reason has the function of interpreting the given tradition; it does not create the tradition. This analogy can help us to understand the Middle Ages much better.

The next step was carried through, less speculatively and very cautiously, by those thinkers who took Aristotle into their theology, especially Thomas Aquinas. They held that reason is adequate to interpret authority. At no point is reason against authority; the living tradition can be interpreted in rational terms. Reason does not have to be destroyed in order to interpret the meaning of the living tradition. This is the Thomistic position even today.

The final step was the separation of reason from authority. Duns Scotus and William of Ockham, the nominalist, asserted that reason is inadequate to the authority, the living tradition; reason is not able to express it. This was stated very sharply in later nominalism. However, if reason is not able to interpret the tradition, the tradition becomes authority in a quite different way; it becomes the commanding authority to which we have to subject ourselves even though we do not understand it. We call this "positivism". The tradition is given positivistically; there it is, we simply have to look at it, accept it, and subject ourselves to it as it is given by the church. Reason can never show the meaning of the tradition; it can only show different possibilities which can be derived from the decisions of the church and the living tradition. Reason can develop probabilities and improbabilities, but never realities. It cannot show how things should be. They are all dependent on the will of God. The will of God is irrational and given. It is given in nature, so we must be empiricists in order to find out how the natural laws are. We are not in the center of nature. We are in the orders of the church, in canon law, so we must subject ourselves to these decisions in a positivistic way; we must take them as positive laws, for we cannot understand them in rational terms.

In Protestantism both things came to an end, the authority of the church and to a certain extent reason. Then reason elaborated itself completely and became creative in the Renaissance. In the Reformation, tradition was transformed into personal faith. But the Counter-Reformation tried to keep reason in bondage to tradition, only this tradition was not so much living as formulated tradition, tradition which became identical with the authority of the pope. This is very important for our present situation. All of us have to deal even today with the problem of living tradition. Living tradition is often confused with authority, and this is wrong. Authority can be natural and factual, without involving a break within ourselves, disrupting our autonomy and subjecting us to a foreign law or heteronomy. In the early Middle Ages authority was natural, so to speak, as our relation to nature is natural. By the end of the Middle Ages the situation was changed. Then that concept of authority arose against which we must fight, an authority which demands subjection to one tradition against other traditions. Today dictators even go to the extreme of excluding all other traditions. The so-called "iron curtains" which we build to a certain extent by not admitting books from the East, etc., are attempts to keep the people in one definite tradition and to prevent it from touching other traditions, because every authoritarian system knows that nothing is more dangerous for a given tradition than contact with other traditions. This places the individual at the point of decision with respect to other traditions. The "iron curtain" method was not necessary in the early Middle Ages because there was no other tradition; one lived in this tradition as naturally as we live in nature.

C. TRENDS IN SCHOLASTICISM

1. *Dialectics and Tradition*

The first form in which autonomous thinking arose in the Middle Ages was dialectics. This word "dialectics" is difficult to use today because of its innumerable meanings; its original meaning had been lost. The original meaning in Greek is "conversation", talking to each other about a problem, going through "yes and no", one representing the "yes" and the other the "no". We have already mentioned how the jurists, who represented the canon law, had to harmonize for practical reasons the different authorities, councils, and theologians. Out of this need there arose the method of dialectics, of "yes and no". This method was applied to theological problems. However, the dialectical method of "yes and no" is something of which the guardians of tradition are afraid, because once a "no" is permitted, one cannot know where it may lead. This is as true today, when you think of our fundamentalists and traditionalists, as it was in the early Middle Ages.

The early Middle Ages were not able to stand many "no's", in view of the primitive peoples to which they had to speak, in view of the fact that the church tradition was the only one in which people lived at that time, and in view of the fact that everything was in the process of transformation and consolidation. So the pious traditionalists arose against the dialectical theologians. Here I am thinking, for example, of Bernard of Clairvaux as the representative of the pious traditionalists, and of Abelard's dialectics. The question was whether dialectics can produce something new in theology, or was it to be used only for the sake of explaining the given, namely, the tradition and the authorities?

2. *Augustinianism and Aristotelianism*

When dealing with Augustine we pointed out that Aristotle was missing in his development. Now in the high Middle Ages the Augustinians came into conflict, or at least into contrast, with the newly arising Aristotelians. The Augustinians were represented by the Franciscan order; the Aristotelians were represented by the Dominican order. We have Augustinians against Aristotelians, or Franciscans against Dominicans. One of the heads of the Franciscan order was Bonaventura, a cardinal of the church, who opposed Thomas Aquinas, the great Dominican theologian. One of the fundamental problems of the philosophy of religion was developed when Augustine and Aristotle, or when Plato and Aristotle—since Augustine was Neo-Platonic in his thinking—met again and continued their eternal conversation, a conversation which will never cease in the history of human thought because they represent points of view which are always valid and which are always in conflict with each other. We have the more mystical point of view in Plato, Augustine, Bonaventura, and the Franciscans, and the more rational, empirical point of view in the line from Aristotle to Thomas Aquinas. From the point of view of the foundation of religion and theology this is perhaps the most important of the trends in the Middle Ages. Almost all the problems of our present-day philosophy of religion were discussed in this conflict which was especially strong in the thirteenth century.

3. *Thomism and Scotism*

A third contrast or conflict was between Thomism and Scotism. In a sense this is a continuation of the other struggle, since Duns

Scotus was a Franciscan and Thomas a Dominican. Yet, it was a new problem, also decisive for the modern world, involving the conflict between intellect and will as ultimate principles. For the Dominicans, for Thomism, that is, for the Aristotelian rationality which Thomas introduced into the church, the intellect is the predominant power. Man is man *qua* intellect. For the Augustinian line which leads to Duns Scotus will is the predominant power which makes man man, and God God. God is first of all will, and only secondarily intellect. And will is the center of man's personality, and intellect is secondary. The world is originally created by will and is for this reason irrational and to be taken empirically. On a secondary level it is intellectually ordered, but this order is never final and cannot be taken in by us in deductive terms. In the modern world this same conflict goes on, for example, when thinkers like Henri Bergson and Brand Blanshard of Yale present contrasting systems in terms of the will and intellect.

4. *Nominalism and Realism*

The fourth of the conflicting trends is nominalism against the so-called realism. In order to make this conflict understandable we must know what realism is. If you want to understand what medieval realism was, then simply translate it by "idealism". Medieval realism is what we call idealism, if we are not thinking of idealism in a moral sense or in a special epistemological sense, but in terms of the ideas or essences of things which have reality and power of being. Medieval realism is almost the exact opposite of what we call realism today, and realism today is almost identical with what medieval people called nominalism. For medieval man the universals, the essences, the nature of things, the nature of truth, the nature of man, etc., are powers which determine what every individual thing, such as a tree, or every individual man will always become when he or it develops. This could be called mystical realism or idealism. *Universalia realia*—the universals are realities; this is medieval realism. Of course, the universals are not things in time and space. That is a misunderstanding which makes it a little too easy to reject universals by saying: "I have never seen manhood; I have only seen 'Paul' and 'Peter.'" This is something medieval people knew as well. However, they maintained, all "Pauls" and "Peters" always have noses and eyes and feet and language. This is a phenomenon which can be understood only in terms of the universal, the power of being, which we call manhood, which makes it possible for every man to become a man with all these potentialities. These potentialities may be undeveloped or even destroyed, but every individual has them.

Nominalism holds the opposite view: Only Peter and Paul, only this particular tree at the corner of 116th Street and Riverside Drive exists, and not "treehood", not the power of treehood, which makes it become a tree. Here you have an example of the difference in feeling. If as a nominalist you look at a tree, you feel: "This is a real thing; if I run against it, I will hurt my head." But it is also possible in looking at it to be astonished that with all the seeds sown in the soil, this particular structure of a tree develops, shooting up and spreading its branches. Then in this big tree you can see "treehood", and not just a big tree. And in Peter and Paul you can see not only these particular individuals, but also the nature of man, manhood, as a power which makes it possible for all men to have this character. This is an important discussion which was carried on in logical terms, and is still being carried on. There is hardly a day that I do not fight against nominalism on the basis of my comparatively medieval realistic kind of thinking, which conceives of being as power of being. That is a sin against the "holy spirit" of nominalism, and thus also very much against the "unholy spirit" of logical positivism and many other such spirits. And I fight this fight because I believe that although extreme realism is wrong, namely, that realism against which Aristotle was fighting in Plato which regards universals as special things somewhere in heaven, there are nevertheless structures which actualize themselves again and again. So I can say, the power of being always resists non-being. For this reason I believe that we cannot be nominalists alone, although the nominalist attitude, the attitude of humility toward reality, of not desiring to deduce reality, is something which we must maintain.

The immediate importance of nominalism was that it disrupted the universals, which were understood not only in terms of abstract concepts but also of embracing groups, such as family, state, friends, craftsmen, all groups which precede the individual. At the same time, the danger of medieval realism was that the individual was prevented from developing his potentialities.

Therefore, nominalism was an important reaction, so important that I would say that without it the estimation of the personality in the modern world—the real basis of democracy—could not have developed. While I am usually critical of our being nominalists, I do praise its emphasis on the fully developed individual and his potentialities, which withstands any danger of our becoming Asiatic. In face of such a danger medieval nominalism must be understood as positively as medieval realism. Medieval realism maintains the powers of being which transcend the individual; medieval nominalism preserves or emphasizes the value of the individual. The fact that the radical realism of the early Middle Ages was rejected saved Europe from Asiatization, that is, from collectivization. The fact that at the end of the Middle Ages all universals were lost resulted in the imposition of the power of the church on individuals, making God himself into an individual who, as a tyrant, gives laws to other individuals. This was the distortion which nominalism brought along with itself, whereas the affirmation of the personal was its creative contribution. Thus, when you read about nominalism and realism in text-books of logic, do not be betrayed into the belief that this is in itself a basically logical problem. Of course, it must be discussed in terms of the science of logic as well, but it really has to do with the attitude toward reality as a whole which expresses itself also in the logical realm.

5. *Pantheism and Church Doctrine*

Partly connected with realism in the Middle Ages is pantheism, the tendency toward the complete extinction of the individual. This was done in different ways. First, it was expressed in what is called Averroism. Averroes, the greatest of the Arabian philosophers, said that the universal mind which produces culture is a reality in which the individual mind participates. But the individual mind is not something independent. This was in line with Asiatization, and Averroes was rejected. Secondly, pantheistic elements were expressed in German mysticism of the type of Meister Eckhart. This was able to dissolve all the concreteness of medieval piety, and led to the philosophy of the Renaissance. The church rejected it in the name of the individual authoritarian God.

D. THE RELIGIOUS FORCES

Next we shall consider the religious forces of the Middle Ages. The greatest and most fundamental of these religious forces was the hierarchy. The hierarchy represented the sacramental reality on which the existence of the church, state, and culture as a whole depended. It administered the Mass which was the central sacramental event. Then the hierarchy carried through the work of educating the Germanic-Romanic tribes which entered the church from their barbaric state. In doing so the hierarchy tried to influence not only the individual through the sacrament of penance, but also the social status of reality. The sacrament of penance was the correlate to the sacrament of the Mass; the Mass is objective, penance subjective. The ecclesiastical hierarchy wanted to control the world. Civil powers, or the secular hierarchies with the emperor at the top, arose and came into conflict with the church hierarchy. The emperor aspired to do the same thing from the secular point of view which the church tried to do from the religious, namely, to establish one body of Christian secular life, a life which is always at the same time both secular and religious, instead of having two separate realms as we do.

By assuming secular functions the hierarchy was always in danger of becoming secularized itself. Other religious forces resisted this tendency, one of which was monasticism. Monasticism represents the uncompromising negation of the world, but this negation was not a quietistic one. It was a negation coupled with activity directed to transforming the world—in labor, science, and other forms of culture, church architecture and building, poetry and music. It was a very interesting phenomenon and has little to do with the deteriorated monasticism against which the Reformers and humanists were fighting. On the one hand, it was a radical movement of resignation from the world, leaving the control of the world to the secular clergy, but on the other hand, it did not fall merely into a mystical form of asceticism, or into a ritualistic form as the Eastern church was in danger of doing; it applied itself to the transformation of reality.

The monks produced the great medieval aesthetic culture, and even today some of the monastic orders represent the highest form of culture in the Catholic Church. The Benedictines, in particular, have preserved this tradition until the present time. The monks were also the real bearers of theological science, perhaps even of all science. The Franciscans and especially the Dominicans produced the greatest theologians. Other monks did agricultural work, irrigation of land, drying up swamps, and all sorts of things needed in the newly conquered countries in central and northern Europe where conversions had been made. These monastic groups were, as we might say today, the active, ascetic vanguard of the church. They were free to perform cultural activities and yet were bound to the fundamentals of the church. Later on attempts were made to introduce this monastic spirit into other groups as well. We can mention two groups, the knights and the crusaders. The knights fought against the pagans and conquered eastern Germany. If you want a sweeping historical statement, consider that these chivalric orders which fought for the Christianization, and also Germanization, of eastern Europe a thousand years ago have now been conquered in this twentieth century, with the help of the Christian nations of the West. That is to say, the Slavic groups have retaken what was taken from them by the military monastic orders of the Middle Ages, and Christianity is now suppressed for the sake of the Communist form of a non-Christian secularism. It was a great world-historical event, as great as the battles of the knights in the Middle Ages, when in the twentieth century, especially in the Berlin Conference of 1945, eastern Europe was surrendered and the Germanic population which had lived there for a thousand years was thrown out. If this situation is seen in perspective, you see a little of the importance of these medieval orders.

The crusades, and the spirit of the crusaders, can be seen as the result of the introduction of the monastic spirit into the lower aristocracy. They were to conquer Palestine and the Byzantine Empire in the East. But in the end they were also repelled.

Sectarianism was another religious force; it should not be understood so much from a dogmatic point of view, as is usually done. Of course, the sects sometimes did have strange doctrines and for this reason left the church. But the real reason was psychological and sociological and much less theological. Sectarianism is the criticism of the church for the gap between its claim and its reality. It is the desire of special groups to represent ideals of consecration, sanctification, and holiness. It is an attempt to carry through some of the monastic radicalism in terms which are anti-hierarchical. To a certain extent the sectarian movements were lay movements. As the word *sectare* means, they "cut" themselves off from the body of the church. However, the non-sectarian way of introducing monastic ideals, at least in part, into secular life was through the so-called *tertiarii*, the "third orders". There was a first order of St. Francis (the order for men), a second order for women, the nuns, and later on a third order was created for the laymen. They did not enter the cloister, nor were they celibate. They subjected themselves partly to the discipline of the monastic orders, and as such produced a kind of lay piety which became stronger toward the end of the Middle Ages, and prepared the way for the Reformation.

Then we must mention the great individuals of church history as bearers of medieval piety. They were not great individuals in the sense of the Renaissance. Rather, they were great individuals as representatives of something objective, namely, of the "holy legend". The holy legend starts with the Bible and continues through all the centuries. "Legend" does not simply mean "un-historical"; it is a mixture of history and interpretation, involving stories which are attached usually to great individuals who themselves had no connection with them. Thus, legendary history is a history of representatives of the spirit of the church. This meant that the Catholic Christian of the Middle Ages was aware of a continuity through all history, going back to biblical times, even back to Noah and Adam in the Old Testament period. This continuity in history was represented by great individuals who are interesting, however, not as individuals but as representatives of the tradition and the spirit in which the people lived. This seems to me more important than the superstitious use of the individuals, for example, by praying to those who had become saints. The holy legend was a reality which, like nature, was something within which one lived. It is a reality in which the living tradition expresses itself symbolically. Those who study religious art will see that up to Giotto the great figures of medieval art are not so much individuals as representatives of the divine presence in a special event or form or character.

Another of the religious forces was the popular superstitions of daily life. The forms of daily life can be called superstitions, if by "superstition" we have in mind the identification of a finite reality

with the divine. Such superstitions permeate the entire Middle
Ages; for example, the relics of the saints, or from the life of
Christ. Another superstition was expressed in the ever-repeated
miracles or in the attitude toward holy objects, which were used
not so much as pointers to the divine but as powers which contain the divine in themselves. The positive side of this was that it
consecrated the daily life. Let me show you this by a picture.
Take a medieval town, the town of Chartres, for instance. Not
only its cathedral is important—which you must look at to understand the Middle Ages—but also the very way in which it stands
on the hill in the middle of a small town. It is a tremendous
cathedral, overlooking the whole surrounding country. In it you
find symbols of the daily life—the nobility, the craftsmen, the
guilds, and the different supporters of the church. The whole
daily life is within the walls of the cathedral in consecrated form.
When people went into it, their daily life was represented in the
sphere of the holy; when they left it, they took with them the
consecration they had received in the cathedral back into their
daily lives. This is the positive side of it. The negative side is
that all this is expressed in superstitious forms of poor pictures,
sculptures, relics, and all kinds of holy objects.

Something else of great importance in the daily life of the
medieval man was the experience of the demonic. This was a
reality for these people. The vertical line which leads up to the
divine also leads down to the demonic. And the demonic is a
power which is present in the cathedral as something already
conquered. Exorcism, expelling the demonic, was one of the daily
practices in the cathedral. When entering the cathedral one
sprinkled oneself with holy water. This had the effect of purifying
oneself from the demonic forces which had been brought along
from the daily life. Baptism was primarily exorcism of the demonic
forces before forgiveness of sins could be received. Demonic
figures are seen supporting the weight of the churches. This is
perhaps the greatest symbol—the power of the divine conquers
the power of the demonic within the daily life. Toward the end
of the Middle Ages, when the Renaissance brought in the demonic
symbolism and reality of the later ancient world, the demonic
prevailed over against the divine in terms of anxiety. The church
of this period lived in a constant anxiety about the presence of
the demonic within itself and in others. This is the background

to the trials of witches and in part also to the persecution of heretics. It is the basis for the demonic persecution of the demonic; there is no better way to describe these witchcraft trials. It is the feeling for the "underground" in life which could erupt any moment in many individuals in terms of neurotic anxiety. At first the churches were able to conquer it, but not at the end of the Middle Ages. So they started the great persecutions of sorcerers, which were even more cruel and bloody than those of the heretics. As in every persecution fear was behind this hostile attitude toward oneself and others, the tremendous anxiety about non-being in terms of demonic symbols.

E. The Medieval Church

It is interesting that in the systems of the medieval theologians there is no special place for the doctrine of the church. This indicates, among other things, that the church was self-evident; it was the foundation of all life and not a matter of a special doctrine. Of course, in the discussions about the hierarchy, the sacraments, and the relation to the civil power, a doctrine of the church was implicitly developed.

Our first consideration is: What was the relation of the church to the kingdom of God in medieval thinking? The answer to this question is the basis on which the other questions about the relation of the church to the secular power, to culture, etc., can be answered. The background to this is what we said about Augustine's interpretation of history. We must review this in order to understand the situation.

In the Augustinian interpretation of history we have a partial identification and partial non-identification of the church with the kingdom of God. They are never completely identified because Augustine knew very well that the church is a mixed body. It is full of people who formally belong to it but who in reality do not belong to it. On the other hand, he identified the church with the kingdom of God from the point of view of the sacramental graces present in the hierarchy. Now, either this identification or this non-identification could become the point of emphasis. This was always the problem of the Middle Ages. The church, of course, tried to identify itself with the kingdom of God in terms of the hierarchical graces. However, it is not correct to think that any medieval representative, whether theologian, pope, or bishop, identified his own goodness or holiness with the kingdom of God, but always his sacramental holiness, his objective sacramental power. The objectivity of this sacramental reality is decisive for understanding medieval thought. On the other hand, the actual church was a mixed body and the representatives of the sacramental graces were distorted. So from this point of view it was possible to attack the church. The discussion in the Middle Ages was carried on in continuous oscillation between these two poles.

Parallel to this there was in Augustine also a partial identification and a partial non-identification of the state with the kingdom of earth, which was also designated as the kingdom of Satan. The partial identification was based on the fact that in Augustine's interpretation of history states are the result of compulsory power. He called them "robber states", states produced by groups of gangsters, who are not considered criminals only because they are powerful enough to take the state into their own hands. This consideration, which reminds one of the Marxist analysis of the state, is contrasted, however, to the idea of natural law that the state is necessary to repress the sinful powers which would lead to chaos if left unchecked.

Here again the emphasis could be either on the identity of the state with the kingdom of Satan, or at least the kingdom of the sinful world, or on the non-identification of the two, stressing the possibility that the state has a divine function to restrain chaos. All of this is understandable only in the kind of period in which Augustine lived, when the Roman Empire, and later the Germanic-Romanic kingdoms, were realms of non-Christian power. Even when Constantine accepted Christianity, the power play was still going on, the substance of the ancient culture still existed, and was not yet replaced by the religious substance of the church. But then the situation changed. With the expansion of Christianity westward the church became the cultural substance of life, the power which determined all the individual relations, all the different expressions of art, knowledge, ethics, social relations, relation to nature, and all other forms of human life. The ancient substance was partly received by Augustine and partly removed, and what was left in it was subjected to the theonomous principles of the church.

In such a situation one could no longer say that the state is the kingdom of Satan because now the substance of the state is the church. So a new situation arose which had consequences not only for the relation of the church to the state, but also for the state itself. How was the Germanic system related to the church? Before the Germanic tribes were Christianized, they had a religious system in which the princes, the leaders of the tribes, represented not only the earthly but also the sacred power. They were automatically representing both realms. This was continued in the Germanic states insofar as the clergy belonged to the feudal order of these tribes. A man like Hinchmar, the great bishop of Rheims in France, represented the feudal protest of a sacred political power—political and sacred at the same time—against the universality of the church. The German kings, who had to give political power to the higher feudal lords, also had to give power to the bishops as higher feudal lords. The church called this simony, from the story of Simon who wanted to buy the divine power. This was connected with the fact that these feudal lords had to give something for what they received. All of this was bound up with the territorial system of the Germanic-Romanic tribes, a system which stood in opposition to the universality of the church.

Opposition against the feudal bishops and the local kings or princes came from three quarters: (1) from the lower clergy; (2) from the popes, especially Gregory VII; (3) from the proletarian masses, which were anti-feudal, especially in northern Italy. The pope used the lower bishops who were nearer to the lower clergy than the pope himself, so in the name of the pope they could resist the feudal clergy in their own territories. This was the situation which finally led to the great fight between Gregory VII and Henry IV. Usually this is called the struggle between church and state, but this is misleading. "State" in our modern sense is a concept which comes from the eighteenth century. Thus, when we speak of the "state" in Greece, in Rome, or in the Middle Ages, we should always put it in quotation marks. What did exist were legal authorities, with military and political power.

The conflict was not due to the state's encroaching upon the rights of the church, as was often the case later. It was a much more fundamental thing. Since the church was the representative of the spiritual substance of everyone's daily life, of every function, craft, business, profession, there was no separation of realms as developed after the Reformation. There was one reality with different sides. Then the question arose as to who should head this one reality. There must be a head, and it is dangerous to have two heads. So both sides, the clergy and the princes or feudal lords, claimed to be the head of this one reality. The "state" represented by the feudal order was conscious of also representing the Christian body as a whole, and the church represented by the pope was conscious of playing the same role. The same position was claimed by both sides, a position which embraced the secular as well as the religious realms. The king aspired and claimed to represent and be the protector of all Christendom. This was especially true when the king became the German emperor and as such the continuation of the Holy Roman Empire. On the other hand, Pope Gregory VII claimed the same thing from the hierarchical side. He made claims which surpassed everything which had been done before. He identified himself with all bishops as the universal bishop. All episcopal grace comes from the pope; in him Peter is present, and in Peter Christ himself is present. There is no bishop who is not dependent on the pope for his episcopal sacramental power. The pope is the universal monarch in the church. But he even went beyond this: the church is the soul of the body, and the body is the secular life. Those who represent the secular life are related to him who represents the spiritual life, as the limbs of the body are related to the inner self which is the soul. As the soul shall govern the limbs of the body, so the pope shall govern the kingdoms and all feudal orders.

This was expressed by the famous doctrine of the "two swords". There are two swords, the earthly and the spiritual. As the bodily existence is subjected to the spiritual existence, so the earthly sword of the king and of the feudal lords is subjected to the spiritual sword of the pope. Therefore, every being on earth has to be subject to the pope at Rome. This was the doctrine of Pope Boniface VIII, in whom the papal aspirations were radically expressed. The emperors fought against this, and compromises were made, but generally speaking the popes prevailed, at least as long as there was this one reality of Christendom about which popes and emperors were fighting.

However, new forces arose in the Middle Ages. First and foremost among them were the national states. The national states claimed independence from both the pope and the emperor. National feeling was behind them. The importance of Joan of Arc was that in her French nationalism first arose and came into direct conflict with the pope. At the end of the Middle Ages the national states had taken over much of the papal power. Again France was leading: Philip the Fair took the papacy to Avignon in France, and the resulting schism between the two popes radically undercut the papal authority. The princes and kings, who gradually became independent and who created the national states, were at the same time religious lords. Thus in England the theory arose that the king represents Christ for the Church of England, as the pope is the vicar of Christ.

Another theory arose which was directed against the pope. The bishops of these developing national states did not want to be simply subjects of the pope; they wanted to regain the position the bishops had at the time, let us say, of the Council of Nicaea. They developed the idea of *conciliarism*; the council of bishops is the ultimate authority of the church. This idea is in contrast to *curialism* (from *curia*, the papal court); the papal court is the monarchic power over church and state. Thus, in alliance with the nationalist reaction against empire and papacy, conciliarism was a radical movement which threatened the pope. In the long run, however, the pope finally had the power to destroy the reform councils in Basle and Constance, where conciliarism had triumphed for a while. The national separations and splits of all kinds, plus the desire of the later Middle Ages to have a unity in spite of everything, made it possible for ecclesiasticism and monarchism to prevail in the Roman Church.

There were also important movements of criticism against the church, the sectarian and lay movements at the end of the Middle Ages. The greatest critic of the church in the theoretical realm was William Ockham, who fought for the German national state against the universal monarchy of the pope. But the most effective was Wyclif of England. Wyclif criticized the existing church in a radical way from the point of view of the *lex evangelica*, the evangelical law, which is in the Bible. He translated the Bible and fought against the hierarchy with the support of the national king. Already at that time the relationship between the king of

England and the pope became very precarious. The pope did not succeed in inducing the king to persecute Wyclif and his followers.

Finally the hierarchy (i.e., as a universal reality) came to an end in the revolutionary movement of the Reformation. The Protestant churches took the form of the territorial church which had long before been prepared under the princes. With the power of the pope and the hierarchy vanishing it happened that the church no longer had a backbone. So the prince received the title of "highest bishop". This means that he replaced the hierarchical, sacramental bishops, and became the highest administrator within the church, as a lay member at that; he was the predominant lay member who could keep the church in order. In this way the Protestant churches became subjected to the earthly powers, and to this day they have this problem. In Lutheranism it was the problem of the church's relation to the princes, their cabinets, and authoritarian governments. In the Calvinist countries, and also in America, it is the socially ruling classes which are decisive for the church and make up its administrative backbone.

F. THE SACRAMENTS

From the point of view of the actual religious life the sacraments were perhaps the most important thing in medieval church history. When we discuss the sacraments in the Middle Ages, if we are Protestants, we must forget everything we have in our immediate experience of the sacraments. In the Middle Ages the sacraments were not things which happened at certain times during the year and which were merely regarded as comparatively solemn acts. The preached word did not need to accompany the sacraments. Thus Troeltsch could call the Catholic Church the greatest sacramental institution in all world history.

Previously we have said that the Middle Ages were dominated by one problem, namely, to have a society which is guided by a present reality of a transcendent divine character. This is different from the period in which the New Testament was written, where the salvation of the individual soul was the problem. It is different from the period of Byzantium (*ca.* 450–950) where mysteries interpret all reality in terms of the divine ground, but not much is changed. It is different from the post-Renaissance period, ending in the nineteenth century, in which the world is directed by human reason, by man as the center of reality. It is different also from the early Greek period in which the mind was looking for the eternal Immovable. All of these periods had their particular problem. The problem of the Middle Ages, accordingly, was the problem of the world (society and nature) in which the divine is present in sacramental forms. In the light of this we can ask: What does "sacramental" mean? It means all kinds of things in the history of the church. It means the deeds of Christ, the sufferings of Christ (the stations of the cross); it means the Gospels, which can be called sacraments; it means symbols in the Bible; it means the symbolic character of the church buildings, and all the activities going on in the church, in short, everything in which the holy was present. This was the problem of the Middle Ages— to have the holy present.

The sacraments represent the objectivity of the grace of Christ as present in the objective power of the hierarchy. All graces— "graces" may be translated as substantial powers of the New Being—are present in and through the hierarchy. The sacraments are the continuation of the basic sacramental reality of God's manifestation in Christ. In every sacrament there is present a substance of a transcendent character. Water, bread, wine, oil, a word, the laying on of hands—all these things become sacramental if a transcendent substance is poured into them. This substance is like a fluid which heals. One of the definitions of a sacrament is: "Against the wounds produced by original and actual sin, God has established the sacraments as remedies." Here in medical symbolism what is meant is clearly expressed: the healing power is poured into the substances.

The question often raised in Protestantism is how many sacraments there are. Up to the twelfth century there were many sacramental activities. It was always more or less clear which of them were the most important, namely, baptism and the Lord's Supper. It took more than a thousand years of church history to discover that seven sacraments are the most important. After this discovery the term "sacrament" in a special sense became reserved for just these seven sacraments. This is unfortunate for the understanding of what a sacrament is. We must keep in mind the universal concept of the sacrament: the presence of the holy. Therefore, *sacramentalia* are being performed in the churches all the time; these are activities in which the presence of the divine is experienced in a special way. The fact that there are seven sacraments has many reasons behind it—traditional, practical, church-political, psychological, and many others. There are seven sacraments in the Roman Church; for a long time there were five. In Protestant churches there are two; in some groups, at least, of the Anglican Church there are actually and theoretically three sacraments. But the number does not matter. The question is: What does sacramental thinking mean? This is what Protestants have to learn; they have forgotten it.

In the Roman Church the main sacraments are baptism and the eucharist; but there is also penance as the center of personal piety. There is ordination which is the presupposition for the administration of all the other sacraments. There is marriage as the control of the natural life. Confirmation and extreme unction are supporting sacraments in the life of the individual. Thus, we see that the *raison d'être* for some of the sacraments is "biographical", while other sacraments stem from the establishment of the church.

Now what is a sacrament? A sacrament is a visible, sensuous sign instituted by God as a medicament in which under the cover of a visible thing the power of God is hiddenly working. The basic ideas are: divine institution, visible sign, medicament (the medical symbol is very important), the hidden power of God under the cover of the sensuous reality. A sacrament is valid if it has a material substance, a form, that is, the words by which it is instituted, and the intention of the minister to do what the church intends to do. These three elements are necessary. The sign (we would say, the symbol) contains the matter. Therefore, the sacrament has causality; it causes something in the inner part of the soul, something divine. But it does not have ultimate causality. It is dependent on God as the ultimate causality. The sacraments mediate the grace. "Grace" should always be translated as divine power of being, or power of New Being, which justifies or sanctifies—these two words being identical in Catholicism, while in Protestantism quite distinct from each other. Grace, or the divine power of the new being, is poured by the sacraments into the essence of the soul, into its very innermost center. And there is no other way to receive justifying and sanctifying grace than through the sacraments. The substance which is poured into the center of the soul has effects upon the different functions of the soul, or mind, as we would say. The intellect is driven toward faith by the sacramental grace; the will is driven toward hope; and the whole being is driven toward love.

The decisive statement is that the sacrament is effective in us *ex opere operato*, by its mere performance, not by any virtue. There is only one subjective presupposition, namely, the faith that the sacraments are sacraments, but not faith as a special relationship to God. It is a "minimum" theory; those who do not resist the divine grace can receive it even if they are not worthy, if only they do not deny that the sacrament is the medium of the divine grace. The theory of *ex opere operato* (by its very performance) makes the sacrament an objective event of a quasi-magical character. This was the point at which the Reformers were most radical.

The whole life stood under the effects of the sacraments. Baptism removes original sin; the eucharist removes venial sins; penance removes mortal sins; extreme unction removes what is still left over of one's sins before death; confirmation makes a person a fighter for the church; ordination introduces one into the clergy, and marriage into the natural vocation of man or wife. However, above them all is the sacrament of the Mass. This is the sacrifice of Christ repeated every day in every church in Christendom, in terms of the transubstantiation of bread and wine into body and blood. This sacrifice is the foundation of the presence of the divine and of the sacramental and hierarchical power of the church. This was, therefore, the sacrament of sacraments, so to speak. Officially it was a part of the Lord's Supper, but objectively it was and is the foundation of all sacraments, for here the priest has the power to produce God, *facere deum*; making God out of the bread and wine is the fundamental power of the church in the Middle Ages.

Penance was in a kind of tension with all the others. It was the sacrament of personal piety. There was much discussion about it. What are the conditions of the forgiveness of sins in the sacrament of penance? Some made them very easy, some more heavy. All believed that a person's repentance is necessary—light or heavy—and, on the other hand, that a sacrament is necessary. But no scholastic gave an answer as to how the sacrament and the personal element are related to each other. It was just at this point that the medieval church exploded, that is, by the intensification of the subjective side in the sacrament of penance. This was the experience of Luther and, therefore, he became the reformer of the church.

G. ANSELM OF CANTERBURY

Next we shall take up two men of the twelfth century, Anselm of Canterbury and Abelard of Paris. The basis of Anselm's theological work was the same as for all the scholastics, the assertion that in the Holy Scriptures and their interpretation by the fathers all truth is directly or indirectly enclosed. His phrase *credo ut intelligam* (I believe *in order to* understand, not I understand in order *to believe*) must be understood in the light of how he understood faith and tradition. Faith is not belief as a special act of an individual, but is participation in the living tradition. This living tradition, the spiritual substance in which one lives, is the foundation, and theology is interpretation built on this foundation.

The content of eternal truth, of principles of truth, is grasped by the subjection of our will to the Christian message and the consequent experience arising from this subjection. This experience is given by grace; it is not produced by human activities. Here the term "experience" becomes important. "Experience" must be distinguished from what we mean by it today, if we mean anything at all, since the term is used so widely that it has become most questionable and almost meaningless. In any case, at that time experience did not mean "religious" experience, generally speaking; such a thing did not exist then. Rather, experience meant participation in the objective truth implicit in the Bible and authoritatively explained by the church fathers. Every theologian must participate in this experience. Then this experience can become knowledge, but not necessarily so. Faith is not dependent on knowledge, but knowledge is dependent on faith. Again we can use the analogy we have used before: Natural science presupposes participation in nature, but participation in nature does not necessarily lead to natural science. On this basis reason can act with complete freedom to transform experience into knowledge. Anselm was a great speculative thinker at a time when the word "speculation" did not yet have the meaning of gazing into the clouds; instead, it meant analyzing the basic structures of reality.

Knowledge based on experience leads to a system. Here we come to one of the features of all medieval thinking. The medieval thinkers knew that in order to think consistently, you must think systematically. In the term "systematic theology" which we use in our teaching there is a remnant of this insight that knowledge must have the character of a system in order to be consistent. On the other hand, people are often attacked today when they use the word "system", just because they want to think systematically, and not sporadically and fragmentarily. But the church cannot afford—as an individual thinker can—to have here an insight and there an insight which have nothing to do with each other or even contradict each other. What would be bad in systematic theology is the derivation of consequences from principles which have no foundation in experience. But this is not the meaning of "system". Its meaning is the ordering of experience cognitively in such a way that the contents of experience do not contradict each other and the whole truth is reached. As Hegel rightly said, the truth is the whole.

Thus, reason can elaborate all religious experiences in rational terms. Even the doctrine of the trinity can be dealt with by reason on the basis of experience. In other words, autonomous reason and the doctrine of the church are identical. Again this is to be compared with our relationship to nature when we say that mathematical structure and natural reality belong to each other. Mathematical reason is able to grasp nature, to order and to make understandable natural movements and structures. In the same way theological reason is able to make understandable and to connect with each other the different religious experiences. This is the courageous way in which Anselm attacked the problems of theology. In saying that even the trinity can be understood in rational terms, he is following the Augustinian heritage. We can call it dialectical monotheism, a monotheism in which movement is seen in God himself. God is a living God; therefore, there is a "yes" and a "no" in himself. There is not a dead identity of God with himself, but a living separation and reunion of his life with himself. In other words, the mystery of the trinity is understandable for dialectical thought. This mystery is included in reason itself and is not against reason. How could it be, since, according to classical theology, God has reason in himself as his Son, the Logos? Reason, therefore, is valid so far as God and the world are essentially considered. Autonomy is not destroyed by the mystery. On the other hand, autonomy is not empty and formalistic. It does not empty the mysteries of the divine life, but only points to it in dialectical terms. The content, the substance and the depth of reason, is a mystery which has appeared in revelation.

This means that Anselm was neither autonomous in an empty formalistic sense, nor heteronomous in subjecting his reason to a tradition which he did not understand, which was almost a magical mystery. Anselm's attitude is what I call theonomous. This is a concept I often use in my own writings and discussions. Whenever you are asked, "What do you mean by theonomy?" then you can answer, "Anselm's way of philosophizing, or Augustine's way, or . . ."—now I hesitate to say it—"Hegel's". I mention Hegel in spite of all my criticism of him. This theonomous way means acknowledging the mystery of being, but not believing that this mystery is an authoritarian transcendent element which is imposed upon us and against us, which breaks our reason to pieces. For this would mean that God would be breaking his Logos to pieces, which is the depth of all reason. Reason and mystery belong together, like substance and form.

There is one point, however, at which I deviate from Hegel and go along with Anselm. Actually, it is more than a point, but a total turning of the whole consideration: the Logos becoming flesh! This is not a matter of dialectical reason. This is not only dialectical, not only mystery, but paradoxical. Here we are in the sphere of existence, and existence is rooted in the freedom of God and man, in sin and grace. Here reason can only acknowledge and not understand. The existential sphere, reason itself, is ruled by will and decision, not by rational necessity. Therefore, it can become anti-reason, anti-structure, anti-divine, anti-human. This means that it is not mystery and revelation which place a limitation upon rational necessity. The mystery of being is preserved by good dialectics, and destroyed by bad dialectics. But beyond mystery and dialectics there is something paradoxical. This means that although man has contradicted himself and always does so, there is a possibility of overcoming this situation because a new reality has appeared under the conditions of existence, conquering it. This is the Christian paradox! It is a matter of serious concern that we do not create a gap between the divine mystery and the divine Logos. Again and again the church has affirmed that they belong together. If one denies that the structure of reason is adequate to the divine mystery, he is completely dualistic in his thinking; then God would be split in himself.

Anselm's theonomous thought is expressed in his famous arguments for the existence of God, or as I like to say, his so-called arguments for the so-called existence of God, because I want to show that they are neither "arguments" nor do they prove the "existence" of God. But they do something much better than this. There are two arguments, the cosmological and the ontological. The cosmological argument is given in his *Monologion* and the ontological argument in his *Proslogion*. I want to show that these arguments are not arguments for the existence of an unknown or doubtful piece of reality, even if it is called "God". They are quite different from this.

The cosmological argument says: We have ideas of the good, of the great, of the beautiful, of the true. These ideas are realized in all things. We find beauty, goodness, and truth everywhere, but, of course, in different measures and degrees. But if you want to say that something has a higher or lower degree of participation in the idea of the good or the true, then the idea itself must be presupposed. Since it is the criterion by which you measure, it is not itself a matter of measure and degree. The good itself, or the unconditionally good—being or beauty—is the idea which is always presupposed. This means that in everything finite or relative, there is implied the relation to an unconditioned, an absolute. Conditionedness and relativity imply and presuppose something absolute and unconditioned. This means that the meaning of the conditioned and the unconditioned are inseparable. If you analyze reality, especially your own reality, you always discover in yourself elements which are finite, but inseparably related to something infinite. This is a matter of conclusion from the conditional to the unconditional, yet it is a matter of analysis which shows that both elements correspond to each other. Reality by its very nature is finite, pointing to the infinite to which the finite belongs and from which it is separated.

That is the first part of the cosmological argument. So far it is an existential analysis of finitude, and to this extent it is good and true, and the necessary condition for all philosophy of religion. Actually, it is *the* philosophy of religion. However, this idea is mixed with a metaphysical realism which identifies universals with the degrees of being. As we discussed before, medieval realism attributes power of being to the universals. In this way a hierarchy of concepts is constructed in which the unconditionally good and great, and being, is not only an ontological quality, but becomes an ontic reality, *a* being besides others. The highest being is that which is most universal. It must be one, otherwise another one could be found; it must be all-embracing. In other words, the meaning or quality of the infinite suddenly becomes a higher infinite being, the highest or unconditionally good and great being. The argument is right as long as it is a description of the way in which man encounters reality, namely, as finite, implying and being excluded from infinity. The argument is doubtful and yields a conclusion which can be attacked if it is supposed to lead to the existence of a highest being.

In the *Proslogion* Anselm himself criticizes this argument because it starts with the conditional and makes it the basis of the unconditional. His criticism is right with respect to the second part of his argument, but not with respect to the first, for in the first part of his argument he does not base the infinite on the finite, but analyzes the infinite within the finite. But Anselm wanted more than this; he wanted a direct argument which does not need the world in order to find God. He wanted to find God in thought itself. Before thought goes outside itself to the world, it should be certain of God. This is what I really mean by theonomous thinking.

This is the argument; it is difficult to follow because it is extremely scholastic and far from our modes of thought. Anselm says: "Even the fool is convinced that there is something in the intellect than which nothing greater can be thought, because as soon as he (the fool) hears this, he understands it; and whatever is understood is in the understanding. And certainly, that than which nothing greater can be thought cannot be only in the intellect. If, namely, it were in the intellect alone, it could be thought to be in reality also, which is more. If, therefore, that than which nothing greater can be thought is in the intellect alone, that than which nothing greater can be thought is some-

thing than which something greater can be thought. But this is
certainly impossible. Therefore, beyond doubt, something than
which nothing greater can be thought exists in intellect as well
as in reality. And this art Thou, our Lord." Now, this last sentence
is remarkable because I have not read such a sentence in any of
our logical treatises in the last few hundred years. After going
through the most sophisticated logical argumentation, it ends
with "And this art Thou, our Lord." This is what I call theonomy.
It is not a thinking which remains autonomous in itself, but a
thinking which goes theonomously into the relationship of the
mind to its divine ground.

I shall now attempt a point-by-point analysis of the meaning of
this argument.

(1) Even the fool—the fool of Psalm 53, who says in his heart,
"there is no God"—understands the meaning of the term "God".
He understands that the highest, the unconditional, is conceived
of in the term "God".

(2) If he understands the meaning of God as something unconditional, then this is an idea which exists in the human mind.

(3) But there is a higher form of being, that is, being not only
in the human mind, but being in the real world outside of the
human mind.

(4) Since being both within and outside of the human mind is
higher than being merely in the intellect, it must be attributed to
the unconditional.

Each step in this argument is such that it can be easily refuted,
and refutations were given already in Anselm's time. For instance,
the refutation is that this argument would be equally valid for
every highest thing, say, for a perfect island. It is more perfect
for it to exist in reality than only in the mind. Moreover, the term
"being in the mind" is ambiguous. It means actually being
thought, being intended, being an object of man's intentionality.
But "in" is metaphorical and should not be taken literally.

To the first criticism Anselm answered that a perfect island is
not a necessary thought, but the highest being, or the unconditioned, is a necessary thought. To the second criticism he could
argue that the unconditional must overcome the cleavage between
subjectivity and objectivity. It cannot be only in the mind; the
power of the meaning of the unconditional overcomes subject
and object, embracing them both. If Anselm had answered in

this way, the fallacious form of the argument would have been abandoned. Then the argument is not an argument for a highest being, but an analysis of human thought. As such the argument says: There must be a point at which the unconditional necessity of thinking and being are identical, otherwise there could be no certainty at all, not even that degree of certainty which every skeptic always presupposes. This is the Augustinian argument that God is truth, and truth is the presupposition which even the skeptic acknowledges. God is identical, then, with the experience of the unconditional as true and beautiful and good. What the ontological argument really does is to analyze in human thought something unconditional which transcends subjectivity and objectivity. This is necessary, otherwise truth is impossible. Truth presupposes that the subject which knows truth and the object which is known are in some way in one and the same place.

However, it is impossible to conclude from this analysis to a separate existence. This touches on the second part of the argument. At this point we cannot follow medieval realism. The so-called ontological argument is a phenomenological description of the human mind, insofar as the human mind by necessity points to something beyond subjectivity and objectivity, and points to the experience of truth. If you go beyond this, you are open to a devastating criticism, as the whole history of the ontological argument proves. The history of this argument is dependent on the attitude toward form or content. If the *content* of the argument is emphasized, as all great Augustinians and Franciscans until Hegel have done, the ontological argument is acceptable. If the argumental *form* is emphasized, as equally great thinkers from Thomas Aquinas to Kant have done, the argument must collapse. It is very interesting that this is an argument which has continued from Plato to the present. And its most classical formulation is that of Anselm.

How is it possible for the greatest of thinkers to be divided on this argument? One can hardly say that Thomas was more clever than Augustine, and Kant more clever than Hegel, or vice versa; they are all supreme minds, and yet they contradict each other. How can the phenomenon be explained that this argument is passionately accepted and rejected by the greatest thinkers? The reason can only be that each side is looking at something different. Those who accept the argument look at the fact that in the human mind, in spite of its finitude, something unconditional is present. The description of this unconditional element is not an argument. I am among those who affirm the ontological argument in this descriptive sense. On the other hand, people like Thomas, Duns Scotus, and Kant reject the argument because they say the conclusion is not valid. And certainly they are right. I try to find a way out of this world-historical conflict—whose consequences are greater than indicated by the scholastic form of it—by showing that these people are doing different things. Its advocates have the correct insight that the human mind, even before it turns to the world outside, has within itself an experience of the unconditional. Its opponents are right when they say that the second part of the argument is invalid because it cannot lead to *a* highest being who exists. Kant's argument that existence cannot be derived from the concept is absolutely valid against it. So one can say: Anselm's intention has never been defeated, namely, to make the certainty of God independent of any encounter with our world, and to link it entirely to our self-consciousness.

I would say that at this point the two ways of the philosophy of religion part company. The one type looks at culture, nature, and history theonomously, that is, on the basis of an awareness of the unconditional. I believe this is the only *possible* philosophy of religion. The other type looks at all this—nature, history, and the self—in terms of something which is given outside, from which through progressive analysis one might finally come to the existence of a highest being called God. This is the form which I deny; I think it is hopeless and ultimately ruinous for religion. In a religious statement I could say that where God is not the *prius* of everything, he can never be reached. If one does not start with him, one cannot reach him. This is what Anselm himself felt when he realized the incompleteness of the cosmological argument.

Anselm is famous in theology also for the application of his principles to the doctrine of the atonement. In his book, *Cur Deus Homo?* (Why a God-man?), he tries to understand the rational adequacy of the substitutional suffering of Christ in the work of salvation. The steps in the doctrine are as follows:

(1) The honor of God is violated by human sin. It is necessary for the sake of his honor for him to react in a negative way.

(2) There are two possible ways to react, either by way of punishment, which would mean eternal separation from God, or by way of satisfaction, giving satisfaction to God so that he can overlook the sins. This is the way in which God in his mercy has decided to solve the problem.

(3) Man is unable to fulfill this satisfaction because he has to do what he can do anyhow, and he cannot do more. Besides, his guilt is infinite, which makes it impossible by its very nature for man to solve the problem. Only God is able to give satisfaction to himself.

(4) On the other hand, because man is the sinner, it is man, not God, who must give the satisfaction. Therefore, someone who is both God and man must do it, who as God *can* do it and who as man *must* do it. The God-man alone is able to do this.

(5) But the God-man could not make satisfaction through his deeds, since he had to do these anyhow out of full obedience to God. He could do it only through his sufferings, because he did not have to suffer; he was innocent. Thus, voluntary suffering is the work through which Christ makes satisfaction to God.

(6) Although our sin is infinite, this sacrifice—since it is made by God himself—is an infinite one; it makes it possible for God to give Christ what he now deserves because of his sacrifice, namely, the possession of man. Christ himself does not need anything; what he needs and wants to have is man, so God gives him man.

Behind this legalistic, quantitative thinking there is a profound idea, namely, that sin has produced a tension in God himself. This tension was felt. Anselm's theory became so popular because everyone felt that it is not simple for God to forgive sins, just as it is not simple for us to accept ourselves. Only in the act of suffering, of self-negation, is it possible at all. Here lies the power of this doctrine of the atoning work of Christ. The church has never dogmatized Anselm's theory. It has wisely restricted itself from doing so, because there is no absolute theory of atonement. Abelard, as we shall see, and Origen as well as others have had different theories of the atonement. The church has never decided, but it is obvious that it liked Anselm's most, probably because it has the deepest psychological roots. This is the feeling that a price must be paid for our guilt, and that since we cannot pay it, God must do it.

Then the question arose: How can man participate? To this the juristic mind of Anselm had no answer. At this point Thomas Aquinas said: It is the mystical union between head and members, between Christ and the church, which lets us participate in all the steps of Jesus himself.

H. Abelard of Paris

We have discussed Anselm of Canterbury as a typically theonomous thinker, theonomous in the sense that he does not crush reason by heteronomous authority, and theonomous in the sense that he does not leave it empty and unproductive, but filled with the divine substance as it is given through revelation, tradition, and authority. Anselm represents the more objective pole in medieval thought, objective in the sense that the tradition is the given foundation, but not exclusive of an intensive personal kind of thinking and searching. On the other hand, in Abelard of Paris we have a representative of the subjective side, if "subjective" does not mean willful but taking into the personal life, as subjective reality. It is unfortunate that the words "objective" and "subjective" have become so indefinite and distorted in all respects. We should not think that if something is objective, it is real and true, whereas if it is subjective, it is willful. "Objective" here refers to the reality of the given substance of the Bible, tradition, and authority. "Subjective" refers to something which is taken into the personal life, and as such experienced and discussed.

Abelard was a philosopher and theologian in the twelfth century, who lived in the shadow of the Cathedral of Notre Dame in Paris. Subjectivity, which characterizes his spiritual attitude and character, is visible in the following points:

(1) Abelard was enthusiastic about dialectical thinking, showing the "yes" and "no" in everything. He was full of contempt for those who accept the mysteries of the faith without understanding what the words mean through which the mysteries are expressed. He did not wish to derive the mysteries from reason, but to make them understandable to reason. Of course, there is always the danger that the mystery will be emptied, but this danger is inherent in thinking itself. Thinking unavoidably destroys the immediacy of life, once it is begun. The question is whether a higher immediacy can be re-established. This is also true of the theological lectures you hear here. To hear them means

being endangered. This is the reason some of the more fundamentalistic people would be very much afraid if their future theologians would be educated in a place like Union Theological Seminary in New York, which likes—as Abelard did—dialectical thinking. But if this danger is not risked, faith can never become a real power.

(2) Abelard represents the type of jurisprudential thinking which was introduced into Western Christianity by Tertullian. He was, so to speak, the lawyer who defended the right of the tradition by showing that the contradictions in its sources—which no one can deny—can be solved. In doing this he was supporting the church; but, of course, the same dialectics which have the power to defend also have the power to attack. Some of the traditional theologians sensed this danger in dialectics, even before the danger became actual. This is also the reason some more or less orthodox theologians do not like apologetics; the same means by which you defend Christianity can be used to attack it.

(3) Abelard was a person of strong self-reflection. This was almost a new event in a period which was so objective in the sense of being related to the contents and not to oneself. In Abelard there was not merely a commitment to truth or goodness, but at the same time to a reflection about his being committed. We all know about this; we have a feeling of repentance and we reflect on having this feeling. We have an experience of faith and we reflect on this experience. This is characteristically modern, and it first appeared in Abelard. From this perspective we can understand his famous autobiography, *Historia Calamitatum* (History of My Misfortunes). The title is in line with Augustine's *Confessions*, but the important difference is that his self-analysis is not made in the face of God, as with Augustine. The self-analysis is done in relation to himself, in relation to what he has experienced. The title reveals the danger in which we all live as modern men. When Augustine spoke of confessions, he related himself to God as he looked at himself. If we speak of "misfortunes" or "calamities", there always remains a feeling of resentment, and resentment is a sign of subjectivity. This in Abelard was supported by his tremendous ambition, his lack of consideration for others, for instance, his teachers, and his continuous attacks on authorities.

(4) This subjectivity is visible also in the realm of feeling.

Abelard was one of those who discovered this as a special realm. An example of this was his romance with Heloise, an event with all the tragedy and greatness of the romantic form of love, although this was much earlier than its development in the period of romanticism. It represents the discovery of *erōs* against two things which had been predominant, first, paternalistic authority, and secondly, simple sexuality, which has nothing to do with the personal relationship, but which the church had allowed and limited and which was used as an element in the paternalistic family. Instead of this, we have in the romance of Abelard and Heloise a relationship in which the sexual and the spiritual dimensions are united. This was something new and threatening in a period in which the barbaric tribes were just becoming educated and receptive of the Christian gospel. Abelard was, so to speak, ahead of his time.

Abelard's book *Sic et Non* (Yes and No) used a dialectical method which was older than Abelard. It came from the canonistic literature (the sacred law literature) in ecclesiastical jurisprudence. The papal lawyers tried to harmonize the decrees of the various popes and synods. The practical problem was that the pope and his advisers had to make decisions, and they wanted these to be based on the tradition of law. So the law had to be harmonized. However, the dogmatic decisions of the popes and synods were a part of canon law, so they too had to be harmonized through "yes and no". When Abelard wrote his book, he tried to harmonize the doctrines, not to show dogmatic differences in order to arouse doubt and skepticism. On the contrary, he wanted to show that a unity is maintained in the tradition which can be proved by methods of harmonization. This was also accepted by the church authorities because they needed it; in fact, all scholastics accepted the "yes and no" method of Abelard. They asked questions, put opposing views against the answers, discussed the opposing views, and finally came to a decision.

The first step in this method is the attempt to deal historically with the texts of the fathers, the synods, the decrees, and the Bible. The question whether the texts in question are authentic had to be raised. Further, one had to show in what historical situation and under what psychological conditions these texts were written. Any changes in the texts had to be examined. The sphere and the configuration in which these changes occur in the same author had to be investigated and described. If all this has been done, then it might be shown that what seemed to be contradictions are not such at all, but only different forms in which the very same idea is expressed. It happens often in the history of thought that statements contradict each other only when taken as isolated statements out of the *Gestalt*, the structure, to which they belong. While appearing contradictory, they may actually say one and the same thing.

The second step is the elaboration of the literal meaning of a word—the philological task. This may lead to the discovery of different senses of a word, even in the same writer. In my lectures I continuously discover that the semantic problem is predominant, that if we use words like "faith" or "Son of God", they have as many meanings as there are people in the room, each with a different nuance. Now, if we ask ourselves: Is there any danger in this method of semantic analysis, or more widely, to what degree can logical calculus, semantic purification and reduction, be applied to the contents of the Christian message?—then I would say there is no absolute possibility of applying it, because when we deal with the existential things of life, every word has an edge which makes it what it is, which gives it its color and power; if that is removed, you leave a bone—a conceptual bone—without flesh and skin. This is why I am not convinced by the criticisms of logical positivists, in spite of my interest in semantics, because I believe that if they have their way completely, all words in realms like theology, metaphysics, ontology, art theory, or history will lose their full meaning and be reduced to mathematical signs from which the real power and meaning of such words escape.

The application of the authority of the Bible as the ultimate criterion is the next step. This sounds very Protestant, like so much biblicism in the Middle Ages, but it really is not. It was not a new experience of the Bible out of which Abelard spoke, as was the case with Luther. It was rather the application of the Bible as a law, as the ultimate legal judge. This is quite different from the Protestant interpretation of the Bible as the place where the message of justification can be found. The legal relationship to the tradition in Abelard is different from the creative traditionalism of Anselm. Though he was less dialectical than Abelard, Anselm was more creative and even more courageous, and at the same time more sensitive to the substance of the tradition.

Abelard shows subjectivity in all his doctrines, ethical and theological. His doctrine of ethical autonomy is connected with the subjective reason. He was a predecessor of Kant, in spite of the tremendous difference in time and situation. He taught that it is not an act in itself that is good or bad, but the intention makes it so. Kant expressed the same idea—nothing is good except a good will. So for Abelard the act itself is indifferent; only the intention is decisive. "In the intention consists the merit." Therefore, what makes us sinful is not nature itself, not even the desire itself, but the intention, the will. The contents of a moral system are not the important thing, but whether or not the conscience follows them. The contents of the moral system are always questionable when applied to a concrete situation. They can never be taken as absolutes, but the conscience must be the guide. The perfect good, of course, is an exact correspondence between the objective norm and the subjective intention, provided the conscience shows what is actually right. But often this is not the case. When it is not, it is better to follow our conscience, even if it is objectively wrong. He says: "There is no sin except against our conscience." In one sense even Thomas Aquinas accepted this notion. Aquinas said: If a superior in my order, to whom I have sworn obedience, asks me to do something which is against my conscience, I shall not do it, although I am obliged to be obedient to him. The conscience was regarded as ultimate judge, though it may be objectively erroneous. The Protestants and Kant were anticipated by these formulations, but in Abelard's time they could not work, because he neglected the educational element. If the uneducated masses are told that they should follow their conscience, but they have no sufficiently strict objective norms, they will wander and go astray. In this respect, as in so many others, Abelard anticipated ideas which later became actual, for example, in eighteenth-century France.

Abelard denied that in Adam all have sinned. Sin is not sensuality, but an act of the will. There is no sin without an agreement of the will, and since we did not agree with our will when Adam sinned, it is not sin for us. Here we see how subjectivity, exactly as in the eighteenth century, dissolves the doctrine of original sin, because this doctrine shows the tragic side of sin, the objective and not the personal, subjective side.

In christology Abelard emphasized the human activity of

Christ, and denied in a radical way that Christ was a transformed God or Logos or higher divine being. For him the personal activity of Christ is decisive, not his ontological origin in God.

He is best known to Protestants and most often quoted for his idea of salvation. As we have seen, Anselm in his doctrine of atonement makes a deal between God and Christ, out of the situation produced by human sin. He describes atonement in quantitative terms of satisfaction. For Abelard, however, it is the love of God which is visible in the cross of Christ; this produces our love. It is not an objective mechanism between transcendent powers which enables God to forgive, as it is in Anselm, but it is the subjective act of divine love which evokes in us a love for him. Salvation is man's ethical—in the sense of personal—response to the forgiving act of divine love. This is one of the types of the doctrine of atonement. It is a doctrine of atonement in the personal center. The mechanism of atonement through substitutionary suffering is ruled out. Anselm's doctrine lies in the mythological realm in which God and Christ trade with each other; Christ sacrifices and gets something back from God in return. In this respect Abelard is pre-Protestant and pre-autonomous. This is subjectivity in the sense of reason and centered personality. Many of these ideas in Abelard were rejected; he was too early for the educational situation in which the church found itself. For instance, if you tell someone whom you want to educate that the act of confession (i.e., repentance) is valid only if it arises out of love toward God, and not from fear, then you undercut the educational effect of the preaching of the law. Abelard as a theologian did not think in terms of what is good for the people, but in terms of what is ultimately true, and what is good for those who are autonomous. Although some of his doctrines were rejected, he became one of the most influential people in the development toward scholasticism, because of the greatness of his dialectical method.

I. Bernard of Clairvaux

Bernard of Clairvaux, a man of the same century as Abelard, fought with him over the possibility of applying dialectics to Christian beliefs. Bernard is the most eminent representative of Christian mysticism. As the foe of Abelard he succeeded in bringing Abelard before a council which rejected him. Yet, it is only half-true to call him an adversary of Abelard, because Bernard was also in favor of the subjective side, subjectivity in terms of mystical experience. He wanted to make the objective Christian doctrines, the decisions of the fathers and the church councils, matters of personal appropriation. The difference was that while Abelard did this in terms of reason, Bernard did it in terms of mystical experience. This experience is based on faith, as with every medieval theologian, and faith is described as an anticipation of the will. This is Augustinian voluntarism which Bernard is expressing. Faith is daring and free, an anticipation of something which can become real personally only through full experience. Certainty is not given in the act of faith; it is a daring anticipation of a state to which one may attain. Faith is created by the divine Spirit, and the experience which follows confirms it.

However, Bernard's mysticism was even more important and influential than these ideas which foreshadow the Franciscan school and much of later medieval thought about faith. In a seminar on Christian mysticism we have dealt with the question, "Can mysticism be baptized?" Can it be Christian? Mysticism is much older than Christianity, and much more universal. What about the relation of Christianity to mysticism? In our seminar we have come to the conclusion that mysticism *can* be baptized if it becomes a concrete Christ-mysticism, very similar to the way it is in Paul—a participation in Christ as Spirit. This is just what Bernard of Clairvaux did. The importance of Bernard is that he is the "baptizing father" in the development of Christian mysticism. Whenever it is said, as some Barthians do, that Christianity and mysticism are two different things, that either one is a Christian or a mystic, that the attempt of almost two thousand years to baptize mysticism is wrong, then one must point to Bernard in whom a mysticism of love is expressed. Only if you have a mysticism of love can you have a Christian mysticism.

Mysticism has two types of content in Bernard. First, there is the picture of Jesus as it is given in the biblical record, through which the divine is transparent. The stress is on participation in his humility, not on an ethical command, although this follows after it. We participate in the reality of God in Jesus. The mystical following of Jesus is participating in him. When we read about how Francis of Assisi and Thomas à Kempis tried to follow Jesus, we should never forget that this was not the way in which a Jew follows Moses; it was not another law, but it was meant as a participation in the meaning of what Jesus is. In this way the mystics of the Middle Ages overcame a legal interpretation of obedience to Christ. We cannot really follow him except we participate in him mystically. This participation is dynamic, not static and legalistic. This concrete, active mysticism of love to Christ is the presupposition of the second type of content in Bernard's mysticism. This is the abstract mysticism; it is called "abstract" because it abstracts from anything concrete. It is a mysticism of the abyss of the divine. This side of the mystical experience is that which Christian mysticism has in common with all other forms of mysticism. There are three steps, according to Bernard:

(1) Consideration (you look at things from outside; they remain objects for your subjectivity).

(2) Contemplation (participating in the "temple", going into the holiness of the holy).

(3) *Excessus* (going outside oneself, an attitude which exceeds the normal existence, one in which man is driven beyond himself without losing himself, it is also described as *raptus*, being grasped).

In the third stage man goes over into the divinity, like a drop of wine which falls into a glass of wine. The substance remains, but the form of the individual drop is dissolved into the all-embracing divine form. One does not lose one's identity, but it becomes a part of the divine reality.

These two forms of mysticism must always be distinguished: concrete mysticism, which is mysticism of love and participating in the Savior-God, and abstract mysticism, or transcending mysticism, which goes beyond everything finite to the ultimate ground of everything that is. When we examine these two forms, we can say that at least for this life Bernard's mysticism stands within the Christian tradition. As for the second type, we can say that this makes love in eternity impossible. But then we must add that Paul said something similar in his statement that God will be all in all. This means that when we come to the ultimate, we cannot think simply in terms of separated individuals, although we must still think in terms of love. And this is no easy task. In any case, the decisive thing is that in Bernard there is something different than in Pseudo-Dionysius, and this is his concrete mysticism, Christ mysticism, love mysticism. It is still mysticism, because mysticism is participation, and participation involves partial identification.

In coming to the end of this discussion on the early Middle Ages, we must briefly consider Hugh of St. Victor, the most influential theologian of the twelfth century. More than Anselm, Abelard, or Bernard, he was a fulfiller of systematic thinking. He wrote a book, *On the Sacraments of the Christian Faith*. The term "sacrament" is used in the broadest sense; all the works of God and everything in which the divine becomes visible are sacraments. He distinguishes two groups of the works of God. He calles them the *opera conditionis*, the works of condition, and the *opera reparationis*, the works of reparation. This offers a deep insight into medieval life. All things are visible embodiments of the invisible ground behind them. Nevertheless, this does not lead to a pantheistic form of theology, because although all the works of God are sacraments, they are concentrated into seven sacraments. If not only bodily realities, but also activities of God are called sacraments, then the idea of sacrament becomes full of dynamism. Thus, we have an interpretation of the world in dynamic sacramental form, centered around the seven sacraments of the church, particularly around the Mass and penance.

J. JOACHIM OF FLORIS

In Joachim of Floris we have an interpretation of history which became extremely influential upon the Middle Ages as well as upon modern thought. Joachim was an abbot of a monastery in Calabria in southern Italy. He wrote a number of books in which he developed a philosophy of history which became an alternative to the Augustinian interpretation of history and formed the background to most of the revolutionary movements in the Middle Ages and in modern times. Augustine's interpretation of history was the basis for most conservative movements during the same time. I want to confront the Joachimist interpretation of history with the Augustinian.

The Augustinian view places the reign of Christ, the thousand-year period, in the present time and identifies it with the control

of this period by the hierarchy and its divine graces. The sacramental power of the hierarchy makes it the immediate medium of
Christ, so that the thousand-year period, the monarchy of Christ,
is the monarchy of the church. Since this is the last period, according to Daniel, there is no future any more; the thousand years are
here and we live in them. Criticism can only be directed to the
church so far as it is a mixed body, not to its foundation, which
is final. In this way Augustine removed the threat of millenari-
anism—the doctrine of the thousand years—which holds that the
millennium is still to come in the future, and in the light of which
the church and its hierarchy could be criticized.

Joachim renewed the idea of the thousand years of Christ
which still lie in the future. He spoke about the three dispensations which unfold in history and which are characterized by
historical figures. The first period runs from Adam to John the
Baptist, or to Jesus Christ; it is the age of the Father. This age is
overcome by the very fact of the Christ. The second period runs
from King Uzziah (Isaiah 6) to the year A.D. 1260. This way of
figuring is arrived at by the fact that according to the genealogies
of the Old Testament, this age is supposed to embrace forty-two
generations. The third dispensation runs from Benedict in the
sixth century after Christ, when Western monasticism started; it
is called the age of the Spirit. It has twenty-one generations after
Christ, which lead up to the year 1260.

This construction seems to be very artificial. The ages overlap;
the second overlaps with the first age from King Uzziah to the
birth of Christ, or to John the Baptist. The second is overlapped
by the third from Benedict to 1260. What does this overlapping
mean? It represents a profound insight into historical developments. Historical periods never start sharply but always unfold
with some overlapping. There is no such thing as "the end of the
Gothic period" and "the beginning of the Renaissance", no "end
of the Renaissance" and "beginning of the Baroque", no "end of
the Baroque" and "beginning of the Rococo", etc. Every new
period is conceived and born in the womb of the previous one.
No one was more aware of this than Karl Marx when he constructed his interpretation of history, describing how each new
period was prepared in the womb of the preceding one—for
instance, the socialist in the womb of the bourgeois period, and
the latter in the womb of the late feudal period. It is like birth;

there is a certain period in which mother and child are together in the same body. According to this idea of overlapping, the germs of the new period are prior to what he called *fructificatio* (fructification), mature realization. A period is never mature when its first beginnings become visible. In this trinitarian scheme applied to history, the succeeding period is always present for a certain amount of time in the preceding one. In this way Christ is one moment in the three periods of history, and history goes beyond him. This is the same problem we have in the Fourth Gospel, whether or not the Spirit goes beyond the Christ. The Fourth Gospel decides in a double way: on the one hand, it decides partly for the Spirit going beyond the Christ when it says that many things cannot be said now, but the Spirit will come and help you; and, on the other hand, the Spirit does not take of its own but from Christ, who is present in the second period, the period of the Son.

These ideas about the meaning of historical development should be taken seriously. They should not be rejected just because of these names in the Old Testament, which are certainly arbitrary. Every historian knows about the arbitrariness of every periodization of history. Historians will tell you that the period which we call the "Renaissance" was shared in by only a few people—artists, scholars, and politicians in Italy, and later by some people in England, Holland, and Germany. The masses of people still lived under the conditions which had prevailed for the past century.

What are the characteristics of these stages? Being a profound observer Joachim knew that the first stage was to be determined sociologically. This is a period in which marriage is the decisive sociological form, work and servitude (slavery, feudalism, etc.) are economically decisive, and which religiously can be identified as the period of law. In the second period the clergy and the organized church are decisive. The sacramental reality makes the law unnecessary; because of grace it is a time for faith instead of good works. It is not an age of autonomy, but one in which the clergy represent for everyone the presence of the divine. The third period is monasticism, when the monastic ideal will grasp all mankind and the birth of new generations will cease. This is, therefore, by necessity the last period. The graces given by the Holy Spirit in this period are higher than the sacramental graces of the second period, and still higher than the law of the first period. Whereas the second period was prepared already in Judaism, which had some sacramental graces, the third period was prepared in church history, with the foundation in monasticism. The inner part of this period is freedom, that is, autonomy, not being subject any more to state or church authorities. The appropriate attitude is contemplation instead of work, and love instead of law.

So we have here a sociological understanding of the different periods of history, but sociology is not the "cause" of everything, as it is in Marxism but it is a necessary condition. At the same time it is an interpretation of religion which shows the difference between works (under the law), grace accepted by faith, and autonomous freedom in contemplation and love. The scheme is trinitarian; the dynamic element which is always implied in trinitarian theology has become horizontal, transferred to the movement of history. It is the historization of the trinitarian idea: Father, Son, and Spirit have different functions in history. Of course, all three are always present—God cannot be divided—but they are present with a different emphasis. This means that something is still ahead. The perfect society, the monastic society, will still come, and when measured by it not only the Old Testament society but also the New Testament society, the church, must be criticized.

Another idea is that truth is not absolute, but is valid for its time—*bonum et necessarium in suo tempore*—the good and necessary according to its time. This is a dynamic concept of truth, the idea that truth changes in history according to the situation. The early church had to apply this principle always to the Old Testament. The truth of the Old Testament is different from that of the New Testament, and yet it also is the divinely inspired Word of God. To account for this theologians spoke about dispensations or covenants. The idea of the *kairos* was used, which means that as the time is different, so the truth is different. This idea was placed against the absolutism of the Catholic Church, which identified its own being with the last period of history, that is, with the ultimate truth. For Joachim there is a higher truth than that of the church, namely, the truth of the Spirit. From this it follows that the church is relative. It is *inter utrumque*, between both the period of the Father and the period of the Spirit. Its shortcomings are due not only to distortions, but also to its relative validity. In this scheme the church is relativized. Only the third period is absolute; it is not authoritarian any more, but autonomous. Every individual has the divine Spirit within himself. This means that the ideal for Christianity lies in the future and not in the past. He called it *intellectus spiritualis* and not *literalis*, that is, a spiritually formed intellect and not an intellect dependent on literalistic laws.

From this it follows that in the future the hierarchy as well as the sacraments will come to an end. They will not be needed because everything will be directly related to God spiritually, and no authoritarian intervention will be necessary. Joachim spoke of a *papa angelica*, an angelic pope, which is more a principle than a man. It is a pope who represents the presence of the Spirit without authority. The hierarchy will be transformed into monasticism, and so will the laity. When this happens the last period will have been reached. In this third stage there will be perfection, contemplation, liberty, and Spirit. This will happen in history. For Augustine the final end is only transcended; nothing new will happen in history any more. For Joachim the new is in history.

Joachim also spoke of the "eternal gospel", which is not a book. The gospel is the presence of the divine Spirit in every individual, according to the prophecy of Joel, which is often used in this context. It is a *simplex intuitus veritatis*, a simple intuition of truth which all can have without intermediate authority. Freedom means the authority of the divine Spirit in the individual. This is theonomy, not rationalistic autonomy, theonomy which is filled with the presence of the divine Spirit. History produces freedom in the course of its progress. The idea is progressivistic; the goal is ahead.

These were revolutionary ideas which understandably Thomas Aquinas fought against in the name of the church. The church has its classical period in the past, not in the future. The classical period of the church is the apostolic age. The church is based on history; history has brought the church about, but the church is itself not in history. It is beyond it because it is at the end of history. Joachim's ideas are important because they had a dynamic, revolutionary, explosive power. The extreme Franciscans used his prophecies and applied them to their own order, and on that basis they revolted against the church. Many sectarian movements, including the sects of the Reformation on which much of American life is dependent, were directly or indirectly dependent on Joachim of Floris. The philosophers of the Enlightenment who taught that there will be a third period of history in which everyone will be taught directly by the inner light—the light of reason —were dependent on Joachim's ideas. The socialist movement rests on the same idea when in its classless society everybody will be directly responsible to the ultimate principles. It is not the case, of course, that all these people knew Joachim and his ideas directly, but there was a tradition of revolutionary thinking in Western Europe, some of the fundamental ideas of which first appeared in Joachim. Much of American utopianism must be understood in the light of this movement in the West. So far as I know none of this revolutionary thinking can be found in the Eastern religions, because by definition they are non-historical religions. In Joachim a new insight into the dialectics of history appeared. His influence was mediated by the radical Franciscan monks.

K. The Thirteenth Century

The thirteenth century is the high point of the Middle Ages. The whole destiny of the Western world was decided at this time in a very definite way. All the scholastics were dependent on Peter Lombard, whom we have not yet discussed, although he belongs to the twelfth century. He was not as original as the others, but he represents the systematic, didactic type of the Middle Ages. He organized the statements of the fathers in a book entitled *The Four Books of Sentences*, which became the text-book of the Middle Ages, if there ever was a text-book. Every great scholastic started by writing a commentary on Lombard's *Sentences*.

The thirteenth century can be described theologically in three steps, represented by three names: Bonaventura, Thomas Aquinas, and Duns Scotus. There are others between them whom we will mention occasionally. Duns Scotus was the greatest of them all as a scholar, and he was also the starting point of new developments on which the whole modern period is dependent. Thomas Aquinas is the classical theologian of the Roman Church, and was established as such again in modern times by the pope.

Bonaventura represents the spirit of Augustine and St Francis, in his being, in his mysticism, and in his theology.

What are the presuppositions of the thirteenth century which made it the high point of the Middle Ages? First, I want to mention the crusades, not because of their political and military significance but because they brought about the encounter of Christianity with two highly developed cultures, the original Jewish and the Islamic cultures. One could perhaps even say that a third culture was encountered at that time, namely, the classical culture of ancient Greece, which was mediated into the medieval world by the Arabian theologians. The fact of an encounter with another, if it is serious enough, always involves a kind of self-reflection. Only if you encounter someone else are you able to reflect on yourselves. As long as you go ahead without resistance, you are not forced to look back upon yourselves. When you encounter resistance, you reflect. This is what Christianity had to do. It began to reflect on itself in a much more radical way. The second presupposition was the appearance of the complete Aristotle in his genuine writings, and with him the appearance of a scientific philosophical system which was methodologically superior to the Augustinian tradition. Thirdly, there was the rise of several new types of monastic orders, the preaching and mendicant orders, which both intensified and popularized the religious substance. They produced world-wide organizations through all countries and contended with each other theologically. Since they were not nationally provincial, they could compete on a world-wide scale and produce theological systems of the highest significance in conflict with each other. Since the thirteenth century these two orders became the bearers of the theological process. They both used Aristotle, but they used him differently. They used the new knowledge of Judaism and Islam, but they used it differently.

This leads us to a description of the two types of orders, the Franciscan and the Dominican, named after two personalities, Francis of Assisi and Dominic. Francis continued the monasticism of Augustine and Bernard. Like them he emphasized personal experience, but he introduced the idea of the active life in contrast to the contemplative life. From the beginning this was always nearer to the Western mind than to the East. Francis also produced a new relationship to nature; not only human hierarchical orders, but also sun and stars and animals and plants belong to the power of the divine life. The best thing to do to understand him is to look at the pictures of Giotto, who painted almost nothing else than the story of St. Francis, who had become the new holy legend. Thus, Francis became the father of the Renaissance; by his feeling of fraternity with all beings, he opened up nature for religion. He opened up nature with respect to its ground of being, which is the same as it is in man.

Francis introduced also the idea that the lay people must be brought into the circle of the holy. In the sacramental system the clergy and the monks were the real representatives, while the laymen were only passive. To bring the laity into the circle he created the so-called "third order", the *tertiaries*. The first is the male order, the monks; the second is the corresponding female order, the nuns; the third is the laymen who remain married and subject themselves to some of the principles of the monastic orders. All of this was placed by Francis under the authority of the pope. Giotto's famous picture, in which Innocent III, the greatest pope, and Francis, the greatest saint of the Roman Church, met each other, depicts a classical moment in world history. Nevertheless, this represented a threat to the hierarchical system. The danger became actual in the revolution of the Franciscan radicals who tried to unite Francis and Joachim, and who became the prototypes of many later anti-ecclesiastical and anti-religious movements. The lay principle was also dangerous because it could spell the end of the absolute authority of the hierarchy. Dangerous also was the new relationship to nature and the vision of the divine ground in it which in the long run would undermine Catholic supernaturalism. Generally speaking, Francis belonged to the Augustinian-Anselmian-Bernardian tradition of the mystical union of Christianity with the elements of culture and nature.

In contrast to Francis, Dominic was not such an original personality. He assumed the task of preaching to the people and of defending the faith. This was something new—defending either by mediation or by conversion or by persecution, that is, either in terms of apologetics or in terms of missions or in terms of church power. In all three ways the Dominicans became the order of the Inquisition and of the Counter-Reformation until, at a later time, the Jesuits took over. The Dominican order produced the classical system of mediation, of apologetic theology, that of Thomas Aquinas, and the greatest preachers, among whom was Meister Eckhart. More than any other school, they brought Aristotle into the West. Their instrument was the intellect, even in their mysticism, whereas the Franciscan-Augustinian tradition laid stress more on the will. Finally, the voluntarism of the Franciscans broke down the intellectualism of the Dominicans, thus opening the way for Duns Scotus, Ockham, and the nominalists.

This was the spiritual background for the tremendous development of the thirteenth century. Without constant reference to these movements, the theology of this period cannot be understood. When we think of Thomas Aquinas, we must understand him as a mediating theologian. He understood, better than anyone else, the mediating function of theology. In German theology the term *Vermittlungstheologie* has been used of the nineteenth century in a derogatory sense. I have come to its defense by saying that all theology is mediation, the mediation of the message of the gospel with the categories of the understanding as they exist in any given period of history.

The dynamics of the high Middle Ages are determined by the conflict between Augustine and Aristotle, or between the Franciscans who were Augustinians and the Dominicans who were Aristotelian. This contrast, however, should not be taken too exclusively. For all medieval theologians were Augustinian in substance. And since the thirteenth century they were all Aristotelian with respect to their philosophical categories. Yet, these schools did have different emphases which have been reflected ever since in the philosophy of religion.

Let us make clear what Aristotle meant for the Middle Ages the moment he was discovered at the beginning of the thirteenth century, with the help of the Arabian philosophers.

(1) Aristotle's logic had always been known, but it was used as a tool and had no direct influence on the content of theology. When the whole work of Aristotle was rediscovered, it was found to be a complete system in which all realms of life were discussed—observations about nature, politics, and ethics. It represented an independent secular world-view, including a system of values and meanings. The question was: How could a world which had been educated in the Augustinian ecclesiastical tradition deal with this secular system of ideas and meanings? It

was similar to the question theology has raised in recent centuries: How can the scientific revolution since the seventeenth century be mediated with the Christian tradition?

(2) Aristotle offered basic metaphysical categories, such as form and matter, actuality and potentiality. He came with a new doctrine of matter, of the relation of God to the world, and on this basis an ontological analysis of reality.

(3) Perhaps the most important thing he gave was a new approach to knowledge. The soul has to receive impressions from the external world. Experience is always the beginning in Aristotle, whereas in the Augustinian tradition immediate intuition was the point of departure. The Augustinians stood, so to speak, in the divine center, and judged the world from there. The Aristotelians looked at the world, and concluded to the divine center.

The whole movement of Augustinianism in relation to Aristotelianism must be viewed in the light of this question of knowledge. The question is: Is our knowledge a participation in the divine knowledge of the world and himself, or must we on the contrary recognize God by approaching the world from the outside? Is God the last or the first in our knowledge? The Augustinians answered that the knowledge of God precedes all other knowledge; it comes first and we must start with it. We have the principles of truth within ourselves. God is the presupposition even of the question of God, as he is the presupposition of every quest for truth. "He is", says Bonaventura, "most truly present to the soul and immediately knowable." The principles of truth are the divine or eternal light within us. We start with them; we begin with our knowledge of God, and from this we go to the world, using the principles of the divine light within us. This divine light or these principles are the universal categories, especially the *transcendentalia*, those things which transcend everything concrete and given, such as being, the true, the good, the one. These are ultimate concepts of which we have immediate knowledge, and this knowledge is the divine light in our soul. Only on the basis of this immediate knowledge of the ultimate principles of reality can we find truth in the empirical world. These principles are present in every act of knowing. Whenever we say what something is, whenever we make a logical judgment about something, the ideas of the true, of the good, of being itself, are present. Bonaventura can say: "Being itself is what first appears in the intellect", and being itself is the basic statement about God. This means that every act of cognition is made in the power of the divine light. The Franciscans said that this divine light and these principles within us are uncreated, and we participate in them. Somehow this means that there is no such thing as secular knowledge. All knowledge is in some way rooted in the knowledge of the divine within us. There is a point of identity in our soul, and this point precedes every special act of knowledge. Or, we could say that every act of knowledge—about animals, plants, bodies, astronomy, mathematics—is implicitly religious. A mathematical proposition as well as a medical discovery is implicitly religious because it is possible only in the power of these ultimate principles which are the uncreated divine light in the human soul. This is the famous doctrine of the inner light, which was also used by the sectarian movements and by all the mystics during the Middle Ages and the Reformation period, and which in the last analysis underlies even the rationalism of the Enlightenment. The rationalists were all philosophers of the inner light, even though this light later on became cut off from its divine ground.

This attitude we call theonomous. The Franciscans tried to maintain a theonomous outlook in spite of the fact that they had to use such Aristotelian concepts as form and matter, potentiality and actuality. So from Augustine to Bonaventura we have a philosophy that is implicitly religious, or theonomous, in which God is not a conclusion from other premises, but prior to all conclusions, making them possible. This is the philosophy which in my article, "The Two Types of Philosophy of Religion" (in *Theology of Culture*), I call the ontological type; it can also be called the mystical type, the type of immediacy. I also like to call it the theonomous type in which the divine precedes the secular.

The opposite type is the Thomist philosophy of religion. Thomas Aquinas cuts off the immediate presence of God in the act of knowing. Of course, he acknowledges that God is the first in himself, but he is not the first for us. Our knowledge cannot start with God, although everything starts with him; but our knowledge must reach him by starting with his effects—the finite world. In starting with the effects of God we can conclude to their cause. In other words, man is separated from being itself, from truth itself, and from the good itself. Of course, Thomas could not deny that these principles are in the structure of man's intellect, but he calls them created light, not uncreated light. They are not the divine presence in us; instead, they are the works of God in us; they are finite. Thus, in the act of knowledge, we do not have God, but with these principles we can attain to God. It is not that we start with the divine principles in us and then discover the finite world, as the Franciscans; but we start with the finite world and then perhaps we can discover God in our acts of cognition.

In opposing this Thomist theory the Franciscans said that this method which must start—in a good Aristotelian way—with sense experience is good for *scientia* (for "science" in the broadest sense of the word) but it destroys *sapientia*, wisdom. *Sapientia* means the knowledge of the ultimate principles, the knowledge of God. One of Bonaventura's followers made the prophetic statement that the moment you pursue the Aristotelian-Thomist method and start with the external world, you will lose the principles. You will gain the external world—he agreed with that because he knew that empirical knowledge can be acquired in no other way—but you will lose the wisdom which is able to grasp intuitively the ultimate principles within yourself. Thomas answered that the knowledge of God, like all knowledge, must begin with sense experience and reach God on this basis in terms of rational conclusions.

The divergence between these two approaches to the knowledge of God is the great problem of the philosophy of religion, and, as I will now show, it is the ultimate cause of the secularization of the Western world—I am using "cause" in the cognitive realm, for there are other causes too. The Aristotelian method is placed against the Augustinian, and gradually this method of starting with the external world prevailed. Thomas knew that the conclusions reached in this way, though they are logically correct, do not produce a real conviction about God. Therefore, they must be completed by authority. In other words, the church guarantees the truth which can never be fully reached merely by an empirical approach to God. The situation is clear: In Bonaventura we have a theonomous knowledge in all realms of life; we have no knowledge whatsoever without beginning with God. In Thomas we have autonomous knowledge, reached by the scientific method, as far as it goes. But Thomas knew that it does not go far enough, so it must be completed by authority. This is the meaning of the heated struggle between the Augustinians and the Aristotelians in the thirteenth century. There was a gap in the Thomist approach, but at that time the gap was not yet visible. By his genius, his power to take in almost everything, his power to mediate, his personal, even mystical, piety, Thomas was able to cover the gap, but the gap was there and had consequences reaching far beyond what Thomas himself realized. This came out in Duns Scotus.

Duns Scotus was not a mediating but a radical thinker. He was one of those who tear up what seems to be united. He fought against the mediations of Thomas Aquinas. On the other hand, he did not follow his own Franciscan predecessors. He followed Thomas by accepting Aristotle, but he realized the consequences which Thomas was able to cover. For Duns Scotus there is an infinite gap between the finite and the infinite. Therefore, the finite cannot reach God cognitively at all, either in terms of immediacy—as the older Franciscans wanted—nor in terms of demonstrations, as Thomas and the Dominicans wanted. He criticized—and insofar as you are nominalists, you will like this criticism—even the *transcendentalia*, the ultimate principles. He says: Being itself (*esse ipsum*) is only a word; it points to an analogy between the infinite and the finite, but only an analogy. The word "being" does not cover God as well as the world. The gap is such that you cannot cover both of them with one word, not even in terms of the *verum, bonum, unum* (the true, good, and one), and that means in terms of being itself. Therefore, there is only one way that is open to receive God, the way of authority, the way of revelation received by the authority of the church.

The result is that in Duns Scotus we have two positivisms: the religious or ecclesiastical positivism, which means that we must simply accept what is given to us by the church since we cannot reach God cognitively, and the positivism of the empirical method, which means we must discover what is positively given in nature by the methods of induction and abstraction. Now the gap of which I spoke has become visible. In Thomas it was closed; in Duns Scotus it was opened up and has never been closed again. It is still our problem, as it was the problem of the thirteenth century.

The gap opened up by Duns Scotus became very large a century later in Ockham, the real father of nominalism. In his view God cannot be approached at all through autonomous knowledge; he is out of reach. Everything could be the opposite of what it is. Therefore, God can be reached only by subjecting ourselves to the biblical and ecclesiastical authorities. And we can subject ourselves to them only if we have the *habitus*, the habit, of grace. Only if grace is working in us can we receive the authority of the church. Cultural knowledge, the knowledge of science, is completely free and autonomous, and religious knowledge is completely heteronomous. The original theonomy of the Augustinian-Franciscan tradition has been broken into complete scientific autonomy on the one side, and complete ecclesiastical heteronomy on the other side. This is the situation which prevailed at the end of the Middle Ages. Since the Middle Ages were based on a system of mediation, they came to an end when these mediations broke down.

If we compare these positions on the traditional question of reason and revelation, we can say: In Bonaventura reason itself is revelatory insofar as in its own depths the principles of truth are given. This does not, of course, refer to the historical revelation in Christ, but to our knowledge of God. In Thomas reason is able to express revelation. In Duns Scotus reason is unable to express revelation. In Ockham revelation stands alongside of reason, even in opposition to it. At the end of the Middle Ages the religious and secular realms are separated, but not in the way in which they are today, for the Middle Ages still wanted to maintain its traditional unity. Therefore, the church developed its radical heteronomous claim to rule over all realms, and thus to control them from the outside. Then the desperate fight between autonomous secularism and religious heteronomy developed. The late Middle Ages should not be confused with the earlier Middle Ages. As long as the tradition retained its force, the Middle Ages were not heteronomous; they were theonomous. But by the end of the Middle Ages, an independent secular realm became established. This led to the question whether the church could control this independent realm. The Renaissance and the Reformation were the means by which the church was deprived of this power.

The theory of double truth appeared at this time. Some people seriously believed—they were not merely being diplomatic, to hide themselves—that in reality a statement on the same matter can be both theologically true and philosophically false, and vice versa. Thus, they could accept the whole heteronomous system of the church and, at the same time, continue to develop their autonomous thought. If a philosophical proposition conflicted with the theological tradition, they could take refuge in the "double truth" theory. For many this was a way of evasion, but it was also a belief that these realms are so separated that you can say in one realm the opposite of what you say in the other.

We have been dealing with the epistemological problem, but behind it there is the problem of God. The medieval idea of God has three levels.

(1) The first and fundamental level is the idea of God as *primum esse*, the first being, or *prima causa*, the first cause. The word "cause" here is not meant in the sense of "cause and effect" in the realm of finitude. And the word *prima* does not mean first in a temporal way, but in the sense of the "ground" of all causes. So the term "cause" is here used more symbolically than literally. God is the creative ground in everything, *creatrix universalium substantia*, the creative substance of everything that is. This is the first statement about God. God is the ground of being, as I like to express it, or being-itself, or the first cause; all these terms point to the same meaning.

(2) This substance cannot be understood in terms of the inorganic realm—as fire or water, as the ancient physicists did—nor in the biological realm as a life process. It must be understood as intellect. The first quality of God as the ground of being is intellect. Intellect does not mean intelligence; it means the point in which God is for himself subject and object at the same time; it means God knowing himself and knowing the world as that which he is not. The ground of being, or in other words, the creative substance, is the bearer of meaning. The consequence is that the world is meaningful; it can be understood in words which have meaning. The *logos*, the word, can grasp it. To understand reality, we must presuppose that it is understandable. Reality is understandable because its divine ground has the character of intellect. Knowledge is possible only because the divine intellect is the ground of everything.

(3) The third point is that God is will. This comes from the Christian Augustinian tradition, whereas the emphasis on intellect comes from the Greek Aristotelian tradition. If the concept of will is applied to God and the world, it refers to the dynamic ground of everything, not to the psychological function which we observe in ourselves. Will is the productive power of the ground of being. This will has the nature of love—in good Augustinian tradition. The creative substance of the world has meaning and love; it is intellect and will, symbolically speaking. Just as we said that God knows himself, so now we must say that God wills or loves himself as the absolute good, indeed, as the ultimate aim of everything. He loves the creatures in giving them in a graded way the good of which he is the ultimate ground. Therefore, all the creatures long for him; he is the object of their love, the love toward that in which every being sees its ultimate good.

That is the medieval idea of God. This God is not called a person. The word "person" was never applied to God in the Middle Ages. The reason for this is that the three members of the trinity were called *personae* ("faces" or "countenances"): the Father is *persona*, the Son is *persona*, and the Spirit is *persona*. *Persona* here means a special characteristic of the divine ground, expressing itself in an independent hypostasis. Thus, we can say that it was the nineteenth century which made God into *a* person, with the result that the greatness of the classical idea of God was destroyed by this way of speaking. Of course, this personal structure, including being, intellect, and will, is analogous to our experience of our own being, so if we call ourselves "persons", we must also speak of God as "person". But this is quite different from calling God *a* person. First of all, he is being itself; he is the ground of being in everything. The personal side is expressed in intellect and will, and their unity. But to speak of God as *a* person would have been heretical for the Middle Ages; it would have been to them a Unitarian heresy, because it would have conflicted with the statement that God has three *personae*, three expressions of his being.

On the question of the relationship between intellect and will in God the same controversy took place as on the epistemological problem. For the Thomist tradition, intellect is characteristic of God and man. Thomas argues that man can be distinguished from an animal only because he has intellect. An

animal would be human if it could intellectually place purposes
before the will. But the animal only wills without purposes, in
the sense in which we ascribe that ability to man. Thus, for
Thomas it is the intellect which makes man human, and which is
the primary characteristic of God. Intellect is the power of insight into the universally true and good. Duns Scotus opposed
this doctrine. For him God and man are will. Will is universally
creative. There is no reason for the divine will other than the
divine will itself. There is nothing which determines the will. The
good is good because God so wills it. There is no intellectual
necessity for the world to be as it is, that salvation should happen
as it does. Everything is possible for God except that he cease to
be God. Duns Scotus spoke of God's *potentia absoluta*, the absolute power of God. God uses his absolute power only in order to
create a given world in which there are definite orders. On this
level he spoke of God's *potestas ordinata*, the ordered power of
God. He distinguishes these two things. The world as we know it,
as well as the plan of salvation as we know it by revelation, is
not *necessarily* as it happens to be; it is as it is by the ordered power
of God. Implied in this distinction is something threatening. The
world is not as it is from eternity; there is no real necessity that it be
as it is. The absolute power of God stands threateningly behind
the ordered power, and may change everything. Duns Scotus did
not believe that this would happen, but it could happen.

What does such an idea mean? It means that we have to accept
the given, that we cannot deduce it, that we have to be humble
toward reality. We cannot deduce the world or the process of
salvation in terms of necessity. Compare this to Anselm's doctrine
of atonement, in which he tried to deduce in terms of necessity
the way of salvation between God and Christ and man. Duns
Scotus would say there is no such necessity; instead, this is a
positive order of God. In this idea of the absolute power of God
we have the root of all positivism, in science as well as in politics,
in religion as well as in psychology. The moment that God became defined as will—determined by his will and not by his
intellect—the world became incalculable, uncertain, unsafe. So
we are compelled to subject ourselves to what is positively given.
All the dangers of positivism are rooted in this concept of Duns
Scotus. So I consider him the turning point in the history of
Western thought.

L. The Doctrines of Thomas Aquinas

We shall discuss a few of the most important doctrines of Thomas Aquinas. The first is his doctrine of nature and grace. His famous statement reads: "Grace does not remove nature, but fulfills it." This important principle means that grace is not the negation but the fulfillment of nature. The radical Augustinians, or more exactly, the Manichaean distorters of Augustine, would not accept this statement. They would say that grace removes nature. For Thomas Aquinas, with whom I am in agreement on this point, nature and grace are not two contradictory concepts. Grace contradicts only estranged nature, but not nature as such. But now Thomas says that nature is fulfilled in supernature, and supernature is grace. This is the structure of reality which has existed from creation. God gave to Adam in paradise not only his natural abilities, but beyond these a *donum superadditum*, a gift added to his natural gifts. This is the gift of grace by virtue of which Adam could persist in a state of union with God.

This a point at which Protestantism deviated completely from Thomas Aquinas. Protestantism said that the perfect nature does not need any additional grace; if we are perfect in our created status, there is no need for any grace to come from above. Therefore, Protestantism removed the idea of a *donum superadditum*. This sounds like a mythological story about whether Adam did or did not get this grace, but that is not the interesting point. These mythological stories express a profound vision about the structure of reality. In Thomism the structure of reality has two levels. For Protestantism creation is complete in itself; the created forms of reality are sufficient. God does not need to add anything to them. This is the same basic feeling toward life that we find in the Renaissance, which sees creation as good in itself, with man and his created potentialities in the center, without a supernatural gift added to him. Thomas has two degrees, nature and supernature. Protestantism says that only because nature is distorted by man's fall, by his estrangement from God, is there a need for another power, the power of grace, whose center is forgiveness. Forgiveness is the *restitutio ad integrum*, the restitution of nature to its full potentialities. This idea is ultimately monistic. The created world is perfect in itself; God does not need to give additional graces to his fulfilled creation. Yet, God must come down into existence to overcome the conflicts in it, and this is what grace does. So in Protestantism grace is the acceptance of that which is unacceptable. In Catholicism grace is a substance, which stands in analogy to the natural substances.

The Thomist principle is valid also for the relationship of revelation and reason. Revelation does not destroy reason but fulfills it. Here again I agree with Thomas. I believe that revelation is reason in ecstasy, that in revelation the depth of reason breaks into the form of reason, driving it beyond itself without destroying it. But I would not accept the Thomist form of the doctrine in which reason exists in one realm and revelation in another realm in which reason is completed. Thus we have two forms here. The Catholic world-view is essentially dualistic— nature and supernature. Catholicism defends supernaturalism with all its power. Protestantism, on the other hand, is united with the Renaissance in the monistic tendency—monistic in the sense of having one divine world and having salvation and re- generation (one and the same thing) as the answer of God to the disruption of this world. But this answer is not the negation of the created structure of this world.

In some sense the Protestant dualism is deeper, but it is not a dualism of substances. It is a dualism of the kingdom of God and the demonic powers which stand against it. It is not an identifica- tion of the created with the fallen world. The fallen world is the distortion of the created world. Therefore, the new being is not another creation, but the re-establishment of the original unity. One of the consequences of this is that in Protestantism the secular world is immediate to God. In Catholicism the secular world needs the mediation through the supernatural substance, which is present in the hierarchy and their sacramental activities. Here again you have a fundamental difference. Protestantism is emphatically for secularity. This is clearly expressed in Luther's words about the value of the housemaid's work in contrast to the monk's. If it is done in fear of God, the maid's work is more valuable than the asceticism of the monks, even if that is done in the fear of God. Here the emphasis is on the secular act as such, which is the revelation of God if done in the right way. One does not have to become a monk, but if in trying it one claims to be in a supernatural realm, this contradicts the paradox of justification, that as a *sinner* you are justified.

From his epistemology it follows that Thomas would reject the ontological argument for the existence of God. The ontological argument holds that in the center of the human mind there is an immediate awareness of something unconditional. There is an *a priori* presence of the divine in the human mind expressed in the immediate awareness of the unconditional character of the true and the good and of being itself. This precedes every other knowledge, so that the knowledge of God is the first knowledge, the only absolute, sure, and certain knowledge, the knowledge not about *a* being, but about the unconditional element in the depths of the soul. This is the nerve of the ontological argument. However, as I said in connection with Anselm, the ontological argument was also elaborated in terms of a rational argument which concluded from this basis to the existence of a highest being. Insofar as this was done, the argument is not valid, as all its critics—Thomas, Scotus, Kant—have clearly shown. As an analysis of the tension in man between the finite and the infinite, it is valid; it is a matter of immediate certainty.

Thomas Aquinas belongs to those who reject the ontological argument because he saw that as an argument it is invalid. The same is true of Duns Scotus. But now in order to fill the empty space created by the collapse of the ontological argument and of the immediate awareness of the divine in man, Thomas had to find a way from the world to God. The world, although not the first in itself, is the first which is given to us. This is just the opposite of what the Augustinian Franciscans said: the first which is given to us is the principle of truth in us, and only in its light can we exercise the function of doubt. So Thomas had to show another way, the way of the cosmological argument. According to this way, God must be found from outside. We must look at our world and find that by logical necessity it leads to the conclusion of a highest being. Thomas had five arguments for it, which appear again and again in the history of philosophy.

(1) The argument from motion. Motion demands a cause. This cause itself is moved. So we have to go back to an unmoved mover, which we call "God". This is an argument from movement in terms of causality. To find a cause for the movement in the world, we must find something which itself is not moved.

(2) There is always a cause for every effect, but every cause itself is an effect of a prior cause. So we go back from cause to cause, but to avoid an infinite regression, we must speak of a first cause. This cause is not first in a temporal sense, according to Thomas, but it is first in dignity; it is the cause of all causes.

(3) Everything in the world is contingent. It is not necessary that something is as it is. It might have been otherwise. But if everything is contingent, if everything that is can disappear into the abyss of nothing, because it has no necessary existence, this must lead us back to something which has ultimate necessity, from which we can derive all the contingent elements.

(4) There are purposes in nature and man. But if we act in terms of purpose, what is the purpose? When we reach that, we must again ask what that is for. So we need a final purpose, an ultimate end behind all the means. The preliminary purposes become means when they are fulfilled. This leads to the idea of a final purpose, of an ultimate meaning, as we would perhaps say today.

(5) The fifth argument is dependent on Plato. It says that there are degrees of perfection in everything that is. Some things are better or more beautiful or more true than others. But if there are degrees of perfection, there must be something absolutely perfect by which we can distinguish between the more or less of perfection. Whenever we make value judgments, we presuppose an ultimate value. Whenever we observe degrees, we presuppose something which is beyond degree.

In all these arguments there is the category of causality. They conclude from characteristics of this world to something which makes this world possible. I believe that these arguments are valid as analysis. Each of them is true as long as it is not an argument but an analysis. In the doctrine of the arguments for the existence of God we have probably the most adequate analysis of the finitude of reality that has appeared in the writings from the past. They include the existential analysis of man's finitude, and as such they have truth. Insofar as they go beyond this and establish a highest being which as a being is infinite, they draw conclusions which are not justified.

In Thomas Aquinas we have the concept of predestination which combines several motives. Predestination was an Augustinian idea taken over by Thomas on the basis of his principle of intellect, which understands the necessities, and can by necessity derive consequences from what has preceded. On the other hand, Duns Scotus emphasized the will so much that the divine as well as the human will become ultimate realities, ontological ultimates, not determined by anything other than themselves. So Duns Scotus and the Franciscans introduced the element of freedom—the Pelagian element. These Franciscan Augustinians introduced a crypto-Pelagianism into medieval theology, whereas Thomas Aquinas, on the basis of his intellectualism, thought in deterministic terms. This shows that Thomas was religiously much more powerful than the Protestant criticism of Scholastic theology admits. It seems that Luther did not know Thomas Aquinas at all. He knew the late nominalistic theologians, who can rightly be said to have been distortions of scholasticism. So Luther fought against them. But he could have found both his and Calvin's predestinarian thinking in Thomas Aquinas.

The ethical teachings of Thomas Aquinas correspond to his system of grades, as do all the realms of his thought. In his ethics there is a rational substructure and a theological superstructure. They are related to each other exactly as nature and grace are related. The substructure contains the four main pagan virtues, taken from Plato: courage, temperance, wisdom, and the all-embracing justice. These produce natural happiness. Happiness does not mean having a good time or having fun, but the fulfillment of one's own essential nature. In Greek the word for happiness is *eudaimonia*, and there is a philosophical school called eudaemonism. Christianity has often attacked it on the grounds that happiness is not the purpose of human existence, but the glory of God is. I think this is a completely mistaken interpretation of *eudaimonia*. This is exactly what Christian theology calls blessedness, except that this is blessedness on the basis of the natural virtues, and Thomas knew this. Therefore, Thomas was not anti-eudaemonistic. *Eudaimonia* is derived from two Greek words, *eu* and *daimōn*, meaning "well" and "demon"—a divine power which guides us well. (Cf. Socrates' *daimōn*.) The result of this guiding is *eudaimonia*, being led in the right way toward self-fulfillment.

According to Thomas Aquinas, the four natural virtues of philosophy can give natural blessedness, *eudaimonia* in the Greek sense. Virtue was not a term with the bad connotations it has today, for example, abstinence from sexual relations. It meant what the Latin term indicates: *vir*, meaning "man", hence, manliness, power of being. In all these different virtues power of being expresses itself, the right power of being, the power of being which is united with justice. What Thomas did was to combine Christian ethics with the ancient ethics of self-fulfillment, with its natural virtues: the courage to be, the temperance which expresses the limits of finitude, the wisdom which expresses the knowledge of these limits, and finally the all-embracing justice which gives to each virtue the right balance in relation to the others.

On this natural basis the Christian virtues of faith, love, and hope are seen. They are supernatural, because they are given not by nature but by grace. So Thomas' ethical system has these two stories, the natural ethic and the spiritual ethic. This is something more than a theoretical speculation; it was an expression of the sociological situation. The acceptance of the virtues of Plato and Aristotle meant that a city culture had developed. The pagan and the Christian virtues had been combined in the period in which the orders of the knights developed, and they had a great influence on the high Middle Ages. They united pagan courage with Christian love, pagan wisdom with Christian hope, pagan moderation with Christian faith. Humanistic and classical ideals were taken in and developed within the universally Christian culture.

The ethical purpose of man is the fulfillment of what is essential for him. For Thomas what is essential for man is his intellect, which means his ability to live in meanings and in structures of reason. Not the will but the intellect makes him human. Man has the will in common with animals; the intellect, the rational structure of his mind, is peculiar to man.

Thomas combined ethics with aesthetics. He was the first one in the Middle Ages to create a theological aesthetics. "The beautiful is that kind of the good in which the soul rests without possession." You can enjoy a picture without possessing it. By their sheer form you can enjoy the woods or ocean or houses or men depicted in pictures without having to possess them. In art, also in music, there is disinterested enjoyment of the soul. Beautiful is that which is pleasurable in itself. This is a motif which leads in the direction of humanism, but it is not an autonomous humanism, but one which is always but the first step toward something which transcends human possibilities.

In similar fashion he dealt with the problem of church and state. There are the values represented by the state, and the higher, supernatural values embodied in the church. The church has authority over the states, the different national governments, because it represents something higher. If necessary the church can ask the people to be disobedient. The Thomistic ethics which we have been discussing have been fully as influential in the Western world as his dogmatic statements. They can be found in the second part of the second section of his *Summa Theologica*.

M. WILLIAM OF OCKHAM

William of Ockham is the father of nominalism. The conflict between nominalism and realism was the destiny of the Middle Ages and is still today the destiny of our own time. Today it continues, at least in part, as a conflict between idealism and realism, whereby realism today is what nominalism was in the Middle Ages, and idealism is what medieval realism was. Ockham criticized the mystical realism of the Middle Ages for regarding the universals as real things, as having an independent existence. If the universals exist apart from things, they simply reduplicate the things. If they exist in the mind only, they are not real things. Therefore, realism is nonsense. Realism is meaningless because it cannot say what kind of reality the universals have. What is the reality of "treehood"? Ockham says it is only in the mind, and so has no reality at all; it is something which is meant, but it is not a reality. The realists of that time said the universal "treehood" which directs every tree in a special way is a power of being in itself. It is not a thing—no realist ever said that—but it is a power of being. The nominalists said that there are only individual things and nothing else. It is against the principle of economy in thinking to augment the principles (cf. Ockham's razor). If you can explain something like the universals in the simplest way, for instance, by saying that they are meant by the mind, then you should not establish a heaven of ideas as Plato did.

This criticism was rooted in the development toward individualism which became increasingly powerful in late medieval life. It was a change from the Greek and medieval moods. The Greek feeling toward the world starts with the negation of all individual things; the medieval subordinates the individual to the collective. So this was not simply a logical game which the nominalists won for the time being. Rather, it represented a change of attitude toward reality in the whole of society. You will find nominalism and realism discussed in books on the history of logic, and rightly so, but that does not give the full impact of what this controversy meant. This was a debate between two attitudes toward life. Today these attitudes are expressed in terms of collectivism and individualism. However, the collectivism of the Middle Ages was only partly totalitarian; it was basically mystical. This mystical collectivism—basically the church as the mystical body of Christ—is different from our present-day collectivism. Yet, it was collectivism. The realists fought for it, while the nominalists dissolved it. And as soon as nominalism became successful, this was the actual dissolution of the Middle Ages.

Now, if only individual things exist, what are the universals, according to Ockham? The universals are identical with the act of knowing. They rise in our minds, and we must use them, otherwise we could not speak. They are natural. He called them the *universalia naturalia*. Beyond them are the words which are the symbols for these natural universals which arise in our minds. They are the conventional universals. Words can be changed; they exist by convention. The word is universal because it can be said of different things. Thus, these people were also called "terminists" because they said the universals are merely "terms". They were also called "conceptualists" because they said the universals are mere "concepts", and have no real power of being in themselves. The significance of a universal concept is that it indicates the similarity of different things, but that is all it can do. All of this boils down to the point that only individual things have reality. Not man as man, but Paul and Peter and John have reality as individuals. Not treehood, but this particular tree on the corner has reality, and all other particular trees. We call them trees because we discover some similarity between them.

This nominalistic approach was applied also to God. God is called by Ockham *ens singularissimum*, the most single being. This means that God himself has become an individual. As such he is separate from all other individuals. He looks at them and they look at him. God is no longer in the center of everything, as he was in the Augustinian way of thinking. He has been removed from the center to a special place at a distance from other things. The individual things have become independent. The substantial presence of God in all of them has no more meaning, because such a notion presupposes some kind of mystical realism. Hence, God has to know things, so to speak, empirically, from the outside. Just as man approaches the world empirically, because he is no longer thought to be in the center, so also God knows everything empirically from the outside, not immediately by being the center in which all reality is united. This is a pluralistic philosophy in which there are many individuals, of which God is one, although the most important one. In this way the unity of all things in God has come to an end. The consequence of their individual separation is that they cannot participate in each other immediately in virtue of their common participation in a universal. Community, such as we have in the Augustinian type of thinking, is replaced by social relations, by society. As a consequence of this nominalism we live today in a society in which we relate to each other in terms of co-operation and competition, but neither of these has the meaning of participation. Community is a matter of participation; society is a matter of common interests, of being separated from each other and working with or against each other.

We do not know each other except by the signs, the words, which enable us to communicate and to have common activities. This was an anticipation of our life in a technological society which developed first in those countries in which nominalism was predominant, as in England and America. Attitudes concerning the relations between man and man, and between man and things, are nominalistic in America and in the traditions of American philosophy, as is largely the case in England and in some West European countries. The substantial unity which was preserved by realistic thinking has disappeared. This means that we have knowledge of each other not through participation but only by sense perceptions—seeing, hearing, touching. We deal with our sense perceptions and the reflections of them in our minds. This, of course, produces positivism; we have to look at what is positively given to us.

Many things follow from all this. A rational metaphysics becomes impossible. For example, it is impossible to construct a rational psychology which proves the immortality of the soul, its pre- or post-existence, its omnipresence in the whole body, etc. If such things are affirmed, they are matters of faith, not of philosophical analysis. Similarly all aspects of rational theology become impossible. God does not appear to our sense perceptions. He remains unapproachable since we have no direct or immediate relationship to him, as we do in Augustinian thought. We cannot have direct knowledge of God. We can have only indirect reflections, but they never lead to certainty, only to probability of a lower or higher degree. This probability can never be elevated to certainty; instead it is very doubtful. It is quite possible that there is not one cause of the world, but many causes. The most perfect being—the definition of God—is not necessarily an infinite being. A doctrine like the trinity which is based on mystical realism—the three *personae* participate in the one divinity—is obviously improbable. These things are all matters of irrational belief. Science must go its way and faith must guarantee all that is scientifically irrational and absurd.

If this is the case, it is easy to see that authority becomes the most important thing. Faith is subjection to authority. For Ockham the authority he has in mind is more the authority of the Bible than that of the church. Ockham dissolved the realistic unity not only in thought but also in practice. He sided with the German king against the pope. He produced autonomous economics as well as autonomous national politics. In all realms of life he was for the establishment of independent spheres. This means that he contributed radically to the dissolution of medieval unity.

N. GERMAN MYSTICISM

Meister Eckhart was the most important representative of German mysticism. What did these mystics try to do? They tried to interpret the Thomistic system for practical purposes. They were not speculative monks sitting alongside of the world, but they wanted people to have the possibility of experiencing what was expressed in the scholastic systems. Thus, the mysticism of Meister Eckhart unites the most abstract scholastic concepts—especially that of being—with a burning soul, with the warmth of religious feeling and the love-power of religious acting. He says: "Nothing is so near to the beings, so intimate to them, as being-itself. But God is being-itself." The identity of God and being is affirmed. *"Esse est deus"*—being-itself is God. This is not a static concept of being. When I have used the concept of being, I have often been attacked for making God static. This is not even true of Meister Eckhart's mysticism. Being is a continuous flux and return; he calls it *Fluss und Wiederfluss*, a stream and a counter-stream. It always moves away from and back to itself. Being is life and has dynamic character.

In order to make this clear he distinguishes between the divinity and God. The divinity is the gound of being in which everything moves and counter-moves. God is *essentia*, the principle of the good and the true. From this he can even develop the idea of the trinity. The first principle is the being which is neither born nor giving birth; the second is the process of self-objectivation, the Logos, the Son; the third is the self-generation, the Spirit, which creates all individual things. For the divinity he uses the terms of negative theology. He calls it the simple ground, the quiet desert. It is the nature of the divinity not to have any nature. It is beyond every special nature. The trinity is based on God's going out and returning back to himself. He re-cognizes himself, he re-sees himself, and this constitutes the Logos. The world is in God in an archetypical sense. "Archetype" is a word which has been revived today by Jung; it is the Latin translation of the Platonic "idea". The essences, the archetypes of everything, are in the depths of the divine. They are the divine *verbum*, the divine Word. Therefore, the generation of the Son and the eternal creation of the world in God himself are one and the same thing. Creaturely being is receiving being. The creature does not give being to itself; God does. But the creature receives being from God. This is a divine form of being. The creature, including man, has reality only in union with the eternal reality. The creature has nothing in separation from God. The point in which the creature returns to God is the soul. Through the soul what is separated from God returns to him. The depths of the soul in which this happens Eckhart called the "spark", or the innermost center of the soul, the heart of the soul, or the castle of the soul. It is the point which transcends the difference of functions in the soul; it is the uncreated light in man. In this way the Son is born in every soul. This universal event is more important than the particular birth of Jesus.

However, all this is in the realm of possibility. Now it must be brought into the realm of actuality. God must be born in the soul. Therefore, the soul must separate itself from its finitude. Something must happen, which he calls *entwerden*, the opposite of becoming, going away from oneself, losing oneself. The process of salvation is that man gets rid of himself and of all things.

Sin and evil show the presence of God, as everything does. They push us into a situation of awareness of what we really are. This is an idea which Luther took over from Meister Eckhart. God is the *nunc aeternum*, the eternal now, who comes to the individual in his concrete situation. He does not ask that the individual first develop some goodness before he will come to him. God comes to the individual in his estrangement. To receive the divine substance, serenity or patience, not moving, is needed. Work is not the means of coming to God; it is the result of our having come to him. Eckhart fought against making the religious relationship a matter of purposing. All this is a strange mixture between quietism—being quiet in one's soul—and a tremendous activism. The inner feeling must become work, and vice versa. This also removes the difference between the sacred and the secular worlds. They are both expressions of the ground of being in us.

This mysticism was very influential in the church for a long time, and is still influential in many people. This Dominican mysticism is a counter-balance to the nominalistic isolation of individuals from each other. One could say that in the religious realm the impulses of German mysticism prevailed. In the secular realm the nominalistic attitude prevailed. Both nominalism and German mysticism were to some degree preparations for the Reformation.

O. The Pre-Reformers

The period prior to the Reformation is quite different from the high Middle Ages. During this period the lay principle becomes important and biblicism begins to prevail over church tradition. Perhaps the most important expression of this situation is the Englishman, John Wyclif. He had a large number of ideas which the Reformers used, and he certainly prepared the soil in England for the Reformation. What the pre-Reformers all lacked was the one fundamental principle of the Reformation—Luther's breakthrough to the experience of being accepted in spite of being unacceptable, which in Pauline terms is called justification by grace through faith. This principle does not appear before Luther. Almost everything else in the Reformation can be found in the so-called pre-Reformers. Thus, when we speak of the pre-Reformers, we have in mind mainly those critical ideas applied against the Roman church which were later also used by the Reformation. If it is argued that they should not be called pre-Reformers, what is meant is that they lacked the main principle of the Reformation, the real breakthrough to a new relationship to God.

Wyclif was dependent on Augustine, but also on Thomas Bradwardine in England who represented an Augustinian reaction against the Pelagian ideas connected with nominalism. Thomas Bradwardine was an important link between Augustine and the English Reformation. The title of his book is characteristic, *De Causa Dei contra Pelagium*, which means the cause of God against Pelagius, not the Pelagius who was Augustine's enemy, but the Pelagianism which he found in nominalistic theology and in the practice of the church. Against this he followed Augustine and Thomas Aquinas with respect to the doctrine of predestination. He says: "Everything that happens, happens by necessity. God necessitates whatever act is done. Every act or creature which is morally evil is an evil only accidentally." This means that God is the essential cause of everything, but evil cannot be derived from him. From this it follows, as for Augustine, that the church is the congregation of the predestined. The true church is not the hierarchical institution of salvation. This true church is in opposition to the mixed body in the church, to the hierarchical institution which, as it now exists, is nothing else than a distortion of the true church. The basic law of the church is not the law of the pope, but the law of the Bible; this is the law of God or of Christ. These ideas were not meant to be anti-Catholic. Neither Bradwardine nor Wyclif thought of leaving the Roman Church. There was only one church, and even Luther needed much time before he separated himself.

There were dangers for the Roman Church in the Augustinian principles. After Augustine a semi-Pelagianism removed the dangers of Augustinianism from the Roman Church. Now these dangers appear again in the name of Augustine, as represented

by Thomas Bradwardine and John Wyclif. The idea of predestination means that many people are not predestined, many of
the hierarchs, for example. This provides a basis for looking for
symptoms in the hierarchy which show that they are not predestined. These symptoms are discovered by applying the law of
Christ, such as the Sermon on the Mount, or the sending of the
disciples—all ideas and laws which are dangerous in an organized
hierarchical church.

From his criticism of the hierarchy Wyclif revised the doctrines
of the church and its relationship to the state. This also has a
long tradition. Since the twelfth century there had been in
England a movement represented by one who was called the
Anonymous of York, a man who wrote on behalf of the king,
making the king the Christ for the British nation. There was an
anti-Roman tendency which favored having a British territorial
church, similar to the Byzantine situation. The king is the Christ
for the nation, depicted in hymns and in pictures as the Christ,
just as Constantine in Byzantium was the Christ for the whole
Eastern church. These analogies are preparations for the revolt
of the crown of England against the pope.

Wyclif differentiated between two forms of human domination
or government, the natural or evangelical domination, which is
the law of love, and the civil domination, which is a product of
sin and a means of force for the sake of the bodily and spiritual
goods. On the one hand, we have the natural law, which in the
classical tradition is always the law of love, and all that it includes.
This is the law which should rule. On the other hand, there is unfortunately a need for civil government, which is necessary
because of sin. Force and compulsion are inescapable means to
maintain the goods of the nation, bodily and spiritually. The first
law, the law of love, is sufficient for the government of the church.
Since the church is the body of the predestined, force is not
needed here. Its content is the rule which Jesus gave, the rule of
serving. The law of Christ is the law of love, which expresses
itself in service. From this it follows that the church must be
poor; it must not be economically and politically in control. It
must be the church which is poor, the church as it was anticipated by the radical Franciscans and originally by Joachim of
Floris.

The church, however, is not entirely holy. For ministers to be wealthy is an abuse which should be removed, by the power of the king, if necessary. If the church responds with excommunication, the king should not fear this, for it is impossible to excommunicate a man unless he has first excommunicated himself. The real excommunication of a Christian is severing himself from communion with Christ. This means that the hierarchy has lost its chief power; it can no longer decide about the salvation of the individual. It can be criticized when it acts against the law of Christ, which is the law of poverty, the law of spiritual rule. From this it follows, further, that there is no dogmatic necessity to have a pope. This was also in the line of Joachim of Floris, who spoke of a *papa angelica*, an angelic pope, which is really a spiritual principle. Wyclif says that if we are ruled by a spiritual principle, it is all right to have a pope, but not necessary. These ideas are in line with the sectarian protest against the rich and powerful church, yet they remain on the whole within the framework of official doctrine. They are not the same as the Reformation protest, because they are based on the principle of law—not the law of the church but the law of Christ—and not on the gospel.

Since the basis of Wyclif's attack was the law of Christ as given in the Bible, he developed the authority of Scripture against that of the tradition and against the symbolic interpretation of the Bible. He even reaches the point, also on biblical grounds, that the *predicatio verbi*, the preaching of the Word, is more important than all the ecclesiastical sacraments. The transition in the Middle Ages from realism to nominalism is accompanied by a transition from the predominance of the eye to the ear. In the early centuries of the Christian Church the visual function was predominant in religious art and in the sacraments. Since Duns Scotus, and even more since Ockham, the hearing of the Word becomes most important, and not the seeing of the sacramental embodiment of the reality. Even before the Reformation the emphasis on the word develops; it came to the foreground in nominalism. Why? Because realism sees the essences of things. "Idea" comes from *idein*, "seeing". *Eidos*, "idea", means picture, the essence of a thing which we can see in every individual thing. Of course, this is an intuitive spiritual seeing, but it is still seeing, and it is expressed in the great art. The great art shows the essence of things, visible to the eye. In nominalism we

have individuals. How can they communicate? By words. Therefore, if God has become the most individual being, the *ens
singularissimum* in Ockham's language, then we receive a communication from him not through a kind of intuition of his divine
essence, as expressed in all his creations, but by his word which
he speaks to us. Thus, the word became decisive in contrast to
the visual function. The importance of the word as over against
the sacraments appears already in Wyclif. This is not yet Reformation theology, because here the word is the word of the law;
it is not yet the word of forgiveness. This is the difference between the Reformation and the pre-Reformation.

If there is to be a pope, he must be the spiritual leader of the
true church, the church of the predestined, otherwise he is not
really the vicar of Christ, the spiritual power from which all
spiritual power is derived. But the pope is a man who falls into
error. He is not able to give indulgences; only God can do that.
This is the first statement against the system of indulgences—
before Luther's Ninety-five Theses. If the pope is not living in
humility, charity, and poverty, he is not the true pope. When the
pope accepts the dominion over the world, as he has done, then
he is a permanent heretic. The pope did just that by means of
the "Donation of Constantine", which was the great foundation
of the political power of the pope, making him the prince of
Rome and sovereign over the Western half of the empire, in spite
of the fact that this document was historically a falsification. It is
heretical for the pope whose power is spiritual to become a prince.
If he does this, he is the Antichrist. This is a term which comes
from the Bible and was used during the Reformation. It has been
used in church history especially by sectarians in their criticism of
the church. They said that if the pope claims to represent Christ,
but is actually a ruler of this world opposed to Christ, then he is
the Antichrist.

I once spoke with Visser 't Hooft, general secretary of the
World Council of Churches, about the Hitler period in Holland.
He said: We Dutch people, and many other Christians, at first
had the feeling that Hitler might be the Antichrist because of all
the anti-divine things he did. But then we realized that he is not
good enough to be the Antichrist. The Antichrist must maintain
at least some of the religious glory of the real Christ, so that it
would be possible to confuse them and to adore him. But Hitler

had none of this. Then we knew, he said, that the end of time had not yet come, and Hitler is not the Antichrist.

This was not a question about a dogma concerning the Antichrist. In these ideas Visser 't Hooft was standing in the real tradition of the sectarian movements. Today if we call someone the Antichrist, it is understood simply as name-calling. But when Luther called the pope the Antichrist, he was not name-calling, but speaking dogmatically; that is, in the very place where Christ is supposed to be represented, everything is done which stands against Christ.

The church's involvement in big business is further evidence of its Antichrist character. The Vatican had become the banking house of the world, especially in Luther's time, but before also. The bishops were bankers in a lesser way, but all this, Wyclif insisted, must be abolished. Even the monks had lost their ideal of poverty and accommodated themselves to the general desire of the church to be wealthy.

These criticisms brought Wyclif to even more radical conclusions. He attacked transubstantiation by saying that the body of Christ is, spatially speaking, in heaven. He is actually, or *virtualiter* (i.e., with his power) in the bread, but not spatially. This contradicts the idea of transubstantiation completely. When the church rejected him, although he knew he was right on biblical grounds, he came to realize that the official church can err with respect to articles of faith. This was also Luther's great experience, that the church rejected a true criticism of its errors. On the basis of the Bible as the real law of Christ, he was able to criticize any decision of the church which was unbelievable. He criticized the number of sacraments and particular sacraments, such as marriage. He criticized the idea in Catholicism that the sacraments have the *character indelebilis* (indelible character), according to which a special character which cannot be lost adheres to those who are baptized, confirmed, or ordained. He even criticized the celibacy of the priests. He criticized the idea of the treasury of the saints, and the superstitious elements in the popular religion. Monasticism should be abolished because it introduces division in the one church. There should not be a division in the status of Christians. There should be a *communis religio*, a common religion, to which everyone belongs. What the Catholic Church calls monastic counsels, such as love of the

enemies, should be fulfilled by all Christians. In terms of the
negative side, one could say that Wyclif anticipated nearly all
the positions of the Reformers. He was supported by the king, because the English crown had for a long time opposed the interference of Rome in the affairs of the nation, not only religiously
but also politically. Wyclif was attacked very much, but always
protected. After his death his movement slowly ebbed away, but
the seeds were in the soil and became fertile when the real
Reformation broke through.

This shows that the Roman Church could not be reformed on
the basis of a sectarian criticism, radical as it was in Wyclif. A
reform could occur only by the power of a new principle, the
power of a new relationship to God. And this is what the sixteenth-century Reformers did.

CHAPTER IV

Roman Catholicism from Trent to the Present

BEFORE taking up the Reformation we are going to discuss the Counter-Reformation from the Council of Trent to the present time. During the Reformation period there were many councils which attempted to overcome the split in the church. The demand for a general council never stopped. When the Council of Trent was convened, instead of being a universal council, it was a council of the Counter-Reformation. At Trent sessions of this council were held during several decades, with many interruptions. The Protestant Reformers were excluded from it.

A. THE MEANING OF COUNTER-REFORMATION

The Counter-Reformation was not simply a reaction, but was real reformation. It was reformation insofar as the Roman Church after the Council of Trent was not what it was before. It was a church determined by its self-affirmation against the great attack of the Reformation. When something is attacked, and then re-affirms itself, it is not the same. One of the characteristic results is that it becomes narrowed down. The medieval church should not be seen in the light of post-Tridentine Catholicism. The medieval church was open in every direction, and included tremendous contrasts, for example, Franciscans and Dominicans (Augustinians and Aristotelians), realists and nominalists, biblicists and mystics, etc. In the Counter-Reformation many possibilities which the Roman Church had previously contained were shut off. The Roman Church tended to become "counter"—the "counter" of Reformation—just as the Protestant church, with its prophetic principle, became the principle of protest against Rome.

This is the unwholesome split of Christianity. The Reformation, instead of becoming the reformation of the whole church, became the dogma of the protesting group, the Protestants. The non-Protestants reformed themselves, but in terms of "counter", in terms of opposition to something, not of immediate creativity. This is always the historical situation: if a group has to resist, it narrows down. Take simply the attack of Communism on the Western world, and you see how the freedoms for which America stands are tremendously narrowed down in defense of these freedoms. The Reformation itself was very wide open. But when all kinds of attacks were directed against the Reformation, the result was a very narrow Protestant Orthodoxy—here we call it "fundamentalism"—which represented a narrowing down of the Reformation in resistance against the attacks.

B. The Doctrine of Authorities

This leads us to a presentation of the doctrine of the authorities which the Council of Trent defined.

(1) The traditional Holy Scriptures and the Apocrypha of the Old Testament are both Scriptures and of equal authority. Luther had removed the Apocrypha of the Old Testament from canonic validity. He would have liked to remove many more books from the biblical canon, e.g., the Book of Esther, and others. Why is it important that he removed the Apocrypha? Because they are characterized by legalism, a legalism in terms of proverbs, to a great extent. This legalistic spirit had been in the Roman Church for a long time, and now was preserved in terms of the authority of the apocryphal books. So we have two Bibles, the Roman and the Protestant, and they are not identical.

(2) Scripture and tradition are equal in authority; the phrase was "with equal piety and reverence accepted". This was the form in which the Council of Trent negated the Scripture principle. What the tradition is, was not defined. Actually the tradition became identical with the decisions of the Vatican from day to day. But the tradition was not defined; the fact it was left open made it possible for the pope to use it in whatever way he pleased. Of course, he was not free to use it absolutely willfully, because there was an actual tradition deposited in the councils and former decisions, but the present decision is always decisive.

And the present decision about what the tradition is lies in the hands of the pope.

(3) There is only one translation which has ultimate authority, the Vulgate of St. Jerome. This was a decision against Erasmus, who had edited a text of the New Testament in terms of higher criticism. Erasmus' text was used by the Reformers. The pope excluded this kind of higher criticism for dogmatic purposes by making the Vulgate the only sacred translation.

(4) When the principle of biblicism prevails, the question always arises: Who interprets the Bible? Trent's unambiguous answer was: the Holy Mother Church gives the interpretation of Scripture. In Protestantism it was the theological faculties. The difference is that the pope is one man, and his decision is final; there were many theological faculties in Protestantism, and since they disagreed with each other so much, their authority in the long run was ineffective.

This doctrine of authorities in the church was a restatement of what the Reformers attacked. It makes the position of the pope unimpeachable; he cannot be attacked or criticized. He is beyond any possibility of being undercut by a competing authority, even the Bible's, because he alone has the ultimate decision in the interpretation of the sacred text.

C. The Doctrine of Sin

The Council of Trent offers an interpretation of man different from that of the Reformers. For Trent sin is a transformation of man into something worse—*in deterius commutatum*—commuted into something worse, or deteriorization. This was said against the Reformers who held that man has completely lost his freedom by his fall. This freedom that is completely lost is the freedom to contribute to one's relationship to God, not the psychological sense of freedom, which no one denied in these discussions. However, for the theology of Trent man's freedom is not lost or extinguished, but only weakened. The sins before baptism are forgiven in the act of baptism, but after baptism concupiscence remains. However, this concupiscence should not be called sin, according to the Roman Church. For the Augsburg Confession sin is a lack of faith; the Roman Church says that although concupiscence comes from sin and inclines to sin, it is not sin itself.

This means that man is not completely corrupted; even his natural drives are not sin. This had one important consequence in that Catholicism—except perhaps in America where from the beginning it has been influenced by the general climate—is not puritan. Catholicism can be radically ascetic, but it is not puritan in the ordinary life. When we Protestants from the northern and eastern sections of Germany went to Bavaria, we had the feeling that we were then in a gay country in comparison to the religious and moral climate in the Protestant areas. This difference had a basis in doctrine. For the Reformers concupiscence is sin in itself; for the Roman Church it is not. Therefore, it can admit many more liberties in the daily life, more gaiety, and more expressions of the vital forces in man, than Protestantism can.

On the other hand, the doctrine of sin in the Reformers was based on the fact that sin is unbelief. Against this the Roman Catholic Church says: No, sin is neither unbelief nor separation from God. Sin is understood as acts against the law of God. This means that the religious understanding of sin was covered over by the Council of Trent. This is another fundamental difference. From this point on, sin was understood in the Roman Church in terms of particular acts which can be forgiven. When Catholics confess their sins to a priest, they receive absolution and are liberated from them. This again contributes to a much fuller affirmation of the vital elements of life in predominantly Catholic countries. By contrast, in Protestantism sin is separation from God; "sins" are only secondary. Therefore, something fundamental must happen. A complete conversion, transformation of being, and reunion with God are necessary. This lays a much greater burden on every Protestant than any Catholic has to bear. On the other hand, the Catholic position is in principle legalistic and divides sin into "sins". When Protestants do this, as they sometimes do, they follow the Catholic and not the Reformation line of thought.

D. The Doctrine of Justification

The central inssue between the Reformers and the Roman Catholic Church was the doctrine of justification by faith alone (*sola fide*), the formula which the Reformers used for polemical purposes. In the Council of Trent the Roman Church repeated the Thomistic tradition on the doctrine of justification, but with a diplomatic tendency. The Catholic Church knew that this was, as the Reformers called it, the *articulus stantis aut cadentis ecclesiae*, the article by which the church stands or falls. Since this was the main point of the Reformation opposition, the Roman Church felt it had to be as conciliatory as possible. It avoided some of the distortions of this doctrine in nominalism which the Reformers had attacked. Nevertheless, it remained clear in the main statement that the *remissio peccatorum*, the forgiveness of sins, is not *sola gratia*, by grace alone. Other elements are added. It speaks of a preparation for the divine act of justification whereby a *gratia praeveniens*, a prevenient grace, is effective in man which can be rejected or accepted, whichever way a man decides. Thus, man must cooperate with God in his prevenient grace. After grace is received by man, it is given to him in the degree of his cooperation. The more man cooperates with God in his prevenient grace the more is the grace of justification given to him.

Justification as a gift contains two things: faith on the one hand, and hope and love on the other. Faith alone is not sufficient. According to the Council's decision, it is even possible that justification may be lost by a Christian through a mortal sin, but that faith still remains. Now the Reformers would say: If you are in faith, you can never lose your justification. But the Roman Church understood faith in terms of its ancient tradition, which defined faith as an intellectual and a moral act. Of course, if faith is an intellectual and a moral act, it can be lost, and nevertheless justification can be there. However, faith for the Reformers is the act of accepting justification, and this cannot be lost if there shall be justification.

Nothing has been more misunderstood in Protestant theology than the term *sola fide*, by faith alone. This has been understood not only by the Romans but also by Protestants themselves as an intellectual act of a man. This act of "faith" forces God to give his forgiveness. But *sola fide* means that in the moment that our sins are forgiven, we can do nothing else than receive this forgiveness. Anything else would destroy the activity of God, his exclusive grace. This central position of the Reformers that grace can only be *received* by faith alone was first misunderstood and then rejected. This means that from this moment on the split in the church became final. No reconciliation was possible between these two forms of religion—the Reformation doctrine which holds that our act of turning to God and receiving his grace is unambiguously a receptive act, one in which God gives something to us and we do not do anything, and the Catholic doctrine which teaches that we must act and prepare for grace, that we must cooperate with God, and that faith is an intellectual acknowledgment, which may or may not be there. All the anathemas of the Council of Trent on this point are based on this misunderstanding of *sola fide*.

E. The Sacraments

While the fathers of Trent tried to approximate the Protestant position on justification to some degree, they made no such effort at all on the sacraments. Here caution was unnecessary because every caution would have undercut the very essence of the Roman Church. So the Council of Trent states: "All true justice starts, and if it has started, is augmented, and if it has been lost, is restituted, by the sacraments." This is the function of the sacraments; it is the religious function altogether.

Not much was said about the way in which the sacraments are effective nor about the personal side in the reception of the sacraments. The formulation was made that the sacraments are effective *ex opere operato non ponentibus obicem*, i.e., by their very operation for those who do not resist. If you do not place an impediment (*obicem*) within yourselves in the way of the effectiveness of the sacraments, then no matter what your subjective state, they are effective by their mere performance (*ex opere operato*). This was another crucial point for the Reformers, that there cannot be a relationship to God except in the actual person-to-person encounter with him in the realm of faith. This is much more than non-resistance; it is an active turning toward God. Without this the sacraments are not effective for Protestants as they are for Catholics.

With respect to the number of the sacraments, which had been reduced by Luther and Calvin to two sacraments, there are seven, all of them instituted by Christ. This is *de fide*, a matter to be accepted on faith for the Catholic. This means no historical doubt is allowed whether they were really instituted by Christ or not. When you read the words *de fide* in connection with a dogmatic formulation in a Catholic book, this means that this is a dogma of the Roman Church which you cannot doubt or deny, except at the risk of being cut off from the Roman Church.

There is no salvation without the sacraments. The sacraments are saving powers, not merely strengthening powers, as in Protestantism. They have a hidden force of their own, mediated to all those who do not resist the grace. Baptism, confirmation, and ordination have an indelible character—another statement against the Reformers' position. One is baptized for life; this had the practical consequence in the Middle Ages that all the baptized fell under the law of heresy. Those who belonged to other religions, such as Jews and Muslims, fell under another law which limits alien religions, but were not persecuted for heresy, as Christians were. The indelible character of a sacrament was a life-and-death matter in the practice of the Roman Church. The same is true of the indelible character of ordination. This meant that the excommunicated priest could perform valid marriages in prison. The sacramental power in him overcomes his state of excommunication as an individual. This stands against the Protestant doctrine of the universal priesthood. In Catholic doctrine not every Christian has the power to preach and to administer the sacraments, but only those who are ordained; being ordained means having received sacramental power. The sacramental power is even embodied in the ritual form of the sacraments. If there is a given ritual formula, no priest, no bishop, can change it or omit something from it without sinning. The sacramental power is communicated from its origin in the actuality of the church to the forms which are used; no arbitrariness is possible.

Infant baptism is valid; the water of baptism washes away the contamination of original sin. To have faith during one's later life in the power of baptism as the divine act which initiates all Christian being, as Luther demanded, is not sufficient for the forgiveness of sins. This means that baptism loses, religiously speaking, its actual power for the later life. It is not a point to which one religiously returns; its meaning lies in the fact of the *character indelebilis*.

The doctrine of transubstantiation was preserved, and wherever it is preserved you always find a clear test of it, namely, the demand to adore the Host. For Protestants the bread is not the body of Christ except in the act of performance. For Catholics the bread and the wine are the body and blood of Christ after they have been consecrated. So when you enter an empty Catholic church—as you do when you travel in European countries, because they are the objects of greatest interest—you come into a sacred atmosphere. You are not coming into a house which is used on Sundays, and sometimes during the week, but a house in which God himself is present twenty-four hours a day, in the holiest of holies, on the altar, in the shrine. This determines the whole mood which prevails in such a church. God is always there in a definite way on the altar. I believe that the reason the attempts of some Protestant churches to remain open for prayer and meditation during the day have a very limited effect on people is that nothing is happening in them. If, however, you go into a Roman Church, something has happened, the effects of which are still there—the presence of God himself, of the body of Christ, on the altar.

On this basis the Roman Church also preserved the Mass against the criticism of the Reformers, not only the Mass for the living, but the Mass—the sacrifice of the body of Christ—for those who have died and are in purgatory. In these respects the Council of Trent made practically no reform at all, nor did it provide a better theological foundation. It simply confirmed and consecrated the tradition.

The attitude toward the sacrament of penance was a little different. This was another point against which Protestantism directed an attack. The sacrament of penance was, generally speaking, maintained as a sacrament, and even the weakest aspect of this sacrament, the doctrine of attrition, which Luther ironically called the repentance evoked by the gallows, the kind of repentance induced by fear, was retained as a necessary preparation. Contrition, the real repentance, *metanoia* in the New Testament, is not sufficient. It is fulfilled only in connection with the sacrament and with the word of absolution. This word does not simply declare that God has forgiven, but itself gives the forgiveness. It is not that the priest gives the forgiveness, but through the priest, and only through the priest, does God grant forgiveness. Moreover, Christians need more than the word of absolution from the priest. They also need satisfactions, because the punishment is not removed with the guilt. Therefore, some punishments must be imposed on the people even after they have taken part in the sacrament. The satisfactions are such things as praying the "Our Father" a hundred times, or giving money, or making a pilgrimage, etc. This was the point with which the Reformers disagreed the most.

Marriage is retained as a sacrament, although in contradiction to this, virginity is evaluated more highly than marriage. This is still the situation in the Roman Church. Now what was still somewhat in flux before the Reformation became fixed. It was fixed against the Reformation. This shows how the Roman Church lost its dynamic creativity. You can sense this when you read the systematic theologies written by Catholic theologians; they deal with very secondary problems, because all the fundamental problems are solved.

The basic doctrine behind all of them is the sacrament of ordination. Here is the point in which all the others are united. The priest does what constitutes the Roman Church as such; he exercises the sacramental power. Preaching is often secondary and even omitted. Sacrifice and priesthood are by divine ordination—sacrifice in the sense of offering up the body of Christ in the Mass. Both are implied in every ecclesiastical law. Both are presupposed; this church of the sacramental sacrifice is the hierarchical church, and the hierarchical church is the church of the sacramental sacrifice. This is Catholicism in the Roman sense.

F. Papal Infallibility

These decisions confirmed the split in Christianity. Rome actually had accepted only external remedies against abuses. But many problems were left. The first was the problem of the pope in relation to councils. This leads us to the development from Trent to the Vatican Council in 1870. At Trent two opinions were fighting against each other. The first was that the pope is the universal bishop, the vicar of Christ. This means that every episcopal power is derived from the power of the pope; every bishop participates in the pope and the pope participates in him, because he is the vicar of Christ. The other opinion was that the pope is the first among equals, representing the unity and the order of the church. This is the point of view of conciliarism; the councils finally have the power to make the ultimate decisions. The former is the point of view of curialism; the Curia, the court of the pope, is the central power of decision. This question was not decided at Trent. It took a few more centuries.

One of the presuppositions for the decision that was to be made at the Vatican Council was that the historical development more and more destroyed those groups which were most dangerous for the pope in the Roman Church; these groups were the national churches. For example, the movement for an independent French church—called Gallicanism—was a real threat to Rome. There were similar movements in Germany, Austria, and other places, where the national churches under the leadership of their bishops resisted many papal aspirations. The civil rulers formed alliances with the national bishops against the pope. But this was undermined by the historical development. One of the reasons was that the rulers, such as the leaders of the French revolution (Napoleon), or the German princes, used the pope against the local ecclesiastical powers. Diplomacy always plays the one side off against the other. The national princes used their own bishops against the encroachments by the pope, and they used the pope against the power of their own bishops. The result of these oscillations was that finally the pope prevailed. In 1870 the Vatican Council made the statement on the infallibility of the pope. This decision has many presuppositions. First, it was necessary to give a definite meaning to the term "tradition". One distinguished now between ecclesiastical and apostolic tradition. The apostolic tradition is composed of the ancient traditions which came into the church through ways which are not given in the Bible. The ecclesiastical tradition is the tradition about which the pope has to decide in the course of the church's history. The ecclesiastical tradition, which was the only living tradition, was identical with the papal decisions. This is the positive statement.

And now its negative side: The Jesuits more and more undercut all other authorities. In contrast to Thomas Aquinas, they undercut conscience and made themselves leaders of the consciences of the princes, and of the other people too. Most of the decisive political personalities surrounded themselves with Jesuits to advise them, as leaders of their conscience. Now if you guide the conscience of a prince, you can apply this guidance to all political decisions, because in all political decisions there are moral elements. This is what the Jesuits did. They turned the consciences of the Catholic princes toward all the cruelties of the Counter-Reformation. Thus, the conscience could no longer serve as an authority.

The authority of the bishops was undercut by the Jesuits. Episcopal power in the councils was undercut by the interpretation given by the Jesuits. The councils themselves and their decisions have to be confirmed by the pope. This meant the complete victory of the pope over the councils. The pope was accepted by the majority of the bishops at Trent as the one who has to confirm the Council of Trent. The result is that no council which is not confirmed by the pope can have validity any more. The pope is removed beyond criticism.

Even the church fathers were undercut by the Jesuits. The Jesuits were especially anti-Augustinian. There is only one father of the church, namely, the living pope. All earlier church fathers are full of heretical statements, of errors, even of falsifications. As you see from this, the Jesuits were very modern people. They knew about the historical problems and used them to undermine the authority of the church fathers. Protestant historiography did the same thing, to make possible the prophetic authority of the Reformers. So both sides used criticism, the Jesuits to give absolute power to the pope, and the Protestants to liberalize the authority of the Bible.

The constitution of 1870, *Pastor Aeternus,* declared the pope to be the universal power of jurisdiction over every other power in the church. There is no legal body which is not subject to the pope. Secondly, he is declared universal bishop. This means practically that through the local bishop he has power over every Catholic, and if this does not work he can exercise direct episcopal power and bring the subjects of a bishop into revolt against him. Thirdly, the pope is infallible when he speaks *ex cathedra.* This is the most conspicuous decision of the Vatican Council, one which brought about the separation of some Catholics, who called themselves the "Old Catholics", from the Roman Church. They remained a small group in Western Germany, and never succeeded in taking over the Roman Church.

The first *ex cathedra* decision since 1870 was made in our generation, in 1950, about the bodily assumption of the Virgin Mary. Before he made this decision the pope asked most of the bishops. The majority was on his side; a minority was opposed to it. The tradition on this point is more than a thousand years old. We have pictures from many periods in church history of Mary being elevated into heaven and crowned by Christ, or received by God. Now the question was: Is this a pious opinion in the church which is to be tolerated, or is it a matter *de fide*? As long as it is a pious opinion, any Catholic can disagree with it, without losing the salvation of his soul. The moment that it is declared *de fide*, as it was done in 1950 by the pope, every Catholic is bound to accept it as truth, and nothing can relieve him of this necessity. Many Catholics were deeply shaken by this, but they subjected themselves to it.

Infallibility of the pope does not mean that there exists a man whose every word is infallible. For eighty years, from 1870 to 1950, no pope had said anything which is infallible in the strictest sense. But then in 1950 he did, which reminded us that this dogma about the infallibility of the pope is taken absolutely seriously, without restriction. From a Protestant or humanist point of view there can be no approach to this doctrine and its implications.

This was finally confirmed in the fourth point of *Pastor Aeternus*: The pope is irreformable by an action of the church. You must compare this with the impeachment proceedings which are possible against any president of the United States; they are rare, but they have happened and can happen again. This sort of thing happened against the popes in the Middle Ages; some were removed and others were put in their place. All this came to an end in 1870, because there is no power which can remove a pope. The pope is in this sense absolute and irremovable. No impeachment is possible. In this way every dogma formulated by the pope is implicitly valid. This means, for instance, that the doctrine of the Immaculate Conception of Mary the Virgin in the birth of Christ, which had been formulated before 1870, now became *de fide*. Prior to this time the Dominicans, who were against the Franciscans on this matter, could say that it is not a valid dogma. It became a valid dogma because of the implication that the pope has accepted it *ex cathedra*.

G. JANSENISM

There was a strong movement in the Roman Church back to the original Augustinianism of the church. This movement is called

Jansenism, named after Cornelius Jansen. The Jesuit, Molina, wrote against the Thomistic Dominicans who taught the doctrine of predestination. The Jesuits opposed this doctrine and fought for human freedom. Now Jansen and the Jansenists, the most important of whom was Blaise Pascal, arose and fought against the Jesuits. But the Jesuits prevailed and the popes followed them. The Jesuit was the modern man in the Roman Church. He was disciplined, very similiar to the totalitarian form of subjection we see today. He was completely devoted to the power of the church, and at the same time nourished on much intellectual education and modern ideas, deciding for freedom and reason.

The Jansenist movement attempted to return to a genuine Augustinian tradition, but was opposed and finally destroyed by the Jesuits. In the process, however, the Jesuits lost a lot of their standing in the public eye, and in the eighteenth century were thrown out of many Catholic countries. One interesting point in the discussion was that if the sentences of Cornelius Jansen are condemned, then this condemnation covers not only the matter of content, but also the question of fact (*question de fait*), whether he really said what he was accused of saying. This seems very foolish, but the important point behind it is that when the pope inquires into someone's text, and then condemns it, he is right not only in rejecting its ideas, but also in his statement that these ideas are really in the text. This means that the pope is the interpreter of every text. If the pope says that this is what the text means, no philological defense in the face of that is possible. Here we see the natural extension of the totalitarian and authoritarian principle even to historical facts. The pope decides what is a historical fact, not only what is true in theological terms.

Jansenism produced other writings. There was a man, Quesnel, who tried to introduce Augustinian principles again and to defend them against the Jesuits. But again the pope took the side of the Jesuits and Augustine was removed from Counter-Reformation Catholicism to a large extent. In the bull *Unigenitus* the pope drove out the best in the Roman tradition. He drove out Augustine's doctrine of grace, of faith, and of love. For instance, it is anathema if someone says with Augustine: "In vain, Lord, thou commandest if thou dost not give what thou orderest." For Augustinianism the commandments of God can be fulfilled only if God gives what he commands. Now, after the Jansenist controversy, somebody who says this in the Roman Church is condemned, and implicitly this means that Augustine is condemned.

When you meet modern progressive Catholics—there are more of them in Europe than in America, where Catholicism, with a few exceptions, has lost its spiritual power—you will find that they always fall back upon Augustine and are always on the verge of being thrown out, of being excommunicated or forbidden to express themselves. In my recent trips to Germany I had discussions several times with Catholic groups and became astonished at how near we were to each other. But these people feel that if they agree with me on Augustinian principles, they are in danger. And they are! This means that the condemnation of Augustinianism in the Jansenist struggle is like a sword which hangs over every form of spiritualized Catholicism.

H. PROBABILISM

The last problem I want to discuss is probabilism. Opinion given by authorities in the Roman Church on ethical questions are probable. The Jesuits said: If an opinion is probable, one is allowed to follow it even though the opposite opinion should be more probable. This means that on ethical matters one has no autonomy; that is something the church would radically deny. One must always follow the guidance of the Roman priest, especially of the confessor. But the confessor himself has many possibilities. Since he must talk to a person, not in the power of his spirit, but on the basis of authorities, and since these authorities always contradict each other, or are at least different, he can advise a person to do something which is probably right, even though other courses of ethical action are more probable. If he can find an acknowledged authority of the church who has said something about a problem, one can follow it, even if it is not safe, even if other things seem to be better. The result of this doctrine was a tremendous ethical relativism, laxity, and chaos. This, of course, was most advantageous in the eighteenth century when the church was following the new morals of an emerging bourgeois society. This was so abused that finally a reaction arose in the Roman Church.

Alfonso Maria di Liguori reacted against it, but did not really overcome it, because he also said that it is not I who can decide, but my confessor. And how can the confessor decide? Finally the principle of the probable triumphed. Another development connected with this was that now every sin becomes a venial sin. Here again Jesuitism and the bourgeoisie—the greatest enemies—joined together to remove the radical seriousness of sin which the Jansenists and the early Protestants maintained.

I. RECENT DEVELOPMENTS

Much more can be said about present-day Catholicism. I have already said a few things about more recent decisions of the pope. Let me refer to one decision which is not so well known as the decision about the bodily assumption of the Holy Virgin. This was the papal encyclical *Humani generis* in which the pope said things which went beyond what was said in the Vatican Council about the infallibility of the pope. In the *Vaticanum* the infallibility referred only to statements made *ex cathedra,* when the pope speaks officially on matters of dogma or ethics. But in the *Humani generis* of 1950 he made statements about philosophies, directing a sharp attack against existentialism. This means that if the pope has decided that a philosophy is unsound, no faithful Catholic can work in line with it any more. This goes far beyond anything which the pope has said before. Thomas Aquinas is then placed in the role of *the* Catholic philosopher. This meant that some of the French existentialists—de Lubac and others—had to give up their teaching positions because philosophically they were existentialists, although they answered the existentialist questions in religious terms.

I recall asking Reinhold Niebuhr in March, 1950: "What do you think? Will the pope make this declaration about the assumption of the Holy Virgin *ex cathedra?*" Then he answered: "I don't think so; he is too clever for that; it would be a slap in the face of the whole modern world and it would be dangerous for the Roman Church to do that today." Only a few months later it was done! This means that even such a keen observer as Reinhold Niebuhr could not imagine that the pope would dare to do such a thing today. But he did it. This means that an authoritarian system has to become more and more narrow in order to fix itself.

It has to do what other totalitarian systems do; they exclude step by step one danger after the other. They try to prevent their subjects from meeting other traditions. The Roman Church had done this right along by means of the "Index of Prohibited Books". These books are forbidden not for the scholars, but for the populace. People are not allowed to read any of the books which appear on the Index, and students have to obtain special permission to read them. But there is another connotation to this papal decision. It meant that the liberal world had become so weak that the pope had no need to fear it. This was our error—Niebuhr's and mine—that we thought the pope would respect the Protestants and the humanists—perhaps even the Communists—all over the world, and not put himself in the position of having almost everybody speak of the superstitious attitude of the Roman Church in making such a dogma. But the pope was not afraid, and probably he was right, because the very weak Protestant resistance against this and similar things cannot hurt the Catholic Church any more. And the humanist opposition is almost nonexistent because it is in a process of self-disintegration. The greatness of the existentialists is that they describe this disintegration, but they themselves are in the midst of it.

Totalitarianism and authoritarianism must be distinguished. Rome is not totalitarian; only a state can be that. But Rome is authoritarian, and it exercises many functions which totalitarian states have exercised. The question which the existence of Catholicism puts before us is whether, with the end of the liberal era, liberalism altogether will come to an end. This leads me to the question, which is very near to my heart, whether with the end of the Protestant era, the Protestant principle will also come to an end. With this we are led to the problem of the Reformation.

We shall have to deal with the Reformation in a brief survey, after having agreed with Professor Handy that in view of the fact that you come from Protestant traditions and are nourished on Protestant ideas, you do not need this as much as you need a knowledge of the ancient and medieval church. But I am not so sure that you do not need it! For the kind of Protestantism which has developed in America is not so much an expression of the Reformation, but has more to do with the so-called Evangelical Radicals. There are the Lutheran and Calvinist groups, and they are strong, but they have adapted themselves to an astonishing degree to the climate of American Protestantism. This climate has been made not by them but by the sectarian movements. Thus, when I came to America twenty years ago, the theology of the Reformation was almost unknown in Union Theological Seminary Reformation was almost unknown in Union Theological Seminary [New York], because of the different traditions, and the reduction of the Protestant tradition nearer to the non-Reformation traditions.

CHAPTER V

The Theology of the Protestant Reformers

A. MARTIN LUTHER

THE turning point of the Reformation and of church history in general is the experience of an Augustinian monk in his monastic cell—Martin Luther. Martin Luther did not merely teach different doctrines; others had done that also, such as Wyclif. But none of the others who protested against the Roman system were able to break through it. The only man who really made a breakthrough, and whose breakthrough has transformed the surface of the earth, was Martin Luther. This is his greatness. His greatness should not be measured by comparing him with Lutheranism; that is something quite different. Lutheranism is something which historically has been associated with Protestant Orthodoxy, political movements, Prussian conservatism, and what not. But Luther is different. He is one of the few great prophets of the Christian Church, and his greatness is overwhelming, even if it was limited by some of his personal traits and his later development. He is responsible for the fact that a purified Christianity, a Christianity of the Reformation, was able to establish itself on equal terms with the Roman tradition. From this point of view we must look at him. Therefore, when I speak of Luther, I am not speaking of the theologian who produced Lutheranism—many others contributed to this, and Melanchthon more than Luther—but of the man in whom the Roman system was broken through.

1. *The Breakthrough*

This was a break through three different distortions of Christianity which made the Roman Catholic religion what it was. The breakthrough was the creation of another religion. What does "religion" mean here? "Religion" means nothing else than another personal relationship between man and God—man to God and God to man. This is why a reunion of the churches was not possible, in spite of tremendous attempts to do this during the sixteenth century and later. You can compromise about different doctrines; you cannot compromise about different religions! Either you have the Protestant relation to God or you have the Catholic, but you cannot have both; you cannot make a compromise.

The Catholic system is a system of objective, quantitative, and relative relations between God and man for the sake of providing eternal happiness for man. This is the basic structure: objective, not personal; quantitative, not qualitative; relative and conditioned, not absolute. This leads to another proposition: The Roman system is a system of divine-human management, represented and actualized by ecclesiastical management.

Now first the purpose: The purpose is to give eternal blessedness to man and to save him from eternal punishment. The alternatives are eternal suffering in hell or eternal pleasure in heaven. The way to accomplish the purpose is through the sacraments, in which a magical giving of grace is the one side, and moral freedom which produces merits is the other side—magical grace completed by active law, active law completed by magical grace. The quantitative character comes through also in terms of ethical commands. There are two kinds, commandments and counsels—commandments for all Christians, and counsels, the full yoke of Christ, only for the monks and partly for the priests. For instance, love toward the enemy is a counsel of perfection, but not a commandment for everybody. Asceticism is a counsel of perfection, but not a commandment for everybody. The divine punishments also have a quantitative character. There is eternal punishment for mortal sins, purgatory for light sins, and heaven for people in purgatory, and sometimes for saints already on earth.

Under these conditions no one ever knew whether he could be certain of his salvation, because one could never do enough; one could never receive enough grace of a magical kind, nor could one do enough in terms of merits and asceticism. The result of this was a great deal of anxiety at the end of the Middle Ages. In my book, *The Courage to Be*, I described the anxiety of guilt as one of the three great types of anxiety, and I related this anxiety of guilt historically and socially to the end of the Middle Ages. This anxiety is always present, of course, but it was predominant then and was almost like a contagious disease. People could not do enough to get a merciful God and to get rid of their bad conscience. A tremendous amount of this anxiety was expressed in the art of that period, and also expressed in the demand for more and more pilgrimages, in the collection and adoration of relics, in praying many "Our Fathers", in giving of money, in buying indulgences, self-torturing asceticism, and everything possible to get over one's guilt. It is interesting to look at this period but almost impossible for us to understand it. Luther was in the cloister with this same anxiety of guilt and condemnation. Out of this anxiety he went into the cloister and out of it he experienced that no amount of asceticism is able to give a person a real certainty of salvation in a system of relativities, quantities, and things. He was always in fear of the threatening God, of the punishing and destroying God. And he asked: How can I get a merciful God? Out of this question and the anxiety behind it, the Reformation began.

What did Luther say against the Roman quantitative, objective, and relative point of view? The relation to God is personal. It is an I-thou relationship, mediated not by anybody or anything, but only by accepting the message of acceptance, which is the content of the Bible. This is not an objective status in which one is; it is a personal relationship which Luther called "faith", not faith in something which one can believe, but acceptance of the fact that one is accepted. It is qualitative, not quantitative. Either a person is separated from God or he is not. There are no quantitative degrees of separation or non-separation. In a person-to-person relationship one can say there are conflicts and tensions, but as long as it is a relationship of confidence and love, it is a qualitative thing. It is not a matter of quantity. Likewise, it is unconditional and not conditioned, as it is in the Roman system. One is not a little bit nearer to God if one does more for the church, or against one's body, but one is near to God completely and absolutely if one is united with him at all. And if not united, one is separated. The one state is unconditionally positive, the other unconditionally negative. The Reformation restated the unconditional categories of the Bible.

It follows from this that both the magical and the legalistic elements in the piety disappear. The forgiveness of sins, or acceptance, is not just an act of the past done in baptism, but it is continually necessary. Repentance is an element in every relationship to God, and in every moment. The magical and the legal elements disappear, for grace is a personal communion of God with the sinner. There is no possibility of any merit; there is only the need to accept. There can be no hidden magical power in our souls which makes us acceptable, but we are acceptable in the moment in which we accept acceptance. Therefore, the sacramental activities as such are rejected. There are sacraments, but they now mean something quite different. And the ascetic practices are rejected forever, because none of them can give certainty. At this point a misunderstanding often prevails. One asks: Now is that not egocentric—I think Jacques Maritain told me this once—if Protestants think about their own individual certainty? However, Luther did not have in mind an abstract certainty; he meant reunion with God, and this implies certainty. Everything centers around this being accepted. This is certain: If you have God, you have him. If you look at yourself, your experiences, your asceticism, and your morals, you can become certain only if you are extremely self-complacent and blind toward yourself. These are absolute categories. The divine demand is absolute. It is not a relative demand which brings a more-or-less kind of blessedness. The absolute demand is: Joyfully accept the will of God. And there is only one punishment, not different degrees of ecclesiastical satisfaction and degrees of punishments in purgatory, and finally hell. The one and only punishment is the despair of being separated from God. Consequently, there is only one grace, reunion with God. That is all! Luther reduced the Christian religion to this simplicity. Adolph von Harnack, the great historian of dogma, called Luther a genius of reduction.

Luther believed that his was a restatement of the New Testament, especially of Paul. But although his message contains the truth of Paul, it is by no means the whole of what Paul said. The situation determined what he took from Paul, that is, the doctrine of justification by faith which was Paul's defense against legalism. But Luther did not take in Paul's doctrine of the Spirit. Of course, he did not deny it; there is even a lot of it in Luther, but that is not decisive. The decisive thing is that a doctrine of the Spirit, of being "in Christ", of the new being, is the weak spot in Luther's doctrine of justification by faith. In Paul the situation is different. Paul has three main centers in his thought, which make it a triangle, not a circle. The one is his eschatological consciousness, the certainty that in Christ eschatology is fulfilled and a new reality has started. The second is his doctrine of the Spirit, which means for him that the kingdom of God has appeared, that the new being in Christ is given to us here and now. The third point in Paul is his critical defense against legalism, justification by faith. Luther accepted all three, of course. But the eschatological point was not really understood.

Luther's breakthrough was externally occasioned by the sacrament of penance. There are two main sacraments in the Roman Church, the Mass, which is a part of the Lord's Supper, and the sacrament of penance, which is the subjective sacrament, dealing with the individual and having an immense educational function. This sacrament may be called the sacrament cf subjectivity in contrast to the Mass as the pre-eminent sacrament of objectivity. The religious life in the Middle Ages moved between these two. Although Luther attacked the Mass, this was not the real point of criticism; the real issue had to do with the abuses connected with the sacrament of penance. The abuses stemmed from the fact that the sacrament of penance had different parts, contrition, confession, absolution, and satisfaction. The first and last points were the most dangerous ones.

Contrition—the real repentance, the change of mind—was replaced by attrition, the fear of eternal punishment, which Luther called the repentance inspired by the imminent prospect of the gallows. So it had no religious value for him. The other dangerous point was satisfaction, which did not mean that you could earn your forgiveness of sins by works of satisfaction, but that you have to do them because the sin is still in you after it has been forgiven. The decisive thing is the humble subjection to the satisfactions demanded by the priest. The priest imposed on the *communicandus* all kinds of activities, sometimes so difficult that the people wanted to get rid of them. The church yielded to this desire in terms of indulgences, which are also sacrifices. One must sacrifice some money to buy the indulgences, and these indulgences remove the obligations to perform the works of satisfaction. The popular idea was that these satisfactions are effective in overcoming one's guilt consciousness. One can say that here a sort of marketing of eternal life was going on. A person could buy the indulgences and in this way get rid of the punishments, not only on earth but also in purgatory. The abuses brought Luther to think about the whole meaning of the sacrament of penance. This led him to conclusions absolutely opposed to the attitude of the Roman Church. Luther's criticisms were directed not only to the abuses but to the source of them in the doctrine itself. Thus Luther placed his famous Ninety-five Theses on the door of the Wittenberg church. The first of these is a classic formulation of Reformation Christianity: "Our Lord and Master, Jesus Christ, saying 'Repent ye,' wished that the whole life of the believers be penitence." This means that the sacramental act is only the form in which a much more universal attitude is expressed. What is important is the relationship to God. It is not a new doctrine but a new relationship to God which the Reformers brought about. The relationship is not an objective management between God and man, but a personal relationship of penitence first, and then faith.

Perhaps the most striking and paradoxical expression is given by Luther in the following words: "Penitence is something between injustice and justice. Therefore, whenever we are repenting, we are sinners, but nevertheless for this reason we are also righteous, and in the process of justification, partly sinners, partly righteous—that is nothing but repenting." This means that there is always something like repentance in the relationship to God. Luther did not at this time attack the sacrament of penance as such. He even thought that the indulgences could be tolerated. But he attacked the center out of which all abuses came, and this was the decisive event of the Reformation.

After Luther's attack had been made, the consequences were clear. The indulgence money can only help with respect to those works which are imposed by the pope, i.e., the canonical punishments. The dead in purgatory cannot be released by the pope; he can only pray for them; he has no power over the dead. The forgiveness of sins is an act of God alone, and the pope—or any priest—can only declare that God has already done it. There is no treasury of the church out of which the indulgences can come, except the one treasury of the work of Christ. No saint can do superfluous works because it is man's duty to do everything he can anyhow. The power of the keys, that is, the power of the forgiveness of sins, is given by God to every disciple who is with him. The only works of satisfaction are works of love; all other works are an arbitrary invention by the church. There is no time or space for them, because in our real life we must always be aware of the works of love demanded of us every moment. Confession, which is made by the priest in the sacrament of penance, is directed to God. One does not need to go to the priest for this. Every time we pray "Our Father", we confess our sins; this is what matters, not the sacramental confession. About satisfaction Luther said: This is a dangerous concept, because we cannot satisfy God at all. If there is satisfaction, it is done by Christ to God, not by us. Purgatory is a fiction and an imagination of man without biblical foundation. The other element in the sacrament of penance is absolution. Luther was psychologically alert enough to know that a solemn absolution may have psychological effects, but he denied its necessity. The message of the gospel, which is the message of forgiveness, is the absolution in every moment. This you can receive as the answer of God to your prayer for forgiveness. You do not need to go to church for this.

All of this means that the sacrament of penance is completely dissolved. Penitence is transformed into a personal relationship to God and to the neighbor, against a system of means to obtain the release of objective punishments in hell, purgatory, and on earth. All of these concepts were in reality at least undercut by Luther, if not abolished. Everything is placed on the basis of a person-to-person relationship between God and man. You can have this relationship even in hell. This means that hell is simply a state and not a place. The Reformation understanding of man's relationship to God abolishes the medieval view.

The pope did not accept the absolute categories in Luther's view of man's relationship to God. Thus the conflict between Luther and the church arose. Let us make clear, however, that this was not the beginning of the schism. Luther hoped to *reform* the church, including the pope and the priests. But the pope and the priests did not want to be reformed in any way. The last great bull defining the power of the pope said: "Therefore, we declare, pronounce and define that it is universally necessary for salvation that every human creature be subject to the Roman high priest." This is the bull which defines most sharply the unlimited and absolute power of the pope.

2. *Luther's Criticism of the Church*

Luther criticized the church when it did not follow his criticism of the sacrament of penance. The only ultimate criterion for Christianity is the message of the gospel. For this reason there is no infallibility of the pope. The pope may fall into error, and not only he but also the councils may err. Neither the curialistic theory that the pope is an absolute monarch nor the conciliaristic theory that the great councils of the church are absolutely infallible is acceptable. The pope and councils are both human, and can fall into error. The pope can be tolerated as the chief administrator of the church on the basis of human law, the law of expediency. However, the pope claims to rule by divine right, and makes of himself an absolute figure in the church. This could not be tolerated for Luther, because no human being can ever be the vicar of the divine power. The divine right of the pope is a demonic claim, actually the claim of the Antichrist. When he said this, the break with Rome was clear. There is only one head of the church, Christ himself, and the pope as he is now is the creation of the divine wrath to punish Christianity for its sins. This was meant theologically, not as name-calling. He was theologically serious when he called the pope the Antichrist. He was not criticizing a particular man for his shortcomings. Many people were criticizing the behavior of the pope at that time. Luther criticized the position of the pope, and his claim to be the representative of Christ by divine right. In this way the pope destroys the souls, because he wants to have a power which belongs to God alone.

Luther as a monk had experienced the importance of monasticism in the Roman Church. A double standard of morality grew out of the monastic attitude; there were the higher counsels for those who are nearer to God, and then the rules which apply to everybody. The higher counsels for the monks, such as fasting, discipline, humility, celibacy, etc., made the monks ontologically higher than ordinary men. This double standard was called forth by the historical situation in which the church grew rapidly. The result was that the masses of people could not take upon themselves, as it was said, the whole yoke of Christ, because it was too heavy for them. So a special group did it, following the counsels of a higher morality and piety. These were the *religiosi,* those who made religion their vocation.

Luther attacked the double-standard morality. The divine demand, he said, is absolute and unconditional. It refers to everyone. This absolute demand destroys the whole system of religion. There is no status of perfection, such as the Catholics ascribed to the monks. Everyone has to be perfect, and no one is able to be perfect. Man does not have the power to produce the graces to do the right thing, and the special endeavor of the monks will not do it. What is decisive is the intention, the good will, not the magic habit (*habitus*) of which the Catholic Church spoke. And this intention, this good will, is right even if its content is wrong. The valuation of a personality is dependent on the inner intention of a person toward the good. Luther took this seriously. For him it was not enough to will to do the good, or the will of God; you must will what God wills joyfully, with your voluntary participation. If you fulfill the whole law, but do not do it joyfully, it is worth nothing. The obedience of the servant is not the fulfillment of Christian ethics. Only he who loves, and loves God and man joyfully, is able to fulfill the law. And this is expected of everyone.

This means that Luther turned religion and ethics around. We cannot fulfill the will of God without being united with him. It is impossible without the forgiveness of sins. Even the best people have within them elements of despair, aggressiveness, indifference, and self-contradiction. Only on the basis of divine forgiveness can the full yoke of Christ be imposed on everybody. This is completely different from a moralistic interpretation of Christianity. The moral act is that which follows—it might or might not follow, although essentially it should do so—and the *prius* of it is the participation in the divine grace, in God's forgiveness and in his power of being. This makes all the difference in the world. It is most unfortunate that Protestantism is always tempted to revert to the opposite, to make the religious dimension dependent on morality. Wherever this is done, we are outside the realm of true Protestantism. If someone says: "Oh, God must love me, because I love him and do almost everything he demands"—namely, what the suburban neighbor demands!—then the religious and the ethical relationship is completely reversed. The center of the Reformation, the meaning of the famous phrase, *sola fide,* is rather put this way: "I know that I do not do anything good, that every-thing seemingly good is ambiguous, that the only thing which is good within me is God's declaration that I am good, and that if I but accept this divine declaration, then there may be a trans-formed reality from which ethical acts may follow." The religious side comes before the ethical.

The phrase *sola fide* is the most misunderstood and distorted phrase of the Reformation. People have taught that it means that if you do the good work of believing, especially believing in some-thing unbelievable, this will make you good before God. The phrase should not be "by faith alone" but "by grace alone, received through faith alone". Faith here means nothing more than the acceptance of grace. This was Luther's concern, because he had experienced that if it is put the other way around, you are always lost, and if you take it seriously, you fall into absolute despair, because if you know yourself, you know that you are not good. You know this as well as Paul did, and this means that ethics are the consequence and not the cause of goodness.

What did Luther have to say about the sacramental element in the Roman Church, which gave it its tremendous power? The Roman Church is essentially a sacramental church. This means that God is essentially seen as present, not as one who is distant and who only demands. A sacramental world-view is one in which the divine is seen as present in a thing, in an act, or in anything which is visible and real. Therefore, a church of the sacrament is a church of the present God. On the other hand, the Roman Church was one in which the sacraments were administered in a magic way by the hierarchy, and only by the hierarchy, so that all who do not participate in them are lost, and those who do participate, even if they are unworthy, receive the sacrament. To this Luther said that no sacrament is effective by itself without full participa-tion of the personal center, that is, without listening to the Word connected with the sacrament, and the faith which accepts it. The sacrament *qua sacrament* cannot help at all. The magical side of sacramental thinking is thus destroyed.

From this it followed that transubstantiation was destroyed, because this doctrine makes the bread and the wine a piece of divine reality inside the shrine and put on the altar. But such a thing does not occur. The presence of God is not a presence in the sense of an objective presence, at a special place, in a special form; it is a presence for the faithful alone. There are two criteria for this: if it is only for the faithful, then it is only an action. Then if you enter a church and the sacrament is spread, you do not need to do anything, because it is pure bread. It becomes more than this only in action, that is, when it is given to those who have faith. For the theory of transubstantiation, it is there all the time. When you enter an empty Roman church, you must bow down before the shrine because God himself is present there, even though no one else is present besides you and this sacrament. Luther abolished this concept of presence. He denounced the *character indelebilis* as a human fiction. There is no such thing as a "character" which cannot be destroyed. If you are called into the ministry, you must minister exactly as everyone else does in his profession. If you leave the ministry, and become a businessman or professor or shoemaker, you are no longer a minister and you retain no sacramental power at all. Any pious Christian, on the other hand, can have the power of the priest in relation to others. But this does not require ordination.

In this way the sacramental foundation of the whole hierarchical system was removed. But most important was Luther's attack on the Mass. The Mass is a sacrifice *we* bring to God, but in reality we have nothing to bring to God, and therefore the Mass is a blasphemy, a sacrilege. It is a blasphemy because here man gives something to God, instead of expecting the gift of God himself in Christ. And nothing more than this is needed.

3. *His Conflict with Erasmus*

The representative of humanism at this time was Erasmus of Rotterdam. At the beginning Luther and Erasmus were friendly toward each other, but then their attacks on each other created a break between Protestantism and humanism which has not been healed up to the present time, in spite of the fact that Zwingli tried to do it as early as the twenties of the sixteenth century. Erasmus was a humanist, but a Christian humanist; he was not antireligious at all. He believed himself to be a better Christian than any pope of his time. But as a humanist he had characteristics which distinguished him from the prophet. Luther could not stand Erasmus' nonexistential detachment, his lack of passion toward the religious content, his detached scholarly attitude toward the contents of the

Christian faith. He felt that in Erasmus there was a lack of concern for matters of ultimate concern.

Secondly, Erasmus was a scholarly skeptic, as every scholar has to be in regard to the traditions and the meaning of the words he has to interpret. Luther could not stand this skeptical attitude. For him absolute statements on matters of ultimate concern are needed. Thirdly, Luther was a radical, in political as well as in other respects. Erasmus seemed to be a man willing to adapt to the political situation—not for his own sake but in order to have peace on earth. Fourthly, Erasmus had a strongly educational point of view. What was decisive for him was the development of the individual in educational terms. All humanism, then and now, has had this educational drive and passion. Fifthly, Erasmus' criticism was of a rational kind, lacking in revolutionary aggressiveness.

The whole discussion between Luther and Erasmus finally focused on the doctrine of the freedom of the will. Erasmus was for human freedom; Luther against it. But this needs to be qualified. Neither Erasmus nor Luther had any doubts about man's psychological freedom. They did not think of man as a stone or an animal. They knew that man is essentially free, that he is man only because he is free. But on this basis they drew opposite conclusions. For Erasmus this freedom is valid also in coming to God. You can help God and cooperate with him for your salvation. For Luther this is impossible. It takes the honor away from God and from Christ and makes man something he is not. So Luther speaks of the "enslaved will". It is the free will which is enslaved. It is ridiculous to say that a stone has no free will. Only he who has a free will can be said to have an enslaved will, that is, enslaved by the demonic forces of reality. For Luther the only point of certainty can be justification by faith, and no contribution of ours to salvation can give us consolation. Luther said that in Erasmus the meaning of Christ is denied and finally the honor of God is denied.

Here we see a fundamental difference between two attitudes. The attitude of the humanist is detached analysis, and if it comes to synthesis, it is that of the moralist, not that of the prophet who sees everything in the light of God alone.

4. His Conflict with the Evangelical Radicals

Luther's conflict with the evangelical radicals is especially important for American Protestants because the prevailing type of Christianity in America was not produced by the Reformation directly, but by the indirect effect of the Reformation through the movement of evangelical radicalism.

The evangelical radicals were all dependent on Luther. Tendencies of this kind existed long before in the Middle Ages, but Luther liberated them from the suppression to which they were condemned. Almost all of Luther's emphases were accepted by the evangelical radicals, but they went beyond him. They had the feeling that Luther stood half-way. First of all, they attacked Luther's principle of Scripture. God has not spoken only in the past, and has now become silent. He always speaks; he speaks in the hearts or depths of any man who is prepared by his own cross to hear. The Spirit is in the depths of the heart, although not of ourselves but of God. Thomas Müntzer, who was the most creative of the evangelical radicals, said that it is always possible for the Spirit to speak through individuals. But in order to receive the Spirit, a man must share the cross. Luther, he said, preaches a sweet Christ, the Christ of forgiveness. We must also preach the bitter Christ, the Christ who calls us to take his cross upon ourselves. The cross is, we could say, the boundary situation. It is internal and external. In an astonishing way Müntzer expressed this in modern existentialist categories. If a man realizes his human finiteness, it produces in him a disgust about the whole world. Then he really becomes poor in spirit. The anxiety of creaturely existence grasps him, and he finds that courage is impossible. Then it happens that God appears to him and he is transformed. When this has happened to him, he can receive special revelations. He can have personal visions, not only about theology as a whole, but about matters of daily life.

On the basis of these ideas these radicals felt that they were the real fulfillment of the Reformation, and that Luther remained half-Catholic. They felt that they were the elect. Whereas the Roman Church offered no certainty to any individual with respect to justification, and whereas Luther had the certainty of justification but not of election, and whereas Calvin had the certainty not only of justification but also to a great extent of election, Müntzer and his followers had the certainty of being elected within a group of the elect; they were the sectarian group.

From the point of view of the inner Spirit, all the sacraments fall down. The immediacy of the procession of the Spirit makes even what was left of the office of the minister unnecessary in the sectarian groups. Instead of that they have another impetus, which could express itself in two ways. One movement would transform society by suffering, and if society could not be changed, they could abstain from arms and oaths and public office and whatever involves people in the political order. Another group of radicals would overcome the evil society by political measures, and even by the sword.

The evangelical radicals are also referred to as enthusiasts. Their emphasis is on the presence of the divine Spirit, not on the biblical writings as such. The Spirit may be present in an individual in every moment, even giving counsels for activities in daily life. Luther had a different feeling. His was basically the feeling of the wrath of God, of God who is the judge. This was his central experience. Therefore, when he speaks of the presence of the Spirit, he does so in terms of repentance, or personal wrestling, which makes it impossible to have the Spirit as a possession. This seems to me the difference between the Reformers and all perfectionist and pietistic attitudes. Luther and the other Reformers placed the main emphasis on the distance of God from man. Hence, the Neo-Reformation theology of today in people like Barth stresses continually that God is in heaven and man is on earth. This feeling of distance—or of repentance, as Kierkegaard said—is the normal relationship of man to God.

The second point in which the theology of the Reformation differs from the theology of the radical evangelical movements has to do with the meaning of the cross. For the Reformers the cross is the objective event of salvation and not the personal experience of creatureliness. Therefore, the participation in the cross in terms of human weakness or moral endeavor to take one's weakness upon oneself is not the real problem with which the Reformation deals. Of course, this is presupposed. We have these same nuances among us today, wherein some of us, following the theology of the Reformation, emphasize more the objectivity of salvation through the cross of Christ, and others more the taking of the cross upon oneself. These two aspects are not contradictions in any way, but as with most problems of human existence, it is more a matter of emphasis than of exclusiveness. It is clear that those of us who are influenced by the Reformation tradition emphasize more the objectivity of the cross of Christ, as the self-sacrifice of God in man, while others coming from the evangelical tradition, so strong in America, emphasize more taking one's own cross upon oneself, the cross of misery.

Thirdly, in Luther the revelation is always connected with the objectivity of the historical revelation in the Scriptures, and not in the innermost center of the human soul. Luther felt that it was pride for the sectarians to believe that it is possible to have immediate revelation in the actual human situation apart from the historical revelation embodied in the Bible.

Fourthly, Luther and the whole Reformation, including Zwingli, emphasized infant baptism as the symbol of the prevenient grace of God, which means that it is not dependent on the subjective reaction. Luther and Calvin believed that baptism is a divine miracle. The decisive thing is that God initiates the action, and that much can happen before the human response. The time difference between the event of baptism and the indefinite moment of maturity does not mean anything in the sight of God. Baptism is the divine offer of forgiveness, and a person must always return to this. Adult baptism, on the other hand, lays stress on the subjective participation, the ability of the mature man to decide.

Luther and the other Reformers were also concerned about the way in which the sects isolated themselves, claiming that they were the true church and that their members were the elect. Such a thing was unthinkable for the Reformers, and I think they were right on this. It is well known that the sects of the Reformation were psychologically lacking in love towards those who did not belong to their sect. Some of you probably have had similar experiences with sectarian or quasi-sectarian groups today. What is most lacking in them is not theological insight, not even insight into their own negatives, but love, that love which identifies with the negative situation in which we all are.

A final difference had to do with eschatology. The eschatology of the Reformers caused them to negate the revolutionary criticism of the state that we find in the sectarian movements. The Reformation eschatology of the coming kingdom of God moved along a vertical line, and had nothing to do with the horizontal line, which was, so to speak, given to the devil anyway. Luther often spoke of the beloved last day for which he longed in order to be liberated, not so much from the "wrath of the theologians" as with Melanchthon, but from the power play which was no nicer then than it is now. This difference in mood is visible in a comparison of the state of things in Europe and America. Under the influence of the evangelical radical movements the tendency in America is to transform reality. In Europe, especially after two World Wars, there is an eschatological feeling—the desire for and vision of the end in a realistic sense—and a resignation of Christians in the face of power plays.

5. Luther's Doctrines

(a) The Biblical Principle

Whenever you see a monument of Luther, he is represented with the Bible in hand. This is somewhat misleading, and the Catholic Church is right in saying that there was biblicism throughout the Middle Ages. We have stressed before that the biblicistic attitude was especially strong in the late Middle Ages. We saw that in Ockham, the nominalist, a radical criticism of the church was made on the basis of the Bible. Nevertheless, the biblical principle means something else in Luther. In nominalistic theology the Bible was the law of the church which could be turned against the actual church; but it was still law. In the Renaissance the Bible is the source-book of the true religion, to be edited by good philologists such as Erasmus. These were the two prevailing attitudes: the legal attitude in nominalism, the doctrinal attitude in humanism. Neither of these was able to break through the fundamentals of the Catholic system. Only a new principle of biblical interpretation could break through the nominalistic and humanistic doctrines.

Luther had many of the nominalistic and humanistic elements within himself. He valued very highly Erasmus' edition of the New Testament, and he often fell back on a nominalistic legalism in his doctrine of inspiration whereby every word of the Bible has been inspired by the dictation of God. This happened in his defense of the doctrines of the Lord's Supper, when a literal interpretation of a biblical passage seemed to support his point of view. But beyond all this Luther had an interpretation of Scripture in unity with his new understanding of man's relationship to God. This can be made clear if we understand what he meant by the "Word of God". This term is used more often than any other in the Lutheran tradition and in the Neo-Reformation theology of Barth and others. Yet it is more misleading than we can perhaps realize. In Luther himself it has at least six different meanings.

Luther said—but he knew better—that the Bible is the Word of God. However, when he really wanted to express what he meant, he said that *in* the Bible there is the Word of God, the message of the Christ, his work of atonement, the forgiveness of sins, and the offer of salvation. He makes it very clear that it is the message of the gospel which is in the Bible, and thus the Bible contains the Word of God. He also said that the message existed before the Bible, namely, in the preaching of the apostles. As Calvin also later said, Luther stated that the writing which resulted in the books of the Bible was an emergency situation; it was necessary and it was an emergency. Therefore, only the religious content is important; the message is an object of experience. "If I know what I believe, I know the content of the Scripture, since the Scripture does not contain anything except Christ." The criterion of apostolic truth is the Scripture, and the standard of what things are true in the Scripture is whether they deal with Christ and his work—*ob sie Christum treiben*, whether they deal with, concentrate on, or drive toward Christ. Only those books of the Bible which deal with Christ and his work contain powerfully and spiritually the Word of God.

From this point of view Luther was able to make some distinctions among the books of the Bible. The books which deal with Christ most centrally are the Fourth Gospel, the Epistles of Paul, and I Peter. Luther could say very courageous things. For instance, he said that Judas and Pilate would be apostolic if they gave the message of Christ, and Paul and John would not be if they did not give the message of Christ. He even said that anyone today who had the Spirit as powerfully as the prophets and apostles could create new Decalogues and another Testament. We must drink from their fountain only because we do not have the fullness of the Spirit. This is, of course, extremely anti-nominalistic and anti-humanistic. It emphasizes the spiritual character of the Bible. The

Bible is a creation of the divine Spirit in those who have written it, but it is not a dictation. On this basis Luther was able to proceed with a half-religious, half-historical criticism of the biblical books. It does not mean anything whether the five books of Moses were written by Moses or not. He knew very well that the texts of the prophets are in great disorder. He also knew that the concrete prophecies of the prophets often proved to be in error. The Book of Esther and the Revelation of John do not really belong to the Scriptures. The Fourth Gospel excels the Synoptics in value and power, and the Epistle of James has no evangelical character at all.

Although Lutheran Orthodoxy was unable to preserve this great prophetic aspect of Luther, one thing was accomplished by Luther's freedom; it was possible for Protestantism to do something which no other religion in the whole world has been able to do, and that is to accept the historical treatment of the biblical literature. This is often referred to by such misleading terms as higher criticism or biblical criticism. It is simply the historical method applied to the holy books of a religion. This is something which is impossible in Catholicism, or at least possible in a very limited way only. It is impossible in Islam. Professor Jeffery once told the faculty that every Islamic scholar who would try to do what he did with the text of the Koran would be in danger. Research into the original text of the Koran would imply historical criticism of the present text, and this is impossible in a legalistic religion. Thus, if we are legalists with respect to the Bible, in terms of the dictation theory, we fall back to the stage of religion which we find in Islam, and we share none of the Protestant freedom that we find in Luther.

Luther was able to interpret the ordinary text of the Bible in his sermons and writings without taking refuge in a special pneumatic, spiritual, or allegorical interpretation alongside of the philological interpretation. The ideal of a theological seminary is to interpret the Bible in such a way that the exact philological method, including higher criticism, is combined with an existential application of the biblical texts to the questions we have to ask, and which are supposed to be answered in systematic theology. The division of the faculty into "experts" is a very unwholesome state of affairs, where the New Testament man tells me that I cannot discuss a certain problem because I am not an expert, or I say that I cannot discuss a matter because I am not an expert in Old or New Testament. Insofar as we all do this, we are sinning against the original meaning of Luther's attempt to remove the allegorical method of interpretation and to return to a philological approach which is at the same time spiritual. These are very real problems today, and students can do a great deal about them by refusing to let their professors be merely "experts" and no longer theologians. They should ask the biblical man about the existential meaning of what he finds, and the systematic theologian about the biblical foundation of his statements, in the actual biblical texts as they are philologically understood.

(b) Sin and Faith

I want to emphasize Luther's doctrines of sin and faith very much because they are points in which the Reformation is far superior to what we find today in popular Christianity. For Luther sin is unbelief. "Unbelief is the real sin." "Nothing justifies except faith, and nothing makes sinful except unbelief." "Unbelief is the sin altogether." "The main justice is faith, and so the main evil is unbelief." "Therefore the word 'sin' includes what we are living and doing besides the faith in God." These statements presuppose a concept of faith which has nothing whatsoever to do with the acceptance of doctrines. With respect to the concept of sin, they mean that differences of quantity (heavy and light sins) and of relativity (sins which can be forgiven in this or that way) do not matter at all. Everything which separates us from God has equal weight; there is no "more or less" about it.

For Luther, life as a whole, its nature and substance, is corrupted. Here we must comment on the term "total depravity" which we often hear. This does not mean that there is nothing good in man; no Reformer or Neo-Reformation theologian ever said that. It means that there are no special parts of man which are exempt from existential distortion. The concept of total depravity would be translated by a modern psychologist in the sense that man is distorted, or in conflict with himself, in the center of his personal life. Everything in man is included in this distortion, and this is what Luther meant. If "total depravity" is taken in the absurd way, it would be impossible for a man to say that he is totally depraved. A totally depraved man would not say that he is totally depraved. Even saying that we are sinful presupposes something beyond sin. What we can say is that there is no section in man which is not touched by self-contradiction; this includes the intellect and all other things. The evil are evil because they do not fulfill the one command to love God. It is the lack of love toward God which is the basis of sin. Or, it is the lack of faith. Luther said both things. But faith always precedes love because it is an act in which we receive God, and love is the act in which we are united with God. Everybody is in this situation of sin, and nobody knew more than Luther about the structural power of evil in individuals and in groups. He did not call it compulsion, as we do today in terms of modern psychology. But he knew that this is what it was, a demonic power, the power of Satan, which is greater than individual decisions. These structures of the demonic are realities; Luther knew that sin cannot be understood merely in terms of particular acts of freedom. Sin must be understood in terms of a structure, a demonic structure which has compulsory power over everyone, and which can be counterbalanced only by a structure of grace. We are all involved in the conflict between these two structures. Sometimes we are ridden, as Luther described it, by the divine compulsion, sometimes by the demonic. However, the divine structure of grace is not possession or compulsion, because it is at the same time liberating; it liberates what we essentially are.

Luther's strong emphasis on the demonic powers comes out in his doctrine of the devil, whom he understood as an organ of the divine wrath or as the divine wrath itself. There are statements in Luther which are not clear as to whether he is speaking of the wrath of God or of the devil. Actually, they are the same for him. As we see God, so he is for us. If we see him in the demonic mask, then he is that to us, and he destroys us. If we see him in the infant Jesus, where in his lowliness he makes his love visible to us, then he has this love to us. Luther was a depth psychologist in the profoundest way, without knowing the methodological research we know today. Luther saw these things in non-moralistic depths, which were lost not only in Calvinist Christianity but to a great extent in Lutheranism as well.

Faith for Luther is receiving God when he gives himself to us. He distinguished this type of faith from historical faith (*fides historica*), which acknowledges historical facts. Faith is the acceptance of the gift of God, the presence of the grace of God which

grasps us. The emphasis is on the receptive character of faith—
nihil facere sed tantum recipere, doing nothing but only receiving.
These ideas are all concentrated in the acceptance of being
accepted, in the forgiveness of sins, which brings about a quiet
conscience and a spiritual vitality toward God and man. "Faith
is a living and restless thing. The right living faith can by no means
be lazy." The element of knowledge in faith is an existential
element, and everything else follows from it. "Faith makes the
person; the person makes the works, not works the person." This
is confirmed by everything we know today in depth psychology.
It is the ultimate meaning of life which makes a person. A split
personality is not one which does not do good works. There are
many people who do many good works, but who lack the ultimate
center. This ultimate center is what Luther calls faith. And this
makes a person. This faith is not an acceptance of doctrines, not
even Christian doctrines, but the acceptance of the power itself
out of which we come and to which we go, whatever the doctrines
may be through which we accept it. In my book, *The Courage to
Be,* I have called this "absolute faith", a faith which can lose every
concrete content and still exist as an absolute affirmation of life
as life and of being as being. Thus, the only negative thing is what
Luther calls unbelief, a state of not being united with the power
of being itself, with the divine reality over against the forces of
separation and compulsion.

(c) The Idea of God

Luther's idea of God is one of the most powerful in the whole
history of human and Christian thought. This is not a God who
is a being beside others; it is a God whom we can have only
through contrast. What is hidden before God is visible before
the world, and what is hidden before the world is visible before
God. "Which are the virtues (i.e., powers of being) of God?
Infirmity, passion, cross, persecution: these are the weapons of
God." "The power of man is emptied by the cross, but in the
weakness of the cross the divine power is present." About the state
of man Luther says: "Being man means non-being, becoming,
being. It means being in privation, in possibility, in action. It
means always being in sin, in justification, in justice. It means
always being a sinner, a penitent, a just one." This is a paradoxical
way of speaking, but it makes clear what Luther means with

respect to God. God can be seen only through the law of contrast.

Luther denies everything which can make God finite, or a being beside others. "Nothing is so small, God is even smaller. Nothing is so large, God is even larger. He is an unspeakable being, above and outside everything we can name and think. Who knows what that is, which is called 'God'? It is beyond body, beyond spirit, beyond everything we can say, hear, and think." He makes the great statement that God is nearer to all creatures than they are to themselves. "God has found the way that his own divine essence can be completely in all creatures, and in everyone especially, deeper, more internally, more present, than the creature is to itself and at the same time nowhere and cannot be comprehended by anyone, so that he embraces all things and is within them. God is at the same time in every piece of sand totally, and nevertheless in all, above all, and out of all creatures." In these formulae the old conflict between the theistic and pantheistic tendencies in the doctrine of God is solved; they show the greatness of God, the inescapability of his presence, and at the same time, his absolute transcendence. And I would say very dogmatically that any doctrine of God which leaves out one of these elements does not really speak of God but of something less than God.

The same thing is expressed in Luther's doctrine of omnipotence. "I call the omnipotence of God not that power by which he does not do many things he could do, but the actual power by which he potently does everything in everything." That is to say, God does not sit beside the world, looking at it from the outside, but he is acting in everything in every moment. This is what omnipotence means. The absurd idea of a God who calculates whether he should do what he could do is removed by this idea of God as creative power.

Luther speaks of creatures as the "masks" of God; God is hidden behind them. "All creatures are God's masks and veils in order to make them work and help him to create many things." Thus, all natural orders and institutions are filled with divine presence, and so is the historical process. In this way he deals with all our problems of the interpretation of history. The great men in history, the Hannibals, Alexanders, Napoleons—and today he would add, the Hitlers—or, the Goths, the Vandals, the Turks—and today he would add, the Nazis and the Communists—are driven by God to attack and to destroy, and in this way God is speaking to us through them. They are God's Word to us, even to the church. The heroic persons in particular break through the ordinary rules of life. They are armed by God. God calls and forces them, and gives them their hour, and I would say, their *kairos*. Outside of this *kairos* they cannot do anything; nobody can apart from the right hour. And in the right hour no one can resist those who then act. However, in spite of the fact that God acts in everything in history, history is nonetheless the struggle between God and Satan and their different realms. The reason Luther could make these two statements is that God works creatively even in the demonic forces. They could not have being if they were not dependent on God as the ground of being, as the creative power of being in them, in every moment. He makes it possible that Satan is the seducer; at the same time he makes it possible that Satan is conquered.

(d) The Doctrine of Christ

What is interesting in Luther's christology is first of all his method, which is quite different from that of the ancient church. I would call it a real method of correlation; it correlates what Christ is for us with what we say about him. It is an approach from the point of view of the effects Christ has upon us. Melanchthon expressed the same idea in his *Loci*. He says that the object of christology is to deal with the benefits of Christ, not with his person and natures apart from his benefits. In describing this method of correlation Luther says: "As somebody is in himself, so is God to him, as object. If a man is righteous himself, God is righteous. If a man is pure, God is pure for him. If he is evil, God is evil for him. Therefore, he will appear to the damned as the evil in eternity, but to the righteous as the righteous, according to what he is in himself." This is a correlative way of speaking about God. For Luther, calling Christ God means having experienced divine effects which come from Christ, especially the forgiveness of sins. If you speak about God apart from his effects, this is a wrong objectifying method. You must speak of him in terms of the effects he can have. The One whose effects are divine must himself be divine—this is the criterion.

What we say about God always has the character of participation—suffering with him, being glorified with him; crucified with him, being resurrected with him. "Preaching the Crucified means preaching our guilt and the crucifixion of our evils." "So we go with him: first servant, therefore now King; first suffering, therefore now in glory; first judged, therefore now Judge. . . . So you must act: first humiliation, in order to get exaltation." "Together condemned and blessed, living and dead, in pain and in joy." This is said of Christ and of us. The law of contradiction, the law of God always acting paradoxically, is fulfilled in Christ. He is the key to God's acting by contradicting the human system of valuation. This paradox is also valid in the church. In its visible form the church is miserable and humble, but in this humility, as in the humility of Christ, there is the glory of the church. Therefore, the glory of the church is especially visible in periods of persecution, suffering, and humility.

Christ is God for us, our God, God as he is in relationship to us. Luther also says that he is the Word of God. From this point of view Protestantism should think through its christology in existential terms, maintaining the immediate correlation of human faith and what is said about Christ. All the formulae concerning his divine and human natures, or his being the Son of God and Son of Man, make sense only if they are existentially understood.

Luther emphasizes very much the presence of God in Christ. In the incarnation the divine Word or Logos has become flesh. Luther's doctrine of the Word has different stages. First, there is the internal Word, which he also calls the heart of God, or the eternal Son. Only this internal Word, which is God's inner self-manifestation, is perfect. As the heart of man is hidden, so the heart of God is hidden. The internal Word of God, his inner self-manifestation, is hidden to man. But Luther says: "We hope that in the future we shall look to this Word, when God has opened his heart . . . by introducing us into his heart." The second meaning of the Word in Luther is Christ as the visible Word. In Christ the heart of God has become flesh, that is, historical reality. In this way we can have the hidden Word of the divine knowledge of himself, although only for faith, and never as an object among other objects. Thirdly, the Word of God is the spoken Word, by prophets, by Jesus, and the apostles. Thus, it becomes the biblical Word in which the internal Word is spoken forth. However, the revealing being of the eternal Word in Christ is more than all the spoken words of the Bible. They witness to him, but they are the Word of God only in an indirect way. Luther was never so bibliolatrous as so many Christians still are today. Word for Luther was the self-manifestation of God, and this was by no means limited to the words of the Bible. The Word of God is in, with, and under the words of the Bible, but not identical with them. The fourth meaning of the Word of God is the word of preaching, but this is only number four. If somebody speaks of the "church of the Word", whereby he is thinking of the predominance of preaching in the services, he is certainly not being a follower of Luther in this respect.

The special character of Luther's doctrine of the incarnation is the continual emphasis on the smallness of God in the incarnation. Man cannot stand the naked Absolute—God; he is driven to despair if he deals with the Absolute directly. For this reason God has given the Christ, in whom he has made himself small. "In the other works, God is recognized according to the greatness of his power, wisdom, and justice, and his works appear too terrible. But here (in Christ) appears his sweetness, mercy and charity." Without knowing Christ we are not able to stand God's majesty and are driven to insanity and hatred. This is the reason for Luther's great interest in Christmas; he wrote some of the most beautiful Christmas hymns and poems. He liked Christmas because he emphasized the small God in Christ, and Christ is the smallest in the cradle. This paradox was for Luther the real meaning of Christmas, that the One who is in the cradle is at the same time the Almighty God. The smallest and most helpless of all beings has within himself the center of divinity. This is Luther's way of thinking of the paradoxical nature of God's self-revelation. Because God acts paradoxically the weakest is the strongest.

(e) Church and State

Anyone who knows the Reformation must ask whether it is possible for a church to live on the basis of the principles of the Reformation. Does not the church have to be a community, organized and authoritarian, with fixed rules and traditions? Is not a church necessarily Catholic, and does not the Protestant principle contradict the possibility of having a church, namely, the principle that God alone is everything and man's acceptance of God is only secondary?

Now, there is no doubt that Luther's doctrine of the church is his weakest point. The problem of the church was the most unsolved problem which the Reformation left to future generations. The reason is that the Catholic system was not replaced and could not be replaced definitively by a Protestant system of equal power, because of the anti-authoritarian and anti-hierarchical form of Protestant thinking. Luther, together with Zwingli and Calvin, chose the ecclesiastical type of church in contrast to the sectarian type of the evangelical radicals. This is a distinction which comes from Ernst Troeltsch, and a very good one. The ecclesiastical type of church is the mother from which we come. It is always there and we belong to it from birth; we did not choose it. When we awaken out of the dimness of the early stages of life, we can perhaps reaffirm that we belong to it in confirmation, but we already belong to it objectively. This is quite different from the churches of the radical enthusiasts, where the individual who decides that he wants to be a member of the church is the creative power of the church. The church is made by a covenant through the decision of individuals to form a church, an assembly of God. Everything here is dependent on the independent individual, who is not born from the mother church, but who creates active church communities. These differences are most noticeable if you contrast the ecclesiastical type of church on the European continent with the sectarian type in America, which is even expressed in the main denominations here.

Luther's distinction between the visible and the invisible church is one of the most difficult things to understand. The main point we must insist on in understanding what Luther means is that they are the same church, not two churches. The invisible church is the spiritual quality of the visible church. And the visible church is the empirical and always distorted actualization of the spiritual church. This was perhaps the most important point of the Reformers against the sects. The sects wanted to identify the church according to its visible and its invisible sides. The visible church must be purified and purged—as all totalitarian groups call it today—of anyone who is not spiritually a member of the church. This presupposes that we can know who is spiritually a member of the church, that we can judge by looking into the heart. But this is something only God can do. The Reformers could not accept this because they knew there is nobody who does not belong to the "infirmary" which is the church. This infirmary is the visible church and is for everyone; nobody can get out of it definitely. Therefore, everybody belongs to the church essentially, even if he is spiritually far away from it.

What is this church? The church in its true essence is an object of faith. As Luther said, it is "hidden in spirit". When you see the actual working of the church, its ministers, the building, the congregation, the administration, the devotions etc., then you know that in this visible church, with all its shortcomings, the invisible church is hidden. It is an object of faith and it demands much faith to believe that in the life of ordinary congregations today, which are by no means of high standing in any respect, the spiritual church is present. This you can believe only if you believe that it is not the people who make the church, but it is the foundation—not the people but the sacramental reality—the Word, which is the Christ. Otherwise we would despair about the church. For Luther and the Reformers the church in its true nature is a spiritual matter. The words "spiritual" and "invisible" usually mean the same thing in Luther. The basis of faith in the church is exclusively the foundation of the church, who is Christ, the sacrament of the Word.

Every Christian is a priest, and thus has potentially the office of preaching the Word and administering the sacraments. They all belong to the spiritual element. For the sake of order, however, some specially fit personalities shall be called by the congregation to fill the offices of the church. The ministry is a matter of order. It is a vocation like all other vocations; it does not involve any state of perfection, superior graces, or anything like that. The layman is as much a priest as any priest. The official priest is the "mouthpiece" of the others, because they cannot express themselves, and he can. Thus, only one thing makes the minister, and that is the call of the congregation. Ordination has no sacramental meaning at all. "Ordaining is not consecrating", he says. "We give in the power of the Word what we have, the authority of preaching the Word and giving the sacraments; that is ordaining." But this does not produce a higher grade in the relationship to God.

In the Lutheran countries the church government very soon became identical with the state government, and in the Calvinist countries with the civil government (trustees). The reason for this is that the hierarchy was removed by Luther. There is no pope, no bishops, no priests any more in the technical sense. Who then shall govern the church? First of all the ministers, but they are not adequate since they have no power. The power comes from the princes, or from free associations within society, as we have very often in Calvinism. The princes were called by Luther the highest bishops of their realms. They are not to interfere with the inner religious affairs of the church; but they have to run the administration—the *ius circa sacrum*, the law around the sacred. The ministers and every Christian are to take care of the sacred matters.

Such a solution was brought about by an emergency situation. There were no bishops or ecclesiastical authorities any more, and the church needed administration and government. So emergency bishops were created, and there was nobody else who could be this except the electors and princes. Out of this emergency situation there began to emerge the state church in Germany. The church became more or less—and I think rather "more" than "less"—a department of the state administration, and the princes became the arbiters of the church. This was not intended, but it shows that a church needs a political backbone. In Catholicism it was the pope and the hierarchy; in Protestantism it had to be the outstanding members of the community who take over, either the princes or social groups, as in more democratic countries.

Luther's doctrine of the state is not easy to deal with because many people believe that Luther's interpretation of the state is the real cause of Nazism. Now, first of all, a few hundred years mean something in history, and Luther is a little bit older than the Nazis! But this is not the decisive point. The decisive point is that the doctrine of the state was a positivistic doctrine; providence was positivistically understood. Positivism means that things are taken as they are. The positive law is decisive, and this is connected by Luther with the doctrine of providence. Providence brings this and that power into existence, and therefore it is impossible to revolt against these powers. You have no rational criterion by which to judge the princes. Of course, you have the right to judge them from the point of view whether they are good Christians or not. But whether they are or not, they are God-given, and so you have to be obedient to them. Historical destiny has brought the tyrants, the Neros and Hitlers.

Since this is historical destiny, we have to subject ourselves to it.

This means that the Stoic doctrine of natural law, which can be used as a criticism of the positive law, has disappeared. There remains only the positive law. The natural law does not really exist for Luther. The Stoic doctrine of the equality and the freedom of the citizen in the state is not used by Luther at all. So he is non-revolutionary, theoretically as well as practically. Practically, he says, every Christian must put up with bad government because it comes from God providentially. The state for Luther is not a reality in itself. It is always misleading to speak of the Reformers' theory of state. The word "state" is not older than the seventeenth or eighteenth century. Instead of that they had the concept of *Obrigkeit*, of authority, superiors. The government is the authority, not the structure called the "state". This means there is no democratic implication in Luther's doctrine of the state. The situation is such that the state must be accepted as it is.

How could Luther maintain this? How could he accept the despotic power of the states of his time inasmuch as he, more than anyone else, emphasized love as the ultimate principle of morality? He had an answer to this, and this answer is very much full of spirit. He says that God does two kinds of work. The one is his own proper work; this is the work of love and mercy, the giving of grace. The other is his strange work; it is also the work of love, but a strange one. It works through punishment, threat, the compulsory power of the state, through all kinds of harshness, as the law demands. People who say this is against love ask the question: How can compulsory power and love be united with each other? And they derive from this a kind of anarchism which we so often find in the ideas of Christian pacifists and others. The situation formulated by Luther seems to me the true one. I believe he saw more profoundly than anybody I know, the possibility of uniting the elements of power and love in terms of this doctrine of God's "strange" and "proper" works. The power of the state, which makes it possible for us even to be here or for works of charity to be done at all, is a work of God's love. The state has to suppress the aggression of the evil man, of those who are against love; the strange work of love is to destroy what is against love. It is correct to call this a strange work, but it is nevertheless a work of love. Love would cease to be a power on earth altogether without destroying that which is against love. This is the deepest insight into the relationship between power and love that I know. The whole positivistic doctrine of the state makes it impossible for Lutheranism, from a theological point of view, to accept revolution. Revolution results in chaos; even if it tries to produce order, it first produces chaos and disorder increases. Thus, Luther was unambiguously against revolution. He accepted the positively given gift of destiny.

Nazism was possible in Germany because of this positivistic authoritarianism, because of Luther's affirmation that the given prince cannot be removed. This provided a great inhibition against any German revolution. But I do not believe that this would have been possible anyway in the modern totalitarian systems. But the negation of any revolution did serve as an additional spiritual cause. When we say that Luther is responsible for the Nazis, we are uttering a lot of nonsense. The ideology of the Nazis is almost the opposite of Luther's. Luther had no nationalistic ideology, no tribal or racial ideology. He praised the Turks for their good government. From this point of view there is no Nazism in Luther. There is a connection only from the point of view of the conservatism of Luther's political thinking. But this is nothing else than a consequence of his basic presupposition. The only truth in the theory which connects Luther with Nazism is that Luther broke the back of the revolutionary will in the Germans. There is no such thing as a revolutionary will in the German people; that is all we can say and nothing more.

It is equally nonsensical for people to say that it was first Luther and then Hegel who produced Nazism. It is nonsense, because even if Hegel said that the state is God on earth, he did not mean the power state. He meant the cultural unity of religion and social life organized in a state. In this sense Hegel could say there is a unity of church and state. But for him "state" is not the party movement of the Nazis, or a relapse to a tribal system. State for him is organized society, repressing sin.

B. HULDREICH ZWINGLI

Zwingli was not as original a theologian as Luther was. He was partly dependent and partly independent of Luther. It is not easy to describe the character of Zwinglian Christianity. Zwingli was very much influenced by the humanists. He remained his whole life a friend of Erasmus. Neither he nor Melanchthon separated themselves from Erasmus as Luther did. They were humanists as well as being Christians. They were Christian humanists. This is especially clear in a man like Zwingli. The authority of the Scriptures in Zwingli is based on the call of the Renaissance: Back to the sources! The Bible is the revelation of God. "God himself wants to be the schoolmaster." Luther could never have said such a thing. For Luther God is much more powerful than a schoolmaster. The decisive difference is that Zwingli had a fully developed doctrine of the Spirit, which was lacking in Luther and the other Reformers. "God can give truth, through the Spirit, in non-Christians also." The truth is given to every individual always through the Holy Spirit, and this Spirit is present even if the word of the Bible is not present. This was in some sense a liberation from the biblical burden which Luther placed upon the people.

Luther had a dynamic form of Christian life. Zwingli, and Calvin too, had a static one; faith is psychological health. If you are psychologically healthy, then you can have faith, and vice versa. Actually, these two things are identical. Faith for Luther is a dynamic thing, reaching heights and depths. For Zwingli it is much more humanistically balanced. It is similar to the bourgeois ideal of health. "Christian faith is a thing which is felt in the soul of the faithful like health in the body." In Luther there is a continual dying and rising of the community with the personal God of wrath and love. In Zwingli the union with God is not dynamic in this way. Zwingli is progressive; Luther is paradoxical. It is difficult to speak of the paradox on Zwinglian soil. Either the paradox is dissolved or it has to be accepted as such. The basic difference, then, between Zwingli and Luther is this: The paradox of the Christian life against the rational progressivism of the Christian life.

The Swiss Reformation is a synthesis of Reformation and humanism. Calvin, whom we shall deal with later, was dependent on both Zwingli and Luther, but in spite of the fact that he turned from Zwingli back to Luther, to a certain extent, he was also humanistically educated and his writings show the classical erudition in style and content. However, whenever liberal theology arose from the seventeenth through the nineteenth centuries, it developed more in line with Zwingli than with Calvin. I have already stated that Zwingli believed that the Spirit is working directly in the human soul, that his ordinary way of working is through the Word of the Bible, but that God can also work in an extraordinary way in people who have never had any contact with the Christian message, with people in other religions and in humanists. Zwingli's examples are taken mostly from the Greek philosophers, such as Socrates, etc.

Yesterday I read a hymn to be sung by a congregation of Southern Negroes or Midwestern peasants which included Socrates in it, besides Christ and Luther. I do not think it wise to bring theology into a hymn in this way. If people like Zwingli and Calvin speak of revelation and salvation in men like Socrates and Seneca, they are making a mistake. The mistake is that they choose only certain representatives of pagan piety. However, pagan piety is exactly the same as Christian piety in this respect that it is just as intensive in the common people who are really pious in their knowledge of God, and people in this class should have been mentioned just as much. But since they were good humanists, they mentioned only their own sociological class, people who were not only great men but who also belonged to the intelligentsia. If you are ministers, it is better to decide not to incorporate such things into a hymn. Although I have given you as much Socrates and Plato as I can, nevertheless, I do not sing to them.

Zwingli defines God as the universal dynamic power of being in everything that is. In this sense you can recognize some of my own theological thinking in Zwingli and Calvin, but also in Luther. However, in the humanistic form in which Zwingli conceived of God, it has a much more rational deterministic character. God works through the natural law. Thus, Zwingli's doctrine of predestination is colored by a rational determinism. The same thing is true of Calvin's doctrine, whereas in Luther there is more of Ockhamism and Scotism, and therefore a sense of the irrational acting of God in every moment, which cannot be subjected to any law.

The law plays a different role in the Lutheran and Zwinglian Reformation. In Zwingli it is not the law which makes us sinful, but the law shows that we are sinful, whereas Luther had the profound insight that we have rediscovered in modern psychology that the law produces resistance, and thus, as Paul said, it makes sin more sinful. This was lacking in both Zwinglian and Calvinistic thinking. The concept of law in them has a very positive connotation. This refers generally to natural law. And natural law means in ancient literature primarily the law of reason, the logical, ethical, and juristic law. Secondly, it is also the physical law. We should not think of physics when we read about natural law in books of antiquity. Usually it means the ethical law within us, which belongs to our being and is restated by the Decalogue and the Sermon on the Mount. It exists by nature, by created nature, and is that which we are essentially. This kind of law is much more in the minds of Zwingli and Calvin than in Luther's. Luther detested the idea that God has established a law between himself and his world, between himself and the finite actions and things and decisions. He wanted everything as nonrational, nonlegal, as possible, not only in the process of salvation but also in the interpretation of history and nature. Zwingli and Calvin accepted nature in terms of law. Thus, when Immanuel Kant defined nature as a realm in which physical law is valid, this was much more Calvinistic and Zwinglian; in any case, it was not Lutheran. For Luther nature is the mask of God through which he acts with mankind in an irrational way—very similarly to the Book of Job. The attitude towards nature in Zwinglianism and Calvinism is much more in accordance with the demands of bourgeois industrialized society to analyze and transform nature for human purposes, while Luther's relationship to nature has much more the sense of the presence of the divine, irrationally, mystically, in everything that is. If I had not known this before, I would have learned it when I came to America.

For Zwingli the law of the gospel is law. It is not only this, of course, since he does accept Luther's doctrine of the forgiveness of sins, as did all the Reformers. At the same time he spoke, however, of a new evangelical law, as the nominalists and humanists did. This law should be the basis of the law of the state. Wyclif and Ockham had the same idea; this shows that at this point there is a Catholic element in Reformed thought, namely, the idea that the gospel can be interpreted as the new law. The term, "the new law", is a very old one, appearing very early in church history. For Luther this would have been an abominable term. The gospel for Luther is grace, and nothing more than grace; it can never be the new law. But for Zwingli this new law is valid not only for the moral situation but also for the state, the political sphere. Politically the law of the gospel determines the laws of the city. If cities do not subject themselves to this law, they may be attacked by other cities which do. This law, Zwingli thought, is against Catholicism, so he started the war against the cantons in Switzerland and died in one of the battles. But the principle remained that the law of the gospel should be the basis of the law of the state. This had a tremendous influence in world history and saved Protestantism from being overwhelmed politically by the Roman Church of the Counter-Reformation.

A deeper element of difference between Luther and Zwingli has to do with the doctrine of the sacraments. The fight between Luther and Zwingli in Marburg in 1529 contrasted two types of religious experience, the one a mystical interpretation of the sacrament, the other an intellectual interpretation. Zwingli said that the sacrament is a "sure sign or seal" which like a symbol serves as a reminder; by partaking of it we express our will to belong to the church. The divine Spirit acts beside the sacraments, not through them. Baptism is a kind of obliging sign, like a badge. It is a commanded symbol, but it has nothing to do with subjective faith and salvation, which are dependent on predestination.

In the controversy on the doctrine of the eucharist, the point at issue was on the surface a matter of translation, but in reality it was a question of a different spirit. The discussion centered on the meaning of the word "is" in the statement: "This is my body." The humanists usually interpret "is" to mean "signifies" or "means". Luther stressed that it must be taken literally; the body of Christ is literally present. For Zwingli it is present for the contemplation of faith, but not *per essentiam et realiter* (by essence and in reality). "The body of Christ is eaten when we believe that he is killed for us." Everything is centered on the subjective side. It is the representation of a past event, not in itself a present event. The present event is merely in the subject, in the mind of the believer. He is certainly with his Spirit present in the mind, but he is not present in nature. Mind can be fed only by mind, or spirit by spirit, and not by nature.

Zwingli maintained against Luther that the body of Christ is in heaven *circumscripte* (by circumscription), that is, in a definite place. Hence, the body of Christ is a particular individual thing; it does not participate in the divine infinity. Just like a man with a body, Christ is finite, and the two natures are sharply separated. The Lord's Supper is a memory and a confession, but not a personal communion with someone who is really present. Luther's emphasis is on the reality of the presence, and to underscore this he invented the doctrines of the omnipresence of the body of the elevated Christ. The presence of Christ is repeated in every act of the sacrament of the Lord's Supper. Historical person and sacramental person are identical. To explain this Luther said: "Where you put God, there you must put humanity; they cannot be severed or separated; it has become one person." To say that the divine character of the bodily Christ is only said in symbolic or metaphoric terms is of the devil. Luther completely rejected the idea that the divinity of Christ is separated from his humanity in heaven. Even in heaven the divinity and the humanity of Christ belong together. He expressed this in the profound and fantastic doctrine of the ubiquity of the body of Christ, the omnipresence of the body of the ascended Christ. Christ is present in everything, in stone and fire and tree, but for us he is present only when he speaks to us. But he can speak to us through everything. This is the idea that God drives toward embodiment or corporeity, and that the omnipresence of Christ's body in the world is the form in which God's eternal power is present in the world. If this is carried through in scholastic terms, and taken literally or superstitiously, it is an absurd doctrine, because it belongs to a body to be circumscribed. But if it is taken symbolically, it becomes a profound doctrine, because it says that God is present in anything on earth. He is always also present with his concrete historical manifestation in Christ. Luther meant this quite primitively, but his meaning is that in every natural object you can have the presence of Christ. In a Lutheran service during the Sundays in spring, you always find a tremendous amount of flowers and things of nature brought into the church, because of this symbol of the participation of the body of Christ in the world.

When the discussion on the Lord's Supper came to an end, the Reformers had reached agreement on many points. They denied the doctrine of transubstantiation; but they could not agree on the ubiquity of Christ's presence. Luther stated that there was a fundamental difference between Zwingli and himself when he said: "They have not the same spirit with us." What does this mean? First of all, it involves the matter of the relationship

between the spiritual and the bodily existence. In Zwingli you
have a humanistic intellectualism which separates the spirit from
the body, a tendency which is ultimately rooted in Neo-Platonism.
Hence, in Calvinism there is a lack of interest in the problem of
expression. For Luther, on the other hand, spirit is present only
in its expressions. The interest is incorporation. Oetinger, the
mystic, said: "Corporeality is the end of the ways of God." Hence,
there followed a great interest in the bodily reality of Christ, in
history and in sacrament. The second spiritual difference has to do
with the religious meaning of nature. In Zwinglian thought nature
is controlled and calculable in terms of regular natural laws. By contrast Luther's dynamic naturalism often goes into the demonic
depths of nature, and is not interested in any laws of nature.

Two Latin phrases were used to express the difference. The
Lutheran formula is *finitum capax infiniti*—the finite is capable of
the infinite. For Zwingli this is impossible. The Reformed formula
is *finitum non capax infiniti*—the finite is not able to have the
infinite within itself. This is a fundamental difference which shows
up first in christology, then is extended to the whole sacramental
life and the relationship to nature.

It is perhaps well to say that in the Swiss Reformation the
sociological background was codeterminative of the particular
form in which these discussions took place. In Germany we have
the form of surviving aristocracy. In Switzerland we have the
large towns like Zürich and Geneva which were centers of trade
and industry. Sociologically the Swiss Reformation drives in the
direction of industrial society. In the Lutheran Reformation,
especially in northern Germany, the pre-bourgeois situation is
retained as much as possible. When you read Luther's *Small
Catechism*, you will see evidences of a paternalistic culture of
small farmers and some craftsmen in villages and small towns. If,
in contrast to this, you read some of the writings of Zwingli and
Calvin, you are with men who have a world-wide horizon, due to
the trading that went on in the centers in which they lived.

C. John Calvin

1. *The Majesty of God*

Calvin's doctrine of God and man is the turning point of all his
other doctrines. Some have said that the doctrine of predestin-

ation is the main point. This, however, is easily refuted by the fact that in the first edition of his *Institutes*, the doctrine of predestination was not even developed. Only in the later editions did it acquire a prominent place. It can also be refuted from more important angles.

The doctrine of God is always the most decisive thing in every theology. For Calvin the central doctrine of Christianity is the doctrine of the majesty of God. Calvin states more clearly than any of the other Reformers that God is known in an existential attitude. For him human misery and divine majesty are correlated. Only out of human misery can we understand the divine majesty, and only in the light of the divine majesty can we understand human misery. Calvin applied to God a word which Rudolf Otto rediscovered—*numen*, numinous. God is a *numen* for him; he is unapproachable, horrifying, and at the same time fascinating. He speaks of God in terms of "this sacred numinous nature". He is distinguished from all idols and from the gods of polytheism. God cannot be spoken of directly because of his radical transcendence. Calvin had a very interesting theory of Christian symbolism. The symbols are significations of God's incomprehensible essence. He said that the symbols have to be momentary, disappearing, and self-negating. They are not the matter itself. I think this self-negating is the decisive characteristic of every symbol with respect to God; if they are taken literally, they produce idols. It is Calvin who said this, and not the mystical theology of a Pseudo-Dionysius. Thus, when we speak of symbolism when referring to God, we can refer to one who is certainly beyond suspicion of being less than orthodox.

The truth of a symbol drives beyond itself. "The best contemplation of the divine being is when the mind is transported beyond itself with admiration." The doctrine of God can never be a matter of theoretical contemplation; it must always be a matter of existential participation. The famous statement of Karl Barth, derived from a biblical text (Ecclesiastes 5:2), that "God is in heaven, and you are on earth", is one that Calvin often made and explained. The heavenly "above" is not a place to which God is bound, but an expression of his religious transcendence. This leads to the central attitude in Calvinism of fear of idolatry. Calvin fought against idols wherever he believed he saw them. For this reason he had no interest in the history of religion, which is practically

condemned as a whole as being idolatrous. Religion cannot avoid
having an element of idolatry in it. Religion is a factory of idols
all the time. Therefore, the Christian and the theologian must be
on their guard and prevent idolatrous trends from overwhelming
their relationship to God.

Calvin fought against having pictures in the churches, and all
kinds of things which can divert the mind from the wholly transcendent God. This is the reason for the sacred emptiness of the
Calvinist church buildings. There is always a fear of idolatry in
the depths of men who have overcome idolatry. So it was with the
prophets, so it was with the Muslims, and so it was now with the
Reformers. Calvinism is an iconoclastic movement, crushing idols,
pictures of all kinds, because they deviate from God himself. This
idea that the human mind is a "perpetual manufacturer of idols"
is one of the most profound things which can be said about our
thinking of God. Even orthodox theology is often nothing more
than idolatry.

On the other side, the human situation is described in much
more negative terms by Calvin than by Luther. "From our natural
proneness to hypocrisy, any vain appearance of righteousness
abundantly contents us instead of the reality", which is our sin.
Man cannot stand his reality; he is unrealistic about himself. As
we say in modern times, man is ideological about himself; he
produces unreal imaginings about his being. This is a radical
attack on the human situation, but it corresponds to God as the
God of glory. When Calvin speaks of the God of love, it is usually
in the context of the elect. Among them he reveals his love. Those
who are not the elect are from the very beginning excluded from
love. If this is true, then is it not also true that for Calvin God
is the Creator of evil? This question has to be answered in connection with the doctrines of providence and predestination.

2. Providence and Predestination

Calvin was well aware that his way of thinking could easily
lead to a half-deistic concept which places God alongside the
world. Several hundred years before the deistic movement arose
in England, Calvin warned against the deistic idea of God beside
the world. Instead of this he conceived of a general operation of
God in preserving and governing the world, so that all movement

depends on him. Deism is a carnal sense which wants to keep God at a distance from us. If God is sitting on his throne without caring about what is going on in the world, that leaves the world to us. This is exactly what the Enlightenment and industrial society needed. They could not tolerate a God who is continually involved with the world. They had to have a God who gives the world its initial movement, then sits beside it without disturbing the businessman in his affairs and the creators of industry. Against this Calvin says: "Faith ought to penetrate further." God is the world's perpetual preserver, "not by a certain universal action actuating the whole machine of the world and all its respective parts, but by a particular providence sustaining, nourishing, and providing for everything which he has made." All this implies a dynamic process of God within the laws he has given. He knew that the doctrine of natural law could easily make God into something beside reality. Therefore, according to Calvin all things have instrumental character; they are instruments through which God works in every moment. If you want to call this pantheism, you do not know what the word means. If you call it panentheism, that could be all right, because this means that everything is in God. Things are used as instruments of God's acting, according to his pleasure. This is very close to Luther's idea. Calvin also has a concept of omnipotence which is against the absurdity of imagining a highest God sitting somewhere and deliberating with himself what he should do, knowing that he could do many other things or anything he wanted. This would be exactly like a woman in the household who decides to do this or that. This is an unworthy view of God, and the Reformers knew it. "Not . . . vain, idle or almost asleep, but vigilant, efficacious, operative, and engaged in continual action; not a mere general principle of confused motion, as if he should command a river to flow through the channels once made for it, but a power constantly exerted on every distant and particular movement. For he is accounted omnipotent, not because he is able to act but does not act, and sits down in idleness." Omnipotence is omniactivity. Providence consists in continuous divine action.

This raised the problem with which Calvin was still wrestling on his deathbed: If this is so, is God not the cause of evil? Calvin was not afraid to say that natural evil is a natural consequence of the distortion of nature. Secondly, he said it is a way to bring the elect to God. But then he made a third assertion: It is a way to show the holiness of God, in the punishment of those whom he has selected for damnation and in the salvation of those who are elected. This says that God has produced evil men in order to punish them and in order to save others who are evil from their evil nature. This exclusively theocentric view which centers everything around the glory of God has understandably been attacked, and Calvin was very sensitive to the charge that he made God the cause of evil.

The suffering of the world is not a real problem for Calvin. Since his first principle is the honor of God, he can show that human suffering is (1) a natural consequence of the distorted, sinful world; (2) a way of bringing the elect to God; (3) a way for God to show his holiness in the punishment of a distorted world. Physical evil here is taken partly as a natural consequence, partly as an educational means, and partly as punishment for sin. But this does not solve the problem of moral evil. Calvin tries to show that the evil acts of Satan and of wicked men are determined by God's counsel. Even Pilate and Nebuchadnezzar were servants of God. God blinds the minds and hardens the hearts of men; he puts an evil spirit in their hearts. Calvin quoted Augustine: "For God, as Augustine says, fulfills his righteous will by the wicked wills of wicked men." "He (Augustine) declares that he (God) creates light and darkness, that he forms good and evil, and that no evil occurs which he has not performed." Such statements which seem to make God the cause of evil are understandable only in the light of Calvin's idea that the world is "the theater of the divine glory". God shows his glory in the scene we call the world. In order to do this, he causes evil, even moral evil. Calvin said that to think that God permits evil because of freedom is frivolous, because God acts in everything that goes on; the evil man follows the will of God although he does not follow his command. By following his will, evil men defy God's command, and that makes them guilty.

This means that Calvin's idea of providence is strictly God-caused; I do not say "determined", but "God-caused". And if—as Calvin realized—some people feel that we cannot say this about God, that this kind of providence is a horrible thing, he answered: "Ignorance of providence is the greatest of miseries; the knowledge of it is attended with the highest felicity." Belief in providence liberates us from anxiety, dread, and care. This period, around the end of the Middle Ages, was one of catastrophes and external changes, and of profound anxiety internally. Calvin's doctrine of providence is not an abstract one; it is supposed to heal anxiety, to give moral courage, and for this reason he praises the divine providence.

Involved with his doctrine of providence is his famous doctrine of predestination. Predestination is providence with respect to the ultimate aim of man. It is providence which leads man through his life to his final aim. So predestination is nothing else than the logical implication and the final fulfillment of providence. What does this doctrine of predestination mean? How does this problem arise? Why is it that most of the great names in religion, from Isaiah, Jesus, Paul, Augustine, to Luther, are adherents of predestination, whereas those who do not adhere to it are nearer to a moralistic interpretation of Christianity than to a strictly religious one? If we deny predestination, we are denying the high line of religious personalities and their theology.

The question behind this doctrine is: Why does not everybody receive the same possibility to accept or reject the truth of the gospel? Not everyone has the same possibility historically, for some have never known Jesus. Not all have the same possibility psychologically; their condition is such that they cannot even understand the meaning of what is said to them. The answer to this question is divine providence, but, as we have said, providence with respect to our eternal destiny is predestination. The moment that Christianity emphasizes the uniqueness of Christ, it must ask why most people have never heard of him, while others who have heard of him are so preconditioned that their hearing has no meaning to them. In other words, all of these who teach predestination have observed something empirically, namely, that there is a selective and not an equalitarian principle effective in life. Life cannot be understood in terms of an equalitarian principle, but only in terms of a selective principle.

Everybody asks questions such as these. Calvin said that we should not suppress such questions out of false modesty; we must ask them. "We shall never be clearly convinced . . . that our salvation flows from the fountain of God's free mercy till we are acquainted with his eternal election, which illustrates the grace of God by this comparison, that he adopts not all promiscuously to the hope of salvation but gives to some what he refuses to others." There is another side to this too. Those who ask this question are given a certainty of salvation because predestination makes salvation completely independent of the oscillations of our human being. The desire for the certainty of salvation is the second reason for the doctrine of predestination in Paul, Augustine, Luther, and Calvin. They could not find a certainty by looking at themselves, because their faith was always weak and changing. They could find it only by looking beyond themselves to the action of God.

The concrete character of divine grace is visible in an election which includes me specifically and at the same time excludes others. This leads to the concept of double predestination. "We call predestination the eternal decree of God by which he has determined in himself what he would have every individual of mankind to become, for they are not all created with a similar destiny; but eternal life is foreordained for some and eternal damnation for others. Every man, therefore, being created for one or the other of these ends, we say is predestined either to life or to death." That is Calvin's definition. What is the cause of this election? Only God's will and nothing else. "If, therefore, we can assign no reason why he grants mercy to his people but because such is his pleasure, neither shall we find any other cause but his will for the reprobation of others." The irrational will of God is the cause of predestination. This introduces us to an absolute mystery. We cannot call God to any account. We must accept it purely and simply and drop our own criteria of the good and the true. If someone says this is unjust, Calvin would say that we cannot go beyond the divine will to a nature which determines God, because God's will cannot be dependent on anything else, not even in him. Here we see the full weight of the Ockhamistic-Scotistic idea that the will of God is the only cause of what God does, and nothing else.

Calvin himself felt the horrible aspect of this doctrine. "I inquire again how it came to pass that the fall of Adam, independent of any remedy, should involve so many nations with their infant children in eternal death, but because such was the will of God ... it is an awful decree, I confess!" Nevertheless, when Calvin was attacked, especially in his last years—in face of his death—he answered in a slightly different way: "Their perdition depends on the divine predestination, in such a manner that the cause and matter of it are found in themselves." Hence, the immediate cause is man's free will. Like Luther, Calvin is thinking on two levels. The divine cause is not really a cause but a decree, something which is a mystery and for which the category of causality is only symbolically and not properly applicable. Besides this Calvin knew, as did the other Reformers and every predestinarian, that it is a man's finite freedom through which God acts when he makes his decree of predestination.

If we should criticize this, we should not say that it is a simple contradiction between God's causality and human freedom. This is too easy, because the levels are different, and there is no possible contradiction on different levels. A contradiction must occur on the same level. There is the level of divine action, which is a mystery because it does not fit our categories, and there is the level of human action, which is a mixture of freedom and destiny. Do not think of the Reformers, or any of the great theologians, in terms of a single level of thought. Otherwise you are faced with all sorts of impossible statements which not only contradict each other, but also result in the destruction of your minds, if by a heroic attempt you try to accept a contradiction. Instead, you can think in terms of two levels. For example, you can say: "I cannot escape the category of causality when I speak of God's action, and when I do so, I derive everything from God, including my eternal destiny." This sounds like a mechanical determinism. But this is not what predestination means. On the divine level causality is used symbolically to express that everything which brings us to God is derived from God.

The question this raises for the individual Calvinist is whether he is elected. What gives him the assurance of election? Thus the search for the criteria, the marks of election, begins. Calvin recognized some of them. The first and most decisive one is the inner relationship to God in the act of faith. Then there is the blessing of God and the high moral standing of a person. These are all symptoms. Psychologically this brought about a situation in which the individual could gain certainty only by producing the marks of election in terms of a moral life and an economic blessing. This means that he tried to become a good bourgeois industrial citizen. He believed that if he were this, he had the marks of predestination. Of course, theologically it was known that predestination could never be caused by such actions. But if they are there, the individual can have certainty. Here lurked the danger in this theology which dealt with the marks of election.

It is remarkable how little Calvin had to say about the love of God. The divine glory replaces the divine love. When he speaks of the divine love, it is love toward those who are elected. The universality of the divine love is denied, and the demonic negation, the split of the world, acquires a kind of eternity in Calvin through his doctrine of double predestination. Therefore, this is a doctrine which contradicts the divine love as that which sustains everything that is, a doctrine which Dante expressed when in his *Divine Comedy* he wrote at the entrance of hell: "I also have been created by divine love." However, if something is created by divine love, it cannot be eternally condemned.

3. *The Christian Life*

I want to make only a few statements about Calvin's doctrine of the Christian life. He said: "When they explain vivification of that joy which the mind experiences after its perturbations and fears are allayed, I cannot coincide with them (i.e., with Luther), since it should rather signify an ardent desire and endeavor to live a holy and pious life, as though it were said that a man dies to himself that he may begin to live to God." For Luther the new life is a joyful reunion with God; for Calvin it is the attempt to fulfill the law of God in the life of the Christian. The summary of the Christian life is self-denial and not love. It is departing from ourselves. "Oh, how great a proficiency has that man made who, having been taught that he is not his own, has taken the sovereignty and government of himself from his own reason, to surrender it to God." What describes the Christian life for Calvin is not Luther's view of the ups and downs, the ecstasy and despair, in the Christian. For Calvin the Christian life is a line going upward, exercised in methodical stages.

There are two other elements in Calvin's view of the Christian life. The world is a place of exile. The body is a valueless prison of the soul. These words are more those of Plato than of the Old or New Testament. Yet, Calvin denied any hatred of life. His asceticism was not of the Roman type which tended to deny life itself or to deny the body by ascetic exercises. It was what Max

Weber and Ernst Troeltsch called an inner-worldly asceticism. It has two characteristics: cleanliness, and profit through work. Cleanliness is understood in terms of sobriety, chastity, and temperance. This has had tremendous consequences in the lives of people in Calvinist countries. It has been expressed in an extreme external cleanliness and an identification of the erotic element with the unclean. This latter is against the principles of the Reformation, but it was the consequence of the Calvinist ethics. The second characteristic of this inner-worldly asceticism is activity in the world to produce tools and, by means of them, profit. This has been called the "spirit of capitalism" by Max Weber (*The Protestant Ethic and the Spirit of Capitalism*). This has been so misunderstood that I would like to make a few comments on it. There are some people who think that great scholars like Max Weber and Ernst Troeltsch have stated that Calvinism produced capitalism. Then these clever people answer Weber— probably the greatest scholar in the nineteenth century in the fields of sociology and the humanities—by pointing out that capitalism existed before Calvin was born, especially in the Lombardian plain in northern Italy, in the cities of northern and southern Germany, in London, etc. What Weber said is that there is something in the spirit of Calvinist ethics and some related sectarian ethics which serves the purposes of investment, an important element in the capitalist economy. In pre-capitalist economy the rich man showed his riches in glorious living, in building castles or mansions or patrician houses. But Calvinism tried to show people how to use their wealth differently. It should be used partly for endowments and partly for new investments. One of the best ways of supporting the capitalist form of economy is to make the profits into investments, that is, into means for more production, instead of wasting the profits in glorious living.

That is what Max Weber wanted to say. If you do not believe he was right, I can tell you that in eastern Germany, before the catastrophes of the twentieth century happened, the cities in which the Protestants lived were the wealthy ones, and the ones in which the Catholics lived were the poor ones. Perhaps the poor were happier than the rich, but the towns and cities influenced by Calvinism produced capitalism in Germany, and not the Catholics, or the Lutherans in the East.

4. Church and State

Calvin's doctrine of the church is like Luther's; the church is the place where preaching is carried on and the sacraments are correctly administered. However, Calvin makes a much more radical distinction between the empirical church and the invisible church. While for Luther the invisible church is only the spiritual quality of the visible church, for Calvin the invisible church is the body of those who are predestined, in all periods of history, and not always dependent on the preaching of the Word. This is connected with the doctrine of the Holy Spirit in Zwingli and Calvin; the Spirit works also apart from the Christian message, and is therefore universally active.

From this point of view the visible church is an emergency situation, an adaptation of God to human weakness. Thus, it is not a matter of believing in the church, but believing that there is a church. The main function of the church is educational. The church always has to bring people into the invisible church, the body of the predestined, by means of preaching and the sacraments. On the other hand, the emphasis on the educational work of the church is much stronger than in Lutheranism. Although the church is ultimately an emergency creation of God, it is actually the only way for most people to come to God at all. The difference between Calvin's and Luther's doctrine of the church is that instead of having two marks of the church—doctrine and sacraments—as Luther had, Calvin has three marks: doctrine, sacraments, and discipline. The element of discipline is decisive. "As some have such a hatred of discipline as to abhor the very name, they should attend to the following consideration. . . . As the saving doctrine of Christ is the soul of the church, so discipline forms the ligaments which connect the members together and keep each in its proper place." The discipline starts with private admonition; it goes through public challenge (this was ruinous socially) and finally to excommunication. But even excommunication is not able to remove one from the saving power of God. Whereas someone who has been excommunicated cannot be saved while in this state, according to the Roman Church, in Protestantism a person will be saved in spite of excommunication if he is among the predestined.

Besides these three marks of the church, there are other things by divine law. There are four offices: pastors or ministers, doctors or teachers, presbyters, and deacons. The pastors and presbyters are the most important of these four offices. All four are by divine order; they must always be there; they are derived from the Bible.

In its mixed status the church has within itself a community of active sanctification. This community is created by the church and becomes manifest in the Lord's Supper. Thus, discipline precedes the reception of the Lord's Supper. Now, I do not want to go into Calvin's doctrine of the sacraments. The main thing is that he tried to mediate between Luther and Zwingli. Against Zwingli, he did not want the Lord's Supper to be only a commemorative meal; he wanted the presence of God, but not a presence which is superstitious and magical, as he saw in Luther's doctrine, where even unbelievers eat the body of Christ. This is magic, and I think rightly rejected by Calvin. Instead, he spoke of the spiritual presence of Christ, and this is also the presupposition for an effective reading of the Bible.

Calvin was a humanist and, therefore, gave to the state many more functions than Luther. Luther gave it practically only one function: to suppress evil and to preserve society from chaos. Calvin used the humanistic ideas of good government, of helping the people, etc. But Calvin never went so far as to say, with the sectarian movements, that the state can be the kingdom of God itself. He called this a Jewish folly. What he said—with Zwingli —is that a theocracy has to be established, the rule of God through the application of evangelical laws in the political situation. Calvin worked hard for this. He demanded that the magistrates of Geneva care not only for legal problems, the problems of order in the general sense, but also for the most important content of daily life, namely, for the church. Not that they shall teach in the church or render decisions as to what shall be taught, but they shall supervise the church and punish those who are blasphemers and heretics. So Calvin with the help of the magistrates of Geneva created the kind of community in which the law of God would govern the entire life. Priests and ministers are not necessarily involved in it. Theocratic rulers are usually not priests, otherwise theocracy becomes hierocracy; rather, they are usually laymen. Calvin says that the state must punish the

impious. They are criminals because they are against the law of
the state which is based on God's law.

Calvinism saved Protestantism from being overwhelmed by
the Counter-Reformation. Calvinism became a tremendous inter-
national power through the alliances of Protestants on a world-
wide scale. Another element in Calvinism is the possibility of
revolution. Certainly Calvin said that all revolution is against the
law of God, as Luther did. But then he made an exception which
has become decisive for Western European history. He said that
although no individual citizen should be allowed to start a revolution, the lower magistrates should be willing to do so if the
natural law, to which every ruler is subject, is being contradicted.
This is a possibility in a democracy such as ours in which all of
us are lower magistrates; we establish the government by our
voting. Under these circumstances revolution is universally
permissible. The situation in Western Europe was that the kings
and queens were mostly on the side of Catholicism, and Protestantism could be saved only by people who believed they could
fight against the rulers in the name of God, rulers who suppress
the true gospel, the purified gospel of the Reformation.

5. *The Authority of Scripture*

The doctrine of the authority of Scripture in Calvin is important
because on its basis biblicism developed in all groups of Protestant faith. The Bible for Calvin is the law of truth. "At length,
that the truth might remain in the world in a continual course of
instruction to all ages, he determined that the same oracles which
he had deposited with the patriarchs should be committed to
public records. With this design the law was promulgated, to
which the prophets were afterwards annexed as its first interpreters." The Bible must, therefore, be obeyed above all. It contains a "heavenly doctrine". Although an adaptation, this was
necessary because of the mutability of the human mind. This
was the necessary way to preserve the doctrines of Christianity.
By writing them down, God's instructions become effectual.
Calvin also spoke of the Bible as the "peculiar school of the
children of God".

All of this can be harmless—or quite the opposite. Much discussion is taking place as to how to interpret Calvin's doctrine of

Scripture. In any case, the answer is that this authority is absolute, but only for those to whom the divine Spirit gives the testimony that the Bible contains the absolute truth. If this happens, we can witness to the whole Bible as an authoritative book. The form of the Bible's authority is derived from the fact that the Bible was composed under the dictation of the Holy Spirit. This term, dictation of the Holy Spirit, led to the doctrine of verbal inspiration which surpassed anything which can be found in Calvin himself, and which contradicts the Protestant principle as such. The disciples were "pens" of Christ. Everything which came from them as human beings was superseded by the Holy Spirit who testifies that the oracles of God are contained in this book. "Between the apostles and their successors, however, there is . . . this difference—that the apostles were the certain and authentic amanuenses of the Holy Spirit, and therefore their writings are to be received as the oracles of God." "Out of the mouth of God" the Bible is written—the whole Bible. Any distinction between the Old and New Testaments, largely disappears. You can find this still today in every Calvinist country.

CHAPTER VI

The Development of Protestant Theology

We shall now give a survey of the rhythm in the development of Protestant theology in the last centuries. This development is important not only from the historical point of view, but also because elements created during this period are profoundly embedded in our minds and souls and bodies. Although we cannot present a history of Protestant theology, we can show the various tides in its development.

A. The Period of Orthodoxy

The immediate wave which followed the Reformation is the period of Orthodoxy. Orthodoxy is greater and more serious than what is called fundamentalism in America. Fundamentalism is the product of a reaction in the nineteenth century, and is a primitivized form of classical Orthodoxy. Classical Orthodoxy had a great theology. We could also call it Protestant scholasticism, with all the refinements and methods which the word "scholastic" includes. Thus, when I speak of Orthodoxy, I refer to the way in which the Reformation established itself as an ecclesiastical form of life and thought after the dynamic movement of the Reformation came to an end. It is the systematization and consolidation of the ideas of the Reformation, and developed in contrast to the Counter-Reformation.

Orthodox theology was and still is the solid basis of all later developments, whether these developments—as was usually the case—were directed against Orthodoxy, or were attempts at restoration of it. Liberal theology to the present time has been dependent on the Orthodoxy against which it has fought. Pietism

was dependent on the Orthodoxy which it wanted to transform
into subjectivism. Past and present restoration movements try to
recapture what was once alive in the period of Orthodoxy. Hence,
we should deal with this period in a much more serious way
than is usually done in America. In Germany, and generally
in European theological faculties—France, Switzerland, Sweden,
etc.—every student of theology was supposed to learn by heart
the doctrines of at least one classical theologian of the post-
Reformation period of Orthodoxy, be it Lutheran or Calvinist,
and in Latin at that. Even if we should forget about the Latin
today, we should know these doctrines, because they form the
classical system of Protestant thought. It is an unheard-of state
of things when Protestant churches of today do not even know
the classical expression of their own foundations in the dogmatics
of Orthodoxy. This means that you cannot even understand
people like Schleiermacher or Ritschl, American liberalism or the
Social Gospel theology, because you do not know that against
which they were directed or on what they were dependent. All
theology of today is dependent in some way on the classical
systems of Orthodoxy.

Orthodox theology also had a political significance, because of
the need to define the status of religion in the political atmosphere
of the post-Reformation period. It was a period which prepared
the Thirty Years' War. Under the German emperor every territory
had to define exactly where it stood, and this was the basis of its
legal acknowledgment within the unity of the Holy Roman
Empire. The theology, furthermore, was a theology of the territorial princes. They wanted to know from their theological faculties exactly what a minister was supposed to teach. They had to
know it because they were the official lords of the church, the
highest bishops, *summi episcopi*. All of the theological problems
at this time involved a legal problem. When in regard to the
Augsburg Confession you read about the *Variata* or *Invariata*, you
might think, "What nonsense!" Not only the unity of Protestantism was threatened, but also people were killed when the *Variata*
(the Altered Augsburg Confession) was introduced in place of the
Invariata (the Unaltered Augsburg Confession) without the permission of the princes. It was more than just nonsense. It was the
difference between Gnesio-Lutheranism and Philippism. Gnesio-
Lutheranism means genuine or original Lutheranism, and was

represented by Flacius, who was also the greatest church historian of Protestantism. Flacius had a point of view similar to the Barthian school today, stressing the total depravity of man. In scholastic terminology Flacius said that the substance of human nature is original sin. This idea, however, was not accepted by Orthodoxy.

Philippism, on the other side, represented the tendency of Philip Melanchthon. It was very similar to Reformed ideas, so that it is even difficult today to find out how much in Philippism is Reformed and how much is Melanchthonian. This group was nearer to what today we would call a moderate liberal theology, against the Gnesio-Lutherans. The result of these struggles at the end of the sixteenth century was the *Formula of Concord* (1580). Many of the territorial churches believed that it contained the pure interpretation of the Augsburg Confession in its unaltered form. The implication of all this is that the doctrinal element becomes much more important in Orthodoxy than in the Reformation, where the spiritual element was more decisive than the fixed doctrines. Luther did not fix doctrines, although he himself could be very tenacious.

1. *Reason and Revelation*

We must deal now with the principles of orthodox thought. One of the first was the relationship to philosophy, a very old issue in Protestantism. Luther, it seems, was disinclined to accept anything from reason, but in reality this is not true. It is true that he made many angry statements against the philosophers, by whom he usually had in mind the scholastics and their teacher, Aristotle. But in his famous words at the Diet of Worms Luther himself said that unless he were refuted either by Holy Scripture or by reason, he would not recant. Luther was not an irrationalist. What he fought against was that the categories of reason should transform the substance of faith. Reason is not able to save but must be saved itself.

It became immediately clear that theology cannot be taught without philosophy, that philosophical categories must be used, consciously or unconsciously, in teaching anything whatsoever. For this reason Luther did not prevent Melanchthon from introducing Aristotle again, and with Aristotle many humanistic elements. However, there were always some who attacked philosophy, humanism, and Aristotle. There was a man, Daniel Hoffmann, who said: "The philosophers are the patriarchs of heresy." This is what some theologians say even today. But when they develop their own theologies, you can easily show from which "patriarchs of heresy", that is, from which philosophers, they have taken their categories. They have said: What is philosophically true is theologically wrong; the philosophers are unregenerated insofar as they are philosophers. This is a very interesting statement because it means that there is a realm of life which in itself cannot be regenerated. This contradicts, however, the emphasis on secularism in Protestantism. "Philosophers", said Hoffmann, "try to be like God because they develop a philosophy which is not theologically given." Hoffmann was not able to carry through this idea, but he produced a continual suspicion against the philosophers in the churches and in theology, a much greater suspicion against philosophy than exists in the Roman Church. And this suspicion is very much alive again in the present-day theological situation.

The final victory of philosophy within theology was the presupposition of all the theological systems in Orthodoxy. Johann Gerhard was the one who developed the classical system in Lutheran theology. He was a great philosopher and theologian, in some ways comparable to Thomas Aquinas for Roman Catholics. He represents the latest flowering of Protestant scholasticism. He distinguished articles which are pure from those which are mixed. Those which are solely revealed are pure; those which are rationally possible as well as revealed are mixed. He believed, with Thomas Aquinas, that the existence of God can be proved rationally. But he was also aware that this rational proof does not give us certainty. "Although the proof is correct, we believe it because of revelation." In this way we have two structures: the substructure of reason, and the superstructure of revelation. The biblical doctrines form the superstructure. What actually happened later—and this is a preview of the centuries which followed—was that the mixed articles became unmixed rationally, and that the substructure of rational theology dispossessed the superstructure of revelation, drawing it into itself and taking away its meaning. When this happens, we are in the realm of rationalism or Enlightenment.

2. *The Formal and Material Principles*

Protestantism in Orthodoxy developed two principles of theology, a formal and a material principle. So far as I know, however, these are nineteenth-century terms. The formal principle is the Bible; the material principle is the doctrine of justification. They are interdependent, according to Luther. What presents the message of justification in the Bible is that which deals with Christ, and this is what is authentic. On the other hand, this doctrine is taken from the Bible and is, therefore, dependent on it. This interdependence of Bible and justification was maintained in Luther's thought in a free, creative, and living way. The attitude of Orthodoxy became different. The two principles were placed beside each other. The result was that the Bible became the real principle in the realm of authority.

What was the doctrine of the Bible in Orthodoxy? The Bible is attested in a threefold way: (1) by external criteria, such as age, miracles, prophecy, martyrs, etc.; (2) by internal criteria, such as style, sublime ideas, moral sanctity; (3) by the testimony of the Holy Spirit. This testimony, however, gets another meaning. No longer does it have the Pauline meaning that we are the children of God ("The Spirit himself beareth witness with our spirit that we are children of God." Romans 8:16). Instead, it became the testimony that the doctrines of the Holy Scriptures are true and inspired by the Spirit. In place of the immediacy of the Spirit in the relationship of God and man, the Spirit witnesses to the authenticity of the Bible insofar as it is a document of the divine Spirit. The difference is that if the Spirit tells you that you are children of God, this is an immediate experience, and there is no law involved in it at all. But if the Spirit testifies that the Bible contains true doctrines, the whole thing is brought out of the person-to-person relationship into an objective legal relationship. This is exactly what Orthodoxy did.

A very interesting discussion about the *theologia irregenitorum* followed from this, the theology of those who are not converted, the unregenerated. If the Bible is the law of Protestantism, it should be possible for all who can read the Bible and interpret it objectively to write a systematic theology, even though they do not participate in the Christian faith. All they have to do is to understand the meaning of the words and sentences of the Bible. This was absolutely denied by the pietists, who said that there can be only a *theologia regenitorum,* a theology of those who are regenerated. If we look at this discussion in modern terms, we can say that Orthodoxy believed in the possibility of a systematic theology which is not existential, while the pietists believed that it is necessary for theology to be existential.

There is something difficult in both positions. The unregenerated man is able to know that what the Church or the Bible says is essential for salvation, but he is unable to apply this to the present situation. The function of the orthodox theologian is independent of his religious quality. He may be completely outside. On the other hand, the pietist theologian can say of himself, and others can say of him, that he is converted, regenerated, and a real Christian. But he has to state this with certainty. Is there anyone who can do this, who can say: "I am a real Christian"? The moment he does it, he ceases to be a real Christian, since he is looking to himself for certainty in his relation to God. This is most certainly impossible. This problem still exists today in all Protestant churches. In my *Systematic Theology* I have solved the problem in the following way. Only he who experiences the Christian message as his ultimate concern is able to be a theologian, but nothing more than this can be demanded. It may be that one who is in doubt about every particular doctrine is a better theologian than many others, as long as this doubt about doctrine involves his ultimate concern. So one does not need to be "converted" to be a theologian—whatever that term may mean. You are not asked to test whether or not you are a good Christian, so that you can say: "Now since I am a good Christian, I can be a theologian." The pietist would tell you: "You must first be converted before you can really be a theologian." Then you should answer him: "The only thing which is 'first' is that the ultimate concern coming from God has grasped me, so that I am concerned about him and his message, but I cannot say more than this. And sometimes I am not even able to express it in these terms, because even the term 'God' disappears sometimes. In any case, I cannot use it as the basis for believing that I am a good Christian and thus possibly a theologian."

The orthodox doctrine of inspiration took some of Calvin's ideas and made them more radical and primitive. The authors of Scripture were the hands of Christ, the notaries of the Holy Spirit, the "pens" by which the Spirit wrote the Bible. The words, and even the pointings in the Hebrew text, are inspired. Hence, an orthodox theologian, Buxtehof, contested the fact that the consonants of the Hebrew text received their vowel pointings in the seventh to ninth centuries A.D.; instead, they must have originated with the Old Testament itself. The prophets must have invented the system of pointing, which was actually invented fifteen hundred years later. This is the consequence of a consistent doctrine of inspiration; otherwise, what would the divine Spirit do with the Hebrew text, for without the vowels, the Hebrew words are ambiguous in many places. Then there is the problem with Luther's and the King James' translations, and with other new translations. One is driven to actual absurdities with this doctrine of inspiration. To maintain it one has to make artificial harmonizations, for there are innumerable contradictions in the Bible on historical as well as on other matters. Such contradictions are made out to be only apparent, and one is forced to be ingenious in inventing ways to harmonize them.

Another deeper principle was the *analogia scripturae sanctae*, the analogy of sacred Scripture, which means that one part must be interpreted in terms of another. By this means creeds could be established on the basis of Holy Scripture. These were the formulae which everybody was supposed to find in the Bible. This was another inescapable consequence of the doctrine of inspiration.

There was another help for people who had to swallow the doctrine of verbal inspiration. The question was: What about the many doctrines we find in the Bible? Are they all necessary for salvation? The Catholic Church had a very good answer. You do not need to know any of them; you have only to believe what the church believes. Only the ministers and educated people need to know the special doctrines. The Catholic layman believes what the church believes, without knowing what that is in many respects. Protestantism could not do this. Since personal faith means everything in Protestantism, the distinction between *fides implicita* and *explicita* (implicit and explicit faith) is impossible for it. But then an impossible task arose: How can every ordinary farmer, shoemaker, and proletarian in the city and the country understand all these many doctrines found in the Bible, which are too numerous even for an educated man to know in his theological examinations? The answer was given by distinguishing between fundamental and non-fundamental articles. Such a distinction is popular even today. In principle this distinction should not be made, because if the divine Spirit reveals something, to what extent can we say it is non-fundamental? In any case, non-fundamentals proved later on to be very fundamental, when certain consequences were drawn from non-fundamental deviations.

Although this was a dangerous thing, it had to be done for educational reasons. Most people are just not able to understand all the implications of the doctrines of the church. Two interests were in conflict with each other. On the one hand, the interest of the systematic theologian is to increase the fundamentals as much as possible; everything is important, not only because he is writing about it, but because it is in the Bible. On the other hand, the interest of the educator contradicts this interest of the systematic theologian. The educator wants to maintain as little as possible, so that what he teaches becomes understandable. He would like to leave out all doctrines of secondary importance. In the end the educator prevails. What we find in the rationalism of the Enlightenment is largely a reduction of the fundamentals to the level of popular reasonableness. Education was partly responsible for the coming of the Enlightenment; it was a central concern of all the great philosophers of that period. Even today the departments of education are usually more inclined toward a theology based on the Enlightenment than the other departments of theology are. The reason for this is that the educational needs bring about a limitation of content, whereas the theological needs call for an enlargement of content.

B. PIETISM

Orthodoxy had one doctrine which was a transition to the next great movement—Pietism. In its doctrine of the *ordo salutis*, the order of salvation, the last step was the *unio mystica*, the mystical union with God. For Luther this is the beginning of the faith in justification. The moment that Orthodoxy accepted from the ecclesiastical tradition the *unio mystica* as a definite state which must be reached, the concept of faith became intellectualized. In Luther both are kept together; in Orthodoxy they fall asunder.

Faith becomes the intellectual acceptance of true doctrine, and communion with God becomes a matter of mystical experience. This splits Luther's thought—especially of the younger Luther— into two pieces; the mystical and the intellectual aspects are placed beside each other.

What is Pietism? The term is much less respectable in America than in Europe. There the words "pious" and "pietist" can be used of people, but hardly in America, because here they carry the connotations of hypocrisy and moralism. Pietism does not necessarily have these connotations. It is the reaction of the subjective side of religion against the objective side. Of course, the subjective side in the order of salvation was dealt with in Orthodoxy, but it did not mean very much. Actually Orthodoxy lived in the objectivity of theological and ecclesiastical organization. Yet, this should not be overemphasized. As the hymns of Paul Gerhardt show—he lived during the highest development of this period— there was always a personal religious relationship to God. But for the masses of people it was the license to become licentious; the state of morality was miserably low, especially in the Lutheran countries, where the doctrinal element was decisive and discipline did not exist.

The pietists, and especially the greatest of them, Philip Jacob Spener, wrote in continual reference to Luther. He showed that all the elements of Pietism were present in the early Luther, and that Orthodoxy had removed them in favor of the objective contents of doctrine. Spener tried to show that Orthodoxy had grasped only one side of Luther. Pietism was justified in this respect. Pietism also had a great influence on culture as a whole. It was the first to act in terms of social ethics. The pietists in Halle founded the first orphanage and started the first missionary enterprises. Orthodoxy held that the non-Christian nations are lost, because they had already received the apostolic preaching immediately after the founding of the church, and rejected it. St. Thomas, for instance, had gone to Asia. So it is not necessary to renew the missionary enterprise. The pietists felt altogether differently about it. Human souls, wherever they may be, can be saved through conversion. So they began their missions to foreign lands, and this gave them world-historical perspectives. A man like Zinzendorf, together with Wesley, looked to America, while Orthodoxy restricted itself to its own territorial churches.

The liturgical realm was also changed a great deal. One of the most important changes was the reintroduction of confirmation as a confirming of the sacrament of baptism.

Pietism is important for theology in three respects. It tried to reform theology, the church, and morals. According to Pietism, theology is a practical discipline. In order to know, one must first believe—an old demand of Christian theology. This demand entails, at the same time, the central importance of exegesis. Old and New Testament theology become decisive, not systematic theology. Wherever biblical theology prevails over systematic theology, that is almost always due to the influence of Pietism. Before the theologian is able to edify others, he must first be educated himself.

The church is not only a body of people which exists to listen to the Word. Not only ministers but also laymen are the bearers of the church. Laymen are to have an active part in the priestly function in different places—sometimes in the church, but mostly in their homes, and in special conventicles of piety, *collegia pietatis*, where they came together to cultivate piety. They spent hours in the interpretation of the Bible, and they emphasized the need for conversion. They emphasized the idea of an *ecclesiola in ecclesia*, a small church within the large church.

Pietism also influenced the morals in the Protestant world. At the end of the seventeenth century the moral situation was disastrous in Europe. The Thirty Years' War brought about dissolution and chaos. The form of life became extremely brutal, unrefined, and uneducated. The orthodox theologians did not do much about it. The pietists, however, tried to gather individual Christians who would accept the burden and the liberation of the Christian life. Its main idea was sanctification, a common emphasis in Christian sectarian movements. Individual sanctification includes, first of all, a negation of the love of the world. The question of the ethical *adiaphora* became important in the discussion with orthodox theology. (*Adiaphoron* means that which makes no difference, having no ethical relevance.) The question was whether there are some human actions of no ethical relevance, which can be done or left undone with equal right. Orthodoxy said there is a whole realm of such *adiaphora*; Pietism denied it, calling it love of the world. As it often happens with such things, Spener was mild in his condemnation, then Francke and the Halle pietists became very radical. They fought against dancing, the theater, games, beautiful dresses, banquets, shallow talk in daily life, and in general resembled the Puritan attitude. In this connection, however, I would like to say that it was not so much the Puritans who produced this system of vital repression so common in America; it was more the pietistic evangelical movements of the mid-nineteenth century which were responsible for this condemnation of smoking, drinking, movies, etc.

The orthodox theologians strongly reacted against the attack of the pietists. One of them wrote a book with the title *Malum Pietisticum*, "The Pietistic Evil". They fought against each other on many points, but in the end the pietistic movement was superior because it was allied with the trends of the time, away from the strict objectivism and authoritarianism of the sixteenth and seventeenth centuries to the principles of autonomy which appeared in the eighteenth and nineteenth centuries.

It is entirely wrong to place the rationalism of the Enlightenment in contradiction to pietistic mysticism. It is popular nonsense that reason and mysticism are the two great opposites. Historically, Pietism and the Enlightenment both fought against Orthodoxy. The subjectivity of Pietism, or the doctrine of the "inner light" in Quakerism and other ecstatic movements, has the character of immediacy or autonomy against the authority of the church. To put it more sharply, modern rational autonomy is a child of the mystical autonomy of the doctrine of the inner light. The doctrine of the inner light is very old; we have it in the Franciscan theology of the Middle Ages, in some of the radical sects (especially the later Franciscans), in many sects of the Reformation period, in the transition from spiritualism to rationalism, from the belief in the Spirit as the autonomous guide of every individual to the rational guidance which everybody has by his autonomous reason. From another historical perspective, the third stage of Joachim of Floris, the stage of the Holy Spirit, is behind the idea among the bourgeoisie of the Enlightenment that they have reached the third stage, the age of reason, in which every individual is taught directly. They go back to the prophecy of Joel, in which every maid or servant is taught directly by the Holy Spirit, and no one is dependent on anybody else for the Spirit.

Thus we can say that rationalism is not opposed to mysticism, if by mysticism we mean the presence of the Spirit in the depths of the human soul. Rationalism is the child of mysticism, and both of them are opposed to authoritarian Orthodoxy.

C. THE ENLIGHTENMENT

Socinianism is one of the sources of the Enlightenment. It was a movement started by Faustus Socinus, who fled from Italy to Poland where he found a haven of security against the Counter-Reformation and the persecutions of some of the Reformation churches. He and his followers wrote the book called *Racovian Catechism*, which presents a predominantly rationalistic Protestant theology. Harnack says in his *History of Dogma* that Socinianism was the end of the history of Christian dogma. Protestantism had preserved some dogmas, at least the early dogmas of the church. Socinianism dissolved all the Christian dogmas with the help of the rationalism and humanism of the Renaissance. This movement is more important than either the repetition of it in English deism, where it was radicalized, or in modern liberal theology, including Harnack himself, where it was carried through.

(1) The Socinians accepted the authority of the Bible, but declared that in non-essential things it may be in error. Furthermore, historical criticism is necessary. Its criterion is that nothing can be a revelation of God in the Bible that is against reason and common sense. And nothing that is morally useless can be the revelation of God in the Bible. Socinus spoke of *religio rationalis*, rational religion, which is given in the Bible and is the criterion for the authority of the Bible.

(2) In the doctrine of God Socinus criticized mainly the dogma of the trinity. The Socinians are the predecessors of the later Unitarian movements. He said—and in this he is historically right —that the arguments for the trinitarian dogma do not exist in the Bible as they were later presented in Orthodoxy. The Bible does not contain the dogma of the trinity, although there are some trinitarian formulations. The Greek concepts, he said, anticipating the Ritschlian criticism of the dogma on which we are all dependent today, are inadequate for understanding the meaning of the gospel and are, moreover, contradictory in themselves.

(3) God created the world out of the given chaos (*tohu wabohu*

in the creation story in Genesis) which the pagan religions and also Greek philosophy presuppose. Man is the image of God because of his reason, which makes him superior to the animals. Adam was not a perfect man, but was primitive and by nature mortal. He had neither original immortality nor original perfection. I believe this is closer to the biblical text in both respects than the later glorification of Adam which makes his fall absolutely impossible to understand. The Socinians derive the fall of Adam from the strength of his sensual impressions and on the basis of his freedom. This freedom is still in man.

(4) Hence, the idea of original or hereditary sin is a contradictory concept. Socinus says that there is no sin without guilt. If we are guilty by birth, then we must have sinned before we were born, or at least at the very beginning of our life, which is a meaningless statement. What is really the truth is that we are historically depraved and that our freedom is weakened. This makes it necessary for God to give us a new revelation beyond natural revelation. Christ has a true human nature, but not a divine nature. On the other hand, he is not just an ordinary man. He is a higher type of man, a "superman", so to speak, in the Nietzschean, not the comic-book, sense. For this reason he can be an object of adoration.

(5) The priestly office of Christ is denied. He is prophet and king. The ideas about a substitutionary sacrifice or punishment or satisfaction for sin are meaningless and self-contradictory, because guilt is always a personal thing and must be attributed to individuals. On the other hand, Christ is king and sits at the right hand of God and is really ruling and judging.

(6) Justification is dissolved into a moralistic terminology. In order to be justified, we must keep the commandments. With respect to the state, he favored passive resistance against the power forms of the state.

(7) Eschatology is dissolved; it is a fantastic myth. What remains and is most important is immortality. This must be preserved by all means.

Many of these ideas anticipate the theology of the Enlightenment and modern liberalism. What really survives from Socinianism are the three theological ideas of the Enlightenment: God, freedom, and immortality. I like to quote from Immanuel Kant's *What is Enlightenment?*: "Enlightenment is man's release from his self-incurred tutelage. Tutelage is man's inability to make use of his understanding without direction from another. Self-incurred is this tutelage when its cause lies not in lack of reason but in lack of resolution and courage to use it without direction from another. *Sapere aude!* 'Have courage to use your own reason!'—that is the motto of enlightenment." Kant goes on to show how much more comfortable it is to have guardians and authorities but he says this comfort has to be given up. Man must stand upon himself; it is his nature to be autonomous.

Rationalism and Enlightenment emphasize human autonomy. "Autonomy" is not used in the sense of arbitrariness, of man making himself or deciding about himself in terms of his individual desires and arbitrary willfulness. Autonomy is derived from *autos* and *nomos* (self-law) in Greek. It does not say that "I am a law unto myself", but that the universal law of reason, which is the structure of reality, is within me. This concept of autonomy is often falsified by theologians who say this is the misery of man, that he wants to be autonomous rather than dependent on God. This is poor theology and poor philosophy. Autonomy is the natural law given by God, present in the human mind and in the structure of the world. Natural law usually means in classical philosophy and theology the law of reason, and this is the divine law. Autonomy is following this law as we find it in ourselves. It is always connected with a strong obedience to the law of reason, stronger than any religious idea that seems to be arbitrary. The adherents of autonomy in the Enlightenment were opposed to anything so arbitrary as divine grace. They wanted to emphasize man's obedience to the law of his own nature and the nature of the world.

The opposite of autonomy is the concept of heteronomy. Heteronomy is precisely arbitrariness. Arbitrariness shows up as soon as fear or desire determine our actions, whether this fear be produced by God or society or our own weakness. For Kant the authoritarian attitude of the churches, or even of God if he is seen in a heteronomous light, is arbitrariness. Arbitrariness is subjection to authority, if this authority is not confirmed by reason itself, for otherwise one is subjecting oneself on the basis of fear, anxiety, or desire. The Enlightenment is the attempt to build a world on this autonomous reason.

Just as autonomy is not willfulness, reason is not calculation.

Reason is the awareness of the principles of truth and justice. In the name of this reason, the Enlightenment fought against the demonic authorities of the *ancien régime* in eighteenth-century France and in Europe generally. This reason is the awareness of the principles of truth and goodness, not the calculating and controlling reason of business. The eighteenth century had some heroic elements in it; reason is always seen fighting against the distortions of humanity under the regime of the French kings and the Roman popes and all who cooperated with them for the suppression of humanity. We should not have contempt for the rationalism of the eighteenth century, if we know what it did for us. It is due to the Enlightenment that we have no more witch trials. It was Cartesian philosophy applied to concrete problems which made such a superstition impossible. The general education we all enjoy in the West is a creation of the eighteenth century. And our democratic ideology had its origin in the same century.

Harmony is a third principle of the Enlightenment, following from the principles of autonomy and reason. If we find the principles of truth and justice in the depths of our being, and if each individual has different interests, how are a common knowledge and common symbols of democracy and economy possible? If autonomous reason in each individual is the ultimate arbiter, is not that the end of a coherent society? The principle of harmony is the answer to this question. This principle does not mean that there is nice harmony between everyone. The eighteenth century knew how terrible life really was. Rather, harmony means that if everyone follows his rational, or even irrational tendencies, there is nevertheless a law behind the backs of everyone which has the effect of making everything come out most adequately. This is the meaning of the Manchester school of economics, the meaning of the pursuit of happiness in the American Constitution and of belief in democracy. In spite of the fact that each one decides for himself about the government, a common will, a *volonté générale*, will somehow result from all of this. This is the belief in ethics and education, that a community spirit will be the result of everyone's becoming educated as a personality. This is the principle of Protestantism, that if every individual in his own way encounters the biblical message, a conformism of Protestant character will be the outcome.

The miracle is that this happened, that actually the prophecy under the principle of harmony was really verified in all these realms. The greatest development in economy happened. A Protestant conformism arose, in spite of the numerous denominations. And democracy has worked and is still working, in spite of the disruptive tendencies that are visible today in America. The modern belief in progress is rooted in this principle of harmony, in spite of any lack of authority.

Tolerance is another concept we must keep in mind when dealing with the Enlightenment. One of the main historical reasons for tolerance is that if intolerance had continued, all Europe would have been destroyed by the religious wars. It could be saved only by a tolerant state which is indifferent toward the various confessional groups fighting against each other. However, when John Locke wrote his letters on tolerance, he was well aware that tolerance can never be an absolute principle. So he limited it in an interesting way. Although a leader of the development toward the Enlightenment, he nevertheless said that there are two groups which cannot be tolerated. They are the Catholics and the atheists. Catholics cannot be tolerated because they are by definition intolerant; they aim to subjugate every nation they can by force to the authority of the Roman Church. Atheists are not intolerant, but they threaten the very foundation of Western society, which is based on the idea of God. The greatest witness to John Locke's point is Friedrich Nietzsche, who said that because "God is dead", the transformation of the whole society is at hand. This is what John Locke wanted to preclude in the name of reason.

English Deism is another movement of great importance for modern theology. The deists used philosophy in a practical way to solve theological problems. Deism was a movement of the intelligentsia, and not so much a real philosophy. They wrote attacks against traditional Orthodoxy. They criticized, as the Socinians had done, the problems of biblical religion. All elements of criticism can be found in them which we now associate with liberal theology. The problems of biblical history, the authority of Jesus, the problem of miracles, the question of special revelation, the history of religion, which shows that Christianity is not something so different, the category of myth, which was invented by the deists two hundred and fifty years before Bultmann's essay on demythologization—these are the problems with which Continental theology has had to deal ever since. The great movement of historical criticism began around 1750. Lessing, who was the greatest personality of the Enlightenment, a poet and a philosopher, was the leader in the fight against a stupid Orthodoxy which stuck to the traditional terms. The great critical line of development in theology, running from D. F. Strauss, Schleiermacher, etc. to Johannes Weiss, Albert Schweitzer, and Bultmann, had its origin back there in the middle of the eighteenth century, which itself was carrying through the ideas of the Socinians and others.

It may seem as if there were one all-embracing development in theology, an ocean which flooded over the continents. But this is not true. There were reactions in all these periods. There were high and low tides. There were the reactions of Methodism and Pietism; there was the reaction of Romanticism at the end of the eighteenth century; there were the revivalistic movements in the mid-nineteenth century, and finally there is the reaction of Neo-Orthodoxy at the beginning of the twentieth century. In all of these movements, one question is predominant: What about the compatibility of the modern mind with the Christian message? There was always an oscillation between an attempt at synthesis, in the Hegelian and Platonic sense, which means a creative unity of different elements of reality. In this sense the two men with the greatest theological influence in the nineteenth century were Hegel and Schleiermacher. Together they produced what I call the great synthesis. They took into themselves all the impulses of the modern mind, all the results of the autonomous development. Beyond this they tried to show that the true Christian message can be maintained only on this basis, and not in terms of either Orthodoxy or the Enlightenment. They rejected both and tried to find a way beyond them, Schleiermacher more from the mystical tradition of his pietistic background (he was a Moravian), and Hegel more in philosophical terms out of the Neo-Platonic tradition. By 1840 both of these forms of synthesis were considered to have broken down completely, and an extreme naturalism and materialism developed. At this time, then, another theological school tried to save what it could. This was the Ritschlian school, the leaders of which, beside Ritschl himself, were Wilhelm Herrmann and Adolph von Harnack, who is the teacher of all of us in many respects. This was a new synthesis on a more modest level, on the level of Kant's division of the world of knowledge from the world of values.

The Ritschlian synthesis broke down at the turn of the century, partly under the impact of inner theological developments. Here I can mention Ernst Troeltsch, my great teacher, and Martin Kähler, my other great teacher, who came from the pietistic and revivalistic tradition of Halle. Primarily, however, it broke down from the impact of the events of world history, the World Wars, which spelled the end of centuries of European life. Again the diastasis against the synthesis of Christianity and the modern mind became real under Karl Barth. My own answer is that synthesis can never be avoided, because man is always man, and at the same time under God. He can never be under God in such a way that he ceases to be human. In order to find a new way beyond the former ways of synthesis, I use the method of correlation. I try to show that the Christian message is the answer to all the problems involved in self-criticizing humanism; today we call this existentialism; it is a self-analyzing humanism. This is neither synthesis nor diastasis, neither identification nor separation; it is correlation. And I believe the whole story of Christian thought points in this direction.

PART II

Introduction: Problem and Method

Our task is to cover in this series of lectures the tremendously large subject of Protestant theology in the nineteenth and twentieth centuries.[1] We can do this only because this course has a definite purpose and particular limits.

The primary purpose of this course is to understand our own problems by seeing their background in the past. I do not intend that you should learn merely a lot of facts which have no meaning for you. Instead I want to show you how we have arrived at the present situation. In view of this purpose it will be possible to draw from a great amount of material.

I hope you will discover that the past can be interesting even in itself, and not merely because it is *our* past, the past from which we come as religious people and theological thinkers. Perhaps the *erōs*, the word for love in Platonic Greek, will be aroused to interest you in some of the events in the past. This would be a beautiful by-product, but I do not know to what extent I will succeed in evoking that *erōs*.

In any case, there always exists this twofold purpose of a course in history, and especially of a course in the history of thought. The main purpose is to understand ourselves; yet there is the other purpose of

[1] Editor's Note: These lectures were delivered at the Divinity School of the University of Chicago during the spring quarter of 1963. They were offered under the course title "Protestant Theology in the Nineteenth and Twentieth Centuries." The class met eighteen times for sessions lasting an hour and a half. All material in the footnotes has been supplied by the present editor.

responding to a fascination for things which have happened in the past. This latter purpose might even be the more important for some of you now; as a rule, however, it is not the main reason for historical research.

This double purpose, especially the primary and basic one of trying to understand ourselves, leads us to emphasize the trends of thought more than the individual personalities who shaped them. We will see how these trends lead into our present situation. Of course, individual theologians will be discussed because they are the bearers of the development, but only those will be discussed more fully who happen to represent the great turning points in the course of events leading to us.

The orientation of this course makes it impossible to limit ourselves to a discussion of theologians. We must relate ourselves also to philosophers. In some cases they are more important than the theologians of their time because their philosophy of religion made decisive inroads into the history of Christian thought. In other cases the scientists will be more significant than the philosophers; also literature and even music— to allude to Karl Barth—will form an important part of the historical development.

I was very much interested and surprised when I read how Karl Barth dealt predominantly with the history of philosophy, and even music, in his beautiful book on the history of nineteenth-century theology.[2] And if Karl Barth does this, considering his attitude toward philosophy, then I certainly feel justified in doing the same thing. I recommend Barth's book as an illustration of the greatest convergence between his thinking and my own. Therefore, we will have to trespass the limits of the theological circle by dealing with philosophers, men of science and literature.

There is another kind of limit that we must trespass in order to understand the problems of the nineteenth century. We will have to go back into the eighteenth century, and occasionally even before that, because the principles of the modern mind were formulated in the centuries preceding the nineteenth. You can find these principles

---

[2] *Die protestantische Theologie im 19. Jahrhundert* (Zürich: Evangelischer Verlag, 1952). The English translation is entitled *Protestant Thought from Rousseau to Ritschl* (New York: Harper & Row, 1959). Unfortunately, only eleven chapters, less than one half, of the German edition are included in the English version.

implicit in all the great thinkers of the Renaissance, and certainly in the great scientific systems of the seventeenth century. But it was only during the eighteenth century that these principles became fully formulated as criticisms of theology. Every university and college worthy of their names are dependent on the thinkers of the eighteenth century and on their fundamental criticisms of the traditions of Orthodoxy and Pietism. And if you should come from Europe to America as I did thirty years ago, you would be astonished at how much more Americans are dependent on the eighteenth century than Europeans. The reason is very simple. America experienced every little of the romanticist reaction against the eighteenth century. Therefore, there is a very strong relationship here to the eighteenth century; thus I will be speaking very much to your situation when I go back to the principles out of which the criticism of orthodox and pietistic theology came.

We must also go beyond the nineteenth century into the twentieth because certain fundamental theological events have taken place in the last sixty years. I will now mention only a few of them in passing: the end of liberalism represented classically by Adolf von Harnack; the great all-embracing victory of the existentialist point of view; then the resurgence of what is called neo-orthodoxy in America and the theology of crisis in Europe. It is unfortunate that the latter is also called dialectical theology, because it is really more antidialectical than dialectical. Finally, there has been an appearance in recent years of what one could call neoliberalism. Now, these four movements have appeared in the twentieth century, and if we did not include them, this course would have no existential conclusion for our situation.

Now, I repeat, this is a large program for a single quarter, but it can be carried out if we select and interpret the material from a particular point of view, or better, from an overarching point of view. This means that we do not simply say that there was Mr. X and he said this, and a little later Mr. Y came along and he said that, and so with all the Xs and the Ys we reach the present time. That is a nonsensical way of dealing with history, even though it might be claimed to be the most "factual." Actually, it has nothing to do with real facts. Of course, there are factual elements in an interpretation of history, otherwise the interpretation becomes a misinterpretation of the course of history. History has an inner *telos*. *Telos* means "end," the "end" toward which something runs. Every period has an inner *telos,* and a given period must be interpreted historically in the light of its "end." Everything in this period receives its significance for us from its relation to the *telos*. In every moment innumerable things happen. In one hour like this more things are happening than all the books in the world could describe if we were to enter into the microcosmic elements in ourselves, in our brains and minds. Therefore, the interpretation of history must be selective; everything depends on the point of view from which we select and on the principle used in establishing what is important. For example, what is most important in church history? The answer is, of course, the Christian Church and its theological work. This also includes Western culture and the relationship of cultural activities to religion. In any case, a point of view in the interpretation of history must be found.

There is a point of view which I want to use, namely, the continuous series of attempts to unite the diverging elements of the modern mind. The most important of these attempts will seek to unite the orthodox and the humanist traditions. If the word "orthodox" seems too narrow for you, then we can speak of the "classical" tradition instead. All modern theology is an attempt to unite these two trends in the recent history of Christian thought. But, of course, this is only a very general formulation. The situation is infinitely richer, both culturally and religiously, than this can indicate. But if we look carefully, we will find that all the theologians, especially the great ones, will try to answer the question: What is the relation between the classical and the humanist traditions? One answer could be: There is no positive relation between them at all; the one simply stands beside the other. There could be the opposite answer: There is a complete unity between them, either in the one direction or in the other. But between these two opposite answers there can be many others, not as onesided as these two, which try to find a vital relationship, filled with many problems, tensions, and possible solutions.

First, I will develop the different elements in this divergent situation which had to be united. After having shown these elements, namely, Orthodoxy, Pietism, the Enlightenment and Romanticism, etc., I will discuss the greatest, the most embracing and effective, but in the last analysis unsuccessful attempts to bring about a union of all of them. I call these *the great synthesis*. *Synthesis* in Greek means "putting together," but in English this word has a negative connotation. Synthetic pearls are not genuine pearls. However, the theology of Schleiermacher and the philosophy of Hegel—these two great representatives of the synthesis in the early nineteenth century—are certainly not artificial pearls. They are very genuine and have had a tremendous impact on the whole history of thought to the present day. Hegel, for example, through the reactions of his pupils, has changed the surface of the earth in the twentieth century, perhaps more than any philosopher has ever done. We have only to think of the Communist Revolution.

These two thinkers, Schleiermacher and Hegel, are the points toward which all elements go and from which they then diverge, later bringing about the demand for new syntheses. We will see how these new syntheses have been attempted again and again, and finally what in my opinion has to be done today. So the whole story has a dramatic character. It is the drama of the rise of a humanism in the midst of Christianity which is critical of the Christian tradition, departs from it and produces a vast world of secular existence and thought. Then there is the rise of some of the greatest philosophers and theologians who try to unite these divergent elements again. Their syntheses in turn are destroyed and the divergent elements collide and try to conquer each other, and new attempts to reunite them have to be made. The Ritschlian school is an example of this, with Harnack as its leading representative. And in our century there is the Bultmann school, and so on.

Thus we really have a drama before us, a drama in which many tragedies are involved. All the disruptions of inner, personal, spiritual life of countless people are involved in the conflicts of this drama—conflicts which do not stop before the sacred doors of theological schools and seminaries. They are inescapable for all of us, whether we like it or not.

There is one thing in what I have said that you might tend to question, namely, the predominance of German theology in the nineteenth and early twentieth centuries. This is simply a fact which I cannot help. The reason for this is that other Protestant countries were not involved in this conflict to the same intense degree. If we look at Great Britain for a moment, we see that there was no great depth of genuine theological interest. The Anglican Church put its main emphasis on liturgical questions, and on questions of political structure and ethical consequences. This is its genius, its greatness, but it is not theology in the strict sense. In the Scandinavian countries there is only one man who made a great difference in the nineteenth century, and he is Søren Kierkegaard. He was not only a religious writer, as Martin Heidegger calls him, but in his religious writings the existentialist philosophy was present. Many modern existentialists have derived their philosophy from Kierkegaard's writings. Kierkegaard was what he was because he had to struggle to overcome his master, Hegel. Hegel's thought permeates his whole work, almost every sentence. And contemporary with Kierkegaard there was another theologian greatly influenced by Hegel, Bishop Hans Martensen of Denmark (1808–1884). He was a theologian of mediation,[3] to use a term dating from the middle of the nineteenth century.

In Holland during the nineteenth century there developed a split between the critical attitude on the one side (the liberal church took into itself all the critical elements of liberalism) and the orthodox Calvinist Church on the other side, which maintained the traditional theology with great tenacity. But during this period there were no new theological solutions in Holland.

In Switzerland the older traditions were preserved, but here there arose certain other influences which were later to shape modern theology. Three names must be mentioned. The greatest of them is Friedrich Nietzsche (1844–1900), whose attack on Christianity had an enormous influence on the whole later theological development. The second is Jacob Burckhardt (1818–1897), the historian, who wrote the beautiful books about the Renaissance and the art of Florence and Rome. And the third one is Franz Overbeck (1837–1905), who declared —something which Barth often mentions—that if Christianity has arrived at the point of nineteenth-century liberalism, then one must ask

[3] The expression "theology of mediation" is a technical term referring to various nineteenth-century efforts to correlate the Christian faith with the modern mind. For a discussion of this *Vermittlungstheologie,* see below, pp. 208–215.

the question: Are we still Christians? and he passionately denied that. He had a great influence on later thought. These are some of the vital new impulses that were experienced in Switzerland, and which played an important role in the theological revolution that occurred in the twentieth century (Barth and Brunner).

In France, which has only a small number of Protestants, the modernist movement was the most interesting, comprising those who represented what was called "symbolofideism." This means literally the "symbolism of faith." Alfred Loisy (1857–1940) is the best known of the modernists. These modernists had an interesting theory of religious symbolism. They were excommunicated by the Pope, but their influence has never ceased. Often I meet Catholic laymen, especially highly educated ones, who take it for granted that most of the dogmas have to be taken symbolically. But officially this is not permitted. The modernistic symbolofideists were condemned by the Pope.

Now the United States followed generally the continental development, first orthodoxy, then pietism, usually called revivalism here, and then liberalism. But there are two differences. The first is that in this country liberalism took the form of a church, namely, Unitarianism. This has never happened in Europe. There liberalism was a theological movement in the established churches, but it never established itself as a church. Perhaps this was a better solution because it seems that Unitarianism in this country suffers from its separation. It tends to be less flexible than liberal theology in Europe because it becomes bound to a church tradition.

The second important difference is the rise of the social gospel movement. There were also social ethical elements in the late nineteenth-century liberal theology represented by Harnack, but they were not essential. Only with the rise of religious socialism, a comparatively small movement after the first World War, did similar things occur in Germany. Before this they had already occurred in Switzerland and in England. But the transformation of all theology from the point of view of social ethics, thus creating a theology of the social gospel,[4] is something original in this country.

[4] Cf. Walter Rauschenbusch, *Theology of the Social Gospel* (New York: The Macmillan Company, 1918).

Now that gives us a broad overview of things. It is enough to show you that the central and most dramatic movements of theology took place in Germany. This also means that it happened on Lutheran soil. This is not strange, because there is no other Protestant church which places such a heavy emphasis on doctrine, on the pure doctrine as it was called in the Reformation period. What Luther called the Word of God over against the Roman Church was embodied in the Lutheran confessions and doctrines. And Lutheranism, at least in some sections, still preserves this tremendous emphasis on the doctrinal side of Christianity. Calvinism lays more stress on the disciplinary, ethical side, and Episcopalianism more on the liturgical side.

All this shows that the kind of history of Christian thought to which I will introduce you is, so to speak, the historical dimension of systematic theology. It is not church history and I am no church historian. And when you ask, Why should I learn all this? Why these studies of the history of Christian thought which only seek to establish dates that can soon be forgotten again?—then I must answer that this is not the way in which I intend to deal with the past.

CHAPTER I

Oscillating Emphases in Orthodoxy,

Pietism and Rationalism

A. The Period of Orthodoxy

First I want to say a few words about what followed the period of the Reformation, namely, the development of orthodoxy. Now the word "orthodoxy" has two meanings. There is both Eastern Orthodoxy and Protestant Orthodoxy. The Eastern Churches which call themselves Orthodox (e.g., Russian and Greek) do so not so much because of their doctrinal interests, but because of their interest in the tradition. The Eastern Orthodox Churches, of course, have fixed liturgical forms and they also have doctrinal statements, but they are very flexible in this respect. They have the good fortune of not having a Pope. Because they feel that they are in continual development, they can work in close relation with Protestantism in the World Council of Churches. The term "orthodoxy" in Greek simply means "right opinion," but in Eastern Orthodoxy it connotes the "classical tradition." The tradition is expressed in the councils, in the creeds, in the acknowledged Fathers, and in the whole liturgical development. This is Eastern Orthodoxy. It is clear that here orthodoxy means something quite different from what it means when we speak of Protestant Orthodoxy.

We must also be sure to distinguish between orthodoxy and fundamentalism. The orthodox period of Protestantism has very little to do with what is called fundamentalism in America. Rather, it has special reference to the scholastic period of Protestant history. There were great scholastics in Protestantism, some of them equally as great as the medieval scholastics. One of them is Johann Gerhard (1582–1637) who in his monumental work[1] developed fully as many problems as the tomes of the medieval scholastics in the thirteenth and fourteenth centuries. Such a thing has never been done in American fundamentalism. Protestant Orthodoxy was constructive. It did not have anything like the pietistic or revivalistic background of American fundamentalism. It was objective as well as constructive, and attempted to present the pure and comprehensive doctrine concerning God and man and the world. It was not determined by a kind of lay biblicism as is the case in American fundamentalism—a biblicism which rejects any theological penetration into the biblical writings and makes itself dependent on traditional interpretations of the Word of God.

You cannot find anything like that in classical orthodoxy. Therefore it is a pity that very often orthodoxy and fundamentalism are confused. One of the great achievements of classical orthodoxy in the late sixteenth and early seventeenth centuries was the fact that it remained in continual discussion with all the centuries of Christian thought. Those theologians were not untheological lay people ignorant of the meanings of the concepts which they used in biblical interpretation. They knew the past meanings of these concepts in the history of the church which covered a period of over fifteen hundred years. These orthodox theologians knew the history of philosophy as well as the theology of the Reformation. The fact that they were in the tradition of the Reformers did not prevent them from knowing thoroughly scholastic theology, from discussing and refuting it, or even accepting it when possible.

All this makes classical orthodoxy one of the great events in the history of Christian thought. I feel that the superiority of the more educated Catholic theologians in our century over the more educated Protestant theologians is largely due to the fact that they know their

---

[1] The reference is to Gerhard's 9-volume work on dogmatics, *Loci theologici* (1610-22). This is a classic expression of the "local" (or topical) method of scholastic theology.

Latin as well as you know your English. They are able to formulate the classical doctrines of Christianity in continuity with the Latin language that in theology goes back at least to Tertullian in the second century. We have in the Latin language something that I sometimes call a philosophical and theological clearing house. Its sharpness of linguistic and logical distinctions overcomes much of the vagueness that is prevalent in Protestant thought. There is no modern language that has this kind of sharpness. Now I would not suggest that you should all speak Latin as well as our theological fathers used to do. They had to write an essay in Latin in order to pass an examination for admission into the university. They had to be able to use Latin freely, without a commentary. Although this ability has been lost—and it represents a great loss of sharpness in theological thinking—we should at least be able to read the Latin texts with a translation running on one side. I hope somebody will take this to heart and write such a book. We could have a compendium, as it was called in Germany in my time, of classical orthodoxy, Lutheran or Calvinist, or better both united in one compendium, where you have on one side the classical formulations in Latin—which you could recognize because there is so much of the Latin language in English—and on the other side the English translations, which are never as good as the Latin.

In this connection I often think of the saying of one of my former teachers, Martin Kähler, who lived in the period immediately following Goethe, and who knew his Goethe as well as the Bible by heart. He used to say that the orthodoxy of the sixteenth and seventeenth centuries is the abutment against which the bridge of all later Protestant theology leans. That is a very good symbol, because all later Protestant theology becomes a bit vague and is suspended in the air if it is not related to the classic formulation of Reformation theology in Protestant Orthodoxy. The vagueness of much theological thinking in modern Protestantism stems from this lack of knowledge of Protestant Orthodoxy.

Friedrich Schleiermacher, the father of modern Protestant theology, was theologically educated within the framework of Protestant Orthodoxy. If you read his dogmatics, *The Christian Faith*,[2] you will find that

[2] Edited by H. R. Mackintosh and J. S. Stewart (Edinburgh: T. & T. Clark, 1928).

he never develops any thought without making reference to classical orthodoxy, then to the pietist criticism of orthodoxy, and finally to the Enlightenment criticism of both, before he goes on to state his own solutions. This is an important procedure for all theological thought.

Orthodoxy is the most objective representation of Protestant theology. Of course, when I use the word "objective," I find that I must always carefully define what "objective" means as over against "subjective." Today the word "objective" means scientifically verified or empirically true. This is not the sense in which I mean it. One cannot simply transpose categories from science to the humanities. When we speak of Orthodoxy as "objective" we have in mind a representation of doctrine as such without particular reference to the individual who accepts or rejects it. The "subjective" element—the word "subjective" does not mean willful or arbitrary as it is usually used today—has reference to the believing subject, construing something in what we today call existential terms. Orthodoxy tried to be as objective as possible, but even this system was open to subjective elements. First of all, there was the subjective element which belongs to all Protestantism, namely, Luther's personal experience, or Zwingli's, or later on Calvin's. All three of them broke through the objectivism of the Roman Church. This breakthrough was an element in the orthodox system itself. This becomes very clear when we look at the two main principles of Orthodoxy. These have been called the "material principle" and the "formal principle."

The material principle of the Reformation is the doctrine of justification by faith, or rather by grace through faith. Excuse me for this slip of the tongue! Never say what I just said by mistake, but always say, justification *by* grace *through* faith. The justifying power is the divine grace; the channel through which men receive this grace is faith. Faith is by no means the cause, but only the channel. In the moment in which faith is understood as the cause of justification, it is a worse work of man than anything in Roman Catholicism. It results in destroying one's own honesty by compelling oneself to believe certain things. This is the consequence of the phrase, justification *by* faith. If faith is a human work which makes us acceptable to God, and if this human work is the basis or cause of salvation, then we can never be certain of our salvation in the sense in which Luther sought for certainty when he asked the question, "How do I find a merciful God?" Therefore, whenever you are dealing with Protestant theology, dismiss forever this distortion of faith —*sola fide* in Latin—which sees faith as a cause instead of as a channel. Luther made this clear repeatedly when he said that faith is always receiving and only receiving; it does not produce anything. Certainly it does not produce the good will of God.

Here the linguistic problem becomes the profoundest theological problem. The great distortions in Protestantism have come from this basic confusion—as if Luther ever said that an intellectual acceptance of doctrines can be the saving power for men. For Luther faith is the result of the divine Spirit, and the divine Spirit and grace are one and the same thing. God gives us grace by giving us the Spirit. It is the Spirit who makes it possible for us to accept the message that our sins are forgiven. It is absolutely contrary to the whole Reformation if somebody should say that before you can be forgiven you must first have belief in God, in Christ and his atonement, plus Luther's doctrines and Catechisms. That is anti-divine and anti-Reformation. The primary thing is to be open for the divine grace, and not the attempt to produce it. The worst form of trying to produce it—at least today—is to try to accept doctrines, to believe in something which somehow we believe is unbelievable, force it upon ourselves and repress honest doubt. That is the worst kind of distortion.

There is the other principle, the "formal principle," on which the system of Orthodoxy was built. This is the principle of Scripture which became fixed and rigid. Is it not possible to rest confidently on this? But we all know that ever since Origen there have been many interpretations of the Bible. Every period of history has a different understanding of what is decisive in the Bible. The Bible is an object of interpretation. If somebody does not believe that, just ask him, "Do you know what the Greek words meant at the time they were written so that you can identify them with the Word of God?" Then very likely he will say, "I don't even know Greek, but I have the King James Bible, and of course, that is the true Word of God. All of the modernistic Bibles should be burned." That is the typical point of view of somebody who simply does not know. It may be a repression of willingness to face the real situation. The Bible is the book which contains the reports of the events which

have happened both in the Old and the New Testaments. It presents
the history of revelation and its fulfillment in the Christ as the foundation of the Christian Church. This is the central event which the Bible
proclaims.

But if we say that this protects us from being subjective, then we
have never tried to translate even one verse of Scripture. The right
translation of all the great passages of the New Testament is dependent
on an understanding of their meaning, and this is a work for which
rigorous scholarship is needed. At the same time, the religious tradition
is at work in the understanding of Scripture when simple believers read
it. Their reading does have saving power for them. This is the meaning
of the Protestant formula *Scriptura suiipsius interpres,"* (Scripture
interprets itself). It does this to every pious layman who reads the Bible;
this does not mean, however, that he may make a theological dogma out
of his ignorance of the situation, as fundamentalism does. So here we
have the principle of subjectivity unavoidably entering in, although the
Reformers tried to prevent it by putting the authority of the Bible in
place of the authority of the church. This is most clear in Calvin. For
Calvin the Bible does not say anything to anyone, either to theologians
or to pious readers, without the divine Spirit. The divine Spirit is the
creative power in which our own personal spirit is involved and transcended. The spirit is not a mechanism for dictating material as in some
forms of the theory of inspiration.

There is another dangerous element in classical orthodoxy to which I
must refer. This is the two-storied character of orthodoxy theology. The
lower story is called "natural theology," which works with reason, and
the upper story is called "revealed theology." The theologians always
had difficulty determining what belonged to each. Naturally, doctrines
like those dealing with the trinity and the incarnation were placed into
revealed theology, but already the doctrines of creation and providence
were doubtful. Where did they belong? Thus Johann Gerhard, of
whom we spoke earlier, distinguished between pure and mixed doctrines
(*doctrinae purae et mixtae*). The pure doctrines are those which can be
deduced only from divine revelation; the mixed doctrines are those
which can be dealt with partly in terms of reason and partly in terms of
revelation.

Such a view is quite unsatisfactory and presupposes a concept of reason that itself is unsatisfactory. Thus it happened that a revolution occurred by the lower story fighting against the upper story. As often happens in society, the lower classes fight against the upper classes. But during the Enlightenment it was the lower story of the building of theology which revolted against the upper story. The lower claimed the right to become the whole building and denied the right to have any independent upper story at all. We call this "rationalism" in theology. There was something in the very structure of Orthodoxy which made it possible for this revolution of rationalism to take place.

B. The Reaction of Pietism against Orthodoxy

Before the revolution of natural theology against revealed theology took place, there was another type of criticism against the orthodox system which had recourse to a subjective element and recalled Luther's personal experience. In the power of the Spirit which speaks through the biblical message Luther had carried out a revolution against the objectivism of the Roman Church. In his earlier development Luther was very much influenced by mystical elements. He was profoundly influenced by the so-called *Theologia Germanica,* the classic of devotional literature from the period of German mysticism. It was Luther's experience of God which produced the explosiveness of his teaching that really transformed the surface of the earth. What was this experience? It was not the criticism of dogma. There had been much of that prior to Luther. Most of his positions had been theoretically formulated earlier by the so-called prereformers. But it was the explosion of a personal relation to God. Was that based on human achievements of an intellectual or moral kind, or was it based on openness for what God gives and in particular *forgives?* The latter was the decisive thing. Thus already in the period of the Reformation there were elements that we must call mystical, and which became pronounced again in the anti-orthodox movement of Pietism. This happened first in Germany in the seventeenth century (Spener and Francke), then in British Methodism (the Wesley brothers), and finally in a great number of sectarian movements in this country which claim for themselves the presence of the Spirit.

Pietism also had its theology, but it was generally a theology which accepted the orthodox tradition, just as the revivalist movement in America did, only making it less theologically relevant by a fundamentalist deviation and primitivization. However, Pietism fought against Orthodoxy on the ground of Orthodoxy; this was a long and often bitter fight. Let me give you an illustration of this. There was a debate on what was called the *"theologia irregenetorum,"* the theology of the unregenerate, of those who are not born again. Orthodoxy maintained the view that since theology is an objective science, it is possible to write a fully valid theology whether we are reborn or not. Pietism said, "No, that's impossible; you must be reborn with respect to everything in which you participate, in all that you talk about; you can be a theologian only if you have the experience of regeneration." The answer of the Orthodox theologians to this was: "How can you state beyond any doubt that you are regenerate? Is any emotional experience to be considered a real rebirth? Is not regeneration a process under the guidance of the divine Spirit which does not permit you to make a clear distinction between before and after?"

Of course there are some people who have a decisive experience. John Wesley had it; August Francke, the German pietist, had it, and Nicholaus von Zinzendorf had it, but these are exceptional cases. The development of the ordinary Christian does not manifest a clear-cut division between before and after, so that he could say with finality: Now I am able to be a theologian because I have really experienced rebirth. Modern theology is still discussing this point. Today we ask instead: Isn't existential participation in theological problems necessary in order to understand and solve them? I think that this way of putting the question can be a formula of union, combining the concerns of the orthodox and the pietist theologians. Existential participation indeed is necessary, but an experience of regeneration at a definite point in time is certainly not. That is impossible. It is enough that we are existentially concerned about these problems, that we participate in them existentially, even though for the moment it may be in the form of doubt. So my answer to the question which became one of the chief points of contention between Orthodoxy and Pietism is that existential participation and ultimate seriousness in dealing with theological questions is necessary. Indeed, this is a presupposition of theology, but by no means does it entail the fixing of a date and pointing to an inner experience of regeneration. The final upshot was that Pietism succeeded in bringing Orthodoxy out of its seemingly unconquerable fortress by appealing to the element of subjectivity in the Reformers themselves. That was the other side of Luther and Calvin which had been neglected in Orthodoxy. Thus Pietism was able to break open this very frozen system of thought.

C. The Rise of Rationalism

The theology of the Reformation created a special educational problem which opened the door to rationalism. In Roman Catholicism you can be saved by believing what the church believes. This is called the *fides implicita* (implicit faith). If you believe what you are taught, then implicitly you receive the truth which the Catholic Church teaches. This was one of the points on which the Reformation erupted, for in place of the *fides implicita* the Reformers taught that everyone must have an experience of grace in faith. Each individual must be able to confess his sins, to experience the meaning of repentance, and to become certain of his salvation through Christ. This became a problem in Protestantism. It meant that everyone would have to have some basic knowledge of the fundamental doctrines of the Christian Church. In teaching these doctrines, you could not carry on the instruction of ordinary people in the same way as future professors of theology are taught, with their knowledge of Latin and Greek, of the history of exegesis and theological thought. How can you teach everybody? By making the teaching extremely simple. This simplification became more and more a rationalization. You must teach what is understandable by reason in your religious education, because it is necessary that everyone should know what is said and meant in the Catechism.

The consequence of this was that the doctrines had to be made more reasonable to become more understandable. This was one of the ways in which religious education served as a preparation for the Enlightenment. Often the people of the Enlightenment had no idea that they were doing anything else than preserving the religious tradition. But they said, "We must do it in a reasonable way so that people can understand." In Protestantism we cannot have people like the masses of Roman Catholic people, who attend church, listen to the mass, perhaps go to confession, and then leave again. Protestants must have a direct personal relationship with God, whether or not they go to church. They must know for themselves, and cannot be led to priests and professors. Therefore, doctrine must be made understandable to the people. Do not forget that this is still a problem for us. Since we are all autonomous in contrast to the Roman Christians who accept what the church teaches, we must know the doctrine for ourselves, whether we are laymen or ministers. Thus liberal education in our time faces this same problem: How can these things be made understandable? That is not the whole problem, but that is the educational side which is very important for the whole development.

We have been discussing the revolt against Orthodoxy from the side of natural theology which Orthodoxy itself had made a part of its two-story system. The substructure of orthodox theology is natural theology, and natural theology is rational theology. Thus the rise of rational criticism of revealed theology came out of Orthodoxy itself. Rational theology is a theology which through arguments for the existence of God, and the like, attempts to build a universally acceptable theology by pure reason. At this point the revolt could take place, the revolt of the substructure against the superstructure. The substructure was built by the tools of rational arguments; the superstructure as revealed theology is based on the sources of revelation. In Protestantism these are virtually equated with the biblical writings, while in Catholicism the tradition of the church is included as well. The whole structure was delicately built and extremely vulnerable from the point of view of the relation between the two stories. It would be possible for reason to revolt against revelation, as it is usually phrased in traditional terminology. But this is a poor way of phrasing it, as I will show later.

This led to the struggle in the eighteenth century between a naturalistic or rationalistic and a supernaturalistic theology. This struggle brought about the weakening of the power of Orthodoxy. Now Pietism and Rationalism had one element in common. Pietism was more modern than Orthodoxy; it was nearer to the modern mind, because of the element of subjectivity in it. If the word "subjectivity" has the connotation of willfulness to you, it should not be used; rather, we should speak of existential participation. This may be a clumsy expression, but at least it avoids the bad connotation of arbitrariness which is usually connected with the word "subjectivity." The common denominator in Pietism, or revivalism as it is often called, and in Rationalism is the mystical element. This is one of the most important insights for understanding the development of Protestant theology after the Reformation to the present time. Therefore, I want to discuss now the relation between the mystical and rational elements in theology.

Rationalism and mysticism do not stand in contradiction to each other, as is so often thought. Both in Greek and modern culture rationalism is the daughter of mysticism. Rationalism developed out of the mystical experience of the "inner light" or the "inner truth" in every human being. Reason emerged within us out of mystical experience, namely, the experience of the divine presence within us. This can be seen most clearly in the Quaker movement. Quakerism in George Fox's time was an ecstatic, mystical movement, as were most of the radical movements of the Reformation and post-Reformation periods. Already in the second generation of Quakerism there developed a moral rationalism from which have come the great moral principles of modern Quaker activities. There never was the feeling on the part of Quakers that their rational, pacifist, and in certain respects, very bourgeois morality stood in conflict with their mystical experience of intuition. Therefore, it is useful to study the development of Quakerism in order to understand the relation between mystical and rational inwardness. Both of them exist within our subjectivity. The opposite of a theology of inwardness is the classical theology of the Reformers, namely, the theology of the Word of God which comes to us from the outside, stands over against us and judges us, so that we have to accept it on the authority of the revelatory experiences of the prophets and apostles.

This whole conflict is of fundamental importance to the movements of theology in the centuries that we wish to discuss. The same conflict occurred in our century, between the liberal theology of Harnack's *What Is Christianity?*[3] and Karl Barth's theology of crisis. To see this conflict you should read the classical exchange of letters between Harnack and Barth. Here we have the modern parallel to the encounter between the theologians of the Reformation and the Anabaptists and other spiritualistic movements. Unfortunately, the terms "spiritualist" and "spiritist" have been stolen by the occultists, and can no longer be used in good theology. In the third volume of my *Systematic Theology*,[4] in the part on "Life and the Spirit," I develop a theology of the Spirit, but I do not use these confusing adjectives. If by chance I do use them, I am not thinking about spiritualism in the sense of entering into communication with souls that have passed beyond death. I would not be interested in that even if it were a reality. The spiritualist movements in the Reformation period are often called "radical evangelical movements." We have this same sort of conflict between Orthodoxy and Pietism, which we have discussed, and in the nineteenth century between German classical idealism and the rebirth of Orthodoxy in the restoration theology of the mid-nineteenth century.

If for a moment I may be allowed to be personal, you see this same conflict going on between my own theology and Karl Barth's, the one approaching man by coming from the outside (Barth) and the other starting with man. Now I believe that there is one concept which can reconcile these two ways. This is the concept of the divine Spirit. It was there in the apostle Paul. Paul was the great theologian of the divine Spirit. It formed the center of his theology. The classical Protestant view has held, along with Luther, Melanchthon, Calvin, and Bucer, that Paul was a theologian of justification by grace through faith. That certainly is not wrong. But this was a defensive doctrine for Paul. He developed this doctrine in his fight against the so-called Judaizers. They wanted to transform the gospel into another law; they demanded that the pagans or Gentiles subject themselves to the Jewish law, and for them Jesus was only another interpreter of the law. Paul had to fight against this, otherwise there could be no Christian Church in the pagan

[3] Adolf von Harnack, *What Is Christianity?* translated by Thomas B. Saunders (New York: Harper & Brothers, 1957).
[4] The University of Chicago Press, 1963.

nations. Christianity would have remained a small Jewish sect. Nevertheless, as important as the doctrine of justification was for Paul, it was not the center of his theology. At the center was his experience and doctrine of the Spirit. Thus he is on the side of those in Protestant theology who stress inwardness. Paul goes so far as to say what many mystics have stressed since, namely, that a successful prayer is not one which obtains what we ask for, but one which attains the Spirit of God. It is God himself as Spirit who prays for us and bears witness with our spirit. You can read this in Romans 8. You will find there that Paul is indeed the theologian of the Spirit.

Although I am not a mystical theologian, I would say that I am more on the side of the theology of experience and inwardness, for I believe that the Spirit is in us. In the concept of the Spirit the highest synthesis is given between the Word of God which comes from the outside and the experience which occurs inside. Now all this has been a digression, but if a systematic theologian teaches history, he cannot help but tell you what he thinks about things. He cannot simply enumerate facts in textbook fashion. You can do that much better for yourself. The problem is the difference between the theology of the Word from the outside and the theology of inner experience, which is frequently but wrongly called "the inner Word." That is not a good term. "Inner light" is better. In modern terminology we speak of "existential experience." The point is that these two things are not mutually exclusive. The concept of the Spirit is the mediating power which overcomes the conflict between outside and inside.

I said that the principles of reason develop out of an originally ecstatic experience which produces insight. This insight can become rationalized. As the principles of reason emerge within us, the original underlying ecstasy can disappear or recede, with the result that the Spirit becomes Reason in the largest sense of the concept. We will develop this later in the lectures on the Enlightenment. Anyway, I hope that you now understand one thing: The opposite of mysticism is not rationalism, but rationalism is the daughter of mysticism. The opposite of mysticism is the theology of the Word in terms of an authority coming from the outside, to which we subject ourselves either by accepting doctrines or by fulfilling moral commands. We should also avoid the distortions of the word "mystical." A person, for instance, is said to be a bit mystical when he is somewhat foggy in his mind. That is not a serious usage of the term. Mysticism means inwardness, participation in the Ultimate Reality through inner experience. In some cases mystics have tried to produce this participation by means of asceticism, self-emptying exercises, and the like. But mysticism should not be identified with these exercises either.

Whatever we may think of abstract mysticism such as we find in Plotinus or in Hinduism, which are very similar to each other, we must nevertheless say that there is a mystical element in every religion and in every prayer. This mystical element is the inward participation in and experience of the presence of the divine. Where this is lacking we have only intellect or will; we have a system of doctrines or a system of ethics, but we do not have religion. In Protestantism, especially in some Protestant groups in this country, we see what happens when the mystical element is neglected and forgotten. Doctrines are not pushed aside, but they are put on the altar or in a box, so to speak. They are taken for granted, and no one is supposed to question them seriously. Theology is not very important. But so-called Christian morals are kept, with the result that the "teachings of Jesus" are misused and Jesus is modeled after the poor image of a teacher. Jesus was more than a teacher; his teachings were expressions of his being, and were thus not teachings in an ordinary sense. Thus Protestantism becomes an unmystical system of moral commandments, and its specifically religious basis, the presence of the Spirit of God in our spirit, is disregarded. The history of Protestant theology refutes such an attitude and shows that it is a complete deviation from the genuine experience of the divine presence.

There are many reasons why rationalism was born out of mysticism both in Greek and modern culture. But we cannot go into them. We can only observe that it happened on a large scale in the late seventeenth and eighteenth centuries. Ecstatic Protestant groups and their leaders were also the leaders of the Enlightenment. This happened in many places and can be understood only on the basis of what I have said about the relation of rationalism to mysticism. The one term which grasps their unity is the term "inner light." It comes from the Augustinian-Franciscan tradition in medieval theology, which was renewed by the sectarian movements in the Reformation period, and underlies much of Protestant theology in America. The inner light is the light which everybody has within himself because he belongs to God, and in virtue of which he is able to receive the divine Word when it is spoken to him.

CHAPTER II

The Enlightenment and Its Problems

A. The Nature of Enlightenment

Now we must go to the fundamental principles of the Enlightenment. We will not be speaking directly of the great thinkers of the eighteenth century, such as Hobbes (really seventeenth century) and Hume in England, Lessing and Kant in Germany, and Rousseau and Voltaire in France, but we will be describing the fundamental principles of the Enlightenment. Most of our academic life is based on these principles.

1. The Kantian Definition of Autonomy

We will be discussing four main concepts, without going into the details of their application. The first of these is "autonomy." In order to introduce this concept, I will indicate how Kant understood it in the latter part of the eighteenth century. Kant defined enlightenment (*Aufklärung*) as man's conquering the state of immaturity so far as he is responsible for it. Immaturity, he said, is the inability to use one's own reason without the guidance of somebody else. Immaturity of this kind is caused by ourselves. It is rooted in the lack of resoluteness and courage to use reason without the guidance of another person. The free use of reason is the essence of enlightenment. Now that is a very adequate description of what autonomy means. Kant pointed out how much more comfortably one lives if one has guardians, of whatever kind they may be, whether religious, political, philosophical, or educational ones. But it was his intention to drive men out of their security under the guidance of other people. For him this security contradicts the true nature of man.

That is the meaning of the idea of autonomy in the light of Kant's words. He could say that this is the fundamental principle of enlightenment, the autonomy of reason in every individual human being. The word "autonomy" needs some interpretation. It is derived from two Greek words, *autos*, which means "self," and *nomos*, which means "law." Autonomy means being a law to oneself. The law is not outside of us, but inside as our true being. This Greek origin of the word shows clearly that autonomy is the opposite of arbitrariness or willfulness. Autonomy is not lawless subjectivity. Kant emphasized this when he said that the essential nature of the human will is the law of reason. Every deviation from it hurts the essential nature of the will itself. It is the law implicit in man's rational structure. It has implications for the theoretical as well as for the practical side of man's activities. It refers to knowledge as well as to the arts, to the development of personality as well as to community. Everything which belongs to man's nature shares in his rational structure. Man is autonomous. The law of aesthetic fulfillment (works of art), of cognitive fulfillment (scientific inquiry), of personal fulfillment in a mature personality, of community fulfillment in principles of justice—all these belong to reason and are based on the autonomy of reason in every human being.

I must warn you about some distorted statements on autonomy. There are theological books of the neo-orthodox movement, for example, which attack autonomy as a revolt against God. They identify it with individual willfulness and arbitrariness. In doing this they distort the meaning of autonomy. Man's autonomy does not stand against the word or will of God—as if God's will were something opposed to man's created goodness and its fulfillment. We could define autonomy as the memory which man has of his own created goodness. Autonomy is man's living in the law of reason in all realms of his spiritual activity. Many philosophers of the Enlightenment identified autonomy with the divine will and were in no way critical of this identification. But for the individual man it means the courage to think; it means the courage to use one's rational powers. This becomes even more clear when we look at the opposite term, namely, "heteronomy."

The word "heteronomy" also comes from two Greek words, *heteros,* which means "strange" or "foreign," and *nomos,* which means "law." Now the whole thing is turned around. It is not autonomy but ultimately heteronomy that involves willfulness and arbitrariness. Why? Because if we should obey a strange authority, even if it were to come from God, it would go against the will of our own created goodness, and we would be subjecting ourselves to something that is not pure reason within us, such as our desires, our strivings, or the pleasure principle, and the like. Then we are looking for the security of a foreign authority which deprives us of the courage to use our reason because of the fear of punishment or of falling into insoluble problems. So we come to the surprising result that heteronomy is ultimately the attempt to escape fear, not by courage but by subjection to an authority which gives us security. In this sense heteronomy indirectly appeals to the pleasure principle and denies our own rational structure. Kant, for instance, was very much aware even before Freud and modern psychotherapy that religious heteronomy also subjects men to strange laws—whether heteronomy in relation to the church or the Bible—and that men follow these laws driven by fear. This means that ultimately they are being driven by the pleasure principle, subverting the created goodness of man's rational structure.

In this sense all religious authority can become heteronomous. Of course, the heteronomy disappears in the moment in which it is transformed into theonomy (divine law). Theonomy implies our own personal experience of the presence of the divine Spirit within us, witnessing to the Bible or to the church. It is very interesting that Calvin who sounds so heteronomously authoritarian in many of his utterances was the one who most clearly stated that the Bible can be our authority only when the divine Spirit witnesses to it (the *testimonium Sancti Spiritus internum*). Where this inner witness is lacking, the authority of the Bible has no meaning. Obedience to its authority would be mere external subjection and not inward personal experience. In autonomy one follows the natural law of God implanted in our own being, and if we experience the truth of this law in the Bible or in the church, then we are still autonomous, but with the dimension of the theonomous in us at the same time. If we do not have this experience, then we follow in authoritarian subjection as immature persons, searching for security by avoiding the anxieties of punishment and danger. Autonomy which is aware of its divine ground is theonomy; but autonomy without the theonomous dimension degenerates into mere humanism.

Heteronomy has been broken in our time, and this is a dangerous thing. Men are always looking for the security of heteronomy, especially the masses of men. The breaking up of ecclesiastical heteronomy means that the masses of people run to other heteronomies, such as the totalitarian systems, sectarian fanaticism, or fundamentalistic narrowness, thus closing themselves off from the whole development of autonomous thought in modern times.

In the light of these principles you can understand why the Enlightenment was one of the greatest of all revolutions. Socially it was a bourgeois revolution. But spiritually it was the revolution of man's autonomous potentialities over against heteronomous powers which were no longer convincing. But don't misunderstand me! As long as people in the Middle Ages lived in these traditions without criticizing them—just as we breathe air without knowing it—then it is still theonomy. But as soon as the human mind began to ask questions at the end of the Middle Ages, then the great problem arose. The church responded by using all its power heteronomously to suppress the questioning mind which was no longer at ease in the atmosphere of ecclesiastical tradition and could no longer regard it as self-evident. Something new had taken place. Man became aware of his power of radical questioning. What should then be done? Should we try to suppress autonomous thought, as the church tried to do by means of the Inquisition, or should we do something else? Should we attempt to find within autonomy the dimension of theonomy, namely, the religious dimension, without weakening autonomous thought? This is what Schleiermacher and Hegel tried to do. The problem is still alive today. We cannot surrender autonomy, but neither can we live in an empty autonomy, because then we are in danger of grasping securities given by false authorities and totalitarian powers.

* * * * * * * * * *

Question:[1] In your definition of theonomy you mentioned the experiences of the presence of the inner divine Spirit which witnesses to the Bible and church. Would you describe this Spirit more fully so that I could recognize it in myself? Or if it is self-authenticating, how does one cultivate or achieve this Spirit?

Answer: Now this is a mixture of theology and counseling. But let me say one thing. It is obvious that if we speak of the Spirit working within us, it is self-authenticating. By what else could it be authenticated? If by some other authority, why would we acknowledge that authority? Because the Spirit tells us to. Then we are back with the Spirit. This was Calvin's idea, for example, when he spoke about the authority of the Bible. The divine Spirit witnesses to the content of the Bible, and in this way the Bible can become an authority. Only through the witness of the Spirit can the Bible cease to be a merely external authority. There is, however, a problem in Calvin's theology at this point. Does the Spirit witness to the particular contents of the Bible, so that this witness is happening while reading the Bible, or does the Spirit witness to the Bible as such, so that after this the Bible becomes in itself an authority? It was the latter understanding which became predominant in Calvinistic Orthodoxy, and from there came into Lutheranism also, and thus became the principle of authority in Orthodoxy as a whole. I can repeat something I said before. If the divine Spirit witnesses to the Bible as such, without any consideration of the particular contents, then in principle anybody can write a theology. This leads us to the idea of a *theologia irregenetorum*, a theology of those who are not reborn. But if it is the particular content that is being attested by the Spirit, then you must be existentially

[1] Editor's Note: As was Tillich's custom, he requested that students submit questions for him to answer before the start of the lecture. His answers invariably would interweave historical and systematic aspects of the subject. The editor has selected a few of the questions and answers, both to allow Tillich to sharpen his own presentation of a subject and to retain the atmosphere of the classroom situation.

involved in the content of the Bible in every moment of reading it. You must at least be participating in such a way that the Spirit works in you and witnesses to the truth of the biblical message. But you also ask, if the Spirit is self-authenticating, what can I do to receive it? This question cannot be answered, for if I did succeed in answering it, then I would be giving you a method for forcing God upon you. But God destroys every such method even as he destroys our moral self-righteousness. The only answer which can be given is to remain open to the impacts of life—which may come from others, or from reading the Bible, or services of the church or acts of love—through which God may work upon us. In listening and waiting we may experience the Spirit, but more than this cannot be said. There is no valid method at all for forcing God upon us.

* * * * * * * * * *

2. Concepts of Reason

Now we come to another equally important concept, the concept of reason. Here also much semantic clarity is needed in order to purify our image of the past. This is a very difficult concept and we can take but a few steps in attempting to interpret what this word means.

It certainly does not mean what is usually implied in all our talk about reason and/or revelation. If I can succeed in preventing you from jumping into discussions about reason against revelation before you clearly define the meaning of the terms, then this lecture will not have been in vain. In ordinary language reason is very highly respected. But it has a much narrower meaning than it had in the Enlightenment and in the previous history of the Western world. Today it means the calculation of the businessman, the analysis of the natural scientist, and the construction of the engineer. These three aspects determine the concept of reason. It would be therefore historically inaccurate to use this modern concept of reason as the model for understanding what the Enlightenment means by reason. When we speak of the "Age of Reason" we cannot restrict reason to its modern analytic and synthetic senses.

I will distinguish four different concepts of reason, and discuss them point by point.

a. Universal Reason: The first concept of reason has the meaning of the universal logos. Logos is the Greek word for reason. But it also means "word." In Heraclitus and in Stoicism logos means both word and reason. The Greeks asked the question how the human word and human language are able to grasp reality. Their answer was that the logos, the universal form and principle of everything created, is both in reality as a whole and in the human mind. The word is meaningful when men use it because it can grasp reality. The opposite is also true. Reality grasps the human mind, so that men can speak to and about reality.

That is the logos concept of reason. This concept appears and reappears everywhere in Christian theology as a first principle. It is a principle of order and structure in all realities. As the Fourth Gospel says, "All things were made through him [i.e., the Logos], and without him was not anything made that was made" (John 1:3, RSV). The Logos is the principle through which God created the world. This is a fundamental insight of all classical theology. Reality and mind have a logos structure. As a structure of reality and mind, logos includes our power of knowledge, our ethical awareness or conscience, and our aesthetic intuition. These are all expressions of the logos in us. (Immanuel Kant wrote the critiques of pure or theoretical reason and practical reason, and the neo-Kantian school added the aesthetic reason as a third, uniting the practical and the theoretical). Reason or logos is therefore in the tree, for instance, as well as in the man who names the tree and describes the image of tree-ness which reappears in every individual tree. This is possible only because there is a structure in the tree which man is able to grasp by his mind, or, since this is always mutual, his mind is grasped by the structure.

The universe has been created by an intelligent power, the divine ground, and since the world has been intelligently built, intelligence can grasp it. We can grasp the world intelligently because it has been created intelligently. It has a structure. This is equally valid in philosophy as well as in theology. There is no conflict here in regard to the theological or philosophical use of this concept of reason. There is a necessary logos element in all theology. Any theology which does not have an understanding of the universal character of the logos structure of the world, and that means of reason in the sense of logos, becomes barbaric and ceases to be theology. When the logos element in theo-logy disappears, theology becomes a fanatical repetition of biblical passages without endeavoring to understand their meaning.

What we have just described is a feature of that dualistic heresy which divorces creation and redemption, and sets them in contradiction to each other. Creation contains the logos, and if redemption contradicts creation, then God contradicts himself. Then we have a good God and a bad God, the good God of redemption and the bad God of creation. The church in the early centuries was almost destroyed in the fight for the goodness of creation, that is, for the logos structure of reality as a whole. The church finally overcame the temptation to accept a dualism by regarding it as a demonic temptation, demonic because the characteristic of the demonic is the split in the divinity between the good and the bad God. Yet this heresy continues to appear in Christianity. It was espe-cially strong in the earlier period of neo-orthodoxy.[2]

But the same thing appears in other less refined or sophisticated forms. There is much of this dualistic heresy in existentialist literature which describes the "question" but does not give an "answer," leaving the world to the devil, so to speak.

b. Critical Reason: The logos concept of reason was not the most important in the eighteenth century, although it was definitely a pre-supposition of that piety which praised the glory of creation. Rather, the second concept of reason, namely, critical reason, was the more effective. In the name of critical reason the way was prepared for the French Revolution, which transformed the world. Before that the American Revolution occurred, uniting religious and rational dimensions in the Constitution. That is its greatness. But in the French Revolution, because of the conflict with Catholicism, reason became radical and even

[2] Editor's Note: Tillich expressed his delight with the apparent turn in Karl Barth's thinking represented in the little book, *The Humanity of God.* He inter-preted this as a hopeful sign of a new attempt to overcome the danger of setting the God of redemption against the God of creation, and also as an emphasis which makes contact with his own thinking that always starts with the human situation.

antireligious. It brought about the destruction of the old institutions controlled by the heteronomous authorities of both church and state.

We must understand what this critical reason was. It was not a calculating reason which decides whether to do this or that, depending on which is more advantageous. Rather, it was a full, passionate, revolutionary emphasis on man's essential goodness in the name of the principle of justice. The revolutionary bourgeois fought against feudalism and the authoritarian churches. Unlike our present-day analytic and critical reason, he had a passionate belief in the logos structure of reality, and was convinced that the human mind is able to re-establish this structure by transforming society. We could therefore call it revolutionary reason as well as critical reason. Because of its religious depths this critical revolutionary reason overcame the prejudices of the feudal order, the heteronomous subjection of people both by the state and the church. It could do so because it spoke in the name of truth and justice. The philosophers of the Enlightenment were extremely passionate. They were not positivists; they were not interested in merely collecting facts which had no meaning for the revolutionary program. They became martyrs for the passion which they felt was given by the divine logos within them. It would be good if both in the East and in the West there would be more of this revolutionary reason. Both in Russia and in America it has been suppressed by the positivistic observation of facts, without that passion for the logos which is the manifestation of the divine in mind and reality.

c. Intuitive Reason: Then I come to a third concept of reason. I call it intuitive reason, which is used by all philosophers somehow or other in all periods. Formerly it was identified with Plato's idea of the intuition of the essences, and particularly of the universal essences of the good and the true. Today we have another term for it. We call it phenomenological. This is a school of philosophy which ultimately goes back to Platonism and which has many roots in the Middle Ages, perhaps especially in the Franciscan tradition. Its basic assumption is that the human mind has power to intuit essences. In looking at a red object at this moment, a red shirt or dress, the mind can experience the essence of redness. The essence of redness appears in a particular object and can be grasped by the mind. This I call intuitive reason.

Today reason and intuition are placed in contrast to each other, but they should not be. Intuitive reason is a nonanalytic reason which expresses itself in terms of descriptions. To understand the structures of life and spirit, we must use this descriptive method. Intuitive reason means looking at meanings, trying to understand them, and not analyzing objects, be it psychical or physical objects. That is another kind of reason. We use intuitive reason all the time in dealing with the world, when we see the universal in the particular, without asking analytic questions, or relational questions, etc. Whenever we are discussing meanings, as we are doing in this very lecture, we are in the realm of intuitive reason, as Plato also was in his dialogues. When he tried to discuss what virtue, courage, or fortitude are, then he used this intuitive method. This is most explicit in his early dialogues. When we want to know what fortitude is, then we look at examples, examples to which an ordinary meaning of the language leads us. We compare these examples, and from these examples we finally get a universal concept which covers the different examples and shows their point of identity.

In modern philosophy this is called the phenomenological method. This method is absolutely necessary for all the humanities. The understanding of meanings in all literature, theology, or philosophy is dependent on the use of this method. Philosophically it has been restated, but not invented, by Edmund Husserl (1859–1938) in his *Logical Investigations*[3] around 1900. He was a predecessor of existentialism. That puts us in the interesting situation that existentialism has been generally accepted, but not its predecessor. Yet we find that today some of the philosophical minds among the psychoanalysts who first accepted existentialism as the philosophical foundation of their work are now going back to phenomenology (or intuitive reason), realizing that without that method, existentialism would not be able to utter one word.

d. Technical Reason: This brings me to the last concept of reason, to its predominant meaning today, namely, to technical reason. It analyzes reality into its smallest elements, and then construes out of them other things, larger things. We see this kind of reason at work in Einstein in terms of mathematical physics. Yet there was also a strong element of

[3] *Logische Untersuchungen* (Halle: M. Niemeyer, 1900).

intuitive reason in Einstein. Einstein himself tried to describe the relation between the intuitive and analytic elements in his own processes of thinking. Besides these there was the critical element, exemplified in Einstein's political activities. Here he followed the eighteenth-century understanding of reason. He knew what justice means from reason, but of course he used a different kind of reason in his scientific discoveries. He also knew of the logos character of reason. In a published discussion between Einstein and myself on the idea of God,[4] Einstein said that the miracle of the structure of reality is what he called the divine. This was 50 per cent of what I would also call the logos concept.

So you see that the greatest representative of technical reason was aware of other dimensions of reason. The power of technical reason is its ability to analyze reality and to construct tools out of it. An extreme example of its use is logical positivism. What it says is merely analytic; it is a tool used mostly in order to produce other tools. We should not despise technical reason. We all live from it. Theologians especially should not despise it if they wish to remain theologians. Even the analytic form of thought used in argumentation must be kept pure. In discussions we should never replace logic by emotion or by a heteronomous acceptance of religious authorities. We must use it equally as fully and rigorously as those who are not aware of the other forms of reason, only we must use it in awareness that there are four fundamental forms of what we call reason.

3. *The Concept of Nature*

Next we turn to the concept of nature. This is necessary in view of the conflict that was going on throughout the eighteenth century between naturalism and supernaturalism. Supernaturalistic theology attempted to save the tradition by means of the same tools which naturalism used in trying to transform the tradition. Therefore, we must ask what this concept of nature meant during these controversies. I can tell you autobiographically that one of my first scientific inquiries into theology—which was my *Habilitationsschrift*—dealt with the concept

4 Cf. Paul Tillich, "Science and Theology: A Discussion with Einstein," *Theology of Culture* (New York: Oxford University Press, 1959).

of naturalism and supernaturalism in the period before Schleiermacher.[5] Out of this study I gained insight into the intricacies of the concept of nature in these discussions, which has influenced my thinking.

There are two fundamental concepts of nature which I distinguish, the material and the formal concept of nature. The material concept refers to things in nature, usually to subhuman or nonhuman things. This is what we usually call nature, all the realities that are the subject matter of physics, biology, botany, etc. The formal concept of nature refers to human beings, but of course man's body belongs as well to the material concept; it is as natural as any animal body. But it contains a different element. It has mind or spirit. Following from man's being as mind and spirit is the fact that man has a history. So nature and history are placed into contrast.

We are using the material concept of nature when we ask questions about whether nature is also fallen, whether nature can be saved, or when we speak about going out into nature, or when we discuss whether nature is only an object of our control, subject to our technical activities, or whether nature is such that man can commune with it. In all these cases we point to the material concept of nature. But there is quite a different concept, and this one has even more theological significance. It is the concept of the natural, coming from Greek thinking, from the word *physis*, which has to do with *growth*. The opposite of this is *nomos*, which is something produced by human will, such as institutions of society, conventional rules and laws, everything that is not produced by natural growth, but produced by people who transform what is grown. This distinction helps us to understand better the social criticism which came out of the critical schools of philosophy after Socrates, the Cynics, Hedonists, and also the Stoics. Their concept of natural law as that which we have within us by birth was the basis for their criticism of all that was arbitrary in society.

In all the literature of the Western world, from the Greek to the medieval sources and perhaps up to the seventeenth century, when you

---

[5] *Der Begriff des Übernatürlichen, sein dialektischer Charakter und das Prinzip der Identität, dargestellt an der supranaturalistischen Theologie vor Schleiermacher* (1915).

see the term "natural law," it very rarely means "physical law," law as discovered by physics. Usually it means rational law, particularly the law of morals or the law of cognitive reason, that is, the rules of logic. All this is called natural law; it is man's true nature. The law of the logos of which I spoke before embraces both nature outside of man and man himself. It is given by creation, and therefore it is called natural.

In order to make meaningful theological statements about nature or naturalism, it is necessary to distinguish these two concepts of nature. Related to the concept of the natural which we have just discussed are two other concepts, the unnatural and the supernatural. The unnatural is simply the perversion of the nature of a given thing. On the other hand, the supernatural is not supposed to be unnatural. It is supposed to be higher in power and value than the natural. It is a higher sphere which can enter into and interfere with the sphere of the natural. The supernatural interferes both with nature outside and with man's mental and spiritual activities. The mind or spirit of man (spirit with a small "s" of course) belongs to the realm of the natural, not in the material but in the formal sense of nature. Man's mind transcends the material sense by the very fact he is able to use language and to create tools.

The concept of the supernatural raises a theological problem. What does it mean to say that there is a sphere higher in power and value than the human sphere? What does it mean to say that the supernatural sphere can interfere with the human sphere? In what sense is the idea of interference justified? If God interferes with the natural which exists by his act of creation, does this not lead to a demonic split in the divine nature? Does God interfere and if so, in what sense? These are problems with which all theology has to deal, including modern theology. They were the problems of Hegel and Schleiermacher, both of whom tried to develop a theology which transcended naturalism and supernaturalism. These problems are also involved in modern theology whether we are discussing the doctrine of God, christology, soteriology, or eschatology.

4. *The Concept of Harmony*

Now we come to a fourth concept, the concept of harmony. This concept is part of the fundamental faith of the Enlightenment. In my terminology we could call harmony its ultimate concern. All the philosophers of the Enlightenment use this concept directly or indirectly, explicitly or implicitly. All of them elaborated their systems under the guidance of this principle. Our first remark about it has to be semantic. Today harmony may have a musical connotation, which it always has had and should have. But it has also deteriorated to mean "nice," when we speak of a nice harmonious family life. Of course, harmony understood in this way was not the ultimate concern of the great philosophers of the Enlightenment.

Harmony in the philosophy of the Enlightenment is a paradoxical concept. This means that it must always be qualified by the words "in spite of." The ancient Pythagoreans spoke of a universal harmony, of a cosmic harmony, but in spite of every individual thing and every individual human being seemingly going their own way. Yet, through all there was an overarching harmony. The Greek word *cosmos* which we translate by universe originally meant beauty and harmony. The Pythagoreans discovered mathematical formulae for the musical harmonies. They believed in the harmony of the sounds produced by the movement of the stars. Therefore they spoke of a cosmic harmony of the spheres, each of which has a different sound, but all together creating a harmonious sound. If you delete the half-poetic, mythological element from such ideas, then you can say that they had a universal, ecstatic interpretation of reality. Of course, the Pythagoreans also knew that there is a split in reality, which they symbolized by the split between the even and the odd numbers. The odd numbers represent the good, the even numbers the bad, because the odd numbers are perfect. They are finished; the even numbers can be divided and are therefore unfinished. For all Greek thinking the finished is the good, the unfinished is the bad.

This concept of harmony was carried into the Platonic–Christian idea of providence. Plato was the first who philosophically made this a central concept. It is also a fundamental concept of Christian theology, and even more of Christian daily life. The daily life of the Christian believer is largely determined by providence. Ordinary Christians find in their faith in providence a kind of ultimate security in the vicissitudes of their lives. But this fundamental Christian idea of providence became secularized in the Enlightenment. Now it was formulated in terms of harmony.

The Christian idea of providence does not contain the mechanical notion that God has ordered everything once upon a time, and that now he sits on his throne and sleeps while the world goes its way. The Reformers had to fight tremendously against this distortion of the idea of providence. Rather, providence means that God is creating in every moment, and directing everything in history toward an ultimate fulfillment in the kingdom of God. Then you have the "in spite of" element. In spite of human finitude, in spite of human estrangement from God, God determines every moment so that in it an experience of the ultimate is possible, so that in the whole texture of good and evil in history the divine aim will finally come to prevail. Providence does not work mechanically, but it directs and guides. For the individual human being, providence means that in every moment of the time process, there is the possibility of reaching toward the kingdom of God. This is the Christian concept, which is so important for the personal life of the religious man and for all Christians everywhere. To anticipate things a bit—this is also a fundamental concept of the Ritschlian theology.

Even when the idea of providence is secularized in the Enlightenment, certain traits of it are preserved, especially the "in spite of" element. Christianity emphasizes that in spite of sin and error, something meaningful can be done in history by the providential guidance of God. The philosophies of the Enlightenment also maintained this aspect. It was applied by them to all realms of life. The first clear expression of this in the secular realm can be seen in the area of economics. It was expressed by Adam Smith (1723–1790) of the Manchester School of Economics in his idea of harmony. The idea is that in spite of the fact that everyone may be motivated by the profit interest, each one out for his own profit, in the end the total aims of production and consumption will be reached according to some hidden law. With many qualifications, this idea also underlies the theory of modern American capitalism. There is this basic belief in harmony. In spite of the fact that producer, seller, and buyer fight with each other, each bargaining for the greatest possible profit or for the best deal, somehow the laws of economics will be at work behind their backs in such a way that the best interests of all concerned and of the whole society will be satisfied.

Of course, history has shown that this seemingly mysterious law of the harmony of interests working behind the backs of individuals in society who act for profit in their economic life has helped to eliminate the poverty which was still existing in the eighteenth century in all Western countries. Without this belief in the hidden law of harmony, the Manchester theory would have never arisen and worked as it did.

The same principle is valid in politics. According to the philosophers of the Enlightenment, democracy presupposes that if every person follows his own reasoning, a general consensus or a majority will can be formed which is to the advantage of all. Then the minority should be prepared to acknowledge that the will of the majority was the true will of the whole, the *volonté générale*—the mystical concept of Rousseau who distinguishes the *volonté générale*, the general will, from the will of all. The majority does not represent the will of all, because there is the opposition, but it represents the general will, the true will which is driving toward the best interests of the group as a whole.

Now you can see immediately the consequence of this belief in harmony. If there is no belief in this harmony, democracy cannot work, for the minority will not accept the validity of the decision of the majority. There is plenty of evidence of this in some of the South American countries. As soon as a democratic majority appears which is disliked by the military leaders, they instigate a *putsch* to overthrow the government. This is the chief characteristic of the negation of democracy. As soon as there is no belief in harmony, that is, in the providential validity of the majority decision, then democracy is impossible.— When I was in Japan, I was often asked by Japanese intellectuals to give lectures on the religious foundations of democracy, because they have the same problem. They have a democracy too, but they know how much it is threatened when a strong minority will not accept the concept of the general will, of providential harmony.

We have the same concept applied in the field of education. Education is necessary to produce the political maturity required for people to acknowledge the principle of harmony in democracy. The belief is that education can develop the potentialities of every individual in such a way that finally a good society will come out of it. This was the belief which induced the people of the Enlightenment to create public schools, which had not existed up to that time. There had been only upper class schools or church schools where the people were subjected to the preaching and teaching of the church. But the Enlightenment created public schools which became the center of culture.—I was astonished when I came to this country to find how seriously education is taken here, much more seriously than in any European country that I know. The reason for this is that the belief in harmony is much stronger.—In any case, public schools were founded under the influence of the philosophy of the Enlightenment.

Even God was pictured as an educator. It was believed that God educates mankind in stages and that now in our great century, namely, the eighteenth century, the century of Enlightenment, the age of maturity has dawned. God has finally reached his educational aim. The classical expression of this idea was given by Gotthold Ephraim Lessing (1729–1781), the German poet, philosopher, and theologian, and the greatest representative of German Enlightenment, in his little book, *The Education of the Human Race*.[6] This book will give you more insight into the Enlightenment than perhaps anything else, from the point of view of the feeling for the meaning of life.

Another area in which the principle of harmony was applied was in epistemology, the theory of knowledge. It is very clear in John Locke (1632–1704) and is behind practically all empiricism. For here there is the belief that the chaotic impressions which come to us from reality will find a way to produce in our minds a meaningful image of reality, making knowledge and action possible. This presupposes a law of harmony working within us. It is interesting to notice how secure, how dogmatically sure many empiricists are that the law of harmony in this respect really works.

The most profound expression of this idea of harmony in philosophy is to be found in Gottfried Wilhelm Leibniz (1646–1716), the German philosopher. The whole classical period of German and European philosophy in general is to a great extent dependent on him. He was great enough at the same time so that he can now be the beloved figure of present-day analytic philosophers because he had the splendid idea of

---

[6] *Lessing's Theological Writings,* translated by Henry Chadwick (Stanford: Stanford University Press, 1957).

describing all reality in terms of a logical calculus! Leibniz used the term "harmony," and spoke of a pre-established harmony which makes the operations of reality in all realms possible. The philosophical background of this idea is the Cartesian (Descartes) separation of extended things or material bodies (*res extensa*) from thinking substances or the ego (soul) (*res cogitans*), raising the question of the possibility of the communication between the two. The answer was found in a third reality, which is God. In God the communication of soul with body takes place. Our soul has no direct communication with our body. Our thinking can influence our body through the medium of the transcendent unity of both body and mind in the divine ground.

Now Leibniz carried through this idea in an interesting fashion. In the history of philosophy you learned about monads, meaning "one" in Greek. Monads cannot communicate directly with each other; they are separated from each other by the body. Nevertheless, we as individual monads can talk to each other. How is this possible? Only by a pre-established harmony which goes to the divine ground of both you and me. Leibniz expressed this idea in the phrase, "Monads do not have windows and doors." This means that the individual human being is closed within himself. This theory of monads has been interpreted—rightly I think—as a symbolic expression of the dissolution of the medieval community into the atomized society of modern times.

In any case the question was: "How is communication of one being with another possible?" The answer was by a pre-established harmony behind our individual lives. Every individual monad, you and I, has the whole universe within himself. Every individual is a microcosm. But each of us embodies the universe in differing degrees of clarity. We are supposed to develop it to the highest possible clarity, but potentially we know and possess everything. The development of this potentiality is the infinite task of every monad. This is Leibniz' idea, his metaphysical formulation of the concept of harmony. This theory, however, which seems somewhat fantastic to us, had a tremendous influence on the thinking of the Enlightenment and on later philosophy.

In Protestantism we have the religious counterpart to this concept of harmony. The Protestant idea was that religion or Christianity has no need of a central authority which gives all the answers, either by councils or popes. On the other hand, the fact that the church held councils was an expression of the principle of harmony, for the assumption prevailed that the majority opinion of the council was the expression of the divine Spirit. Of course, Protestantism also had an authority, one formal principle as it was called later on, namely, the Bible. The idea that the Bible can have an impact on every individual reader through the divine Spirit is an expression of the principle of harmony. The principle of harmony is at work behind the backs of the individual Bible readers, making possible a universal harmony and the existence of the church. In spite of the numerous denominational differences and theological conflicts in Protestantism, it is believed that there is still such a thing as Protestantism. There is, to be sure, no visible form of unity, despite the World Council of Churches; Protestants are divided, and yet it is possible to distinguish Protestantism from Eastern Orthodoxy, or Roman Catholicism, or humanism, and from all other religions. There is some kind of unity; this belief is an expression of the principle of harmony, but it is always accompanied by an "in spite of" qualification.

After running through all of these applications of the principle of harmony, I hope you can see that when the central supernatural authority was removed, and the individualizaton and conflict in reality remain, then the only possible answer there can be, both in religion and culture, both in economics and politics, both in epistemology and physiçs, is the principle of a presupposed harmony which produces indirectly what was supposed to be produced directly by a divine inter-ference or by an inner-historical, all-uniting authority such as existed in the medieval Roman Church. This supernatural authority was now replaced by the principle of harmony. This finally led to another question: What if the harmony does not work? This is the existentialist question which began with the second period of Romanticism in the beginning of the nineteenth century, and runs throughout the nine-teenth and twentieth centuries.

We still have in the majority of our intellectuals, the bearers of our intellectual life, this kind of paradoxical optimism that is identical with the concept of harmony. We have it in Freudianism and Marxism; we have it in our ordinary democratic humanism; we have it in everything that is called liberalism in economics and politics. Yet, it is not the same as it was in the eighteenth century. Many things have happened in the meantime. The theological development of the last century and a half has been looking for an answer to the question: What if the principle of harmony does not work?

* * * * * * * * * *

Question: Please distinguish between your definition of reason in the sense of universal logos and the Enlightenment concept of harmony.

Answer: These two do not lie on the same level so it is difficult to make a distinction. But I can speak about the relation between them. The logos type of reason refers to the intelligible, meaningful structure of reality in its essential character; the concept of harmony refers to the dynamics of actual existence, that is, the way in which different tendencies in time and space are united in terms of harmony. That is, in spite of the arbitrariness of individuals, the universal outcome of the historical movement is positive and meaningful. So roughly we can say that while logos deals with the formal structure of reality in its essential nature, harmony deals with the dynamics of existence in time and space with all its ambiguities. Very simply, the one is structure, the other is dynamic movement.

Question: You have stated that one of the key doctrines of the Enlightenment was the harmony of man's mind with the eternal Logos. In what respects is this doctrine similar to or different from the romantic doctrine of the infinite within the finite? If they are similar, to what extent is the romantic movement a return to the basic Enlightenment doctrine after its destruction by Kant?

Answer: Now here there is a presupposition which is simply not factual. I have stated that one of the key doctrines of the Enlightenment was the harmony of man's mind with the eternal Logos. I think you must have misunderstood it by 180 degrees. What I really said was that the harmony of the Enlightenment is not the harmony of the mind and has nothing to do with what we call harmony today, harmony in the sense of the restfulness of the mind, of sitting in a beautiful garden, looking at the flowers and feeling harmony between oneself and nature. This question perhaps shows that I was not emphatic enough in distinguishing this concept of harmony in the Enlightenment from its sentimentalization. So I must try again.

Now harmony is a paradoxical concept. You are *not* harmonious. There is no harmony in your mind at all. You are not in harmony with God. You are in opposition to him and you fight with him. But nevertheless, behind your back destiny or providence is guiding reality in such a way that it turns out best for you in the end. This means that you are brought back to God or to yourself in spite of everything. The principle of harmony in the Enlightenment can only be understood in terms of this "in spite of." It is best to think of the Manchester School of Economics for an illustration. Both the seller and the buyer fight for their own profits. The two meet in the market, and in their struggle for their own profit, a kind of transitory equilibrium results which brings about the greatest profit for the whole society. The individual is thinking of his own advantage, but the whole society is being served "in spite of" that. Therefore we have the idea that private vices are public benefits. Although you are very greedy, and you don't want to pay a penny more to this seller than you have to, and although he has the same feeling toward you and fights against you, somehow behind your backs a harmony is brought about through the guidance of providence. This is the paradox of providence. Destiny or God, or the dialectical process in Hegel or Marx, does something of which you are not aware. Although you are greedy and disagreeable, the outcome is finally the best for all concerned. I gave you examples of this in all the other realms. In democracy, for example, despite all the name-calling in the political campaigns and all the promises made by candidates which they don't for a moment intend to fulfill, there is a *volonté générale* that emerges. Although nobody knows what the true will of society is, through the democratic process such a thing emerges. After the voting has been completed, the majority decision represents the true and general will of the society as a whole.

So the idea of harmony has nothing to do with niceness. Nor does it mean that the human mind and the eternal Logos are identical. The Enlightenment had no such idea at all. It only had the idea that reason, the logos type of reason, shows man the fundamental principles of justice. And if these fundamental principles of justice are violated, as the Enlightenment felt they were violated in the feudalistic society, then the Enlightenment fought against social abuses in the name of the principles of natural law which belong to the human mind. But there was no mystical union of man and God, no presence of the infinite in the finite as in Nicholas of Cusa.

Only one thing in this question is right, namely, that mysticism and rationalism are not contradictory, but that rationalism lives from the fundamental mystical principle of identity, the principle of the presence of the structure of truth in the depths of the human mind. This point in the question is indeed right. There is such a relationship. But no enlightened philosopher would have accepted Spinoza. They all rejected Spinoza, and Spinoza is the real heir of Nicholas of Cusa and the mystical tradition of the Western world. For Voltaire, Rousseau, and other representatives of the Enlightenment, the subject-object scheme is decisive. However, they realized that in man's natural structure there is an awareness of justice. In the name of this justice they could fight against the distortions in society.

* * * * * * * * * *

B. The Attitude of the Enlightened Man

After having dealt with four great concepts of the Enlightenment—autonomy, reason, nature, and harmony—we will discuss the attitude of the men of the Enlightenment, of the great bearers of the development of the Enlightenment and its consequences up to the present time.

1. *His Bourgeois Character*

First let me make a sociological statement. The enlightened man is a bourgeois. *Bourgeois* is a French word, the French equivalent of the *Bürger* in German, which means "he who lives inside the walls of the town." He is quite different from the medieval man. He is supposed to be calculating and reasonable. In the Middle Ages the self-confidence, self-consciousness, and self-evaluation of a human being were not rooted in his rational powers—reason in the largest sense—but rooted instead in his ability to deal with the situation into which he was put by a transcendent destiny. The medieval man had his particular place in society, whether as emperor or as beggar or as someone who occupied a station in life between these two extremes. Each place had a direct relationship to ultimate reality. The function of the emperor was to unite the body of Christendom all over the known world. The function of the beggar was to give the people an occasion for acts of charity and in this way help to save their souls. Everyone in between had the same feeling of having a special place. This was a hierarchical order of society—holy orders one above the other, represented both in heaven and on earth. This concept came from the great mystic, Dionysius the Areopagite (ca A.D.500). It was taken into the Middle Ages by the scholastics in order to describe the place where everyone stands in life, including not only the ecclesiastical hierarchy but also the secular, political, and social hierarchies. The corollary of this in the Lutheran Reformation was the concept of vocation. Everyone had his place by divine calling (vocatio) where God placed him. There he shall stay and not try to break out of this situation.

This vertical orientation of the totality of life in the Middle Ages stands in direct opposition to the horizontal outline of the bourgeois society of the Enlightenment. The bourgeois wants to analyze and transform the whole of reality in order to control it. The horizontal line is decisive in his work, and he wants to control it by calculation. As a businessman he must calculate. If he does not, he loses. This calculation means that he must go beyond the place where he happens to find himself now. He does not accept the status quo. This again demands knowledge of reality. Reality far beyond his limited place must be known in order to be calculated and controlled. One must presuppose that nature is regular and that reality has some calculable patterns. So the bourgeois had a calculating attitude, and to him nature and reality as a whole appeared to be made up of regular patterns on which he could rely and which make his business decisions possible.

2. His Ideal of a Reasonable Religion

Irrational elements which interfere with a calcuable pattern of reality must therefore be excluded. This means that the irrational elements of religion must be eliminated. The bourgeois needs a reasonable religion which views God as lying behind the whole of life's processes. God has made the world and now it follows its own laws. He does not interfere any more. Every interference would mean a loss of calculability. No such interferences are acceptable and all special revelations have to be denied.

Thus all the boundary-line concepts of life were denied because they disturb the calculating and controlling activities of man in relation to reality. For instance, death is removed as an interfering power in the progressive thought of controlling reality. The classical understanding of death in the vertical line, which views man's life as coming from eternity and going back to it, had to disappear. In the bourgeois theological preaching, even in Roman Catholicism in the early eighteenth century, the preaching on death was removed. The great conflict between Pascal and the Jesuits involved the issue of the victory of the bourgeois society in removing death and guilt and hell from preaching. The Jesuits were on the side of bourgeois society. Jesuitism at that time gave the bourgeoisie a good conscience in breaking out of the vertical line into the horizontal by removing the boundary-line situations in classical theology. Traditional threats in terms of death and ultimate judgment were omitted. They were not in good taste. It is not in good taste to speak to people about death. In modern American society too one avoids speaking of death. One does not die; one just passes away. Death is not convenient for progressive society. It means the end of man's control and calculations and the end of inner-worldly purposes.

An even stronger attack is made on the idea of original sin. There was not only the very justifiable criticism of the superstitious and literalistic way this doctrine had been preached in connection with the story of Paradise, but it was also criticized because it conflicted with the belief in the progressive improvement of the human situation on earth. Most of present-day humanism still follows the Enlightenment in this criticism. It was a great event in theology when Reinhold Niebuhr succeeded in making an inroad on this prevailing view of humanism. Of course, he received support from the existentialist style of the twentieth century in which we are living. Despite that, the humanistic assumption of a progressive improvement in the human situation is still very much alive.

The fear of hell was also dismissed. The fear of death is actually the fear of hell; therefore, this concept was removed. Its symbolic meaning disappeared. The consequence of this was that its opposite was also removed, not only the mythological symbolism of heaven, but also the idea of grace as such. Grace is an action which comes from outside man's autonomous activities, and therefore for Kant it was an expression of something heteronomous. For since it comes from outside, it undercuts the autonomous power of man. What remained then was a reasonable religion, as Kant called it.[7] In this reasonable religion prayer was also removed, because prayer relates one to that which transcends oneself. This relationship fell under strong suspicion by the enlightened people. Kant said that if someone is caught by surprise while praying, he would feel ashamed. He felt that it was not dignified for autonomous men who control the world and possess the power of reason to be found in the situation of prayer.

Thus the existential elements of finitude, despair, anxiety, as well as of grace, were set aside. What was left was the reasonable religion of progress, belief in a transcendent God who exists alongside of reality, and who does not do much in the world after he has created it. In this world left to its own powers moral demands remain, morals in terms of bourgeois righteousness and stability. Belief in the immortality of the soul also remains, namely, the ability of man to continue his improvement progressively after death.

3. *His Common-sense Morality*

A basic element of the morality of the enlightened man is tolerance. The enlightened bourgeois man is tolerant. His understanding of tolerance was conditioned by the religious wars. His profound disgust of the murderous and destructive forms of these wars—which in Germany killed half of the population during the Thirty Years' War (1618–1648)—caused him to deny the absolute claims of the church. The spirit of tolerance was perhaps first produced by the Reformation. But it was not until after the bloody religious wars had demonstrated the

---

[7] Cf. Immanuel Kant's book, *Religion within the Limits of Reason Alone,* translated by T. M. Greene and H. H. Hudson (New York: Harper & Brothers, 1960).

impossibility of reuniting the churches that the secular powers took over and forced tolerance upon them.

A second reason for tolerance besides the political one arose out of the sectarian, spiritualistic movements of the Reformation period. They placed strong emphasis upon the belief that every individual is immediately related to God. No one type of relationship has the right to deny other possible types of relationships with God. This same feeling underlies much of American religious life. The Bible and tradition become secondary in comparison with the divine Spirit with whom each individual is immediately related.

A third reason has to do with the rise of the secular state. The state became increasingly secular because it had to transcend the split between the churches. It could not succeed in identifying itself with one of them. Now an interesting problem arose, which is stated clearly by John Locke. Could there be a complete tolerance? Can one be tolerant of the Catholics, for example, when they are on principle intolerant, especially when they possess the power? John Locke said no. Catholics should not be tolerated. Nor should atheists be tolerated, he thought. For the whole system of morality in society is based on the belief in God as the moral lawgiver and judge. If this belief disappears then the whole system collapses. Here we see that basic limits are set to tolerance even by its champions.

We were discussing tolerance as an element in the attitude of eighteenth-century bourgeois society, classically expressed in Locke's writings on tolerance. We pointed out that tolerance has its background in the experience of the seventeenth century, the century of the terrible religious wars which almost destroyed Europe. When it was seen that neither the Protestants nor the Catholics could gain a decisive victory, the secularized state had to intervene, identifying itself with neither religious group. Tolerance toward different religious traditions grew out of this experience of the cruel and destructive religious wars. Such wars are always the most bloody because in them an unconditional concern expresses itself in a particular way, and this particular way then assumes the ultimacy which is supposed to be expressed by that concern, but which is not identical with it. This results in the demonization of religion in its worst form.

We have the same phenomenon in our century, the struggle of the quasireligions with their tendency of totally eradicating the enemy on account of an absolute, unconditional faith in the concrete and particular expressions of their ultimate concern. The wars between Nazism and Communism within the nations and between the nations, as well as the spirit of absolutism which runs through the cold war between liberal humanism in the West and totalitarianism in parts of the East—these are modern forms of this phenomenon. We see the horror resulting from the demonic elevation of something finite to absolute validity. I call it demonic because individuals and nations become possessed and are driven to destroy everything which stands in their way. And since this is done on a finite basis, they are themselves ultimately led to self-destruction. These are the dialectics of the demonic. The demonic expresses itself first in the realm of the concrete religions, in France between the Catholics and the Huguenots and in all the rest of Europe between Catholics and Protestants. Each side is unaware of the fact that God is greater than any particular form in which his manifestation appears. Against this situation it is understandable that the idea of tolerance should arise, and be championed by the secular power. In a Europe which was almost destroyed, the secular state brought salvation from religious fanaticism, and was supported in this principle of tolerance by the religious mystical idea of the immediacy of each individual before God. So much for the idea of tolerance, which was not an unlimited tolerance, as we said, because, at least for Locke, the Catholics and the atheists had to be excluded, the Catholics because they were intolerant on principle, and the atheists because they denied the religious foundations of tolerance.

We come now to another characteristic of the bourgeois moral life, the element of discipline. The whole bourgeois culture is based on the repression of those elements which were allowed in the aristocratic society of feudal times. In part this sense of moral discipline goes back to Calvinism. Calvinism itself came from a city, Geneva, in which the factor of discipline was fundamental. In the aristocratic society, at least in the upper classes—but also among the peasants as the works of the Dutch painters of peasant scenes in the seventeenth century show—there was an acceptance of enjoyment in life, an expression of vitality in the more primitive directions of erotic play, the desire for intoxication to elevate the feeling of vitality, but also the sense of beauty in the arts and the glory of nature as in ancient Greece. The more aristocratic a position someone held, the greater possibility he had of expressing all forms of heightened vitality. The aristocrats were not only the big land owners, but also the patricians in the medieval and late medieval cities.

In bourgeois society all this was denied, partly in the name of religion and partly—and these are always interdependent—in the name of the needs of the sociological and economic structure of the bourgeois order. All this had to be restricted and repressed for the sake of the purpose of transforming reality through work. This work required discipline and self-control. This is connected with Protestantism also in another way. Protestantism had abolished the monastic form of asceticism. It was the monumental attack on monasticism by Luther and Calvin and all the Reformers which destroyed the monastic form of asceticism as a valid religious order of life. But now in Protestantism a different form of asceticism arose, an inner-worldly—not extra-worldly as in monasticism —asceticism of labor and of laboring people who produce the technical means for transforming reality in the service of mankind. It was Max Weber (1864–1920), the great German sociologist, who described this inner-worldly form of Protestant asceticism.[8] The idea of the kingdom of God, so important for Calvinistic thinking, took on the connotation of working for the transformation of nature for the sake of mankind.

In this light we can understand such things as the fourteen-hour workday, both by those workers who received only the minimum of subsistence and by the owners who worked even harder and longer but received the profits. Thus work, discipline, and self-control formed the heart of the ethical principles of bourgeois society. The forms of economic existence of bourgeois society were undergirded by this inner-worldly asceticism for the sake of the kingdom of God.

It is instructive to study those cases where this type of bourgeois self-discipline disintegrates. As soon as it starts to disintegrate, the whole system begins to crumble. We have economic-historical inquiries into nineteenth-century Germany showing what happens with the gradual

[8] *The Protestant Ethic and the Spirit of Capitalism* (New York: Charles Scribner's Sons, 1930).

victory of the bourgeois society. This victory was delayed in Germany, for Germany was under feudal power much longer than France, England, Holland, and Belgium, but finally toward the end of the nineteenth century the bourgeoisie became victorious also in Germany. There one can see the following sociological law at work, although such laws are never strict because human freedom can change them. First of all, the producers of the great corporations and enterprises were as a rule subjected to a strict discipline of work. In the second generation this discipline was continued, but now on a more luxurious basis. Then the third generation, enjoying a much higher standard of living, became what is known as playboys in this country. In Germany they sought the luxuries of life, giving expression both to the sensual and artistic forms of vitality. Perhaps they collected paintings or built great mansions. This law of the three generations which helps to analyze bourgeois society shows that when repression is not enforced any more and when there exists simultaneously an ascetic form of dedication to labor, you have the beginning of the disintegration of the pillars of this society.

4. His Subjective Feeling

One of the words we meet most often in the literature of the eighteenth century is the word "tears." Everybody weeps; everybody cries in ecstasy of despair or happiness. Whenever scenes of happiness are described, people shed tears; they cannot help it. What does this mean? This was the century of reason, and yet there was sentimentality. How are they related to each other? There is an alliance of two poles. People wept about everything which remained after the principles of reason were actualized. Rationalism says that emotional elements should be excluded from rationality. Emotions are irrelevant to the serious things of life, such as the production and merchandising of bourgeois industry. So when the emotions are excluded from reason and are not subject to the criteria of logic, the result is that they run wild and end in all kinds of uncontrolled emotionalism. This happens in human beings of the twentieth century too. People who are complete rationalists in the realm of thought fall into uncontrolled emotionalism in their personal life. If man is split into two parts, into the rational and the emotional, the result will be the absence of reason from his emotions. A dangerous situation develops when emotionalism is connected with ignorance. One of the dangers in this country is all of the ignorant emotionalism that has been created by the cold war propaganda, for one day it may explode in the wrong way and destroy many of the democratic institutions. This is the danger of all the fascist movements from McCarthyism to its current forms. We should also realize that if the philosophers remain in their closed spheres of mere logical inquiry of logic, and do not go into the relevant problems of life, then they abandon the reality of our existence to movements which unite emotionalism and ignorance.

C. Intrinsic Conflicts of Enlightenment

Now we must deal with conflict within the Enlightenment itself. It is important to see these to understand the concurrent theological development. There are conflicts in the Enlightenment, and our usual gray image of the period is not at all true. In reality the period of the Enlightenment is infinitely more rich than our gray image of it would indicate. Actually no period in history should be seen as monolithic. If we look at the Renaissance and think that every peasant in southern Bavaria was a bearer of the sixteenth-century Renaissance, then we are imagining a ridiculous thing. There were only a few thousand people in all Europe who brought about the Renaissance. But these were the people who were conscious of the situation and who became the intellectual leaders of the future. So neither the Renaissance nor any of the following periods was monolithic.

In the period of the Enlightenment there were continually underground movements, underground because only occasionally did they come clearly to the surface and revolt against the surface situation. But these reactive movements never became really dominant; they were never able to prevent the final victory of the bourgeoisie, either in the intellectual life or in the economic life, which was the most important in bourgeois society, either in political revolutions or in religious consequences. They did not overcome the optimistic and progressivistic attitude of the Enlightenment. Nevertheless, they were there and made their appearance when the victorious bourgeoisie suffered internal conflicts, preparing the way for the new situation of the twentieth century. We must mention them also because they played a tremendous role in later theological discussions.

1. *Cosmic Pessimism*

The first one I want to mention is the underground of cosmic pessimism in the whole Enlightenment. This was the reaction to natural events of catastrophic proportions. What was the attitude of the eighteenth-century theologians? It was what I would call teleological optimism. *Telos* means aim or purpose in Greek. There was a basic optimism toward the divine purpose in creating the world. What was the purpose of God? It was to make the universe in such a way that all things would work together for the good of man. The descriptions of the Enlightenment theologians of the divine wisdom always portrayed God as a wonderful technician who made the best possible machine for the glory and well-being of man. For this purpose he created the sun and the moon. He took care that the sun does not shine at night so man can sleep. In every least little thing one saw the wisdom and goodness of God in creating the best possible world for man's purpose. Everything was teleological and had a purpose for the human race. Why should one not be optimistic and progressivistic and enjoy everything that God in his wisdom created for man's good?

But then something happened. That was the earthquake of Lisbon in the middle of the eighteenth century which killed quite a number of people. Compared with the horrors of the twentieth century that perhaps cannot mean very much to us. But at that time, when there were fewer human beings and a higher culture, that is, a higher evaluation of human beings, it came as a tremendous shock. Sixty thousand people were killed by this earthquake in Lisbon. This was a catastrophe of unimaginable dimensions to a period in which God was considered as having created the world for the purpose of serving man. This event was in part responsible for the shaking of the optimism and progressivism of the eighteenth century. Also it symbolized in a dramatic way what everyone knew can happen at any time, but which can easily be glossed over.

It is interesting to see how the philosophers were shaken. It was an event which greatly influenced Goethe (1740–1832) in the early years of his life. It was after this earthquake that Voltaire (1694–1778), the classical representative of the French Enlightenment, wrote the deeply pessimistic novel, *Candide,* which ends with the advice to retire to one's garden and withdraw from the horrors of world history.

Such things were not able to inhibit the continuing progress of bourgeois society out of which later came the evolutionary ideas of the nineteenth century. In any case this pessimism was latent and could come into the foreground as a powerful philosophical movement, as it did in the later Schelling (1775–1854) and Schopenhauer (1788–1860). But the dominant philosophy of the Enlightenment was basically optimistic, and was most characteristically expressed by Leibniz in his principle of theodicy. The word "theodicy" comes from the two Greek words, *theos* meaning God and *dike* meaning justice. Theodicy thus means "justifying God for the evils in the world."

Leibniz' theodicy was, however, much more profound than the use of it by the optimistic philosophy of the Enlightenment. His idea was that if God would create a finite world, he would not be able to overcome the limits connected with finitude. God had to accept these limits of finitude and the various types of evil that go along with it. This is a risk he had to take. Assuming then that God was to create a world at all, it would naturally be—as our world actually is—the best of all possible worlds. This phrase became a slogan, and when the pessimistic reactions set in, this phrase was used ironically. Look at Lisbon and the sixty thousand dead people, and who will speak of the best of all possible worlds? This was the reaction. But of course it was unfair to a great philosophy. This often happens. The same thing happened to Hegel. What Leibniz really meant was not that the world was all good, but that if there is to be a world at all, then this is the least evil or the best possible world, because God cannot make a finite world absolutely good. That is to say, finitude has within itself the necessity of evil.

This fundamental philosophical problem will reflect itself in all the theologians of the nineteenth century. They will deal with the problem of theodicy. The world that God created is good, but because it is finite, the world cannot be perfect. Leibniz' phrase was singled out, distorted and placed against him with bitter irony.

2. *Cultural Vices*

Another question: How does progress come about in bourgeois society? Here a very interesting paradox was seen by some of the philosophers of the Enlightenment, and in particular by Rousseau (1712–1778). In his first book[9] Rousseau dealt with the question: Have the sciences and the arts contributed in a positive way to the morals of society? The question itself was formulated by the Academy of Sciences for a literary contest, and Rousseau won the prize. The question itself indicated that some skepticism about the glory of civilization had cropped up among the intellectuals of French society. Rousseau's answer was, No, the arts and sciences have not contributed either to the morality or to the happiness of mankind. What they really do is to advance immorality, not in the narrow sense in which we often use it, but in the wider sense of ethical development and sensitivity, or rather, their opposites, antiethical development and insensitivity.

Rousseau alleged that in the new state of society the increase in the pleasure of a few has become the basis for the misery of the many. He did not have in mind only the bourgeois society, but instead the whole development of civilization since primitive times. The advance of the sciences and technical productivity has produced a much sharper division in society between the "haves" and the "have nots" in comparison with the earlier period. The earlier period becomes the "lost paradise" for Rousseau, and the seemingly progressive culture becomes the negative state. This situation has been brought about by the establishment of private property, which is something that did not exist in the earlier period. So Rousseau gave a vivid description of the eighteenth-century political and economic situation before the French Revolution, namely, on the one hand luxury and laziness, and on the other hand exploitation and misery. Therefore Rousseau questioned the belief in the progressive development of morality through civilization. Is cultural progress good?

[9] *Discours sur les sciences et les arts* (1750).

No! Is modern progressive society better because it has the arts and sciences in comparison with the natural state of the savages, the noble savages as they were later called? And many answered with Rousseau, No! So let us go back to the primitive state of nature.

In these views Rousseau proved to be a double prophet. In his political writings he was the father of the French Revolution and the spokesman of the bourgeois society. Nobody foreshadowed the French Revolution so powerfully and representatively as Rousseau. But with his critical attitude toward progress in civilization, he became the predecessor of Romanticism, the period which followed the Enlightenment and which fought to overcome it. The interesting thing is that Rousseau represented both at the same time. Indeed, the great fulfillers of the Enlightenment were at the same time the conquerors of it. There was David Hume in England, Immanuel Kant in Germany, and Rousseau in France. As great representatives and fulfillers of the Enlightenment, they were somehow at the same time its conquerors. Therefore, we have been speaking of the intrinsic conflicts of the Enlightenment. It is especially clear in the case of Rousseau. The father of the French Revolution was at the same time the predecessor of Romanticism.

3. Personal Vices

Then another problem arose. If we have a society of economic exchange that is dependent on selling and buying, it happens that human desires must be aroused to make such selling and buying possible. Thus an antipuritan principle developed in the midst of the Enlightenment and bourgeois discipline. If everybody should work and no one should buy and use the products of industry, there would soon be no work to do and the whole system would collapse. Therefore, it is not only good but essential to arouse in people the desire for goods. This resulted in the introduction of the pleasure principle as a dynamic into bourgeois society in opposition to the original Calvinistic and early bourgeois principle of work with its ascetic character. To put it in a formula one can say that *private vices are public goods*. We will see how this was exhibited in England by Mandeville.

We must say something about the philosophical presupposition of the ethics of eudaemonism which developed after the ascetic period of bourgeois society. Often we use the word "materialism." It is used today in cold war propaganda, for the Communists are considered to be materialists. The people who use this term in propaganda do not bother with its meaning, otherwise their passion for propaganda might decrease—and that would be a pity! But here in an academic room we must try to find out what materialism really means.

There are many different forms of materialism. Marxist materialism, for example, is entirely different from the French materialism of the eighteenth century. This latter is a particular type, namely, an ontological or metaphysical materialism—one of the ideas against which Marx fought most ardently. But there was an eighteenth-century philosopher very much worth studying because theological ethics up to today has tried so hard to refute ideas like his. This man's name is Helvétius (1715–1771), which in Latin simply means "Swiss." Helvétius was a Frenchman and a representative of materialism. He had the idea that the only principle by which man acts is that of self-love. He does not try very hard to analyze what this self-love is, but basically it means that nobody desires objects for their own sake. Helvétius' psychology was that every person loves things only for his own pleasure. There is no foundation for the idea of a moral conscience which distinguishes between good and bad. The conscience is the result of punishment. So he formulated the thesis: "Remorse begins where impunity ends." That means that you repent for what you have done only if you are punished, but if you get away with it, there is no remorse. Psychologically, this is true to a great extent, but it is not always true, and it is not true as a matter of principle. According to Helvétius the greatest men are those with the greatest passions and with the power to satisfy them. Even if everything were equal in education, opportunity, and talent, there would remain the difference in passion. This power of passion would make all the difference in the world.

This element of power is one of the most important underground elements of the Enlightenment. It was largely repressed and kept underground. Machiavelli (1469–1527) was taboo in the eighteenth century as in the two preceding centuries, not because he was wrong but because those who acted according to his principles suppressed his theory. All possible forms of power were allowed, even poison and murder, with recourse to the ideological consolation that it is good for the state. All of the politicians were Machiavellian, but his ideas were not expressed. If they had expressed his ideas, they would have undercut their own power. It is only effective when it is done without talking about it. So the struggle for power was a real underground element of the eighteenth century. A nineteenth-century philosopher came along and did what Machiavelli did, not in a diplomatic political form, but in a more universal metaphysical form. This was Friedrich Nietzsche with his idea of "will to power." Nietzsche blew the lid off the Enlightenment and brought this power element out into the open. He was one of the main forerunners of the existentialist philosophy of the twentieth century.

Of course, on this basis religion was denied. The power of the priest is based on the stupid credulity of the masses. Nietzsche also had to deny the church because it condemned passion as sin; whereas for him the great passions are what accomplish the most. The really great virtues which finally do the most for everybody are virtues of passion. Religion contradicts these passions and pleasures which are accessible to everyone; religion demands repression, so drop religion.

4. *Progress Based on Immorality*

Out of the underground of the Enlightenment a demonic naturalism arose, but could not come to the surface before the end of the eighteenth century. A large part of it was expressed in sexual ideas. In England it was expressed in a more philosophical way: Progress is based on immorality, on the negation of ethical principles. This idea was also in Helvétius, but it was formulated philosophically by Bernard de Mandeville (1670–1733). Like the Manchester theory of economics he held that because of necessity of economic exchange, it is best for the whole society if everyone follows his own pleasure instincts. Progress depends on those people who have a great desire for luxury and who are able to buy items of luxury for themselves. If we keep in mind that these ideas developed on the soil of English puritanism which for a long time had suppressed pleasure, we can appreciate the intrinsic conflict which resulted from now glorifying the strivings for luxury out of economic necessities. If the groups which indulged in luxury were to be eliminated, all social progress would break down. If privilege and status were negated, economy would be retarded. Thus the proposition was advanced that the private vices of the powerful individuals who desired luxury, glory, and social status are the forces which keep the whole machinery of capitalistic society moving.

If we study these things, we see that the eighteenth-century society was anything but monolithic. The problems which we have come to know under the label of the existentialist analysis of the human predicament were part of the underground of the Enlightenment, and were there ready to come to the foreground later.

D. The Fulfillers and Critics of Enlightenment

Now let us deal with the three men to whom we referred earlier as the fulfillers and conquerors of the Enlightenment, Rousseau, Hume, and Kant.

1. *Rousseau, the French Revolution, and Romanticism*

I do not think I need to say much more about Rousseau as the father of the French Revolution. His principles led both to the American and to the French Revolution. They were the principles of natural reason. It was the use of critical reason, as I called it, derived ultimately from the Stoics, which made Rousseau the philosopher of the French Revolution. It was the application of the belief in harmony, that the will of the majority is the true will of society and the best for it. But in Rousseau we also have the other concept of nature. You remember that I spoke of the two concepts of nature, the material and the formal. The material concept of nature refers to nature outside of man, but includes man's physical body. The formal concept refers, for instance, to man's natural spirit. Rousseau as the father of the French Revolution was using the formal concept of nature when he identified nature with reason. He derived his notion of the natural or the rational from the idea of an original paradisiacal state of mankind, the state of original communism. He did not use the word "communism" but spoke rather of the "absence of private property" among the savages. Here nature existed in prerational form, in the form of the natural community of all beings together —a nature-produced ecology, as it is called today, where man is a part of the whole nature. This notion was intensified by the sentimentality about which I spoke, this longing to go back to nature. You can see this illustrated in Versailles if you visit the Petit Trianon which was built in order to play shepherd and shepherdess. This is a mixture of frivolity and a longing to escape civilization. It was Rousseauism that was expressed in these impressive buildings. One can see a strange combination of the two concepts of reason. There is the critical reason which laid the foundation for the revolutionary philosophy of the French Revolution, as well as for some of the fundamental principles of the American Constitution, and alongside of this there is the romantic sentimental longing for nature outside of men in which, as he believed, the "natural" was embodied thousands of years ago before the beginning of civilization. With this second aspect of Rousseau's thinking, the Enlightenment philosophy which undergirded the French Revolution was conquered by the Romanticism of the following period. So we have in Rousseau both the fulfillment and the conquest of the principle of reason in the eighteenth century.

2. *Hume, the History of Religion, and Positivism*

Now we come to the second thinker in whom I see the fulfillment and conquest of the Enlightenment. He is David Hume in England (1711–1776). The trends of the Enlightenment which were expressed in classic form by John Locke came to an end in Hume. In his epistemology he criticized the confidence of the Enlightenment in its rational principles. He undercut the certainty of belief in the validity of what we have called the intuitive and critical concepts of reason. And along with this he undercut the metaphysical foundations of natural law on which the Enlightenment depended.

The main religious concepts of the Enlightenment theology were God, freedom, and immortality. Hume undercut them by his fundamental epistemological skepticism. He represented a way of criticizing the rational certainty of the Enlightenment, which in England was felt like a death blow. Hume defeated the great attempt of modern men to treat all the problems of life on the basis of reason in its different meanings. In this respect he can be considered an important point of departure for what we call positivism in modern philosophy.

The bourgeoisie had conquered its foes in the various revolutions and was now increasing its position of power. If the principles by which the bourgeoisie gained power would still be valid in this situation, they could become threatening to the victorious bourgeoisie itself. Therefore, critical reason was replaced by a positivistic acceptance of observing and calculating reason. This signifies the great change from the critical passion of the great thinkers of the Enlightenment to the positivism of nominalistic philosophy in modern times. What does positivism mean after all? It means accepting what is positively given as such, observing and describing it without trying to criticize it or without trying to make a constructive system out of it. We have then in Hume a great change which became important also for the continent of Europe through Hume's impact on Kant.

This changed orientation is significant for the situation in the three countries which were the leading contexts of modern philosophical development: France, Great Britain, and Germany. In the France of Rousseau's time we have reason fighting and struggling against tradition up to the French Revolution. France was Catholic and the Enlightenment was nourished in part by the critical attitude of Freemasonry. Even today it splits the French mind into those who follow the Catholic Church and those who fight against it. The great struggles in the beginning of this century between church and state in France, the radical separation in every respect, and the inner division of the whole nation are understandable only on the basis of the leading ideas of the Enlightenment which conflicted with the authoritarian system of the Roman Church, and not only with its authority, but also with its content. There are not many symptoms in the last fifty years of French history which suggest that this tremendous split can be overcome through a synthesis. That is the French situation even today.

The British situation is determined by Hume's positivistic attitude. Hume never attacked the established church, but he did attack the belief that you can justify it by reason. From the point of view of reason there was a thoroughgoing skepticism over against all the symbols of Christianity, but without that radical and hateful attack which took place in France. This also characterizes the situation in England today. We have there two attitudes which do not openly fight against each other, but which run beside each other, almost without touching each other. On the one hand, there is the established church with all its traditions and symbolism guarded over by the Queen, the symbol of the empire, of the past, but not a real power. On the other hand, there is the majority of the intelligentsia which goes its own way without really attacking the established church but also without uniting with any of its traditional symbols. No synthesis is attempted. That is why the contribution of the established church in Great Britain to systematic theology is almost nonexistent. For some reason this does not apply equally to the Scottish Church. But in French Catholicism, especially in some of its apologetic works, a great contribution was made to theology. Also nineteenth-century German theology made a great contribution because of its urgent need to find a synthesis.

Now in these days there is an interesting thing happening in England, something which I have become aware of recently because in a way I am involved in it. A book has appeared written by Bishop John Robinson of Woolwich, with the title *Honest to God*.[10] Those of you who read the section on religion in *Time* magazine have no doubt heard of it. This was also the way in which I first heard of it before the Bishop sent me the book. He develops theological thoughts which were born in the German situation and which seek an answer to the conflicts between the religious tradition and the modern secular mind. Robinson refers a great deal to my writings and to the writings of Bonhoeffer, the theologian martyred by the Nazis, who wrote letters from prison.[11] In these letters Bonhoeffer dealt with the same problem that I have dealt with in all my books, namely, the problem of seeking a solution to the conflicts between the religious tradition and the modern mind. Robinson's formulations provoked much resistance because they undercut the traditionalism of the church. The church never took seriously the prob-

---

[10] Philadelphia: The Westminster Press, 1963.

[11] Dietrich Bonhoeffer, *Letters and Papers from Prison,* translated by Reginald H. Fuller (New York: The Macmillan Company, 1953).

lem of finding a union of tradition with the modern mind and of showing the significance of the traditional symbols to modern man. And so a great shock was produced in the church by this book. Of course, in the British situation there have been some rare exceptions, like Archbishop Temple, who tried to take in some of the basic ideas of continental theology. But on the whole what has been characteristic of the British situation is the unwillingness to sacrifice the security of its liturgically founded tradition for the sake of radical theological thought. Therefore, it has not given answers to the questions implied in the existence of modern man.

3. *Kant, Moral Religion, and Radical Evil*

I must now concentrate on Germany which has done far more than any other country for Protestant theology in the nineteenth and twentieth centuries. Of course, I must include Switzerland because linguistically and theologically it belongs to the same situation. Karl Barth, for example, was for many years a professor of theology in Germany before he went back to Switzerland.

The man who was decisive for the theology of the nineteenth century, perhaps even more than Hegel or Schleiermacher, is Kant (1724–1804). He is the third of these three great figures who fulfilled and conquered the Enlightenment.

Kant followed Hume in his epistemological criticism of a philosophy which assumes that the religious ideas of God, freedom, and immortality can be established by rational arguments. This is impossible for the basic reason that man is finite. The finite mind is not able to reach the infinite. Almost everyone in the nineteenth and twentieth centuries accepted this criticism as a presupposition. You will not find a theologian who has not accepted it, or modified it, and attempted to save what could be saved of natural theology after Kant's tremendous attack on it. Even a man like Karl Barth who is so firmly rooted in the classical tradition has fully accepted the Kantian criticism of natural theology.

The basis of this criticism of natural theology is Kant's doctrine of the categorical structure of the human mind. The categories of thought and the forms of intuition, time and space, constitute the structure of man's finitude, and therefore these categories are valid only for the understanding of the interrelations of finite things. If one transcends the finite things and their interrelations, then the categories of causality, substance, quantity and quality, etc., are not valid. The immediate consequence of this is that you cannot make God a first cause or a universal substance. These categories are valid for physical or other scientific calculations; they must be presupposed. In fact, they are presupposed by everybody. Even Hume who criticizes them presupposes them in his criticism. Nevertheless, you cannot go beyond them. The category of causality, for example, is a description of the interrelation of finite experiences. Time is the main form of finitude by its transitoriness, by the impossibility of fixing it in one moment. If you fix this moment, time is already gone. If the categories are not used in the realm of phenomena, those things which appear in time and space, they cannot be used at all. This means that the use of the concepts of God, freedom, and immortality is impossible in terms of rational structure, as natural theology tried to do.

This criticism is so fundamental and radical that Kant has been called the destroyer of the whole rational theology of the Enlightenment. But there is another implication in it. The first philosophical lecture I heard in my life was delivered by Julius Kaftan (1848–1926), the systematic theologian of the University of Berlin. I was perhaps sixteen years old and still in the *Gymnasium*. In Germany there is no college, but there is a *Gymnasium* which takes you till the eighteenth year, and then you go directly into the university. I was fascinated by this lecture and never forgot it. It was an oversimplification, but a very impressive one which had a great deal of truth in it. Kaftan at this time was the leading authority of the Kantian-Ritschlian school of theology. He said that there are three great philosophers and there are three great Christian groups: The Greek Orthodox whose philosopher's name is Plato; the Roman Catholics whose philosopher's name is Aristotle; and the Protestants whose philosopher's name is Kant. Now this alone would be very interesting because now in the ecumenical movement Plato, Aristotle, and Kant may come together to join in a heavenly disputation. However this may be, what is the basis for the statement that Kant is the philosopher of Protestantism? The real basis is the fact that he is the philosopher who saw most clearly and sharply the finitude of man and man's inability of breaking through the limits of his finitude to that which transcends it, namely, to the infinite.

Kant's doctrine of categories and of time and space as the structure of man's mind, a structure which construes the world of the finite for him but beyond which man cannot go, is what gives him a certain kind of humility before reality. This humility is also found in empirical philosophy which accepts the empirically given phenomena. But in Kant it goes much deeper existentially than in ordinary empirical philosophy.

We are finite and must therefore accept our finitude. The Protestant idea that we can come to God only through God, that only grace can overcome guilt, sin, and our estrangement from God, and not we ourselves, and no good works can help us, this idea can be extended also to the realm of thought. We cannot break through to God even in the realm of thought. He must come to us. This was a very fundamental change in contrast to the metaphysical arrogance of the Enlightenment which believed in the power of reason—all the different forms of reason —to place man immediately in the presence of the Divine. Now men were in a prison, so to speak. Kant had placed man in the prison of finitude. All attempts to escape—which characterize both mysticism and rationalism—are in vain. The only thing we can do is to accept our finitude. Certainly in this way Kant represents to a great extent the attitude of Protestantism.

But could this be all? Is man nothing more than finite? Can philosophy even speak of finitude if there is not a point at which man transcends it? Animals are finite, but they do not know it. They are not above finitude at any point. Then Kant wrote his second critique, the critique of practical reason. This dealt with the idea of the moral imperative. He called it the categorical or unconditional imperative. Here there is a breakthrough, not in the realm of theoretical thought but in terms of the experience of the unconditional command of the moral imperative. The breakthrough does not go directly to God. Kant gave an argument for the existence of God which falls under his own criticism and was never really accepted. But he showed one thing, that in the finite structure of our being there is a point of unconditional validity.

This point is the moral imperative and the experience of its unconditional character.

So we have no certainty about God or freedom or eternal life, but we have the certainty of belonging to something unconditional which we can experience as such. It is obvious that Kant did not have in mind particular contents of the moral imperative. He was educated enough in terms of ethnology to know the vast differences of content in the moral imperative from culture to culture. But the commanding form of this imperative, its unconditional character, is independent of any particular content. Thus not the content of the moral imperative but its radical form is what gives Kant the feeling of a breakthrough to that which transcends the prison of finitude in which the human mind has been placed by theoretical reason.

Another thing appeared in Kant's philosophy which came as a shock to his contemporaries, even to people who, like Goethe, had transcended the Enlightenment. The unconditional command of the moral imperative is given to us. But we who live in time and space have not taken it into our actual will. Although it is our essential will, that which makes our will the true will, our actual will is perverted. The principle of action or the maxim, as Kant called it, according to which we act is perverted. This he called the radical evil in man. Now remember that the most passionate point of attack of the Enlightenment against Christianity dealt with the doctrine of original sin, or of radical evil, as Kant called it, or of universal tragic estrangement, as I prefer to call it. Radical evil means that evil goes to the *radix,* meaning "root" in Latin. Radical evil means that in the root of human existence there is a perversion of man's essential will.

Kant's idea of radical evil was an unforgivable sin from the point of view of the Enlightenment. Kant was attacked very much because he said this. But Kant was followed later on by several who even deepened it and carried it through to the early sources of existentialism, namely, the second period of Schelling the philosopher. Here we find in Kant a deviation from the Enlightenment that is very radical. Kant elaborated these ideas in his book, *Religion within the Limits of Reason Alone,* into a whole philosophy of religion. Or I would simply call it a little systematic theology. This systematic theology underlies much of what is going on in America even today, for Kant's ideas were developed further by Ritschl and his school and were transmitted into American theology by Walter Rauschenbusch (1861–1918) and the Social Gospel movement. This movement was still very powerful up to the years before the second World War when Reinhold Niebuhr attacked it.

We must now briefly present a picture of Kant's theological ideas. Kant conceives of history as the ongoing struggle between evil, radical evil, and good. The good principle is present in mankind; it is identical with man's essential nature, which is good. It has appeared in the Christ who represents this essential goodness of men over against its perversion by radical evil. In the Christ the perversion was overcome; the unity of God and man was re-established. The victory over the evil principle by Jesus is the beginning of the kingdom of God on earth. The church is the invisible body of those who are determined by essential reason and who take into themselves the power of reunion with God. The transition from the invisible church to something very mixed in the empirical churches is unavoidable. But the empirical church must always be criticized by the standard of the essential church of pure reason. For Kant this criticism is very radical, so radical that it is actually a negation of the empirical church. The empirical church is seen by him as a group ruled by superstitions and subjected to ecclesiastical authorities. Therefore every individual belonging to the essential church should try to overcome this visible church which destroys autonomy by heteronomous authority and destroys reason by superstitions. Everybody should try, and the church as a whole should try, to overcome these elements.

The sharpest attack was made against the priestly rule of the church. This for Kant was the absolute opposite of the autonomous rule of reason. From Kant's point of view all elements of immediacy between God and man were to be eliminated. I indicated this already when I spoke of his criticism of the arguments for the existence of God. Now we can see that there is a certain religious type which expresses itself here in Kant. He allows no room for the presence of the divine Spirit in the human spirit with its ecstatic implications. The mystical presence of the divine is radically denied. In the Ritschlian school which was influenced by Kant, the most radical attack on mysticism ever made in the history of Christianity was carried out by Ritschl and his disciples, including Harnack, the greatest figure of this school. What we are left with is a consistent type of finitude in which only the moral imperative elevates man above animal existence. Morality gives him dignity, and the struggle between good and evil is a moral one in which elements like grace and prayer are denied.

Grace supposedly devaluates man's autonomous freedom for good and evil, and prayer is an ecstatic experience of which one would be ashamed if someone caught him in the act by surprise. This was Kant's fundamental feeling. And, of course, ecstasy in nature itself, for which we have the word miracle, is an encroachment upon the universal essential structure of reality. What remains is a philosophy of the kingdom of God. This kingdom is identical with the establishment of the moral man on earth. This notion includes not only individual morality, but also social justice and peace on earth. Kant wrote a classic little book on eternal peace which became the basis of the religion which influenced the Social Gospel movement at the end of the last and the beginning of this century.

Kant wrote a third critique, the *Critique of Judgment*. Here he tried with great caution to escape the prison of finitude. His followers in the classical period of German philosophy took it as a way out. From Kant's point of view it would be better to say that he was only enlarging and beautifying the prison, but not really breaking through it. But his followers considered it a breakthrough. In this *Critique of Judgment* Kant tried to bring together the two divergent critiques of reason, theoretical and practical reason. He showed possible unions between the two. These cannot, however, be affirmed assertively, but only in terms of possibility, or better, as a human vision of realities without knowing that the realities really correspond to the vision.

In this *Critique* Kant developed his notion of nature. Thereby he became the father of modern *Gestalt* theory reflected in all forms of organicism, and in the arts. In these two realms Kant saw that judgments are possible, the judgment that nature is an organism as a whole and in the organic structures and the judgment that in art there is an inner aim in every representation of meaning. Kant did not say that nature is actually like this, but always added a qualification in terms of an "as if" (*als ob*). He was completely overwhelmed by the Newtonian natural laws, by the mathematical, scientific approach to nature. But he said that although the real nature with which we have to deal is the nature of Newtonian physics, we can nevertheless consider nature *as if* there were structures, meaningful structures, or organisms, and *as if* the whole universe had the character of an organic structure of this kind.

So Kant, with caution and great restriction, introduced a principle which was picked up by Romantic philosophy as a main principle for its philosophy of nature, only minus the "as if." That is the big difference. From the presuppositions of Kant's prison of finitude you can only say "as if," but if at several points you can break through this prison, then you might be able to say what nature or reality really is like. This was the watershed between critical philosophy and later ontological philosophy.

Thus Kant stands like Rousseau and Hume as a fulfiller and critic of German Enlightenment. His greatness is that he understood man's creaturely finitude, of course, on the basis of his half-pietistic Protestantism. The pietistic element was removed, but existentialism and pietism have much to do with each other. I am reminded of the atheistic sermon which Heidegger once gave us in his pietistic categories. At any rate Kant was praised by all the theologians of the nineteenth century for establishing the insight into man's creaturely finitude, or as we would say today, into man's existential situation. But the human mind and the human soul could not remain on this level. Therefore, all movements of the nineteenth century, although based on Kant, would try to go beyond him. In my student years there was a slogan often repeated: Understanding Kant means transcending Kant. We all try to do this, and I will be showing you various ways in which theology has tried to do it.

CHAPTER III

The Classic-Romantic Reaction
against the Enlightenment

We have discussed two figures from France, Voltaire, the classical representative, and Rousseau, the fulfiller and conqueror of the Enlightenment; and two from England, the classical figure, John Locke, and then the fulfiller and conqueror, David Hume. From Germany I have presented only the fulfiller and conqueror of the Enlightenment, Kant, but not the classical figure, Gotthold Ephraim Lessing.

A. LESSING, HISTORICAL CRITICISM, AND THE REDISCOVERY OF SPINOZA

Lessing's was a very universal mind. He was a poet, dramatist, philosopher, and theologian. He stirred up one of the greatest storms in the history of Protestant theology, when as a librarian in a small German town he edited a book written by a historian, Reimarus.[1] Reimarus started this modern search for the historical Jesus. Lessing, the librarian, published certain of Reimarus' fragments of research on the

[1] Hermann Samuel Reimarus' studies were published by Lessing after the death of Reimarus in 1768, in a collection called the *Wolfenbüttel Fragments*. The English translation is entitled *The Object of Jesus and His Disciples, as Seen in the New Testament*, edited by A. Voysey (1879). Cf. also Albert Schweitzer's book, *The Quest of the Historical Jesus*, the original German title of which is *Von Reimarus zu Wrede*.

life of Jesus which he had conducted by applying radical historical criticism. It was very dangerous to publish them. Reimarus had already died, but his manuscript was in the hands of Lessing. The storm was tremendous when these fragments were published. The chief pastor of Hamburg, Goetze, tried to defend orthodoxy, with some good and some bad arguments. But the whole intellectual climate was irreversibly changed. No theologian could thereafter approach the documents of the story of Jesus without being aware of the questions asked by Reimarus concerning the reliability of the Synoptic Gospels.

Thus the fundamental problem of historical criticism arose in the middle of the eighteenth century. People were shocked in that time just as many lay people were shocked today when the Dead Sea Scrolls were published. Except for the fact that we know more about first-century Palestine, the situation is not basically different so far as theology is concerned. Lessing's courage to edit these radical fragments of research was one of the things which made him great.

Another important thing about Lessing is his classic expression of progressivistic thought about philosophy and religion in his little book, *The Education of the Human Race*. His idea was that mankind has arrived at the age of reason. The description of this reason as autonomous is very similar to the idea of the great prophet of the twelfth century, Joachim de Fiore, who prophesied the coming of an age of the divine Spirit in which everyone will be taught directly by the Spirit and no authorities will be needed any more. I told you about the intimate relation between this kind of spirit-mysticism and rationalism. Well, Lessing is a great representative of this unity. The age of reason is for Lessing the actualization of the age of the Spirit. He refers directly to the movement of Joachim de Fiore as among his predecessors.

Another fascinating idea comes up in Lessing, as in other enlightened people of that age. That is the idea of reincarnation of men. People who had died before the age of reason had dawned would return so that they could participate in the fulfillment of true humanity. What seems to be a very irrational idea is used to answer a difficult problem for all progressivistic thinking. If we say that in the future sometime there will be an age of reason and peace and justice etc., we must ask about those who die before the coming of that age. Are they excluded from fulfillment?

If there is no transcendent fulfillment, they are excluded. And for the people of the Enlightenment, of course, there was no fulfillment. At least, it was not as unambiguous as it was in the Christian tradition. So they had to answer in terms of time and space. The idea of rebirth or reincarnation was the only one which could help them.

Perhaps we can add still another thing about Lessing. He wrote a play, *Nathan the Wise,* which has been translated and often performed. In this play he describes the encounter between Islam, Christianity, and Judaism. The wise Jew is the hero of the whole play. The theme of the play is the relativism of religions. In the history of Christianity it was the encounter with Islam which brought the question of the relativism of Christianity itself to the fore. Christianity became fanatical because now it was threatened. Paganism did not represent a real religious threat, but Islam did, and conquered the eastern half of Christianity. This raised the question of the relation between these two historical religions.

Then a last point. On his deathbed, Lessing had a conversation with the philosopher Jacobi (1743–1819)[2] who played an important role at that time. After Lessing's death Jacobi published that in this conversation Lessing had acknowledged a great admiration for Spinoza. According to this report Lessing even went so far as to call himself a Spinozist. This was a scandal. At that time spiritual things were taken so seriously that the idea that a man like Lessing, the great figure of the Enlightenment, should have been a Spinozist came as a great shock. Spinoza was taboo, not only to Christian and Jewish Orthodoxy—he had been thrown out by the Jewish congregation in Amsterdam—but also to the Enlightenment, because the innermost center of Spinoza's thought, the volcano beneath his frozen geometrical system, was Jewish mysticism of the Middle Ages. This can be traced historically. If you read Spinoza's ethics not in terms of the validity of his definitions and conclusions which were given *more geometrico* (in geometrical fashion), as he called it, but in terms of the underlying passion, in terms of the highest aim which is placed before man, namely, to participate in the eternal love with which God loves himself, then you see how pertinent it is to

[2] F. H. Jacobi followed Kant in removing religious certainty from the sphere of reason to that of faith. He is often quoted for claiming to have been a "pagan with his head, but with his heart a Christian."

speak of a mystical volcano hidden beneath a geometrically frozen surface.

The eventual result was that Spinoza was received more and more widely. Schleiermacher even wrote a hymn to Saint Spinoza. He really was a "saint" in his life as much as any Catholic saint ever was. Schleiermacher asked his contemporaries to sacrifice in thought and in feeling to this saint who was a lonely man, and in his loneliness was one of the deepest and greatest thinkers of all times. Yet all these men were Kantians. Kant's Copernican revolution, as he himself called it, had shaken all the philosophical foundations. How could Spinoza then be received on a Kantian basis?

B. THE SYNTHESIS OF SPINOZA AND KANT

The relation between Spinoza and Kant became the philosophical and theological problem. Why should this be so difficult? Well, on the one side is Spinoza's mystical pantheism, as it has sometimes been called. This is the idea that there is one eternal substance, and that everything that exists is but a mode of this substance. This universal substance has innumerable attributes, but we know only two of them, mind and extension, as Descartes, Spinoza's teacher, had said. This one substance is present in everything. Here we have what I would call the principle of identity. Everything has a point of identity in the eternal divine substance which underlies everything. The identity between the finite and the infinite is complete. It was this mystical background which accounts for the fascination which thinkers in the following periods up to today have had in Spinoza's philosophy. This is true of Goethe who was perhaps even closer to Spinoza than Lessing was.

Now against this mystical pantheistic system stands Kant's philosophy, which emphasizes the principle of distance, the principle of finitude which man must accept, the transcendence of the divine beyond man's grasp and lying outside his center. This finitude of man and his inability of ever reaching the infinite is the motive in all Kant's criticisms. So all of Kant's followers and the whole continental philosophy faced this problem: How to unite mysticism and the Protestant principle; how to unite the principle of identity, the participation of the divine in each of us, and the principle of detachment, of moral obedience, without participation in the divine.

My doctoral dissertation was about this tension. It focused on one particular man, Schelling, the predecessor, friend, and later enemy of Hegel. I tried to discover how Schelling sought to solve the problem of this tension. The title of my book was *Mystik und Schuldbewusstsein in Schellings philosophischer Entwicklung*, 1912.[3] Here you see these two things. More abstractly you can express it by the principle of identity in relation to the principle of contrast, or even of contradiction, in a moral sense at least. Here we have the fundamental motives in attempting to create the great synthesis following Kant. It started in part already during his lifetime, and then was fully developed after his death, coming to its conclusion in Hegel and Schleiermacher. Later the great synthesis was destroyed, partly at least in the name of the slogan "back to Kant." The slogan meant that we should give up the principle of identity, accept finitude and have a religion of moral obedience.

I call this the great synthesis of Kant and Spinoza, a synthesis which, of course, includes many other things. This is the synthesis of the principle of identity and the principle of detachment or contrast. The philosophers of Romanticism, and above all Schleiermacher, the great theologian of Romanticism, are all characterized by this attempt at synthesis. They were Protestant theologians; they had learned about Kant's destruction of natural theology; nobody doubted this any more. On the other hand they came from mystical traditions. For instance, Schleiermacher came from the tradition of Zinzendorfian pietism. All these theologians had the task of uniting these seemingly irreconcilable contrasts.

The dynamo of the history of theology ever since, going through the whole nineteenth century, is the tension between these two things. If you take a seminar on Karl Barth, you will see again the protest against mysticism, against any form of the principle of identity. But there are also theologies which come from the union of Kant and Spinoza.

---

[3] *Mysticism and Guilt-Consciousness in Schelling's Philosophical Development* (1912). This book has not been translated into English.

C. The Nature of Romanticism

Before we deal with Schleiermacher, we have to discuss what Romanticism is, in order to understand what people mean when they speak of Schleiermacher as a romantic philosopher. Karl Barth, who dislikes Romanticism very much, has said that we are all romantics. That means that he was fair enough to acknowledge even his own dependence on the great anti-Enlightenment romantic tradition of the nineteenth and twentieth centuries.

In order to speak about the nature of Romanticism I first need, as always, to make a semantic statement. When I came to America, I heard Reinhold Niebuhr, my friend and colleague at Union Theological Seminary in New York speak of Romanticism in terms of what I usually called utopianism. Utopianism is the idea of a fulfilled society in the future and of an original, just society along the lines of Rousseau's idea of the noble savages. Niebuhr called this Romanticism. In continental Europe nobody would have referred to utopianism by the term Romanticism, although certain elements in Rousseau, such as the sentimental desire of returning to nature, had a relation to actual Romanticism. But the Romanticism of the main countries in which it appeared, of France, England, and Germany, is really quite different. Now I want to show you what some of the constitutive elements of Romanticism are, by asking, what made theologians and philosophers like Schelling, Schleiermacher, Schlegel, and Rothe all romanticists? What produced the great romantic poetry in Germany? How did Romanticism influence the naturalistic philosophy of the late nineteenth century of men like Nietzsche? And—this should not be forgotten—what produced the romantic music in people like Schubert and Schumann and up to Brahms?

1. The Infinite and Finite

Our first consideration has to do with the relation of the infinite to the finite. Here we have to go back to the early Renaissance, to Nicholas of Cusa, cardinal of high standing in the Roman Catholic Church, who

was born in 1401 at Cues (Cusa) on the Moselle. He is a very important man, but better known in the twentieth century than in the nineteenth. In the nineteenth century under the power of neo-Kantian
philosophy, Descartes was almost exclusively regarded as the founder of
modern philosophy. But in our century it has become clear that we need
to know more than merely the creator of the method of modern philosophy, namely, Descartes, who influenced both empiricism and rationalism. We also need to know the one who represents the metaphysical
foundations of the modern mind, and this man is Nicholas of Cusa.

The philosopher who helped to rediscover Nicholas of Cusa is Ernst
Cassirer,[4] who also came to this country with the help of Hitler. I
myself learned of Nicholas of Cusa very early in my thinking through
the influence he had on the line of thought which led to Schelling.

Very much like Descartes, this man was basically mathematically
minded, but he used his mathematical education not in a methodological
but in an ontological direction. His main principle was the *coincidentia
oppositorum* (the coincidence of opposites), the coincidence of the finite
and the infinite. In everything finite the infinite is present, namely, that
power which is the creative unity of the universe as a whole. And in the
same way the finite is in the infinite as a potentiality. In the world the
divine is developed; in God the world is enveloped. The finite is in the
infinite potentially; the infinite is in the finite actually. They are within
each other. He expresses this in geometrical terms by saying that God,
or better, the divine, is the center and the periphery of everything. He is
in everything as the center, although he transcends everything; but he is
also the periphery because he embraces everything. They are removed
from him and at the same time he is in them.

It is very interesting that Martin Luther in his discussions of the
presence of the divine in the sacramental materials of bread and wine
used similar formulations, probably without any dependence on Nicholas of Cusa. It is doubtful that Luther knew him, but he had similar
earlier sources available to him, that is, in German and ultimately neo-

---

[4] Ernst Cassirer's books on the Renaissance and the Enlightenment are entitled:
Individual and Cosmos in the Philosophy of the Renaissance (1927); *The Platonic
Renaissance in England* (1932); and *The Philosophy of the Enlightenment*
(1932).

Platonic mysticism. Luther said that God is nearer to everything than anything is to itself. He is fully in every grain of sand, but the whole world cannot comprehend him. He transcends everything finite, although being in it. So we have here a common development and this common development underlies the modern mind in its ultimate concern, so to speak, in the fundamental principles of interpreting God and the world.

This represents a tremendous change from the common view that God is in heaven, but only his active powers are on earth. For Nicholas and for Luther on his mystical side—a mysticism which at first was open, but later hidden—they are within each other. The modern mind overleaps the strict dualism of a divine sphere in heaven and a human sphere on earth which developed in the later ancient world. The divine is not in some place alongside of the world or above the world, but is present in everything human and natural. In some respects one can say that modern naturalism was born out of the mystical idea of the coincidence of opposites. This was not simply a methodological approach to reality, rationalistic or empiricistic. Behind it was an experience that nature is not outside of creative reality, but is potentially before the creation in God—of course this is not meant temporally but logically— and then after the creation the divine is within it. This means that the finite is not only finite, but in some dimension it is also infinite and has the divine as its center and ground.

This principle of the relation between the finite and the infinite is the first principle of Romanticism on which everything else is dependent. Without it Romanticism and a theologian like Schleiermacher become completely unintelligible.

Now let me briefly indicate the line of thought coming from the early Renaissance (Nicholas of Cusa) and going into the eighteenth and nineteenth centuries. The next person whom we must mention is Giordano Bruno (1548–1600), the martyr of this Renaissance naturalism. His was an ecstatic naturalism, not a calculating naturalism of subjecting nature to analysis and technology. Bruno repeatedly spoke about the enthusiasm for the universe, and this brought him to his death by the Inquisition. This could happen because the whole system of authority was based on the principle of detachment, of nonparticipation, the principle of authority, of mediation between God and man. The mystical inwardness of Nicholas of Cusa was not accepted.

Nicholas of Cusa was able to be one of the most influential cardinals in Rome without being attacked, although he wrote something which was even more dangerous than almost anything that Giordano Bruno wrote, namely, *De Pace Fidei*.[5] In this book he wrote about the peace of faith in heaven where there is an assembly in which it is taught that the Logos, the divine word, is present in every religion—in accordance with the interpretation of Paul—and that therefore the struggle between the religions is unnecessary. This idea of a peace based on something that transcends the particular expressions of the religions was a dangerous idea. It touched on an issue which had become burning ever since the encounter with Islam and the continuing theological discussion with Judaism in medieval Christianity. Nicholas could get away with holding such ideas in the early Renaissance, but Bruno became a victim of the counter-Reformation, perhaps because the church felt that his enthusiastic naturalism would remove the divine out of reality.

In England we have Shaftesbury (1671–1713), a great representative of the principle of harmony, who applied it to an organismic interpretation of nature. In Germany the most representative of this line of thought was not the philosopher Schelling, but the poet Goethe. Here again we see an enthusiasm for nature. Goethe expressed this not only in his poetry but also in his natural scientific inquiries which anticipated to a large extent the modern *Gestalt* theory. According to this theory nature is not a causal assemblage of isolated atoms, but is composed of structures. One must look for these structures, these original phenomena, in nature. In the psychological realm these are the archetypes of Hume. Both these original phenomena of Goethe and the archetypes of Hume go back to Plato's ideas or essences which transcend every empirical reality.

So we can say that in Goethe the motifs of Nicholas of Cusa, Giordano Bruno, and the Earl of Shaftesbury were combined to form an image of reality which was overcome in the second half of the nineteenth century by the empirical sciences. But there were continual reac-

5 *On the Peace of Faith.*

tions to the empirical sciences in the nineteenth and twentieth centuries. There was Nietzsche, for example, an ecstatic naturalist like Giordano Bruno, but without the mystical elements.

In Goethe the idea of the infinite in nature was certainly present, but it was present in a balance between the infinite and the finite. We call this the classical attitude of Goethe, a development which is altogether against the Enlightenment. In Goethe's attitude toward nature the Greek spirit is still alive, namely, the balance of elements in the classical form. Of course, in one sense this was not possible any more. All attempts on the basis of Christianity to return to Greece have proved to be failures. You cannot return. Modern humanism is and remains Christian humanism, and the most anti-Christian of the humanists, people like Nietzsche, often happen to be sons of Protestant clergymen, as Nietzsche actually was. The Christian substance cannot be wholly lost. It is not by chance that many of the classical thinkers, like Schelling and others, came from the homes of Protestant ministers. The Protestant ministers in the rather barbaric Protestant countries in Northern Europe were the bearers of the higher culture. Often they were grasped by the spirit of Greece to such a degree that they wanted simply to return. But this is never possible.

In any case, the problem of the infinite and the finite was solved during Goethe's brief classical period. This was not the period of the later or early Goethe, but the middle-aged Goethe. It is an interesting thing that the classical periods are always like the upper edge of a roof; there is much which goes on before they can appear. There must be Enlightenment as in Greek sophism; there must be *Sturm und Drang* (storm and stress), a youth movement, then an intellectual movement. Only after these stages could Goethe come to his classical period. The same thing was true of Plato. The classical Plato is to be found in the middle dialogues. We find the same thing in Greek sculpture. The classical period endures only a short time between the archaic and the naturalistic period. Thus the classical period was represented only during a short period of Goethe's life. Then Romanticism broke through. Romanticism broke the classical balance of the infinite and the finite, by the dynamic power of the infinite which transcends every finite form.

Here we have another characteristic of fully developed Romanticism. In this sense we are all romantics, because our thinking is dynamic and does not want to bind itself to any given form. Behind this is Kant's doctrine of freedom which had a great influence on Romanticism, especially in the form in which it was interpreted by Fichte (1762–1814) in his philosophy of the absolute ego. The ego is creative, and everything in the world is only a limit to the ego; but the innermost nature of reality is freedom. This he learned from Kant and his doctrine of practical reason. Fichte construed the whole world as a fight between the principle of freedom in every individual self and the resistance of a nonego, an "id" as Freud would call it, against that freedom. This fight is going on all the time. Here you have the romantic dynamics breaking through every particular form. This has certain implications. Take, for instance, a social structure in which one lives today, a suburban structure in America in the 1960's. How can one get beyond this structure? By imagination. Romanticism is a philosophy of imagination. He who is not able to transcend the given situation in which he lives through his own imagination finds himself imprisoned in that situation.

America never had a real period of Romanticism. It imported something from England, but very little of Romanticism influenced the whole life of the educated people. This has had the consequence of underestimating the imagination, of drying out the imagination which alone can transcend the given state of things and conceive the infinite potentialities given in every moment. So you have here another consequence of the victory of the infinite over the finite. But this infinite was not, as it still was in Nicholas of Cusa, in the dimension of going up and going down, with the presence of the divine in the individual in a more or less static way, even if there was an enthusiasm for the cosmos. But modern Romanticism has behind itself the baroque period of the modern world, which had the dynamics which drive into the horizontal line. So this is not only the infinite *above,* but also the infinite *ahead,* presenting in each new moment an infinite variety of possibilities for new creativity. The idea of creativity, of cultural creativity, is a romantic element which has entered this country also. It is the Fichtean and generally romantic idea that culture is human creativity, and that this creativity is infinite in the horizontal line.

We have here then the breaking through of the infinite against the balance it had in the classical criticism or negation of the Enlightenment, the romantic breakthrough of the balance into the horizontal line. This must be understood if we are to understand the basis for the rediscovery of history in Romanticism. The whole understanding of history is something which has to do with Romanticism. Before dealing with this we must deal with another point, the emotional and aesthetic elements in Romanticism.

2. *The Emotional and the Aesthetic Elements in Romanticism*

Romanticism is, as I said, against the Enlightenment. There is no lack of emotion in the Enlightenment, but it is subjective or sentimental emotion. We have the tears which are shed all the time. Romanticism is not sentimental because it does not have to complement, so to speak, the rationality of Enlightenment, the calculating and fighting critical reason. If the infinite is in everything finite, then the awareness of the infinite in the finite is intuitive. This is complete mysticism, or natural mysticism. Mystical intuition is not divorced from emotion; it objectifies emotion by taking it into the very act of intuition. In Romanticism there is the emotion which is not sentimental, but which is revealing and has the character of the Platonic *eros*. It is no mere coincidence that Schleiermacher was the great romantic translator of Plato. If you read this, you will see that it is a romantic interpretation of Plato. It is a sound translation, but translation is always interpretation.—Probably you have to be born German in order to feel this in the language which Schleiermacher uses.—It is the language of *eros* which runs through all of Schleiermacher's translation of Plato. It is the creative *eros* in which the emotional and the cognitive elements are united in the intuition of the infinite in the finite.

This has immediate consequences for the aesthetic element in Romanticism. Romanticism looks at the world through aesthetic categories. Kant had the natural scientific analysis of nature together with the moral imperative with its categorical or unconditional character. In his third critique, the *Critique of Judgment,* Kant found a principle for uniting the theoretical and the practical reason in the aesthetic intuition of reality. In this he found that which transcends the scientific consideration of nature, the Newtonian as it was called at that time, as well as the moral principles. The moral always commands while the theoretical analyzes. Is there a union between them? Is there something in nature which, so to speak, fulfills the commands of the moral imperative and transcends the mere scientific analysis of nature? He discovered, as I told you, the organic in nature and the aesthetic in culture. It is what at that time could still be called the beautiful, but I would call it the expressive, in which the two are united.

Romanticism, therefore, used Kant's *Critique of Judgment* more than anything else because there Kant offered the possibility of accepting the fundamental restrictions of his previous *Critiques* and at the same time of going beyond them.

This means that romantic philosophy replaced religion by aesthetic intuition. Whenever you find the statement made by artists or in works on art that art is religion itself, you are in the sphere of the romantic tradition. For Schelling, in his aesthetic period, art is the great miracle, the unique miracle in all history. It is a miracle which would have to appear only once in the world to convince us of the presence of the ultimate. He calls this the identity transcending subject and object, transcending the theoretical and the practical. We find the same aesthetic intuition of the universe in Schleiermacher's *Speeches on Religion.* Aesthetic intuition as participating intuition takes art seriously as revelatory.

3. *The Turn to the Past and the Valuation of Tradition*

The idea of the presence of the infinite in the finite gave Romanticism the possibility of a new relationship to the past. Here the conflict with Enlightenment was especially great. For the Enlightenment the past was more or less in bondage to superstition. Now that the age of reason has appeared the superstitions of the Middle Ages have disappeared. This was the Enlightenment's view of history. If you read Lessing's little writing on the education of mankind, you will find this idea that at the present time the age in which reason is victorious has begun. Romanticism, on the other hand, had a very different attitude toward the past. The infinite was also present in the past periods of history through expressive forms of life and their great symbols. They had their revelatory character also. This means that history, the historical past, be taken seriously. Tradition could be important for Romanticism, whereas the Enlightenment was merely the critic of tradition, as Protestantism also was in some respects.

This new attitude toward history was very important for historiography. The great nineteenth-century historians were influenced by these romantic ideas. In the past the infinite is present; it has revealed itself in the Middle Ages as well as in Greece, and therefore the idea of a totally new beginning now in the age of reason appears fantastic. Goethe ridiculed this idea in his *Faust,* and so did all the romantics. Many of them, tried to go back to the Middle Ages to re-establish its culture. They also applied their philosophical concept of the organic to society. They had the idea of an organic society. The French religious socialist, Saint-Simon (1760–1825), distinguished critical and organic periods in history. It was very easy to show that the Middle Ages formed an organic period. Everything had its special place and function in the organism. The eighteenth-century Enlightenment, on the other hand, formed a critical period in which the organic structures were attacked, because of their deterioration in terms of tyranny, superstition, etc. Saint-Simon and the religious socialists expected the coming of a new organic period. Most of the later European religious socialist movements—and there have been many of them—have been dependent on this idea of an organic society over against the atomized mass society. This was the idea of Saint-Simon and his school; this was the idea of the later religious socialists in the various European countries, including the religious socialist movement in which I participated.[6]

Without the rediscovery of the organic in society and the presence of the divine in the past periods of history, these developments could not have happened. Here again I see something characteristic for the American situation which has had an almost unbroken tradition of Enlightenment up to today. Romanticism never really broke through into the American tradition. It has appeared in some literary manifestations, but it has never been a transforming power as in Europe. What in

6 See below, for a discussion of Religious Socialism, pp. 234–239.

Europe was seen as politically conservative is here extreme liberalism, and what is here called liberalism is closer to socialism in Europe. The terminology and the feeling toward life are different. One of the consequences of this is that history has not been taken as seriously as it has been in Europe. Even the empirical historians of today do not take it very seriously; seriously means existentially significant for our own existence here and now. When the romantic historians dealt with classical Greece or the Middle Ages, they of course also wanted to discover the facts, but this was not their main interest. Their chief interest was in the meaning of past history for the self-interpretation of man today.

If these existential questions are not asked, the study of history merely deals with the facts of the past instead of dealing with our own situation in terms of the past. I believe that the resistance of American students against taking history seriously is due in part to the fact that Romanticism has never had a profound influence in this country. The American Constitution is a great political document of the Enlightenment; you do not find many romantic elements in it. This is not by chance. The Enlightenment feeling that a new beginning has been inaugurated is part of the American experience.

Therefore, the concept of conservatism is very ambiguous. In Europe conservatism is always associated with a romantic affirmation of the past. It means keeping the traditions, finding the infinite in the religious and cultural traditions of the past, longing for the Middle Ages, for primitive Christianity or Greek culture. The word "conservatism" in this country, on the other hand, does not have the same traditional meaning. It has more to do with the individualism of the capitalistic society. This would never be called conservatism in Europe. Thus it can happen that the term "conservatism" can be used for simple fascist movements, like the John Birch Society, as I learned during my two months in California. These movements have nothing to do with conservatism. They are based on the mass culture of the present and wish to exclude all liberal elements, not for the sake of the Middle Ages, or some similar epoch in the past, but for the sake of maintaining the rule of the upper classes in capitalistic society. It helps to know history to understand the meaning of terms we use so freely.

4. *The Quest for Unity and Authority*

I said that Romanticism is a longing to return to the Middle Ages and its organic structure, but this organic structure is always identical with a hierarchical structure. It is interesting that there is some degree of nonauthoritarianism in the organic character of the larger cities, and only to a limited extent could we call it organic. On the whole the organic has a hierarchical character, which can easily be derived from the concept of the organic in nature. Man as an organism is also hierarchically construed; his centered self is the top of the hierarchy which directs everything. So the idea of the re-establishment of authority was a powerful element in Romanticism, and out of this came the reaction against the democratic tendencies of the American and French Revolutions. We see that reaction very clearly in the German type of Romanticism, but also in France. If you want to understand a figure like Charles de Gaulle, you must understand the romantic traditions and the desire for a hierarchically ruled organism which have broken out again and again in France.

The hierarchy was understood not so much as an isolated political hierarchy, but as a religious political hierarchy, a return to the reunion of the political and religious realms. Richard Rothe (1799–1867), for instance, a pupil of Schleiermacher, was very much interested in the idea of a culture in which church and state become identical again, just the opposite of the American principle of separation of church and state. The state would become the comprehensive form of all culture. We have the same thing in Hegel when he called the state the divine on earth. But this must not be misunderstood. If such men speak of the state as the divine on earth, or if Bonhoeffer speaks of the secular world and not the religious sphere as the real manifestation of the divine, then they are not thinking of the state as an administration in the hands of politicians. That is the liberal democratic concept of the state, presupposing a separation of church and state. Instead they are thinking of the state as the unity of all cultural activities. This is a cultural concept of the state. The political side is less decisive than the religio-cultural side.

Obviously, if you have this concept of state in mind, you can go back romantically to the Greek city-state in which there was no religion alongside political life. The whole political life was permeated with the presence of the gods and the functionaries of the city were also the priests. If you read the early fragments of Hegel, you will find a romantic description of the Greek city-state, involving the identity of state and church as a most important part of the whole idea. Novalis (1772–1801), one of the romantic poets, wrote a famous pamphlet or essay entitled *Die Christenheit oder Europa*[7] in which he described this reunion of everything cultural within the religious in all Europe, overcoming the boundary lines separating European countries, and the re-establishment of a Europe in terms of a religio-political authority similar to the pope. Here in this essay Novalis described the image a romantic man had of the future society.

5. *The Negative and the Demonic in Romanticism*

Now let me say a few things about the negative and demonic side of Romanticism. The first thing that we must emphasize is that there are two periods in Romanticism. I learned this very early through my study of Schelling who in his own development is the prototype of these two lines. Schleiermacher and the early Schelling belong entirely to the first part, but then the later Schelling and Kierkegaard belong to the second part. Perhaps one can say that in the twenties of the nineteenth century the transition from the first to the second half occurred. The first period of Romanticism stressed the presence of the infinite in the finite. We will see what that means for Schleiermacher's development. In the second period something else happened. The depth dimension, the dimension of the infinite, reaches not only up to the divine, but also down to the demonic. This discovery by romantic poets and philosophers is extremely important for our situation because in this second period of Romanticism we have the pre-formation of almost all the ideas of twentieth-century existentialism.

The existentialism of the twentieth century lives not only in terms of

[7] *Christianity or Europe,* untranslated.

Kierkegaard, but also and primarily in terms of the second period of Schelling, who had a decisive influence on Kierkegaard and many others. Here the darkness in man's understanding and in the human situation becomes manifest. The concept of the unconscious is of decisive importance for the whole following century into our time. This concept is not an invention of Freud, as I think all of you know. It is actually older than the second period of Romanticism. We have it indirectly in people like Jacob Boehme and Franz Baader and others, but most important perhaps was its rediscovery and expression in Schelling's philosophy of nature. He construed the whole philosophy of nature as a conflict between an unconscious and a conscious principle. From this point much of Schopenhauer's philosophy of the unconscious will developed, and Freud discovered this category of the unconscious in Eduard von Hartmann (1842–1906), Schopenhauer's pupil. Then Freud developed it further in his psychological and empirical methods, bringing it into the center of our attention today. But the real discovery of the unconscious, and its expression in powerful philosophical terms against the Cartesian philosophy of consciousness, were the work of the second period of Romanticism.

Now the negative element became in Romanticism a demonic element. It reveals the demonic depths of the human soul, something of which the Enlightenment was only dimly aware. After the presence of the infinite in the finite was formulated, then the presence of the demonic in the finite was expressed. The struggle between the good and the bad principles in Kant's philosophy of religion now became the struggle between the divine and the demonic. In spite of all the naturalism which runs through the whole nineteenth century, we have a tremendously intense awareness of the demonic forces in reality during this same period, often in a way that was prophetic of the radical outbreak of these forces in our century.

* * * * * * * * *

Question: You spoke of Romanticism as the breaking-through of the infinite against the classical balance in the horizontal line. What do you mean by the horizontal line?

Answer: This question reminds me of the fact that I neglected to speak on one particular aspect of the romantic thinking, namely, the concept of irony. There is especially one man who is important for this. His name is Friedrich Schlegel (1772–1829), a friend of Schelling and a member of the Berlin circle of romanticists. Something typical of the romantic period was expressed in his attitude. That was irony. The word "irony" means that the infinite is superior to any finite concretion and drives beyond to another finite concretion. The ego of the romanticist in Schlegel's sense is free from bondage to the concrete situation. A concrete situation means both the spiritual situation, a concrete form of faith, and the situation in relation to human beings, for instance, sexual relations which played a great role in the romantic attitude, or the experience of ecstatically transcending any particular finite situation. All these things were implied in the romantic concept of irony. It must be understood in terms of the fundamental principle of the relation between the infinite and the finite. I said that in Goethe's classical period we have a balance, the desire to have a form in which the infinite is actualized in the finite, whereas Romanticism drives beyond any particular actualization of the infinite in a finite situation.

Now this romantic irony breaks through the sociological forms, for instance, the traditional Lutheran paternalism, the idea of the family, the relation of parents to children, the political stability, etc. All these forms now became questionable. Every special content in the traditions of the European countries became a matter of "yes" and "no." Irony does not mean simply an attack; there is a "yes" in it, but the "no" is predominant. It always says "no" as well to a concrete solution to life's problems.

In these avant-garde romantic groups there was an ironical transcending, a going beyond, the given forms of social existence. A consequence of this was the dissolution of traditional ethics. Wherever you find this, it has to do with this romantic ironical elevation of the individual subject beyond the given forms. But if this happens, then with the loss of concreteness a sense of emptiness sets in. Schlegel had the feeling that by undercutting the forms of life, the beliefs, the ethical ties to family, etc., a situation arises in which there is no content, no obligatory contents. This results in a feeling of emptiness with respect to the meaning of life. You see now that the central problem of the twentieth century, namely, the question of the meaning of life, the problem of emptiness in the younger generation, is not as original in our century as we are inclined to believe. It also came out very strongly in the second period of Romanticism. I can formulate the result in one sentence. Schlegel, the most refined critical representative of romantic irony, became a Roman Catholic. This means that out of the feeling of emptiness he gained the desire to subject himself to an authoritarian system in which the contents were already given to him. This is a radical situation which has been repeated again and again among the European intelligentsia, both in the nineteenth and twentieth centuries, especially after the World Wars, after the great catastrophes in Europe. Many people out of a sense of meaninglessness or lack of any contents which are normative, binding, and productive of community, etc., returned to the Roman Catholic Church as the embracing and protecting mother. This is what I meant by the breakthrough of Romanticism into the horizontal line. It is this dissatisfaction with any concrete situation, this ironical undercutting of everything, not in terms of a direct revolutionary attack, and not in order to transform reality as bourgeois society tried to do, but in terms of questioning, undercutting, etc., in terms of "yes" and "no."

We have much of this in Kierkegaard too. He was far from being a revolutionary. Politically he was conservative. But his ability to question every state of life he learned from the basic ironic attitude of Romanticism.

*   *   *   *   *   *   *   *   *   *

D. The Classical Theological Synthesis: Friedrich Schleiermacher

We will devote a lecture or more to the discussion of Friedrich Schleiermacher (1768–1834). Everything we have lectured on so far is a necessary presupposition for understanding him. If you do not have this presupposition firmly in mind, but simply pick up some phrases from the textbooks, it would be better for you to forget about him altogether. Then it is meaningless; you cannot defend him and you cannot attack him either. If you attack him, it is all wrong, and if you try to defend him, you have no power to do so. You must understand an idea out of the sources from which it comes. You must know the negative implications, the struggle in which a person was involved, the enemies against which he fought, and the presuppositions which he accepted. If you do not know these things, everything becomes distorted when dealing with an important figure like Schleiermacher. That is the reason I did not begin with him in lecturing on Protestant theology in the nineteenth and twentieth centuries. He is the father of modern Protestant theology. This is his official title during the nineteenth and twentieth centuries, until neo-orthodox theology tried to disinherit him, deprive him of his fatherhood, and make out of him a distorter of theology.

Now this is a serious problem, because in this conflict over Schleiermacher which took place during and after my student years, theology was faced with having to make a basic decision, whether the attempt to construct a synthesis out of all the elements in theology we have described is the right way, or whether a return to the orthodox tradition with some modernizations is the right way. If the latter method is followed, then of course Schleiermacher has to be abolished; but if the former, then Schleiermacher remains the founder of modern Protestant theology. So you have to make a decision about this. My decision, if I may anticipate, is thoroughly on the side of Schleiermacher, but with one qualification. Neither he nor Hegel, who was even greater and who tried the same thing, really succeeded. From their failure the orthodox groups of the nineteenth century and the neo-orthodox groups of the twentieth century have drawn the conclusion that it is impossible. But I draw the conclusion that it must be tried again, and if it cannot be tried again, then we had better abandon theology as a systematic enterprise and stick to the repetition of Bible passages, or at best, limiting theology to an interpretation of the Old and New Testaments.

But if systematic theology is to have any meaning, we must try again after the breakdown of the syntheses of both Schleiermacher and Hegel. In fact, it has been tried again, both later in the nineteenth century and now in the twentieth century, and even if we have here a continuous history of failures, that is no argument against systematic theology. This is part of the human situation which implies failure wherever there is risk and courage. Besides, out of these failures more insight has come than through the unfailing repetition of orthodox phraseologies. This is not said against Barth who has written a beautiful book about the theology of the nineteenth century, and also about philosophy and music in the eighteenth century. In this book he has wonderful sections on both Mozart and Schleiermacher. He is much more fair than all his neo-orthodox pupils and opponents. So this is not directly against Barth, but indirectly it is, because he has produced those pupils who do not share his greatness and have only inherited some elements of his earlier dictatorial attitude.

1. *The Background of Schleiermacher's Thought*

Schleiermacher represents what I call the great synthesis in the theological realm. Out of this attempt proceeded the whole of later Protestant theology, including its failures. But there is only one alternative to life with failure, that is lifelessness without failure. Schleiermacher is supposed to be the victor over the Enlightenment in the theological realm. He did not deny the enlightened philosophy, but tried to overcome it on another level. For instance, he said that a true philosopher can be a true believer. He can combine piety and philosophy, and there was much piety in Schleiermacher from his early Moravian associations. He can combine piety with the courage of digging into the depths of philosophical thought. Or another word: The deepest philosophical thoughts are completely identical with my most intimate religious feeling.

This means that when we speak of him as the conqueror of the Enlightenment, we are not to think that he separated theology from philosophy, that he despised philosophy and excluded it from the theological enterprise. Enlightenment had reduced religion to the knowledge of God in terms of the arguments for his existence, or more exactly, to natural theology and to morality. The moral side was still very strong in Kant. Kant's philosophy of religion is an appendix to his philosophy of morals, and is determined by his practical philosophy. Religion is only a tool for the fulfillment of the moral imperative. Also the emphasis on knowledge in religion, the emphasis on natural theology, is an element which contributed finally to the failure of Hegel's great and embracing synthesis.

The basis of the theology of the Enlightenment was the separation of God and the world, God and man. This was foreshadowed by English deism. The deism of the early eighteenth century in England followed the philosophy of John Locke. Deism was a philosophy of religion in which the existence of God was established by natural theology, but in such a way that he would not interfere with the activities of the bourgeois society. This was a necessary prerequisite for admitting the existence of God at all. If God interfered in some way, he could not be acknowledged. So he was placed alongside the world as the creator or as the watchmaker—to use other imagery—and after the watch has been made, it runs by itself without the continual intervention of the maker. The deists left men—that means the intellectual representatives of the producing and trading bourgeois society—to their own reason, and in particular to their calculating reason. If this is done, it is possible that by means of calculating and critical reason, the Christian tradition can be criticized. This they did in a radical way, even before Rousseau and Voltaire did it in France. Deism preceded them; it also preceded Hume's positivistic attitude of placing religion as the established church and the critical mind beside each other without scarcely ever touching.

These deists were a very interesting bunch of people, bunch, I say, because that is the way they were considered in England by the representatives of the aristocratic groups which cooperated with the high bourgeoisie and which did not like this kind of critical attitude. They were considered vulgar. It is still vulgar in England to criticize religion in the name of reason. You accept it as something positively given; perhaps you describe it sociologically, but you do not criticize it. It is not noble and aristocratic to do so. The consequence of this attitude was that the deistic thinkers, Toland and Tindal *et. al.*, were considered to be operating on a lower level of reason, of reason that has run wild. And they did run wild. The title of one of the main deistic books, for instance, is *Christianity Not Mysterious* (1696) which removes all supernaturalistic and miraculous elements. They criticized the biblical literature and in a way were the inaugurators of historical criticism, producing results which anticipated much of the historical-critical theology in the modern time. Reimarus, for example, the man whose fragments Lessing published, was dependent on the English deists, and he created the revolution in thinking about the biblical sources in Germany. The rational idea of God in Voltaire and the French Enlightenment also came from the English deists. These deists were part of the background of Schleiermacher's theology. So you will find that he quite often refers to such typical theologians of the Enlightenment.

But there was another side. We spoke about this in connection with Spinoza. The fundamental principle that God exists alongside the world is shared by both the consistent rationalists and the supernaturalists. Against the deistic principle of God existing beside the world, either never interfering with it, as the rationalists said, or occasionally interfering with it, as the supernaturalists said, we now have the principle of *deus sive natura* (God or nature) coming from John Scotus Eriugena, the great theologian of the ninth century who mediated mystical theology to later medieval theology. This principle reintroduced a quite different form of thinking about religion, the real antithesis to the Enlightenment. In discussing Romanticism we called it the principle of the infinite within the finite, the principle of the mutual within-each-otherness.

Spinoza, of course, was modified. It was not the geometrical Spinoza. Those who know a little about Spinoza know that he called his main work *Ethics*,[8] but ethics *more geometrico*, ethics written by the use of the geometrical method. As a title this is in itself of greatest interest. He tried to use the all-powerful mathematical methods in discussing such subjects as metaphysics, ethics, and politics. All of this is presented in a way which makes the world into a geometrically describable whole. This was a very static concept of the world and of the divine ground of the world. He called this "the substance." In any case, this idea was founded on the principle of identity over against the principle of detachment and separation in the Enlightenment. God is here and now. He is in the depths of everything. He is not *everything*, as this much abused term "pantheism" says. Nobody has ever said that. It is absolute nonsense to say such a thing. It is better to avoid the term itself, but if it means

[8] Edited with an introduction by James Gutman (New York: Hafner Publishing Co., 1949).

anything at all, it means that the power of the divine is present in everything, that he is the ground and unity of everything, not that he is the sum of all particulars. I do not know any philosopher in the whole history of philosophy who has ever said that. Therefore the word "pantheism," which you can translate as "God is everything," is downright misleading. I would wish that those who accuse Luther or myself of pantheism would define the term before using it. And, of course, Nicholas of Cusa, Schelling, Hegel and Nietzsche, and many others, are accused of pantheism. As if everybody who is not a supernaturalistic deist or a theist—and theism as the term is used in America today is nothing else than a supernaturalistic form of deism—is a pantheist. Whenever some people hear about the principle of identity, they say this is pantheism, which supposedly holds that God is this desk.

Now, of course, Luther would say that God is nearer to everything than it is to itself. He would say this even about the desk. You cannot deny that God is the creative ground of the desk, but to say that God is the combination of all desks and in addition all pens and men—this is absolute nonsense. The principle of identity means that God is the creative ground of everything. What I dislike is the easy way in which these phrases are used: theism is so wonderful and pantheism so horrible. This makes the understanding of the whole history of theology impossible.

2. His Concept of Religion as Feeling

The principle of identity in contrast to the principle of duality gave Schleiermacher the possibility of creating a new understanding of religion. This new understanding was first expressed in his famous book, *On Religion, Speeches to Its Cultured Despisers.*[9] This book is apologetic theology of the clearest kind. "Apologize" in Greek means answering, answering before the court. For instance, if you are accused, an apology is what you say in your own defense. So apologetic theology is answering theology. I would say that every theology must somehow answer the questions in the human mind in every period, and the

[9] Translated by John Oman (New York: Frederick Ungar Publishing Co., 1955).

apologetic element should never be neglected. Historically, Christian theology was created out of the apologetic needs of the church in the Roman Empire, politically answering the attacks of the pagans during the persecution of the Christians, and theologically answering the criticisms of the philosophers. This was answering theology, and the apologists who formed a particular school of theology in the second century represent more than a particular school. They represent the answering character of all Christian theology up to Augustine.

That is what Schleiermacher also did. He answered the despisers of religion among the cultured people, as the title of his book states. Then out of this apologetic theology new systematic possibilities arose. The argument of Schleiermacher's *Speeches* is as follows: Theoretical knowledge of the deistic type—whether rationalistic or supernaturalistic—and moral obedience of the Kantian type presuppose a disjunction between subject and object. Here I am, the subject, and over there is God, the object. He is merely an object for me, and I am an object for him. There is difference, detachment, and distance. But this difference has to be overcome in the power of the principle of identity. This identity is present within us. But now Schleiermacher made a great mistake. The term he used for the experience of this identity was "feeling." Religion is not theoretical knowledge; it is not moral action; religion is feeling, feeling of absolute dependence. This was a very questionable term, because immediately the psychologists came along and interpreted Schleiermacher's concept of feeling as a psychological function.

But "feeling" in Schleiermacher should not really be understood as subjective emotion. Rather, it is the impact of the universe upon us in the depths of our being which transcends subject and object. It is obvious that he means it in this sense. Therefore, instead of speaking of feeling, he could also speak of intuition of the universe, and this intuition he could describe as divination. This term is derived, of course, from "divine" and means awareness of the divine immediately. It means that there is an immediate awareness of that which is beyond subject and object, of the ground of everything within us. He made the great mistake of calling this feeling. And it is regrettable that a man like Hegel should misunderstand him, in view of the fact that both he and

Schleiermacher were pupils of Schelling and both had experienced the meaning of the principle of identity. Hegel and Schleiermacher, who were both at the University of Berlin, did not like each other. Hegel did what German philosophers and theologians have done so often: they interpret the foe, the one whom they attack, *in pejorem partem,* which means according to the worst possible meaning of what a man has said.

In this country, on the other hand, I have had the impression that the moderateness of the British spirit in theoretical discussion has produced the desire to understand the one with whom we disagree *in meliorem partem,* that is, in the best possible light. For this reason it is much easier to be a member of a theological faculty in America than in Germany. But it does have some shortcomings. Occasionally one has the feeling that theological matters are not taken as seriously as in Germany. This is perhaps the single qualification I have to make, but I would say, from the point of view of *agape,* I prefer the American attitude.

At any rate, the best evidence that when Schleiermacher spoke of feeling he did not mean subjective emotion is the fact that in his systematic theology, in *The Christian Faith,* he uses the expression "feeling of unconditional dependence." In the moment that these words are combined, the feeling of unconditional dependence, the psychological realm has been transcended. For everything in our feeling, understood in the psychological sense, is conditioned. It is a continuous stream of feelings, emotions, thoughts, wills, experiences. On the other hand, the element of the unconditional, wherever it appears, is quite different from subjective feeling.

Therefore, his own phrase, feeling of unconditional dependence,[10] is a phrase which makes it quite apparent that this feeling is not the subjective feeling of the individual and that Hegel's criticism is unfair. The consequence of this in the German churches was an unfortunate misunderstanding also, for when religion was preached as feeling, the male section of the German congregations stopped going to church. When they were told that religion is not a matter of clear knowledge and moral action, but of feeling, they reacted. I can tell you this from my own participation in the nineteenth-century situation. The churches

[10] In German, *"das Gefühl der schlechthinnigen Abhängigkeit."*

became empty. Neither the youth nor the men were satisfied with feeling. They looked for sharp thought and moral significance in the sermons. When religion was reduced to feeling and weakened by sentimental hymns—instead of the great old hymns which had religious power of the presence of the divine—people lost interest in the churches.

Schleiermacher's concept of religion as feeling had unfortunate consequences in this country too. When I discuss theology with antitheological colleagues, they are very happy if they can quote somebody who puts religion into a dark corner of mere subjective feeling. Religion is not dangerous there. They can use their scientific and political words, their ethical and logical analysis, etc., without regard to religion, and the churches can be removed to one side. They do not have to be taken very seriously for they deal with the realm of subjective feelings. We do not participate in such things, but if there are people who do have such desires, let them go to church. We do not mind. But in the moment in which they are confronted by a theology which interferes very much—not from the outside but from the inside—with the scientific process, political movements, and moral principles, and which wants to show that within all of them there is an ultimate concern, as I call it, or an unconditional dependence, as Schleiermacher called it, then these people react. Then they want to put religion back into the realm of feeling. And if theology itself, or religion itself, allows them to do this, they are doing a disservice. Such a preaching of religious feeling does a great disservice to religion.

Schleiermacher did not sufficiently protect himself from the criticism that this feeling is merely, as Freud called it, an oceanic feeling, that is, the feeling of the indefinite. It is really much more than this, and Schleiermacher has another point which makes this as clear as possible. He distinguishes two forms of unconditional dependence. The one is causal, which simply means being dependent on someone as a baby is dependent on its mother, or as we are dependent on the weather to some extent; the other is teleological dependence, which means, from the Greek *telos*, directed toward an aim, namely, the moral fulfillment of the moral imperative. This is important inasmuch as he classifies Christianity as a teleological type of religion, and not the ontological type like the mystical religions of Asia. Teleological dependence has the unconditional character of the moral imperative. Now both elements are present, but according to Schleiermacher the dominant element in Western religion is the teleological-moral element. Here the Kantian influence is quite visible, and thus it is even more unfair to say that Schleiermacher's "feeling" is indefinite. It is very definite in the moral sense; it is also definite in the mystical sense. It is not subjective oceanic feeling.

This is the essence of what is called religious experience, the presence of something unconditional beyond the knowing and acting of which we are aware. Of course, it also has an emotional element in it as everything does when a total person is involved, but this emotional element does not define the character of religion.

On this new basis Schleiermacher proposed that the discussion between the Enlightenment and Orthodoxy, between rationalism and supernaturalism, which was the modified form of Orthodoxy, could come to an end. Both sides are wrong on the basis of this new principle. Supernaturalism is wrong. Things like miraculous interventions of God, special inspirations and revelations are beneath the level of real religious experience. Those are objective events which can be looked at from the outside concerning the existence or nonexistence of which one can debate, but religion itself is immediacy, an immediate relation to the divine. Such external, objective events do not add anything to this fundamental experience of unconditional dependence or divination of the divine in the universe.

Consequently, the authorities which guarantee such supernatural interferences are also unnecessary. Every authority in religion, whether biblical or ecclesiastical, which makes such statements about interferences is removed. This liberates modern science from religious interferences. The supernaturalistic statement about the suspension of the laws of nature for the sake of miracles collapses completely.

But other things also collapse on this basis. The idea of an existing person called "God" and the idea of a continuation of life after the death of a conscious person, or the idea of immortality, collapse as well. This whole supernaturalistic heritage is denied by Schleiermacher in his *Speeches*. The way in which he restates the essence of this heritage in *The Christian Faith* is a question to which we will return later.

The first radical and fundamental apologetic statement made by

Schleiermacher is the following. The unity with God, participation in him, is not a matter of immortal life after death; it is not a matter of accepting a heavenly lawgiver; instead it is a matter of present participation in eternal life. This is decisive. Here he follows the fourth Gospel. The classical German philosophers called this the true Gospel, not because they thought this Gospel contained, historically speaking, reliable reports about Jesus—very soon they learned that this was not the case at all—but because the Gospel of John came closest to expressing principles which could overcome the conflict between rationalism and supernaturalism. This idea that eternal life is here and now, and not a continuation of life after death, is one of the main points they stressed. It is participation in eternity before time, in time, and after time, and that means also beyond time.

This same criticism turned against all mediators between God and man. The principle of identity and all mysticism were always very dangerous for the hierarchical systems, for priestly mediation between God and man. This was the case both in Catholicism and Protestantism. The Protestant Churches were just as hostile as the Roman Church was to the mystical groups, to the Quakers, for example, in whom the principle of identity was affirmed in some way. They were suspicious of mysticism because it offered men the possibility of immediate unity with the divine apart from the mediation of the church. So Schleiermacher reacted against priests and authorities; they were not necessary, because everybody is called to become a priest and to be filled with the divine Spirit. From this point of view you can understand the resistance of the church against all spirit-movements, against the movements in which the individual is immediate to God and driven by the Spirit himself. You can also understand the reason for the subjection of the Spirit, wherever it appears, to the letter of the Bible. The Reformers who originally fought against the Roman Church in the power of the Spirit soon had great difficulties of their own in their struggle against the spirit-movements of the Reformation period. It is a good thing there were countries like Great Britain, the Netherlands, and America to which these representatives could flee from the severe persecutions of both the Roman and Reformation Churches.

Instead of seeing religion as something mediated by the functions of the church, Schleiermacher saw it as the musical accompaniment of the special melodies of every life. In this poetic way he expresses the presence of the religious concern, the ultimate concern, in every moment of life. It is, one may say, the typical idealistic anticipation of eternal life in which there is certainly no religion but in which God is present in every moment. He expresses the ideal which in the New Testament is spoken of as "praying without ceasing." If this is taken literally, it is nonsense. But if it is taken as it is meant, it makes a lot of sense. It means considering every moment of our secular life as filled with the divine presence, not pushing the presence into a Sunday service and otherwise forgetting it.

In order to experience the presence of the divine in the universe as Pythagoras did when he spoke of the harmony of the spheres in musical terms, each of which, while making a different tone, contributes symphonically to the harmony of the cosmos, we must first find that presence in ourselves. Humanity, of which each individual is a special and unique mirror, is the key to the universe. Without having the universe in ourselves we would never understand it. The center of the universe and of ourselves is divine, and with the presence of the infinite in ourselves we can *re*-cognize (I purposely underline the first syllable) in the universe the infinite which is within us. And what is the key to this in ourselves? He says it is love, but not love in the sense of *agape,* the Christian concept of love, but love in the Platonic sense of *eros.* Eros is the love which unites us with the good and the true and the beautiful and which drives us beyond the finite into the infinite.

Every period of human history expresses this encounter between the infinite in ourselves and in the whole universe in different images. The uniqueness of every individual and every period makes it necessary that there be many religions. The manifoldness of religions and the differences in the same religious tradition during its different periods in history are basically the result of the infinite mirroring itself in ourselves and in the universe in always different ways. So the romantic spirit of Schleiermacher caused him to emphasize the concreteness of the historical religions. This was a tremendous step beyond the enlightened idea of natural religion which reduced all religions to three principles: God, freedom, and immortality. The deistic views, whether of the rationalistic or supernaturalistic types, were overcome through the rediscovery of the richness, concreteness, and fullness of the particular religions. In this way Schleiermacher conquered by his principle of the immanence of the infinite in the finite the naturalistic, rationalistic, and supernaturalistic ways of abstracting from the concrete religions some principle which is supposed to be valid for all religions and which obliterates everything concrete in them.

Without the valuation of individuality in the Renaissance and without the element of ecstatic intuition in Romanticism, all this would not have been possible. This is what enabled religious thought to find its way back to the positive religions. The whole Enlightenment was an extinction of the meaningfulness of the concrete or positive religion. Only abstract religious principles were left. On the basis of this rediscovery of the concrete, positive religions—positive means "historically given"—Schleiermacher proceeded further to emphasize a positive Christianity.

Schleiermacher's *Speeches on Religion* (1799) were so successful that when the third edition (1821) was issued, he wrote in his introduction that instead of having to defend himself any more against the enlightened despisers of religion, he now had to fend off the orthodox fanatics who in the name of his defense of Christianity returned to the pre-Enlightenment orthodox tradition, and tried to extinguish the whole development on which Schleiermacher had based his work.

3. *His Positivistic Definition of Theology*

Romanticism generally speaking was the bridge to an appreciation of the positively given. This was quite different from the English type of positivism. David Hume was a positivist out of empirical scientific considerations, out of a critical epistemology in which he thought that we have only given data or sense impressions. In continental Europe positivism was a child of Romanticism which valued the historically and traditionally given. When Schleiermacher wrote his book, *The Christian Faith,* it is significant that he called it *Glaubenslehre* (the doctrine of faith). He did not call it "doctrine of God" which is what "theology" means. He did not dare to give it such a title, for what is positively given is the Christian faith as such. That is a given reality. You can find it in Zinzendorf's Moravian groups of piety to which he belonged for a period in his life, and you can find it in the churches everywhere. Thus systematic theology is the description of the faith as it is present in the Christian churches. That is a positivist foundation of theology. You do not first have to decide about the truths or untruths of religion in general or of Christianity in particular. You find Christianity given as an empirical fact in history, and then you have to describe the meaning of the symbols within it.

Theology is then positive knowledge of a historical reality. Schleiermacher made a very sharp distinction between this empirical positive theology and the so-called rational theology of the Enlightenment. And he goes even further. He says that Christian theology is the totality of those theoretical insights and practical rules without the possession and use of which no church government is possible. Now this definition is something unheard of in the development of theology. It is the clear transition from all kinds of rational theology to positive theology. In this definition the question of truth is completely absent. It is a highly positivistic conception of theology. I would call it a positivistic description of some group which you find in history, whose existence you cannot deny. You can describe the ideas which are important in it and the rules which are accepted. Then you can educate young theologians who are called to be leaders in the church in the knowledge of those things which they are to practice later on. This is a positivism in which the question of truth is left out.

This positivistic character of theology becomes even more pronounced in the following idea. He distinguished philosophical, historical, and practical theology even as we do today, but with one difference. The difference is that dogmatics and ethics belong to historical theology, not to philosophical theology. They belong to historical theology because they are the systematic development of the doctrine which exists in the church or in a particular denomination at a given time. You cannot be more positivistic than that. This doctrine exists today, and the historian has only to describe it. This he calls systematic theology. This is a most conspicuous expression of positivism, and I can add that although it has

not survived, it has been very influential. Now we have both philosophical theology and systematic theology, and both are distinguished from
historical and practical theology. We have these four, or else we may
take philosophical theology into systematic theology.

* * * * * * * * * *

Question: Granted that by feeling Schleiermacher did not mean
subjective emotion, nevertheless, his *Speeches* are not unemotional in
character, and having emotion is an undeniable part of being human.
What is the role of the emotions in the religious life for you and
Schleiermacher?

Answer: This is a very valid question in view of the ambiguity of the
term "feeling" in Schleiermacher and much theology later on. Nevertheless, it is obvious that Schleiermacher is here in the same situation as
we all are. Nobody can exclude the element of feeling in any experience
in which the total personality is involved, and in religion this is perhaps
more true than in any other realm. It is certainly true that the response
of our whole being in immediacy—which might be the right definition
of feeling—can be seen in an earnest prayer or in the worship service of
a community, or in listening to the prophetic word. This emotional
element is there. Let us take an example from the arts. You are deeply
grasped by a painting at which you are looking while visiting an art
gallery; you are taken into it; you live in it and your emotions are
strongly awakened. But if someone should say that your aesthetic
experience is only an emotion, you would answer that it is more than
that. If it were only emotion, it would not have this definite character
which is given through this kind of painting. I recognize, in this
moment in which I am emotionally moved, a dimension of reality of
which otherwise I would never be aware, and a dimension in myself
would never be opened up except through participation in the painting.

I would say the same thing about music. Music is often said to be
completely in the realm of feeling. This is true, but it is a very special
kind of feeling which is related to the particular musical figures and
forms which make music a work of art. This also reveals to you a
dimension of being, including your being, which would otherwise not
be revealed if there were no musical impact on you. So we can say that

although the emotional element is always present in experience of whatever kind, you cannot say that a certain experience is only emotion. Take the experience of love. You cannot say that love *is* emotion. Love has an element of emotion in it and very much so, but it is not an emotion. It is a reunion, as I would call it, of separated entities that belong to each other eternally. This experience cannot be identified with the personal reaction which we call feeling.

What Schleiermacher calls unconditional dependence in religion is certainly connected with a strong element of feeling. This feeling has been described by Rudolf Otto (1869–1937) in his *The Idea of the Holy*[11] as a feeling of being both fascinated and overwrought at the same time. These contrasting feelings are present. But they do not constitute the religious act as such. The appearing of the unconditional to you in the religious act is what constitutes the religious act. Usually I call it the unconditional concern in your very existence. This is a concern also of your mind; you ask about the truth of it; it is a concern of your will; you must do something if you experience it. It changes your whole existence. All these dimensions are implied. If it were only a feeling, it would be a detached aesthetic pleasure, and that would be all. Sometimes Schleiermacher has been misunderstood in this way, but that is not the real Schleiermacher.

In answering the question about Schleiermacher, I also answered the question about my own thinking, because I believe that his "unconditional dependence" is only a slightly narrower way of saying "unconditional concern." Unconditional concern does not emphasize the element of dependence in the way Schleiermacher does. However, it also tries to go beyond the subject-object scheme. It has the same basic motives and is an expression of a total experience, the experience of the holy. There is not a dogmatic difference, but chiefly a difference of connotation, between ultimate concern and feeling of absolute dependence.

* * * * * * * * * *

In our last discussion about Schleiermacher we dealt with his positivistic conception of Christian theology. We pointed out the astonishing fact that he subsumed dogmatics and ethics under historical theology

[11] Translated by J. W. Harvey (New York: Oxford University Press, 1923).

because they are the systematic development of the doctrine as it exists in a particular church at a particular time. This we call positivism; it is theology as a description of the empirically given reality of the Christian religion. But if this were all, then Schleiermacher would not have been a systematic theologian; he would have been a church historian dealing with the present conditions of the church.

But this positivistic feature is counterbalanced—in a logically unclear way—by the fact that Schleiermacher begins with a general concept of religious community as it is manifested universally in the history of humanity. From this he derives a concept of the essence of religion. This is no longer positivism. It is a philosophical analysis of the essence of a thing. This presupposes constructive judgment about what is essential and what is not. His concept of the feeling of unconditional dependence is certainly a concept of a universal and philosophical type. He subjects Christianity to a concept of religion which at least by intent was not derived from Christianity but from the whole panorama of the world's religions. Actually, of course, the derivation which a philosopher of religion makes is always largely determined by the door through which he enters this panorama of religious reality in the world. In his case it is pietistic Christianity. In every philosophical concept of religion we can observe the traces of this entry way, namely, the philosopher's own religion. Nobody can abstract this subjective element from his definition, for in order to derive a concept from reality, one must be able to participate in the life of this reality. For example, one cannot develop a concept of the arts without being able to experience works of art.

The consequence of this is that Christianity becomes a religion among the religions. There are other religions besides Christianity. Usually, then, on this basis Christianity is described by Christian theologians as the highest, the truest, the most fulfilling of all religions. This is a very important point which has been to the fore in theological discussions during the last fifty years because of the Barthian challenge. When we look back into the history of Protestantism we find a book by Zwingli, the Swiss reformer, entitled *De vera et falsa religione*[12] in which he describes Christianity as the true religion over against the false religions which have distorted the divine revelation (cf. Romans 1). But Paul in

[12] Huldreich Zwingli, *On the True and False Religion*.

Romans did not speak of the Christian religion. He spoke of Christ. He would not say that the Christian religion is the decisive thing. It would be well to read Paul's letters to see how he attacked the Christian religion as it existed in his time. He attacked the Jewish-Christian (legalism) as well as the Gnostic distortions (lawlessness). This means that while Paul criticized all religions, he does not exempt Christianity from criticism. He does not put Christianity against the other religions. Rather, he puts Christ against every religion, even against the actual Christian religion as this was expressed in the congregations which he founded.

Now in Zwingli, also in the Reformers in general and in most orthodox theology, we find that this distinction between Christ and Christianity is not clearly carried out. If Christianity is put on the top, then one is bound to ask whether it does not stand under the same judgment as all other religions, in view of its own distortions. If we look at the history of idolatry, we will find that much of it has occurred in the name of Christianity. Actually, the absoluteness of Christianity, as Troeltsch called it, is not the absoluteness of the Christian religion, but of the Christ over against all religion. The superiority of Christianity lies in its witnessing against itself and all other religions in the name of the Christ. Barth has seen this difficulty, and for this reason he tends to avoid the concept of religion and does not want to apply it to Christianity. But if this is done, it is another way of elevating the Christian religion, and not only the Christ above the other religions. I doubt that Barth really intends to do that.

However that may be, the concept of religion is needed because there is the empirical religious reality; there is a great similarity in all the actual religions. If you reject the word "religion," you must simply find another one in naming the given religious reality, the word "piety" or something like that. The term "religion" is, however, unavoidable. I can tell you of my own experience. In the early twenties I wrote an article with the title "The Conquest of the Concept of Religion in the Philosophy of Religion."[13] This was very much in line with Barth's thinking, but even at that time I was aware that this can be done only if Chris-

[13] "Die Überwindung des Religionsbegriffs in der Religionsphilosophie," *Kant-Studien.* Berlin, XXVII, No. 3/4, 1922, 446–469.

tianity also is conquered as a religion in the philosophy of religion, and if there is something in religion which stands against religion. If this is not seen there is no real conquest. But the impact of Barth on Germany was so great that when I returned to Germany in 1948, I was immediately criticized by my friends for still using the word "religion." It had been, so to speak, eradicated from the theological discussion in Germany.

This situation has changed but there is still a resentment against the concept. I believe that this resentment is a self-deception, for then other terms are only substituted for the term "religion." What we need, however, is to be aware of the fact that the method of Schleiermacher, Troeltsch, Harnack, and others, is not sufficient, namely, first defining Christianity as a religion, and then saying it is the highest or absolute religion. What the Barthians do is equally wrong, to say that Christianity is a revealed religion over against the others which are merely human attempts to come to God and are not based on revelation at all.

If we are to try to conquer the concept of religion which seems to relativize Christianity, we have to do it by putting the Christ against every religion, or God as manifesting his judgment in the cross against every religion, but not by elevating Christianity as a particular religion.

Now we have to deal with Schleiermacher's understanding of the essence of religion. In all histories of theology he is regarded as the conqueror of the Enlightenment distortion of religion, where it was intellectualized and moralized. The negative side of Schleiermacher's definition of religion was that it is not essentially a thinking and an acting. The positive side is that religion is the feeling of unconditional dependence, the immediate consciousness of the unconditional in one's self, the immediate existential relation prior to the act of reflection, the immediacy of the awareness of the unconditional in our consciousness. All these terms point to the same reality of religious experience. Knowledge and action are consequences. Religious knowledge and religious action follow from this immediate awareness, but they are not the essence of religion. The immediate awareness of unconditional dependence transcends the mixed feelings of partial freedom and partial dependence which we have in our relation to the world. In all our relations to the world and to others there is this mixed feeling of freedom and dependence. If we are vitally powerful, we feel very much free in dealing with reality; if this feeling of freedom is reduced, then we feel our dependence on others and on all kinds of finite things. Now this whole realm of the experience of the finite is transcended in the awareness of the unconditional. If we speak of God, we can only say that this is the name for the whence of our unconditional dependence. Then God is not conceived of as an objectively given reality as another galaxy of stars. He transcends every finite relation and he is the ground of all of them. They are all unconditionally dependent on him.

If God were an object besides other objects, we could act upon him in terms of knowing and acting. This would mean that God could be proved. Such proofs could be verified and God could be moved by our activity. But God is not an object besides other objects. He is present in our immediate consciousness and all that we say about him are expressions of this immediacy. Schleiermacher is afraid that the term "person" as applied to God would make him an object subject to our cognitive and active dealings. So he uses the term "spirituality" instead of "personality." Of course, in spirituality the personal element is implied. There is no spirit which is not at the same time the bearer of the person. But the concept of spirituality is better suited than personality in removing the danger of an objectifying distortion of the idea of God.

4. *His Interpretation of Christianity*

That is the philosophical concept of religion which underlies Schleiermacher's whole description of Christianity. In the long run this proved to be stronger than the positivistic element, that is, the mere acceptance of Christianity as an empirical reality to be described. Now we come to a section in his thought where he breaks through the positivistic element. This is his christology. When he explains why he thinks Christianity is the highest manifestation of the essence of religion, he says it is because Christianity has two characteristics which distinguish it from other religions. The first is what he calls ethical monotheism. This means that the unconditional dependence in religion is not primarily a physical dependence thought of in materialistic terms. It is not a mechanical dependence as in some of the distortions of the idea of predestination in Calvinist theology in which the religious symbol of predestination is confused with mechanical causality. This is not Schleiermacher's idea, although his idea of dependence has been clearly traced to Calvinistic influences. Christianity is not a religion in which the relation to God is that of physical or mechanical dependence, but is that of teleological dependence, a dependence on God as the giver of the law and showing the goal toward which we have to go. This teleological dependence means that God is the whence of our unconditional moral imperative. Here you see clearly the Kantian element in him. It is not as in Schelling's philosophy of nature where men are dependent on the ultimate through nature.

The other thing which makes Christianity the highest religion is that everything is related to the salvation by Jesus of Nazareth. Salvation has a very definite meaning for him. It is the transformation of a limited, inhibited, or distorted religious consciousness into a fully developed religious consciousness. That person is saved who has a fully developed religious consciousness. He is in continuous conscious communion with God. This is salvation. All eschatological symbolism is removed or must be reinterpreted. This work of salvation, this liberation of our religious consciousness from inhibition, limitation, and distortion, is done by Christ, who himself has the fully developed religious consciousness. Since he does not need salvation, he can become the Savior.

This does not mean that Jesus is a mere example for man. Rather, he is the *Urbild*, the archetype, the original image, the representative of what man essentially is in unity with God. Here we have surprisingly high christological statements in Schleiermacher when we consider the universal concept of religion from which he started. This was possible because his own personal piety and his positivistic affirmation of Christianity came to fulfillment. It is interesting that Emil Brunner in his book on Schleiermacher[14] says that Schleiermacher's christological thinking is an interlude in his dogmatics; it does not fit into the whole system. It is a case of his piety breaking through his systematic principles. I do not think this is true because the positivistic element in Schleiermacher is genuine. It is one of the ways of escaping the

[14] *Die Mystik und das Wort. Der Gegensatz zwischen moderner Religionsauffassung und christlichem Glauben* (Tübingen: J. C. B. Mohr, 1924).

problems of philosophy of religion which, on the other hand, are inescapable. Brunner is right only insofar as one can say generally of all Schleiermacher's thinking that there is a tension between the purely philosophical and the more positivistic approaches to Christianity. All the later schools had the same difficulty. The whole Ritschlian school, which was dependent on Schleiermacher, was strongly positivistic and biblical, on the one hand, and yet dependent on Kant's epistemology, on the Kantian philosophy of religion, on the other hand.

Without going into details concerning the individual doctrines of Schleiermacher, we can say a few words about the method which permeated the whole system. His theological method was to describe the content of the religious consciousness of the Christian as it is determined by the appearance of the Christ. Systematic theology or the system of doctrine is rational insofar as it creates a consistent system of thoughts which do not contradict each other, but are interdependent. He does this with all the means of refined theological dialectics. When he deals with special problems, such as Bible, Christ, sin, salvation, atonement, or whatever it may be, he first discusses the two opposing views, the one which is given in the classical tradition which he knew as well as a Protestant theologian must know it, and the other which is the Enlightenment criticism of seventeenth-century Orthodoxy. Then he tries to find a solution to the problem by looking at the Christian consciousness, which is of course determined by his own concept of religion.

The methodologically decisive thing is that theological propositions about God or the world or man are derived from man's existential participation in the ultimate, that is, from man's religious consciousness. These are valid statements, but not in the sense that everybody could make such statements about the latest discovery in physics or astronomy. The form of the statements is quite different. The difference in form arises from the fact of existential participation, as we would say today. This means that the qualities or characteristics which we attribute to God are expressions of our relation to him. As a follower of Calvin, he said that we cannot say anything about the *essentia dei,* God in his true essence. We can say something only on the basis of his relation to us which is manifest through revelatory experiences. This has implications for the doctrine of the trinity. A doctrine of an objective trinity as a transcendent object is impossible. The doctrine of the trinity is the fullest expression of man's relation to God. Each of the *personae—you* should not say *persons* because that means something else—is a representation of a certain way in which God is related to man and the world. Only in this way do the *personae* make any sense. Therefore he places the trinitarian symbols at the end of the whole system. The doctrine of the trinity stands at the end as the completed doctrine of God, after all particular relations—such as those dealing with sin and forgiveness, creation and death and eternal life, the presence of the Spirit in the church and in the individual Christian, etc.—have been positively described from the religious consciousness of Christians. After this has been done, the lines can be drawn up to the divine as such, which yields to us trinitarian statements.

I follow the same method as Schleiermacher, but with one difference. I have two stages in drawing these trinitarian lines to God. The first is from the doctrine of the living God. The living God is always the trinitarian God, even before christology is possible, before the Christ has appeared. He who speaks of the living God is trinitarian even though he calls himself unitarian. In discussions with Unitarian students and colleagues at Harvard, I did not start with christology, but with the symbol of the living God. He is not a dead oneness in himself, a dead identity, but he goes out and returns. This defines the process of life everywhere. If we apply this symbolically to God, we are involved in trinitarian thinking. The numbers two or three or four—all of them appear in the history of Christian theology—are not decisive. But the movement of the divine, going out and returning to himself—this is decisive if we speak of a living God.

Now Schleiermacher did not use this possibility. He saw trinity only in relation to christology. But I believe that if one does not see it in connection with the idea of a living God, then the trinitarian symbolism, because it would be applied too late, becomes almost impossible to use. In being bound to the single event it easily becomes superstitious; in being related only to the historical Jesus it becomes only something to be observed.

I will give you an example of why this is significant. If we today imagine the possibility of spiritual beings existing in other parts of the universe, the question arises as to the meaning of Christ for them. Then people who have an exclusively christologically oriented conception of the trinity would say that we must bring them the message of Jesus of Nazareth as the Christ. This seems to me absurd. Instead, I would say that the divine Logos, the eternal Logos, the principle of God going out and manifesting himself, appears wherever there are spiritual beings, appears in their history as he has appeared in the center of human history. But what appears precedes human history. "Before Abraham was, I am."[15] This means that the universal Logos, the principle of the divine self-manifestation, is present in Jesus of Nazareth.

In spite of this limited criticism of Schleiermacher, I would say that the fundamental methodological notion that the trinity is not an *a priori* speculation about God is valid. The experience of the living God and the experience of the saving God both give rise to the trinitarian idea. This idea follows from the revelatory experience and cannot precede it. My main criticism of the Barthian method in his *Church Dogmatics*[16] is that he jumps, so to speak, directly into the doctrine of the trinity without starting from the human question. Here I am on the side of Schleiermacher in spite of my limited criticism.

Another point that must be mentioned is Schleiermacher's doctrine of sin. This was very influential. In this he followed the general trend of German classical philosophy and certainly of the Enlightenment. According to this trend, sin is a shortcoming. It is not a "no" but a "not yet." Sin arises because of the discrepancy between the great speed of the evolutionary process in the biological development of mankind and the slower pace of moral and spiritual development of man. The biological development is far ahead of man's spiritual development. Sin is the "not yet" of man's spiritual development within an already fully developed bodily organism. The distance or the gap between these two processes is what we call sin. This condition is universal. It is the state of mankind universally. The Christ is then an anticipation of a state which lies ahead for all mankind. This makes sin in some way necessary and unavoidable. The idea of the fall is swallowed up by the idea of the

15 John 8:58.
16 Karl Barth, *Church Dogmatics*, Vol. I, Pts. 1 and 2 (New York: Charles Scribner's Sons, 1936).

evolutionary necessity of estrangement or sin. At this point later theologians went back instead to Kant's idea of the original transcendent fall and the existentialists developed this on the basis of Schelling's doctrine of freedom.

In many later developments, however, Schleiermacher's relativization of sin was predominant. I said that for Schleiermacher salvation is the presence of God in man, in man's consciousness, which is determined by the divine presence in all its relativities. Here we see the mystical background in Schleiermacher's philosophy, mystical not in the sense of "foggy" but in the sense of the presence of the infinite within the finite. So the Savior takes the faithful, those who belong to him and participate in him, into the strength of his consciousness of God. And the church is the community in which this consciousness of God is the determining power. However relative it is, however distorted and limited, the church has this as its principle. This brings us to the end of our discussion of Schleiermacher's theology. Of course, it would be very interesting to go point by point into his various doctrines, but then this would be a course on Schleiermacher and not on the history of Protestant theology.

E. The Universal Synthesis: Georg W. F. Hegel

I must now come to the man who produced the great synthesis in philosophical terms. Schleiermacher is the great synthesis in theological terms. His colleague, Hegel, at the University of Berlin in the beginning of the nineteenth century, was the fulfillment of the synthesis in the philosophical realm. Both of these in their appearance and in their effects were immediately supraprovincial. Of course, their roots were in the German development, but the effects they had on others transcended the German limits and provincialisms. Schleiermacher's influence on all Protestant theology is also visible in this country, and Hegel's influence extended not only into religion but into the political transformation of the world in the twentieth century; even the rise of existentialism against him bears the imprint of his thinking. So we can say that his great synthesis is the turning point for many of the actual problems of today, including world revolution and the East-West conflict. Neither Marx, nor Nietzsche, nor Kierkegaard, nor existentialism, nor the revolutionary movements, are understandable apart from seeing their direct or indirect dependence on Hegel. Even those who opposed him used his categories in their attacks on him. So Hegel is in some sense the center and the turning point, not of an inner-philosophical school or an inner-theological way of thinking about religion, but of a world-historical movement which has directly or indirectly influenced our whole century.

1. *The Greatness and the Tragic* Hybris *of Hegel's System*

When we speak of Hegel's great synthesis in the realm of philosophy, this can be understood in two ways: first, the great synthesis of the cultural elements present in Western culture, and secondly, the synthesis of the conflicting polarities present in religious thought. I will describe him in both ways.

Before I can do that, however, the distorted image of Hegel must be removed. It would be far better for you to know nothing of Hegel than simply to know the usual caricature. If you have only this image of the noisy mill whose wheels are turning all the time—thesis, antithesis, synthesis—then it would be better not to know anything about him. When I gave my first lecture course in Frankfurt on Hegel, I spent the whole academic year, four hours a week, and got through only half of the material. At that time the early fragments of Hegel were discovered.[17] These fragments offer the best help in purging our minds of the distorted image of Hegel. In Frankfurt at that time I tried to show my students that every great philosophy combines two elements. The one is its vitality, its lifeblood, its inner character; the other is the emergency situation out of which the philosophy grows. No great philosopher simply sat behind his desk, and said, "Let me now philosophize a bit between breakfast and lunch time." All philosophy has been a terrible struggle between divine and demonic forces, skepticism and faith, the possibility of affirming and of negating life. The question of

[17] G. W. F. Hegel, *Early Theological Writings*, translated by T. M. Knox, with an introduction, and fragments, translated by Richard Kroner (Chicago: University of Chicago Press, 1948).

the mystery of existence stands behind all who became creative philosophers and were not merely analysts or historians of philosophy.

In Hegel's fragments one thing stands out quite clearly, namely, that religion and politics formed the lifeblood of Hegel's thinking. It was religion of a supernatural kind in conflict with rationalism which he found disrupting the souls of students of theology and philosophy while he was a seminary student living in the *Stift* in Tübingen, Württemberg. Besides religion there was the political situation determined by the French Revolution, on the one hand, and the tyranny of the German princes, on the other hand. And across the Channel there were the democratic beginnings of the British constitution.

These two things, religion and politics, came together very early in Hegel's philosophy of life. If you want to know what "philosophy of life" means in continental terminology—*Lebensphilosophie* in German can hardly be translated into English—you can read Hegel's fragments. Here among others you have a fragment on love which offers one of the deepest insights into the dynamics of the love relationship, not only on the human level, but in all living reality.

That is the one side in Hegel's thinking. But there was another element in Hegel as in every philosopher, namely, the method which became more and more predominant. His work on logic was in itself great, but its consequence was that gradually the earlier "philosophy of life" was covered over by a logical mechanism of thesis, antithesis, synthesis. It is a great tragedy in the history of philosophy that this logical element became the decisive thing. For instance, in his encyclopedia we have the impression of a mill which always makes the same noise and goes through the same rhythm so that if a concept goes into the mill you know ahead of time what will come out of it. This is a strong element, and a disagreeable one, in Hegel. And I do not wish to hide it. But it is also fair to see what is the lifeblood and its consequences in a man's thinking. For Hegel this was in the religious and political realms.

After these introductory words we will discuss the different periods which he wanted to unite in a great synthesis. Coming from the Enlightenment he witnessed the great struggle between the tradition of Orthodox Protestantism and the rationalistic criticism of it. So he had the problem of uniting traditional Christianity and the Enlightenment. But this was by no means all. He was also living in the period which we called the classical period. We spoke about it in connection with Goethe. It was a direct attempt to return to classical Greece both in the arts and in philosophy, and then indirectly in theology. This element of classicism was very strong in the early writings of Hegel when he described, for example, the ideal political system. He always described the ideal of the Greek *polis,* the city-state, in which religion and culture were united and in which the individual participated democratically in the whole life. So this had to be put into the right place in the great synthesis.

Then he went to the romantic period. He himself was strongly romantic in the beginning and dependent on Schelling. But because of his sober mind, he very soon separated himself from many of the emotional elements of Romanticism and even criticized them in his greatest published work, *The Phenomenology of Mind.*[18] This title is an unfortunate translation of *Die Phänomenologie des Geistes,* for *Geist* in German means "spirit." There we see another element being introduced, namely, the cause of the French Revolution. The students of the theological school in Tübingen participated in the French Revolution to the great anger of the ruling prince of Württemberg. Yet, they did not become revolutionaries because that is not the German temperament. Only in spirit did they become revolutionary, but not in a political way. Later on the revolutionaries came from another world, but using Hegelian categories.

If you look at all of these elements, you see how much is involved: Christian tradition, classical Greece, the Enlightenment, the movement of Romanticism. All these things had to be united into a universal synthesis. Nobody has attempted this so radically and with such a power of synthesis as Hegel. Although Kant was a more profound thinker in his critical way—this is a difficult judgment to make, but still possible— than Hegel, it was Hegel who more than Kant created an epoch in the history of philosophy, in the history of religion, and in politics.

Therefore, the breakdown of this great synthesis was a historic event. It was not simply an inner struggle between philosophical schools. This

18 Translated by J. B. Baillie (New York: The Macmillan Company, 1910).

happens all the time, but sometimes such struggles can become of world-historical importance, as did the theological controversies of the fourth and fifth centuries. The events which surround the rise and fall of Hegel's system transcend the situation of a conflict between schools. This is the greatness of Hegel's system, but often greatness and *hybris* go together. *Hybris* is a Greek word which is often translated as pride. But it should not be so translated because pride is a particular moral or antimoral attitude. It is possible to be without pride and full of *hybris*, extremely humble but in this humility remain in a state of *hybris*. The best translation is "self-elevation toward the realm of the divine." That is what it means in Greek tragedy. The great heroes are those who fall into *hybris*, who try to elevate themselves to the life of the gods, and who then are cast down by the tragic reaction of the divine powers.

This is the case with Hegel's system. It does not have primarily to do with the personal character of Hegel. There are others who have much more of this *hybris*, Schelling, for instance. It is in his fundamental idea itself in which the *hybris* is expressed, the idea that world history can possibly come to an end with one's own existence. The reason that Hegel was attacked from all sides and removed from the throne of providence on which he had placed himself was that the finished system cut off all openness to the future. Only God is on that throne and only God is able both to understand the past and to create the future. When Hegel tried to do both, then he was in the state of *hybris*, and this *hybris* was followed by the tragedy of his system.

Here you see that the history of philosophy is more than the history of some interesting ideas which people find to contradict in each other. The history of philosophy is the history of man's self-interpretation, and any such self-interpretation stands not only under the judgment of logic but also under the judgment of the meaning of existence as a whole. This is the responsibility of thinking and at the same time its greatness.

2. The Synthesis of God and Man (Mind and Person)

The synthesis of the divine and the human in Hegel's system is expressed in the doctrine of the absolute and the relative mind or *Geist*. Mind is a poor translation of *Geist*, but the word "spirit" is also full of difficulties. The word "spirit" has been reserved for religion and attributed to God and divine things alone. Man has been deprived of spirit, and has been divided into mind and body. This mutilation of the doctrine of man has had tremendous practical and theoretical consequences, making almost impossible a sound doctrine of man. We have psychology, we have biology, but we have no doctrine of man. And generally anthropology is—at least when I came to this country—a doctrine about the bones which have been left by the human race on the surface of the earth. Now we have in addition cultural anthropology. But this does not say anything about the essence of man, but only about the stages through which our former ancestors passed. It is also characterized by an especially disagreeable dogmatism regarding the concept of culture itself. Everything which man has created is explained in terms of a particular given culture. Since man is only a product of his culture, we cannot say anything about man universally nor anything about what distinguishes men from animals. But no cultural anthropologist tells you who has produced the culture, why cultures have changed, and what has happened in the context of the culture. So on the doctrine of man as man we are faced with special difficulties today.

Perhaps one of the ways in which we can try to overcome such difficulties is by reintroducing the concept of spirit, with a small "s" and not use this term for God alone with a capital "S." For if you cannot experience what spirit is in yourself, you cannot apply it symbolically or analogically to God either. When we have a doctrine of man as spirit, we must define spirit as the unity of mind and power, the unity of creativity—which makes human culture possible—and vitality—which is the life-power of man. Spirit is a dynamic concept. If you take away the power element of spirit, as you do by using only the concept of mind, what is left is simply intellectual movement. The intellectualization of the mental side of man results in placing the emotional element outside the intellect, in depriving us of what we find in Plato's doctrine of *eros*, namely, the unity of the emotional, the volitional, and the intellectual elements in the person as a whole; it results also in a loss of what is meant in the Christian concept of *gnosis*, as Paul used it, which means both knowledge and union. Knowing God means a union of man's spirit with the divine Spirit. It does not mean *episteme*, that is, detached scientific knowledge, inquiry into the structure of finite things. *Gnosis* always means union, and if the word were not so distorted today, we could say, mystical union, as Protestant Orthodoxy was still able to do. Mysticism means the experience of the union of the divine and the human.

So although Hegel's phenomenology of *Geist* has been translated as phenomenology of *mind*, we will, despite the terminological difficulties, translate *Geist* as *spirit*. For Hegel God is absolute spirit and man is relative spirit; or God is infinite spirit and man is finite spirit. To say that God is Spirit means that he is creative power, not creative power in a naturalistic sense of a mere objective process, but creative power united with mind, or perhaps better, with meaning. This creative power in union with meaning produces in men personal self-consciousness and creates through men culture, language, the arts, the state, philosophy, and religion. All these things are implied in the concept of the spirit. But if you speak of absolute mind, then you have to think of some highest intellect somewhere, a bodiless intellect, so to speak, a mind without power. However, according to the religious tradition, both Jewish and Christian, as well as many other religions, God is first of all the Almighty. He is power. He is unrestricted. He is infinite power. He is the power in all other powers, and he gives them the power to be. This element of power belongs to the concept of spirit. If you take this away by translating *Geist* with mind, it becomes impossible to understand the history of Protestant theology, or Hegel's system and his theological successors.

I have often said that I am a crusader for the rescuing of the word "spirit" with a small "s." We need the word. All other languages have it. In French we have *esprit*, in German *Geist*, in Hebrew *ruach*, in Latin *spiritus*, and in Greek *pneuma*, but in English this word has been more or less lost, in part due to British empiricism and in part due to Descartes' division of man into intellect and body. In spite of all Descartes' greatness in creating the method of modern scientific and philosophical analysis, we must say that from the standpoint of the doctrine of man he has omitted the real center of man, which is between mind and body. Formerly this was called "soul"—a word which is now forbidden by the watchdogs of language in every university, because this word is connected with sentimentality and has no scientific value; this despite the fact that it is the central concept in Aristotle's doctrine of man, namely, *psyche,* which must be translated by *anima* (Latin) or soul.

In any case, this is the bad situation in which we find ourselves, which makes it difficult to understand Hegel at this central point. Spirit is the creator of man as personality and of everything which through man as person can be created in culture, religion, and morality. This human spirit is the self-manifestation of the divine Spirit, and God is the absolute Spirit which is present and works through every finite spirit. To understand this we must go back to what I said about Hegel as a philosopher of life, of life processes. All life processes are manifestations of the divine life, only they appear in time and space whereas in God they are in their essential nature. God actualizes his own potentialities in time and space, through nature, through history, and through men. God finds himself in his personal character in man and his history, in the different forms of his historical actualization. God is not a person besides other persons. The absolute Spirit of which Hegel speaks is not a being beside the finite spirit, but in God its essential reality is given. In time and space it becomes actualized, yet at the same time estranged from its essential character.

Here we have the whole vision of the world as a process of the self-actualization of the divine essences in time and space. Therefore, everything in its essential nature is the self-expression of the divine life. This world process goes through nature and through the various actualizations of spirit. In man's spirit, particularly in man's artistic, religious, and philosophical creativity, God finds himself as he essentially is. God does not find himself in himself, but he comes to himself, to what he essentially is, through the world process, and finally through man and through man's consciousness of God. Here we have the old mystical idea that in man's knowledge of God, God knows himself, and in man's love of God, God loves himself. We found these ideas also in Spinoza, and therefore I emphasize so much that Spinoza is a geometricized Jewish mystic. In Hegel, however, we have these mystical ideas in a dynamic creative form and not in Spinoza's static geometrical form.

Hegel sees God as the bearer of the essential structures of all things. This makes him the great representative of essentialist philosophy, a philosophy which tries to understand the essences in all things as expressions of the divine self-manifestation in time and space. The later existentialist protest can only be understood as the reaction to this essentialist philosophy. Modern existentialism was born as a protest against Hegel's essentialism. Therefore, we must understand Hegel's essentialism, the essences as manifestations of the divine life. God in himself is the essence of every species of plants and animals, of the structures of the atoms and stars, of the nature of man in which his innermost center is manifest. All these are manifestations of the divine life as it is manifest in time and space.

Hegel cannot, therefore, conceive of God as a person beside other persons. Then he would be less than God. Then the world process, the structure of being, would be more than he, would be above him. God would then have a fate; he would be thrown into reality like the Greek gods who are subject to fate, who come and go, who are immortal with respect to a special structure of the cosmos, but who are born and die with this cosmos. But the God of Christianity is not less than the structure of reality. He has it in himself; it is his life. This fundamental change liberates the Christian man from the anxiety of destiny. You can observe the fight against this idea already in the Greek tragedians who were fighting against gods who themselves were subject to fate and who therefore were inferior to man, because man is able to resist the universal fate in the power of the logos. Man is beyond the fate and therefore beyond the gods. So God is not a person. He is spiritual, as I told you in connection with Schleiermacher, but he is not a person because that would subject him again to the fate of the Greek gods.

There is a point of identity between God and man insofar as God comes to self-consciousness in man, and insofar as man in his essential nature is contained together with everything in the inner life of God as potentiality. The process in which God creates the world and fulfills himself in the world is the means whereby the infinite abundance of the divine life grows in time and space. God is not a separate entity, something finished in himself, but he belongs to the world, not as a part of it, but as the ground from which and to which all things exist. This is the synthesis of the divine and the human spirit. It was the point most attacked by the nineteenth-century theology of religious revivalism, which wanted to emphasize the person-to-person relationship and the difference between God and the world.

3. *The Synthesis of Religion and Culture (Thought and Imagination)*

Another synthesis which Hegel constructs is the synthesis between religion and culture. As a result of the basic idea of the relation of the absolute and the relative spirit, religion has a double meaning in Hegel. In one sense everything in its essential nature is rooted in the divine. In order to understand Hegel's synthesis of religion and culture, we must know what "nature" meant to him. Nicholas of Cusa's basic idea of the coincidence of the divine and the human in everything was certainly present in all of Hegel's philosophy. In nature the absolute Spirit is present. But it is present in terms of estrangement. Here we come to the very important twentieth-century concept of estrangement. It is the existentialist concept for what in religious symbolism is called the fall. This idea is applied by Hegel to nature. Nature is spirit, but estranged spirit, spirit not yet having achieved its true nature. God leaves himself, so to speak, in order to go over into estrangement. The important thing historically is that this concept which Hegel created was later used by his pupils against him. For Hegel developed a philosophy of reconciliation, as we shall see, but his pupils said that there is no reconciliation. This statement that there is no reconciliation is the basic statement of existentialism. The world is not reconciled. The greatness of Hegel is that he created the categories in terms of which others could attack him. The tremendous importance of the concept of estrangement in Karl Marx's interpretation of capitalism is derived from Hegel, but then used against him. You cannot understand Marxism and its significance for the philosophical spirit of the nineteenth and twentieth centuries without knowing that he took the concept of estrangement from Hegel only to attack him by means of it. Against Hegel he said, estrangement, yes, but reconciliation, no! The class situation shows that there is no reconciliation. Hegel said that in the state (Prussia) the political reconciliation and the social reconciliation do exist. Against this the existentialist revolt began.

Now in Hegel's system there is a transition from natural philosophy to logic. In Hegel's logic something interesting happens, which you must know in order to understand Kierkegaard's attack on Hegel's system. In his logic Hegel develops the essences of reality in terms of their logical abstraction. He does not speak of men, but man as an essence appears in Hegel's logic. He does not speak of quantities in reality, but the category of quantity appears in his logic. He does not speak of animals, but the category of animal life appears in his logic. So he has in his logic a fully developed system of the essential structure of reality without going into the actualization of these essences in time, space, and history. It is, so to speak, the description of the inner divine life. For this he even uses the symbolism of the trinity, God going out and returning to himself in his eternal life, in the life of the eternal essences, before anything has happened in time and space, before the categories and essences became actuality.

It is clear that we have here a philosophy of the inner divine life under the name of logic. Logic is here not semantics; it is not analytic logic, that is, a subjective power of man's mind. But like Aristotle's logic, it is a description of the structure of reality. However, in Aristotle as in all Greek thinking, it was a static description—the hierarchy of abstractions, and then the conclusions. Hegel's logic describes the structure of the dynamic process of the inner divine life in which all realities in their essence are present, before they are actually in time and space.

Then the question arose: How does this all come to actuality? Here Hegel unites the idea of creation with the idea of the fall, and speaks of nature as the alienated or estranged spirit. The two words "alienation" and "estrangement" went on to play a great role in existentialist philosophy. In my opinion the two words mean the same thing, but I know that some philosophers prefer the word "alienation," perhaps because it is a bit more abstract. I myself have preferred to use the word "estrangement" because it contains the imagery of the stranger and the separation of people who once loved each other and belong essentially to each other. I think it is a more powerful term.

When Hegel says that nature is estranged spirit, estranged does not mean annihilated or altered. So the whole world process is seen by Hegel as a process of divine self-estrangement. This divine self-estrangement reminds us very much of the risk God took, according to Christian theology, when he created the world with the possibility of man's fall. Christian theology would say that God created the world in spite of the fact that he foresaw its estrangement and fall. In Calvinist theology God is said to have even decreed the fall. At any rate, this is the religious substance of Hegel's more logical statement of the alienation of the divine Spirit in nature.

Man's spirit develops out of nature going through many processes. In his encyclopedia Hegel presents a lengthy philosophy of nature. This is largely dependent on Schelling who on the basis of the synthesis of Kant and Spinoza, of which I spoke, developed the romantic element of nature. Schelling showed the inner powers of nature, the conscious and the unconscious. He was the first to use the term "unconscious" in philosophy, and through a special line of thought Freud received this term, and used it for empirical psychological purposes. But actually it comes from Schelling's philosophy of nature. What the romantic philosophers of nature wanted to show is that in nature spirit is struggling for its full actualization in man. You have the same idea in Teilhard de Chardin, the Jesuit, who wrote *The Phenomenon of Man.*[19] It has many analogies to the romantic philosophy of nature and even to the classical if we consider Goethe a representative of the classical philosophy of nature. The great problem of this philosophy of nature was to show its relation to scientific research which had been going on vigorously ever since Galileo and Newton, first in astronomy, then in biology and physics. Hegel tried to take the results of scientific research into his system, as did also Schelling, who personally knew many of the best scientists of his time. But the danger is that if a preliminary result of scientific research is used in the formation of philosophical or theological statements, it tends to become fixed as something metaphysically true. Then the scientists resent this use of their scientific results because they know of the preliminary and tentative character of these results. The same day on which the philosopher writes down his philosophical interpretations of physics or biology, new insights are already being discovered in some laboratory which upon publication will make the philosopher's interpretations

[19] Translated by Bernard Wall, with an Introduction by Julian Huxley (New York: Harper & Row, 1959).

obsolete and invalid. This difficulty is always present. On the other hand, I know from personal encounter with physicists that they desire very much to have a philosophical evaluation and interpretation of what they are doing. So philosophy has a difficult task, but most contemporary philosophers settle for logical analysis of the scientific method, so as not to prejudice any results. But even this is precarious, for it may be that some new result will make necessary a change in method. So the only thing we can do is to say that the vision of a special level of considering nature must remain independent of the progress of natural sciences. This is what Teilhard de Chardin has done. He himself was a member of the expedition which discovered the skull of Pekin man or Sinanthropus, one of these prehistoric beings not yet man but in the series of development toward man. In spite of his very strict scientific training and work, he dared to have such a vision. In the third volume of my *Systematic Theology* I have tried something like this from the philosophical point of view, but I am aware of how precarious and dangerous it is. If, on the other hand, we do not try this, we remove God from nature, and if God is removed from nature, he gradually disappears altogether, because we are nature. We come from nature. If God has nothing to do with nature, he finally has nothing to do with our total being.

For Hegel man is born out of nature, and in man another phenomenon occurs; spirit comes to itself. In man God finds what he essentially is, namely, absolute spirit himself in a relative being, in a being which is biologically conditioned, but with the dimension of the spirit, of self-consciousness. Hegel distinguishes three dimensions or levels of spirit: (a) the subjective spirit, which is man's personal inner life. Psychology, for example, belongs to the doctrine of the subjective spirit; (b) the objective spirit, which is society, state, and family. The subject of ethics belongs here; (c) the absolute spirit, which is the full manifestation of God on the human level. Art, religion, and philosophy belong here.

This is very interesting in many respects. One dangerous thing in it is that ethics appears as philosophy of society. Ethics is connected with family, society, and state. Hegel's ethics is an objectivist ethics. It was at this point that Kierkegaard's most radical attack occurred, for Hegel understood ethics only from the point of view of the essential structure of man in society. He did not understand it as the decision of the individual personality with relation to himself and his society. Against this Kierkegaard placed his concept of the ethically deciding individual person. Because Hegel had no personal ethics in his system, Kierkegaard emphasized so much the decision of the individual personality. Hegel had only a system of social ethics in which the ethical relations of the individual person were developed, but the free, deciding individual did not appear in the system.

The next point has to do with the relation of religion to philosophy. Religion stands between aesthetics and philosophy. This also is important. In a special period of Schelling's development, the aesthetic was the great miracle of the divine self-manifestation. In the aesthetic vision the Kantian dualism between theoretical and practical reason was overcome. Even the state for Schelling was the great work of art, and the artistic creation was regarded as the real manifestation of the divine. Hegel saw that this is impossible because in all art there is an element of unreality. There is a seeming reconciliation, but only in the image, not in reality itself. So Hegel places art as a stage prior to religion, and religion beyond it as the substance. In his philosophy of religion—which was unfortunately never published by Hegel but is available only through several transcripts made by students of Hegel—we find one of the greatest evaluations of religion. Religion is for him the substance and center of life, that which makes everything sacred and gives everything its depths and heights.

But now something interesting happens. Philosophy is put above religion. To understand in what sense, you must first understand one thing in Hegel. In Hegel's hierarchy of natural philosophy—the subjective spirit, the objective spirit, the absolute spirit—the higher level never abolishes the lower one. Man as spirit is still under the law of physics, the law of chemistry, the law of biology. These are three forms which he also distinguishes. You can see immediately how impossible this is from the point of view of modern atomic physics in which the distinction between the chemical and the physical is almost extinguished. Be that as it may, for Hegel the higher does not abolish the lower. But the higher is an expression of the more perfect actualization of the absolute spirit in time and space. And so, if philosophy is higher than religion, it does not abolish religion. Religion remains for Hegel the substance of spiritual reality, that is, the relation to the absolute mind. Here he develops a whole history of religion in which all religions are put in their right place, and Christianity as the revealed religion is given the highest place.

What then is the difference between religion and philosophy? The difference lies in the form of our awareness of the relation to the absolute. In religion we think in images, in *Vorstellungen,* as he called them. Today we would speak rather of myths and symbols. Philosophy is able to interpret these images or symbols in terms of concepts (*Begriffe.*) The conceptualization of the religious contents is the highest aim of philosophy. In this respect Hegel is very near to the way in which Western philosophy has always developed. We can follow this development with marvelous clarity in early Greek philosophy. First there were the myths, theogonies, stories of the genesis of the gods, then cosmogony, the genesis of the world, and then out of these religious myths the first great philosophical concepts were born. The history of philosophy shows this. So Hegel also believed that the philosophical concepts were universally born out of the mythological symbols of religion. In a real sense his own philosophy is philosophy of religion; but in a narrower sense philosophy of religion, connected with the church tradition, symbols and myths, has a special place in his system. In this way he unites the critical mind of philosophy with the intuitive symbolizing mind of religion by having philosophy provide the conceptual form for the symbols of religion.

4. *The Synthesis of State and Church*

The third synthesis of which I want to speak is in the political realm, the synthesis of state and church. If you hear the word "state" used by Hegel and in romantic philosophy generally, you should not think of what is called "state" today in liberal democracy, that is, an abstract system of government. Therefore, the idea of keeping the state away from the economic and cultural contents of life is in this country quite different from what it was for all European countries. In Hegel's understanding state is the synthetic unity of all communal activities in a nation. It is the directing center of education, the arts, religion, economy, defense, administration, law, and of all things which belong to the realm of culture. If you take state in this sense you can better understand the expression Hegel once used that the state is the divine on earth. If you identify state, however, with the central administration, then this is almost blasphemy. It is an unfortunate expression, and has often been used against Hegel. What it means is the presence of God's self-realization in all cultural realms in time and space. The centered unity of this is the state, in the largest sense. If you take it in this sense too, the state is actually the church, because the state is not merely the administration, but the cultural life in all directions, including religion. Then it can be called the body of God on earth, so to speak.

But this expression is so unfortunate because it has been used consciously or unconsciously by the totalitarian ideologies as they developed in Germany, Russia, Italy, and elsewhere. So Hegel is often referred to in order to justify a centralist control of all political and economic life. This is not what Hegel meant at all. Administration is only one of the functions, and law is another, but none of them is meant in a totalitarian way, although there lurked this danger in his formulation. For us the most important is the relation to the church. If we take Hegel's definition of state, then of course church and state are identical. Some of the theologians who followed Hegel thought it was clear that there should not be a particular church at all. The life of the nation and of the church should be identical. The influence of classicism is clear here because in the Greek city-states there was no independent "church" or cult separated from the life of the *polis*. So this became the ideal both for the philosophers and the theologians. One of the theologians, Wilhelm De Wette (1780–1849), said that the destiny of Christianity is no longer dependent on the church, but on the substance given in society and expressed in the form of the state. Substance stands here for spiritual substance, the creative ground out of which the life of a nation grows. Therefore state and church are no longer separated.

These ideas should not sound so strange. In public addresses in America we often hear, "We are a Christian nation." What does this mean? Certainly we are not a Christian nation in any empirical sense. We are extremely unchristian, as every nation is. Perhaps it means that in all our secular life and in the several expressions of our national life, there is a substance which has been shaped by Christianity. If understood in this sense, it can be right, but it is also very dangerous, especially when used in our anti-Communist propaganda. Then it is wrong, for no nation is ever simply Christian or godless, whatever theory its leaders may hold. Neither the one nor the other is true.

We are still involved in this problem as is most evident in some of the statements that Bonhoeffer made in his letters from prison. In these letters he stated that man has come to maturity, that the separation of the religious and cultural spheres should not be maintained any longer, that the church should know that it is not the only representative of the divine in history, but that the secular culture has an equal claim, and perhaps a more genuine claim in our time. This is the Hegelian concern repeated in these ideas. Is culture something which stands beside the church? Shall the church stand aside from the autonomous development of culture? Should it be pushed into a corner where it loses its relevance for all of culture? Or should we instead understand the religious element in culture and the cultural element in religion, and attempt to drive toward a new unity as this existed in former centuries and cultures. This is the deeper meaning of the expression that the state is the divine on earth or of the identity of state and church.

5. Providence, History, and Theodicy

There is another point, a very important and decisive one, at which Hegel tries the great synthesis. That is the interpretation of history in terms of providence and theodicy, which is justification of God for the kind of world this is. Hegel followed Leibniz and the Enlightenment with their concept of the harmony of the universe. Harmony is a paradoxical concept also in Hegel. In spite of the contradictions of reality, in spite of individual willfulness and irrationality, the ultimate outcome of history is positive and is in line with the divine purpose. One can say that Hegel's interpretation of history is the application of the idea of providence in a secularized form, in a form in which the philosopher, so to speak, sits on the throne of God, looking into his providential activities and describing them. In everything which happens Hegel can see the self-actualization of the absolute spirit, the divine ground of being itself. This means that somehow everything in history is divine revelation. He can say that history is reasonable, but reasonable according to the logos concept of reason, according to the principle of the divine self-manifestation in history, according to the universal principle of form in which the divine ground manifests itself.

On this basis Hegel made a statement which has been very much abused, misunderstood, and attacked by very clever philosophers. This is the statement that everything real is rational. Now every eight-year-old boy knows that not everything that is real is rational, but it took sixty-year-old philosophers at the end of the nineteenth century to show with their immense wisdom how to refute Hegel. Then they could express with great feeling how superior they were to Hegel because they knew that there are many things in reality which are not reasonable. But they were not superior; they were only unable to understand the profound thought of the great mind. What Hegel said must first of all be thought of as a paradox. It is the paradox that in spite of the immense irrationality in reality, of which he could speak again and again, there is nevertheless a hidden providential activity, namely, the self-manifestation of the absolute Spirit through the irrational attitudes of all creatures and especially of people. This providential power in history works behind human activity, willing, and planning, and through man's rationality and irrationality. This idea has the same paradoxical character as the Christian doctrine of providence. In spite of tragic occurrences which Hegel also knew about, he did not despair of providence; nor did the early Christians under horrible persecutions. It is only if you speak of providence unparadoxically that you must despair. If you speak of it paradoxically, you can say that in spite of this or that, the mystery of life is behind everything that happens. Every individual is immediate to God in every moment and in every situation, and can reach his own fulfillment in time and above time.

But while the paradoxical element in Hegel's statement is obviously there, Hegel did not accept the mystery in the way in which Christianity has always accepted it. Hegel *knew* why things happened as they did. He *knew* how the process of history unfolds. Therefore, he missed the one element in the Christian affirmation of the paradox of providence, the mystery about the particulars. He did not even discuss the particulars, but he believed he knew the general process as such. He constructed history as the actualization of the eternal essences or potentialities which are the divine life in their inner dialectical movement, the play of God within himself, so to speak. Here he developed the trinitarian symbolism within the divine life. These eternal essences are actualized in the historical process in time and space.

But how are they actualized? Here Hegel's almost tragic feeling in regard to history comes out in a way usually overlooked by his interpreters. He said history is not the place for the happiness of the individual. The individual cannot be happy in history. History does not care about the individual. History goes its grand way from one idea or essence or potentiality within the divine life, actualizing itself, to the others. The bearers of these ideas are the social groups, the nations, and the states. Each nation, each cultural group, has its time in which a particular eternal idea, as it has been spelled out in Hegel's logic, becomes actual in time and space.

He said all this happens by passion and interest. Nothing in history happens without passion and interest. Here we have an insight of the existentialists which they received from Hegel and by means of which they attacked him. The term "interest" was used especially by Kierkegaard in his attack against Hegel, while "passion" and, in the larger sense, will-to-power and economic will, were used by anti-Hegelians like the early Marx and Nietzsche. They were all dependent on the one against whom they fought, even in their use of terminology.

Hegel had a concept which gives strong expression to the "in spite of" character of his doctrine of history. This concept is "the cunning of the idea," a very mythological-sounding phrase. The cunning of the idea is the divine trick, so to speak, working behind the backs of those who are acting in history and bringing into existence something that is in line with a meaningful development of history. This idea makes it possible to understand figures like Hitler. In this respect Hegel is very near to Luther who understood figures like Attila the Hun and the leaders of the Turks during the invasions at the time of the Reformation as the "masks of God." They are the masks through whom God works out his purposes in history. This is also mythological imagery, similar to the cunning of the idea. Both point to the paradoxical character of the divine activity. By paradox we mean it in its original Greek sense, namely, against all expectation, contrary to our normal belief and opinion. In this sense Hegel's cunning of the idea and Luther's masks of God in world history are in the same line. So Hegel could say that he views history as the divine theodicy, the justification of God for the horrors of world history. Hegel said that there is no easy explanation of the negativities in history. We are not able to justify God, but the historical process justifies him. Or God justifies himself by the historical process in spite of the fact that this historical process is full of events which seem to contradict the divine purpose.

There is another important point in Hegel's interpretation of history, of the world process, and even of the inner dialectics of the divine life. It is the principle of negativity. I warned you about seeing Hegel chiefly in terms of the triadic dialectic: thesis, antithesis, synthesis. This can be a caricature of Hegel, but it happens to be a caricature for which he is largely responsible in his later writings, especially in his encyclopedia where it becomes often intolerable. Behind this there is Hegel's idea of the negative element in every life process. The negation drives the positive out of itself and reveals its inner potentialities. This, of course, is another idea taken up by existentialism. The problem of nonbeing in existentialism and in Heidegger is already in Hegel. The difference is that in Hegel the negative is not the continuous threat against the positive, but is overcome in the fulfilled synthesis. Here again Hegel is sitting on the throne of providence, always knowing the outcome. This is the *hybris* which brought Hegel's synthesis, despite its greatness, to its final dissolution. According to Hegel no life is possible without negativity, otherwise the positive would remain within itself in dead identity. Without alteration there is no life. The continuous process of life which goes out of itself and tries to return to itself has in itself the principle of negativity. Here is the deepest point in his theodicy, the necessity of the negative as an implication of life. It is also necessary to know this to understand the rise of existentialism later, and its opposition to essentialism.

6. The Christ as Reality and Symbol

Hegel tried to combine all the elements of his period with the basic Christian affirmation that Jesus is the Christ. The universal synthesis between Christianity and the modern mind stands and falls with the christological problem. For Hegel and all essentialists the problem is particularly difficult because Jesus, who is called the Christ, is first of all an individual. But at the same time he is supposed to be the universal individual. So the question arose: Can an individual be at the same time universal? This is the fight that has been going on since Hegel, and in some way also before him in the Enlightenment and mysticism. The problem has not been fully solved even today.

But Hegel tried to solve this problem. For him the essential identity of God and man in spite of actual separation and hostility is embodied in this one man Jesus who is for that reason called the *Logos*. He developed a christology in line with that principle formulated by Nicholas of Cusa of the mutual inherence of the finite and the infinite. In Jesus as the Christ the infinite is completely actualized in the finite; its very center is present in the center of this one finite man Jesus. Jesus therefore gave expression to that which is universal and which is potentially and essentially true of every human being, and in some way of every being. He is the self-manifestation of the absolute mind. Later revivalist or pietistic theology in Europe was to fight against this because for it the unique individuality and the personal relation to this individuality stand in the very center.

Several days ago I had a very interesting christological discussion with a colleague over the question: Is Jesus important for us as *Mitmensch,* that is, as a fellow human being with whom we can have a common relationship as human beings? Or is he important for us as the bearer of the Spirit? Now, it is my personal opinion that on this question Hegel is nearer to the understanding of Paul and the early church than the pietists with their jesuological way of being related to him. In any case, the problem brought up by Hegel is still a living problem and probably will remain so as long as there is a Christian Church.

7. *Eternity against Immortality*

General piety very aggressively attacked Hegel's mystical and philosophical understanding of immortality. This attack is psychologically understandable. For it is obvious that individual immortality could not be affirmed within the system; it could not agree with the consistency of the system. We participate in the divine life as individuals through the historical process, and to the degree in which we participate in it, we participate in the divine life. This participation was called eternal life by Hegel, as well as by Schelling and the classical German philosophers. They understood this concept of eternal life in opposition to individual immortality. They certainly could claim biblical support for this notion that immortality belongs to God alone, that man has no immortality in himself, not even before the fall according to biblical mythological symbolism. In paradise he could gain immortality only by eating from the tree of life, even as the gods themselves in the myths which underlie the biblical version.

So Hegel here expresses an idea which is in conflict with the feelings and desires of every individual, however profound it might be and however much it might be stressed in mysticism and philosophy. For this reason the philosophical criticism of Hegel found a great deal of popular support.

CHAPTER IV

The Breakdown of the Universal Synthesis

I have shown you the parts which were brought into Hegel's great synthesis. I did not go into the several philosophical elements, how much of Kantianism, how much of Spinozism, how much of the Goethe-Schelling dynamic transformation of Spinoza, how much of Romanticism, etc., are to be found in Hegel. They are all there. But for the purposes of this course I dealt predominantly with the synthesis so far as it had a bearing on the Christian tradition. I have tried to stress how important it was for him to try to create this synthesis. It is a question which is still with us. Can we be schizophrenic forever, living with a split consciousness? Can we be split between the Christian tradition, on the one hand, and the creative concepts and symbols of the modern mind, on the other hand? If that is impossible, how is a genuine synthesis possible? After the breakdown of Hegel's synthesis numerous new attempts were made to reconstruct a synthesis, all of them dependent on Hegel, but none possessing the universality and historical power of Hegel's system.

A. THE SPLIT IN THE HEGELIAN SCHOOL

How did the split in Hegel's school take place? Hegel's interpretation of Christ took for granted the historical reality of the biblical image of the Christ. He did not doubt it. His interpretation also stressed the symbolic meaning of the universal essential unity between God and man. So his interpretation included both reality and symbol. Something happened, however, which seemed to undercut the historical side of that interpretation. The question arose: Can we rely on the historical reports concerning the Christ? Such historical criticism was much older than the period in which Hegel lived. Historical criticism existed since the deistic movement in England, and since the eighteenth-century conflict between rationalism and supernaturalism. But now a new element was introduced by Hegel.

1. *The Historical Problem: Strauss and Baur*

In the eighteenth century the question was whether the reports about the life of Jesus were true or false. The Christian theologians were bent on showing that much of the historical material could be vindicated in face of historical criticism. Some of the critics tried to show that almost nothing remains as historically reliable. Others argued on the basis of Hegel's point of view that even though the reports are not historically reliable, they do not for that reason lose their religious value. It does not matter if there is so much uncertainty regarding the biblical records of the life of Jesus, they may nevertheless have symbolic value. The concept of symbol came from Schelling and Hegel, and was not intended to prejudice the historical question. It was simply a different kind of language from ordinary empirical language.

David Friedrich Strauss (1808–1874) drew out all the consequences from previous historical criticism when he wrote his *Life of Jesus* (1835).[1] It came like lightning and thunder striking the great synthesis and all those who felt safe in it. Strauss showed that the authors of the Gospels were not those traditionally thought to be the authors. But more, he tried to show that the stories of the birth and the resurrection of Jesus are symbols expressing the eternal identity of what is essential in Jesus and God. This was felt as a tremendous shock. For decades later scholars tried to refute Strauss's *Life of Jesus*, and, of course, there were many points in it that proved to be invalid in the light of more research.

[1] *The Life of Jesus, Critically Examined,* translated from the 4th German edition by George Eliot (London: Chapman Brothers, 1846).

But the problem which Strauss raised to the fore in the life of the church could never be removed.

A footnote on Strauss's later development: It contains something tragic. Later he wrote another *Life of Jesus*,[2] this one for the German people, as he said. Here he developed the typical world view of the victorious bourgeoisie, not of the great aggressive bourgeoisie of the eighteenth century, but of the positivistic materialistic bourgeoisie which had become victorious in the nineteenth century, and which he represented. This is characterized by a calculating attitude toward the world, a basic materialistic interpretation of reality, and moral rules derived from the bourgeois conventions. I mention this because of the tremendous attack which Friedrich Nietzsche made against Strauss in the name of the forces of creative life. He attacked this bourgeoisie resting undisturbed in its own finitude.

This has a lot to do with Gospel criticism, for from his bourgeois point of view Strauss eliminated the in-breaking of the divine into the human, of the infinite into the finite. The infinite was adapted to the finite. The image of Christ which Strauss and many later biographers produced was that of a domesticated divinity, domesticated for the sake of the untroubled life of the bourgeois society in calculating and controlling the finite reality. Here Nietzsche was the prophetic victor over Strauss, even more than any theologian.

But this was not the end of the story. The development was furthered by a pupil of Hegel, Ferdinand Christian Baur (1792–1860), who founded the Tübingen school which dealt especially with New Testament research. He tried to apply the Hegelian concepts of thesis, antithesis, and synthesis to the early development of Christianity. The thesis was the early Jewish-Christian communities; the antithesis the pagan, Christian, Pauline line of thought (he emphasized very much the struggle between Peter and Paul over the necessity of circumcision, in which Paul prevailed, opening the way for Christianity to conquer the pagan world); the synthesis of the Petrine and the Pauline types of Christianity was the Johannine. In this point Baur was very much in

[2] *Das Leben Jesu für das deutsche Volk bearbeitet* (Leipzig: 1864). The English translation is *The Life of Jesus for the People* (London: Williams and Norgate, 1879).

the tradition of classical German philosophy. All of these philosophers, Kant, Fichte, Schelling, and Hegel, were great lovers of the fourth Gospel, because of the gnostic terminology in this Gospel, especially the *logos* term. Baur's interpretation of Christianity was very important and influential, however justifiable or unjustifiable his theory may be from a historical point of view. In the face of the orthodox view of a literally inspired Bible, Baur showed how these biblical writings were created in an historical way. The idea of a creative development which was going on in the church and which produced the Scriptures has changed our whole relation to the Bible. The whole development of historical criticism was later to maintain some form of Baur's sense of the historical emergence of the biblical writings over against the view of a mechanically dictated and inspired Word of God, as if God were dictating to a stenographer at a typewriter.

2. *The Anthropological Problem: Ludwig Feuerbach (1804–1872)*

It was Feuerbach who launched an anthropological criticism against Hegel's philosophy of religion. He himself was very much influenced by Hegel before turning against him. Hegel had said that man is that being in whom God recognizes himself. In man's knowledge of God, God comes to know himself. There is thus no knowledge of God apart from that knowledge of him which is in man. Now Feuerbach, under the influence of Western naturalism, materialism, and psychologism, said that Hegel must be turned around. God is nothing else than a projection of man's awareness of his own infinity. You see that this is simply turning Hegel upside down. For Hegel God comes to himself in man; for Feuerbach man creates God in himself. These are two quite different views. Here we have Feuerbach's theory of projection. The word "projection" is widely used today. All education deals with methods of projection; Freudian thought interprets God as a human projection, as a father image, etc. But Feuerbach was much profounder. I recommend to all of you who have just discovered Freud's theory of projection to go back to Feuerbach; he had a real theory of projection.

What does projection mean in a technical sense? It means putting an image on a screen. In order to do this, you need a screen. But I always miss the screen in modern thinking about projection. Granted, God is the projection of the father experience in us; he is the image of it. But why is this image itself God? Who is the screen onto which this image is projected? To this Feuerbach has an answer. He says that man's experience of his infinity, the infinite will to live, the infinite intensity of love, etc., makes it possible for him to have a screen upon which to project images. This, of course, makes sense, and from the point of view of the philosophy of religion one can agree with all projection theories which are as old as Xenophanes, almost six hundred years before Christ. This means that the concrete image, the concrete symbolism applied to the infinite, is determined by our situation and by our relation to our own infinity. This is meaningful. Of course, it is not sufficient, but in any case Feuerbach saw much better than so many seemingly educated people of today that if you have a theory of projection, you must explain why the images are projected on just this screen, and why the result is something infinite, that is, the divine, the unconditional, the absolute. Where does that come from? The father is not absolute. Nothing that we have in ourselves, in our finite structure, is absolute. Only if there is an awareness of something unconditional or infinite within us can we understand why the projected images have to be divine figures or symbols. So in the terms of the greatest theoreticians of projection, I criticize the modern theories of projection which circulate in popular unreflective thought. Here you have a weapon with which to face this popular talk about projection.

Feuerbach did something here which Marx acknowledged as the final and definitive criticism of religion. We cannot understand Karl Marx without understanding his relation to Feuerbach. He said that Feuerbach solved the problem of religion once for all. Religion is a projection. It is something subjective in us which we put into the sky of the absolute. But then he went one step beyond Feuerbach. He said that Feuerbach did a great job, but he did not go far enough. He did not explain why projection was done at all, and this, Marx said, cannot be explained in terms of the individual man. This can only be explained in terms of the social existence of men, and more particularly in the class situation of men. Religion is the escape of those who are oppressed by the upper classes into an imaginary fulfillment in the realm of the absolute. Marx's negation of religion is a result of his understanding of the social condition of man.

Here you see the great influence these ideas have had. The anti-religious attitude of almost half of present-day mankind is rooted in this seemingly professorial struggle between Hegel, Feuerbach, and Marx, with both of the latter coming from Hegel. Feuerbach turned Hegel upside down, and then Marx introduced the sociological element. The projection of the transcendent world is the projection of the disinherited in this world. This was such a powerful argument that it convinced the masses of people. It took more than one hundred years before the labor movements in Europe were able to overcome this Feuerbach-Marxian argument against Hegel's attempt to unite Christianity and the modern mind.

These people whom I have mentioned are called the Hegelian left wing. Against them stood theologians who belonged to the Hegelian right wing: Marheineke, Biedermann, Pfleiderer. They tried to show that it is possible under Hegelian presuppositions to have a tenable and justifiable Christian theology.

B. Schelling's Criticism of Hegel

We have been discussing some of Hegel's critics, people like Feuerbach and Marx. I come now to that critic whom I consider to be the most fundamental philosophically and theologically, and perhaps most important for our intellectual life today. The first great existentialist critic of essentialist thinking since Blaise Pascal (1623–1662), who was in a way the predecessor of all existentialists, was Friedrich Schelling (1775–1854). We have to remember that he was prior to Kierkegaard. In fact Kierkegaard attended Schelling's Berlin lectures in the middle of the nineteenth century, and used many of Schelling's categories in his fight against Hegel.

I know that the name of this man Schelling is almost unknown in this country. There are several reasons for this. One of the reasons is that Schelling, together with Fichte, is a bridge between Kant and Hegel. After you have reached the other side of the bridge, you tend often to forget the bridge itself. Kant is the one who began German classical philosophy, and Hegel is the end. All this happened in no more than half a century. But during this half century Fichte and Schelling were working, first continuing Kant, and then giving basic thoughts to Hegel. Of course, they were not mere bridges between Kant and Hegel. They were independent philosophers having an influence reaching beyond Hegel up to our time. I recall the unforgettable moment when by chance I came into possession of the very rare first edition of the collected works of Schelling in a bookstore on my way to the University of Berlin. I had no money, but I bought it anyway, and this spending of nonexistent money was probably more important than all the other nonexistent or sometimes existing money that I have spent. For what I learned from Schelling became determinative of my own philosophical and theological development.

I have told you already how Schelling synthesized or combined Kant's critical epistemology and Spinoza's mystical ontology. But Schelling was more than this synthesis. In some way Goethe did that too. But Schelling became the philosopher of Romanticism. He represented not only the beginning of romantic thinking in the philosophy of nature. There were elements of this already in Fichte and even in Kant's third *Critique* where he introduced the *Gestalt* theory of biological understanding of life. But Schelling kept pace with the different changing periods of Romanticism, and the decisive turning point was when Romanticism started to become existentialism. In this sense Schelling is far more than a bridge between Kant and Hegel. Long after Hegel's death, he was the greatest critic of Hegel. In Schelling the second phase of Romanticism became existentialist. He arrived finally at an understanding of reality which radically contradicted his former period. This happened through philosophical experiences, understanding of religion, and profound participation in life within himself and around him. He did not, however, abolish what Hegel and he had done before. He preserved a philosophy of essence. Against this he put the philosophy of existence. Existentialism is not a philosophy which can stand on its own legs. Actually it has no legs. It is always based on a vision of the essential structure of reality. In this sense it is based on essentialism, and cannot live without it. If you say that man is evil, you must have a concept of man in his essential goodness, otherwise the word "evil" would not make any sense. Without the distinction between good and evil the words themselves lose their meaning. And if you say that man's structure is distorted in time and space, or that it is "fallen," then you must have something from which he is fallen. You must have some structure which is distorted in time and space. So mere existentialism does not exist. But it can be the main emphasis of a philosophical work and even of a whole period in philosophy. In Schelling's later years it was the main emphasis, although essentialism was presupposed, but not developed. This is also true of our philosophers and poets. I can best illustrate this in terms of the present-day saint of existentialism, the novelist Kafka. In him you will not find that essentialism is explained, but you will always find that it is implicit and presupposed. For without this he could not even describe the futile search for meaning in the novel, *The Castle,* or the horrible experience of a guilt of which he is not conscious in his other novel, *The Trial.* The essentialist understanding of the human situation is behind it, behind the existentialist description. You find this everywhere. If in T. S. Eliot you have the age of anxiety described, this presupposes the possibility of not having anxiety in the radical sense in which he describes it. Thus all existentialism presupposes that from which it breaks away, namely, essentialism. You have it wonderfully expressed in Pascal who relates the God of Abraham, Isaac, and Jacob to both man's greatness and his misery.

Now in his earlier periods, Schelling developed to the extreme the Spinozistic principle, the principle of the ontological unity of everything in the eternal substance. This principle of identity is very hard to understand by people educated in nominalistic thinking, as you all are, whether you know it or not. The nominalistic mind is a mind which sees particulars and relations of particulars, and which uses exclusively logical and scientific methods to get at particulars. The very question of an ultimate identity is very difficult to comprehend. But at least one historical fact should be realized, namely, that by far the greatest part of mankind is not nominalistic, that all Asian religions are based on the principle of identity, and that Greek philosophy from the very beginning started with it when Parmenides said, "Where there is being, there is also the logos of being." This means that the word can grasp being, that the rational structure makes it possible for us to speak about being, and we can use words meaningfully.

Now this fundamental principle underlies the whole history of Christian thought. All the church fathers presupposed this Parmenidean idea, only enriching it by trinitarian symbolism. Where God is, there is his *Logos*, and they are one in the dynamic creativity of the Spirit. It is a necessary idea because it explains something which all thinking presupposes. The presupposition is that there is truth and that truth can be reached by us. In order to have truth, in order to make a true judgment, the subject who makes the judgment and the thing about which the judgment is made must, so to speak, be at one and the same place. They must come together. We use the word "grasp" for this. You must "grasp" the structure of reality. But in order to reach the object, there must be a fundamental belongingness of the subject to the object. This is the one side of the principle of identity, namely, that subject and object are not absolutely separated, that although they are separated in our finite existence, they belong essentially together. There is an eternal unity between them.

The other side of the concept of identity is the problem of the one and the many. This is the great Platonic problem. How is it possible that the many are diverse, but nevertheless form the unity of a cosmos, of a world, of a universe? Even in the word "universe" the word "one" is contained. How is that possible? Again the answer is that there must be an original unity of the one and the many. The principle of identity says that the one substance—Spinoza calls it substance, a very powerful and originally Aristotelian and Scholastic term—makes togetherness possible in the same time and the same space. Without the one substance there could not be causal connections between things, and there couldn't be substantial union and separation of different substances. This latter point is emphasized especially in the Asian religions. I remember a really Spinozistic argument used by a high priest in a Buddhist monastery. In discussing the question of how community is possible between human beings, he said that if every human being has his own substance, then community is impossible. They are eternally separated. I answered that human community is possible only if individuals have their independent substance—substance means, of course, standing upon oneself—otherwise there is no community, but only identity. Where there is no separation, there is no community either. It was with this argument that I left Japan, in the last important discussion I had there.

The philosophers of identity argued that there must be an underlying identity. I would never deny this, for if we were absolute strangers to each other, if there were no element of identity in the common substance of our being human, we could not speak to each other. We would not be able to have any form of community. It is the emphasis on diversity which separates the Western from the Eastern world. It was of the greatest importance that Christianity came from Judaism. In Judaism the individual personality has personal responsibility before the eternal God, and is not dissolved into the identity of everything as in Asia.

These problems in the history of religion are also the problems which preoccupied a philosopher like Schelling. Under the influence of Spinoza he was grasped by the one substance, by that which is beyond subject and object, beyond spirit and matter. His whole philosophy of nature was an attempt to show the indwelling of the potential spirit in all natural objects and how it comes to its fulfillment in man. The romantic philosophy of nature is nothing else than a carrying out of the program of Nicholas of Cusa, the presence of the infinite in the finite, and the program of Spinoza, the one substance in all its modifications, and Schelling's own program, the presence of the spiritual in the material. Thus the philosophy of nature becomes in Schelling a system of intuitions, in a half-philosophical, half-aesthetic way, of the power of being in nature, a power which is beyond the separation of the spiritual and the material.

Now a modern scientist might say that this is all imagination or aesthetic fancy and has nothing to do with his work. But not all modern scientists would say this. I know scientists in biology and psychology of the *Gestalt* school who follow in the line of Schelling, although they have to reject his concrete results. In any case Schelling is the initiator of this romantic philosophy of nature, and because of it he became famous in his mid-twenties. At that time he was the most famous of the German philosophers, with the exception of Fichte, and was better known than Hegel who started much later and developed quite slowly.

In Schelling's philosophy nature is construed dynamically and thus also anti-Spinozistically. In Spinoza nature is presented geometrically whereas in Schelling it is presented partly biologically and partly psychologically. In this construction the process of nature proceeds from the lowest to the highest forms of nature, and finally to man in terms of a contrast of two principles. He called the one principle the unconscious and the other the conscious. He tried to show how slowly in all different forms of nature consciousness develops until it comes to man where it becomes self-consciousness. Then a new development starts, the development of culture and history. Schelling's discovery of the unconscious was, however, a rediscovery, because the philosophers of nature in the Renaissance, Paracelsus and Boehme, around A.D. 1600 already knew about the unconscious element in man and even applied it to both God and nature.

Many of you probably believe that the unconscious is the discovery of Freud. Freud's merit is not the discovery of this concept, but the application of it in terms of a scientific method derived from medical psychology. The concept itself goes back to Schelling, not directly, but by way of Schopenhauer, the voluntaristic philosopher and critic of Hegel, and by way of Eduard von Hartmann who wrote a whole book on the philosophy of the unconscious. And it is possible to show that this book was known to Freud. This is then one element in Schelling's philosophy of nature which has survived and is still valid. In Kant and Fichte you find the predominance of practical reason, of the moral imperative. Religion is only an appendix to the moral imperative. It is at best a tool to express the unconditional character of the moral imperative. The philosophy of Fichte is concerned with the morally deciding self, the ego, the "ich" as he called it, which is completely separate from nature. Nature is only the material which man must use in himself, in his body which is nature, and outside of himself in his surroundings, in order to actualize the moral imperative. Nature has no meaning in itself. So here with a kind of holy wrath Schelling turned against Fichte and said, "It is a blasphemy of the Creator to think that nature is only there in order to be the material for our moral glory; nature has the divine glory in itself." In this way he was brought to the philosophy of nature.

But there is an even deeper consequence of this term. This is the turn toward the concept of grace over against the concept of law. If nature, which makes no conscious decision and has no moral imperative, has within itself the divine presence, then the divine presence is not only dependent on our moral action. It is prior in the development of reality, and it is also subsequent to our moral action. It is below and above the moral imperative. Schelling's philosophy or theology was very much a doctrine of grace, stressing the given divine reality before our merits and before our moral acts. So natural philosophy was a way of rediscovering grace over against the moralism of the Enlightenment. This was one of the great achievements of Romanticism for theology. Here I would say that because American Protestantism has never had a romantic period, aside from a few individuals, it has preserved up to today a religion in which the enlightened moralistic attitude is predominant, and the concept of grace is quite strange. The teachings of Jesus are moral or doctrinal laws. You will not hear very much in sermons in this country about the presence of the divine preceding all that we do. Another consequence of this is the disappearance of sacramental feeling. Sacramental thinking is meaningful only if the infinite is present in the finite, if the finite is not only subject to the commands of the infinite but has in itself saving powers, powers of the presence of the divine. This is a rediscovery of Romanticism. Of course, it was present in the whole sacramental experience of the early church, but to a great extent it was lost in the Reformation criticism, and then finally lost in the Enlightenment which based itself only on the imperative.

So now we have a whole new vision based on the principle of identity. Later Schelling went beyond the philosophy of nature to a philosophical understanding of reality through the arts. The aesthetic element broke through in full power. During his period of aesthetic idealism he made the arts the substitute for religion. Artistic intuition is the way in which we see God. The divine comes to us through the arts. Neither the biblical miracles nor any other are the manifestation of God, but every work of art is the great miracle of the full revelation of the divine substance.

After Schelling had become famous for his philosophy of nature, then developed his philosophy of aesthetic intuition, he finished this period by something which he called the philosophy of identity. Here the principle which was underlying all his periods was expressed, not in a geometrical but in a logical way, and in a way which was the extreme fulfillment of what Spinoza intended. This represented the end of essentialism in Schelling's development. For Schelling 1809 was an important year because of the death of Caroline Schlegel, the wife of his friend Schlegel, the famous translator of Shakespeare. Schelling married her. She was one of the great women of Romanticism. Her letters are a classical document of that period. Her premature death was a tremendous catastrophe for Schelling. Shortly after this two things came out. One was the dialogue *Clara* in which he used the Platonic form of the dialogue to develop the idea that eternal life means the essentialization of what we are in our essential being as seen by God. It is not a continuation of existence in time and space but participation in eternity with what we are essentially. But more important for the history of man's spiritual life was his writing on human freedom.[3] This is probably his most important work because here the concept of freedom breaks into the concept of identity. Freedom, of course, presupposes the possibility of choice. Identity as such is eternally fulfilled. So David Friedrich Strauss could say of Schelling that the principle of freedom drove him out of the restfulness of the principle of identity, which was spelled out in his *System of Philosophy*, as he called it. Here he had spoken like Spinoza of the eternal restfulness, not running for a purpose, but receiving the power of being directly by contemplation.

But then something happened. If you read the two books, *The System of Philosophy*, which is his philosophy of identity, and then *Of Human Freedom*, you feel that you have entered a new world. What had happened was his personal experience of the death of Caroline. But the logic of thought also played a part, the necessity of explaining manifoldness and diversity, and life itself which goes out of identity into alteration and wants to return to itself. How could this be explained? How can we explain that we are living here in time and space in continuous action, as we do, if there is an eternal ground in which the substance which is in all of us lies in eternal rest. The explanation was given in terms of freedom. Freedom breaks out of identity. Here he used

[3] Friedrich W. J. Schelling, *Of Human Freedom*, translated by James Gutman (Chicago: The Open Court Publishing Co., 1936).

the imagery of his philosophy of nature. He construed two or three principles in the ground of the divine, the unconscious or dark principle, the principle of will which is able to contradict itself, on the one hand, and the principle of logos, or the principle of light, on the other hand. There is here the possibility that the unconscious will, the drive in the depths of the divine life, might break away from the identity. But it cannot do so in the divine life itself. The spiritual unity of the two principles keeps them always together. But in man, in the creature, it can break away. In the creature freedom can turn against its own divine substance, its own divine ground. So the myth of the fall is interpreted by him, following the line of Plato, through Origen and Boehme, as the transcendent fall. The fall is not something which happened once upon a time, but something which happens all the time, in all creatures. This fall is the breaking away from the creative ground from which we come in the power of freedom.

This was expressed by Schelling in terms of the problem of good and evil. He showed that the possibility of good and evil is given in God. Evil is possible because the will in the divine ground is able to contradict itself. But in God it never comes to a disruption. Only the free decision of the creature to turn against its created ground accounts for evil. The principles are eternally in union in God, the abysmal depth in the divine life, the prerational development of the will, the principle of the logos or light or reason or structure or meaning, and their unity which he calls the spirit. These three principles are in the divine life, but in the divine life the finite which is present is unable to break away. The unity of the principles can be disrupted only in creatures. This is something which you can find in empirical terminology in Freud and in every modern psychotherapeutic book of profound formulations. You can find it most openly expressed in Jung's writings, and more hiddenly in Freud when he speaks of *eros* and *thanatos*, love and death. In Schelling it appeared in the highest abstraction in the fundamental vision of the nature of the will in relation to the nature of the structure. If you run ahead into the nineteenth century, you will discover the influence of these ideas everywhere. The whole of French voluntarism up to Bergson was dependent on these ideas; in Germany Schopenhauer and Nietzsche were equally dependent on them, and they have had a great effect on the philosophy of Whitehead up to the present time, especially in Charles Hartshorne, the main representative of the Whiteheadian school. So these ideas have had a great influence on history-making personalities.

The influence on theology was not less decisive. Some of the great theologians in the nineteenth century worked in the line of Schelling. But Schelling never rested. After this breakthrough he became silent for many years. In his old age he was called to Berlin in order to fight against the left-wing Hegelians. Many important people attended these lectures in the middle of the nineteenth century. The most important was Søren Kierkegaard, a transcription of whose notes on Schelling's Berlin lectures is to be found in the Copenhagen library in Denmark. This latest period reflected in Schelling's Berlin lectures is a tragic period. These lectures were prematurely published by an enemy of his and, of course, poorly published, which made him many critics, some of them even contemptuous of his work. But what he did is nevertheless worthy of careful study because there is hardly one category in twentieth-century existentialist poetry, literature, philosophy, and indirectly the visual arts, which you cannot find in these lectures. They are to be found in the last four volumes of his collected works. And when people like Friedrich Trendelenburg (1802–1872) and Kierkegaard criticized Hegel's logic, and his confusion of dialectics and history, they were doing what Schelling had done more fully in his latest works.

In these latest writings you will find a distinction between two types of philosophy, negative and positive philosophy. Negative philosophy is philosophy of identity or essentialism. He called it negative because it abstracts from the concrete situation as all science has to do. It does not imply a negative evaluation of this philosophy, but refers to the method of abstraction. You abstract from the concrete situation until you come to the essential structures of reality, the essence of man, the essence of animals, the essence of mind, of body, etc. Negative philosophy deals with the realm of ideas, as Plato called it. But negative philosophy does not say anything about what is positively given. The essence of man does not say anything about the fact that man does exist in time and space. The term "positive philosophy" expresses the same thing that we call existentialism today. It deals with the positive, the actual situation in time and space. This is not possible without the negative side, the essential structure of reality. There could not be a tree if there were not the structure of treehood eternally even before trees existed, and even after trees go out of existence on earth altogether. The same is true of man. The essence of man is eternally given before any man appeared on earth. It is potentially or essentially given, but it is not actually or existentially given. So here we are at a great turning point of philosophical thinking. Now Schelling as a philosopher described man's existential situation. We are then in the second period of Romanticism. The unconscious has pushed toward the surface. The demonic elements in the underground of life and of human existence have become manifest. This can even be called a kind of empiricism. Schelling sometimes called it higher empiricism, higher because it takes things not simply in terms of their scientific laboratory appearances, but in correlation with their essential nature. Thus he arrives at all these categories now current in existentialist literature. We have the problem of anxiety dealt with, the problem of the relation between the unconscious and the conscious, the problem of guilt, the problem of the demonic, etc. Here the observation of things, and not the development of their rational structure, becomes decisive.

What is said against much of twentieth-century existentialism can be said of his philosophy. It is pessimistic. But the term "pessimism" should be avoided because that refers to an emotional reaction. Philosophy cannot be pessimistic. Only a person can be pessimistic in his psychological attitude. This philosophy describes the situation, the conflict between essence and existence, and this conflict is expressed in the concepts of existentialist literature.

But Schelling not only asks the existentialist questions; he also tries to give religious answers to them. This he does in terms of the classical Christian tradition. He is much nearer to Orthodoxy, whereas Kierkegaard is nearer to Pietism and the theology of revivalism, if we can use that term. In any case, for Schelling it is Lutheran Orthodoxy which offers the answers to the existentialist questions. This answer is given in a powerful vision of the history of religion. Here he has given a key, to me and many others, to the meaning of the history of religion. The history of religion cannot simply be explained in psychological terms. It has to do with powers of reality which grasp the unconscious, or which come out of the unconscious and grasp the consciousness of men and produce the symbolism in the history of religion. Of course, he had to use the limited knowledge available to him at that time about the history of religion. He knew much more of this than Hegel, and was himself responsible for the later intensive development in the religious-historical studies of Friedrich Müller (1823–1900). But what Schelling did know was interpreted by him not in terms of meaningless imagination or in terms of subjective psychological projection, but in terms of powers of being which grasp the human mind itself. These go through man's psyche, his soul, through his conscious and unconscious mind, but they do not derive from it. They come from the roots men have in the depths of reality itself.

So the different types of religions express the different powers of being by which men are grasped. The terrible sacrifices in religion, the tremendous seriousness in the history of religions, the fact that religion is the most glorious and the most cruel part of man's history, all this is understandable only if religion is not a matter of wishful thinking, but is a matter of powers of being which men encounter. In this light he explains the inner struggle, the terrible struggles in the history of religion.

This brings my consideration of Schelling to an end. You see that he can be considered the main and the most powerful critic of Hegel, not a critic who breaks out into a merely naturalistic or secularistic opposition to the great synthesis, but one who offers motives for a new synthesis on the basis of his criticism.

C. The Religious Revival and Its Theological Consequences

Most of the theological movements in the nineteenth century began as critical theology, critical of the great synthesis. Theologies and philosophies do not fall like hailstones from heaven, but are prepared in the movement of history, and in all the realms of this movement, sociological, political, as well as religious. Now I come to the religious background of the conservative criticism of Hegel.

1. The Nature of the European Revival

There was around 1830 a movement called the "awakening movement"[4] which swept throughout Europe like a storm. It was not confined to Europe, for at about the same time there was the revivalist movement in America. It touched France, Germany, and Switzerland. In England it was somehow connected with the revival of the Catholic element in the Church of England. Everywhere individuals and small groups were grasped by a new understanding of the problem of human existence and the meaning of the Christian message for them. Usually they would gather around the Bible in small groups. This movement was not restricted to any special sociological groups, although by this time the labor movement was heading in a different direction. It was very strongly represented among the landed aristocracy in East Germany and in Europe generally, among the small peasants in southwestern Germany, and among bourgeois people in other European countries; it was often connected with romantic reactions against the Enlightenment; it was rooted in what I would call the law of nature, valid in both physical and spiritual dimensions, the law, namely, that there can be no vacuum, no void. Where there is an empty space, it will be filled. The Enlightenment with its consequences, especially its materialistic trends in France and later in Germany, created a feeling of a vacuum in the spiritual life. The preaching of the Enlightenment was a kind of lecturing on all possible subjects, agricultural, technical, political, or psychological, but the dimension of the ultimate was lacking. So into this empty space an intense pietistic movement stressing conversion entered and filled it with a warm spirit of vital piety. When I began my studies in the University of Halle in 1904, now in the East Zone of Germany, I was a pupil of the greatest personality of this faculty, Martin Kähler. He was an unusual personality, standing within the classic-romantic tradition. He told us that when he was a young man he knew his Goethe by heart. He was filled with the traditions of German classical poetry, literature, and philosophy. Then this movement of revivalism grasped him, and he was converted in the literal sense of "being turned

4 In German, *die Erweckungsbewegung.*

around." He became a biblical theologian with the highest spiritual power over us. There in Halle one could see the influence of this movement. In the student corporations at the University—what are called fraternities here—the leading activities centered around dueling and drinking. Revivalism changed all this. Some fraternities were set up on definitely Christian principles, forbidding excessive drinking and dueling between students. This was the great side in the revivalist movement. This was still visible in the fraternity of which I became a member in 1904. The Christian principles were taken in utter seriousness. One of the most common topics of discussion was: Can you be a member of such a group if you are in doubt? In one of the meetings of all the Christian fraternities all over Germany and Switzerland I formulated the statement that the foundation is not dependent on us, but on the Christian principle. The individual person doubts, or he does not doubt, and his doubt might even be very radical, but if he takes very seriously the problem of his doubt and his faith, and struggles with the problem of the loss of faith in him, then he is a member of our fraternity. Ever since as a professor of theology I have told my students that faith embraces itself and the doubt about itself. Younger and older ministers have had to be told the same thing. When Martin Kähler was in his seventies and lecturing on the principle of justification by grace through faith, he told us: Do not think that at my age one becomes a fully serene, mature, believing, and regenerated human being. The inner struggle is going on to the last day no matter how old one becomes. This means that his pietism was not a perfectionist pietism, as it often became on Calvinist soil. Rather it was a typically Lutheran type of pietism in which the paradox of justification by grace through faith, God's acceptance of the unacceptable ones, is a fundamental principle.

So here is a motive for theology which looks a bit different from others we have discussed. Out of this some interesting things came. In this second wave of pietism, as in the first one (cf. Zinzendorf and the Moravians, the Wesley brothers and the Methodists) the missionary interest became important. It is interesting that in both the original pietist reaction against Orthodoxy and the second pietist reaction against the Enlightenment there arose a renewed missionary zeal. In the power of their experience those grasped by the revivalist movements wanted to communicate that power to paganism all over the world. So in the thirties a new theology of missions arose. It was a limited one. The main idea was still as in early pietism to save souls out of all nations. Just as the conversion experience was an individual one, so the missionary activity was individualistic in character. It had the idea of converting as many pagans as possible to rescue them from eternal damnation. There was, however, one new element in the nineteenth-century missionary zeal. It was directed not only to the pagans outside of Christendom, to non-Christians and Jews, but also to those at home. This was home missions or "inner missions," as it was called in Germany. This was particularly interesting because it was connected with a strong feeling of social responsibility for the disinherited people.

The way in which this idea of social responsibility developed was interesting. On Lutheran soil it was impossible to have revolutionary movements as could happen on Calvinist or radical-evangelical soil. Yet, this Lutheran pietism was very much interested in the social conditions of the masses in the beginning of the industrial revolution. But it did not have the revolutionary idea of changing the structure of society. It only worked to help the victims of the social conditions. The revolutionary idea was taken over by the socialists, and later in the twentieth century, by the communists. We find the germ of this revolutionary idea already in Thomas Münzer, the leader of the peasant revolt in the Reformation period. Thomas Münzer is a very interesting phenomenon. He did not say that we must change society as such, but that we must give the poor people who are enslaved in work, day and night without interruption, the possibility of reading the Bible, and of having spiritual experiences, experiences of the Spirit. He had observed in the small towns of Saxony where some early capitalist forms of production were used in the factories that these people had no Sunday, insufficient hours of rest and sleep, no chance for an education, no schools, no reading or writing. His socialist ideas came out of this observation of the spiritual situation of the urban working classes, and of the peasant classes.

The reasoning of the nineteenth-century revivalist movement was the same. The healthy part of society should give help to the sick part. The sick part is composed of the laboring people who were exploited in those victorious days of a ruthless capitalism. But home mission was still basically conceived of as conversion of those who were estranged from the church. Indeed the laboring masses were completely estranged from the churches. There was no call for revolution. Revolution was out of the question on Lutheran soil. But there was the call to assume the responsibility of helping the other classes to understand spiritual values of which they were being deprived by their life situation. I cannot develop here all the sociological background—the conditions of the agricultural workers, out of which all the city workers originally came, because there was no industry, and when the industry started, they came from the villages, but in the villages the lowest classes were already estranged from the churches, because the churches were always on the side of the upper classes.

This sense of social responsibility was certainly important, but it was not enough. The members of the church were given the feeling that it was enough to exercise personal charity toward unfortunate individuals. This in itself, however, served to estrange church people from a real understanding of the new sociological situation created by the industrial revolution. Therefore, in spite of the feeling of revivalism and social responsibility for the disinherited people, the rise of socialism and communism could not be prevented in Europe, because it was not seen that individual help was entirely fruitless in relation to the masses of industrial workers who soon numbered in the millions. No individual help could possibly cope with this situation.

To anticipate what happened much later, I would like to say a few words about the religious socialist movement of the twentieth century. This movement tried to combine two elements: on the one hand, a sense of social responsibility for the laboring, disinherited masses, which characterized the theology and piety of the awakening movement, and on the other hand, taking seriously the transformed sociological situation, by not thinking only in terms of individual relations, but accepting the analyses of the social situation of the French and German socialists, especially the profoundest of them made by Karl Marx. So the religious socialist movement combined the heritage of nineteenth-century revivalism and the rise of socialism. When we founded this movement in

Germany after the first World War, we were deeply aware that the social attitudes of the revivalist people and of the Ritschlians, who thought on an individualistic basis, were inadequate to the new situation described by the socialist writers as a complete dehumanization, a *Verdinglichung,* a thingification, an objectification of the masses of people. They were transformed from being persons into being objects of working power which could be bought. They had to sell themselves in order to survive. The quarters in which they lived were not slums in the modern sense, but they were bare of anything human. I remember my horror when I went into the living quarters of the working people in cities like Berlin or in the Ruhr country where the largest industry is concentrated, and saw the kind of dehumanized existence these people endured. Our response to this situation came in the form of combining the revivalist tradition of social responsibility and the sociological analysis of the socialist writers, especially Marx and Engels.

2. *The Theology of Repristination*

There were still other consequences of the awakening movement, especially a revival of traditional theology. The pupils of Schleiermacher, Hegel, and Schelling had produced a theology of mediation, which combined the rediscovered biblical reality with the concerns of the modern mind. But alongside of this theology of mediation there arose a theology of restoration or of repristination, or as we would call it today, a conservative theology as over against a liberal theology. This repristination theology was a radical return to and rediscovery of the orthodox tradition. The theologians in this movement did not produce many new theological thoughts, but they did one valuable thing for us. They opened up the treasures of classical Orthodoxy. I say this even though I am completely opposed to a theology of repristination, for I wish that every student would learn in Latin the classical formulations of Protestant Orthodox theology. Then he would be as educated as the Roman Catholic theologians who know their Thomas Aquinas or their Suarez or some other classical theologian. Then, of course, one can go beyond that. But to go beyond without having been within Orthodoxy is not a wholesome attitude. But this is what has happened more and more. So I say now that the one good thing that the theology of re-pristination did for us was to show forth the treasures of the past as matters which still concern us. It still concerns me what Johann Gerhard or other great Protestant scholastics said about a given doctrine. They knew many of our problems and offered solutions which we should not simply forget. Besides, they were not unlearned as our present-day fundamentalists who are direct products of revivalism, but without theological education. It is a fundamentalism based simply on piety and on biblical interpretation which is ignorant of the way in which the Bible was written and came into existence. So you cannot compare classical Orthodoxy with fundamentalism. But in any case, a repristination theology could not last, because history does not run backward but forward.

This restoration theology was an expression of the dissolution of the great synthesis. These forms of Orthodoxy despised what had happened since the Enlightenment. They went back to classical Orthodoxy. They did not accept the historical criticism of the biblical literature. They took the Bible literally. They even believed that the Pentateuch was written by Moses, even though one of the books tells about his death. Such absurdities are always the consequence of the doctrine of literal inspiration. This view could not and did not last. The real bearers of the development in theology were the theologians of mediation, people like Martin Kähler and the theologians of the Ritschlian school.

3. *Natural Science and the Fight over Darwinism*

Another attack against the great synthesis came from the direction of modern science. Schelling's philosophy of nature and Hegel's mechanical application of the categories of man's spirit to nature produced the great reaction of empirical science. Empirical science followed the method of analysis and synthesis, as we have it in the physical sciences, the mathematical structure of nature as a presupposition, the mechanical movement as the metaphysical background, the Newtonian ideas about natural laws, in short, a mechanical naturalism in all realms, especially in physics and medicine. This movement came to its direct expression in Darwinism, which is worth considering from the point of view of Christian theology.

This mechanical or mechanistic naturalism threatened Christian theology and so Christian theology had to do the work of defense.—There are other kinds of naturalism, the vitalistic naturalism of Nietzsche, the dynamic naturalism of Bergson and Whitehead. This mechanistic naturalism we sometimes call materialistic, but the term "materialism" itself has three different meanings, so I do not use it here.—In any case, Christian theology became a theology of retreat and defense in the face of this mechanistic naturalism. This was true of the Ritschlian theology, the theology of mediation or apologetic theology, and of most of the theological books that were written in the second half of the nineteenth century. Christian theology was like an army retreating in face of an advancing army. With every new breakthrough of the advancing army, in this case modern science, Christian theology would attempt to protect the Christian tradition which still remained intact. Then a new breakthrough would make the previous defense untenable, and so another retreat and setting up a new defense would be necessary. This went on and on.

This whole spectacle, this fight between science and religion, has brought contempt upon the term "apologetic." It was a poor form of apologetic. The first great shock which had to be accepted was the Copernican world view. Galileo, the greatest representative of this idea, was forced by the Inquisition to recant, but his recanting did not help the church at all. Soon the theologians had to accept the Copernican world view. Then there was Newton's mechanics of bodies moving according to eternal natural laws; the concept of natural law was established and philosophically formulated by Kant. This prevented thinking about interferences of a divine being; God was placed alongside the world, and not permitted to interfere with it. Then theology came to the defense of miracles, the idea of the possibility of divine interferences, which of course presupposes a miserable concept of God who would have to destroy his creation in order to do his work of salvation. But this was the apologetic situation. Then another retreat was required because the defense of miracles in this way was untenable. A further shock came with the idea of evolution. Then a six-day creation was defended, then abandoned. Evolution said that life has developed out of the inorganic realm. Then where is God? According to the traditional idea of creation God has created the organic forms; they have not developed out of the inorganic forms. Therefore, a particular work of God's creation must be postulated and on this thin thread the whole apologetic position was suspended. There was the lacuna in scientific knowledge, for science was not able to show how the organic developed out of the inorganic. Theologians enjoyed this lacuna, for they could place God in this gap left by science. Where science could not work any more, God was put to work, so to speak. God filled the gaps left by science.

That was an unworthy idea of God. The position was indefensible so theologians had to withdraw again. But one last point was kept. That is the creation of man. Here the Roman Church still sticks to the idea that even if the evolutionary process is as presupposed by biology today, there is still one point that cannot be explained biologically, namely, the immortal soul which God has given man, the higher animal, at some moment in the process of evolution. This was and still is a last defense against science, but this last defense is not tenable either, for it presupposes a substance, the soul, which is a separate form from the form of the body. But in the Aristotelian sense, the soul is the form of the body and you cannot separate them. Moreover, the concept of eternal life has nothing to do with such a dualistic construction of an immortal soul put at one moment into man's body. When this last defense is given up, science has conquered all apologetic positions. And this is a good thing. Then the situation must be seen in an absolutely new way. Science lives and works in another dimension and therefore cannot interfere with the religious symbols of creation, fulfillment, forgiveness, and incarnation, nor can religion interfere with scientific statements. No scientific statement about the way in which living beings have come into existence or how the first cell developed out of large molecules can have direct bearing on theology. Indirectly, of course, everything is a concern of theology. For when science describes the way in which life is construed and is developed, then indirectly it says something about God, the creative ground of life, but not in terms of an interference of a highest being in the processes of nature.

This whole struggle between science and religion is no doubt in the past for you. But it was not so when I began the study of theology. At that time apologetic theology was full of confidence that science would never find a way of showing the development from, let us say, the original mud to the first cell. But science can show this to a great extent, perhaps not fully, but this is a matter of experiment. Theology does not need to put God to work to fill an empty space in our scientific knowledge.

The struggle over Darwin dealt not only with this general evolutionary idea, but more concretely with the genesis of man. The "monkey trial" was a last remnant of this struggle which was so prominent in the nineteenth century. It was a great shock which the church had to absorb after the initial shocks of the Copernican revolution and the Newtonian idea of natural law. I may be wrong, but I believe that aside from some literalists in the South or in the Bible belt no one in the younger generation or among theologians is involved in this conflict any longer. People presuppose that science has to go its way, and that the religious dimension is different from the scientific. But in the nineteenth century this affair disrupted the faith of millions of people. The laborers who read the socialist literature decided negatively against religion; they looked at religion as always interfering in the arena of scientific discussions. And when religion did this, it was a lost cause. It has taken over a half a century to overcome the antireligious attitude among the scientists and the antiscientific attitude among the religious people. If we are out of this situation now, I hope we never return to it. And we should avoid remnants of this kind of apologetics today. For instance, we should not try to base our doctrine of freedom on Heisenberg's principle of indeterminacy, as if to say that since there is some element of indeterminacy in nature, we can speak of freedom. Perhaps tomorrow this principle will be replaced by another, and then your whole wonderful apologetic collapses, and you join the retreating army of apologists. The theologians of the twentieth century should learn this lesson from the nineteenth century. You cannot apologetically establish symbols which belong to the dimension of the ultimate upon a description of finite relations.

You can speak of the structure of nature, as I have done in the third volume of *Systematic Theology,* through all the realms of the natural. But this is not done for apologetic purposes, but is in line with Thomas Aquinas' statement that he who knows anything, knows something about God. Whatever we know in any realm bears witness to the creative ground of it. In this sense we must deal with statements of science. But we must do so also in another sense. For the work of the scientists is of the highest theological interest insofar as it reveals the logos of being, the inner structure of reality, which is not in opposition to the Logos which has appeared in the Christ, but is the same Logos. Therefore, in this sense the witness of science is the witness to God. This is the right relationship and is not one of fighting against each other in terms of unjustified interferences.

D. Kierkegaard's Existential Theology

Søren Kierkegaard must also be dealt with as a contributor to the breakdown of the universal synthesis, although his greatest influence has been exercised in our time rather than in his own. He made a new start based on a combination of an existentialist philosophy and a pietistic, revivalistic theological criticism of the great synthesis. More specifically, he combined Lutheran pietism of the revivalist type, including the orthodox content of revivalism, with the categories of Schelling's existentialism. Although he denied Schelling's solution, he took over the categories. His criticism, together with that of Marx and Nietzsche, is historically most important. But none of these three became influential in world-historical terms in the nineteenth century. Kierkegaard was largely a forgotten individual in his century. I recall with pride how as students of theology in Halle we came into contact with Kierkegaard's thought through translations made by an isolated individual in Württemberg. In the years 1905–1907 we were grasped by Kierkegaard. It was a very great experience. We could not accept the theological orthodoxy of repristination. We could not accept especially those "positive"—in the special sense of "conservative"—theologians who disregarded the historical-critical school. For this was valid science which was carried on by this school. It cannot be denied if honest research is conducted into the historical foundations of the New Testament.

But on the other hand we had a feeling of moralistic distortion and amystical emptiness, an emptiness in which the warmth of the mystical presence of the divine was missing, as in the whole Ritschlian school. We were not grasped by this moralism. We did not find in it the depths of the consciousness of guilt as classical theology had always had. So we were extremely happy when we encountered Kierkegaard. It was this combination of intense piety which went into the depths of human existence and the philosophical greatness which he had received from Hegel that made him so important for us. The real critical point would be the denial that Hegel's idea of reconciliation is a genuine reconciliation. Man is not reconciled by the reconciliation in the philosopher's head. We will hear the same thing from Marx later on.

We could discuss Kierkegaard in connection with the existentialist movement of the twentieth century, because he became effective only in our own century. Nevertheless, in the structure of this course I prefer to place him in his own historical place where he represents one of the decisive criticisms of Hegel's great synthesis. We will discuss him fairly thoroughly, and you can take this discussion not only as a treatment of nineteenth-century theological thought, but also of twentieth-century theology, for while he wrote in the nineteenth century, his real influence has been significant in the twentieth century. Later we will see similar situations with regard to two other thinkers who were not inner-ecclesiastical representatives of theology, but anti-ecclesiastical representatives. They are Marx, especially in his earlier existentialist protest against Hegel, and then Friedrich Nietzsche, who followed Schopenhauer.

You may be a little surprised that I do not deal more with the theological movements within the church of this period. The reason I do not is that they are not as important as the great critics of Hegel for our own situation. These critics are more fundamental for our theological situation today than are the theologians of mediation. There are some rare exceptions, as for example my own teacher Martin Kähler in Halle. The real impact came from people outside. Of course, Kierkegaard was religiously inside, but as a critic of the church he was perhaps even more radical than Marx and Nietzsche put together.

Kierkegaard has become the fashion in three respects: (a) Reli-

giously, which is most justified, because his religious writings are as
valid today as they were when they were written. (b) As the inspiration
for the dialectical theology, called neo-orthodoxy in this country. In
Europe it is usually called dialectical, which shows its relation to Hegel,
for this term is the main principle of Hegel's thinking. (c) As the
inspiration for Heidegger, the philosopher who has given the name
existentialism to the whole movement which derives from Kierkegaard.

1. Kierkegaard's Criticism of Hegel

As in the case of most of the anti-Hegelians, Kierkegaard's criticism is
based on the concept of reconciliation. For Hegel the world is reconciled
in the mind of the philosopher of religion who has gone through the
different forms of man's spiritual life: the subjective spirit (which is the
psychological side), the objective spirit (the social-ethical and political
side), and the absolute spirit (art, religion, and philosophy). The
philosopher lives in all of them. He is deeply in the religious realm; he
lives in the aesthetic realm; and on the basis of the religious realm he
conceptualizes what is myth and symbol in religion. Out of all this he
develops his philosophy of religion. In this way he mirrors in his mind
the final synthesis after the whole world process has gone through thesis,
antithesis, and synthesis. The divine mind, the absolute mind, comes to
its rest on the basis of religion within the mind of the philosopher who
achieves his highest power when he becomes a philosopher of religion,
conceptualizing the symbols of the religious life. This is for Hegel
reconciliation. This reconciliation in the mind of the philosopher was
the point attacked by all those whom I have mentioned—Schelling,
Feuerbach, pietists, and natural scientists. They all said the world is
unreconciled. The theologians went back to Immanuel Kant and said
the prison of finitude is not pierced, not even by Hegel's great attempt.
The reconciliation of the finite and the infinite has not yet happened.

Kierkegaard did the same thing in a particular way. In the system of
essences reconciliation might be possible, he argued, but the system of
essences is not the reality in which we are living. We are living in the
realm of existence, and in the realm of existence reconciliation has not
yet happened. Existence is the place of decision between good and evil.

Man is in the tragic situation, in the tragic unavoidability of evil. This contradiction in existence means that Hegel is seen as confusing essentialist fulfillment with existential unfulfillment or estrangement. I told you that estrangement or alienation is one of the terms which Hegel created, but which is then turned against him. Nature is estranged spirit for Hegel; the material reality is self-estranged spirit. Now Kierkegaard said that mankind is in this state of estrangement, and Hegel's construction of a continuous series of syntheses in which the negativity of antithesis is overcome in the world process is true only with respect to the essential realm. Symbolically we could perhaps say that it goes on only in the inner life of God. But Kierkegaard emphasized that estrangement is our situation. Only in the inner divine life is there reconciliation, but not in our situation.

Hegel had described the inner divine life in his great logic. The logic is the science of essences in their highest abstraction and their inner dialectical relationship. Then the logicians came along. The man who is very important for the criticism of all essentialism is Trendelenburg. Kierkegaard was dependent on him for his logical criticism of Hegel. His criticism was that the logical process is not a real process; it is not a process in time; it is only a description of logical relations. What Hegel did was to confuse the dialectical process of logic with the actual movement in history. While reconciliation is always a reality in the dialectical process of divine life, it is not a reality in the external process of human existence. So from the logical point of view Hegel was criticized for his fundamental confusion of essence and existence.

Hegel was not able to understand the human situation in terms of anxiety and despair. Kierkegaard could not follow Hegel; all his life he possessed a melancholic disposition. This melancholy of which he often spoke was associated with a curse which his father made against God, and he felt that the reaction to this blasphemy of his father was upon him and never left him free. The point is that such a personality was able to discover things which were not so deeply felt by a character as Hegel, who existed in a bourgeois situation, who felt psychologically more safe and was able to conquer the negative and tragic elements of life which he saw.

2. Ethical Existence and the Human Situation (Anxiety, Despair)

One of the main points connected with Kierkegaard's melancholic personal condition and his feeling of unreconciled reality was his experience of the lonely individual. Here again we have an anticipation of present-day existentialism. The individual stands in solitude before God and the process of the world cannot liberate him from the tremendous responsibility by which he lives in the situation. Again and again he said that the last reality is the deciding individual, the individual who in freedom must decide for good or evil. We find nothing of this in Hegel. It is very interesting that Hegel who was so universal in his thinking and all-embracing never developed personal ethics. His ethics are objectivist; he subsumed ethics under philosophy of history and philosophy of law. Ethics of family, ethics of state, of community, of culture, all that is in Hegel, but not ethics which has to do with the personal decision of the individual. This was already an element in Schelling's attack against Hegel, but it was stressed more by Kierkegaard than by anybody else.

What is the reason for this experience of solitude? It is due to human finitude in estrangement. It is not the finitude which is identical with the infinite, but it is separated finitude, finitude standing upon itself in the individual person. As long as the identity principle was decisive, it was possible to overcome the anxiety of finitude, of having to die, by the experience of being united with the infinite. But this answer was not possible for Kierkegaard. So he tried to show why we are in anxiety because of being finite and in despair because of being in separated finitude. The first is his description of anxiety and the second is his description of despair. There are two writings which every theologian must read. Both are comparatively short: *The Concept of Dread* and *The Sickness Unto Death*.[5] I have always criticized the title of the English translation of *The Concept of Dread*, because dread is different from anxiety. Dread has in it the connotation of something sudden,

---

[5] Søren Kierkegaard, *The Concept of Dread*, translated by Walter Lowrie (Princeton: Princeton University Press, 1944); and *The Sickness Unto Death*, translated by Walter Lowrie (Princeton: Princeton University Press, 1941).

whereas what Kierkegaard describes is an ontological state of man. But now in English the term "anxiety" has generally replaced "dread" to describe this state which Kierkegaard has in mind. *The Concept of Dread,* in any case, is a fundamental book on the theory of anxiety. It has been more fully developed by others, so that now there is a vast literature on the subject, including the works of people like Freud, Rollo May, *et al.*

Kierkegaard wrote about two kinds of anxiety. The first is connected with his theory of the fall. He symbolized this with the biblical myth of Adam and Eve, and found profound psychological insight there. This is the anxiety of actualizing one's own freedom, which is a double anxiety: the anxiety of not actualizing it, of being restricted and of not coming into real existence, and the anxiety of actualizing it, with the knowledge of the possibility of losing one's identity. This is not a description of an original historical Adam, but of the Adam in every one of us, as the word "Adam" means. In this double anxiety of actualizing oneself and of being afraid to actualize oneself, every adolescent finds himself with respect to sex, his relation to his parents, to the political tradition in which he lives, etc. It is always the question of actualizing or not actualizing one's potentialities.

Finally the decision is made for actualizing oneself, and this is simultaneously the fall. But after the fall there is another anxiety, because the fall, like every trespassing of limits, produces guilt. The anxiety of guilt at its extreme point is despair. This despair is described in *The Sickness Unto Death.* This sickness unto death is present in all human beings. This condition is described with the help of many Hegelian categories, as the conflict between spirit and matter in man, man having finite spirit, man experiencing the conflict in himself, having the desire to get rid of himself, and of being unable to commit suicide because the guilt consciousness makes it clear that suicide cannot help you to escape the situation in which you are. One thing ought to be kept in mind, and that is that the term "guilt" means both the objective state of *being* guilty for something that is wrong, and the subjective state of *feeling* guilty. To confuse these two states can be very bad, for example, when many psychoanalysts say that we must abolish guilt. That is very ambiguous, for what they really have to overcome is misplaced guilt feeling, which is one of the worst mental diseases. But this can be done only if they manage to bring the patient to the point where he faces up to his real state of being guilty, his true guilt in the objective sense. We must make a clear distinction between guilt and guilt feeling. Guilt feelings may be very misleading. In neurotic and psychotic conditions they are always misplaced. One of the defenses of the neurotic is to insist on misplaced guilt feeling because he cannot face reality and his own real guilt. This real guilt is his estrangement from the ultimate that expresses itself in actual acts directed against his own true being.

3. *The Nature of Faith (the Leap and Existential Truth)*

There is no escape from the sickness unto death; therefore, something must happen which cannot be mediated in logical terms. You cannot derive it from anything in you; it must come to you; it must be given to you. Here the doctrine of the "leap" appears in Kierkegaard. It has already appeared, in fact, in his description of the fall. Anxiety brings man before a decision, for or against actualizing himself. This decision is a leap; it cannot be logically derived. Sin cannot be derived in any way. If it is derived, then it is not sin any more but necessity. Here we can recall what I said about Schleiermacher for whom sin is the necessary result of the inadequacies of our spiritual life in relation to our physical life. That makes sin a necessity, and thus takes the sharpness of guilt away from sin. Kierkegaard repudiates this notion of sin. For him the fall of man is a leap of an irrational kind, of a kind which cannot be derived in terms of logical necessity.

But there is the opposite leap, the leap of faith. You cannot derive this either from your situation. You cannot overcome the sickness unto death, the anxiety of estrangement. This can only be done by faith. Faith therefore has the character of a nonrational jump in Kierkegaard. He speaks of the leap from the point of view of the individual. He is so well nourished on Hegelian dialectics that he builds up a dialectic of spheres. Between these spheres there is a leap. That is non-Hegelian. But the spheres themselves follow each other hierarchically, and that is truly Hegelian. There are three steps or spheres. You can also call them stages, but they are not so much stages following each other in time as levels lying above each other in space, and coexisting all the time in ordinary human beings. These levels or stages are the aesthetic, the ethical, and the religious. Man lives within all of them, but the decisive thing is how they are related to each other and which one is predominant for him.

Kierkegaard's description of the aesthetic stage was perhaps the most brilliant thing he did. His *Diary of the Seducer,* often abused for other purposes, is the most complete description of the aesthetic stage in its complete actualization. Also his analysis of Mozart's *Don Juan* is a great work of literary criticism, philosophy, and theology all in one. The characteristic of the aesthetic stage is the lack of involvement, detachment from existence. It has nothing to do with aesthetics as such or with the arts. Of course, this attitude of mere detachment and of noninvolvement in the situation can take place in relation to music, literature, and the visual arts; but it can also be found in the theoretical or in the cognitive relation to reality. Cognition can have the merely aesthetic attitude of noninvolved detachment. I am afraid this is seen as the ideal even in many humanities courses in the universities. To be sure, there are elements of mere detachment in every scholarly inquiry; detachment will be necessary when dealing with dates, places, and connections, etc., but as soon as you come to interpretation, detachment will be reduced by existential participation. Otherwise you cannot understand reality; you do not "stand under" the reality.

Hegel was regarded somehow as a symbol of the aesthetic attitude, and so were the romantics. Because of their aesthetic detachment they took all the cultural contents on the basis of a nonexistential attitude, a lack of involvement. When I came to this country and first used the word aestheticism in a lecture, a colleague of mine at Columbia University told me not to use that word in describing Americans. That is a typical European phenomenon. Americans are activists and not aestheticists. Now I do not believe this is true. I think there is quite a lot of this aesthetic detachment even in popular culture. It is present in the buying and selling of cultural goods—I spoke about this on the occasion of *Time* Magazine's fortieth anniversary—in which you often see a nonparticipating, nonexistential attitude. Here Kierkegaard's criticism would be valid. Perhaps on the whole this is not a very great danger among the American intelligentsia. My observation has been that they jump very quickly out of the detached aesthetic attitude—in all lectures and discussions, in philosophy and the arts—to the question, "What shall we do?" This attitude was described by Kierkegaard as the attitude of the ethical stage.

In the ethical stage the attitude of detachment is impossible. Kierkegaard had a concept of the demonic which means self-seclusion. This belongs to the aesthetic stage, not going out of oneself, but using everyone and everything for one's own aesthetic satisfaction. Opposed to this demonic self-seclusion is love. Love opens up and brings one out of self-seclusion, and in doing so conquers the demonic. This character of love leads to the relations of love. Here Kierkegaard accepted Hegel's objective ethics—the ethics of family, of vocation, of state, etc. In the aesthetic stage sex produces isolation; in the ethical stage love overcomes isolation and generates responsibility. The seducer is the symbol of irresponsibility with respect to the other one, for the other one is manipulated only aesthetically. Only through responsibility can the ethical stage be reached.

It is interesting as a biographical fact that Kierkegaard never reached two of the decisive things that he attributed to this stage, that is, family and vocation. He lived from some income as a writer, but he never had an official vocation, either in the church or outside of it. And he had this tragic experience with his fiancée, Regina Olson, whom he loved dearly. But because of the inablity to transcend his self-seclusion, his melancholic state, he finally dissolved the relationship, and never really overcame the guilt connected with it.

Then Kierkegaard dealt with the religious stage. The religious stage is beyond both the aesthetic and the ethical and is expressed in relation to that which interests us infinitely or which produces infinite passion. You recall that I told you about Hegel's two concepts: interest and passion. Hegel's critics took these terms from him and then used them in their criticism of him. Hegel said that without interest and passion nothing great has ever happened in history. This notion was now taken over by Kierkegaard into the religious situation and by Marx into the quasi-religion of the nineteenth-century revolutionary movement.

Religion has within itself two possibilities, identity and contrast. The principle of identity is based on mysticism, the identity of the infinite and the finite; and the principle of distance is based on estrangement, the finitude and the guilt of the human situation. We have discussed this often in these lectures. We saw this especially in the contrast between Spinoza and Kant, Spinoza the representative of the principle of identity and Kant the representative of critical detachment. This duality which permeates all human existence and thought is also present in Kierkegaard's description of the two types of religion. He calls these two types "religiousness A" and "religiousness B," but a more powerful way of expressing the same thing is to use the names of "Socrates" and "Jesus." Both of them have something in common. Both of them are existentialists in their approach to God. Neither is simply a teacher who communicates ideas or contents of knowledge. They are the greatest teachers in human history because they were existential. This means they did not communicate contents, but did something to persons. They did not write anything, but they have produced more disciples than anybody else who has ever written anything. All four Greek schools of philosophy were pupils of Socrates who never wrote a thing, and Christianity is the result of Jesus who never wrote anything.

That alone shows the person-to-person situation, the complete existential involvement of these two types of religiousness. But then there arises the great difference. Religiousness A or the religion of Socrates presupposes that truth is present within every human being. The fundamental truths are in man himself. The dialectical or existential teacher has only to evoke them from man. Socrates does this in two ways. The one is irony. This concept is in the best tradition of Romanticism of which I spoke. This means that every special content of which a person is sure is subjected to radical questioning until its insecurity is revealed. Nothing remains as self-evident. In Plato's dialogues Socrates is the leader of the discussions, and he applies irony to the Sophists who know everything, who are the scholars of their time. The Socratic questioning undercut their scholarly self-consciousness, their belief in their infallibility. Socrates did the same thing with the craftsmen, the businessmen, and the aristocratic people who were his followers. The other way is midwifery. This means that the existential teacher brings to birth what is already inside a person, helps him to find the truth in himself, and does not simply tell him the truth. This presupposes the Platonic idea that man's soul has an eternal relation to all the essences of things. So knowledge is a matter of memory. The famous example given in Plato's dialogue *Meno* is of the slave who is asked about the Pythagorean proposition of the three angles of a triangle, and although he is completely uneducated, he is able to understand it because of the mathematical evidences within him. This is not produced in him by external teaching. This is indeed true of geometry and algebra. Everyone can experience in himself the evidence of such things, but this is not true of certain other things. This then led to the resistance of the empirical school against Socrates and Plato, on the one hand, and leads to the other religious type represented by Jesus, on the other hand.

Both Socrates and Jesus communicate indirectly, as Kierkegaard says, but they do not have textbook knowledge of any kind. By indirect communication Socrates brings to consciousness what is in man. Therefore, he is called a religious teacher. I am in full agreement with that. I think it is ridiculous to say that Socrates is a philosopher and Jesus is religious, or perhaps a religionist, a really blasphemous term. Both of them deal with man in his existential situation from the point of view of the meaning of life and of ultimate concern. They do it existentially. In this sense we can call Socrates the founder of liberal humanism, as one of the quasi-religions. Now, if the difference between Socrates and Jesus is not that of the difference between philosophy and religion—which is absolute nonsense here—then what is the difference? The difference is that the indirect ironical teacher, Socrates, does not transform the totality of the being of the other person. This is done only in religiousness B, by the teacher who is at the same time the Savior, who helps the person whom he teaches in terms of healing and liberating. Here another type of consciousness comes into existence. According to this idea, God is not in man. Man is separated from God by estrangement. Therefore God must come to man from outside, and address him. God comes to man in the Christ.

God is not the paradoxical presence in the individual, but he is present outside of man in the Christ. Nobody can derive the coming of the Christ from the human situation. This is another leap, the leap of

God into time through the sending of his Son. This cannot be derived from man, but is given to him. This makes Jesus the teacher into the Savior of men. While Socrates is the great existential teacher, Jesus is both the teacher and the Savior who transforms man.

In this way the religious stage has within itself a tension. Hegel's interpretation of the Christ was in the line of Platonism. In Hegel the eternal essential unity of God and man is represented in a complete way in the Christ, but it is also present in every individual. For Kierkegaard God comes from the outside or from above. Here you see immediately the starting point of Karl Barth. According to him, you cannot start with man, not even in terms of questioning. You must start with God who comes to man. The human situation is not such that you can find in man's predicament the question which may lead to the religious answer. In terms of this conviction Barth criticizes my own systematic theology, which in this sense is un-Kierkegaardian. This idea of God coming to man totally from the outside had great religious power, but I would say that its religious power is disproportional to its philosophical power, to the power of thought. It cannot be carried out in such a way. But that is not the point here. The point is that you see the bridge from Kierkegaard to Barth and neo-orthodoxy in the idea of God coming to man from above and from outside him, with no point of contact in man. When Emil Brunner wanted to say that there must be some point of contact, Barth answered with his passionate "No"—this famous essay in which he defends his idea of the absolute otherness of God outside of man. Now, I do not believe this idea can be maintained, but, in any case, negatively speaking, it had great religious power.

This is connected with a concept of truth that has to do with the metaphor of leap. This truth is quite different from the objective truth in the scientific sense. So Kierkegaard makes the following statement, which gives the gist of all his philosophical and theological authorship: "Truth is the objective uncertainty held fast in the most personal passionate experience. This is the truth, the highest truth attainable for the existing individual." Here he defines faith as well as truth, for this is just the leap of faith. A very important element is what he calls the objective uncertainty. This means that theology is not based on objective certainty. A merely objective certainty, as Hegel wanted to reach, is not adequate to the situation between God and man. This would be possible only if the individual had already entered the system of essences, the essential structure of reality. But he has not; he is outside of it, as God is outside of him. Therefore, objective certainty in religion is impossible; faith remains objectively uncertain. Truth in the realm of the objective scientific approach is not existential truth. Kierkegaard would not deny the possibility of scientific truth, but this is the truth of detachment. It is not the truth of involvement; it is not existential truth. Existential truth is objective uncertainty and personal, passionate experience or subjective certainty, but a certainty which can never be objectified. It is the certainty of the leap.

This subjective certainty of the leap of faith is always under criticism and attack, and therefore Kierkegaard speaks of holding fast to it in a passionate way. In personal existence there is passionate inner movement, and in the power of this passion we have the only truth which is existentially important for us. This is the most significant thing in the world, the question of "to be or not to be." It is the ultimate concern about man's eternal destiny, the question of the meaning of life. This is, of course, different from the truth we approach in terms of approximative scientific objectivity. If we use the term "subjectivity" in connection with Kierkegaard's idea of existential truth, then please avoid the mistake of equating it with willfulness. This is the connotation the word has today. Therefore, it is so difficult to understand a man like Kierkegaard and practically all classical philosophers. Subject means what it says, something standing upon itself, *sub-jectum,* that which underlies. Man is a *sub-jectum,* one who stands upon himself, and not an *objectum,* an object which is in opposition to a subject looking at it. If man is this, then he becomes a thing. This is the sickness of our time. The protest of subjectivity does not mean the protest of willfulness. It means the protest of freedom, of the creative individual, of personality, of man who is in the tragic situation of having to decide in a state of estrangement, in the human predicament. In these ideas we have almost the whole summary of Kierkegaard's theology.

But then Kierkegaard goes beyond this to the question: What can be done to give content to this situation? With respect to the content we must say that not much can be found of it in Kierkegaard. He was not a constructive theologian, and he could not be, because one can be a constructive theologian only if he is not only existentially interested and passionate, but also has an essentialist vision of the structure of reality. Without this, systematic theology is impossible. So we find very little content in the theological or religious writings of Kierkegaard. We have only a continuous repetition of the term "paradox"—leap is simply another word for paradox, that which cannot be derived, that which is irrational and surprising.

There is, however, one content to which he refers all the time, and this is the appearance of the Christ. Thus the leap which is necessary to overcome the situation of doubt and despair is the leap into the reality of the Christ. He states this in a very unusual, paradoxical, and theologically questionable form. He says that only one thing matters: In the year A.D. 30 God sent the Christ for my salvation. I do not need any more theology; I do not need to know the results of historical criticism. It is enough to know that one thing. Into this I have to leap. Then we must ask: Can we solve the problem which historical criticism has opened up by a theology of the leap? I do not believe it is possible. Philosophically the question is this: In which direction am I to leap? You can leap in all directions, but if you have a direction in mind, you already have some knowledge, so it is not a pure leap anymore. If you are in complete darkness and jump without knowing in what direction you are jumping, then you can land anyhere, maybe even on the place from which you jumped. The danger in this concept is asking someone to jump without showing him the direction. Then we have more than subjectivity and paradox; we have willfulness and arbitrariness; we have complete contingency. But if you already know in which direction to jump, in the direction of Christ, for example, then you must have a reason for this. This reason may be some experience with him, some historical knowledge, some image of him from church tradition, etc., but in any case, you have some content. The mere name alone does not say anything. And if you have these things, you are already in the tradition of theology and the church, and it is not a sheer leap any more. This is a problem which we have to say Kierkegaard left completely unsolved. His statement that you have to leap over two thousand years to the year A.D. 30 is simply unrealistic, because nobody can do that. The intellectual leap, or the emotional-intellectual leap, which you are supposed to make with your whole self, is conditioned by two thousand years of church and cultural history. You cannot do that without using contemporary language, and you use language even though you are silent, for internally you speak whenever you are thinking. When you make such a leap, you are using the language of the 1960's, and so you are dependent on the two preceding millennia. It is an illusion to think we can become contemporary with Christ insofar as the historical Jesus is the Christ. We can be contemporary with the Christ only in the way described by the apostle Paul, that is, insofar as the Christ is the Spirit, for the Spirit is present within and beyond the intervening centuries. But this is something else. Kierkegaard wanted to solve the problem of historical criticism by this concept of contemporaneity. You can do this if you take contemporaneity in the Pauline sense of the divine Spirit present to us, and showing the face of Jesus as the Christ. But you cannot escape historical criticism by becoming contemporaneous with Jesus himself. This is the fundamental criticism which we must make from a theological point of view.

4. Criticism of Theology and Church

We have still to discuss Kierkegaard's critical attitudes toward theology and the church.[6] One can almost say that when Kierkegaard deals with the church or theology, the image which he presents is more a caricature than a fair description. In particular the ecclesiastical office was an object of criticism. He attacked the fact that the minister becomes an employee like all other employees, with special duties and economic securities. This position of the minister, especially its bourgeois elements, of having a career, getting married, raising children, while at the same time proclaiming the impossible possibility of the Christ is for Kierkegaard involved in a self-contradiction. But Kierkegaard does not indicate how this conflict might be solved. Certainly it is a reality, and for Kierkegaard a reality which contradicts the absoluteness of the essence of Christianity. One cannot take this as an objectively valid criticism,

---

[6] Cf. Kierkegaard's *Attack upon 'Christendom,'* translated by Walter Lowrie (Princeton: Princeton University Press, 1944).

because if one did, then one would have to abolish every church office. If the office is not abolished, it is inevitable that the laws of sociology will make themselves felt and influence the form of the office and those who hold it.

The same thing is true of his attacks on theology. He attacks theology because it is an objectifying attempt to construct a well-formulated system out of the existential paradox. Here again the inadequacy of the situation of the theologian is marvelously expressed, but in terms of a caricature. On the other hand, the question is whether theology is a necessary service of the church. If it is—and it has always been that as long as Christianity has existed; there is theology in Paul and John—then the question arises: Can the theological task be united with the paradox of the Christian message in a different way? When Kierkegaard speaks about the theologian in his attack on theology, he sarcastically suggests: Since Christ was born, let us establish a chair in theology dealing with the birth of Christ; Christ was crucified, so let us make a full professorship for the crucifixion of Christ; Christ has risen, so let us make an associate professorship, etc. This kind of comical attack on theology makes a great impact on anyone who reads it, whether he is a theologian or not. But if it is taken as more than a reminder, if it is taken as a prescription, it means the abolition of theology.

The truth which we can gain from this kind of criticism of theology is the truth of the inadequacy of the objectifying attitude in existential matters. This refers both to the ministry and to theology. In the ministry there is the objectifying factor, the factor of a sociological structure in analogy with all sociological structures. In theology there is a structure of thought in analogy with all structures of thought. This reminder is, of course, of great importance. The minister and the theologian should be forever reminded of the inadequacy, and not only that but also of the necessity of what they are doing. The impossible possibility, as Reinhold Niebuhr, I believe, following Kierkegaard has expressed it, is incarnated in the position of the minister and the theologian. For something which is a matter of paradox, contrary to all expectation, is brought into a form of existence comparable to any other object in time and space. But this is the whole paradoxical situation of the church in the world. You can also express it by saying that the Christian religion is one of the many sections of human culture, but at the same time stands vertically in relation to everything which is culture. From this you can draw the conclusion that Christianity should be removed from every cultural relationship, but if you try to do that, you will find it impossible. The very words you use in order to do it are dependent on the culture from which you will try to detach Christianity. On the other hand, if you do not see the vertical aspect, if Christianity is merely for a class of human beings who are blasphemously called religionists and becomes merely a part of the whole culture, this may be very useful for undergirding patriotism, but the paradox is lost.

Here we face a conflict which is as real, permanent, and insoluble for us as it was for Kierkegaard. Since in Denmark at Kierkegaard's time there was a sophisticated theology of mediation, the prophetic voice could hardly be heard any more. Kierkegaard became the prophetic voice. The prophet always speaks from the vertical dimension and does not care about what happens in the horizontal dimension. But then Kierkegaard became a part of the horizontal; he became the father of existentialist philosophy, of neo-orthodox theology, and of much depth psychology. Thus he was taken into culture just as the prophets of Israel who, after they had spoken their paradoxical, prophetic word out of the vertical, became religious reformers, and were responsible, for example, for the concentration of the cult in Jerusalem because of the cultic abuses in other places. So out of the vertical there comes a new horizontal line, that is, a new cultural actualization of the prophetic word. This cannot be avoided. Therefore, there is need for the prophetic word again and again which makes us aware that the situation of every servant of religion is a paradoxical one and is in a sense impossible. Kierkegaard's word was not accepted widely in his time, but when people in the beginning of the twentieth century realized the coming earthquake of this century, Kierkegaard's voice could be heard again.

* * * * * * * * *

Question: You summarized Kierkegaard's understanding of Socrates. Do you consider this a correct interpretation of Socrates, or does it contain features peculiar to Kierkegaard?

Answer: First, I would say that it contains features peculiar to Plato.

We do not know how much it has to do with the historical Socrates. It is parallel to the relation between the Synoptic Gospels and the fourth Gospel. The fourth Gospel has its analogy in Plato, and the Synoptic Gospels in Xenophon. Perhaps neither is right from a strictly historical point of view. But this is the way that a great historical figure appears to us. What is historically decisive is the impact a figure has on those who are with him. So here is a strict analogy between Socrates and Jesus, neither of whom wrote anything.

We know them only through their impact on their disciples, and this impact makes them not only historically significant, but also symbolic figures, figures in whom a symbol or archetype is embodied. Through this elevation to the status of a symbol the figure continues to influence history.

Now the Socrates of Plato certainly does what Kierkegaard says in connection with the Socratic irony and the Socratic maieutic or mid-wifery. The irony destroys that which one believes he knows, and the maieutic method is a way of bringing thoughts out of someone which are implicit in the depths of his soul. These two parts are certainly there in the Socrates whom Plato presents. How high the probability is of the historical accuracy of Plato's picture of Socrates is something that has been discussed for two thousand years. It cannot be said with certainty how much of Plato's image of Socrates is based on the actual Socrates himself. Scholars try to determine that, and with our modern methods of historical research we can perhaps come very near to the historical truth. We find that it is likely that the historical Socrates was not as banal as Xenophon makes him, but neither was he a pupil of Plato; it was the other way around.

But Kierkegaard is right in making another fundamental distinction. We spoke about religiousness A and religiousness B. Religiousness A is a religion in which the divine is present in every human being immediately and can be found in the depths of his being. This is basically a mystical form of religious experience, with God in us, the infinite within the finite. We showed how the whole modern development is dependent on this principle which was most sharply expressed by Nicholas of Cusa, the principle of the coincidence of the infinite and the finite in every finite thing. On the other hand, in religiousness B the basic point is the separation, the estrangement. This means that there is a gap between the divine and the human, so that man needs more than a midwife like Socrates who brings out of us what we already have within us; something new must come from the outside. The Savior or the Christ must come. This is the difference between Jesus and Socrates. Jesus is not only the existential teacher as Socrates; he is also the Savior who overcomes the gap between God and man. I think you have realized that the dialectic between these two principles is important in my own theological lectures, the dialectic between the principle of identity or the coincidence of the infinite and the finite in every person and the principle of a revelatory communication from outside, which is both revelatory and saving or transforming. Revelation in Kierkegaard's sense is not the communication of doctrines or knowledge *about* God. That is a badly distorted concept of revelation. But revelation is the self-manifestation of the divine to a human being which has transforming power. Both the symbolic and the doctrinal statements which arise out of the revelatory experience are secondary.

* * * * * * * * * *

E. Political Radicalism and Its Theological Significance

What I will do now is perhaps surprising to you. I want to give you here the theology of the most successful of all theologians since the Reformation, namely, Karl Marx. I will consider him as a theologian. And I will show you that without doing this, it is impossible to understand the history of the twentieth century and large sections of the late nineteenth century. If you consider him only as a political leader or as a great economist, which he also was, or as a great sociologist, which he was even more, then you cannot understand from what sources the power came which transformed the whole world and conquered nearly half of it in the twentieth century. How can Marx have been a theologian in view of the fact that every word he said is connected with the split in humanity which he is largely responsible for having produced? Yet, there is a deep gap between the original Karl Marx and what is going on now in Russia or China, although the historical effects of his work are manifest in these countries.

1. *The Bourgeois Radicals*

There was in the time that Marx was starting his work a group of people whom we can call liberal radicals. On the basis of the principle of autonomy in bourgeois society a liberal radicalism developed. A man whose name you should at least know is Max Stirner (1806–1856) who wrote a book entitled *The Individual and His Right*.[7] In this very radical book he tried to remove all the overarching norms which traditional society, including the Enlightenment, had imposed on people. Very similarly to Kierkegaard he placed the individual in the center, but unlike Kierkegaard it was the individual without any relationship to God, but only to himself, and therefore without any norm. This was one of the things which produced the resistance of Marx. For this reason I must mention Max Stirner here. He was a neurotic personality and an extremist. Of course, as a mere individual he could not survive for one day without being dependent on others who provided for him. But this is not important for him; he forgets it. The absolute autonomy of the individual is described by him in almost ecstatic words.

Now you can imagine that Marx with his analytic knowledge of society would be full of aggressive irony against such an idea. He knew of the economically productive society, about the peasant and the grocery store, etc., and could not abstract from them as the neurotic bohemian could do so easily. And the beatniks of today who attack society forget the fact that it is the basis of their whole existence every minute. The same is true of Kierkegaard. The church which he attacked so radically, with its tradition within culture, was the basis of his statement that in the years A.D. 1–30 God came to man. Without the tradition of the church which produced both the Bible and the church nothing would have come to Kierkegaard, and his whole relationship to God would not have been possible. This is an idea that you should remember when someone attacks "organized religion"—a bad term—and says, I am very religious, but I am against organized religion. That is nonsense. It is nonsense because in his personal religiousness—excuse this terrible word—he is dependent on the tradition of the church for

[7] Max Stirner is the pseudonym of Johann Kasper Schmidt, author of *Der Einzige und sein Eigentum* (Leipzig: O. Wigand, 1901).

every word, every symbol that he might use in prayer, in contemplation or mystical experience. Without the community of speaking, there is no speaking whatsoever, and without an inner speaking, there is no spiritual life whatsoever. In this way it is easy to refute these attacks against organized religion. You can and should attack the forms and the ways in which it may be organized, but to use the term "organized religion" as name-calling is totally senseless. It simply shows lack of thought, and is usually rooted in bad experiences in childhood or more likely in Sunday School, which is one of the great laboratories in which Christian faith is expelled from children.

2. *Marx's Relation to Hegel and Feuerbach*

Now we must start with Marx's relation to Hegel and Feuerbach. He was a pupil of Hegel. Feuerbach, another pupil of Hegel, had put Hegel on his feet after he had been standing on his head, as Marx said. Hegel believed that reality is identical with the head of the philosopher. Feuerbach showed that the philosopher like everybody else is dependent on the material conditions of life. So Feuerbach developed a materialistic or naturalistic doctrine of man—man's dependence on his senses, etc. Marx said that Feuerbach had done the main thing; he had criticized Hegel's explanation of religion. Marx felt that he did not have to do that any more. But he had to criticize Feuerbach's materialistic ontology, and Feuerbach's idea that being is individual being, that the individual as such is the one who is decisive for the whole situation. Marx's criticism of Feuerbach held that materialism is not much better than idealism. It is a little bit better because idealism is merely ideology without any basis in reality. Materialism is closer to reality. But if only the individual is considered in the materialistic philosophy, then it is as bad as idealism. For its universal concept of man is abstracted from the individual and overleaps the social conditions in which man finds himself.

So Marx attacked both the materialists and the idealists. In regard to the term "Marxist materialism" it would be much better to leave that to the propagandists who use and confuse three different meanings of materialism in order to carry on their propaganda. But that has nothing to do with historical truth and an academic education. So it is better for you to understand that there are three meanings of materialism.

a. The one is the ontological or metaphysical materialism. You find this in Feuerbach who derives everything in nature from the movements of atoms in terms of calculable mechanical causality. It is a theory which has not often been represented in history. Present-day naturalism in America is certainly not materialism. Metaphysical materialism is also called reductionist naturalism, whereby reductionism means reducing everything to the mechanical movement of atoms and molecules. This is an obsolete philosophy. It existed in Europe at the end of the nineteenth century; also it existed in France at the end of the eighteenth century in the French encyclopedists of the pre-Revolution period; and it has existed only very rarely in this country. But on the whole it is a philosophy which has been overcome, and is very remote from Marxism.

b. Then there is ethical materialism, which means being interested only in material goods, in money, etc. When someone is called a materialist in propaganda, no clear distinction is made between ethical and metaphysical materialism. If Marxism is called materialistic, for example, the trick of propaganda is to leave the impression of an ethical materialism. In reality, however, the original socialist movement and also the kind of communism you find in the original Marx attacked the materialism of the bourgeois society, where everything was dependent on buying and selling, on profit, etc. So Marxism was just the opposite. Now the critics of the materialism of the bourgeois society are called materialists, usually with the connotation of ethical materialism, of being interested only in material goods.

c. Historical materialism is the third type. This means that the whole historical process is ultimately dependent on the ways of economic production. This is Marxist materialism. It should be called historical or economic materialism. It is quite different from the other two meanings.

Marx deals with the question of the individual and society. This was not so new in France, England, and Holland, but it was very new in Germany. In Germany the social structure was always taken for granted as something ordained by God. This was in accordance with Lutheran doctrine. Sociological analysis was avoided. Sociology had been fully developed in France in the nineteenth century before German scholars even started to think sociologically. Marx received his sociological view partly from France and partly from his insight into the miserable social conditions of large sections of people in Europe. Man is not man as an individual. The idea of the individual existing by himself is an illusion. This sounds quite different from Kierkegaard and Stirner. But Marx saw that we are really members of a social group. It is impossible to abstract ourselves from sociological reality. So he criticized Hegel and Feuerbach because they did not see individual men as members of a social structure. What is needed is an analysis of the social structure and the individual's place within it.

3. Marx's View of the Human Situation (Alienation)

Like Kierkegaard, Marx speaks of the estranged situation of man in the social structure of the bourgeois society. He uses the word "alienation" (Entfremdung) not from the point of view of the individual but of society. In Hegel estrangement means the absolute Spirit goes over into nature, becoming estranged from itself. In Kierkegaard it means the fall of man, the transition by a leap from innocence into knowledge and tragedy. In Marx it means the structure of the capitalist society.

Marx's description of modern society is of great importance. If we as theologians speak of original sin, for example, and are not aware of the problems of estrangement in the social situation, then we cannot really address people in their actual situation in everyday life. For Marx estrangement means that the social situation results in dehumanization. When he speaks of mankind in the future, he speaks of true humanism. He looks forward to a situation in which true humanism is not a pleasure merely for the cultured few; humanism is not the possession of cultural goods either. He looks for the re-establishment of a true humanity to replace the dehumanization in an estranged society. The main thing in the idea of dehumanization is that man has become a cog within the great process of production and consumption. In the process of production the individual worker has become a thing, a tool, or a commodity which is bought and sold on the market. The individual must sell himself in order to live.

These descriptions imply that man is essentially not an object, not a thing, but a person. Man is not the tool but the highest end or aim. He is not a commodity but the inner *telos* for everything that is done. Man is the inner meaning and aim. Marx's description of dehumanization or the particular form of estrangement that existed in capitalist society completely contradicts what he had inherited from classical humanism. He saw no reconciliation. In historical reality there is only dehumanization and estrangement. Out of this came the power to change the situation. When Marx in the *Communist Manifesto* spoke about the liberation of the masses from their chains, these chains were the powers of dehumanization produced by the working conditions of capitalist society. Consequently, the essential character of man is lost. Man on both sides of the class conflict is distorted by the conditions of existence. Only if these conditions are removed can we know what man truly is. Christian theology says that we can know what man essentially is because essential man has appeared in the conditions of existence in the Christ.

Estrangement refers not only to human relations, characterized by the cleavage between classes, but also to the relation of man to nature. The eros element has been taken away. Nature is only the stuff out of which tools are made, and by means of the tools consumer goods are manufactured. Nature itself has ceased to be a subject with which we as subjects can be united in terms of eros, the love which sees in nature the inner power of being, the ground of being which is creatively active through nature. In the industrial society we make nature only the material out of which to make things for buying and selling.

4. *Marx's Doctrine of Ideology and His Attack on Religion*

Ideology is another extremely important concept for theology. What is ideology? The word itself is older than Marx. It was used, for instance, by Napoleon when he criticized professors for being ideologists instead of being practical statesmen and generals. The word has a history which remains ambiguous even today. Ideology can be a neutral word, meaning simply the system of ideas which one can develop. Every group or class has such a system of ideas. But ideology can also mean—becoming then the most dangerous weapon in the class struggle—the unconscious production of ideas which justify the will-to-power of a ruling group. This is mostly an unconscious production, but it can be used in a conscious way.

Marx used this word "ideology" as a weapon. It was probably his sharpest weapon against the ideas of the ruling classes with which the churches were allied. All the great European churches, the Orthodox, the Lutheran, and the Episcopalian, were on the side of the ruling classes. The Roman Catholic Church was better in this respect for it had preserved a tradition of social feeling and social analysis from its classical medieval period.

A term which we used in our daily language that is very close to the meaning of ideology is rationalization. We speak of the rationalization of individuals who use ideas to justify the power they hold over other persons or to justify their indulgence in certain kinds of pleasures. Applied to social groups rationalization becomes ideology. This is a very important theological concept. Every Christian and every church should always be suspicious of their own ideologies which they use to justify their own traditional self-satisfactions. Every church should be suspicious of itself lest it formulate truths only as an expression of its will-to-power.

This notion of ideology is used by Marx to supplement Feuerbach's criticism of religion. He says that in principle Feuerbach succeeded in removing religion, but his criticism was not founded on sociological analysis. Marx says that the religious symbolism of a transcendent fulfillment (of heaven or immortality) is not merely the hope of every human being, but is the invention of the ruling classes to prevent the masses from seeking fulfillment in this life. Their attention is diverted to a so-called life hereafter. This is formulated in the famous phrase that religion is the opiate of the people. He simply means that if you have the assurance of an eternal fulfillment, you will not fight in a revolutionary way for the temporal fulfillment of man on earth.

Now I do not think that this is true. It is very similar to the way that Kierkegaard criticized the church of his time. It is the radicalism of the prophetic word. But then, of course, this same idea has to be applied to Marx himself and to all the movement which followed him. Then we must ask: What about the ideological character of the ideologies of the victorious revolutionary movements? Are they not also expressions of a new will-to-power? When we see what has happened to the Marxist ideas in Soviet Russia, we must immediately answer in the affirmative. The ruling classes in Russia maintain ideologies derived from Marx to keep themselves in power, although their ideas have only an indirect connection with Marx. There is the ideological element in the will to maintain themselves in power. The reason for this is that Marx lacked a vertical criticism against himself. This is the same situation that we have in all Communist countries, the lack of a vertical criticism. On the horizontal they have a lot of truth, but they cannot put this under the criticism of the vertical, because they have cut it off. Nobody can do that completely, but they have done it to a great extent. The danger in our culture is that we do the same thing with less radical and revolutionary methods, but with the more refined and sophisticated methods of mass culture.

A great gap between the churches and the labor movements in Europe developed. The churches were the representatives of the ideologies which kept the ruling classes in power over against the working masses. This was the tragic situation. It is a great thing that in America this tragedy has happened on a much smaller scale. But in Europe it has led to the radical antireligious and anti-Christian attitudes of all labor movements, not only of the Communists but also of the social democrats. It was not the "bad atheists"—as propagandists call them—who were responsible for this; it was the fact that the European churches, Orthodox, Lutheran, and Episcopalian, were without social sensitivity and direction. They were directed toward their own actualization; they were directed toward liturgical or dogmatic efforts and refinements, but the social problem was left to divine providence. The Czarist ruling classes, the German imperial ruling classes, and the British ruling classes were not in contact with what was going on in the working classes either. In Great Britain the situation was much milder, and therefore Great Britain never had a Marxist revolution. Nevertheless, the situation was very similar.

This situation can be seen the world over. On the one side there is a theology of mere horizontal fulfillment, with the kingdom of God being identified with the classless society or with a continuous transformation of society as in the British Labor party and in German social democracy. On the other side are the churches with their theology which has a vertical dimension. But a few things have happened which attempt to bridge the gap. In England there was a religious socialist movement very early; whether it called itself by that name or not, its ideas were the same. Then in Germany there was a religious socialist movement which came from some prophetic personalities in Switzerland. But nothing of this existed in Germany before the first World War.

I remember the great churches in the workers' quarters in Berlin. Workers did not enter the church except for baptism, marriage, and the funeral. The churches provided some glorification of these events. But any inner relation to the churches did not exist. To a typical Lutheran minister of that time I said: The workers cannot hear the Christian message. You must do it differently. You cannot expect that they will come into the churches. His answer was: They hear the church bells ringing every Sunday morning, and if they do not come to the church services, they will feel guilty. But they did not hear anything, and they did not know anything. They had no relation to the religious symbols of the tradition. The Lutheran attitude was that the people can come to hear the Christian message in the church. At least the people hear the bell ringing, and that is enough. If they do not come, they will be rejected by God. Fortunately, this attitude has ceased to exist. But it was this kind of attitude which produced the tremendous gap between the church and the laboring classes. Religious socialism tried to close that gap.

5. *Marx's Political Existentialism*

The existentialist element in Marx is very great. His concept of truth has a similarity to Kierkegaard's. Truth is truth for human existence, truth which concerns our life-situation. We said that Kierkegaard defined truth as an objective uncertainty passionately held. Marx defines truth in terms of the gap between theory and practice. That is to say, truth must be related to the social situation. A philosophical theory which is not involved in the social situation is not true. We have something of this in pragmatism and in John Dewey. There are in fact great similarities between existentialism and pragmatism. One of the things which has made John Dewey the great educator in this country is his insistence that all knowledge must be united with practical activities in the educational process. This was even more basic for Marx. We cannot know the truth about the human situation without existential participation in the social structure in which we are living. We cannot have truth outside the actuality of the human situation. Therefore, in our period of history one must participate in the proletarian situation in order to understand the depths of estrangement. Here we must cautiously avoid a mistaken idea. In Marx there is no glorification of the proletariat. The revolutionary movements made the proletariat the messiah, the savior, so to speak, not because the proletarians are such wonderful people—Marx never believed that; he knew them—but because they stood at a particular point in history which involved them in a class struggle, and through this struggle a new reality might come into existence. Marx knew that the class split distorted both sides in the situation. Men were made into objects. The leading bourgeois and the working masses are in the same boat with respect to dehumanization. But the proletariat had one advantage. They experienced the estrangement in such a way that they would be forced to revolt. The proletarians are the blessed, in the sense of the Beatitudes, for they exist on the extreme negative edge of the class situation. So in the Marxist criticism of society a biblical truth has been applied to an analysis of the social situation. When one speaks about the saving power of the proletariat, this does not mean that the proletariat is good and the others are bad. Marx's friend Engels was a big businessman, a capitalist. But the structure of the situation puts the proletariat on the lowest level where the need for revolution is felt. Through its revolutionary role it is thought to be the saving power.

6. The Prophetic Element in Marx

We cannot miss the messianic note in Marx's writings. Especially in the earlier writings we hear the voice of a modern secular prophet. He speaks like the old prophets of Israel. Marx as a Jew was in the tradition of Jewish criticism which had lasted through the millennia. His wrath

against the reality as he saw it had something of the old prophetic wrath
in it, although it was distorted by propagandistic elements as happens in
every political leader. Nevertheless we cannot overlook the prophetic
element in his whole work. When the prophets spoke to Israel, even
when they spoke about the other nations, the whole weight of their
attack was directed also against their own nation. They saw that their
word did not transform their own nation. So, they said, the wrath of
God would strike Israel. Especially Jeremiah was aware of this. But
there is also the promise of God. It could not come to naught; it would
come to fulfillment. So the prophets had the idea of the remnant, the
small group which would be the bearer of the divine promise.

The idea of a remnant is not the idea of only the prophets. Everybody
who speaks prophetically to a large group or to a nation has such an
idea. Without such an idea you would be driven to despair and forced to
give up. But you do not need to give up, because there is the remnant.
The word "remnant" means those who are left over, those who do not
adore the idols, who do not do injustices, etc. In the larger sense this
word means those few within the group who are conscious of the situation and who therefore become the bearers of the future development.
This idea of the remnant restricts to a certain extent the messianism of
the proletariat. In the last analysis it is not the whole proletariat, but the
leading groups in it, the vanguards, who are decisive. So a simple
identification of the proletariat with messianism is limited by the fact
that it is those who are the vanguards who have a messianic role. These
vanguards are not always even members of the proletariat. They are
people like Marx and Engels who come from the intelligentsia or the
upper classes and have broken through their own ideological self-
seclusion. They have learned what is going on in history and can join
the vanguards.

The difference between Marx's secularized prophetism and that of
the Jewish prophets is that the latter always kept in mind the vertical
line and did not rely either on human groups or on logical or economic
necessities of development, as Marx did. They ultimately relied on God,
and this was lacking in the modern secularized movement. Certainly,
this movement is quasi-religious. It is not pseudo-religious, for pseudo-
religious means "deceptive" or "lying." But it is quasi-religious because it

has in itself the structure of prophetism, but with one difference—the transcendent, the vertical line, has been lost.

The tragic thing is that the revolutionary movements in Europe, Asia, and Africa originally came from a prophetic message, but when they became victorious, they did not apply their own criticism against themselves. They could not do it, because they had nothing above themselves. The Communists in Russia answer all the problems in the East-West discussion without showing the element of ultimate self-criticism. Of course, there is much self-criticism in individual groups in Communist countries. There are individuals who confess they have sinned. But they have always sinned against the party; there is nothing higher than the party; the party cannot err; the party is infallible. The lack of the transcendent line is the reason for the tragic situation that the revolutionary movement which set out to liberate a whole social class has resulted in a new slavery, the totalitarian slavery as we have it today in the Communist systems. This is a world-historical tragedy. Similar things have happened before in history. Consider, for example, how the movement of Jesus Christ resulted in the church of the Inquisition in the later Middle Ages. All these tragic transformations come about because of the lack of the self-criticism derived from the vertical line. When the church did not judge itself any longer in terms of the vertical line, something like the Inquisition could happen. The Marxist movement was not able to judge itself because of its whole actual structure, and so it could become the social group which we now identify as Stalinism. In this form everything for which the original groups were struggling became suppressed and distorted. It is in our century that we can best see the tragic reality of man's estrangement in the social realm.

F. VOLUNTARISM AND THE PHILOSOPHY OF LIFE

Now I come to the last of the movements which contributed to the collapse of the great syntheses of Schleiermacher and Hegel. This movement is voluntarism, a term derived from *voluntas*, the Latin word for "will." Voluntarism is a philosophy in which the element of will is decisive. It began in the nineteenth century with Schelling who in his earlier years was a philosopher of the will before he became the philosopher of nature. For him will is original being. It is being itself. We can describe being most adequately in terms of will. Being is not a thing; it is not a person; it is will. This idea of will refers to what is often called today "unconscious instinct." But the word "instinct" should be dropped if you are translating Freud. The word "drive" should be used instead. Man has no death instinct. That is a misuse of the word "instinct." But man does have the death drive in himself.

Voluntarism is one of the great lines of thought in the history of philosophy and theology, which has been in continual tension with the other great line of thought which goes back to Aristotle and includes among others Thomas Aquinas, the nominalists, the British empiricists, Kant, to a great extent Schelling and Hegel, and modern language analysis. These two lines of thought have made the Western philosophical movements full of life and tension. In naming Thomas Aquinas we should also mention immediately Duns Scotus and William of Ockham as his voluntaristic opponents.

1. Schopenhauer's Idea of the Will

From Schelling we come to Schopenhauer. What impressed him was not Hegel's great synthesis nor Schelling's philosophy of identity, but rather Schelling's doctrine of will. Usually he is considered as the first representative of voluntarism in nineteenth-century thought. He combined with his voluntarism a deep pessimism. He is always quoted if one speaks of philosophical pessimism. But voluntarism is not necessarily pessimism, as we shall see in Nietzsche, his great pupil and critic.

Not only Schopenhauer's temperament but also his personal destiny must be kept in view. He lived in the overwhelming shadow of Hegel and never really came into his own during his lifetime. His famous book, The World as Will and Idea,[8] became known only very late. It had a tremendous influence in the second half of the nineteenth century and through Freud in our own century. The most important pupil of Schopenhauer was Nietzsche. The line then runs from Nietzsche to Bergson, the French voluntarist, Heidegger and Sartre, and to White-

[8] Translated by R. B. Haldane and J. Kemp (London: Trübner and Co., 1883–86).

head, the great metaphysician of our century. All this came from the powerful voluntaristic element in Schelling, but became generally influential only later through Schopenhauer and Nietzsche.

To understand this nineteenth-century movement it is helpful to go far back for a moment. Where does voluntarism come from? Its first clear appearance is in Augustine, who embodies the element of will in his own personal character in a much more dynamic way than it appears in most of the Greek philosophers and writers. Augustine is the philosopher of will, and especially of that will which is love. The substance of all reality for him is will. He could have written Schelling's statement that original being is will, but since it deals with the creation of God he calls it love. Love is original being; the power of love is the substance in everything that is. This love (*amor*) loves itself (*amor amoris*), the self-affirmation of the will which is divine love.

In the Middle Ages Augustine's ideas were represented by the great Franciscan theologians, while the Dominican theologians represented Aristotle's ideas. The tensions between these two in the thirteenth century represent the high point in medieval thought. In the Franciscan school will precedes intellect. In the Aristotelian-Thomistic school, or Dominican school, intellect precedes will. This is not a vague statement about man's psychology; it is always meant ontologically. That means that in God himself, in the creative ground of being, either will or intellect is the primary power. In this course we have dealt mainly with people who represent the primacy of the intellect. This is very much the case in German classical philosophy. It is also predominant in the eighteenth century, with some exceptions. The priority which Kant gave to practical reason represents a breakthrough of the element of will. In Schelling we have a complete breakthrough, and also in Fichte. But throughout that period the emphasis on intellect was predominant. Now in the thirteenth century Bonaventura was one of the great Franciscans in whom will was the decisive thing, that is, will as love. He was a great mystic and also an early general of the Franciscan order. This mysticism of love goes back also to Saint Francis. Standing in radical opposition to Thomas Aquinas was Duns Scotus, himself a Franciscan, and the greatest critical mind of the whole Middle Ages and one of the most important philosophical minds of the Western world. Both Thomas and

Scotus lived in the thirteenth century. Scotus defined God as will and nothing other than will. In another Franciscan, William Ockham, this became an irrational will. Ockham is the father of nominalistic philosophy of the later Middle Ages. There was an earlier nominalistic movement about which Abelard and Anselm of Canterbury were fighting.

If God is sheer will, he can do what he wants. He has within himself no intellectual limits. There is no logos structure which would prevent him from doing what he wants. The world is in every moment dependent on something absolutely unknown. Ultimately nothing in the world can be calculated. Only insofar as it is ordered by God can it be calculated, but God can withdraw both the natural and the moral orders. If he wanted, he could make murder good, and love bad. The theology of Martin Luther was influenced by nominalism, although not really dependent on it. Luther himself was a voluntarist and had in himself much of the Dionysian awareness of the underground of life in man. He was a great depth psychologist before our present-day depth psychologists. He had insight into the demonic forces in the world and in man. As the legends tell us, he had to fight continuously against the demonic forces in himself, during the attacks which he called *Anfechtungen*. When he described these demonic attacks—perhaps the best translation of *Anfechtungen*—he said that one moment in this situation of absolute despair, which is an element of the demonic attack, is worse than hell itself.

I must mention several other bridges to nineteenth-century voluntarism. There was the philosopher and shoemaker, Jacob Boehme, who saw in his visions the full demonic power, the will element, in God himself. He called it the nature of God and saw that element in God which contradicts the light in God, the logos in God, the wisdom and truth in God. He understood the conflict in the divine life, the tension between these two elements. This tension makes the divine life not simply a sheer actuality (*actus purus*) as in Aristotle, but a dynamic process with the potentiality for conflict. In God this inner conflict is always victoriously overcome, but in creatures it breaks out destructively as well as creatively.

Boehme had a great influence on Schelling's ideas concerning the inner life of God. If all this sounds very mythological, then read the books of Charles Hartshorne, A. N. Whitehead, and Henri Bergson. They were all influenced by Boehme (who himself was dependent on Luther's voluntarism) and Schelling. Even Hegel was to some extent dependent on Boehme.

One of the ways in which you can envisage the Western world in its philosophical and theological developments is in terms of this tension between the merely Apollonian—this means putting intellect over against will as the decisive thing in man—and the combination of the Apollonian and the Dionysian—which puts the will in the center and the intellect as a secondary force over against will. If this is said about man, it is also said about God, both in the Middle Ages and in modern theology. So we have here a very dynamic picture of Western philosophical development. It is important for us to know about this, because we are still in the midst of it. This struggle is still going on, for example, between the Whiteheadian school and the philosophy of logical analysis.

That gives you the historical perspective. But let us go into a few other considerations here. First the term "will." It is very important that in all these men you understand what the idea of will means. If you examine a text on psychology, you will find that usually will is derived from other elements, the vital drive, on the one hand, and the intellect, on the other hand. It is presented as a secondary phenomenon and primarily as a conscious phenomenon. If will is taken in this way, it is impossible to understand how will can be identified with being itself. How can there be will in stones and crystals and plants and animals? They have no consciousness; they have no purpose which is directed by an intellect expressing itself in language, using universals, etc. But this is not what will means if it is understood in an ontological sense. Will is the dynamics in all forms of life. Only in man does it become conscious will. If I decide to go to my office after this lecture, that is a conscious act of my will. In voluntaristic philosophy will is not restricted to a conscious psychological act. You cannot derive the meaning of will from man's psychological experience of himself as a consciously willing being. Nevertheless, the word must be used. Will for these ontologists appears in man as conscious will, in animals as instinct or drives—these appear also in man—in plants as urges, and in material reality as trends such as gravitation, etc. If you understand will as the dynamic element in all reality, then it makes sense.

The term "intellect" is also subject to misunderstanding. The idea as the ontologists have used it does not refer to the I.Q. of the college boy. Intellect comes from the Latin *"inter-legere,"* to read between. To read between means to be in something, to be in the reality and reading it, being aware of it. That means participating in the form of things. Readable things have a form. The substance, the dynamics, you cannot read; they are dark; they are the drives. Reading, which is here meant metaphorically, is only possible where there is form. The word "understanding" has a similar metaphorical meaning. Standing under or reading between have the same meaning. They refer to a position in which we are in the reality itself and are able to become aware of its particular form. This awareness we call cognition.

Schopenhauer's idea is that will, unconscious will, drives toward the actualization of that which it is willing, and since it can never reach it, it reacts with the desire for death. This is a concept which we also find in Freud's death tendency or death drive which is derived from the always unsatisfactory fulfillment of our will. The will never gets what it wills. Out of this the dissatisfaction with life arises. According to Schopenhauer this drives the will to ever new attempts to fulfill its desire and ever new impossibilities of doing it. Life is a restless driving toward fulfillment which can never be attained. The result is the disgust of life, a deep dissatisfaction with every fulfillment. In all the voluntarists the sexual drive plays a great role—from unfulfillment to fulfillment, then to ever new fulfillment. The restlessness of these drives leads finally to a desire to come to rest by not willing any more.

With this idea something very important for the history of Western civilization occurred. Schopenhauer discovered Buddhism and in it the idea of the will to self-negation, the will to bring one's will to rest by not willing any longer. Of course, Schopenhauer was not a historian but a philosopher and as such identified his own philosophy with the fundamental Indian idea that blessedness is the resignation of the individual will, the overcoming of the self in a formless self, as the Zen-Buddhists call it, or the return into the Brahman principles, the eternal ones, as the Hindus call it. From this the ascetic tendency in life is derived. Schopenhauer did not follow along in this point, but anyway he introduced these ideas into the Western world where they have had an influence up to now.

Schopenhauer made one exception to his general view, and this placed him in line with the romantic philosophy of his time. He said that when we hear music we are able to come to rest in time and space. Music was for him the anticipatory salvation of the restless will. In music the will comes to rest, but since one cannot always be listening to music, one must finally tend toward the ultimate salvation which happens only in the moment of death. Schopenhauer is to be considered as the man who overcame in many people the progressivistic optimism of Hegel and prepared the way for the existentialist pessimism of the twentieth century.

2. *Nietzsche's Idea of Will-To-Power*

Even more important than Schopenhauer for the twentieth century and the theological situation is Friedrich Nietzsche. He was a pupil of Schopenhauer. He used the word "life" rather than "will." Life is essentially will, but a special kind of will. It goes in quite the opposite direction from Schopenhauer's will. It is not the will which brings itself to rest and ceases to will, but it is the will which Nietzsche calls will-to-power.

First we must say something about this word "power." I have already had to rescue the word "will" from the misunderstanding that it is merely a psychological phenomenon; rather, it is the universal driving dynamics of all life processes. Now I must rescue the word "power" in Nietzsche from a similar misunderstanding. For him power is the self-affirmation of being. Will-to-power means will to affirm one's power of living, the will to affirm one's own individual existence. In man this will-to-power becomes will to personal and social power. That is not the primary concept, but it is a part of the whole concept. This power has nothing to do with Nazism, with its irrational power. It is the power of the best; only the power over oneself can give one social power. If one is not able to exercise the aristocratic self-restriction, then one's power will decay. So the abuse of it by the vulgar Nazi movement has nothing to do with Nietzsche's vision of will-to-power. It is one of the tragedies that this great symbol created by Nietzsche should become something devilish in the mouths of vulgar people.

Nietzsche's style is oracular in contrast to Hegel's dialectical philosophy. He is one of the great fragmentists in the history of literature. Fragments can be very powerful. In the pre-Socratics we have almost only fragments. In part this is an accident of history, for much of the early pagan literature was destroyed by Christian fanaticism and later by Islamic fanaticism. But in any case these fragments are in themselves complete, understandable, and full of mystery. The same is true of the fragments of Nietzsche. He tells us that he wrote them at a time of an inspired state of mind. He also wrote great poetry.

Nietzsche knew of the ambiguity in all life. He knew of the creative and destructive elements which are always present in every life process. If you want to find out about his idea of God, do not look first to his statement that "God is dead." Read instead the last fragments of *The Will To Power*,[9] which is a collection of fragments. It is not a book in itself. The last fragment describes the divine demonic character of life in formulations which show the ambiguity, the greatness, and the destructiveness of life. He asks us to affirm this life in its great ambiguity. Out of this he then has another kind of God, a God in which the demonic underground, the Dionysian underground, is clearly visible. The victory of the element of rationality or of meaning is not as clear as in other philosophers like Kant or Hegel, Hume or Locke, but there is an opening up of vitality, and its half-creative, half-destructive power.

3. *Nietzsche's Doctrine of Resentment*

Now where do the norms of life come from? Nietzsche has a theory very similar to that of Feuerbach and Marx. This is his theory of resentment. The Jewish-Christian idea of justice, the Greek-Christian idea of logos, and the Christian idea of love are all ideas which result from the resentment of the masses against the aristocratic rulers. It is the revolution of resentment. This is the same type of thing that Marx

[9] Translated by Anthony M. Ludovici (London: T. N. Foulis, 1913–14).

called ideology when he derived the Christian and generally religious ideas and values from the state of negativity of the masses of people to whom the upper classes promised a fulfillment in a transcendent heaven. Marx used this word as a powerful weapon in the revolution. And psychoanalysis shows how individuals use rationalization to justify drives in themselves which they want to maintain or fulfill. So Nietzsche added a third concept, that of resentment. These three concepts have had tremendous power because they are really revealing of the human situation. The concept of *rationalization* shows how the individual man tries to give reasons in a system of values for his natural drives of eros and will-to-power. Freud with his empirical methodology discovered how little our conscious life represents what we actually are. This was a revolution in our climate of thought in the twentieth century; it undercut the bourgeois and puritan moralistic conventions in all Western countries, and in particular the Protestant-dominated countries. Most of you belong to the third generation of this revolution, but I belonged to the first generation; I tried to show what it means for Protestant theology that not the surface consciousness but the underground of human existence is decisive in human experience and relations. The concept of *ideology* revealed the interest of the ruling classes in preserving their power by producing a transcendent system to divert the masses from their immediate situation of disinheritance. We see the same thing today going on in the underdeveloped countries where there are revolutionary tendencies. They often look at our democratic ideas, which are rooted partly in Stoicism and partly in the Old Testament, as an ideology of the Western world to maintain its predominance and to introduce its values.

In Nietzsche's psychology of resentment all the ideas of justice, equality, democracy, liberalism, etc., are born out of the resentment of the masses, and the most powerful bearers of this resentment are the religions of Judaism and Christianity. Therefore, this resentment functions in the exact opposite way from Marx's notion of ideology. The ideas produced by resentment are an attack against the ruling classes, while in Marx the ideological system is a weapon of the ruling classes to keep the others down.

One especially interesting idea in Nietzsche is his attack on the

Christian idea of love. The idea of love is indeed a great problem. First of all, in the modern languages we do not have the distinctions we have in Greek. *Epithumia* is the vital drive (in Latin this is *libido*, the word used by Freud); *philia* is the friendship type of love, the person-to-person relationship; *eros* is the creative, cultural love toward the good, the true, and the beautiful; *agape* is the word used in the New Testament meaning the acceptance of the other one as a person, which includes the principle of justice. It is the power of reuniting with the other person as one standing on the same ultimate ground, and therefore he is the object of acceptance, forgiveness, and transformation. That is the Christian idea of *agape*.

Now this *agape* was sentimentalized long before our time. It was sentimentalized in Romanticism. The concept of Christian love could hardly be distinguished from sentimental desire or from pity. Especially pity was identified with the Christian idea of love. So charity replaced love in the sense in which I have just defined it. Against all this Nietzsche fought with the will to the self-affirmation of life. He is the greatest critic, not of the Christian idea of love, although he thinks it is the Christian idea of love, but of the sentimentalized idea of love, where love is reduced to compassion. In the name of power, the will-to-power, self-affirmation of life, he fights against this idea which undercuts the strong life.

Nietzsche made a good point which we ought to remember in our preaching of love. He said, you speak of selfless love and want to sacrifice yourself to the other one, but this is only a way for the weak person to creep under the protection of somebody else. Erich Fromm, the psychoanalyst, has called this wrong kind of love which Nietzsche attacked "symbiotic love"—from *syn* and *bios*, meaning "living together." This is a love of the weak man for the other one who once lived from his strength, and it is a form of love which exploits the other one. This kind of self-surrender has the unconscious desire for exploitation. This is what Nietzsche was actually fighting against. We should not forget this when speaking of love in Christianity. Love can mean any of these four things which are distinguished in Greek, and therefore it does not mean anything unless we explain in what sense we are using the word. Usually it is connected with a sentimentalized type of love.

Nietzsche was also interested very much in music. He was a great friend of Richard Wagner, the great composer and bridge to modern music. But one of the most interesting events was the break between Nietzsche and Wagner. They were friends, but gradually Nietzsche noticed in Wagner the restoration of a religion of sentimentality. As far as I remember the final break happened in connection with Wagner's *Parsifal*, the romantic sentimentalization of the myth of the representative suffering. Here Nietzsche with his will-to-power, the will of self-affirmation of life, reacted with radicalism and intensity. If you keep in mind that Hitler was a great lover of Wagner's music, you have a clue to how far away Nazism is from Nietzsche's philosophy, although words like "will-to-power" and "superman" sound as if they were a preparation for Nazism. Somehow they actually were, but not in the mind of Nietzsche, just as Marx was a preparation for Stalin, but not in the intention of Marx. These are tragedies in history.

4. The "Death of God" and the New Ideal of Man

The concept of the "death of God" is a half-poetic, half-prophetic symbol. What does it mean? Ordinarily one would think that it means simply the spread of atheism, whatever that word means. But this is not the point in interpreting Nietzsche. Nietzsche did not repeat the atheistic or naturalistic criticism of the theistic idea of God. He accepted just as Marx did Feuerbach's criticism of religion. But Nietzsche meant that when the traditional idea of God falls, something else must fall along with it. The system of ethical values on which society is based fell, and this is the important consequence of this symbol of the death of God. Of course, this is a symbol, for it can only mean that God is dead as far as man's consciousness of him is concerned. The idea that God in himself is dead would be absurd. The idea is rather that in man the consciousness of an ultimate in the traditional sense has died. The result is—and this confirms this interpretation—that somebody else must replace God as the bearer of the system of traditional values. This is man. In the past man had to hear the "thou shalt" and the "thou shalt not" as that which is derived from God or an objective system of values. But now this is gone. So in place of this Nietzsche put man who says "I will." Man no longer says "I shall" because of God, but he says "I will" because I will. I act because I will and I decide what is good or evil.

This idea has many implications. One of them is Nietzsche's famous phrase, "the transvaluation of all values." All the traditional values must be replaced by other ones. Not any transcendent authority does this, but man does it. Who is this man? Does this not imply a tremendous over-estimation of man's greatness? Certainly Nietzsche did not think very highly of man. The mass man who appeared with the industrialization of the European countries was full of resentment; he was weak; he surrendered to the powerful; he produced ideologies which promise him happiness in heaven because he cannot have it on earth. That is man as Nietzsche knew him. So it is not this man, this mass man, who can say "I will." It is the superior man. Nietzsche speaks of the *Übermensch,* which could be translated as superman, except that this has become a character in the funny papers. Other suggestions have been made: higher man or superior man, or simply using the foreign word *Übermensch.* Perhaps superior man is the best.

Where does this superior man come from? He comes from the development of mankind in a Darwinian sense. When you study Nietzsche you should not forget that this was the time in which Darwinism reached its high point. He simply accepted Darwin's idea of the selective process of life in which the weaker species are annihilated and the stronger ones survive to produce still stronger ones. This evolutionary idea of Darwin is the background to Nietzsche's idea of the superior man. Of course, in all evolutionary thinking there is an image of a higher man, of mankind being on a higher level. But Nietzsche did not think merely of an educational, spiritual development of mankind from lower to higher levels of moral education and ethical life, as has usually been thought of in the Western world. Nietzsche would accept this idea too, but he took Darwin in a much more literal and naturalistic way. The superior man is also stronger physically. He is a man straight in body and soul, as he said. In some of his metaphors, this man is even the wild beast, but the wild beast on the human level, not irrational, but powerful, representing a new type of existence in which man is not like the mass man of the present day.

The question has often been asked whether if there is evolution, does the evolution cease with man? Why should it cease with man, and not go beyond him? There are two possible answers. The one answer is that in man the biological possibilities on earth are exhausted; no higher developments can follow. If there is to be any further development, then it must happen in the realm of the mind or soul or spirit of man. But in any case, it is an inner development of man, and not of a bodily kind. Of course, logically this cannot be proved. It presupposes that there is no possibility of a higher bodily development on earth. If this presupposition is not accepted, Nietzsche would be justified. The superior men are the strong ones, full of unbroken vitality, shaped by strict self-discipline, indeed the very ideal of the aristocratic personality. In contrast to them there is the one symbolized in his expression "the last man." His description of the last man is the antitype to the superior man. He is the man who knows everything, but does not care for anything—half-sleepy, half-indifferent, completely conformist, and full of abandoned creativity. He is like the caricature of the "organization man" described in current sociological literature. The mass man avoids at all costs being controversial; therefore he accepts subjection to conformism in all respects. He is disinterested, without any ultimate concern, bored, cynical, empty. All of these descriptions are given in a poetic way by Nietzsche. This is what he calls the nihilism toward which our culture is running.

These ideas have had world-historical consequences. Not only Nazism, but also Fascism used the symbol of the powerful man with the strong self-affirmation of life in himself and in his group. When Fascism and Nazism and early Communism used Nietzsche's categories, they did it with the feeling that the coming nihilism of which Nietzsche spoke would make mankind into a herd of higher animals without creativity, satisfied merely with food and clothes, etc. So this ideology was welcomed by the Fascists and the Nazis. They often used Nietzsche, but they left out one thing. They left out the spiritual aspect. Nietzsche's idea of the superior man includes the bodily and the spiritual or the mental. One of the Nazi leaders said that when he hears the word "spirit" he takes out his pistol, because he felt that this implied the diminution of vitality and creativity. Such ideas were behind the Nazi movement. But do not imagine that we can derive Nazism from

Nietzsche, or from Luther or Hegel for that matter, although some of Nietzsche's formulations have a similarity to the Nazi ideology. But this was only a vulgarization and distortion of ideas which these great men had.

For Nietzsche the idea of the higher race is the aristocratic idea which you can find in all races and nations. It is the vertical idea of racial superiority. It comes from the medieval ideal of the aristocratic personality shaped by strict self-discipline. But in Nazism there was the horizontal idea of race, the idea that a particular biological race is superior to others. Then a particular nation or a particular race, like the Nordic race, becomes the group of superior men. Everything becomes vulgar. In this light you can understand better the quasi-religious demonry of Nazism. It was in opposition to the danger of the industrial society symbolized in the idea of the last man who only looks at things with cynicism and without eros.

Nietzsche's affirmation of life goes beyond all this to a classical metaphysical idea, or mythological idea, expressed by the Stoics, the idea of the eternal return. This is the idea that history does not run ahead but returns to its beginning. This is the classical Greek idea of eternal return. It means that everything that happens now happens an infinite number of times. In *Thus Spake Zarathustra* he described the moment as a door which opens in both directions. In every moment there is a repetition of infinite moments. Everything that happens happens an infinite number of times. This again is symbolic and mythological. If we ask about its meaning, it means the eternalization of the moment. The moment is eternal, not by the presence of eternal life in it, however, as in Schleiermacher and in my own thinking, following the fourth Gospel's idea of eternal life, but for Nietzsche it is a circle. The eternalization of transitory moments means that everything has happened before and will happen again an infinite number of times. It is one of the attempts to understand eternity on the basis of a non-mechanical dynamic naturalism. Religiously it is an affirmation of the eternal meaning of every moment and of everything in every moment. It is eternity not in terms of a hereafter, not in terms of the unique moment into which the eternal breaks, but in terms of any point in a circle from which the circle may start and to which it may return. This is the famous idea of the eternal return. What is decisive in it is the affirmation of life. Nietzsche expresses this by having Zarathustra teach his disciples to say that in the experience of death they will affirm every moment of it. This is Nietzsche's eschatology; this is his hope. Although his life was full of misery, in opposition to this he affirmed it infinitely.

All these ideas have had a great influence on the thinking of our time insofar as it deals with problems of ultimate concern. They have influenced many theologians, at least insofar as they try to answer this form of eschatology by some other form, and to show the difference. They have had infinite importance for all preaching which contains apologetic elements. For here was a man who was not holding to a mechanistic, materialistic form of naturalism. It was an ecstatic naturalism. When we use the word "naturalism" we should be clear about what type we have in mind. Today we call the mechanistic or materialistic typ. of naturalism a reductive naturalism in which everything is reduced to the movement of atoms. It denies that mind and life have any independent reality. They are supposed to be epiphenomenal; *phenomenal* because they exist and you cannot deny that there is life and spirit; and *epi* because they are secondary and superficial, and not a part of any substantial reality. That is not a profound philosophy at all. But it is only one form of naturalism. Nietzsche represented quite another one which was great, although presented in a half-demonic form.

*   *   *   *   *   *   *   *   *   *

Question: You have given a description of Nietzsche, but not a criticism of him. Would you please do so?

Answer: I would like to do so, although this would be a long story if my criticism would take in all the elements of his thought. But let me start with his concept of the will-to-power. I told you that Nietzsche's idea of the will-to-power does not use the terms "will" and "power" in the ordinary sense. Rather, it is the urge toward life in everything that is, even beyond the organic life. It is a metaphysical concept. For the nonhuman dimension the word "urge" would even be more adequate. And "power" is not social, political, or economic power, but rather the self-affirmation of life, not only in the sense of preserving life, but of the further development of life. In this respect, Nietzsche's idea is an adequate description of life processes as we can observe them in ourselves and in nature, so no criticism is needed. But insofar as the world of norms in relation to the will-to-power is lost in Nietzsche, criticism proves to be necessary. It is precisely this lack of normative principles which has made it possible for the Nazis to misuse Nietzsche. Nietzsche himself had the aristocratic norms. His ideal was the republic of Venice in the sixteenth and seventeenth centuries. The strict self-discipline which was characteristic of all members of the aristocratic class was his ideal. So there was not only arbitrariness but also discipline. But this discipline had no norms which could be applied to men as a whole. Therefore, people like Heidegger could simply replace the older norms which, according to Nietzsche himself, have disappeared with the death of God. I spoke about this last time. Heidegger replaced them by the resolve, the decision to do something without any norm, as Nietzsche also did. Since there is no norm, there is only my will, and this is the highest norm. This "I will" of Nietzsche, his highest norm, is not able to provide criteria for good and evil, so Nietzsche could write his little book, Beyond Good and Evil. This is the one criticism, the lack of norms. The result of this lack is apparent, for it provided the possibility of misusing Nietzsche's idea for the sake of an irrational will-to-power as in a phenomenon like Nazism.

I would also have to criticize his doctrine of the eternal return. His idea is a return to the classical circular notion of repetitious time. There is a lack of novelty, of the really new. True, Nietzsche did have a strong emphasis on the new in history. He could speak of the renewal of all values, the transvaluation of values, and the coming of the superior man. There the concept of the new is present. But this happens only within a particular segment of the circle. Nothing absolutely new is created. A symbol such as the kingdom of God as the aim of history is very remote from Nietzsche. Nietzsche denied Augustine's idea that time is running toward something and not toward a point from which it has started. That is, time is going in circles. This was a relapse in Nietzsche, and an inconsistent relapse because he also had the Darwinian notion of movement from lower to higher forms of life in history.

A third criticism would have to focus on the idea of the superior man. The biological increase of perfection in man would not increase the heights of man's spirit. The biological development of man has come to a point from which a new development has started, namely, the development of man's spiritual self-realization in terms of culture, religion, and ethics. This new series of developments cannot be enhanced by any further improvement of bodily existence. One could say that with respect to nature, man is an end, just as with respect to history, the kingdom of God is an end. Nietzsche was driven by naturalism to a misunderstanding of the new beginning which was inaugurated in life when the first man used the first word to describe the universal.

Then we can also say that his idea of the death of God is only relatively true. For the God of the tradition is still alive and Nietzsche himself introduced another God, this divine-demonic being which he called life. I referred you to the last collection of fragments in his *Will to Power*. It gives an ecstatic vision of the irrationality and paradoxical character of life as a whole, and calls for obedience to this life by affirming it as it is. He certainly is not atheistic in the popular nonsensical term. But he has a different God than the God of the religious tradition, especially of the Christian tradition. This holds true as well of the Asian tradition. He denied the Asian tradition when he denied Schopenhauer who introduced the Asian tradition into the Western world. He denied both traditions. Yet, I would say that the presupposition of his negation is an awareness of eternity, and this awareness of eternity was as much alive in him as in every human being.

I could also go into his theory of resentment and theory of morality, which is self-contradictory, because the aristocratic groups which imposed their ethics upon the masses had their own ethical norms independent of individual willfulness. Nietzsche is an irrational prophet, a naturalistic prophet. But Christian theologians can learn very much from him. I regretted nothing so much as the fact that he could be so misused by Nazism. For this reason he lost much of his significance in Germany, and probably also in other countries.

CHAPTER V

New Ways of Mediation

What we have just been dealing with has been the reaction to the great synthesis, the attempt to overcome the cleavages in the modern mind. There is an interesting fact that at the end of the nineteenth century people who sensed very deeply what was happening through the destruction of the great synthesis, the distortion of its elements, the approaching nihilism, etc., all seemed to live on the boundary line of insanity. Nietzsche himself was on this boundary line and was finally completely encompassed by it. So was a man like Baudelaire, the French poet, and Rimbaud and Strindberg. They could not deal with the *fin de siècle* (the situation at the end of the nineteenth century). And painters like Van Gogh and Munch were afflicted in the same way. They are all expressions of the disturbing and destructive consequences of the breakdown of the great synthesis. Their inability to find a roof for themselves drove them into this situation. Or one can say that people who because of their makeup were in danger of falling into insanity could become the prophets of the coming catastrophe—because of their intense sensitivity—and at the same time the representatives of the new situation. These men were lonely geniuses who anticipated the catastrophes of our century and also contributed to the catastrophes by destroying the unifying traditions of the Western world and the syntheses of Hegel and Schleiermacher.

Now we must deal with a large group of highly intelligent, scholarly, and pious theologians who are usually classified in general as theologians of mediation. The term "theology of mediation" (*Vermittlungs-theologie*) can be understood in two ways. It can be understood as something merely negative, by identifying mediation with compromise. It is very easy to accuse a theologian of compromising the message with the modern mind. This places him before the alternative of simply repeating the given tradition or of mediating the tradition to the modern mind. If he simply repeats he is superfluous, because the tradition is there and everyone has access to it, whether or not he understands it at all. But if he is not to be superfluous, he becomes a theologian of mediation, mediating the tradition. And this is the second sense, and something positive. We could say that theology by definition is mediation. The term "theology of mediation" is almost a tautology, for a theology that does not mediate the tradition is no theology. In this sense I would defend every theologian who is accused of being a theologian of mediation, and I myself would cease being a theologian altogether if I had to abandon the work of mediation. For the alternative to it is repetition, and that is not theology at all.

The critical undertone in the term "theology of mediation"—for the term has taken on a negative connotation—is directed against those who tried to rescue as much as possible in Schleiermacher's theology and in Hegel's philosophy (and vice versa)—for both were philosophers and theologians—and to make them more adequate to the religious tradition. The theology of mediation did not represent a new breakthrough, a new beginning, but more an attempt to save what could be saved, and to combine parts of the tradition of Hegel and Schleiermacher with the Christian tradition.

Most of these theologians of mediation are not known even by name in this country, and since they do not have any direct influence here, we will for the most part bypass them. This is not true, however, of the famous attempt to go back to Kant as a help in the situation. This battle cry, this signal of return or retreat, as I like to call it, was sounded by Ritschl and his group. This had great influence in this country. When I came to this country Ritschlianism was dead in Germany, but here to my great surprise it was very much alive.

Let us look at some of the types of theology of mediation. The problem they all had was to gain certainty about the contents of the

Christian message, after the critical movements of the eighteenth and nineteenth centuries had arisen. Everything fell under criticism. Everything was in doubt. The traditional forms had no power of resisting historical criticism or philosophical criticism, even if they would be repeated again and again by the theologians of restoration. So it was necessary to answer this fundamental question: Is there a way of reestablishing certainty in the religious realm?

A. Experience and the Biblical Message

One of the answers to the fundamental questions of certainty was given through a return to Schleiermacher's concept of religious consciousness. The word "experience" was used rather than "consciousness." But it was obviously dependent on Schleiermacher's idea of religion. We can see many theologians in whom the problem of religious experience was in the center of their thinking. In this country there was a theology of experience, the so-called empirical theology. For the moment I want to speak of some of these important theological schools of mediation.

1. *The Erlangen School*

There was the Erlangen school in Germany which preserved a strong attachment to the Lutheran tradition. In this school Schleiermacher's idea of the religious consciousness was enlarged in significance under the heading of the concept of experience. The religious experience meant everything. Let us look at this word. Experience can mean many things. During my first years in America, in the thirties and forties, the atmosphere around Columbia University was influenced by Dewey's pragmatism to such an extent that the word "experience" was used for almost everything. Then I realized that it was simply another word for "reality." For the objective reality was questioned and experience expressed the going beyond of subjects and objects. This word was used so much that I finally had the feeling that the word had become useless. Probably this is still the situation. For this reason I have tried to introduce the word "encounter" which is taken from Buber's concept of the I-Thou encounter.

In any case, the theologians following Schleiermacher asked the question: How can we attain to certainty about God, about revelation, about Christ, about the divine Spirit, etc.? Kant had criticized every way of reaching God by arguments. These theologians of experience accepted Kant's criticism. Nor could they go along with the speculative theology which followed Hegel, using much more refined arguments. Then there was the way of historical research. But this way was closed because historical research, so far from giving contents, actually removed them or made them doubtful, and questioned the whole historical foundation of Christianity. How can we reach a history which happened two thousand years ago when we know so little about it in terms of sound historical research? If this is the case, there is only one possible answer left. There must be a point of immediate participation, and for this the word "experience" was used. The experience of the divine reality must be the presence of the divine reality in us, and this must be the only possible assuring element. Then, however, the question arose: How can the inner experience which we have in our century guarantee anything which has happened hundreds of years ago? The answer to this question was: The reality of the past event is guaranteed by the effect it has on me.

A man named F. H. R. Frank (1827–1894), professor in Erlangen, produced a whole system of theology in which he tried to show how my status here and now as a Christian is dependent on the witness of the Old and New Testaments to what has happened. All the biblical stories, including creation, ultimate fulfillment, the coming of Christ, even the miracles, are guaranteed by my personal experience here and now. It is a kind of projection of my experience into the divine-human reality of the biblical peiod. Such a method was very impressive and was at that time the only way out. But, of course, it was not difficult for the critics to reply that everything that you project out of your own experience has been given to you originally by the Bible and the tradition, and that therefore you cannot escape being dependent on them. So you cannot guarantee the contents by your own experience. But if not, then in what way is it possible? This brings us to the fundamental problem with which modern theology is still wrestling. We cannot accept as the Roman Catholics do the authority of councils and popes. Of course, ultimately they cannot do that either, that is, without having within themselves the experience of the spiritual power of the Roman Church. As long as they do not ask questions, there is no problem, but if they ask questions, then their answer is also experiential. It is based on the experience of the glory, the truth, and the power of the Roman Church and that to which it witnesses. In other words, even the authoritarian Roman Catholic Christians are not able to escape that element of subjectivity which we call experience. But this experience does not give them any contents. All the contents come from the church, its tradition, and the Bible. The fact that they accept *these* contents is due to their participation in the spirit of the church.

The same thing can be true with Protestants. As I mentioned before, Kierkegaard had the idea of becoming contemporaneous with Jesus by leaping over two thousand years. How is that possible? It is a matter of question what Kierkegaard really meant, but perhaps he meant what Paul said when he said that we do not know the Christ any longer according to the flesh but according to the Spirit. We are in Christ (*en Christo*) insofar as he is the Spirit. This is immediate participation. Here you see a theological problem which arose out of the dissolution of the great synthesis. How much can experience guarantee? Can it guarantee any of the contents in space and time? I do not believe that this is a settled question. We are still in the midst of this situation. When today we ask, What guarantees the Christ-character of Jesus of Nazareth? we cannot give a merely historical answer, because the historical scientific answer leaves us in a state of doubt, of degrees of probability or improbability, and does not carry us beyond this. But if we say that something has happened to me, we speak in terms of experience. This thing which has happened to me is related to an event which must have happened in history, because it has had an impact on my own historical existence. This is something which certainly can be said and must be said. Then there remains the question as to how much can actually be guaranteed by religious experience? I leave you with this question, the question with which all the theologians of mediation struggled in trying to overcome the gap between subject and object which was opened up during the Enlightenment, which was seemingly closed in the great synthesis, but then opened up again. And so it stands wide open today, with some new attempts to close it being made at the same time.

2. Martin Kähler

At this time another theologian appeared who dealt with the same problem, but tried to answer it in a different way. He was Martin Kähler, also a theologian of mediation. He found an answer which became very important and which will be discussed for a long time to come, but mainly, no doubt, in the form which Bultmann has given to it. The impact of Kähler was very great in many directions. In his time his impact was limited by the Kant-Ritschlian school which dominated the European universities. Today the situation has changed and the lifework of this theologian has become visible again.

What Martin Kähler did for us—now I speak half-historically and half-autobiographically—was of twofold significance. First, he understood the problem of doubt; he understood the question: How can the subject in religion come to the object? How can they be reunited after having been separated by the criticism of the Enlightenment and the subsequent events? And he answered: This doubt is an element in the continuous human situation which we cannot simply overcome by putting everything into the subjectivity of experience. We must combine the subjectivity of experience, which he also had to accept like everyone else, with the objectivity of the biblical witness. So he pointed to the reality which is described in this witness, not only its central manifestation, namely, the Christ and all that is connected with him, but also the reality of the divine in nature and history, and beyond nature and history, in creation and fulfillment. But how can these two things come together, the subjective and the objective? His answer was that they cannot in an absolute way. They can come together only in a way which accepts the limits of our finitude. This means that we cannot reach absolute certainty. He placed this in analogy to the Protestant message of justification by grace through faith, namely, the acceptance of man in spite of his disrupted inner life and estrangement, which can never be fully overcome. This is the Lutheran idea of the impossibility of being a saint without being at the same time a sinner (*simul iustus et peccator*).

Now Kähler applied this message of justification not only to the inner moral acts of man, but also to his inner intellectual acts. Not only he who has sinned in the moral sense of the word, but also he who has doubted—the intellectual form of sin—is accepted by God. The doctrine of justification is applied to thoughts and not only to morality. This means that doubt does not necessarily separate us from God. This is what I learned from Kähler at that time and developed further in my own theology. But the first impact came from the theology of mediation rooted in the fundamental principle of the Reformation, and then applied to the situation of the split between subject and object since the beginning of the modern period. That is the one thing which came out of this theology of mediation. Similar ideas have become increasingly common in both Europe and America because of the enduring split between the objectivity of the Bible and tradition, and the subjectivity of experience. They come together, but never fully. The split remains, and so doubt remains.

The other point in Kähler's impact on us had to do with historical criticism. Historical criticism is a way of approaching the objective side, namely, those events which we say have had a transforming impact on us. How can we become certain of those events? They are the events that are responsible for our inner experience of being saved in spite of being sinners and doubters. Kähler's answer to the problem of the historical treatment of the Bible was given in terms of a sharp distinction between the historical Jesus and the Christ of faith. His famous book, *The So-called Historical Jesus and the Historic, Biblical Christ*, is coming out in English translation, with an introduction to Kähler and his theology by a former student of mine, because it is so relevant to our own situation.[1]

What is the relationship between the historical Jesus and the Christ of faith? Can we separate them? Must we accept the idea that Christ can never be reached by us apart from faith? Is there anything that can

[1] Translated, edited, and with an Introduction by Carl E. Braaten (Philadelphia: Fortress Press, 1964).

be done about the doubts produced by historical research into the biblical writings? Kähler himself did not believe that the two must be separated. For Kähler the Jesus of history is at the same time the Christ of faith, and the certainty of the Christ of faith is independent of the historical results of the critical approach to the New Testament. Faith guarantees what historical research can never reach. How can faith do this? What can faith guarantee? There lies the problem today, a problem which has been sharpened in the meantime by people like Bultmann and his whole school. The first real view of this situation in its radical aspects, however, we owe to Kähler, who came from the great synthesis, lived in it during a certain period of his life, then was transformed by the awakening movement and became one of the leading theologians of this period. But, as I told you, this position of Kähler was not decisive for the situation in the nineteenth century. He was a prophetic forerunner of what developed more fully only in the twentieth century. The heritage of Martin Kähler has been rediscovered only in the present-day discussion in view of the radical criticism, and not only in Europe but also in this country.

B. The "Back To Kant" Movement

Now I want to deal with the Kant-Ritschl-Harnack line of thought which led to Troeltsch in Germany and to Rauschenbusch and the so-called liberal theology in this country.

Why did a certain theological group suddenly raise the cry "back to Kant" after the great synthesis crumbled and they were surrounded by its many pieces? Why Kant and nobody else? None of these people said "back to orthodoxy" or "back to pietism." There were philosophers as well as theologians in the neo-Kantian school which was dominant at the time that I was a student. It was the Ritschlian school which introduced Kantianism into theology. You recall what we said about Kant's prison of finitude. Kant's critical epistemology determined that we cannot apply the categories of finitude to the divine. But, there was one point of breakthrough in the sphere of practical reason, namely, the experience of the moral imperative and its unconditional character. Here alone can we transcend the limits of finitude. But we cannot do it theoretically. We cannot prove God or speak of God directly, but only in terms of "as if." We call this a regulative way of speaking, not a constitutive way which can affirm something directly of God.

This retreat to Kant goes in the opposite direction of that other slogan which I used before: "Understanding Kant means transcending Kant." This was the idea of Fichte, Schelling, Hegel, and Schleiermacher. The Ritschlians argued that the result of this transcending Kant was the ruins of the great synthesis which now lay before them, like the broken pieces of the Tower of Babel. But the Ritschlians did not believe that these pieces could be put back together in the way that the other theologians of mediation tried to do. Nor was a return to Orthodoxy or Pietism or biblicism possible as the theologians of restoration tried to do. So another way had to be found. This way was a withdrawal to the acceptance of our finitude as we have it in Kant's critical philosophy. The Ritschlians said that Kant is the philosopher of Protestantism. Protestantism does not aspire to climb up to the divine, but keeps itself within the limits of finitude. The attempt of the great synthesis is ultimately a product of mysticism, of the principle of identity between the divine and the human. Therefore, this "back to Kant" movement was extremely hostile to all forms of mysticism, including the theologies of experience, because there is a mystical element present in Schleiermacher's idea of religious consciousness and the other forms of experiential theology. Experience means having the divine within ourselves, not necessarily by nature, but yet given and felt within our own being. But this was not admitted by the neo-Kantian school. They protested not only against genuine mysticism, but also against every theology of experience. What then was left? Only two things. The one is historical research. This is the greatness and at the same time the shortcoming of liberal theology. It is the greatness insofar as it dares to apply the historical method to the biblical literature; it is the shortcoming insofar as it tries to base faith on the results of historical research. That was what they tried to do. There is thus a positive and a negative side in this school.

But there must be a second factor, for how can there be religious certainty? According to the Ritschlians, Kant has left but one window out of our finitude, and this is the moral imperative. The real basis of certainty is the moral point of view. We are certain of ourselves as moral personalities. This is not the experience of something mystical outside of ourselves; this is the immediate personal experience, or more exactly, the experience of being a person as such. Religion is then that which makes us able to actualize ourselves as moral persons. Religion is a supporting power of the ethical. These defenders of Christianity tried to save Christianity with the help of the moral principle, but in doing so they aroused the wrath of all those for whom the mystical element in religion is decisive. So here we have a religion argued for on the basis of the ethical experience of the personality. Religion is the help toward moral self-realization. So the two sides of the Ritschlian theology are: objective, scientific research and the moral principle or experience of the ethical personality.

The great synthesis about which we have been speaking dealt seriously with the question of truth. Christianity's claim was that it mediated truth, truth about God, the world, and man. That means there is ontological, cosmological, and anthropological truth. Both Schleiermacher and Hegel wanted to affirm the truth in connection with the whole of reality. The critics of Hegel and the Hegelians denied that a satisfactory synthesis had been achieved between Christianity and philosophical knowledge about man, nature, the universe as a whole, and the divine source and ground of the universe. So the neo-Kantians and the Ritschlians gave up the claim to truth in this sense. They withdrew to Kant's critique of practical reason and said: The divine appears through the moral imperative and nowhere else. The problem of truth was replaced by the moral answer. The function of Christianity is then to make morality possible. From this point of view all ontological questions were dropped so far as possible. Of course, it is never fully possible for anyone to do that. In the neo-Kantian school itself there arose people at the beginning of this century who showed that there are always ontological presuppositions in every epistemology. It is self-deception to believe that you can answer the famous question, "How do you know?" before you know something, before you answer questions, and then put them under criticism. Epistemology cannot stand on its own feet because knowing and the reality which is known are both ontological concepts. You cannot escape definite presuppositions if you deal with knowledge. The same is true of modern analytic philosophy. It analyzes man's logical and linguistic structures, but it always has a hidden presupposition about the relation of logic and language to reality, even if it does not acknowledge it. Sometimes this relation is completely negative when it is said that we do not know anything about reality, and that our logical and linguistic structures have nothing to do with reality. But this must then be proven, and if somebody tries to prove it, he is an ontologist. Or if there is a positive relation, they have to do what philosophers have always done: they have to show how language and logic are related to reality.

So Ritschlianism was a withdrawal from the ontological to the moral. The whole religious message, the message of Jesus which had to be described in historical terms, is a message which liberates the personality from the pressures of nature both outside of and within man. The function of salvation is the victory of spirit or mind over nature. The way this happens is through the forgiveness of sins. This is the inner meaning of the Ritschlian theology of retreat. It was a theology which could fortify the strong development of the bourgeois personality in the middle and the end of the nineteenth century. In an article in the book, *The Christian Answer*,[2] edited by Van Dusen, formerly president of Union Theological Seminary, New York, I have given a long description of this development of the personality ideal from the Renaissance to the end of the nineteenth century, by showing some works of the visual arts. There you can see what a bourgeois personality is. The Ritschlian theology provided the theological foundation for this development of the strong, active, morally disciplined individual person. It was connected with liberal elements in the social and political structure, with autonomous thinking in the sciences and with the rejection of all authority. It was compatible with the mood of the time, the liberal personalistic mood, but this was not to last long into the twentieth century.

The Ritschlian negation of ontology was joined with another concept which is still being discussed in modern American philosophy, although not as much now as thirty years ago when I came to this country. This is the concept of value judgments. Instead of making ontological statements, it was alleged that Christianity makes value judgments. This means that everything is related to the subject who makes value

[2] "The World Situation," *The Christian Answer*, edited by Henry P. Van Dusen (New York: Charles Scribner's Sons, 1948).

judgments. This was a typical device of escape. It was taken from Rudolf Lotze, (1817–1881), an important figure in the history of philosophy in the middle of the nineteenth century. How could man's spiritual life, man's personality, be saved in the face of the increasing naturalism which dissolves everything into a constellation of atoms? The answer was that although we are unable to make ontological judgments, we can make value judgments. On the basis of value judgments, we can evaluate Christianity as that religion which can overcome the forces of the natural and secure us as personalities of disciplined moral character.

You can see an analogy to this in the secularized puritanism—not the original puritanism—of this country. This was the reason for Ritschl's influence in this country long after it had died out in Germany. It was mediated through pupils of Ritschl himself or of Wilhelm Herrmann (1846–1922) in Marburg under whom many Americans studied. He was a man in whom liberalism was connected with a profound piety and a strong desire to liberate Christianity from all authoritarian ties.

Out of the Ritschlian antiontological feeling came a doctrine of God in which the element of power in God was denied or reduced almost to nothing. It tried to overcome the polarity of power and love in God, and to reduce the idea of God to love. The message of salvation was reduced to forgiveness. The symbol of divine wrath and judgment was removed from practical piety. This was in line with the Enlightenment, with Kantianism and the whole humanistic tradition. It was also very successful. But a criticism is necessary. When we pray, we usually start our prayers with "Almighty God." In doing so we immediately attribute might and power to God. The divinity of God lies in his being the ultimate power of being. This was one of the weakest points in the Ritschlian theology, and at this point the criticism set in.

C. Adolf von Harnack

The greatest figure in the Ritschlian school was Adolf von Harnack (1851–1930). He was a very impressive figure, basically a church historian. His greatest achievement was the *History of Dogma*,[3] still a classical work in this area of research. Any student of the history of

3 Seven vols., translated by Neil Buchanan (New York: Dover Publications, 1900).

Christian thought must reckon with it. Those of you who come from very conservative traditions may have the feeling, without admitting it, that the dogmas sort of fell down from heaven. If you read Harnack's *History of Dogma*, you will see how the great creeds—the Apostles', the Nicene, and the Chalcedonian—came into existence, how much historical drama, how much of human passions, and also how much divine providential guidance were involved in this development. You will see that the ecumenical councils of Nicaea and Chalcedon used a lot of terms from Greek philosophy in formulating the trinitarian and christological dogmas. Harnack saw in this development a second wave of Hellenization. The first wave was gnosticism, and the second wave was the formulation of the ancient dogma. The first was rejected by the church; the second was accepted and used by the church.

Harnack's research into the history of dogma raised a lot of problems which are still being discussed in theology today. The relation of Christianity to gnosticism is still a live issue. Perhaps the most important book on gnosticism is the one written by Hans Jonas, entitled *Gnosis und spätantiker Geist*.[4] His interpretation of gnosticism is based on existentialist categories as used by Heidegger and other existentialists. It shows you that the speculations of the gnostics were not all nonsense, but were based on the human situation in the late ancient world, which—like our own situation—was one of complete disruption and meaninglessness. There was the longing for salvation, the continual looking for saving powers in a deteriorated world at the end of the Roman Empire. Gnosticism was an attempt to express the saving forces and describe the human situation in categories very like those of the present-day existentialist philosophers.

But Christianity rejected gnosticism for one reason. These gnostics were anti-Old Testament. That means they were against the idea of creation, that the world is created good, that there is no matter from which one must be liberated, etc. Liberation according to Christianity is liberation from finitude and sin, and not from matter in which we are involved. In other words, the dualistic form of gnosticism was rejected, the dualism between a highest God and a counter God. The church

[4] Göttingen: Vandenhoek & Ruprecht, 1934. Cf. Hans Jonas, *The Gnostic Religion* (Boston: Beacon Press, 1958).

succeeded in rejecting this gnostic dualism. But the church nevertheless used the concepts of the hellenistic world. You should not call them Greek pure and simple, for classical Greek did not last far beyond the second century before Christ. Hellenism followed this, and Hellenism is a mixture of Greek, Persian, Egyptian, Jewish, and even Indian elements, and mystical groups of all kinds. It is a mixed religiosity in which the Greek concepts were used, but in a religiously transformed sense.

In order to be received the Christian message had to be proclaimed in categories which could be understood by the people who were to receive it. The Christian Church did this without fear. Harnack's criticism was that in this way Christianity became intellectualized. But Harnack was wrong in this respect. My main criticism of him has been right on this point. The more our knowledge of the gnostics and the whole Hellenistic culture has increased in the last fifty years, the more we see how wrong he was in this respect. He considered Hellenism as identical with intellectualization. This is not at all true. This is not even true of Plato, or Aristotle and the Stoics. Every great philosophy is rooted in an existential emergency, in a situation of questioning out of which saving answers must come. If you read Plato and Aristotle you will find that this is certainly the case with them. But in Hellenism this is manifestly so, because the whole period from B.C. 100 to about A.D. 400 is a period in which the question of salvation from distorted reality stands in the center. The Greek concepts already had a religious tinge when they were used by the Christian dogmas. So Harnack was right in saying that Hellenization had taken place, but wrong in defining this as intellectualization.

According to Harnack a foreign element entered into Christianity when terms like *ousia* and *hypostasis* were used in constructing the official dogma of the church. This process began not only in the fourth- and fifth-century councils, but already in the apostolic fathers, and that means in the generation which is contemporaneous with the latest biblical writings. Then this process received a strong impetus from the apologists who elaborated the logos concept in theology. All this can be called Hellenization, but how else could it have happened? The pagans were not Jews, and so the Jewish concepts could not be used. Besides, the Jewish concepts were not used so much even in the circles in which

Jesus and John the Baptist arose. If you read the Dead Sea Scrolls, you will find that the Old Testament concepts are there, but even more you will find elements from the apocalyptic movements from the intertestamental period. Even Judaism had adapted to the new situation. It could not have been done in any other way if Judaism or Christianity were to survive.

Harnack's greatness is that he showed this process of Hellenization. His shortcoming is that he did not see the necessity of it. Those of us who studied under the influence of Harnack's *History of Dogma* sensed a tremendous liberation. It was the liberation from the necessity of identifying Hellenistic concepts with the Christian message itself. On the other hand, I would not accept the idea which one hears so much that all the Greek elements must be thrown out and only the Old Testament terms should be used. Christianity, it is suggested, is basically a matter of the Old Testament language and a continuation of Old Testament theology and piety. If this were to be done consistently, at least two-thirds of the New Testament would have to be ruled out, for both Paul and John used a lot of Hellenistic concepts. Besides, it would rule out the whole history of doctrine. This idea is a new bondage to a particular development, the Old Testament development. Christianity is not nearer to the Jews than to the Greeks. I believe that the one who expressed that was the great missionary to the Greeks and to the Hellenistic pagan world.

There is another side to Harnack which was much more impressive for the masses of educated people at the turn of the century. He himself once told me that in the year 1900 the main railway station in the city of Leipzig, one of the largest in Central Europe, was blocked by freight cars in which his book *What Is Christianity?* was being sent all over the world. He also told us that this book was being translated into more languages than any other book except the Bible. This means that this book, which was the religious witness of one of the greatest scholars of the century, had great significance to the educated people prior to the first World War. It meant the possibility of affirming the Christian message in a form which was free from its dogmatic captivity and at the same time very much rooted in the biblical image of Jesus. But in order to elaborate this image, he invented the formula which distinguished sharply between the gospel of Jesus and the gospel about Jesus. He stated that the gospel about Jesus does not belong in the gospel preached by Jesus. This is the classical formula of liberal theology: the gospel or message preached by Jesus contains nothing of the later message preached concerning Jesus.

Such a statement presupposes the reduction of the gospel to the first three Gospels, then the elimination from these Gospels of all that shows the influence of Paul. Baur's theory of the conflict between Paul and Jesus is revived here in a more refined, modern way, namely, that Paul interpreted Jesus in a way which is very far removed from the actual historical Jesus. This idea of course has some contemporary followers. Only it is not Paul who is so much at the center of the discussion, but the early community, which existed before Paul. This early community, on the basis of the resurrection experience, produced the doctrines about Jesus, doctrines which cannot be found in the original message of Jesus himself. This original message is the message of the coming kingdom, and the kingdom is the state in which God and the individual member of the kingdom are in a relation of forgiveness, acceptance, and love.

Again someone might say, you have merely presented this, but have not criticized it. So I will anticipate this question and say, I don't believe that this is a possible approach. I believe that the whole New Testament is united, including the first three Gospels, in the statement that Jesus is the Christ, the bringer of the new eon. I think this fundamental statement overcomes the split between Jesus, on the one hand, and the early community, or Paul or John, on the other hand. That the differences are there no one who views the literature historically can deny or conceal, but whether the differences are of absolute significance systematically is quite another question. My criticism of the whole liberal theology, including Harnack, is that it had no real systematic theology; it believed in the results of historical research in a wrong way. Therefore, its systematic utterances were comparatively poor. But at that time they had meaning for many people.

D. MISCELLANEOUS MOVEMENTS IN THEOLOGY

Now a few other movements must be dealt with very sketchily.

1. *The Luther-Renaissance*

The Luther-Renaissance was a movement which happened within the Ritschlian school itself, and gave to this school a greater dimension of depth. When Luther was rediscovered, it became clear that Luther's God was not the moralistically reduced God of liberal theology. Luther's God is the hidden God, the unknown God, the God in whom the darkness of life is rooted as well as the light, the God who is seen in terms of the voluntaristic line of thinking to which we referred in a previous lecture. This was very important for it liberated the figure of Luther from a kind of popular distortion; it showed the tremendous inner forces in the great revolutionary, the first reformer whose breakthrough was the root of all the reformatory movements, including Zwingli's and Calvin's and those of the radical evangelicals. This all happened on the basis of the Ritschlian school, but it resulted in an inner deepening of it.

2. *Biblical Realism*

There was another school which was in a certain respect a biblicistic reaction against Ritschlianism, but it was not a biblicism bound to the inspiration doctrine and other fundamentalist tenets. The inspiration doctrine had been given up except by a few fundamentalists in Germany. Rather, it was a biblical realism which was much more adequate to human nature, just as Luther was much more relevant to the human nature than the moralistically determined individual personality of the late nineteenth century ever could imagine. One of those responsible for this biblical realism was Martin Kähler, and along with him were his friends Adolf Schlatter, Wilhelm Lütgert, and Hermann Cremer.

Their weakness was that in spite of their biblical realism and their understanding of the deeper aspects of human nature in the light of the

Bible, they resisted the historical criticism. It was not possible to justify this resistance, because historical criticism was a matter of scientific honesty. Whether one was more conservative or more radical in the historical investigation of the biblical literature, the methods had to be accepted in the long run. I myself experienced a real crisis in my development after I left Halle where this kind of biblicism was firmly established, and began independently to study the history of biblical criticism. It was especially in studying Albert Schweitzer's history of research into the life of Jesus[5] that I became convinced of the inadequacy of the kind of biblicism in which the historical questions are not taken seriously. This experience prevented me from remaining silent about the historical critical problems in face of the Barthian influence during the years of the church struggle in Germany. Barth silenced these problems almost completely in his own school, and when I came to America theologians here were not worried about them either.

But genuine problems cannot be ignored in the long run. The explosion produced by Bultmann was not so much due to anything new that he did, but to the fact that he brought to the surface problems which had been suppressed by the Barthian school. Of course, Bultmann had his own particular kind of radical criticism, but there was nothing methodologically new in the situation ever since historical criticism arose two hundred years ago. The explosion came when Bultmann wrote his article on demythologizing, "New Testament and Mythology."[6] This shock might have been much less severe if the German theologians—and others too—had realized all along the impossibility of disregarding the historical approach in New Testament interpretation.

3. Radical Criticism

The increase of radicalism in historical criticism undercut the presuppositions of Harnack and the whole liberal theology. The presupposition of Harnack's *What Is Christianity?* was that one can arrive at a

[5] *The Quest of the Historical Jesus*, translated by W. Montgomery (London: Adam & Charles Black, 1910).
[6] Rudolf Bultmann, *Kerygma and Myth*, Vol. I, edited by H. W. Hartsch, translated by Reginald Fuller (London: S.P.C.K., 1954).

fairly accurate picture of the empirical man, Jesus of Nazareth, guaranteed by the methods of historical science. One can arrive, that is, at a
definition of original Christianity by deleting all the additions of the
early congregations and of Paul and John. But it turned out that this
was not possible.

Radical historical criticism began first with the Old Testament. Previously the Old Testament had been read in the old Luther Bible in
which certain passages had been printed in large letters. These were the
consoling passages or those specially related to the New Testament
fulfillment of prophecy. The confidence in this way of reading the Old
Testament was broken by the Wellhausen hypothesis. This was an
event of great religious significance. Now the Old Testament could be
read not as a collection of edifying words printed in big letters, but as a
real development in history, as the history of revelation, in which the
divine and the human are both involved.

New Testament criticism proceeded in an even more radical way. If
Harnack could speak about Jesus in terms of God and the soul, as he
did, then the problem was: What about the inner self-consciousness of
Jesus? What was Jesus' understanding of himself? The answer to this is
largely dependent on the "Son of Man" concept in the Gospels. What
did this mean in Jesus' own mind? Did he apply it to himself, and if so,
in what sense? And if not, what did the early Christians mean by it?
The two possible ways of answering this question were presented by
Albert Schweitzer in the conclusion of his book, *The Quest of the
Historical Jesus*. One of the ways is presented and defended by
Schweitzer himself. It is the solution of thoroughgoing eschatology.
Jesus considered himself as an eschatological, apocalyptic figure, identifying himself with the Son of Man in the sense of Daniel. Here the
Son of Man is an emissary of God standing before the divine throne,
then leaving it to descend into the evils of this eon and to bring in a new
age. Then Schweitzer goes on to describe the catastrophe when Jesus
cried out from the cross, feeling that God had abandoned him. Jesus had
expected that God in his power would intervene to save him and the
world, but to no avail. This is the one version.

There are many other versions. But the other one that Schweitzer
contrasted with his own is that of radical historical skepticism, represented by Wilhelm Wrede and later by Bultmann himself. Skepticism

here does not mean doubt about God, the world, and man, but doubt about the possibility of reaching the historical Jesus by our historical methods. My own heritage has been this school of historical skepticism. If Schweitzer's apocalyptic interpretation of Jesus is not right, we must admit that we are in a position where we cannot know very much about the historical Jesus. This radical situation is the background for my own attempt to answer the systematic question how we can say that Jesus is the Christ if historical research can never reach a sure image of the historical Jesus. The second volume of my *Systematic Theology* is an attempt to draw out the consequences for systematic theology created by this skeptical attitude to the New Testament generally and to the historical Jesus in particular.

4. *Rudolf Bultmann*

We can deal with a certain aspect of Bultmann's work while we are on this subject of historical criticism. If you read his *History of the Synoptic Tradition*,[7] you will see the radicalism of his skepticism, and why he is unable to reach conservative results. But for systematic theology the question is not whether the results are more or less conservative or radical. Historians who oppose Bultmann because they are a bit more conservative use the same method he does. The two poles of conservatism or radicalism in criticism do not mean a thing for systematic theology, because a conservative criticism, as much as a radical criticism, can never get beyond probabilities on historical matters. Whether we are offered more positive or more negative probabilities does not make any difference for the fundamental problem of systematic theology.

In this connection we can make some remarks about the so-called new quest of the historical Jesus carried on by some of Bultmann's followers. They are obviously more optimistic with respect to the probabilities, but no change results for the systematic situation. Our knowledge of the historical Jesus never gets beyond probabilities of one kind or another.

Bultmann has combined his radical historical research with a systematic attempt. He calls this systematic attempt "demythologization." He means by this expression that we must liberate the biblical message from

[7] Translated by John Marsh (New York: Harper & Row, 1963).

the mythological language in which it is expressed so that the modern man who does not share the biblical world view can honestly accept the biblical message. This, as I said, amounted to a real explosion in the theological world because the Barthian influence had suppressed the radical critical questions of biblical interpretation. So Bultmann's name became central in the theological debates.

Since you all know what Bultmann is trying to do, let me give you here merely my mild criticism of it. I feel that on most points I am on Bultmann's side. But he does not know the meaning of myth. He does not know that religious language is and always must be mythological. Even when he says that God has acted in Jesus in order to confront us with the possibility of decision for or against authentic existence, this is a symbolic or mythological way of speaking. He resists admitting this; he cannot go beyond it. I have often stated that he should speak not of demythologization but of deliteralization, which means not taking the symbols as literal expressions of events in time and space. This is something indeed that has to be done because the possibility of presenting the Christian message to the pagans of our time depends on it, and all of us are among these pagans by virtue of at least half of our education. We are all on the boundary line between humanism and Christianity. We cannot even speak to ourselves honestly in biblical terms unless we are able to deliteralize them.

While this is the importance of Bultmann, he is not able to bring this into a real systematic structure, not even with the help of Heidegger's existentialism. But this existentialism does help him to show the existential character of the New Testament concepts. The existentialist interpretation of the New Testament deals with the concepts of anxiety, care, guilt, and emptiness, and this is important. I have also applied an existentialist interpretation of biblical texts in all the sermons I have preached. But Bultmann is not able to present all this in a real systematic structure.

5. The History-of-Religions Approach

Hermann Gunkel (1862–1932) was the first great critic from the point of view of the history of religions. He was primarily an Old Testament scholar, but his method and results had implications for New

Testament scholarship. In Germany we call the movement in which he participated the *Religionsgeschichtlicheschule*, one word for the "school of the history of religions." This was not a school in the sense that there was special interest in the living religions like Islam, Buddhism, Hinduism, etc., but it was a method of analyzing the contents of the biblical writings. It tried to discover the extent to which both the Old and New Testaments are dependent on the religious symbolism of the surrounding religions. This, of course, excludes the Asian religions as well as Islam, which came much later, but it includes the religions of Persia, Egypt, and Assyria; it includes the primitive forms of religion and especially the mystery religions which grew up in the Hellenistic world. To what extent are the biblical writings dependent on these pre-Jewish and pre-Christian religious movements?

Gunkel's approach and discoveries had a tremendous influence. I believe that Gunkel's *Commentary on Genesis*[8] is still the classic work which shows the influence of the pagan religions on the Old Testament books. It traces the motifs of the primitive pagan religions which appear in the Genesis stories. It demonstrates how the Jewish spirit, how prophetism and later the priestly writers transformed the pagan myths and purified them under the impact of the prophetic spirit. All this has given us a much better understanding of the Old Testament.

The same thing was done with the New Testament. The surrounding contemporary religions influenced the writers of the New Testament. The influence from the apocalyptic period is obvious. Certain concepts are related to the mystery religions. The term "Lord" (*kyrios*) itself may have some connection with the mystery religions. Nobody can deal with the New Testament today in a scholarly way if he is not aware of this situation. There are always differences of scholarly opinion on these questions, but the approach itself must be taken seriously.

* * * * * * * * *

Question: It seems that most of the systematic theologians that we have studied this quarter have faltered at the point where they talk about or fail to talk about the problem of sin. Can such a generalization

---

[8] *Genesis übersetzt und erklärt* (Göttingen: Vandenhoek and Ruprecht, 1901). Cf. his *The Legends of Genesis,* translated by W. H. Carruth (Chicago: The Open Court Publishing Co., 1901). This book is a translation of the Introduction to the author's *Commentary on Genesis.*

be made in any true sense, and if so does it have any particular significance for the theological enterprise?

Answer: This is not true of the theologians of mediation. We did discuss Schleiermacher's doctrine of sin and pointed out its shortcomings. He derived sin in an evolutionary way from the inadequacies of man's mental development in contrast to his bodily development. In the Ritschlian school too sin did not receive its full significance because it was described in a similar way as the conflict between man's selfhood and his natural basis. Salvation was then conceived of as the spiritual power of man overcoming his natural basis. For the Ritschlian school salvation was especially forgiveness of sins, but not transformation, for the idea of the Spirit being present in man and transforming him was very remote from Ritschlian thinking. So the generalization is true with respect to the leading theologians whom we discussed. But this is not true of the theologians of mediation, some of whom we touched on very briefly. I left out one theologian who is very important on the doctrine of sin. His name is Julius Müller (1801–1878). He earned for himself the additional name sin-Müller because he wrote a very large and classical work on the doctrine of sin,[9] especially in terms of Schelling's philosophy. And, of course, when we dealt with the existentialist philosophers and theologians, we showed their grasp of the situation of human estrangement. Kierkegaard especially was discussed in this connection; his idea that sin presupposes itself, his concept of the transition from innocence to guilt and the problem of sickness unto death are all profound aspects of the reality of sin. There is a strong tradition of understanding the depth of sin in the theologians of mediation, much profounder than in both Schleiermacher and Ritschl.

* * * * * * * * * *

6. *Ernst Troeltsch*

With only one lecture left, we are going to have to limit ourselves to a few remarks on four subjects. The first is the thought of Ernst

[9] *The Christian Doctrine of Sin,* translated by William Urwick (Edinburgh: T. & T. Clark, 1868).

Troeltsch, who was formerly my colleague in the University of Berlin and whom I consider in a special way as one of my teachers, although I never heard him lecture. Secondly, I want to talk about the foundations of religious socialism in Germany. Thirdly, about Karl Barth, and fourthly about existentialist motifs.

I will speak first of Troeltsch as a philosopher of religion. His main problem dealt with the meaning of religion in the context of the human spirit or man's mental structure. Here Troeltsch followed Kant by accepting his three critiques, but he said that there is not only the theoretical *a priori*, man's categorical structure, as Kant developed it in the *Critique of Pure Reason*, not only the moral, as Kant developed it in the *Critique of Practical Reason*, and not only the aesthetic, as he developed it in the *Critique of Judgment*, but there is also a religious *a priori*. This means that there is something which belongs to the structure of the human mind itself from which religion arises. It is essentially present, although always only potentially as with the other three structures. Whether it becomes actualized in time and space is another question, but if it is actualized it has its own kind of certainty as the others have. It is an *a priori*. To say that it is *a priori* does not mean that it is to be understood temporally, as if all the Kantian categories are clear in the consciousness of a new born baby. This is not what *a priori* means. What it means is that if somebody has the character of man, if he has a human mind and human rational structure, then these categories develop under the impact of experience. This is what Troeltsch tried to show in regard to the religious *a priori*. I would say that on this point he stands in the great tradition of the Franciscan-Augustinian school of the Middle Ages. It is impossible for me to understand how we could ever come to a philosophical understanding of religion without finding a point in the structure of man as man in which the finite and the infinite meet or are within each other.

In his book, *The Absoluteness of Christianity*,[10] Troeltsch criticizes Harnack's famous book, *What Is Christianity?* He asks, What is the essence of Christianity and whence do we derive it? Is it the classical period of Christianity, the period of the apostles? Is it an abstraction

[10] *Die Absolutheit des Christentums und die Religionsgeschichte* (Tübingen: J. C. B. Mohr, 1929).

from all the periods, by using the Aristotelian method which abstracts from all the concrete realities in order to reach the essence? In either case we are confronted by impossibilities, because in history there is not such an essence. History is open toward the future. If one wants to speak of an essence, one can do so only by anticipating the entire future, which is impossible. For this reason he denied the possibility of finding an essence.

Troeltsch was not only a philosopher of history; he was also a man with great historical vision. I remember the excitement which was aroused when he published a great essay on the meaning of Protestantism in relation to the modern world.[11] In this particular article he wrote about the medieval character of early Protestantism and challenged the idea that Protestantism had brought an end to the medieval world. He tried to show that early Protestantism had all the medieval characteristics. Instead, the Middle Ages came to an end only with the Enlightenment. This, of course, was a fundamental expression of what one usually calls liberal Protestantism.

Troeltsch's philosophy of history is rooted in a negative attitude toward what he calls "historism," or perhaps in English one might call it "historicism." In any case, it is an attitude of relativism toward history. For historicism, history is mere observation of the past. It is not an attitude of participation in history and of making decisions which are decisive for the course of history. At the end of the nineteenth century under the influence of historicism history was at best an interesting subject to be observed with a detached attitude. I know people who have carried this attitude with them into the twentieth century and have remained historicists in this respect. Now, Troeltsch tried to overcome this by an interesting construction. He asked the question: What is the aim of history? Toward what is history running? That aim would determine the meaning of history. But he denied the possibility of knowing or giving such an aim. He said that we can only speak of the concrete historical structure in which we are living. This was certainly an

---

[11] *Protestantism and Progress: A Historical Study of the Relation of Protestantism to the Modern World,* translated by W. Montgomery (Boston: Beacon Press, 1958); translated from the German edition of 1911, *Die Bedeutung des Protestantismus für die Entstehung der Modernen Welt.*

advance over historicism. He was not only an observer; he also wanted to transform history. But he did this in a limited way. He said that our task is to care for the immediate next stage of history, and he called this Europeanism. It coincides with what we today call the Western world. He included the United States as well, of course. He did not use our expression of the Western world, because at that time the conflict between East and West had not started. Europeanism is a combination of Christian, Jewish, Greek, Roman, and Germanic elements. Christianity is the religion of Europeanism; it belongs to the Western world. Therefore, missions cannot have the intention of converting people in the Eastern world, but instead of fostering the interpenetration of the great religions. He was the president of a special missionary society guided by the liberal theology, and as president of this society, he developed his concept of missions, namely, the interpenetration of cultures and religions. This means that the idea of the absoluteness of Christianity—whatever this questionable concept may mean—would have to be given up. Christianity was relativized by limiting it to the Western culture, by making it the religion of Europeanism. Christianity and Western culture belong to each other, but with respect to the Eastern culture, the best that we could hope for is the interpenetration of the religions.

The next point we wish to discuss is of the highest importance for theology. The history of theology in the past had usually been discussed as the history of dogma or of the doctrinal statements of the church. This was the case in Harnack too. But Troeltsch was influenced by Max Weber (1864–1920), the great sociologist and perhaps the greatest scholar in Germany of the nineteenth century. So Troeltsch now posed the question: What about the social teachings of the Christian churches?[12] That, in fact, is the title of his great work. Should we not look at the dogmatic statements in the light of the social doctrines of the churches? Perhaps we might understand the dogmatic statements better in this light, rather than dealing with them apart from their relation to social reality. This method was influenced by the methodological principles of Marxism, but in a way that was counterbalanced by Max

[12] *The Social Teachings of the Christian Churches,* translated by Olive Wyon (New York: The Macmillan Company, 1931).

Weber's own interpretation of the relation of thought to social reality. For instance, Max Weber tried to show that Calvinism had a tremendous influence on the way in which the capitalistic rulers gained their fortunes and ran their factories by a personal inner-worldly asceticism as called for by the Calvinist ethic.

Troeltsch's method was thus a two-way street. On the one side was the understanding that all doctrines are dependent on social conditions and cannot be understood apart from these social conditions. This was the Marxist side. But on the other side was the equally important insight that the way in which the social conditions are used by people is largely dependent on their ultimate concern, by their religious convictions and their ethical implications. In this way he together with Max Weber tried to give a new key to the interpretation of the history of religion.

These are the main points in dealing with Troeltsch, and, as I told you, I have been deeply influenced by these ideas. But in two respects I already belonged to a new generation. Many of us were not satisfied with the way in which Troeltsch tried to overcome historicism. We felt that he himself was still under its power. The other point at which we departed from Troeltsch had to do with the existentialism that arose in the meantime. Troeltsch was not at all in touch with these existentialist ideas. Ultimately he came from the Ritschlian school, and the Ritschlian school was a rationalistic essentialism. While attempting to overcome these limitations of Troeltsch, we remained always grateful for the often devastating criticism which he leveled at many traditional forms of Christian theology. He taught us a kind of freedom which transcended the often narrow biblicistic attitude of the Ritschlian school and of liberal theology, which despite its liberalism often hangs on to a pietistic biblicistic element.

7. Religious Socialism

Religious socialism can be seen as an attempt to overcome the limitations of Troeltsch's effort to overcome historicism. I would like to have had time to trace the underlying sources of religious socialism. These sources are in the line of development that includes men like Boehme, Schelling, Oetinger, and generally a tradition of biblical realism which was neither orthodox or fundamentalist, on the one hand, nor pietistic, on the other hand, and which transcended the doctrinal Lutheranism by its closeness to social and political realities. The fundamental ideas in this line have become very important in our days again. Accordingly, we emphasize that God is related to the world and not only to the individual and his inner life and not only to the church as a sociological entity. God is related to the universe, and this includes nature, history, and personality. May I add that Martin Kähler and Adolf Schlatter were also in this line of thought. They stressed the freedom of God to act apart from the church in either its orthodox or pietistic form. They were also emancipated from the moralistic transformation of religion in the escapist theology of Ritschlianism.

There are two names we must mention, the Blumhardts, father and son: Johann Christoph Blumhardt (1805–1880) and Christoph Blumhardt (1842–1919). Both of them were ministers, and the son later became a political leader of the socialist movement. The father Blumhardt, as he is called, was a man who felt he had the power to expel demonic forces. He practiced healing in his parish in Bad Boll in Württemberg. He did it in a way that the Synoptic stories say that Jesus did it, not with faith healing, which is mostly a matter of magical concentration, but with the power of the divine Spirit radiating from him. From this experience he came to the realization that God is a healing God, that he has something to do with the world and all the dimensions of reality and not only with the inner conversion of the human soul.

The son Blumhardt applied these ideas to the social realities. His special emphasis was that God loved the world, not only the church and not only Christians. He fought against the egocentricism of the individualistic type of religion which characterized pietistic Lutheranism at that time. For this reason he participated in the socialist movement which was becoming more powerful at the turn of the century. He did this in terms of an inner historical understanding of the kingdom of God, without giving up the transcendent fulfillment of the kingdom of God, as the social gospel theology in this country often tended to do. He could say that the works of those who do not know God are often greater works for God than those which are done in the church by Christians in the name of God.

These are the ideas which we later developed in the religious socialist movement, and I remember that we represented them also at the Oxford Conference in 1937, which was one of the important conferences of the modern ecumenical movement. At that time I was chairman of a small committee which included among others some Eastern Orthodox theologians. Our task was to make a statement about the relation of the church to socialism and communism. We presented a report under rather dramatic conditions to the plenary assembly of the conference, in which we stated that often God speaks to the church more directly from outside the church, through those who are enemies of religion and Christianity, than within the church, through those who are official representatives of the churches. We related this to the revolutionary movements of the nineteenth and twentieth centuries, and especially to the socialist movement. This was accepted almost without any changes by the Oxford Assembly. Although this was a step of great significance, it was too early for it. Today if the National Council of Churches or the World Council of Churches should make such a statement, it would be heard and understood, and perhaps attacked by some. But at that time this type of statement was so far in advance of the actual situation that it was almost forgotten. Thus, out of the experience and insight of people like the Blumhardts a new understanding of the relation of the church to society was opened up in an unheard-of way in most of the European churches. Religious socialism was one of the movements which mediated this new power and vision.

In this connection we might say something about Pope John XXIII. He was able to criticize the church, his own church, and could declare publicly how the church had become irrelevant for many people in our time. He has shown us that the spirit of prophetism which can criticize the religious group in which the prophet lives has not completely died out in the Roman Church. It is still there and surprisingly has been voiced from the top of the hierarchy from where one would least expect it. The other thing that he has done is to make it possible to reach out to those outside the churches, not only to the "separated brethren" outside the Roman Catholic Church, but to the secularists and even to those who are enemies of the church and Christianity. On the basis of my own religious socialist past I feel a kinship with him. He shares the prophetic self-criticism which is open to the truth which has been forgotten in the church and which is now represented against the church by the secular and the anti-religious movements of our time.

The immediate predecessors of the religious socialist movement were in Switzerland, Hermann Kutter (1869–1931) and Leonhard Ragaz, (1868–1945), both of whom you will learn about in every biography of Karl Barth. Both fought for justice and peace in the name of Christianity, Kutter more prophetically and Ragaz more politically. It is important to remember that Karl Barth himself was a part of the religious socialist movement before he made his great break with all such movements. We tried to develop a special type of religious socialism in Germany after the first World War which took into account the particular historical situation in Germany. With the revolution of 1919 in Germany, the country was split into the labor movements and the traditional churches, which were practically all Lutheran, except in the West where there is some Calvinist influence. The problem we faced after the first World War was how to overcome the split between Lutheran transcendentalism and the secular utopianism in the socialist groups. The Lutheran idea was that the world is somehow in the hands of the devil, and that the only counter-power here is the authority of the state. Therefore revolutionary movements were entirely denied and the idea of transforming society in the name of God received no response in the German Lutheran tradition. The secular idea was that the revolution is right around the corner. Its coming is a matter of scientific calculation; it does not even require much political action. This secular idea has nothing transcendent in it, but only believes that if socialism is achieved, all human problems will be solved.

These were the two poles between which we moved as religious socialists at that time. Our answer to the situation was given in terms of some basic concepts. The first was the concept of the *demonic*. Our interpretation dealt with the demonic structures of evil in individuals and social groups. When we first used the concept of the demonic in the early twenties, nobody had heard of it except in history books in connection with the superstitious kinds of belief in demons. We used the word "demonic" to describe the structures of destruction which prevail over the creative elements. The experiential basis of this was the psychological description of the compulsive powers in individuals and the sociological description as given in the Marxist analysis of the bourgeois society. The structures in society are creative and destructive at the same time.

Then we went on to say in terms of the concept of *kairos* that when the demonic power is recognized and fought against, there takes place a breakthrough of the eternal into history. *Kairos* means time, the right time, the qualitative time in contrast to *chronos,* clock time, quantitative time. The idea of the *kairos* is a biblical idea attached in particular to the biblical messages of John the Baptist and Jesus and to Paul's interpretation of history. For us this concept was the main mediating concept between the two extremes. Against the Lutheran transcendentalism *kairos* means that the eternal can break into the temporal and that a new beginning can take place. Against utopianism we knew of the fragmentariness of historical achievements. No perfect end is reached in history free of the demonic. We expressed this sometimes in the symbol from the book of Revelation, the idea of the millennium; the demonic forces are banned for a thousand years, but they are not overcome. They will return from their prison in the underworld. This is highly mythological, but yet profound. It says that the demonic can be conquered for a time; a particular demonic structure can be overcome. But the demonic always returns, just as Jesus described in the case of the individual into whom more demons rush after the one has been cast out.

The third concept was the idea of theonomy. We said that the aim of the religious socialist movement was a theonomous state of society. Theonomy goes beyond autonomy, which is empty critical thought. It goes beyond heteronomy, which means authoritarianism and enslavement. Theonomy is the union of what is true in autonomy and in heteronomy, the fulfillment of a whole society with the spiritual substance, in spite of the freedom of the autonomous development, and in spite of living in the great traditions in which the Spirit has embodied himself. This was our answer. And we found that in the twelfth century of Europe there was something very close to theonomy, represented especially by the Franciscan-Augustinian school in theology.

Do not misunderstand me! We never said like the romantics that the Middle Ages was such a great period. People were evil then as always. But the structure of society had elements of theonomy in it. The entire life was concentrated in the great cathedrals; the whole of daily life was consecrated in the cathedral. This is what I mean by theonomy. If you go to Europe and see the genuinely creative products of this theonomy —not the pseudo-Gothic imitations that we have elsewhere in the world—then you can see how the whole life in these little towns—like Chartres near Paris—was arranged under the vertical line which drives up to the ultimate.

The religious socialist movement never was a movement for higher wages, etc., although there was much to be done in this respect. This was an incredibly exploitative situation. But it tried to re-establish the vertical line in new forms. In this respect I would say that the situation has not changed since 1920. The same problem exists in this country, not in the same social structure, but in the same spiritual structure. There is still a lack of the vertical line, the lack of a theonomous culture.

When religious nationalism arose in the context of the Nazi movement, it used at the beginning some of the ideas of religious socialism in order to make the demonic elevation of a finite reality to ultimacy religiously acceptable in Germany. In the first years of Hitler—when it was still possible to fight intellectually—I had to resist this misappropriation of concepts that we had used for a different purpose. If we had time we would also like to deal with religious pacifism and the social gospel movement in this country. Largely, the form of pacifism which I found when I came to this country in 1933 has been overcome because of the second World War in which only power could resist the demonic elevation of Nazism, and because of the type of theological interpretation given by Reinhold Niebuhr of the complex human situation.

8. *Karl Barth*

We will deal especially with the beginning of the development of Karl Barth. As I said, he came out of the religious socialist movement in Switzerland, but he did not join this movement in Germany. On the contrary, he recognized the danger, which was a real danger as the abuse of religious socialism by religious nationalism showed, that the Christian message will be identified with a particular political or social idea. Whether it be nationalism, or socialism, or democracy, or "the American way of life," which happens to be identified with the Christian message, Karl Barth would see these things as idolatrous. He saw the danger of idolatry much more clearly than the other danger of a divorce between church and society which we saw when we started the religious socialist movement. Therefore, he attacked all these movements, including religious socialism. In a sense this was itself a dangerous thing to do, because the Lutheran students in Germany were only too willing to leave the social problems alone to retreat into problems of systematic theology and biblical research. He broke the attempt to bridge the gap from the side of theology between the revolutionary labor movement and the church in Germany. This break became very clear to me when I saw, while a professor in Marburg, how the students after the first World War turned away from the great social problems created by the catastrophes of the War and settled back in their sanctuaries of theological discussions.

Nevertheless, in view of the situation which came later, what Barth did was providentially significant, for it saved Protestantism from the onslaught of the neo-collectivistic and pagan Nazism. Barth's theology is also called neo-Reformation theology, and is related to the rediscovery of Luther in the Ritschlian tradition, but it goes considerably deeper than the Ritschlians in the understanding of Luther and the doctrines of sin and grace. His theology was also called in the beginning the theology of crisis. Crisis can mean two things. In the one sense it means the historical crisis of bourgeois society in Central Europe after the first World War. Some of this was in Barth's theology, but very little. He elevated this occasional crisis, which happens at a given time in history, into a universal crisis of the relationship between the eternal and the temporal. The crisis is always the crisis of the temporal in the power of the eternal. This is the human situation in every period. But in this way too the interest in the social elements in the post-War period waned in the Barthian school in favor of the doctrinal elements.

Barth did all this in the name of his fundamental principle, the absoluteness of God. God is not an object of our knowledge or action. He expressed this in his commentary on Paul's letter to the Romans,[13] a book of great prophetic paradoxes; it was received in Germany and in all Europe as a prophetic book. It is not exegesis of Romans measured by strict historical standards, and he admitted this. But it was an attempt to restate the paradoxical character of the absolute transcendence of God which we can never reach from our side, which we can never bring down to earth by our efforts or our knowledge, which either comes to us or does not come to us. All our attempts to reach God are defined as religion, and against religion stands God's act of revelation. Here began the fight against the use of the word "religion" in theology.

When I returned to Germany in 1948 after the Hitler period, I was immediately attacked when I used the word "religion" in my writings or speeches, because religion was still felt after Barth's struggle with the Nazi Christians as an expression of human arrogance, a human attempt to reach up to the divine. In the meantime, however, it has come to be understood that revelation can reach man only in the form of receiving it, and every reception of it, whether more inwardly religious or more openly secular, is religion, and as religion is always humanly distorted. But in the earlier period Karl Barth did not acknowledge this; he identified revelation with the Christian message, and denied the revelatory character of everything except the Christian revelation. Therefore, he denied all natural theology. His famous controversy with Emil Brunner about the point of contact in man was the occasion for his most outspoken rejection of natural theology. It was not so much an attack on the whole system of Thomistic natural theology, for this was not necessary to do. But the idea which he attacked was that there is something in man as man which makes it possible for God to be recognized as God by man. What Troeltsch tried to formulate with his idea of the religious *a priori* was the object of his attack. Barth claimed that the image of God in man is totally destroyed. This immediately involved him in an attack on mysticism, following here the line of Ritschl and Harnack. He negated every point of identity between God and man, even in the doctrine of the Spirit who might be dwelling in man. He

[13] *The Epistle to the Romans,* translated by Edwyn C. Hoskyns (New York: Oxford University Press, 1933).

said not that I believe, but that I believe that I believe; the Spirit is not in me, but is against me. But the question how can God appear to man at all remained unanswered in these ideas.

Barth's theology has also been called dialectical. But this word is very misleading. In its prophetic beginnings it was paradoxical, and later its conceptualization became supernaturalistic. But it is not dialectical. Dialectic involves an inner progress from one state to another by an inner dynamics. From this position there follow a number of other antiliberal doctrines. The Word of God is stressed in antithesis to Schleiermacher's idea of the religious consciousness, and to any form of pietistic or mystical experience. The classical christology is accepted, and the trinitarian dogma becomes his starting point. Karl Barth starts from above, from the trinity, from the revelation which is given, and then proceeds to man, and in his latest period, even very deeply into man, when he speaks of the "humanity of God."[14] Whereas, on the other hand, I start with man, not deriving the divine answer from man, but starting with the question which is present in man and to which the divine revelation comes as the answer.

A few more words about Barth's relation to historical criticism and to social political movements. He silenced the problems of historical criticism completely. The question of the historical Jesus did not touch him at all. But problems cannot be silenced. So it happened in almost a tragic way that when Bultmann wrote his article on demythologizing, a split in theology opened up, and the silenced questions broke out into the open all over the theological world. Bultmann saved the historical question from being banished from theology. This is his importance. He showed that it cannot be silenced, that our whole relationship to the Bible cannot be expressed in paradoxical and supernaturalist statements, not even if it is done with the prophetic power of Karl Barth. But we have to ask the question of the historical meaning of the biblical writings.

In regard to the political and social movements he detached himself not only from religious socialism, but also for a time from the political side of Hitler's power. He accepted it and did not speak against it in the

[14] The Humanity of God, translated by John N. Thomas (Richmond: John Knox Press, 1960).

name of religion, although there were many occasions for doing so. For instance, on April 1, 1933, when the first great attack against the Jews was made, with the destruction of a vast amount of life and property, the churches kept quiet. They did not speak up until they themselves were attacked by Hitler. This is one of the great shortcomings of the German churches, but also of Karl Barth. But then Barth became the leader of the inner-churchly resistance against National Socialism. He finally came to a point where he recognized something which he had formerly rejected, namely, that the movement headed by Hitler is a quasi-religious movement which represents an attack on Christianity. So he wrote his famous letter to the Christians in England, asking them in the name of Christ to resist Hitler.[15] This was quite different from his earlier position.

Today Barth is more or less neutral, and in accordance with his fundamental principles does not want to identify the cause of Christ with the cause of the West. For this reason he is very seriously attacked by Western churches. He would not apply his criticism of Islam and Hitler to Communism in the same way, and thus has returned to his original position of detachment.

9. Existentialism

We have already spoken very much about existentialism in connection with Schelling, Kierkegaard, Nietzsche, and Feuerbach, whose revolts against Hegel gave rise to existentialist elements in their thought. They are the sources of present-day existentialism. But existentialism is not only a revolt; it is also a style. Existentialism has become the style of all great literature, of the arts and the other media of our self-expression. It is present in poetry, in the novel, in drama, in the visual arts, and it is my opinion that our century will in historical retrospect be characterized as the period of existentialism.

We must first try to define the term. It is a way of looking at man. But there are two possible ways of looking at man. The one way is essentialist which develops the doctrine of man in terms of his essential

[15] This Christian Cause, A Letter to Great Britain from Switzerland (New York: The Macmillan Company, 1941).

nature within the whole of the universe. The other way is existentialist which looks at man in his predicament in time and space, and sees the conflict between what exists in time and space and what is essentially given. Religiously expressed, this is the conflict between the essential goodness of man, the highest point of which is his freedom to contradict his essential goodness, and man's fall into the conditions of existential estrangement. This is a universal situation, and at the same time man is responsible for it.

Existentialist philosophy is a revolt against the predominance of the essentialist element in most of the history of Western philosophy. It represents a revival of the existentialist elements of earlier thought in Plato, in the Bible, in Augustine, Duns Scotus, Jacob Boehme, etc. In the great philosophers of the past we usually find a preponderance of the essentialist approach, but always with existentialist elements within them. Plato in this regard is a classical figure. His realm of ideas or essences is a realm of essentialism, of essentialist description and analysis. But Plato's existentialism appears in his myth of the human soul in prison, of coming down from the world of essences into the body which is its prison, and then being liberated from the cave. The essentialist element became most powerfully expressed in Hegel and in the great synthesis. But there were also hidden existentialist elements in Hegel which his pupils brought out finally against him and thus inaugurated the generations of existentialism in revolt. And finally, in our century existentialism has become a style. Therefore, to repeat, first existentialism appears as an element, then as a revolt, and finally as a style. That is where we are today.

This rediscovery of existentialism has a great significance for theology. It has seen the dark elements in man as over against a philosophy of consciousness which lays all the stress on man's conscious decisions and his good will. The existentialists allied themselves with Freud's analysis of the unconscious in protest against a psychology of consciousness which had previously existed. Existentialism and psychotherapeutic psychology are natural allies and have always worked together. This rediscovery of the unconscious in man is of the highest importance for theology. It has changed the moralistic and idealistic types which we have discussed; it has placed the question of the human condition at the center of all theological thinking, and for this reason it has made the answers meaningful again. In this light we can say that existentialism and Freud, together with his followers and friends, have become the providential allies of Christian theology in the twentieth century. This is similar to the way in which the Marxist analysis of the structure of society became a tremendous factor in arousing the churches to a sense of responsibility for the social conditions in which men live.

Often I have been asked if I am an existentialist theologian, and my answer is always short. I say, fifty-fifty. This means that for me essentialism and existentialism belong together. It is impossible to be a pure essentialist if one is personally in the human situation and not sitting on the throne of God as Hegel implied he was doing when he construed world history as coming to an end in principle in his philosophy. This is the metaphysical arrogance of pure essentialism. For the world is still open to the future, and we are not on the throne of God, as Karl Barth has said in his famous statement: God is in heaven and man is on earth.

On the other hand, a pure existentialism is impossible because to describe existence one must use language. Now language deals with universals. In using universals, language is by its very nature essentialist, and cannot escape it. All attempts to reduce language to mere noises or utterances would bring man back to the animal level on which universals do not exist. Animals cannot express universals. But man can and must express his encounter with the world in terms of universals. Therefore, there is an essentialist framework in his mind. Existentialism is possible only as an element in a larger whole, as an element in a vision of the structure of being in its created goodness, and then as a description of man's existence within that framework. The conflicts between his essential goodness and his existential estrangement cannot be seen at all without keeping essentialism and existentialism together. Theology must see both sides, man's essential nature, wonderfully and symbolically expressed in the paradise story, and man's existential condition, under sin, guilt, and death.

Index of Names

Index of Subjects